CATACLYSM

THE WAR ON THE EASTERN FRONT 1941–45

Keith Cumins

CASEMATE

Philadelphia & Oxford

Dedication – To the untold victims of Hitler's war in the east;
also to my wife, Merryl, for her patience during the writing of this book.

First published in the United Kingdom by Helion & Company in 2011.
Reprinted in the United States of America and Great Britain as a paperback in 2019 by
CASEMATE PUBLISHERS
1950 Lawrence Road, Havertown, PA 19083, USA
and
The Old Music Hall, 106–108 Cowley Road, Oxford OX4 1JE, UK

ISBN 978-1-61200-752-6

A CIP record for this book is available from the British Library

Printed and bound in the United States of America

For a complete list of Casemate titles, please contact:

CASEMATE PUBLISHERS (US)
Telephone (610) 853-9131
Fax (610) 853-9146
Email: casemate@casematepublishers.com
www.casematepublishers.com

CASEMATE PUBLISHERS (UK)
Telephone (01865) 241249
Email: casemate-uk@casematepublishers.co.uk
www.casematepublishers.co.uk

Contents

List of Illustrations

In photo section.

German Commanders:
 Fedor von Bock
 Hermann Hoth
 Ewald von Kleist
 Erich von Manstein
Soviet Commanders
 I S Konev
 K K Rokossovsky
 A M Vasilevsky
 G K Zhukov
(all above images from the collection of David M. Glantz)
A knocked-out Soviet OT-26 flamethrower tank, Russia, 1941. (Marek Tuszyński)
A dead Soviet soldier, Russia, 1941. (Marek Tuszyński)
Germans inspecting Soviet aircraft, Russia, 1941. (Marek Tuszyński)
Russia 1941 – a destroyed Soviet Mikoyan-Gurevich MiG-3 fighter. (Marek Tuszyński)
Soviet prisoners, Russia, 1941. (Marek Tuszyński)
Destroyed Soviet and German aircraft, Russia 1941. (Marek Tuszyński)
German tankers struggle to free their tank from the clutching mud after rain, autumn 1941 (Lev Lopukhovsky)
A German Junkers Ju 52 transport plane, winter 1941/42. (Imperial War Museum)
Soviet troops counter-attack, December 1941. (Imperial War Museum)
A Soviet Pe-2 crew receive their mission, Kalinin Front, early 1942. (Svetlana Gerasimova)
Two German despatch riders relax with cigarettes on the Eastern Front, 1942. (Imperial War Museum)
German despatch riders dig out their Zundapp motorbike, Spring 1942. (Imperial War Museum)
Marines of the Soviet Northern Fleet, 1942. (Imperial War Museum)
German tanks pause in their advance to Stalingrad, September 1942. (Imperial War Museum)
German infantry move into the outskirts of Stalingrad, September 1942. (Imperial War Museum)
A German signpost in Stalingrad. (Imperial War Museum)
Soviet soldiers fire on a German-held block of flats in Stalingrad, Autumn 1942. (Imperial War Museum)
Advancing elements of the Soviet 158th Rifle Division, Kalinin Front west of Rzhev, November 1942. (Svetlana Gerasimova)

List of Maps

In colour section.

Introduction

The Second World War has been described as the greatest self-inflicted wound that the human race has ever suffered, and nowhere was the trauma greater than in the vast expanse of Eastern Europe between the Elbe and Volga; the infamous Eastern Front. Here lay tales of incredible courage, barbarism, endurance, brilliance, stupidity and waste. But of these, the enduring sense of most participants was the waste, for on the Eastern Front the waste was on a truly prodigious scale.

Most accounts of the conflict in Eastern Europe that were published in English in the decades following the Second World War were based largely on German archival material since access to Soviet archives was denied to all but a select circle of official Soviet military historians. In the early 1990s this began to change and since then some excellent accounts of what became known in the Soviet Union as the Great Patriotic War have been published in the West; but these accounts, based on the newly available material, have tended to explain the conflict from a largely Soviet perspective. Relatively few accounts of the conflict have been produced that place a broadly equal weight on the perspectives the two main combatants. This is an account that focuses almost exclusively on the military aspects of the war, particularly ground operations. An account that attempted to include the political, social, demographic and economic aspects of the war, and to place them in context with contemporaneous global events, could run to several volumes.

A common problem in writing an account of the military events in a war as long and complex as that on the Eastern Front is balancing the need to explain, and place in context, the development of a battle or series of battles in a particular theatre, while simultaneously providing a chronological account of unfolding events across all theatres. Since the fighting that took place on any part of the Eastern Front was almost always influenced by and influential on events elsewhere on the front, in this narrative a generally chronological account of the war has been adopted. However this approach makes delineation of the narrative difficult since there were few occasions in the conflict when there was a general pause in operations across the entirety of the front.

Using a modern map to following the events described in the text can prove frustrating due to a common practice in Eastern Europe in the decades following the Second World War of changing place names. This practice was particularly common in the former Soviet Union and Poland, as well as those parts of Germany, such as East Prussia, which found themselves under Soviet hegemony. Perhaps the best-known examples are Leningrad and Stalingrad, modern day Saint Petersburg and Volgograd respectively, but there are numerous others. In this account of the conflict the place names in common use at the time are used. Where names have changed significantly, the modern usage is tabulated in Appendix I.

A detailed account of combat operations on the Eastern Front inevitably involves reference to the large number of military units involved. Unit identification usually includes, not only a unit's number designation, but also its organisational status, its operational nature, and its nationality. Hence an individual unit's identification can be quite lengthy. Due to the frequency of reference to such units, the longer of the more commonly used terms have been abbreviated. Appendix II contains a list of these abbreviations, and includes a list of the abbreviations used for senior ranks. As a further aid to clarifying the account of combat operations, German army number designations are identified with Latin numbering, whereas Soviet army number designations use Arabic numbering. Hence the German Sixth Army is identified as VI Army, and the Soviet Sixth Army as 6 Army. Corps units are distinguished in a similar manner.

1

Prelude to Disaster

The primary cause of the Second World War in Europe was Hitler's determination to achieve German territorial expansion by any means. Yet the sequence of events that enabled Hitler to bring Europe by the late summer of 1939 to the brink of a catastrophic war is long and complex, and the relative significance of those events is still a matter of much debate.

Long before he came to power Hitler had, in common with many Germans, a vision of a 'Greater Germany'; a nation that would be dominant in Europe, that would encompass all the German speaking peoples of the continent, and that would acquire significant additional territory to the east – living space or *Lebensraum*. This additional territory included regions lost by Germany under the terms of the Versailles Treaty. Yet, what for many Germans was merely an aspiration, Hitler saw as the nation's destiny and he was convinced that fate had chosen him to set Germany on the path to its fulfilment. Furthermore, Hitler's vision of the Greater Germany was more expansive than most: the German-speaking peoples of Europe would be united under a single all-powerful leader; the eastward expansion would bite deep into the territories of the Soviet Union, expunging communism from the region in the process; and in the newly occupied territories the indigenous population, the Slavic 'sub-humans' or *Untermenschen* of Nazi racist creed, would be displaced or made available for German economic exploitation. At the same time a programme of racial purification would expunge the *Untermenschen*, primarily Jews, from the gene pool of the Reich. For Hitler the ultimate objective of this activity would to be to enable purebred Aryan families and communities to occupy the vacated lands where their industry and efficiency would ensure that the agricultural potential of the region could be fully exploited, thereby creating the conditions for a prolonged period of German prosperity and population growth. Clearly, to secure this Arcadian future Germany would be required to undergo a preliminary period of militarisation and increased industrialisation in order to ensure that resistance to German territorial expansion could be overcome by force, or by the credible threat of force.

To this end, soon after his accession to power in 1933 Hitler initiated an extensive rearmament and weapons development programme, and army commanders were encouraged to develop concepts for the prosecution of mobile offensive operations. The final result was what the world came to know as lightning war or *Blitzkrieg*; the close coordination of concentrated armour, mobile infantry and tactical air support directed at key breakthrough points, the effect of which was to confuse and demoralise forces on the flanks of these points. By 1938 Germany had acquired much of the military hardware to successfully conduct such operations, and the armed forces had been expanded considerably from their modest scale of five years earlier. In early 1938 Hitler abolished the German War Ministry and appointed himself Commander in Chief of the Armed Forces. At that time he created an armed forces headquarters, the

Oberkommando der Wehrmacht or OKW, which became, for all practical purposes, his personal military staff. Wilhelm Keitel was appointed chief of the OKW, a role he was to occupy throughout the war, and Alfred Jodl (as head of the OKW Operations Staff) effectively occupied the role of Armed Forces Chief of Staff. The head of the army and head of the Army High Command (*Oberkommando des Heeres* or OKH) was Walter von Brauchitsch with Franz Halder as his Chief of Staff.

In pursuit of his objectives Hitler, from the earliest days of the formation of the Nazi Party[1], embarked on a series of actions that many considered to be reckless gambles. Yet those actions were often carefully considered and behind them lay Hitler's belief that he was being guided by fate; a belief reinforced by the fact that most of his gambles paid off. To his acolytes, one of Hitler's greatest pre-war successes was the Munich Agreement, which included an acknowledgement by Britain and France that Germany had the right to occupy the German-speaking areas of western Czechoslovakia. Hitler, however, was less than delighted with the agreement since it denied him the opportunity to secure the entire country on the pretext of defending an oppressed German minority. Within months Hitler had breached the terms of the Munich Agreement, occupied the Czech regions and created a puppet state in Slovakia. That the Western Powers had entered into the Munich Agreement at all, and that they failed to act when Germany breached its terms, convinced Hitler that Britain and France would not intervene militarily to defend an eastern European state. In Moscow Stalin drew the same conclusion and began to take steps to further secure the Soviet Union's western frontiers. Logical though the two dictators' conclusions about the intentions of the Western Powers may have been, they were wrong. Britain and France were determined to oppose any further German territorial expansion, and Hitler's demonstration that he was prepared to ignore Germany's treaty obligations convinced politicians in Britain and France that further German expansion could not be constrained through negotiation. Hitler's non-aggression pact with Stalin prior to the German invasion of Poland meant that any military intervention by the Western Powers to directly assist the Poles would be ineffectual and, despite the unequivocal guarantees to Poland by Britain and France, the evidence suggests that Hitler was genuinely surprised by the wider war that resulted from his invasion of Poland in September 1939. Yet there is little to indicate that even if Hitler had been aware that Britain and France would declare war following a German attack on Poland he would have been diverted from his chosen course. The occupation of western Poland would be a necessary first step in the eastward expansion of the Reich.

Easy Victories

The Second World War began on 1 September 1939 when German forces crossed the Polish frontier. For the invasion of Poland Hitler deployed five field armies and two panzer groups. The panzer groups included six panzer divisions, each with 240 tanks. The speed of the German success against the Poles was due to a number of factors; the absence of any plan within the Polish military to respond to the new German *Blitzkrieg* tactics; the relatively poor combat effectiveness of the Polish air force; the relatively poor mobility of Polish ground forces; their lack of effective armoured forces; and the fact that by 1939 much of Poland had become a salient into German occupied

---

1   The party's formal name was the National Socialist German Workers' Party.

territory. The Soviet invasion of eastern of Poland later in the campaign was the final deciding factor. German armour at this time was not particularly good, consisting primarily of Mk I and Mk II panzers (PzKpfw I and PzKpfw II). Only five percent of the German tanks were Mk IIIs and only ten percent were the infantry support Mk IV Ds. But the panzers were fast, in radio communication with each other and, in the capable hands of commanders like Guderian and Kleist, their use with other arms was highly co-ordinated and effective. These same tactics were to be repeated less than a year later with even more spectacular success in France and the Low Countries. Prior to that, in February 1940 German forces occupied Denmark in a largely bloodless invasion and defeated British and French forces in northern Norway after a rapid and skilful occupation of the south of the country.

For the invasion of France and the Low Countries on 10 May 1940 Hitler deployed nine field armies and ten panzer divisions. By then the German tank park had improved, with a greater proportion of the machines being Mk IIIs and Mk IVs, and with a significant number of Czech PzKpfw 38Ts. Yet the German armoured strength was more than matched by that of the French. In the French tank park were 500 of the 20-tonne Somuas and 320 of the 32-tonne Char Bs, all of which were virtually immune to the standard German 3.7cm anti-tank gun. The French tactics and training were, however, inferior to the Germans. The French were further disadvantaged by having less mechanically reliable tanks that were unable to communicate by radio.

One key to the German success was the early capture by paratroops of the Belgian fort of Eban Emael, which allowed a panzer corps to bounce the Dyle, thereby making effective defence of northern Belgium impossible. Another key to the German success was the deployment through the Ardennes of an entire panzer group with the subsequent bouncing of the Meuse at Sedan and at Dinant against weak French opposition. This move outflanked the Maginot Line, confused the Allies about German intentions, broke open the Allies' backstop line, and threatened a flanking move against the Allied forces in Belgium. The disasters that subsequently befell the Allied forces in northern France in June 1940 may have been worse but for hesitancy in the German High Command at the rate of advance of their panzer forces. The final phase of the defeat of France began on 5 June and was concluded less than three weeks later.

Soviet Preparation

The potential threat presented by Nazi Germany to the Soviet state was not lost on the pre-war Soviet military planners. Certainly by the late 1930s Stalin had concluded that a war between the Soviet Union and Nazi Germany was inevitable, and after the Munich agreement between Germany and the Western Powers he had taken steps to try to ensure that the Soviet Union was in the most advantageous possible position prior to such a conflict. In some respects Stalin's foreign policy manoeuvrings after the Munich agreement had, despite their negative international repercussions, put the Soviet Union in a strong position. During the spring of 1939 Stalin had increasingly come to view overtures from Britain and France as insidious attempts shift onto the Soviet Union the military burden of constraining Germany's expansionist ambitions. During the summer of that year Stalin and Hitler had each come to the conclusion that a pragmatic interim arrangement between the Soviet Union and Germany on matters of mutual territorial interest in Eastern Europe should be pursued. The result had been the German-Soviet non-aggression pact, signed on 23 August 1939. A secret protocol in the pact had facilitated the Soviet occupation of eastern Poland. In 1940 the Red Army had completed the military occupation of Estonia, Latvia and Lithuania thereby securing Russia's northern flank. Similar action had been taken in the south where Bessarabia, Rumania's eastern province between the Dniester and Prut rivers, had been secured together with additional Rumanian territory to the north of Bessarabia.[2] These territorial acquisitions meant that a potential enemy in the west would need to strike much deeper into Soviet held territory before it could imperil the Soviet state. In addition to the Red Army's defences, an invasion from the west would face two formidable natural obstacles. One of these was the Carpathian mountain range. The frontier ran along the northern reaches of this range and no rapid mechanised invasion of Soviet territory could be contemplated through the mountains. The second natural barrier was the Pripet Marshes, effectively dividing the population centres of Belorussia from the Ukraine. The marshes were totally unsuited to mechanised warfare with few lateral roads or railways. Consequently there were only three broad invasion routes for the Germans and their potential allies into Soviet territory; through Bessarabia into southern Ukraine; through the gap between the northern edge of the Carpathians and the southern fringes of the marshes (the region of Galicia) into northern Ukraine; and north of the marshes into Belorussia and the Baltic States. Yet, though Soviet war games in early 1941 had envisaged a German invasion by this northern route, Soviet strategy was almost exclusively offensive in nature and it was the general view in the Soviet Union that if a conflict arose, little of the fighting would take place on Soviet soil.

Despite these assumptions, Stalin had reason to be concerned about the outcome of an imminent war with Germany. The rapid defeat of France had demonstrated that Germany had developed a devastatingly effective military machine in which the elements required for operational success had been acquired and honed. Conversely the abysmal performance of the Red Army in the Winter War of 1939/40 with Finland had demonstrated serious deficiencies in the Red Army's conduct of offensive operations; deficiencies in supply, command and control, tactics, training, equipment and leadership. In particular Stalin's purge of the armed forces that began in 1937 had decimated the officer corps and had left large sections of the Red Army dangerously short of qualified and experienced commanders. The deficiencies had been identified and were in the process of being addressed but it would be several years before they could be adequately rectified and by 1941 the reforms, such as they were, had been arbitrary, inconsistent and, on occasions, contradictory. Additionally the acquisition of new territory to the west had created a number of problems for the Red Army. The construction of forward defensive positions along the new frontier was far from complete and many of the defences that were in place had been acquired by stripping the so-called Stalin Line – the Western strategic defence line, much of which ran along the 1939 border – a defence line that the Soviet Union had spent much of the 1930s constructing. In Soviet-occupied Poland, the city of Brest on the Soviet side of the new frontier had become a formidable fortress, but much of the Soviet-occupied territory was within the Białystok salient; a triangular wedge of territory that thrust

2   Only in Finland, which the Soviet Union invaded on 30 November 1939, did the Red Army encounter serious resistance.

deep into German occupied Poland with the town of Białystok at its centre. This salient, though perfect for launching a future offensive strike into German held territory, was conversely very vulnerable to encirclement from armoured thrusts deep into its northern and southern shoulders. Consequently in 1940 and 1941 Stalin was anxious to do everything possible to placate Hitler in order to defer for as long as possible the inevitable clash of arms. Yet Hitler, flushed with success in the West and dismissive of Britain's continued resistance, in July 1940 ordered the military planning for an invasion of the Soviet Union, and at the end of that month set May 1941 as the start date for the campaign. Final approval for the deployment of forces for the invasion was given on 18 December 1940 with a start date for the offensive, codenamed Barbarossa, of 15 May.

Balance of Forces
The extent to which the German invasion of Yugoslavia and Greece in the spring of 1941 affected the commencement date and subsequent outcome of Operation Barbaossa has been much debated. It has been argued that the operations against Yugoslavia and Greece fatally delayed the commencement of the attack on the Soviet Union and it is certainly true that the diversion to the Balkans of two field armies with their four panzer divisions was not envisaged in the early planning stage of Barbarossa. Yet operations against regular enemy forces on the Balkan mainland were largely concluded by the end of April enabling key armoured and command units to be transferred north to Poland and East Prussia during May, and the prevailing weather and ground conditions in the Soviet frontier areas in the early summer of 1941 made it unlikely that Barbarossa could have commenced before June.

Operation Barbarossa involved 3,050,000 German and 1,000,000 other Axis personnel. OKH assembled 19 panzer divisions, 13 motorised divisions, and 101 infantry divisions; of which two panzer divisions and 20 infantry divisions were reserves. Additionally the Rumanians contributed four divisions and six brigades to the offensive with a further nine divisions and two brigades in reserve. Due to the relatively poor provision of divisional artillery, the combat capability of Rumanian divisions was considered to be inferior to that of German divisions, as was that of the two Slovakian divisions that represented the Slovak state's initial contribution to the invasion. Along the Carpathian mountain range a Hungarian corps defended the Hungarian – Soviet border. In north-eastern Norway OKW had positioned a further four divisions for an offensive towards Murmansk, and the Finns had deployed 16 divisions, most of which were to be used in offensives on either side of Lake Ladoga.

The structure of the panzer divisions had been modified since the invasion of France, the number of tanks in each division having been reduced by a third to an average strength of around 160, though in practice the number of tanks in each of the panzer divisions assembled for Barbarossa varied considerably. A summary of the structure of a panzer division at this time, together with structure summaries of the German infantry division and motorised division, is given in Appendix III. Key to the German operational planning was the deployment of four panzer groups, essentially mechanised armies, that would repeat the *Blitzkrieg* tactics at selected points along the Soviet frontier. Each panzer group was structured differently but the operational concept envisaged a formation of two panzer corps and a supporting army corps.[3] The panzer corps in turn typically comprised two panzer divisions and a motorised division. The motorised division comprised fully mobile motorised infantry battalions and motorised artillery. Of the motorised divisions, four were *Schutzstaffel* combat formations or *Waffen SS*.[4] These formations were generally disliked by the regular army; they had their own uniforms and command structure and ultimately they were answerable to Hitler through Himmler and not through the OKH/OKW chain of command. Himmler also ensured that his *Waffen SS* units were lavishly supplied with the best weapons and that they wanted for nothing when it came to transport and mobility on the battlefield. Yet for the bulk of the German ground forces, the men in the infantry divisions and rear services, transport and manoeuvre could only be accomplished by methods that would have been all to familiar to their fathers in the First World War; trains, horses and old-fashioned 'foot slogging'. The *Luftwaffe* strength along the frontier, organised into three air fleets, was 2,770 aircraft out of a total *Luftwaffe* front line strength of 4,300. This was a weaker force than had been employed in the invasion of France, losses in the Battle of Britain and commitments in the Balkans having taken their toll. The OKH headquarters for Barbarossa were located at Rastenburg in East Prussia and the OKW headquarters were moved from Berlin to secret bunkers in a heavily forested area near the railway line half an hour east of Rastenburg, the so-called 'Wolf's Lair'.

On the eve of Barbarossa the land forces of the Red Army comprised 198 rifle divisions, 61 tank divisions, 31 motorised rifle divisions and 13 cavalry divisions, a total of 303 divisions. Of these, 237 divisions including 45 tank divisions were in the 'Western theatre' between the Baltic Sea and the Black Sea, and a further 21 divisions, including 4 tank divisions, were positioned on the Finnish and Norwegian borders. Not all of the 258 divisions in the West were near the front; 42 rifle divisions, 10 tank divisions and 5 motor rifle divisions were part of the High Command Reserve, and the other 201 divisions were divided between the frontier armies and the operational reserve (see below). Based on the authorised strengths, a Red Army rifle division at combat readiness was only slightly smaller than its German counterpart (14,483 personnel compared to 17,734), but in practice most Soviet rifle divisions at the outbreak of hostilities contained only around 10,000 personnel, reflecting their peacetime authorised strength of 10,921 personnel. Although the bulk of the Red Army was organised into divisional units, the land forces also included 16 airborne brigades, five independent rifle brigades, an independent tank brigade and 57 Fortified Districts, the latter typically consisting of around 5,000 troops in relatively fixed positions and independent of the corps/army structure. Of the airborne brigades, one was in the Far East and the rest were organised into five airborne corps. In numerical terms an airborne corps was equivalent to a fully manned rifle division. Outside the army chain of command were a significant number of NKVD (internal security) divisions. These were responsible for border security, transport security and the protection of key

---

3   The term panzer corps is used throughout, though in fact until 21 June 1942 the correct designation for these corps was motorised corps.

4   The *Waffen SS* was but one branch of the *Schutzstaffel*, an organisation which, under the command of Heinrich Himmler, developed from Hitler's personal bodyguard to acquire primary responsibility for meeting the *Führer*'s ever increasing requirements in matters of security enforcement and the centralisation of power.

infrastructure assets. As the war progressed such divisions were increasingly used in a conventional combat role. A typical Soviet army structure is show in Appendix IV.

Almost all of the Soviet Union's 20 mechanised corps, typically composed of two tank divisions and a motorised rifle division, were in the 'Western theatre'. The mechanised corps were untried formations that had been created just a year earlier in response to the clear success of the German panzer corps concept. Yet the Soviet mechanised corps lacked the sophisticated command, communication and logistic support elements of their German counterparts. Additionally the Red Army suffered from a chronic shortage of trucks and the motorised rifle divisions generally had insufficient mechanised transport to be worthy of the 'motorised' designation. Equipment reliability and maintenance was also a key failing in the Soviet tank park where the operational reliability of the Soviet tanks could often be measured in hours rather than days or weeks. Of the multiplicity of Soviet tank types in June 1941, only the KV1 and T34 could battle the German panzers on better than equal terms. Both were new models, plagued with teething problems, and they constituted only a small proportion of the Red Army's 10,000-vehicle tank park. The BT tank was fast and had a good range, especially on metalled roads, and it was more than a match for the German light tanks, but it was relatively thin-skinned and vulnerable when faced with the German Mk IIIs and Mk IVs. Most of the rest of the Red Army's tank park was composed of the T26 light tank. Designed in the 1920s, as late as 1935 the T26 still had claim to being the best light tank in the world, but by 1941 it had become obsolete, slow and vulnerable compared to the competition. Another crucial weakness of the Soviet tank forces was the absence in most vehicles of radios and many of the vehicles that did have radios only had receivers without the ability to transmit.

Soviet divisions were relatively well provisioned with artillery. Each rifle division typically had fifteen four-gun batteries under its direct control and additional artillery support could be supplied at corps and army level. Artillery design ranged from 19th Century models to the relatively modern, but transport for most guns relied on horse power. Indirect fire control was also relatively unsophisticated in the Red Army, relying almost exclusively on field telephone systems. The artillery arm at the outbreak of war also suffered from shortages of some types of ammunition, the ammunition for the 45mm anti-tank gun, the army's standard anti-tank weapon, being in particularly short supply.

In 1940 the Soviet Union produced more than 10,000 aircraft but less than 100 were of 'modern' design; sixty-four Yak-1 fighters, twenty MiG-3 high altitude fighters and a couple of Pe-2 dive-bombers. Too much preference was given to the production of slow short-ranged bombers that had virtually no protection against fighters. However in the first half of 1941 the Soviet Union's production of aircraft of modern design had increased to 1,946 fighters, 458 Pe-2s and 249 Il-2 (*Shturmovik*) ground attack aircraft. Yet even the best of the new Soviet fighters, the Yak-1, was inferior to the standard German fighter of the time, the Me-109. Additionally, in comparison with the *Luftwaffe*, the command and control of the Soviet air force was somewhat diffuse. A significant number of fighters were controlled by the strategic air defence command, which was also responsible for the operation of anti-aircraft guns and barrage balloons. Control of most of the remaining aircraft was subordinated to individual army commanders or Front commanders of which there were 17 in the frontier areas of the Western theatre.

Soviet military strategy in the West envisaged the employment of three strategic layers or echelons from the Baltic to the Black Sea. The first and most westerly was the 'tactical echelon', consisting of ten frontier armies together with a few 'tactical reserve' armies deployed a couple of hundred kilometres back from the frontier. These armies were grouped within Special Military Districts that would be redesignated 'Fronts' on the outbreak of hostilities. A Front was the Red Army equivalent of an army group. Behind the tactical echelon would be six or seven armies of the operational reserve, the 'operational echelon' which could support the tactical echelon as required to grind down and weaken an opponent until the third echelon, the strategic reserve, could be mobilised and brought into play to totally destroy an enemy and drive deep into central Europe.

End of Illusion

The extent to which Soviet forces were surprised by the German attack has been a matter of some debate. Stalin was in denial over the imminence of a German attack almost until the eve of the opening barrage. He was certain that Hitler would not risk an attack against the Soviet Union until Germany had settled the conflict with Britain. For months he had been grasping at reports that suggested German troop movements near the frontier were designed to extort trade concessions from the Soviet Union, or were part of a plan to deceive the British over the *Wehrmacht*'s cross-channel invasion plans. At the same time he deprecated credible evidence in relation to the Barborossa plan and its timing, preferring to interpret it as a British plot to embroil the Soviet Union in conflict. Consequently the tactical echelon was placed under strict orders to avoid any action that could be interpreted by Germany as a provocation, and in consequence it was severely constrained in its ability to prepare for the onslaught. One mitigating factor in the Soviet uncertainty was the absence of a German offensive on 15 May, the day that Soviet intelligence reports suggested would be start date for an attack. Stalin had found this intelligence information sufficiently credible to authorise the raising of seven new armies from the internal Military Districts in order to create an operational echelon along the Dnieper and Dvina rivers. Over the subsequent five weeks there were other reports of imminent German attacks, all of which proved to be incorrect. With frontline commanders confused by the contradictions between the clear evidence of German preparations on the frontier, a series of false alarms, and the reassuring advice they were receiving from Moscow, at the end they were left surprised by the offensive they had been expecting.

If Stalin was unsure about when war would come, of one thing he was certain, when the fighting started all strategic operations would be controlled from the centre. For that purpose a High Command Headquarters was created on 23 June 1941. On 10 July this was transformed to the Supreme Command Headquarters and on 8 August Stalin became the Supreme Commander of the Red Army, and the Supreme Command Headquarters was renamed the Supreme High Command Headquarters. These strategic headquarters are generally referred to as STAVKA, an abbreviation of the Russian for general headquarters or general command staff (*stavka verkhovnogo glavnokomandovaniya*). Initially STAVKA consisted of seven members and was chaired by the Soviet Defence Commissar, Marshal S K Timoshenko. Other members included Stalin, Marshals Budenny and Voroshilov and General G K Zhukov. Zhukov was also Chief of the General Staff. His deputies were Lt-Gen N F Vatutin, head of the operations section and Lt-Gen F I Golikov head of military intelligence – the GRU. Also on Zhukov's staff were Col-Gen N N Voronov, an artillery specialist who at that time was head of the air defence command – the PVO, and Major-Gen A M Vasilevsky the head of the General Staff Directorate. STAVKA appointed thirteen permanent councillors, membership of which included Voronov, Vatutin, Marshal Shaposhnikov and Marshal Kulik.

2

Barbarossa

For the offensive against the Soviet Union, the *Wehrmacht* organised its ground forces into three army groups. These three army groups acquired the collective title of the Eastern Army or *Ostheer*. A detailed German order of battle is given in Appendix V, but can be summarised as follows:

Field Marshal Ritter von Leeb's Army Group North was composed of Col-Gen Georg von Kuechler's XVIII Army, Col-Gen Ernst Busch's XVI Army and Col-Gen Erich Hoepner's IV Pz Group. Hoepner had two panzer corps, XLI Pz Corps commanded by General Georg-Hans Reinhardt, and General Erich von Manstein's LVI Pz Corps. Army Group North's objective was to strike to the northeast from East Prussia through the Baltic States towards Leningrad.

Field Marshal Fedor von Bock's Army Group Centre was composed of Col-Gen Hermann Hoth's III Pz Group, IX Army commanded by Col-Gen Adolf Strauss, Field Marshal Hans Gunther von Kluge's IV Army, and Col-Gen Heinz Guderian's II Pz Group. Hoth had two panzer corps, XXXIX Pz Corps commanded by General Rudolf Schmidt, and General Adolf Kuntzen's LVII Pz Corps. Guderian had three panzer corps, General Heinrich von Vietinghoff's XLVI Pz Corps, General Joachim Lemelsen's XLVII Pz Corps, and General Geyr von Schweppenburg's XXIV Pz Corps. Army Group Centre's objective was to surround the Soviet armies in Western Belorussia and to strike to the east through Minsk to Smolensk.

Field Marshal Gerd von Rundstedt's Army Group South was composed of Field Marshal Walter von Reichenau's VI Army, Col-Gen Ewald von Kleist's I Pz Group, General Karl-Heinrich von Stuelpnagel's XVII Army and Col-Gen Eugen Ritter von Schobert's XI Army. Kleist had three panzer corps, General Eberhard von Mackensen's III Pz Corps, General Gustav von Wietersheim's XIV Pz Corps and General Werner Kempf's XLVIII Pz Corps. Army Group South's primary objective was to strike east and southeast from the Galicia region into the northern Ukraine to take Kiev and to secure bridgeheads over the middle Dnieper. On Rundstedt's right flank XI Army would strike east from Rumania across the rivers Prut, Dniester and Bug into the southern Ukraine to prevent an orderly withdrawal of Soviet forces across the lower Dnieper.

A detailed Soviet order of battle is given in Appendix VI but it can be summarised as follows:

Northwestern Front commanded by Col-Gen F I Kuznetsov faced Army Group North and the left flank of Army Group Centre. Northwestern Front was composed of Lt-Gen P P Sobennikov's 8 Army and Lt-Gen V I Morozov's 11 Army on the frontier and Major-Gen N E Berzarin's 27 Army north of Riga. To defend the Baltic States Kuznetsov had 369,000 personnel and 1,500 tanks in 19 rifle divisions, 4 tank divisions, 2 motorised rifle divisions and an airborne corps.

General D G Pavlov's Western Front faced the bulk of Army Group Centre. Western Front was composed of Lt-Gen V I Kuznetsov's 3 Army, Major-Gen K D

Golubev's 10 Army and Major-Gen A A Korobkov's 4 Army on the frontier with Col-Gen P M Filatov's 13 Army Headquarters near Minsk. In reserve Pavlov had a further four rifle corps and two mechanised corps. For the defence of Belorussia Pavlov had 671,000 personnel and 2,900 tanks in 25 rifle divisions, 12 tank divisions, 6 motorised rifle divisions, 2 cavalry divisions and an airborne corps.

Army Group South was opposed by Southwestern Front and 9 Separate Army. Southwestern Front was commanded by Col-Gen M P Kirponos and was composed of 5 Army commanded by Lt-Gen M I Potapov, 6 Army commanded by Lt-Gen I N Muzychenko, 26 Army commanded by Lt-Gen F I Kostenko and 12 Army commanded by Major-Gen P G Ponedelin. To defend the northern Ukraine and the Carpathians Kirponos had 26 rifle divisions, 6 mountain rifle divisions, 16 tank divisions, 8 motorised rifle divisions, 2 cavalry divisions and an airborne corps. Col-Gen Y T Cherevichenko's 9 Separate Army of 6 rifle divisions, a mountain rifle division, 4 tank divisions, 2 motorised rifle divisions and 2 cavalry divisions was formed from the Odessa Military District and was in position to defend the Odessa region along the Rumanian border. In the Ukraine the Red Army deployed in excess of 900,000 personnel with more than 5,000 tanks.

Hundreds of kilometres east of the frontier, the operational echelon was completing its deployment. It consisted of Major-Gen M F Lukin's 16 Army, Lt-Gen I S Konev's 19 Army, Lt-Gen F N Remezov's 20 Army, Lt-Gen V F Gerasimenko's 21 Army, Major-Gen F A Ershakov's 22 Army, Major-Gen K I Rakutin's 24 Army and Lt-Gen V I Kachalov's 28 Army, though the latter, raised from the Archangel Military District, had not deployed to its designated area on the Desna north of Bryansk by the outbreak of hostilities. In the north were Lt-Gen V A Frolov's 14 Army in the Murmansk area, Lt-Gen F D Gorolenko's 7 Army in Russian Karelia and Lt-Gen M N Gerasimov's 23 Army in the Karelian Isthmus.

On the eve of the conflict an order was issued for the formation of an additional army, designated 18 Army, based on the Kharkov Military District Headquarters staff. This army was assigned four corps from the existing forces of Southwestern Front and 9 Separate Army.

'The World Will Hold Its Breath'

The scale and significance of the German invasion of the Soviet Union dwarfed anything that had gone before. It was a clash of social systems, a clash of economic systems, a clash of cultures, and ultimately it was the cataclysmic clash between the pre-eminent emergent political ideologies of the age. In military terms it was a clash of titans in which Germany planned the elimination of Bolshevism in Europe, the destruction of the Red Army as an effective military force, and the occupation of European Russia and the Ukraine. Little wonder that Hitler was moved to predict that at the operation's commencement, "The world will hold its breath".

In the final planning for Barbarossa it was envisaged that once Army Group Centre had reached Smolensk, it would turn part of its mechanised force north to assist in the capture of Leningrad, and it would turn the bulk of its remaining mechanised forces south to outflank any attempt by the Red Army to make a stand on the middle Dnieper. The role of Army Group Centre was seen by all as the key to the campaign. Hoth's III Pz Group followed by IX Army, and Guderian's II Pz Group followed by

See Map 1

IV Army, were to strike deep into Belorussia north and south of the Białystok salient respectively, to meet near Minsk 300km behind the front. The southern flank of Army Group Centre was covered by 1st Cavalry Division, which was assigned the task of moving along the northern edge of the Pripet Marshes and guarding against a Soviet thrust from the south. These operations were designed to achieve the primary German objective of the destruction of the Soviet field armies west of the Dvina/Dnieper river barriers in order to avoid the risk of having to pursue powerful Soviet forces into the depths of Russia. Having achieved the destruction of the Soviet field armies, the primary objectives would be Kiev, Smolensk and Leningrad. The capture of Moscow was specifically identified as an objective for a second phase of operations once the first phase objectives had been achieved. Yet, from the first, many senior German commanders saw the capture of Moscow as the primary purpose of the invasion. The OKW/OKH plan for the attack on Russia, which had been submitted to Hitler on 17 December 1940, had included Moscow as one of the key objectives. To the surprise of the General Staff, Hitler's authorisation for Barbarossa (Directive 21), issued the next day, set only Leningrad as the key objective in the north, as its capture would deprive the Soviet Union of access to the Baltic Sea. To support the attack on Leningrad, the Finnish Army, acting independently, would attack south on both sides of Lake Ladoga. In the Arctic, an Army of Norway force[1] led by General Eduard Dietl was to attack out of northern Norway and Finland toward Murmansk to secure the nickel mines at Petsamo.

Advance planning for the maintenance of supplies to the advancing German armies was undertaken with meticulous care. From the start, German military planners recognised the potential difficulties of movement and supply into the depths of the Soviet Union. The whole of the Soviet Union had only 80,000 km of railway, all of broader gauge than the railways of Eastern Europe; only 65,000km of road was hard surfaced, and of the remaining 1.3 million kilometres of roads, more than 85% were little more than cart tracks. In any case, less than one-fifth of Army Group Centre's manpower was mechanised and the army would need to rely heavily on horses for mobility and supply.

However constrained the mobility of the German army may have been, that of its opponents was constrained even more tightly. Neat and carefully structured though the Soviet order of battle on the eve of Barbarossa may have been, within days it began to sink into confusion as Soviet divisions were decimated, engulfed or simply swept away by the German advance; and of all the factors that caused the Red Army such grief, lack of mobility was chief among them. Within weeks dozens of Soviet divisions had disappeared from the order of battle of the tactical echelon, and even the order of battle of the operational echelon started to become unrecognisable as forces were juggled around and newly-raised divisions from the strategic reserve were thrown into the mix to try to stem the German tide.

That tide began to flow on Sunday 22 June 1941. Soon after midnight of that day Stalin, faced with mounting evidence of German intentions, including the testimony of deserters from the German lines, approved the issuing of a warning to the frontier forces of the possibility of an imminent German attack. This warning continued to

---

1   Two German and one Finnish corps under OKW command – later designated XX Mountain Army after the introduction of a third German corps.

stress the need for Soviet forces not to be provoked into actions that might cause 'major complications'. As the warning was being received at the various Front commands, German aircraft were approaching the frontier at high altitude, and German Special Forces were beginning the process of securing intact the key bridges over the frontier rivers. At dawn German artillery began a devastating bombardment of Soviet forward positions while to the Soviet rear, airfields, communication hubs, fuel depots and ammunition dumps were obliterated by air strikes. The German action engendered a degree of operational and command paralysis in Western Front and Northwestern Front, a paralysis that was exacerbated by continued demands for restraint from Moscow. Kirponos was somewhat better prepared, having maintained close contact with the NKVD border guards who were in little doubt about what the Germans were planning. Kirponos was also better equipped to fight off the panzers than his colleagues to the north. Pre-war Soviet planning had assumed that any Soviet offensive to the west would take place from the Ukraine, and that any invasion of the Soviet Union from the west would most likely be targeted at the Ukraine. Consequently the bulk of the Soviet mechanised forces had been deployed in Southwestern Front, but to tackle them Rundstedt had been allocated only one-fifth of the panzers available to the *Ostheer*. While Army Group North and Army Group Centre made good progress in the opening hours and days of the offensive, progress by Army Group South was relatively slow. On the extreme southern flank there was little activity. Schobert's 175,000 strong XI Army did not possess any mechanised forces, and it faced the two mechanised corps of Cherevichenko's army. German strategy had been to delay the opening of the offensive by XI Army in the expectation that Cherevichenko's tank divisions would be diverted to the north to face I Pz Group.

Due to his experiences with Soviet tank forces in the Spanish Civil War, Pavlov was considered to be the Soviet Union's armoured warfare expert, and during the evening of 22 June he was ordered to counter-attack the invaders. A thrust against II Pz Group from the Kobrin area toward Brest by 14 Mech Corps was undertaken the next day. See Map 2 This was dispersed by continuous German air and artillery bombardment that prevented the divisions of 14 Mech Corps from being employed in a unified fashion. As a result, 4 Army was forced back along the northern edge of the Pripet Marshes, and divisions from the Front reserve had to be fed in piecemeal to plug the worst of the gaps. On Pavlov's right flank III Pz Group punched a gap into the boundary between Western Front and Northwestern Front. The advance of III Pz Group was greatly assisted by the capture intact of key bridges over the Neman in 11 Army's rear area on 23 June, and XXXIX Pz Corps reached Vilno that evening. Northwestern Front was experiencing the same difficulties as Western Front; communications up and down the chain of command were erratic at best; unrealistic orders were arriving at Front Headquarters from STAVKA and, with an eye to possible future courts-marshal, were being passed directly on to lower commands; and the speed of the German advance was preventing Soviet commanders from making a coordinated operational response. The confusion in the Soviet command structure might have been considerably worse had it not been for a short-wave radio net command headquarters in Leningrad that remained intact and proved invaluable in collecting reports from cut-off Red Army units.

Leeb's army group, the smallest of the three, had the shortest frontline, but had the farthest to go. From Leeb's centre, IV Pz Group hit the left flank of 8 Army from north of the Neman, and quickly broke through the Soviet frontier defences. Hoepner's instructions were clear: Advance as quickly as possible to Leningrad via Dvinsk, Pskov and Novgorod; flank protection to be provided by Busch and Kuechler. Only at Taurage on XLI Pz Corps' left flank did IV Pz Group encounter significant Soviet resistance on the first day. Advancing eastwards along the northern bank of the Neman, LVI Pz Corps threatened the right flank of 11 Army south of the river and then took a key viaduct at Ariogala on the Dubysa. Once across this northern tributary of the Neman, Manstein's panzers could threaten the 'fortress town' of Kovno 40km to the southeast. On 23 June Northwestern Front tried to concentrate its two mechanised corps against XLI Pz Corps' north-easterly advance along the Koenigsberg – Riga road. The result was a two-day tank battle during which 3 Mech Corps virtually ceased to exist. Mechanical breakdown and empty fuel tanks meant that, as in the Western Front area, scores of Soviet tanks were abandoned on the battlefield to be destroyed at leisure by German engineers, and the poor Soviet communication system meant that the actions of the tank divisions were never properly coordinated. With the panzers in Vilno and across the Dubysa, Morosov took the decision to pull 11 Army back from the frontier and to the north of Kovno, a decision that would effectively abandon the town to the Germans. By 24 June, elements of 8 Pz Div had reached Ukmerge on the Kovno – Dvinsk road. This, and the defeat of the two mechanised corps on the Riga road, meant that Northwestern Front could only abandon Lithuania and pull back to the Dvina in central Latvia in compliance with Timoshenko's order to establish a 'stubborn defence' along the river.

In the Army Group Centre zone, II Pz Group, advancing to the northeast along the northern fringes of the Pripet Marshes towards Baranovichi, had, by 24 June, cut off 4 Army from further direct retreat eastwards. On the same day a major armoured offensive by Pavlov's mechanised corps was conducted against the German penetration of Western Front's right flank. This offensive involved 11 Mech Corps and 6 Mech Corps in the area of Kuznica, and it hit XX Corps of IX Army. It caused some delay in the advance of IX Army and caused considerable consternation at OKH, but the offensive succumbed to a combination of effective German anti-tank defences, air attacks, poor Soviet armoured force coordination and wholly inadequate logistic support. As a result, forces in the Białystok salient found themselves threatened with encirclement by IX Army and IV Army, while the rest of Western Front was being threatened with a deeper encirclement by the two panzer groups advancing on Minsk from the northwest and the southwest. In response Pavlov assigned 21 Rifle Corps and 50 Rifle Div from Front reserves to Filatov's 13 Army Headquarters, and he ordered Filatov to gather retreating forces to defend the approaches to Minsk. To the north there was no longer any semblance of a frontline. Between 13 Army in the Minsk area, and 11 Army withdrawing northeast towards Dvinsk, there were virtually no Soviet forces. Furthermore a yawning gap was opening between 11 Army and 8 Army, the latter withdrawing north towards Riga.

The capture of Vilno by III Pz Group on 23 June seemed to Bock to open the way for the early capture of Vitebsk and the 'land bridge' to Moscow between the upper reaches of the Dvina and the Dnieper. Hoth, with the support of Bock and Guderian, wanted to push on to the east in a vast encircling move around Smolensk, but he was ordered by Field Marshal Brauchitsch at OKH to turn south to close the Minsk pocket from the north. Brauchitsch was swayed by Col-Gen Halder's opinions and, though Halder was as keen as the Army Group Centre commanders on the 'Moscow option', he was concerned about closing the Minsk pocket and supporting IX Army, which was becoming detached from III Pz Group with some Soviets units and their key equipment escaping through the gap. On 25 June Hitler forbade the conduct of armoured operations by Army Group Centre and Army Group South too far to the east without proper precautions being taken to secure the rearward areas. Halder's response to this was to placate Hitler and to remedy the serious difficulties facing IX Army by ordering a double envelopment; at Białystok by IX and IV Armies, and at Minsk by the two panzer groups. By 25 June II Pz Group had reached Baranovichi, while lead elements of III Pz Group reached the outskirts of Minsk the next day. In order to keep the option of a further deep thrust to the east open, Halder activated Col-Gen Maximilian Freiherr von Weichs' II Army Headquarters, which OKH had originally intended to keep in reserve until Smolensk had been reached. Halder planned to place most of IV Army's divisions under II Army, leaving IV Army, with VII Corps and IX Corps, to assume command responsibility for the two panzer groups. This process was not completed until 3 July when IV Army became temporarily Fourth Panzer Army. Kluge and Guderian disagreed both over the need to secure the Minsk pocket and the need to push farther east. Guderian, a favourite of Hitler's, was also highly resistant to attempts to remove any mechanised units from his command, and 'faulty reception' of transmitted orders on 2 July meant that 17 Pz Div, instead of moving west to help secure the Minsk pocket, was moved east to Borisov on the Berezina. This river had been reached at Bobruisk on 28 June by 3 Pz Div, prompting Hitler the next day to voice his concern to OKH that the wide-ranging panzer operations were endangering the success of the large encirclements, and prevailing on Brauchitsch to instruct Army Group Centre not to allow Guderian to advance beyond Bobruisk but rather have him hold the city "only for security". Halder, however, in possession of intelligence information that estimated the Red Army's residual strength in Belorussia and the Baltic States at just 26 divisions, hoped that Guderian would use any opportunity to move on and cross the Dnieper at Rogachev and Mogilev, thereby opening the way to Smolensk and the approach to Moscow.

The most coordinated Soviet response to the German offensive was that made by Southwestern Front where, between 23 June and 26 June, Kirponos attempted to implement a STAVKA Directive, issued late on 22 June, requiring the encirclement and destruction of German forces moving east towards Dubno and Lutsk. The main weight of the German offensive had fallen on the left flank of 5 Army, and Kirponos initially attempted to use 22 Mech Corps from 5 Army and 15 Mech Corps from 6 Army to counter-attack the flanks of the German penetration. An attack was mounted by 15 Mech Corps against XLVIII Pz Corps on 23 June but it was conducted by only part of one division and was totally ineffective. A more robust attack was mounted the next day but ran into effective anti-tank defences. Rundstedt was able to move an infantry division from VI Army's XLIV Corps into position to defend against further attacks from 15 Mech Corps while XLVIII Pz Corps continued to move on Dubno, the town falling to 11 Pz Div on 26 June. On 24 June 22 Mech Corps mounted a somewhat more effective attack against III Pz Corps on the northern flank of the German penetration. This attack, to the east of Vladimir-Volynsky, involved some

See Map 3

fierce fighting, but it resulted in heavy Soviet losses and it did not prevent III Pz Corps, reinforced with 13 Pz Div from Rundstedt's reserves, from pushing on to Lutsk and taking the town on 26 June.

By 26 June Kirponos was ready to launch a counter-offensive on a significantly larger scale. Reinforced by 19 Mech Corps from Southwestern Front's reserve, 5 Army's 9 Mech Corps attacked I Pz Group between Lutsk and Dubno while 15 Mech Corps, supported by 8 Mech Corps from 26 Army, attacked Kleist's right flank near Dubno. The powerful 4 Mech Corps from 6 Army was unable to contribute significantly to these offensives since its divisions had become widely dispersed in earlier stopgap defences. The attack on Kleist's right flank hit 57 Inf Div of Kempf's XLVIII Pz Corps and forced it back some 10km, but, in attempting to push on to Dubno, 8 Mech Corps ran into 16 Pz Div of XIV Pz Corps. During 27 June a combination of tank battles, air attacks and artillery fire halted any further advance by 8 Mech Corps, and the corps' structure began to lose cohesion. The accompanying attacks by 15 Mech Corps, conducted through difficult terrain and under concerted air attack, accomplished little. The offensive in 5 Army's sector against the spearhead of I Pz Group was opened by 19 Mech Corps on 26 June before the corps' motorised rifle division could reach the battlefield. The two Soviet tank divisions hit both 11 Pz Div and 13 Pz Div, but were pushed back towards Rovno. The next day 9 Mech Corps joined the offensive, but it too suffered heavy losses. Ordered on 28 June to resume the offensive, the corps commander Major-Gen K K Rokossovsky, having lost contact with 19 Mech Corps, decided instead to place his corps on the defensive to the west of Rovno. From these defensive positions 9 Mech Corps was able to ambush the lead elements of 13 Pz Div as they approached the town, and it inflicted heavy losses on the panzer division. After a further two days of steadily increasing German pressure, 9 Mech Corps was ordered to abandon Rovno and to withdraw to the east. To the south 8 Mech Corps had been surrounded and it was not until the beginning of July that the remnants of the corps were able to fight their way out to Soviet positions. As a consequence, Soviet forces lost Brody, which in turn rendered the defence of Lvov untenable and risked the possible encirclement of the frontier armies to the south. On 30 June, with XVII Army fighting its way into Lvov, STAVKA ordered the withdrawal of Southwestern Front to the 1939 border – the 'Stalin Line'. This withdrawal was far from uneventful. The Front's three southern armies were under constant threat of encirclement by Kleist's mechanised forces. Kirponos ordered a series of counter-attacks which had the effect of slowing the German advance, but by 7 July the 'Stalin Line' of fortifications south of Novograd-Volynsky had been breached, with 11 Pz Div reaching Berdichev, thereby forcing a wedge between 5 Army and 6 Army. By 9 July Rundstedt's forces had taken Berdichev, and had also taken Zhitomir and Novograd-Volynsky.

On 25 June STAVKA created a new Front in southern Ukraine. Designated Southern Front, it was commanded by Col-Gen I V Tyulenev and was composed of the newly-created 18 Army and Cherevichenko's 9 Army. On the creation of Southern Front, 9 Army lost its 'Separate' status, and 18 Army Headquarters acquired two rifle corps and a mechanised corps from Southwestern Front and a mechanised corps from 9 Army. Lt-Gen A K Smirnov was appointed to the command of this army. By early July the Rumanian contingent in XI Army had been increased. XI Corps received 1 Rum Pz Div and 6 Rum Inf Div; XXX Corps received 13 Rum Inf Div; XXX Corps lost 5

Rum Cav Bgd but this unit was combined with 6 Rum Cav Bgd to form the Rum Cav Corps under Schobert's command. Schobert also lost the Rumanian Mountain Corps to III Rum Army, which was positioned on XI Army's left flank. On Schobert's right flank IV Rum Army moved to the Prut while II Rum Corps moved into the Danube delta. On 2 July Southern Front was attacked along its entire length. III Rum Army was tasked with the reoccupation of Northern Bukovina; XI Corps moved on Mogilev-Podolsky, XXX Corps moved on Beltsy, LIV Corps attacked towards Dubossary, III Rum Corps attacked towards Kishinev, V Rum Corps attacked towards Bendery, while II Rum Corps attacked along the coast from the Danube delta. Tyulenev obtained permission to pull Southern Front back from the Prut. His intention had been to set up a new defence line on the Dniester but, in the event, he was able to achieve a temporary stabilisation of the front west of the Dniester.

By 28 June Guderian's forces had linked up with III Pz Group near Minsk, leaving large parts of 3, 10 and 13 Armies trapped in the Białystok, Volkovysk and Novogrudok pockets west of the city. During the next two nights large groups of Soviet forces tried to break out from the Slonin – Derechin areas. By 30 June the panzer forces had taken the Belorussian capital, but the German cordon on the eastern fringes of the encirclement was stretched thin in places, and autonomous armed groups of Soviet troops, predominantly from 4 Army and 13 Army, continued to filter east and southeast, occasionally making co-ordinated assaults on the attenuated German lines. Additionally, thousands of troops from 4 Army outside the encirclement were able to filter east through the northern fringes of the Pripet Marshes towards Soviet positions on the Dnieper. Some pockets of prolonged resistance remained in the German rear such as in the fortress of Brest where 3,500 Soviet defenders held out for several weeks, holding up a full German infantry division until the beginning of July. Nonetheless by the end of June three-quarters of Western Front was surrounded and the rest was in a parlous state of disarray.

In Latvia Hoepner's panzers, racing north from Lithuania, captured Dvinsk on 26 June and, over the next few days, secured several other viable bridgeheads over the Dvina before Northwestern Front was able to organise a viable defence. Dvinsk was a key communications hub over the Dvina and, despite attempts by Northwestern Front to retake the town with 5 Abn Corps, elements of 27 Army and 21 Mech Corps, the latter recently released from STAVKA reserve, the town remained under German control. To try to fill the gap between Northwestern Front and Western Front, STAVKA took the decision on 27 June to release 22 Army from operational reserve to defend the Dvina between Dvinsk and Vitebsk. Ershakov's 22 Army came under the operational control of Western Front on 29 June. This was just one of the seven armies of the operational echelon that had been almost completely invisible to German military intelligence prior to the launch of Barbarossa. On 1 July XVIII Army took Riga and the next day Hoepner's panzers broke out from their bridgeheads over the Dvina. Manstein's LVI Pz Corps advanced from Dvinsk towards Opochka, and XLI Pz Corps, from its bridgeheads at Jekabpils some 50km downriver from Dvinsk, advanced towards Ostrov. Manstein's forces failed to reach Opochka, difficult terrain rather than Soviet resistance being the main impediment. Permission was granted for Manstein to turn the bulk of his corps north towards Ostrov, the town having been taken by 1 Pz Div of Reinhardt's XLI Pz Corps on 4 July.

On 1 July Timoshenko was appointed to the command of Western Front and Marshal Shaposhnikov took over as Defence Commissar. Pavlov, who had been replaced by Lt-Gen A I Eremenko as commander of Western Front just two days earlier, was arrested and subsequently shot together with his chief of staff. In Northwestern Front, F I Kuznetsov, criticized for having failed to organise a credible defence anywhere, was also relieved, to be replaced by Sobennikov on 4 July; Lt-Gen F S Ivanov taking command of 8 Army. Vatutin was sent from STAVKA at the end of June to take over as Northwestern Front's chief of staff, his post as head of the General Staff Operations section being taken by Lt-Gen G K Malandin. With German mechanised forces in central Belorussia across the Berezina at Bobruisk, and about to cross at Borisov, Timoshenko's first tasks were to make some order out of the communications and administrative chaos at Front Headquarters, and to organise a credible defence on, or west of, the Dnieper. For the latter task 20 Army and 21 Army, already deployed on the Dnieper, were released from STAVKA reserve on 8 July and F I Kuznetsov was appointed to command 21 Army.

On 1 July Army Group Centre's two panzer groups were ordered to the Polotsk – Vitebsk – Orsha – Mogilev – Rogachev line. By 3 July Hoth's panzers, having raced 200km east from Vilno since the beginning of the month, had cleared the southern bank of the Dvina below Polotsk, and the next day they crossed the river at Disna, some 30km downriver from Polotsk. On 5 July, after having had some success in re-establishing a functioning Front Headquarters, Timoshenko ordered 20 Army to launch a counter-attack with 5 Mech Corps and 7 Mech Corps from north of Orsha and southwest of Vitebsk toward Senno and Lepel, a counter-attack to be supported by 2 Rifle Corps and 44 Rifle Corps attacking from the area east of Borisov. These attacks were launched on the morning of 6 July and were carried out by a total of nearly one thousand Soviet tanks. III Pz Group's 7 Pz Div bore the brunt of these assaults, along with 17 Pz Div on the northern flank of II Pz Group. While this fighting was in progress, 20 Pz Div crossed the Dvina on 7 July and began to move on Vitebsk.

Operational Echelon

By the second week of July the border battles were effectively over and the Soviet pre-war strategy was in ruins. Instead of being available to conduct powerful counter-strikes against the invader, the operational echelon was being employed piecemeal to act as the nation's primary defence in place of frontier armies that no longer existed. Golubev's 10 Army, entirely lost west of Minsk, was formally disbanded on 4 July; much of the headquarters staff of 3 Army escaped the encirclement but most of its combat units did not; the forces of 4 Army that had escaped encirclement were scattered from Brest to Rogachev and few were in communication with Army Headquarters. The three armies of Northwestern Front were still in the field and fighting, but the Front had lost ninety thousand troops and more than a thousand tanks.

On 8 July Halder was able to report that the counter-offensive by Western Front west of Orsha had been contained, and he presented to Hitler the latest, still over-optimistic, OKH estimates of residual Red Army strength. These estimates, and the speed of the *Ostheer*'s territorial gains, prompted Hitler to lay out his vision for the future conduct of the war. This included Army Group Centre employing pincer movements to break the last Soviet resistance north of the Pripet, thereby forcing the way open to Moscow; the destruction of Moscow and Leningrad from the air; a push to the Volga; and the construction of winter barracks. Yet, despite the successes and the nearly 290,000 Western Front personnel in German prison camps, the news from the front also held dark portents. Although, by 9 July 17 Pz Div had destroyed a hundred Soviet tanks coming from the direction of Orsha, losing few of their own, III Pz Group had nonetheless suffered heavy loss of life. This fighting also prompted a subsequent concentration of Soviet reserves at Velikie Luki where they were in a position to operate against either the north-eastern flank of III Pz Group or the south-eastern flank of IV Pz Group. To the south elements of II Pz Group had crossed the Dnieper near Rogachev on 4 July but were unable to maintain their bridgehead against determined opposition from 21 Army's 63 Rifle Corps. For all Halder's predictions of its imminent collapse, the Red Army was still organised and still fighting. In fact, in early July, STAVKA created five new armies from the strategic reserve. These armies, numbered 29 through 33, were formed predominantly from NKVD border guards and People's Militia from the Moscow region, though 29 Army was based on 30 Rifle Corps. German losses on the Eastern Front up to that point had been 92,000, more than a quarter of them fatalities; small by the standards of the Red Army's losses, but by no means insignificant.

On 10 July STAVKA appointed three commanders-in-chief of 'Direction' to co-ordinate the actions of the Fronts. Marshal Voroshilov was appointed to the Northern and Northwestern Fronts.[2] On 4 July, with the defence of the Baltic States in disarray, Northern Front had been ordered to prepare a precautionary defence line on the Luga between the Gulf of Narva and Lake Ilmen. The prospect of having to defend the southern approaches to Leningrad was the last thing Popov needed since, on 30 June, Finnish forces had crossed the frontier into territory lost to them in the Winter War. Timoshenko remained in command in the centre, and Eremenko, who had been acting as Timoshenko's deputy, resumed formal command of Western Front. In the south Marshal Budenny coordinated the actions of Southwestern Front and Southern Front. In practice these appointments served little purpose since the 'Direction' commanders had no reserves or forces of their own, and they simply added another layer of bureaucracy to the chain of command.

Despite the failure of 20 Army's offensive against III Pz Group, by 10 July Timoshenko had re-established the cohesion of Western Front, the units of which were along a line stretching from north of the Dvina to south of Gomel. On the extreme See Map 4 northern flank was 22 Army. This army, after having been heavily engaged with III Pz Group, occupied a 210km front from Idritsa to Drissa and along the Dvina. Slightly to the rear and to the south was 19 Army. This army had been brought by rail to the Rudnia – Demidov – Vitebsk area. As soon as they had detrained, its divisions had been thrown into an attack against III Pz Group in an attempt to hold Vitebsk, and in the process 19 Army had suffered heavy losses. Vitebsk fell to 20 Pz Div on 10 July but the attacks from 19 Army had delayed somewhat Hoth's subsequent push towards Orsha. In the area from Vitebsk to Orsha was 20 Army with fifteen divisions including the remnants of the two mechanised corps that had begun the ill-fated counter-offensive

---

2   Northern Front had been created on 24 June in anticipation of a declaration of war from Finland, a declaration that came the next day. The Front was commanded by Lt-Gen M M Popov and it controlled 14 Army, 7 Army and 23 Army.

in the Lepel – Orsha area on 6 July. Despite its losses, this army was in good shape and was well deployed, each division having not more than 12km of front to defend. Deployed in the city of Smolensk was 16 Army with just two rifle divisions that had been brought hurriedly north from the Ukraine. Southwest of Smolensk along the line Shklov – Mogilev – Stary Bykhov was Filatov's 13 Army, the condition of which was not good. Many of its troops had just managed to escape from the encirclement around Minsk, and its single mechanised corps had no tanks remaining. Behind 13 Army southeast of Smolensk, occupying the high ground around Elnia, was 24 Army. Rakutin's forces had had weeks to familiarise themselves with the terrain and were in position to offer a stout defence. Rakutin's neighbour to the south along the Desna was 28 Army. On the extreme southern wing of the Western Front, along the line Stary Bykhov – Rogachev – Rechitsa, and also around Gomel, was the powerful 21 Army that had been shielded from the west by the Pripet Marshes. With three rifle corps placed in two echelons, 21 Army held a 140km sector of the frontline. Also filtering east were strong elements of 4 Army that had escaped the Minsk encirclement and were retreating, often under fire, toward 13 Army and 21 Army.

On 10 July, as Timoshenko was adjusting to his new role, II Pz Group began to cross the Dnieper. Guderian was unable to cross at the most favourable points such as Zhlobin, Rogachev, Mogilev, and Orsha since these were heavily fortified, and he was obliged to make the crossings at Stary Bykhov to the north of Rogachev, and at Shklov and Kopys between Mogilev and Orsha in 13 Army's sector. Nonetheless Guderian was confident of success, and a few days earlier he had told his corps commanders to ignore the flanks and drive for Smolensk. Screening units were placed around the Soviet strong points and, in the early hours of 11 July, 29 Mot Div of XLVII Pz Corps crossed the river and headed straight for Smolensk. The river crossings had left Soviet forces at Mogilev and Orsha surrounded, and the crossing at Stary Bykhov by XXIV Pz Corps had opened a gap between 13 Army and 21 Army. In the 13 Army area Filatov was killed on 8 July. He was replaced briefly by Remezov (Lt-Gen P A Kurochkin assuming command of 20 Army), and later in the month Lt-Gen V F Gerasimenko was appointed to the command of 13 Army. After III Pz Corps had secured Vitebsk, Hoth ordered XXXIX Pz Corps to swing around Smolensk from the north through the line Lesno – Surazh – Usiavits toward the northeast, hoping that the heaviest enemy resistance would thus be skirted, but destroyed bridges and mines in the roads reduced the speed of the motorized units to that of the infantry.

On 12 July STAVKA ordered Timoshenko to prepare a defence of Mogilev and to launch a counter-attack from the direction of Gomel toward Bobruisk in order to hit the rearward areas of the advancing II Pz Group. By 12 July a significant concentration of Soviet forces had been achieved in the Gomel area, based on 21 Army, which posed a powerful threat to the flank of any further eastward movement by Army Group Centre. The counter-attack by 21 Army began on 13 July with a force of about twenty divisions, and it achieved some initial success by forcing the Dnieper, retaking Rogachev and Zhlobin, and pushing on toward Bobruisk against the southern flank of XXIV Pz Corps. At the same time III Pz Group's left flank came under pressure from Velikie Luki, and much of Halder's optimism of five days earlier began to evaporate after captured Soviet documents showed new armies being positioned east of Orsha and Vitebsk, and a column of Soviet infantry 100km long was observed marching north from Gomel. Yet the situation did not look so bad to Guderian and Hoth. Guderian shrugged off Schweppenburg's concerns about the threat to his corps' lines of communication, and lead elements of Hoth's XXXIX Pz Corps reached Demidov and Velizh. The next day, 14 July, 12 Pz Div of XXXIX Pz Corps reached Lesno and then turned in a more easterly direction toward Smolensk. Despite being checked near Rudnia after being hit by Soviet attacks from three sides, 12 Pz Div managed to hold fast to the Demidov highway northwest of Smolensk while Guderian's northerly XLVII Panzer Corps crowded up toward Orsha. This left a great conglomeration of Soviet troops more or less boxed in from three directions to the north and west of Smolensk. On 14 July a new 'Front of Reserve Armies', which included 24 Army at Elnia and 28 Army on the Desna, was created under Lt-Gen I A Bogdanov. Bogdanov's command also included four of the new armies from the strategic reserve, 29 Army, 30 Army, 31 Army and 32 Army. These new armies were in a parlous state and were held in the rear in the areas northwest and southwest of Moscow.

In the north Leeb's IV Pz Group, operating far in advance of the infantry divisions of XVIII Army and XVI Army, began to move north and northwest from Ostrov See Map 5 along the only two available roads. The terrain between Lake Peipus and Lake Ilmen was predominantly marsh and forest, constraining the ability of Hoepner's mobile forces to manoeuvre. OKH had made clear its preference for an advance on Leningrad by IV Pz Group via Novgorod, but on 7 July it approved Hoepner's proposal for a simultaneous advance towards Luga. Reinhardt's corps, advancing to the north, took Pskov on 8 July, but Manstein's corps, operating on the Novgorod axis, made only slow progress towards Porkhov. Hoepner therefore decided to concentrate his effort on the left wing, and to approve Reinhardt's proposal that XLI Pz Corps should advance directly north through weakly defended territory east of Lake Peipus towards the more suitable tank country of the lower Luga. Until 9 July the Luga line had been only weakly defended, but with the continuing advance of Army Group North from Pskov, Popov increased the defences to include six rifle divisions, two tank divisions and three divisions of People's Militia (DNOs). The latter, raised from the Leningrad populace and composed largely of enthusiastic volunteers, were poorly equipped and even more poorly trained, and few Red Army commanders had any illusions about their combat ability. Designated the Luga Operational Group, these Soviet forces were commanded by Popov's deputy, Lt-Gen K P Piadyshev, though in the defence of the approaches to the upper Luga forces of Northwestern Front were under Vatutin's direct command. By 14 July Reinhardt had established two bridgeheads over the Luga, at Sabsk and at Porietchye, but, at the end of an inadequate supply line and facing increasingly ferocious resistance from the Soviets' Luga defences, he would need time to accumulate the resources for a final thrust on Leningrad.

Yet time was a luxury that Reinhardt did not have. In the second half of July Leeb's priority was the army group's right wing, which was subjected to Soviet attacks from Luga to Nevel. Leeb was particularly concerned about the risk of a flank attack on the right of XVI Army from Soviet forces in the Velikie Luki area. XVI Army's II Corps had become involved in a battle near Nevel on the XVI Army / IX Army boundary and had become over-extended. Busch's two other corps were fully committed in the Novorzhev area. At Soltsy 8 Pz Div was surrounded for four days after a counter strike by 11 Army, and this required Hoepner to divert forces from Reinhardt's XLI Pz Corps on the Luga to restore the situation in Manstein's LVI Pz Corps sector. In response to the increasing Soviet pressure on his right, Leeb transferred I Corps and XXXVIII Corps from XVIII Army to Pskov and subordinated them to Hoepner; but in doing so he left XVIII Army only with sufficient strength to clear 8 Army from Estonia, a process that was to take until the end of August, and he weakened the ability of his army group to crush the Luga defences.

By 15 July lead elements of 29 Mot Div had reached Smolensk, and by the end of the next day had taken the city. Guderian then made a critical decision. He elected not to turn XLVI Pz Corps toward the area west of Yartsevo to link up with Hoth northwest of Smolensk and instead he aimed for the heights of Elnia 80km southeast of Smolensk. Determined to secure a springboard to Moscow, he forfeited the chance to forge a strong wall around the Smolensk pocket. Elnia was taken by 10 Pz Div on 19 July against fierce resistance from 24 Army, which was amply supported by artillery. That day Guderian ordered a halt to further eastward offensive operations, but he reinforced 10 Pz Div in what had become the Elnia salient with 2 SS Mot Div (*Das Reich*). With strong pressure exerted against Hoth's left wing from Velikie Luki; on Smolensk from both east and west, by 24 Army against XLVI Pz Corps in the Elnia salient; against XXIV Pz Corps by the remnants of 13 Army and 4 Army along the Sozh; and against II Army from 21 Army between Zhlobin and Bobruisk, Army Group Centre did not have the strength to both defend its perimeter and close the Smolensk pocket at Dorogobuzh. The consequent availability of an opening leading out of Smolensk to the east at Dorogobuzh saved the divisions of 20 Army and 16 Army from complete disaster. This was, however, a period of enormous confusion at STAVKA, with little accurate information emerging from the battlefront. On 20 July Stalin appointed himself Commander in Chief of the Red Army, and ordered all military units to "purge unreliable elements". Part of this order required commanders to detain escapees from German encirclements so that they could be interrogated by the NKVD. A degree of confusion was also evident in the German command system when Army Group North and Army Group Centre failed to coordinate their actions to capture potentially surrounded Soviet forces, which were in the process of retreating from XVI Army, from breaking out through the lines of LVII Pz Corps south of Velikie Lukie. Within Velikie Lukie 19 Pz Div was under considerable Soviet pressure, and on 20 July was ordered to abandon the town and to pull back to Nevel. Also by that date Western Front had formed five special groups under Lt-Gen S A Kalinin, Lt-Gen V I Kachalov, Lt-Gen I I Maslennikov, Major-Gen V A Khomenko and Rokossovsky, to mount a counter-offensive to encircle Smolensk and aid the trapped Soviet divisions west of the city.

On 21 July, the day German bombers attacked Moscow for the first time, infantry divisions of IX Corps began to relieve II Pz Group forces in the Elnia salient, and along Army Groups Centre's right flank east of the Dnieper at Propoisk, 10 Mot Div, under considerable pressure from Soviet forces on the Sohz, requested support from II Army's forces. Guderian's forces could do no more in the area south of Smolensk without reinforcement from II Army. Yet Weichs, his army still fending off attacks from 21 Army in the Zhlobin area, had few forces to spare.

Strategic Review

On 19 July Hitler issued a Directive, made in conformity with pre-invasion plans for when Smolensk had been taken, that required Army Group Centre to commit part of its mechanised forces to move north to assist Army Group North in its assault on Leningrad. The Directive also required most of the rest of Army Group Centre's mechanised forces to move south into the Ukraine in an attempt to encircle the forces of Southwestern Front east of the Dnieper. Any continued advance on Moscow was to be conducted with infantry formations only. Despite its spectacular success, by the fourth week of July the Barbarossa plan was beginning to unravel. In the Ukraine, Army Group South was only just beginning to achieve the sort of success that the other two army groups had experienced from the start. According to the Barbarossa timetable Leningrad should have been taken by 21 July, yet Army Group North was still battling against ferocious Soviet resistance in the Lake Ilmen area, and on 26 July Leeb formally reported to OKH the terrain difficulties that an approach to Leningrad from the south and west would encounter. In the centre the Barbarossa timetable had anticipated the capture of Moscow by 15 August. Yet this objective, still 300km distant, was beginning to seem unattainable. Timoshenko's counteroffensive against Smolensk was unleashed on 23 July with 28 Army striking from the Roslavl area, and 30 Army and 24 Army attempting to advance westwards from the area Belyi – Yartsevo. A large group under Rokossovsky, with armour, helped some units of 16 Army and 20 Army to break out across the Dnieper from south of Yartsevo. At the same time 17 Inf Div of XIII Corps arrived to assist 10 Mot Div at Propoisk, but the pressure from Soviet forces was so great that Guderian had to retain XXIV Pz Corps in the Propoisk – Cherikov area where it could prepare for a possible push on Roslavl, the capture of which would be necessary to secure his flank prior to any advance towards Moscow. By this time Halder had come to the conclusion that defeating Soviet armies by encirclement would not of itself lead to the rapid defeat of the Soviet Union, and that henceforth, German offensives should concentrate on defeating the Soviet Union economically. To this end he proposed to Hitler that II Pz Group and the infantry divisions of Fourth Panzer Army should push south to Kharkov, and then to the Volga/Caucasus while III Pz Group should combine with Army Group North for an offensive against Moscow. Hitler was sufficiently convinced to issue, on 23 July, an addendum to his Directive of 19 July that required Kleist's and Guderian's panzer forces to combine east of the Dnieper to capture the industrial region around Kharkov, and to then cross the Don into the Caucasus. After supporting Army Group North in the advance to Leningrad, III Pz Group would return to Army Group Centre to support an advance to the Volga, and VI Pz Group, after having been stripped of much of its equipment, would return to Germany.

In response to the extension of the length of Western Front's line, on 24 July a new Central Front, consisting of 21 Army and 13 Army, was formed under F I Kuznetsov; Lt-Gen M G Efremov taking command of 21 Army. Kuznetsov's new command was based on 4 Army Headquarters, 4 Army being formally disbanded on 26 July. Central Front's role was to protect the seam of Western Front and Southwestern Front in the Gomel area and the Sohz river sector as far as the area east of Mitslavl.

Despite the continued pressure on the flanks of Army Group Centre and on the Elnia salient, Bock was finally able to find the resources to close the Smolensk pocket on 27 July, Hoth's 20 Mot Div of XXXIX Pz Corps linking up with Guderian's XLVII Pz Corps. Yet the surrounded Soviet forces of 20 Army, 16 Army and part of 19 Army, all subordinated to Kurochkin's command, continued to escape, and the pressure on Bock's flanks did not diminish. LIII Corps of II Army was unable to cross the Dnieper due to the strong Soviet pressure in the Rogachev – Zhlobin area and on 28 July the corps was subjected to 14 hours of artillery bombardment west of Rogachev. On the same day, after taking over from XXIV Pz Corps in the Krichev bridgehead, the forces of II Army's XIII Corps were subjected to intense artillery bombarded and ferocious infantry attack. On 29 July Soviet forces assaulted almost the whole front of IX Army and, despite IX Army having been reinforced with XXIII Corps (two infantry divisions) from the OKH strategic reserve, the Soviet offensive achieved a breakthrough southwest of Belyi. Consequently, towards the end of July, the German High Command was faced with the tactical necessity of securing the flanks of Army Group Centre before contemplating any further advance to the east. Even Guderian, the most committed advocate of the 'forward to Moscow' school, acknowledged, despite his bombast to the contrary earlier in the month, that the Soviet forces on the flanks of Army Group Centre, at Velikie Luki in the north, and around Gomel in the south, had to be dealt with. Plan Barbarossa would need to be modified still further to deal with the threat to Army Group Centre's flanks from new Soviet armies that the *Wehrmacht* had never expected to encounter. On 30 July, with II Army forced to suspend its offensives over the Dnieper and the Sohz because of ammunition shortages, Hitler issued a new Directive to take account of the realities on the ground on the Moscow axis, and he also called a halt to the offensive against Murmansk by the Army of Norway that had begun on 29 June.[3] Bock's mechanised forces were to be given ten days to 'restore and refill their formations'. Consequently there would be a delay in any mechanised support from Army Group Centre to Army Group North in its advance on Leningrad. Army Group Centre was to go over to the defensive except for an offensive against Gomel, where Central Front still presented a major risk to Bock's right flank. West of the Dnieper, Central Front had been badly mauled by II Army during July, but had been reinforced on its left flank in the Pripet Marshes north of Mozyr with a revived 3 Army. Still under the command of V I Kuznetsov, 3 Army was composed of some units from the strategic reserve and other units that had emerged from the Army Group Centre pockets. Meanwhile in Moscow Zhukov had been digesting the information emanating from the front. It was clear to him that the eastward advance of Army Group Centre had stalled, and that the greatest strategic threat to Soviet forces lay in the Central Front sector where a push south by German mechanised forces could threaten Southwestern Front with encirclement. On 29 July Zhukov advised Stalin that any German advances against Moscow or Leningrad were unlikely to succeed, but that the Gomel area was the Red Army's key strategic weak spot. He recommended that Central Front should be reinforced with artillery and by an army from the strategic reserve, and that it be assigned two additional armies, one each from Western and Southwestern Fronts. Crucially, he also recommended that Soviet forces should be pulled back behind the Dnieper, and that Kiev should

---

3   Dietl's offensive had stalled on the Litsa, and a supporting offensive farther south had stalled east of Salla. In September Dietl renewed his attempt to advance on Murmansk but, after several weeks of abortive effort, finally abandoned the offensive.

be abandoned. To Stalin, who perceived the main risk to be from a renewed German offensive towards Moscow, this advice seemed both dangerous and defeatist, and the idea of abandoning Kiev was anathema. The next day Zhukov was dismissed as Chief of the General Staff to be replaced by Shaposhnikov. All Soviet forces facing Army Group Centre were ordered to undertake vigorous offensive action, and a new Reserve Front, based on 24 Army, 31 Army, 32 Army and 33 Army, was created from the Front of Reserve Armies, with orders to move into the Rzhev – Vyazma line to back up Western Front in the defence of the Moscow axis. At the end of July Timoshenko assumed direct command of Western Front, Eremenko becoming his deputy, and Lt-Gen V D Sokolovsky assumed nominal command of Western Direction. By this time 22 Army and 29 Army had begun to fortify a line from the upper reaches of the Lovat to Velikie Luki to Lake Dvina, a line that was to hold throughout August.

The Uman Pocket

By 4 July Rundstedt had decided to redirect his main effort into the southern Ukraine and had begun to restructure his forces accordingly. Only one of I Pz Group's panzer corps would be left to continue the advance on Kiev. The rest of Kleist's panzer group would turn to the south towards Kirovograd. The purpose of this redeployment was to try to cut in behind Southwestern Front west of the Dnieper and to encircle the bulk of Southwestern Front between I Pz Group and XI Army. VI Army was divided in two, one half to support the advance on Kiev, and the other to support Kleist's main effort.

See Map 3

Yet, with the loss of Berdichev to 11 Pz Div, and the advance of 13 Pz Div towards Zhitomir, at the end of the first week in July Kirponos and STAVKA were preoccupied with the defence of the approaches to Kiev. On 9 July Kirponos launched a major counter-offensive by 5 Army and 6 Army against the German penetration to the east. From Popotov's 5 Army, 9 Mech Corps, 19 Mech Corps and 22 Mech Corps, supported by 31 Rifle Corps, struck German forces in the area of Novograd-Volynsky. The objective was to cut off the German penetration to Zhitomir, and it involved a significant concentration of T34 tanks used to attack 13 Pz Div (with 25 Mot Div and 14 Pz Div in its wake). Despite intense Soviet efforts, Kleist's forces were able to hold open what had become the 'Zhitomir Corridor', and after four days of heavy fighting Soviet forces were unable to achieve any significant territorial gains. Muzychenko, under pressure on his left flank from XVII Army (which had been reinforced at the beginning of July with a Hungarian corps), was unable to coordinate the actions of 6 Army's mechanised forces with those of 5 Army. On 12 July Kirponos pulled Kostenko's 26 Army Headquarters out of the front line and divided 26 Army's forces between 6 Army and 12 Army. Kostenko was ordered to take command of all Soviet forces to the east and northeast of Belaia Tserkov, and to re-establish a link with 5 Army by mounting an offensive to the northwest.

Meanwhile Rundstedt, whose spearhead forces from 13 Pz Div had stalled on the river Irpen some 110km east of Zhitomir, had abandoned plans for an early capture of Kiev. Recognising that his left flank would remain potentially at risk from Potapov's mechanised forces, he turned his northern grouping to face north in order to deal with 5 Army, and he directed two corps from his southern grouping to attack Kostenko's forces. Kleist's main effort continued to be to the south, and it was not until 15 July, when German forces took Kazatin, that Kirponos recognised Rundstedt's intentions and the consequent potential risk to 12 Army and to much of 6 Army. Two days later, and without STAVKA's formal permission, he began to prepare plans for 6 Army and 12 Army to pull back to the Dnieper. On 18 July XI Army crossed the Dniester at Mogilev-Podolsky and at Soroki. The risk of encirclement of 6 Army, 12 Army and 18 Army was clear, and STAVKA ordered these armies to pull back to the line Belaia Tserkov – Gaisin, but before the withdrawal could be carried out, much of this fall-back position had already fallen into German hands.

On 21 July, with I Pz Group north of Uman, and XVII Army advancing in parallel on the right bank of the Bug, Kostenko was given revised orders; he was to turn 26 Army to the southwest to assist the withdrawal of 6 Army and 12 Army. Kostenko was able to present a significant threat to Kleist's left flank and Kleist was only able to spare XLVIII Pz Corps to continue the move to the south to attempt to link up with German forces approaching the Bug south of Vinnitsa. This link up was prevented by 2 Mech Corps, which had been moved north from the Southern Front area on 19 July. The virtually encircled forces were placed under Ponedelin's overall command and ordered to break out to the east to link up with 26 Army. Ponedelin had 130,000 men and nearly 400 tanks, but his supply lines to Southwestern Front had been cut and his exhausted troops were low on supplies. As Kleist reinforced XLVIII Pz Corps with two infantry divisions, Ponedelin broke off the breakout attempt and reported to Kirponos that his armies were experiencing an almost complete loss of combat capability.

On 25 July command of the two armies was transferred from Southwestern Front to Southern Front and Tyulenev, in compliance with instructions from STAVKA, ordered the forces to move to the Uman area and to try to break out to the east from there. This was despite the fact that there was a viable escape route for Ponedelin's forces to the southeast into 18 Army's area, an escape route that remained open until early August, but poor communication between the armies, the Fronts, Budenny's 'Southwestern Direction' Headquarters and STAVKA prevented the appropriate orders being issued for its use. By 2 August Ponedelin's forces were completely encircled when I Pz Group and XVII Army linked up near Pervomaisk. Several attempts were made over the subsequent five days to break out, but by 12 August, when fighting in the pocket had ceased, more than 100,000 prisoners, including Ponedelin and Muzychenko, were in German hands.

The Uman encirclement left STAVKA with no choice but to begin a withdrawal to the Dnieper. Orders to that effect were issued to Southern Front before the end of July, becoming known in Soviet circles as the Tiraspol – Melitopol Defensive Operation, and by 4 August the whole of Tyulenev's right wing between the Dnieper and the Bug was disintegrating. On 6 August Tyulenev signalled STAVKA, "The availability of Southern Front forces, due to losses and wear as a consequence of six days of operations, makes it quite out of the question for those lines – particularly at the junction with Southwestern Front at Kirov-Znamensk and Kremenchug – to be firmly held by our forces". In the Southwestern Front zone, 26 Army had pulled back to the Dnieper by the beginning of August. To try to plug the gap in Southwestern Front's lines created by the loss of the armies at Uman, 38 Army, based on 8 Mech Corps under Lt-Gen D I Riabyshev and all available units in the Cherkassy area, was activated on 4 August. Six days later, when 6 Army and 12 Army were formally disbanded, a new 37 Army under Major-Gen A A Vlasov was also activated. These armies were deployed on the Dnieper from Kiev to Kremenchug.

In the northern Ukraine fierce fighting continued through the second half of July and into August. Hitler was concerned about the threat that 5 Army presented to the left flank of Army Group South and, potentially, to the vulnerable deep right flank of Army Group Centre north of the Pripet. Rundstedt was continually urged to deal with this threat, and he used XVII Corps and LI Corps to try to defeat Potapov's forces between Kiev and Olevsk. Yet 5 Army, reinforced by 1 Abn Corps from Front reserves, was, by 4 August, able to launch an offensive of its own against VI Army. This offensive proved to be costly and achieved little, forward elements of VI Army reaching the outskirts of Kiev on 6 August. However Rundstedt was ordered to halt his offensive on Kiev and to turn Reichenau north to deal with 5 Army. Kiev was to be to left to the *Luftwaffe* for destruction from the air. On 8 August XVII Corps took Korosten, after which 5 Army began to withdraw towards Kiev. Two days later 5 Army had begun to reach the relative safety of the Kiev defences and German forces had reached the Dnieper south of the city.

The Approaches to Leningrad

By the end of July Finnish forces in Karelia had pushed 7 Army back some 50km down the eastern side of Lake Ladoga, and were advancing east towards Lake Onega. At that time the Finnish army began a major offensive against 23 Army in the Karelian Isthmus, the objective being to secure former Finnish territory to the 1939 border and, subsequently, to assist German forces in taking Leningrad. Towards the end of July 8 Army in Estonia was split into two by XVIII Army's attacks; 10 Rifle Corps withdrawing towards Tallinn, and the rest of the army pulling back towards Narva to be placed under Northern Front's command. In the Northwestern Front area, after the fighting around Soltsy had subsided, 11 Army and 27 Army withdrew to a line south of Lake Ilmen from Staraia Russa to Kholm. By 6 August the pursuing XVI Army had taken both towns, and Busch had a continuous front from Lake Ilmen to Velikie Luki. Yet the rate of advance of Leeb's forces had slowed considerably. From an average of nearly 30km per day in the advance from East Prussia to Pskov, it had fallen to nearly one-tenth of that in the subsequent advance to secure the Luga line and the region south of Lake Ilmen, and Leningrad, Leeb's ultimate objective, was still 100km away. Leeb planned to launch his final drive on the Soviet Union's second city on 10 August. At the northern end of the Luga Line near Kingisepp, XLI Pz Corps, supported by XXXVIII Corps, would attack along the most direct route to Leningrad. In the centre LVI Pz Corps would attack through Luga, while to the south I Corps and XXVIII Corps would attack along the north-western shore of Lake Ilmen towards Novgorod and Chudovo. South of Lake Ilmen, XVI Army would launch an offensive eastwards towards the Valdai hills. Busch's right flank XXIII Corps would be protected by III Pz Group which, after its pause for resupply, was scheduled to be transferred to Leeb's command.

See Map 5

That a final German push towards Leningrad was in prospect was not lost on Voroshilov, Vatutin or Popov. Under command of Major-Gen I I Pronin, 34 Army was made operational from the forces of the strategic reserve on 30 July, and by 8 August it had moved to the Staraia Russa sector of Northwestern Front between 11

Army and 27 Army. On 7 August another new Soviet army, 48 Army under command of Lt-Gen S D Akimov, was made operational and moved to Northwestern Front's right flank north of Lake Ilmen. Additionally, on 9 August, Krasnogvardeisk, 50km south of Leningrad, and Kingisepp were each reinforced by Northern Front with two divisions. To disrupt the German preparations, Vatutin was ordered to launch an offensive on both sides of Lake Ilmen with his four armies, his objective being to reach the Utorgosh – Soltsy – Dno line, and, in the process, envelop and destroy X Corps on XVI Army's left flank. This pre-emptive strike was scheduled for 12 August but was itself somewhat pre-empted by Leeb's offensive two days earlier. To the north XLI Pz Corps, which had been defending its Luga bridgeheads for more than three weeks, began its offensive on 8 August. After several days of intense effort, Reinhardt's forces broke through the Luga Operational Group's defences upriver from Kingisepp, and, on 11 August, cut the Kingisepp – Krasnogvardeisk railway.[4] From there XLI Pz Corps turned east towards Krasnogvardeisk, while XXXVIII Corps turned to the west to attack Kingisepp. Reinhardt's forces encountered stiff resistance on the approaches to Krasnogvardeisk, but the fall of Kingisepp on 12 August prompted the withdrawal of 8 Army's forces from Narva to the Luga, and Krasnogvardeisk was taken on 17 August.

Vatutin's plans for an offensive north of Lake Ilmen were disrupted by the advance of I Corps and XXVIII Corps towards Novgorod on 10 August, but his offensive south of Lake Ilmen went ahead as planned on 12 August. Two days later 34 Army had pushed 40km into the German lines, threatening both to envelop X Corps and to cut the supply lines to I Corps and XXVIII Corps farther north. In response, Leeb was obliged to divert the bulk of LVI Pz Corps south from Luga to deal with the threat, and the newly available XXXIX Pz Corps from III Pz Group was moved to Dno. As a consequence of diverting LVI Pz Corps to the Lake Ilmen area, Leeb weakened the German advance across the Luga, but north of the lake the advance of I Corps and XXVIII Corps towards Novgorod was able to continue. German forces reached Novgorod on 16 August and took Chudovo four days later. By the end of the third week of August the danger to German forces southwest of Lake Ilmen had been contained as Vatutin's offensive floundered in difficult terrain, and by 23 August, with much of 48 Army surrounded, Vatutin's personnel losses had risen to nearly 200,000 from an initial force of 327,000. The offensive by I Corps and XXVIII Corps isolated 48 Army from the rest of Northwestern Front prompting its reassignment to Northern Front on 23 August. This transfer was of marginal benefit to Popov since Akimov was at that time in command of little more than 6,000 men. At the same time Northern Front was divided into Karelian Front, commanded by Lt-Gen V A Frolov and comprising 14 Army and 7 Army, and Leningrad Front under Popov comprising 23 Army, 8 Army, the former Luga Operational Group forces and 48 Army. On 26 August STAVKA ordered the evacuation of Tallinn, bringing to an end the Red Army's defence of Estonia. Two days later Tallinn was abandoned, the Baltic Fleet withdrawing to Kronstadt. During the evacuation by sea of Soviet troops from Tallinn, many thousands were drowned when the majority of the evacuation ships were sunk by bombs and mines. By 25 August 11 Army and 34 Army had been

---

4   The original unitary Luga Operational Group was disbanded on 23 July and divided into several smaller operational groups to defend the upper, middle and lower Luga.

pushed back to the Lovat after suffering heavy losses. South of Luga the weakened LVI Pz Corps, reduced to just 3 Mot Div but supported by XVI Army's L Corps of one infantry division and 4 SS Mot Div (*Polizei*), took until 24 August to take the town. The next day, XXXIX Pz Corps, having joined I Corps and XXVIII Corps in the offensive north of Lake Ilmen, took Lyuban. From Lyuban Schmidt divided his corps into its three divisional units and simultaneously attacked towards Kirishi, Kolpino and Volkhov. By 29 August XXXIX Pz Corps had taken Kirishi and Tosno, and had reached Mga, but farther west the withdrawal of 8 Army from Estonia threatened the flank of XLI Pz Corps, and it took until the beginning of September before XXVI Corps and XXVIII Corps were able to push a much diminished 8 Army to the north and into a coastal strip based on Oranienbaum west of Leningrad.

Meanwhile III Pz Group's LVII Pz Corps was being used to support the advance of XVI Army's II Corps and XXIII Corps in their eastward offensive towards Valdai and Ostashkov, and at the end of August 19 Pz Div took Demyansk while 20 Pz Div supported II Corps in surrounding a large Soviet force west of Ostashkov. As a result of these reverses Sobennikov was sacked from command of Northwestern Front, and the Front was placed under the direct command of STAVKA.

On 27 August STAVKA abolished the Northwestern Direction command and appointed Voroshilov to command Leningrad Front. Two days earlier it had made 52 Army and 54 Army operational from the strategic reserve, and had assigned them to the Volkhov to prevent a possible link-up between German and Finnish forces, the latter continuing to push 7 Army back towards the Svir. By the end of August, with German forces on the Neva 16km southeast of Leningrad; much of the former Luga Operational Group surrounded south of Krasnogvardeisk; and the Finns along the 1939 border in the Karelian Isthmus 30km north of Leningrad, Popov's defences were in tatters. Leningrad Front reorganised its available forces in the south into two armies; the newly operational 55 Army commanded by Major-Gen I G Lazarov, and 42 Army, which, having been made operational on 4 August, was placed under the command of Ivanov and subsequently redeployed from Reserve Front. For the defence of the coastal sector west of the city, Popov had the remnants of 8 Army, Major-Gen V I Shcherbakov having taken over command from Ivanov. In the Karelian Isthmus 23 Army defended the northern flank against the Finns. On 4 September, as German heavy artillery began to shell the city, the Finnish Army renewed its offensive against 7 Army east of Lake Ladoga towards the Svir, where it expected to make contact with German forces coming from the southwest. On 8 September, after a week of heavy fighting, Schmidt's forces took Schlusselburg at the source of the Neva on Lake Ladoga thereby severing Leningrad's land connections with the Russian interior. On that day the *Luftwaffe* began heavy air raids against the city. The epic siege of Leningrad had begun.

From the Sohz to the Desna

After the Smolensk pocket had been nominally closed on 27 July, it was clear that the panzer corps of Kluge's Fourth Panzer Army would need to be withdrawn for a period of rest and re-supply before any further major offensives could be conducted. In fact Fourth Panzer Army was disbanded on 29 July; its component parts, IV Army, II Pz Group and III Pz Group, re-emerging as independent army formations. At that time,

See
Map 4

despite the furious ongoing Soviet attacks against Army Group Centre's perimeter, Guderian was ordered to prepare an offensive against Roslavl using the infantry divisions of VII Corps and IX Corps. Yet the infantry formations in Army Group Centre were also in need of rest and resupply. By the end of July the *Ostheer* had suffered 213,000 casualties, disproportionately borne by Army Group Centre, and had received less than a quarter of that number as replacements. In the Smolensk area Hoth's 7 Pz Div and 20 Pz Div were unable, due to intense Soviet artillery fire and some well dug-in KV1 heavy tanks, to eliminate Rokossovsky's river crossings around Yartsevo. This allowed Kurochkin's forces to continue to escape from the Smolensk encirclement. On 2 August German air reconnaissance reported to Army Group Centre that the Soviets had built a bridge on the eastern side of the pocket and that their troops were "streaming out to the east". More groups escaped over the subsequent few days after Rokossovsky's group forced open the Dnieper crossing at Solovev on 4 August. What was left of 16 Army, including its headquarters staff, joined Rokossovsky's group, which after 5 August took on the designation '16 Army', though effectively the original 16 Army was lost. Additionally 19 Army and 20 Army had been severely mauled, and by 5 August Army Group Centre had taken 100,000 Soviet prisoners in the area between Orsha and Smolensk.

On 3 August Zhukov took command of Reserve Front and prepared plans to increase the pressure being applied by 24 Army on German forces in what had become an embattled salient at Elnia, where German casualties had been mounting inexorably. On 6 August the newly-formed 42 Army, based on 50 Rifle Corps, was placed under Reserve Front's command and the next day the newly-formed 49 Army and 43 Army, the latter made operational at the end of July and based on 33 Rifle Corps, were also assigned to Zhukov.

By the beginning of August Guderian was ready to launch his offensive towards Roslavl. The initial move was undertaken by XXIV Pz Corps advancing southeast across the Sohz to attack Roslavl from the south and east, and the next day forward elements of IX Corps crossed the Desna near Bogdanovo to close in on Roslavl from the northeast. By 4 August Kachalov's operational group from 28 Army had become surrounded in the Roslavl area, and Roslavl itself fell to Guderian's forces two days later. On 8 August, despite a breakout by some of Kachalov's forces on 5 August, II Pz Group took 38,000 prisoners in the Roslavl pocket, and the remnants of 28 Army were broken up by Guderian's forces, Kachalov being killed at Starinka. Kachalov was denounced as a traitor by Lev Mekhlis, head of the Main Political Directorate of the Red Army, and 28 Army was formally disbanded on 10 August.

After taking Roslavl, Guderian wanted to push farther east to Vyazma, leaving II Army to deal with the Soviet forces in the Gomel area where, by 3 August, the resistance of 21 Army was beginning to crumble. However, such a move would have been contrary to Hitler's instructions of 30 July, instructions that by 6 August Army Group Centre had begun to carry out. Furthermore, II Army required assistance to stabilise its northern front along the Sohz. Weichs was fully stretched, and his army's reserves were down to one infantry regiment and a cavalry division. He also had to maintain XXXV Corps in the area southwest of the Berezina to protect Army Group Centre's right flank from a possible strike north by 5 Army from Mozyr. Guderian's II Pz Group was required to assist by taking Krichev, a task that was begun on 9 August

See
Map 6

by XXIV Pz Corps and 7 Inf Div of XIII Corps, but not finally accomplished until 14 August when a further 16,000 Soviet prisoners were taken. The fall of Krichev meant that 21 Army was under threat of being outflanked by a further German push on Gomel, and it prompted F I Kuznetsov to take the decision to abandon Gomel and Rogachev, and to retreat southeast towards Novozybkov after a strong rearguard had been left in Gomel.

Four of II Army's five corps were already engaged in an encircling move around Rogachev – Zhlobin. Zhlobin fell to LIII Corps on 14 August and the bridges over the Dnieper to the east of the town, though damaged, were taken in usable condition. XII Corps, moving east of the threatened encirclement, was turned to the west to prevent a breakout of Soviet forces from Rogachev. Rogachev was taken by II Army the next day and a sizable Soviet force, predominantly from 63 Rifle Corps, became trapped in the resultant pocket. After crossing the Dnieper, XIII Corps' southward push towards Gomel was halted temporarily by a counter-attack with tanks against 17 Inf Div, and XLIII Corps (also moving towards Gomel) was halted by an attack from a Soviet rifle division on 267 Inf Div, an attack that succeeded in pushing through German lines between Rudenka and Zavod. Furthermore, an attempt by XXIV Pz Corps to build on II Army's success to push rapidly on to Gomel from the east failed when 4 Pz Div ran into strong resistance at Kostiukovichi.

On the day that Zhlobin fell, STAVKA issued orders for a new Front, designated Bryansk Front, to be created based on a headquarters drawn from staff of the disbanded 20 Rifle Div and 25 Mech Corps. Its task would be to cover 230km of front from south of Roslavl to Novgorod-Severski between Reserve Front and Central Front, and in particular to fill the gap that was opening up between Reserve Front and Central Front by Guderian's advance to the south. Since this advance was dividing 13 Army from 21 Army, 13 Army, then under the command of Golubev, would be assigned to the new Front. Bryansk Front, under the command of Eremenko, became operational two days later on 16 August. In addition to the eight rifle divisions, two cavalry divisions, the airborne corps and the tank division of 13 Army, Eremenko would also have the newly-formed 50 Army commanded by Major-Gen M P Petrov, which was based on 2 Rifle Corps, and initially consisting of seven rifle divisions and a cavalry division. At that time the command of Central Front also changed. F I Kuznetsov was reassigned to command the newly-formed 51 Army in the Crimea. Eframov took command of the two remaining armies of Central Front and Major-Gen V N Gordov assumed command of 21 Army. As Eremenko was taking command of his new Front, 3 Pz Div captured the Mglin crossroads, and Guderian, under orders to contain the eastward withdrawal of 21 Army from Gomel, sent XXIV Pz Corps farther south through Unecha towards Starodub. The next day, 17 August, despite strong pressure on the western flank of XXIV Pz Corps, 10 Mot Div and 3 Pz Div broke through 13 Army's lines and cut the Gomel – Bryansk railway, placing the entire Bryansk Front, a Front that was barely formed, in a difficult position. These events prompted Budenny to notify STAVKA of his concerns for 5 Army, then northwest of Kiev, and he requested permission to pull 5 Army back to the Dnieper.

By 18 August 50,000 Soviet prisoners had been taken by II Army in the Zhlobin – Rogachev area. Advancing from the north behind Central Front, II Pz Group reached Starodub on 18 August, but the next day units of Lt-Gen Walter Model's 3 Pz Div at

Unecha were hit hard from the west and surrounded. As a result, forward elements of the division were required to reverse their course and head back to the north from Starodub. Yet the road from Mglin to Unecha remained blocked, and XXIV Pz Corps' advance was stalled for a further five days during which, part of XXIV Pz Corps had to be supplied by air.

On 18 August Zhukov, still a member of STAVKA despite his 'demotion' at the end of July, warned Stalin that II Pz Group was likely to move south against Southwestern Front rather than east against Moscow. The German goal, he asserted, would be to destroy Central Front and push to the region of Chernigov, Konotop and Priluki, and to hit Southwestern Front from the rear. After the fall of Kiev, German mobile units would be able to bypass the Bryansk forests and push on Moscow from the south and also, at the same time, strike toward the Donets Basin. Zhukov proposed that a powerful group be concentrated in the area Glukhov – Chernigov – Konotop in the northern Ukraine along the Desna and Seim rivers, which would be in a position to hit Guderian's eastern flank as his panzer group moved south. This additional force, he argued, should consist of a dozen rifle divisions and a thousand tanks. Stalin replied the next day, reassuring Zhukov that the creation of Bryansk Front and 'other measures' would guard against the potential threats to Kiev. Nonetheless on 19 August STAVKA approved Southwestern Front's request to pull back to the Dnieper, subject to 37 Army remaining on the west bank of the river to defend Kiev, and it ordered Kirponos to hold the line south from Loev and to cover the Chernigov – Konotop – Kharkov approach. The approval for a withdrawal was of particular significance to 5 Army where the imminent loss of Gomel rendered its position around Mozyr untenable.

As 21 Army and 3 Army pulled back to the southeast, Gomel fell to XIII Corps on 20 August after heavy street fighting with 21 Army's rearguard, but the rearguard ensured that the last of the Sohz bridges was blown before German forces could secure them. As Efremov attempted to comply with his instructions to pull back 3 Army and 21 Army, and to secure the junction of his Central Front with Bryansk Front, Bryansk Front was given the additional task of planning the destruction of II Pz Group, and Southwestern Front was ordered to create a new army along the Desna near Novgorod-Severski between 21 Army and 13 Army.

On 21 August 5 Army, which had been withdrawing steadily eastwards since the fall of Korosten on 8 August, began to retreat east from Mozyr in what Potapov had planned would a four-day phased withdrawal towards the Dnieper. This withdrawal came as a great relief to the German High Command, since the presence of a significant Soviet force in the deep flank of both Army Group Centre and Army Group South had been causing concern. Weichs had been required to commit XXXV Corps to an offensive north of Mozyr, and the withdrawal of 5 Army eased the pressure on both Bock and Rundstedt. Despite Popatov's planning, on 24 August mistakes by 27 Rifle Corps on the right flank of 37 Army enabled LI Corps to secure a viable bridgehead over the Dnieper at Okuninovo that compromised 5 Army's proposed defences.

On 24 August Guderian was ready to renew his offensive south from Starodub. Eremenko and STAVKA, waiting for the blow to fall on Bryansk Front's northern flank, were surprised when II Pz Group hit the left flank of 50 Army at Pochep instead. Leaving one corps to cover his left flank against Bryansk Front, the next day Guderian turned the rest of II Pz Group south. At the same time II Army began an offensive south towards Chernigov. Yet Stalin remained convinced that any movement south by II Pz Group would be in preparation for a thrust through Bryansk to Moscow. In any case, Stalin argued, if II Pz Group continued to the south instead of the east, Bryansk Front could attack its left flank instead of its right. Neither Zhukov nor Budenny believed Kiev could be held if II Pz Group continued its march to the south but, for better or worse, Stalin insisted that Southwestern Front do everything it could to defend the central Ukraine. On 25 August Central Front was disbanded, and the forces remaining in 3 Army and 21 Army were combined under 21 Army, placed under the command of V I Kuznetsov, and assigned to Bryansk Front. The headquarters of 3 Army were moved northeast to the right flank of 13 Army where, under Major-Gen I G Kreizer's command, it began to re-form from forces from the reserve.

On 25 August STAVKA ordered an intensification of the Soviet offensives along the entirety of Army Group Centre's front in order to tie down Bock's forces and so prevent any further move south towards the Desna. At this time the armies of Western Front stretched from Toropets to Yartsevo and consisted of 22 Army, 29 Army under Maslennikov, 30 Army under Khomenko, together with the battered but still extant 16 Army, 19 Army and 20 Army east of Smolensk. During the last week of August and the first week of September these forces engaged in furious battles with the left flank of Army Group Centre, specifically III Pz Group and IX Army. Losses on both sides were high, but for Timoshenko's forces particularly so, and for a time 22 Army, after an audacious advance by 19 Pz Div, was surrounded near Velikie-Luki. The town fell to German forces on 26 August and 34,000 Soviet troops were taken prisoner. On 22 August IV Army formally took command of XX Corps and IX Corps in the Elnia salient and of VII Corps on the upper-Desna front to the south. Five days later Kluge visited the salient and unsuccessfully recommended to Bock that the positions be given up due to the high losses being incurred in ground unfavourable to defence. Just three days later, on 30 August, a reinforced 24 Army renewed its attacks against IV Army's positions around Elnia in an offensive that had been carefully planned by Zhukov and Rakutin. It was coordinated with action on other sectors of the front, and it made use of combined arms assault groups that attempted to encircle the German forces in the eastern extremity of the salient. Rakutin's forces took the town of Elnia on 6 September, drove IV Army back across the Desna, and by 8 September reached the Ustrom and the Striana where they were stopped by prepared German defences. During a subsequent inspection of the Elnia battlefield, Zhukov was impressed with the devastation of German defensive positions caused by the new *Katyusha* rocket artillery. The offensive towards Roslavl, conducted by Lt-Gen P A Kuznetsov's 43 Army on Rakutin's left flank, was less successful, despite its actions being coordinated with an offensive by Bryansk Front's 50 Army northwest towards Zhukovka. As in the Western Front fighting, Zhukov's forces suffered heavy casualties and at the beginning of the second week in September both Western Front and Reserve Front were ordered to end their offensives. From 10 July to 10 September Western Front lost nearly 470,000 of 579,400 troops initially engaged, while Reserve and Central Fronts lost an additional 210,000.

On 26 August the new army required by STAVKA in the Southwestern Front area was formed. Designated 40 Army, and commanded by Major-Gen K P Podlas, it was based on 27 Rifle Corps and units first brought to the Kiev area during the previous two weeks, and initially it comprised just two rifle divisions and an airborne corps. With this, Podlas was required to block, along a defence line that ran from north of Bakhmach and Konotop to Shostka and from there along the Desna to Stepanovki, the two panzer divisions, two motorised divisions and cavalry division that constituted Guderian's vanguard. Forward elements of II Pz Group approached Shostka and Korop on 26 August after succeeding in establishing a bridgehead over the Desna south of Novgorod-Severski. This crossing threatened 40 Army before it had fully formed and it continued to divide 21 Army from 13 Army. The next day, while STAVKA issued orders to Eremenko to "destroy the enemy in Starodub and close up 21 Army's and 13 Army's flanks", V I Kuznetsov ordered a continuation of the retreat of his 21 Army across the Desna in order to avoid encirclement. Yet he failed to advise Podlas on his right and, as a result, 40 Army was unable to mount an early counter-attack from Konotop against the German bridgehead. In consequence 40 Army was forced to retreat to the southeast on 28 August, and most of Kuznetsov's command found itself cut off from the rest of Bryansk Front. Meanwhile 5 Army, in withdrawing across the Dnieper and trying to establish defences on the east bank of the river from Loev to Okuninovo, failed to use its right flank to defend the approaches to Chernigov from the northwest.

On the southern flank of Bryansk Front, 13 Army was under constant pressure from XLVII Pz Corps, and by 28 August was still struggling to form a line from Pochep to south of Starodub and then along the Sudost. In desperation STAVKA ordered Eremenko to conduct continuous air attacks to try to stop Guderian's move to the south. The air attacks continued until 4 September without significant success. Success was also lacking on the ground. By the end of August up to 300 tanks had been engaged in fighting near Trubchevsk alone, but 13 Army had been so badly mauled by XLVII Pz Corps that it was forced to pull back behind the Desna. Eremenko, frustrated with Golubev's performance, replaced him at the end of August with Major-Gen A M Gorodniansky who, until that time, had only commanded a division. Stalin, frustrated with Eremenko's performance, could only urge him to greater efforts.

The Kiev Encirclement

Towards the end of August as Southern Front and the left flank of Southwestern Front completed their planned withdrawal to the Dnieper, Rundstedt's forces closed up to the river along most of its length through the Ukraine. Opposing him Rundstedt faced 9 Army and 18 Army from the Black Sea coast to the bend of the Dnieper south of Zaporozhye. Covering the Zaporozhye area was 12 Army, reconstituted from reserves on 25 August and commanded by Major-Gen I V Galanin. Defending the Dnepropetrovsk sector was 6 Army, also reconstituted on 25 August and commanded by Major-Gen R I Malinovsky. The Kremenchug sector was covered by 38 Army, 26 Army protected the area between 38 Army and the southern approaches to Kiev, while 37 Army covered the Kiev sector. Formidable though the Dnieper may have been as a natural barrier, Rundstedt was well aware that if it could be breached, particularly north of its great bend between Zaporozhye and Kremenchug, then any subsequent offensive to the north could compromise the Soviet defence of the north-eastern Ukraine and, if a link up with the continued push to the south by II Pz Group could be effected as planned, had the potential to ensnare the whole of Southwestern Front. Consequently

Rundstedt urged his forces to make every effort to establish viable bridgeheads on the Dnieper's left bank. On Rundstedt's right wing Schobert's forces needed no urging. Tyulenev and Cherevichenko had botched the retreat to the Dnieper in the Kherson area, and elements of XI Army made a successful crossing of the river on 22 August against virtually no opposition. Schobert began to expand his hold on the left bank and pushed towards the Sea of Azov, threatening to isolate Soviet forces in the Crimea, and on 30 August, after Tyulenev was wounded, Riabyshev was appointed to command Southern Front. On 31 August in the XVII Army zone elements of LII Corps established a viable bridgehead across the Dnieper at Derievka 30km southeast of Kremenchug. Stuelpnagel acted quickly to reinforce and enlarge this lodgement, and within days the bulk of LII Corps' infantry division and two light divisions were across. By 10 September half of XVII Army was within the bridgehead, and elements of Kleist's I Pz Group began to join them the next day.

By early September Stalin's certainty that Guderian's offensive was ultimately aimed at Moscow was starting to wane. On 31 August Major-Gen N V Feklenko, the new commander of 38 Army, reported the crossing of the Dnieper by XVII Army. If Guderian continued to move south, the three-quarters of a million men in Southwestern Front together with its 100,000 reserves were clearly at risk. Feklenko was ordered to eliminate the German bridgehead and, with Stalin's admonishment for the failure to retake Pochep and Starodub still ringing in his ears, Eremenko tried again to stop Guderian. Between 2 September and 12 September Bryansk Front launched a series of counter-attacks against Guderian's eastern flank. The initial attacks, at STAVKA's insistence, were by 50 Army and 3 Army toward Roslavl with the help of four rifle divisions from Zhukov's Reserve Front to the north. Simultaneously 21 Army and 13 Army attempted to converge on Semenovka to encircle and destroy the main force of II Pz Group in the Pochep – Starodub – Novgorod-Severski region, and a Front Mobile Group of 108 Tank Div, 141 Tank Bgd and 4 Cav Div commanded by Eremenko's deputy, Major-Gen A N Ermakov, was to advance through Pogar to Novgorod-Severski. By the evening of 2 September 108 Tank Div was half-encircled and the next day II Pz Group seized bridgeheads over the Desna at Korop and Novgorod-Severski. On 5 September Eremenko requested permission to form "blocking detachments" – rear formations authorised to fire on Soviet forces retreating without orders.

Bad though the situation for Soviet forces in Bryansk Front may have been, they were potentially much worse for those on the right flank of Southwestern Front. By the beginning of September Kirponos had recognised the vulnerability of Chernigov on 5 Army's right flank, and ordered Potapov to defend the town. Potapov attempted to comply, but only parts of 15 Rifle Corps were available for the task. The next day, 2 September, STAVKA ordered Budenny to secure Chernigov but Budenny had no resources available. On 3 September Major-Gen K S Moskalenko was given command of 15 Rifle Corps with the task of defending 5 Army's right flank on the Desna, but that day II Army captured a bridgehead over the river east of the town. This threatened to separate 5 Army from 21 Army and on 4 September Budenny formally reported a grave threat to his flanks. By this time 21 Army, still part of Bryansk Front, found itself fighting between 5 Army and 40 Army, both under the command of Southwestern Front. This anomalous situation was resolved on 6 September when 21 Army was transferred to Southwestern Front. On that date 21 Army was ordered to stop retreating and to attack the lines of communication of II Pz Group from the west. These attacks were unsuccessful, not least because Bryansk Front was unable to support 21 Army's attack by mounting a simultaneous attack from the east. By 7 September II Pz Group had crossed the Seim, had reached Konotop, and was preparing to drive towards Romny. This put 40 Army in a desperate position in the Konotop area, and left 21 Army trapped between II Army and Guderian's panzers. For V I Kuznetsov's army, continued retreat to the south was its only means of escape, and by that time 5 Army was also almost surrounded, Chernigov falling to II Army on 8 September.

During the second week in September Stalin shuffled his senior Red Army commanders. With the offensives by Western Front and Reserve Front coming to an end, Zhukov was sent north to end Voroshilov's brief tenure as commander of Leningrad Front. Timoshenko replaced Budenny as commander of the Southwestern Direction, Konev assumed command of Western Front, and Budenny took command of Reserve Front. At STAVKA, Vasilevsky had taken over from Malandin on 25 August as Deputy Chief of the General Staff responsible for the Operations Department.

As Zhukov was preparing to take his leave for Leningrad on 8 September, Stalin queried him about what he thought the Germans would do next. Zhukov replied that he expected Army Group South to strike out from its Dnieper bridgehead near Kremenchug to link up with II Pz Group, and he again advised Stalin to abandon Kiev and deploy all available reserves in the Konotop area for use against Guderian. Yet Stalin was still reluctant to abandon Kiev. He was determined that the Ukrainian capital should not be given up without a fight, and was concerned that a retreat by Southwestern Front would turn into a rout. The next day STAVKA conceded that the right wing of 37 Army defending Kiev must be withdrawn to the eastern bank of the Dnieper, and that it should combine with 5 Army to turn their fronts to face the direct threat from the north.

By 11 September 3 Pz Div, XXIV Pz Corps' lead division, had reached Romny, and only 170km separated Army Group Centre from Army Group South. At the same time a 60km gap had opened up between Bryansk Front and Southwestern Front. The next day Major-Gen Hans-Valentin Hube's 16 Pz Div broke out of the left flank of Army Group South's Kremenchug bridgehead. For nearly two weeks Feklenko had tried in vain to contain and eliminate the bridgehead, but it had expanded to a depth of 25km and a breadth of 50km. During the first day of its breakout 16 Pz Div advanced 20km to the north. The next day it raced farther north to Lubna where it was stopped by determined Soviet resistance. However, on 13 September Hube's division was joined by 14 Pz Div on the left flank and 9 Pz Div on the right. In the II Pz Group sector, 3 Pz Div advanced a further 40km south on 13 September to approach Lokhvitsa. As 14 September dawned, just 40km separated the two panzer groups, but still Kirponos was being denied permission to withdraw. Nonetheless a significant portion of 21 Army was able to escape eastwards through gaps in II Pz Group's lines between Priluki and Piriatin. On 16 September Kleist's forces pushed farther north to make contact with 3 Pz Div near Lokhvitsa, trapping 26 Army, 37 Army, 5 Army, part of 21 Army and part of 38 Army. Only then did Timoshenko give verbal permission, made without STAVKA authorisation, for a withdrawal of Southwestern Front from the Dnieper to the Psel. Kirponos was reluctant to act on verbal orders when STAVKA had been so insistent on the continued defence of Kiev, and he insisted on receiving the orders in writing before he would act. This Timoshenko was not able to procure until the early hours of 18 September. By then it was too late. Although the German trap was not closed tight, during the third week of September just a handful of panzer divisions were available to secure more than 100km of the eastern edge of the encirclement, the relatively immobile Soviet forces on the Dnieper were already 200km from safety. Over the next few days the encirclement of Southwestern Front tightened and simultaneously German forces pushed the frontline farther to the east; in the north a panzer corps from II Pz Group moved east from the Belopolie area; farther south 10 Mot Div and 4 Pz Div from XXIV Pz Corps advanced eastwards towards Sumy; and 14 Pz Div and 16 Pz Div from I Pz Group advanced east from Mirgorod. Still farther south LII Corps and XLIV Corps from XVII Army broke out of the Kremenchug bridgehead to advance east and northeast towards Poltava. The encirclement of Southwestern Front was tightened by VI Army, II Army and XI Corps of XVII Army, while 3 Pz Div and 9 Pz Div covered the encirclement's eastern extremity. Some 450,000 Southwestern Front personnel were trapped in the final encirclement. Kirponos was killed on 21 September and Potapov was captured. Of the trapped Soviet armies, 5 Army, 26 Army and 37 Army were formally disbanded on 25 September, and organised Soviet resistance within the encirclement ended the next day. Thereafter Soviet forces in the encirclement broke into small groups and tried to escape to the east. By the end of the month only around 15,000, mainly from 5 Army and 21 Army had done so, but they included Timoshenko, Kostenko, Vlasov, Moskalenko and also V I Kuznetsov with most of his 21 Army Headquarters staff. In the battle for Kiev, Southwestern Front lost in excess of 600,000 personnel killed, missing or taken prisoner, and German commanders could claim the greatest battlefield victory in history.

By the end of September the Red Army had lost in excess of 2.1 million personnel, of whom 430,000 were fatalities and the rest were taken prisoner or missing. A further 688,000 were wounded sufficiently badly to require hospitalisation. In all, this represented more than half the pre-war strength of the Soviet armed forces. Comparable German losses were 551,000 killed, missing and wounded.

3

Ebb Tide

During the last week of July 1941 Halder had concluded that German offensives in the East should be geared to economic rather military objectives, and he had persuaded Hitler to that view. Yet Halder had maintained throughout that Moscow was a key economic as well as a political objective in the war against the Soviet Union, and despite the diversion of most of Army Group Centre's mechanised forces to north and south through most of August, he never lost sight of Moscow as a key target. On 7 August he convinced Jodl, who had considerable influence with Hitler, that Moscow should remain a primary objective in combat operations into the autumn. The next day OKH assessed Red Army strength facing the *Ostheer* at 143 divisions. This figure, despite the Red Army's horrendous losses during July, was nearly twice that estimated by OKH just one month earlier. On 11 August an OKH report acknowledged that, though Soviet forces were badly armed and led, the Soviet strategic preparation had been good and the military strength of the Soviet economy had been underestimated. This confirmed Halder's view that the *Ostheer* should concentrate on economic targets. Yet it did not diminish his enthusiasm for a strategic offensive against Moscow, which he envisaged could be conducted simultaneously with the offensive into the Ukraine. His views were expressed in a formal OKH proposal that argued in favour of a Moscow offensive as a priority target for early September as soon as the Gomel and Velikie Luki flanks had been dealt with. Yet this proposal quickly received a series of blows. On 21 August Hitler ordered XXXIX Pz Corps from Hoth's III Pz Group to remain in Army Group North's sector to assist in the attack on Leningrad, and he ordered II Army to join II Pz Group in a deep thrust south into central Ukraine. The next day, on advice from Jodl and Hermann Goering,[1] he rejected OKH's proposals for a limited strengthening of Army Group Centre's flanks before a resumption of the Moscow offensive. Halder's proposal would have required the dismemberment of II Pz Group, something that Guderian convinced Hitler on 23 August would be unwise. Since the whole of II Pz Group was committed to an offensive to the south, and only one panzer corps was left on the Moscow axis, there could be no possibility of a Moscow offensive in September. Despite Halder's lobbying, Hitler was content that, as envisaged in the original Barbarossa plan, Kiev, not Moscow, must be the next strategic goal.

Yet Halder did not give up. He argued that if an offensive against Moscow could not be mounted in September, preparations should be made to launch the offensive as soon as the Soviet defences on the Dnieper had been breached. Instead of IV Pz Group being returned to Germany, it should be moved to Army Group Centre where it should join with III Pz Group for a final offensive on the Moscow axis before the onset of winter. By 5 September Hitler had come to agree, having concluded that the Soviet Union could not be beaten unless Moscow was taken. The next day, with the

---

1   Goering, with the unique rank of *Reichsmarschall*, was Hitler's deputy and head of the *Luftwaffe*.

threats to Army Group Centre's flanks seemingly satisfactorily resolved but with the offensives by Western Front and Reserve Front still raging, Hitler issued a new and wide-ranging Directive. It called for the capture of Leningrad, a link up with Finnish forces east of Lake Ladoga, the capture of Kiev, Kharkov and the Crimea, and, crucially, it required Army Group Centre to, "go on the offensive in the general direction of Vyazma and to destroy the enemy located in the region east of Smolensk by a double envelopment employing powerful panzer forces concentrated on the flanks." Ten days later Bock, designating the operation 'Typhoon', modified the plan to include a third thrust, this time by II Pz Group along the Tula axis south of Bryansk to attack Moscow from the south. This proposal, accepted by OKW, ended any prospect of a further strategic offensive in the south towards the lower Volga and the Caucasus.

Leningrad – The Start of the Siege

Even before Schlusselburg on Lake Ladoga was captured by German forces on 8 September, thereby isolating Leningrad from ground communications with the rest of the country, Leningrad was seen as becoming, in Halder's words, "a secondary theatre of operations." Hitler's Directive of 6 September required Leeb only to encircle the city. By 15 September LVII Pz Corps, XLI Pz Corps, and the headquarters of LVI Pz Corps were to be transferred to Army Group Centre. The only mechanised force that would be left to Leeb would be XXXIX Pz Corps with 12 Pz Div, 18 Pz Div and 20 Mot Div, though 8 Pz Div, refitting after suffering heavy losses, would also become available for a time. In the Karelian Isthmus the Finns had stopped on the 1939 border and were clearly unwilling to participate in an assault on the city. Hitler had no wish to see heavy German casualties in street fighting and most certainly did not wish to commit mechanised formations to an urban conflict.

Leningrad was landlocked but not completely isolated. Soviet forces still controlled much of the eastern and southern shore of Lake Ladoga, and it would be possible for supplies to be shipped across the lake to the south-western shore held by Leningrad Front. If Leeb was to encircle the city in conformity with Hitler's Directive and thereby avoid a protracted siege of the southern Karelian Isthmus, he would need to use the mechanised forces of IV Pz Group before the middle of September to achieve a decisive success in the narrow isthmus to the east of the city. See Map 5

To defend Leningrad against the Leeb's offensive, Voroshilov had thirteen rifle divisions, five DNOs, three tank brigades and a few independent infantry formations that were altogether equivalent to another rifle division. In addition, Voroshilov had 23 Army defending the northern approaches to the city from the Finns. Yet since he had no information on Finnish intentions, he could not afford to lower his guard to the north. From west to east Voroshilov had 8 Army defending the coastal strip stretching some 50km west of Leningrad, 42 Army defending the south-western approaches to the city, 55 Army defending the south-eastern approaches from Krasnogvardeisk to the Neva, and two divisions under Voroshilov's direct command defending the Neva. East of the German salient from Mga to Lake Ladoga, the so-called Schlusselburg corridor, the newly-raised 54 Army, commanded by Marshal Kulik, was assembling behind the battered remnants of 48 Army.[2] On 9 September Kulik was ordered to

---

2   By that time 48 Army was under the command of Lt-Gen M A Antoniuk.

mount an offensive against the Schlusselburg corridor and to re-establish contact with Leningrad Front.

Leeb launched his offensive against Leningrad Front's defences on 9 September with XLI Pz Corps, supported on its flanks by XXXVIII Corps and L Corps, attacking north towards the Baltic coast in order to isolate 8 Army from the city. At the same time XXVIII Corps attacked towards Pushkin from the east, and XXXIX Pz Corps attempted to widen the Schlusselburg corridor east of the Neva. After two days of fierce fighting, Reinhardt's forces took Dudergov and began to break the Soviet resistance at Krasnoe Selo. As Voroshilov committed the last of his reserves to hold the German offensive, Zhukov was ordered to fly to Leningrad to replace him. Stalin was not only disappointed that Voroshilov had been unable to conduct a more effective defence of the approaches to Leningrad, he was concerned over what he perceived as signs of defeatism, and was incensed that Voroshilov had not informed STAVKA promptly of the loss of Schlusselburg. On 12 September XLI Pz Corps took Krasnoe Selo and reached Pulkovo near the south-western outskirts of the city. The next day Zhukov arrived in Leningrad with Lt-Gen M S Khozin and Major-Gen I I Fedyuninsky as his assistants. They arrived to find a seemingly hopeless situation.

Reinhardt's forces were just 10km from the coast and were continuing to push north towards Uritsk; German attacks to the south of the city in the Pushkin – Krasnogvardeisk area were making progress; Front and Army command staff seemed to have accepted the inevitability of the city's capture; Voroshilov had virtually no reserves; and to the east Kulik's offensive had achieve little. Zhukov responded with a flurry of orders. He appointed Khozin as Front Chief of Staff, cancelled Voroshilov's instructions for the destruction of key infrastructure assets, issued a 'not one step back' order to all troops, replaced Ivanov with Fedyuninsky as commander of 42 Army, organised the preparation of an additional inner defence ring, and ordered the raising of additional reserves – a rifle division from NKVD personnel, a sixth DNO, two rifle brigades from naval personnel and a rifle brigade from PVO personnel. Such reserves as could be immediately scraped together were sent to Uritsk to try to keep XLI Pz Corps from reaching the coast. The next day Shcherbakov was ordered to attack the left flank of the German penetration towards Uritsk, and when he complained that he didn't have the resources for such an offensive, he was replaced by Lt-Gen T I Shevaldin.

Yet Leeb was not without problems either. Overhanging all his considerations was the impending withdrawal of XLI Pz Corps to Army Group Centre. The first of Reinhardt's forces departed on 15 September and the withdrawal was largely completed by 20 September. Leeb had received an infantry division to compensate for this loss, and two other infantry divisions, including the Spanish 250 'Blue' Division, were being made available, but in mid-September he was struggling to find the resources to comply with Hitler's Directive. On 16 September his forces reached the coast, isolating 8 Army in the Oranienbaum salient; two days later they took Pushkin and Pavlovsk, and advanced on Pulkova just 12km from the city centre, but furious Soviet defence of the Pulkova Heights prevented any further advance.

To the east Kulik's offensive against the Schlusselburg corridor had been a shambles. His 54 Army had incorporated the forces of 48 Army, the latter being formally disbanded on 20 September, but far from penetrating the Schlusselburg corridor, 54 Army had been pushed back towards Volkhov by XXXIX Pz Corps.

For his incompetent handling of his forces, Kulik was replaced by Khozin and was subsequently demoted. Nonetheless much of the Lake Ladoga shoreline remained in Soviet hands and the Finns, having reached the Svir, were unable to advance further. During the fourth week of September the front line around Leningrad achieved a degree of stabilisation. Militarily the worst of the crisis of Leningrad was over; but for the civilian population the ordeal had barely begun.

East of the Dnieper

During the final days of September STAVKA engaged in a flurry of frantic activity to respond to the disaster that had befallen Southwestern Front. As reserves were rushed to the eastern Ukraine, Major-Gen V V Tsyganov was appointed to command 38 Army in place of Feklenko, and on 26 September Cherevichenko was moved from 9 Army to command 21 Army, Major-Gen F M Kharitonov assuming command of 9 Army. At the end of September Southwestern Direction was disbanded, the Western Direction command having been disbanded a few days earlier on 27 September, and Timoshenko was appointed to command the residual 147,000 troops of Southwestern Front. His new command was bolstered by the inclusion of 40 Army, transferred from Bryansk Front, on his right flank, and by 6 Army, transferred from Southern Front, on his left flank. At the beginning of October Timoshenko could deploy thirteen rifle divisions and eight cavalry divisions, but they had to cover a front of more than 600km, and there was little prospect of them preventing a concerted German mechanised thrust to the east.

On 12 September Schobert was killed and command of XI Army passed to Manstein, General Ferdinand Schaal assuming command of LVI Pz Corps. Manstein's task was to take the Crimea and to secure Rostov. Riabyshev's Southern Front had been struggling to contain the eastward advance of XI Army, which by mid-September had reached the Sea of Azov, thereby isolating 51 Army in the Crimean peninsula. An attempt by LIV Corps to drive through the Perekop Isthmus and to break into the Crimea off the march was unsuccessful, but the fighting in the isthmus continued for several weeks. On 24 September Smirnov's 18 Army and Kharitonov's 9 Army mounted a counter-offensive against Axis forces north of the Sea of Azov in an effort to re-establish contact with 51 Army. The heaviest blow fell on III Rum Army holding the line between XI Army and XVII Army. Soviet forces penetrated the Rumanian lines in several places and Rundstedt was only able to stabilise the situation through the diversion of German forces to the area. The diverted forces included XLIX Mtn Corps, which Manstein had intended to use to support LIV Corps. Disconcerting though this offensive may have been to the German High Command, and though it relieved the pressure on 51 Army, it failed to achieve its primary objective, and by the end of the month Manstein had pushed 9 Army back towards Melitopol. On 29 September Stalin agreed to the evacuation of Odessa and the use of the forces there to reinforce 51 Army in the Crimea. Odessa had been invested by IV Rum Army since 5 August, and its stubborn defence had been used by Soviet propaganda to counter some of the disasters elsewhere along the front.

By the end of September VI Army occupied the northern flank of Army Group South's front on the west bank of the Psel. Concentrating his forces southeast of Lokhvitza, Reichenau prepared for an advance east on the Belgorod – Kharkov axis.

On his right, southeast of Poltava, XVII Army was deploying for an advance east on the Kharkov – Lozova axis. Farther south, I Pz Group occupied the bridgeheads that had been established by XVII Army at the Dnieper's eastern extremity, Kleist concentrating his forces east of the Samara/Dnieper between Dnepropetrovsk and Novomoskovsk. The rest of line south to Genechesk was held by the newly arrived Italian Corps (three divisions), the Hungarian Corps, a Slovak light division, III Rum Army and part of XI Army. At this time STAVKA did not know where the German mechanised forces would strike next. The encirclement and destruction of Southern Front by Kleist's and Guderian's mechanised forces acting in concert from the Poltava area was just one of a number of potentially disastrous scenarios that STAVKA could envisage in the Ukraine. The two panzer groups could strike east through Kharkov to the industrially vital Donbas region and beyond; they could strike northeast through Kursk on the Tula axis to threaten Moscow from the south; or the two panzer groups could divide to try to achieve two strategic objectives simultaneously. Soviet High Command did not have to wait for long to learn what its German counterpart had decided.

Operation Typhoon Begins

At the end of September Army Group Centre had nearly two million men and fifteen hundred tanks organised into 44 infantry divisions, 14 panzer divisions, 8 motorised divisions and a cavalry division, plus a further 10 divisions for 'mopping up'. After a pause of six weeks in offensive operations and a relatively quiet three weeks after the cessation of the attacks by Western Front and Reserve Front, most of Bock's command was fully rested and refitted. A notable exception was II Pz Group which, after being in almost continuous action throughout August and September, only had around half its normal complement of tanks.[3]

See Map 7   Operation Typhoon was launched on 30 September with II Pz Group's three panzer corps thrusting from Glukhov towards Orel with the objective of enveloping Bryansk Front. This was to be achieved in conjunction with a thrust from II Army's two southern corps towards Bryansk from north of Starodub, with Sukhinich as the objective of its left flank XIII Corps. The offensive by II Army, together with the rest of Operation Typhoon, began on 2 October. Hoepner's IV Pz Group, which, since 26 September, had been subordinated to Kluge's IV Army command, attacked with LVII Pz Corps and XLVI Pz Corps from Roslavl in an encircling move towards Vyazma – Gzhatsk, while General Georg Stumme's XL Pz Corps, recently transferred to theatre from the Balkans, attacked towards Yukhnov on IV Pz Group's right flank. The offensive by IV Pz Group was undertaken in conjunction with an encircling thrust from III Pz Group's XLI Pz Corps and LVI Pz Corps attacking towards Sychevka from south of Prechistoe. South of the Dnieper, IV Army's three corps, between Roslavl and Smolensk, struck towards Elnia as IX Army's two right flank corps struck the Soviet frontline north of the Smolensk – Moscow highway. On Bock's left flank, IX Army's XXIII Corps attacked towards Olenino in order to simultaneously secure the left flank of III Pz Group's advance and maintain contact with Army Group North's right flank as it moved east to the Ostashkov lakes.

---

3   Guderian had lost Vietinghoff's XLVI Pz Corps to IV Pz Group but had acquired Kempf's XLVIII Pz Corps. This left Kleist with just two panzer and two motorised divisions as I Pz Group's mechanised strike force.

STAVKA had been expecting Bock to launch an offensive on the Moscow axis but had been unable to anticipate its scale or direction. To face the main weight of the offensive, Western Front, commanded by the newly-promoted Col-Gen I S Konev, and Budenny's Reserve Front, had altogether one million men and 770 tanks in 67 divisions. These forces were organised into twelve armies. On the right flank Major-Gen V A Iushkevich's 22 Army covered the frontline in the Andreapol area; Maslennikov's 29 Army covered the Zapadnaya sector; and Khomenko's 30 Army was southwest of Belyi. In the frontline sector along the most direct route to Moscow, the Smolensk – Moscow highway, STAVKA had concentrated three armies with 17 divisions. Lukin, who had taken command of 19 Army when Konev was promoted to the command of Western Front, was north of Yartsevo; Rokossovsky's 16 Army covered the Yartsevo sector; and Ershakov's 20 Army was east of Dorogobuzh. Reserve Front's 24 Army under Rakutin covered the Elnia sector; and Sobennikov's 43 Army was between Roslavl and Spas-Demensk. As second echelon, under Budenny's command, was Major-Gen V N Dolmatov's 31 Army between Olenino and Rzhev; Lt-Gen I G Zakharkin's 49 Army west of Sychevka; Major-Gen S V Vishnevsky's 32 Army west of Vyazma; and General D P Onuprienko's 33 Army at Spas-Demensk. Bryansk Front had nearly a quarter of a million men and 220 tanks organised into 17 divisions in three armies and an operational group. West of Bryansk, and linking with 43 Army to the north, was M P Petrov's 50 Army; east of Pochep was Kreizer's 3 Army; and east of Novgorod-Seversky was Gorodniansky's 13 Army. On Bryansk Front's left wing, and linking with Southwestern Front's 40 Army, was Ermakov's operational group that at the end of September was preparing for an offensive towards Glukhov, and was consequently not configured for defensive operations.

The force and shock of Guderian's offensive threw back Ermakov's five divisions and two tank brigades on the first day to expose the left flank of 13 Army. By the end of the next day Guderian's forces had isolated two of Gorodniansky's divisions, and had cut off Ermakov's group from the rest of Bryansk Front. The next morning III Pz Group struck the junction of 30 Army and 19 Army, while IV Pz Group penetrated 43 Army's lines to reach the defences of 33 Army. Konev and Eremenko both tried to respond to the German incursions by deploying reserves to block the German advance but, as had happened on numerous other occasions, the Soviet manoeuvres were too slow to be effective. By 3 October III Pz Group had penetrated 50km east to the north of Vyazma; IV Pz Group had penetrated 80km northeast towards the south of Vyazma; and from II Pz Group Lemelsen's XLVII Pz Corps was approaching Karachev in 13 Army's rear, while Schweppenburg's XXIV Pz Corps was approaching Orel, some 200km from its jumping off point of three days earlier. With the last of the fighting in the Kiev encirclement just a week old, an encirclement of comparable magnitude was unfolding west of Moscow.

Konev formed an operational group of three divisions and two tank brigades under the command of his deputy Lt-Gen I V Boldin with orders to counter-attack III Pz Group from the south in conjunction with an attack on Hoth's left flank by 30 Army. These attacks, carried out on 3 October and 4 October, slowed Hoth's advance, but in the Reserve Front sector IV Pz Group, by 4 October, had shattered both 43 Army and 33 Army, and, by advancing towards Vyazma, was threatening the rear of 24 Army and Western Front's 20 Army. Yet, despite the obvious danger, STAVKA did not give permission for a withdrawal of 24 Army and the left flank armies of Western Front until late on 5 October. Until then Stalin had been more concerned with the apparent threat from Guderian's advance from the southwest, and on 1 October he ordered Zakharkin's 49 Army and the newly-formed 1 Gds Rifle Corps under the command of Major-Gen D D Lelyushenko to deploy to protect Orel. Only on 5 October did STAVKA's priorities change after a Soviet fighter pilot reported a column of German tanks 20km long on the Yukhnov road northeast of Spas-Demensk. This report was not believed by STAVKA until confirmed by two other pilots later in the day.

Zhukov was ordered back from Leningrad, Fedyuninsky assuming command of Leningrad Front. Reserve Front's 31 Army and 32 Army were transferred to Western Front command, and reserves from Northwestern Front were diverted to the Moscow area. Additionally, reserves that during the second half of September had been allocated to support Southwestern Front, were diverted north to Moscow. Responding to STAVKA's belated authorisation to begin the withdrawal of his threatened forces, Konev ordered Rokossovsky to transfer command of 16 Army's frontline forces to Ershakov, and to move his 16 Army Headquarters to Vyazma to organise the defence of the town. But by then it was too late; Vyazma fell to German forces on 6 October and the next day 16, 19, 20 and 24 Armies together with much of 32 Army were encircled west of the town. Stalin was furious, and only Zhukov's intervention prevented Konev from being arrested and shot.

Farther south the situation for Soviet forces was barely less disastrous than that in the Vyazma area. Orel fell to XXIV Pz Corps on 4 October. The next day Schweppenburg's forces pushed on along the Tula axis, 3 Pz Div towards Bolchow and Major-Gen Willibald Freiherr von Langermann's 4 Pz Div towards Mtsensk. On its approach to Mtsensk Langermann's lead formation, 5 Pz Bgd commanded by Col Heinrich Eberbach, reached an intact bridge over the Lisiza near the village of Kamenewo, 25km northeast of Orel. The next morning Eberbach's five panzer companies rushed the bridge, took it intact, and destroyed a defending Soviet force of infantry, T26 tanks and anti-tank guns. But as Eberbach's forces advanced beyond the ridge line on the east bank of the river, they were ambushed by a tank brigade of KV1 and T34 tanks under the command of Col M E Katukov, part of Lelyushenko's 1 Gds Rifle Corps. In the resultant battle Eberbach's forces were pushed back from the ridgeline and Guderian's advance on Tula became stalled on the Lisiza. Eberbach only lost ten tanks and a handful of heavy artillery pieces in this engagement, but the outcome was considered sufficiently serious by OKH that an enquiry into the events at Kamenewo was ordered. Katukov lost eighteen tanks in the engagement but he completely disrupted Guderian's timetable for the advance to Moscow. The action at Kamenewo, and the subsequent Soviet defence of the Tula road, delayed the taking of Mtsensk by German forces until 24 October. On 6 October XLVII Pz Corps, approaching Bryansk, crashed into Eremenko's Front Headquarters. Eremenko and most of his staff escaped to the northeast, but for several days Eremenko was out of contact with his subordinate armies. By the time he was able to restore contact with his command he found that a link up at Karachev between XLVII Pz Corps and II Army's LIII Corps on 9 October had encircled 3 Army and 13 Army. An advance farther north towards Belev by II Army's XLIII Corps had also put 50 Army at risk of encirclement, though much of M P Petrov's army was able to withdraw to the east, becoming available for the subsequent defence of Tula.

Still farther south, since I Pz Group was not required for Typhoon, an encirclement of Southern Front was planned by Rundstedt and Kleist in an offensive to Osepenko that would be supported by XI Army in a thrust along the coast. Kleist's forces struck out on 30 September from Novomoskovsk through 12 Army's left wing towards the southeast. They made rapid progress, placing Southern Front's centre and left wing at risk of encirclement. On 5 October Riabyshev was replaced as commander of Southern Front by Cherevichenko, and F I Kuznetsov was moved from 51 Army to command 21 Army once again. The continued advance of I Pz Group to the southeast, the Italian Corps mopping up in its wake, left only infantry formations from VI Army and XVII Army to mount an offensive against the forces of Southwestern Front, and Timoshenko's Front began a long withdrawal to the east easily avoiding encirclement by the German infantry divisions. With no immediate threat to Kharkov, and a German offensive against the Crimea appearing imminent, F I Kuznetsov was returned to 51 Army on 10 October and command of 21 Army again reverted to its long-standing chief of staff, Major-Gen V N Gordov. By 6 October Kleist's panzers had linked up with advance units of XI Army's XXX Corps near Osepenko, leaving both 9 Army and 18 Army surrounded southeast of Orekhov. Elements of 9 Army, including Kharitonov, broke out to 12 Army's positions at Stalino, and elements of 18 Army broke out to Taganrog, but a further 100,000 Soviet prisoners were taken and Smirnov was killed.

See Map 8

On 5 October a number of changes were made in the *Ostheer* command structure. Hoth replaced Stuelpnagel as commander of XVII Army, and Reinhardt assumed command of III Pz Group. Model, perhaps the most effective and certainly the most successful of the *Ostheer*'s divisional commanders, was promoted and appointed to Reinhardt's former command at XLI Pz Corps. Bock reallocated forces between II Army and II Pz Group to bring the more forward elements of II Army under Guderian's command, while placing those of Guderian's forces still south of Orel under II Army. With a minimum of force redeployment, this allowed Guderian's command, redesignated II Pz Army, to continue northeast towards Tula, while II Army, moving east from the Orel area towards Elets, protected Guderian's right flank.

Since Bock's forces during the first week of October had smashed several Soviet armies and had surrounded half a dozen more, there was a widespread belief at all levels of the German command that the capture of Moscow was imminent, and that the war would soon be over. Understandable though this optimism may have been, it was misplaced. The Red Army still had considerable reserves, and its morale, despite its horrendous losses and devastating setbacks, remained equal to the task of offering a stiff defence of the capital. During September rumours had begun to emerge of widespread massacres of civilians in Minsk. Subsequently those Russians who had grown to hate Stalin's regime and who, in the early weeks of the war, might have been prepared to suppress their innate patriotism in order to achieve a change of regime, increasingly came to doubt whether life under German rule would be any better.

Stalin had been expecting a renewed German offensive on the Moscow axis since the conclusion of the battles in the Smolensk area in early August, and considerable effort had been expended in preparing the capital's defences in a series of concentric belts, the most important of which was the Mozhaisk Line half way between Moscow and Vyazma. On 12 October the rate of work on these defences underwent a quantum change with the mobilisation of hundreds of thousands of Moscow citizens for defence construction work on the close approaches to the city. Another factor working against German ambitions was time. Combat operations in Russia have historically been constrained by two annual 'seasons of mud'. One of these occurs during the autumn rains before the winter freeze can harden the ground. The other occurs in the spring during a period of spring rains and snowmelt. At these times the unmetalled Russian roads are rapidly churned into impassable channels of mud, and off-road movement becomes highly problematic. Thereafter military manoeuvre and supply is largely restricted to the relatively few all-weather metalled roads and to the railways. As Bock's forces, still more than 300km from Moscow, completed the Vyazma encirclement, the rains began in earnest and they were to continue throughout October.

On 10 October the remnants of Western Front and Reserve Front were combined under Zhukov's command, Konev becoming the deputy Front commander. The encircled forces in the Vyazma area were placed under Lukin's command, and Lukin was ordered to break out to the east. However Bock, having learned the lessons of previous encirclements, ensured that there was an effective barrier in place to prevent any significant movement of Soviet forces to the east, and half a dozen panzer divisions were committed to the task. Unlike at Smolensk, STAVKA did not have resources immediately available to mount a break-in effort against the encirclement, and the forces inside the pocket, low on supplies and with their mobility impeded by the rains, were unable to mount an effective defence. The Vyazma pocket was eliminated by the middle of October, though isolated groups continued to tie down some German forces to the end of the month. The surrounded Soviet forces at Vyazma included four field army headquarters, forty-two divisions, nine tank brigades and thirty-one heavy artillery regiments; a force equivalent to nearly two-thirds of the combined initial strength of Western and Reserve Fronts. On 10 October, 24 Army was disbanded, the formal disbandment of 32 Army following two days later. Only around 85,000 troops, mainly from 19 Army and 20 Army escaped from the encirclement, the majority to be assigned to Rokossovsky's command. Both 19 Army and 20 Army were formally disbanded on 20 October. In the Bryansk encirclement the German cordon was less tight. A substantial part of 13 Army managed to fight its way out to the southeast, while Kreizer and a substantial part of 3 Army broke out to east. Yet heroic escape notwithstanding, the opening phase of Operation Typhoon was a disaster for the Red Army on an even greater scale than Kiev, with 658,000 Red Army personnel being taken prisoner.

To the Mozhaisk Line

During the 'season of mud' STAVKA was able gather more reserves for the defence of the approaches to the capital; 14 rifle divisions and 16 tank brigades. Most of these came from the Far East; well trained, well-equipped and with high morale. On 10 October, 26 Army, disbanded after the Kiev encirclement, was reformed based on Lelyushenko's 1 Gds Rifle Corps. This new army, commanded by Lt-Gen G G Sokolov, was charged with the defence of the Mtsensk – Tula axis. The next day 5 Army, also disbanded after the Kiev encirclement, was reformed and placed under Lelyushenko's command. The task of 5 Army was to defend the direct route from

Vyazma to Moscow at Mozhaisk. Zakharkin's 49 Army, which had been moved to the southeast from the Sychevka area at the beginning of October, was ordered to the southern end of the Mozhaisk line to defend the Kaluga axis. STAVKA's defensive task was made somewhat easier by an OKH decision on 10 October to divert III Pz Group away from the Moscow axis towards Kalinin. This decision was taken in support of an ongoing offensive by Army Group North against Northwestern Front. Since IX Army was also involved in this turn to the north, it left only IV Pz Group and IV Army available for the continuation of the eastward offensive towards Moscow. The rationale behind this OKH decision was that the Soviet central defensive axis had been fatally weakened, that the destruction of Northwestern Front would precipitate the surrender of Leningrad, and that from Kalinin III Pz Group could, by attacking to the southeast, link up east of Moscow with II Pz Army advancing to the northeast from Tula. Given the huge distances involved and the appalling state of the transport network, this was a hugely ambitious strategy, but it was taken by a German High Command brimming with confidence at its own abilities. Those abilities were amply demonstrated by Reinhardt who broke through 29 Army's defences south of Rzhev and, despite the difficult ground conditions, advanced more than 200km with 1 Pz Div in the van to take Kalinin on 14 October. STAVKA responded by ordering Vatutin, Northwestern Front's Chief of Staff, to organise an operational group to retake the town. Zhukov ordered his left flank forces to pull back north of the Volga, and he sent Konev to oversee the withdrawal. The fall of Kalinin, and the rapid progress of German forces along the western approaches to the capital, prompted a degree of panic in Moscow that over a four-day period bore portents of civil unrest, prompting a formal declaration of a state of siege in the capital on 19 October.

On 17 October Zhukov's four right flank armies, 22 Army, 29 Army, 31 Army and 30 Army, together with Vatutin's group, were subordinated to a new Front under Konev's command. Kalinin Front was based on the headquarters of 10 Army, which, having been reconstituted just two weeks earlier as an operational army, was again disbanded. Konev's subsequent efforts through the second half of October to retake Kalinin were unsuccessful, but they prevented any German exploitation from the town that may have threatened Northwestern Front. From 24 October Bock, having largely completed the mopping up in the Vyazma area, was able to move much of IX Army to Kalinin and so relieve III Pz Group for further offensive action to the east.

On the central Moscow axis Bock's forces began to reach the Mozhaisk Line on 11 October. Three days later 10 Pz Div and 2 SS Mot Div (*Das Reich*) from IV Pz Group reached the Napoleonic battle site at Borodino some 10km west of Mozhaisk, but were held from any further advance by the newly arrived and heavily reinforced 32 Rifle Div of Lelyushenko's 5 Army. The defence of the Borodino area by 32 Rifle Div delayed Hoepner's advance on Moscow for a crucial seven days. On 5 Army's right flank Rokossovsky's 16 Army covered the Volokolamsk area and linked with 30 Army falling back from Koslovo. Between 5 Army at Mozhaisk, and 49 Army at Kaluga, the remnants of 43 Army, in the process of being reinforced from the strategic reserve, was positioned east of Medyn to defend Maloyaroslavets.

During the second half of October, in vicious and often confused fighting, IV Army and IV Pz Group pushed the Soviet defenders out of Volokolamsk, Mozhaisk, Marolaroslavets, Borovsk and Kaluga to reach to within 100km of Moscow, while to the south II Pz Army pushed northeast from Mtsensk reaching the outskirts of Tula on 26 October. Yet, compared with the spectacular successes of the first half of October, Army Group Centre found progress through the second half of the month to be slow and grinding.

Sevastopol, Kharkov and Rostov

The evacuation of Odessa began on 2 October and was completed by 16 October. In its planning, execution and outcome it was a successful example of a combined-arms operation, and has been described as a minor Dunkirk. With little loss, the Black Sea Fleet transferred almost the entire Odessa garrison and most of its equipment to the Crimea where the garrison forces were subordinated to F I Kuznetsov's 51 Army. Kuznetsov's forces had been defending the Crimea against XI Army's LIV Corps since mid-September, and the reinforcement from Odessa left Kuznetsov with a substantial force of sixteen divisions.

During the second week of October the bulk of XI Army withdrew from the Melitopol area, XLIX Mtn Corps being transferred from Manstein's command to I Pz Group. Manstein's army, supported by III Rum Army, was to prepare for a larger scale offensive into the Perekop Isthmus in the second half of October. Kuznetsov anticipated a major German offensive but, concerned that Manstein might launch an amphibious assault, spread his forces thinly around the coast. When Manstein launched his offensive down the Perekop Isthmus on 18 October, the forces available to stop him were insufficient. Once XI Army, with III Rum Army in its wake, had broken into the Crimea, a general defence of the peninsula by Soviet forces became highly problematic. On 22 October Kuznetsov was relieved of command of 51 Army and replaced by Lt-Gen P I Batov. By the end of the month Manstein had pushed 51 Army out of eastern Crimea across the Kerch Straits to the Taman Peninsula. Only around the port of Sevastopol in the southwest of the peninsula did a substantial Soviet force of more than fifty thousand troops remain. This force, designated the Coastal Army, and under the command of Major-Gen I E Petrov, could be supplied and reinforced by the Black Sea Fleet, and at the end of October another epic siege began.

After the encirclement of 9 Army and 18 Army at the end of the first week in October, Rundstedt believed that he had largely destroyed Southern Front's combat effectiveness, but in fact, despite their heavy losses, Cherevichenko's armies were still in being and his forces, in the process of being reinforced, were still capable of offering a stiff defence. Consequently I Pz Group did not have the luxury of time to rest and refit in mid-October, and combat continued throughout the month. Stalino was not taken by Kleist's forces until 20 October and, after 100,000 Soviet miners had been mobilised for its defence, it was not until 29 October that Rundstedt could claim to have secured the entire Donbas region. Farther north VI Army and XVII Army continued to push Southwestern Front steadily to the east, but a combination of poor roads, lack of mechanised transport and wet weather meant that the German advance was only 2-3km per day. Kharkov was taken by VI Army on 24 October but there was no 'bag' of prisoners as Southwestern Front continued to retreat towards the Donets.

Kleist's primary objective during November was Rostov. A key communications hub near the mouth of the Don, its possession by German forces would open a range of temping possibilities for OKH, none of which would involve another major river crossing. From the city, Army Group South could move down the Black Sea coast to seize the last of the Black Sea Fleet's ports and to secure to the oilfields of Maikop; it could move southeast to the oilfields of the Caspian Sea; or it could move northeast towards the Volga and Stalingrad. By the end of October Kleist's forces, redesignated I Pz Army on 25 October, required several days to rest and refit before an assault on Rostov could begin, but by 5 November I Pz Army was ready for the next stage of its seemingly unstoppable advance to the east.

STAVKA prepared for the German offensive towards Rostov by reinforcing 9 Army, which was primarily responsible for the defence of the approaches to the city, and by preparing a series of defensive barriers along the most likely approach routes. On 17 October Remezov's 56 Army was activated and, operating independently of Southern Front's command, was moved by STAVKA to the left bank of the Don south of Rostov, and subsequently into the city for its direct defence.

By the end of October I Pz Army, reinforced during October with an additional panzer division, was across the Mius. On Kleist's right wing III Pz Corps had pushed to within 30km of Rostov along the coast of the Sea of Azov, but was stopped from any further advance by formidable defences on the western approaches to the city. Kleist decided to attack farther north across the Tuzlov and east towards Shakhty in order to be able to turn and advance on Rostov from the northeast. Yet this was no lightning advance. It took I Pz Army's XIV Pz Corps six days of difficult combat to reached Shakhty, at which point Kleist, short of supplies and at the end of a tenuous supply system, required a six-day pause to reorganise his forces. During this time Cherevichenko was not idle. By shortening his lines of defence elsewhere, sufficient forces were released – ten rifle divisions and two cavalry corps – to enable 37 Army to be reconstituted and deployed in the Shakhty area. Under the command of Major-Gen A I Lopatin, 37 Army became operational on 15 November, by which time 56 Army was taking up defensive positions in and around Rostov. Two days later Kleist struck towards the city. Despite constant attacks on their left flank from 37 Army, Kleist's forces took Rostov on 21 November. Cherevichenko responded by mounting a series of furious but poorly coordinated counter-attacks; 18 Army and 37 Army from the north, 9 Army from the east and 56 Army from the south across the frozen Don. Kleist found himself under threat of encirclement and, his position becoming increasingly untenable, he withdrew I Pz Army to the west. Rundstedt, who had throughout most of November been requesting from OKH a halt to further offensive operations until his forces could be reinforced and adequately supplied, insisted that Army Group South's right flank be withdrawn to the Mius and that his forces assume the defensive. When Hitler refused to sanction a withdrawal to the Mius, Rundstedt resigned. He was replaced by Reichenau on 1 December, the newly-promoted General Friedrich Paulus subsequently assuming command of VI Army.[4] The change of command at Army Group South came too late to reverse the ongoing withdrawal of the army group's right flank, and it was along the Mius that the front line stabilised during the winter of 1941/42.

---

4   Paulus, as a senior OKH staff officer, had been closely involved in the overall planning for Operation Barbarossa.

Tikhvin

Having failed to isolate Leningrad from Lake Ladoga during September, Leeb's only remaining option was to try to isolate Lake Ladoga and the whole of Leningrad Front from the rest of Russia. For this task he still had Schmidt's XXXIX Pz Corps which, together with XXXVIII Corps from XVIII Army, was ordered to mount an offensive to the northeast towards Volkhov and Tikhvin in order to link up with Finnish forces on the Svir. Meanwhile attacks were to be mounted on either side of Lake Ilmen for an advance through Kesttsy, Valdai and the Ostashkov lakes towards the upper Msta.

As Leeb was planning his offensive, STAVKA was preparing offensive plans of its own. On 25 August another new army, designated 52 Army, had been formed from forces of the strategic reserve, and was subsequently moved to the Volkhov area. To deal more effectively with Finnish forces on the Svir, General K A Meretskov, a former Chief of the General Staff, was released from a brief but brutal period of incarceration in an NKVD prison, and was appointed on 24 September to the command of 7 Army. On 26 September, 4 Army was reconstituted from 52 Army Headquarters staff and from forces of the strategic reserve, and, under the command of Lt-Gen V F Yakovlev, was positioned on the left flank of Khozin's 54 Army. At the same time 52 Army, commanded by Lt-Gen N K Klykov, was ordered to defend the line east of the Volkhov in the Malaia Vishera area. Both 4 Army and 52 Army were placed under STAVKA's direct control between Leningrad Front and Northwestern Front.

STAVKA had planned to mount a renewed offensive to restore contact with the isolated forces of Leningrad Front, but Leeb struck first. On 16 October Schmidt's forces broke through Soviet lines between 52 Army and 4 Army east of Chudovo. Within a week Malaia Vishera had been taken, and to the northeast the panzers pushed towards Tikhvin from Budogoshch. Four Soviet divisions were transferred across Lake Ladoga from Leningrad Front to support 54 Army and 4 Army, and a division was transferred from Northwestern Front to reinforce 52 Army. Throughout October the Finns tried repeatedly to break through Meretskov's defences on the Svir, but without success.[5]

On 24 October Fedyuninsky, considering himself to be too junior in rank, asked to relieved of command of Leningrad Front, and he exchanged roles with Khozin. On 8 November, as an operational group from XVIII Army approached Volkhov from the south, Schmidt's forces took Tikhvin, severing the last rail link to Lake Ladoga from the Russian interior. STAVKA responded by appointing Meretskov to command 4 Army, command of 7 Army reverting to Gorolenko; it transferred five rifle divisions and a tank brigade from the right flank of 4 Army to 54 Army for the defence of Volkhov, and it demanded a speedy counter-offensive from Fedyuninsky, Meretskov and Klykov.

The three armies attacked as ordered but were unable to coordinate their actions. Yet Leeb's forces were having problems of their own. Temperatures plummeted as the Russian winter set in and German troops struggled to cope with unfamiliar combat conditions for which they were ill equipped. On 12 November Klykov's forces attacked southeast of the Volkhov. The Soviet offensive achieved little in terms of territorial

---

5   Finnish commanders had to take account of mounting reluctance among the rank and file within the army to advance deeper into Russia. In November this reluctance, on a number of occasions, came close to mutiny.

gain, but it was of an intensity that obliged Leeb to divert forces from the Tikhvin area to the south. On 19 November Meretskov's forces struck in the Tikhvin area in a rolling offensive that continued for more than two weeks. Four days earlier, on 15 November, Schmidt had left XXXIX Pz Corps to assume temporary command of II Army, and Lt-Gen Hans-Jurgen von Arnim, commander of 17 Pz Div, replaced him as corps commander. By early December Arnim had concluded that the continuing attenuation of his combat units was rendering his defence of Tikhvin untenable, and in this conclusion he was supported by Leeb. Leeb, like Rundstedt in the south just a week earlier, was unable to obtain permission for a withdrawal of his forces from an impossible position. In defiance of Hitler's explicit instructions Leeb authorised preparations for the withdrawal of German forces from Tikhvin. On 8 December XXXIX Pz Corps, with Hitler's belated and reluctant acquiescence, abandoned the town, and the centre of Army Group North began to withdraw to defensible positions on the Volkhov, a process that was completed by the end of the month. On 10 December STAVKA created Volkhov Front to cover the Lake Ladoga – Lake Ilmen sector of the front south of Leningrad Front's 54 Army. Meretskov was appointed as Front commander, Lt-Gen P A Ivanov assuming command of 4 Army. Volkhov Front initially incorporated 4 Army and 52 Army but was subsequently reinforced with two further armies redeployed from the Moscow area.

The Gates of Moscow

By the end of October the *Ostheer*'s casualty list had grown to more than 685,000, and Operation Typhoon had effectively ground to halt. Army Group Centre, and indeed the entire *Ostheer*, was experiencing a noticeable diminution of combat effectiveness as a result of these losses. Infantry divisions were typically operating at less than two-thirds of authorised strength and the situation in the panzer divisions was even worse. Bock needed time to reorganise his forces and to recast his plans. It was clear that a grandiose strategy involving a vast encircling move around Moscow by III Pz Group and II Pz Army was unrealistic. If the city was to be taken, it would have to be by a closer encirclement than originally envisaged, and it would have to wait until the ground had frozen sufficiently to enable rapid movement of mechanised forces. This reality was recognised by OKH and at the end of October Hitler ordered strikes by panzer forces on the flanks of Western Front in order to achieve a close encirclement of Moscow. The renewed offensive by Army Group Centre's 31 infantry divisions, 13 panzer divisions and 7 motorised divisions, was to begin in mid-November. In its final form Bock's plan required IX Army's right flank to support III Pz Group in an attack eastwards through Klin to the Volga canal north of Moscow. At the same time Strauss was to maintain contact with Army Group North and to advance to the Volga dam southeast of Kalinin. On its right flank III Pz Group would be supported by IV Pz Group, which was still under IV Army's command. In the centre Kluge's infantry formations, which in mid-November were fully committed in defence in front of Moscow, would mount an assault along the central axis towards Moscow when the panzer attacks had drawn Soviet forces away from the centre. On the south-western approaches to the capital II Pz Army would strike through Tula and Kashira. On Guderian's right flank II Army was too far behind to help with the offensive against Moscow, and was charged with operating on the deep flank of II Pz Army providing flank cover and linking with Army Group South. Almost all of Bock's depleted divisions were committed to the offensive, with just two divisions retained as army group reserve.

During the period of fighting for the Mozhaisk Line, Soviet forces experienced a number of senior command changes. Some were made in response to combat injuries and fatalities, but most were made in an attempt to ensure that the Red Army's most able commanders were in place on the key approach routes to the capital. On 12 October Eremenko was severely wounded, and Major-Gen G F Zakharov assumed command of Bryansk Front. On the same day, Ermakov assumed command of 50 Army after M P Petrov was killed in the retreat from Bryansk. On 13 October Lelyushenko was transferred north to replace Khomenko at 30 Army, Lt-Gen L A Govorov assuming command of 5 Army. On 17 October Akimov replaced Sobennikov at 43 Army as the army prepared to defend Maloyaroslavets. On 21 October Iushkevich was transferred from 22 Army to command 31 Army, and Major-Gen V I Vostrukov was appointed to the command of 22 Army. On 25 October, with 50 Army retreating to the Tula area from the west and 26 Army retreating towards Tula from the southwest, STAVKA took the decision to disband the recently reconstituted 26 Army. Onuprienko was replaced by Efremov at 33 Army and on 29 October Golubev assumed command of 43 Army after Akimov was killed.

The manpower difficulties faced by the *Ostheer*'s commanders at the end of October were as nothing compared to those faced by their Soviet counterparts. The Red Army in the west had half a million troops less than the *Ostheer*. This was an unprecedented situation that was not to last for long, but at the beginning of November, though the *Ostheer* still faced nearly 270 divisions and scores of brigades, those divisions generally contained less than 5,000 personnel and in many the manpower strength could be measured in the hundreds. During October and November a significant number of Soviet divisions were transferred from the Far East, and the strategic reserve continued to generate thousands of newly-trained troops each day; but for a time, Western Front was in a weak position that Army Group Centre might be able to exploit.

During the second week of November, with temperatures along the central axis below zero, the ground hardened sufficiently for Bock's offensive against Moscow to be resumed. Based on the available intelligence, Zhukov concluded that Bock would launch his main offensives from Volokolamsk and Tula where the German mechanised forces appeared to have been concentrated. On 10 November Bryansk Front was disbanded and 50 Army at Tula came under Western Front's command, while 3 Army and 13 Army facing II Army were transferred to Southwestern Front. To face the German offensive in mid-November, Zhukov had at his disposal Rokossovsky's 16 Army on the right flank in the Volokolamsk area, Govorov's 5 Army east of Ruza, Eframov's 33 Army in the Naro-Fominsk area, Golubev's 43 Army between Kresty and Kalugino, Zakharkin's 49 Army in the Tarusa area, and Ermakov's 50 Army holding on tenaciously to Tula. South of Tula, in Southwestern Front's area, was Kreizer's 3 Army and, on Rokossovsky's right in the Koslovo area, was Kalinin Front's 30 Army commanded by Lelyushenko. Against Zhukov's firm advice, on 14 November Stalin ordered spoiling attacks against what were clearly the final German preparations for an offensive against Moscow. Rokossovsky attacked at Volokolamsk, and Zakharkin attacked IV Army's right flank from north of Tula. These operations had little effect on German preparations but weakened Soviet defences, and in 16 Army's zone Soviet cavalry forces suffered particularly heavy losses. Farther south Soviet attacks were having more of an impact. During the second week of November, 49 Army and 50 Army attacked the forward units of II Pz Army in the Tula area and thwarted an attempt by XLIII Corps to cut the Tula – Moscow road. As the fighting around Tula continued into the second half of the month, Guderian, on 17 November, had to report the rout of one of LIII Corps' infantry divisions under attack from Soviet cavalry, infantry and armoured forces near Stalinogorsk southeast of Tula. The situation was quickly restored by the corps' other infantry division, but it was an ominous portent of the potential fragility of German morale in the face of prolonged and determined Soviet resistance in increasingly adverse climatic conditions for which German forces were materially and psychologically ill-prepared.

On 15 November III Pz Group, spearheaded by Schaal's LVI Pz Corps, attacked east towards Klin from northeast of Lotoshino, driving a deep wedge between 16 Army and 30 Army. On Reinhardt's right, Hoepner's IV Pz Group attacked from south of Volokolamsk; XLVI Pz Corps attacking to the northeast moving south of Teryayevo towards Klin, and XL Pz Corps striking east directly towards Istra and the northern suburbs of Moscow. Zhukov formed a combat group based on two tank brigades, two cavalry divisions and a rifle division and placed it under Zakharov's command with orders to seal the breach between 19 Army and 30 Army, and on 17 November 30 Army was transferred from Konev's to Zhukov's command. The next day Lelyushenko's 30 Army received reinforcement from 16 Army in the form of 58 Tank Div; a 'division' that consisted of 350 men, 15 light tanks and 5 guns. Lelyushenko, pursued by IX Army, withdrew to defences on the upper Volga north of the Volga dam, but Strauss managed to secure several bridgeheads on the left bank of the river before going over to the defensive himself. On 19 November IX Corps, on the right flank of IV Pz Group, hit the right flank of 5 Army east of Ruza to prevent 5 Army offering support to 16 Army. With Zvenigorod as their objective, IX Corps' three infantry divisions made slow but significant progress. The mechanised forces of III Pz Group and IV Pz Group, battering 16 Army back through a series of fixed defences, did not take Klin until 23 November, by which time temperatures had begun to plummet. The next day XLVI Pz Corps' 2 Pz Div, advancing to the east south of Klin, took Solnechnogorsk. After the loss of Klin and Solnechnogorsk, Rokossovsky was permitted to withdraw to the Istra, while 5 Army pulled back to a line from Istra to Zvenigorod, and on 28 November, after ferocious street fighting, XL Pz Corps took Istra.

On 18 November Guderian, with Kolomna, some 50km to the northeast of Kashira, as his distant objective, renewed his attempts to take Tula by encirclement. By 22 November Tula was surrounded on three sides and Boldin, days after reaching Soviet lines after a prolonged escape from the Vyazma encirclement, was dispatched from Moscow to assume command of 50 Army. Guderian's forces took Stalinogorsk on 24 November and pushed on, north towards Venev, and east towards Mikhailov. Boldin formed an operational group from the left flank forces of 50 Army with orders to defend Venev but the town fell to XXIV Pz Corps on 25 November and the next day the corps' 17 Pz Div approached Kashira, threatening the deep rear of both 50 Army and 49 Army. Instead of taking the undefended town off the march, 17 Pz Div stopped at Pyatnitsa some 6km to the south. A composite Soviet force based on Major-Gen P A Belov's 2 Cav Corps, reinforced with armour, combat engineers and rocket artillery, was designated 1 Gds Cav Corps and ordered from the Serpukhov area to stop Guderian's advance on Kashira. Belov, his force under Boldin's overall command, attacked on 27 November, penetrated the thinly-manned German lines, and pushed back XXIV Pz Corps towards Venev, thereby relieving much of the pressure on the embattled troops in Tula.

North of Moscow elements of LVI Pz Corps' 7 Pz Div managed to cross the Volga-Moscow canal on 29 November, and from Solnechnogorsk 2 Pz Div had, by 30 November, advanced to within artillery range of Moscow's northern suburbs. In the centre IX Corps continued to make progress towards Zvenigorod, and by late November Zhukov was compelled to move a rifle division from 33 Army to support Govorov. The movement of Western Front's forces from the centre to the flank was the signal for IV Army to begin an offensive, with the main effort coming from XX Corps and the left wing of LVII Pz Corps against 33 Army in the Naro-Fominsk sector. The offensive hit well-prepared and vigorously defended Soviet lines and such penetration as was achieved, XX Corps reaching to within 40km of Moscow, was repelled on 3 December by Soviet reinforcements. In the south, after the failure of a final attempt by II Pz Army on 2 December to encircle Tula, Guderian requested permission for his army to go over to the defensive.

Counter-Strike

During the second half of November, as the final German push on Moscow closed on the capital, Stalin seeped reserves to the front a battalion at a time – enough to slow the German advance to a crawl. By 4 December IX Army was on the Volga between Kalinin and the Volga dam; III Pz Group was on the Volga canal south of Dmitrov; IV Pz Group was to the northwest of Moscow, 2 Pz Div having advanced to within 25km of the Kremlin; Kluge's IV Army forces were still at Naro-Fominsk unable to make any progress to the east; Guderian's forces were on the defensive in the Tula – Venev – Mikhailov area; and II Army could not progress beyond the Tim – Elets – Efremov line. This was the high-water mark of the German offensive against Moscow, as both sides seemed to be nearing the end of their combat capability with regiments often operating with the combat strength of a company. For Army Group Centre the exhaustion and lack of reserves were real enough, but on the Soviet side all was not as it seemed. Between 23 November and 2 December three new Soviet armies became operational in the Moscow area; a reconstituted 20 Army, developed from an operational group commanded by Major-Gen A I Lizyukov, a third incarnation of 10 Army under the command of Golikov, and, based on elements of 19 Army Headquarters staff that had escaped from Vyazma, 1 Shock Army under the command of V I Kuznetsov. The 'shock army', constituted primarily for offensive operations, was essentially a normal rifle army with permanent additional heavy artillery and a degree of armoured support. The existence of these reserves, which included six tank brigades, was unknown to German military intelligence; indeed they were largely unknown to many of the frontline commanders in Western Front. On 3 December the German assessment was that the Red Army was down to its last battalions. Yet, as the three new armies in the Moscow area were being made operational, an additional dozen Soviet armies were being organised. Three were to be deployed in the Caucasus as a precaution against possible hostilities by Turkey, but the others were forming east of Moscow. One was subsequently deployed to Southern Front, two were not made operational until later in the war, and two others, 59 Army and a third incarnation of 26 Army, were deployed to Volkhov Front on 18 December, but the remaining four, 60 Army, a reconstituted 24 Army, 61 Army and 39 Army, were to be deployed against Army Group Centre during December.

Yet before even the first of the dozen new armies could become operational, the Red Army had to deal with the immediate threat to Moscow. After III Pz Group crossed the Volga-Moscow canal on 29 November, STAVKA had been obliged to commit two of 1 Shock Army's seven rifle brigades to a counter-attack, and it then released 1 Shock Army and 20 Army to Zhukov in order to fill the gap between 16 Army and 30 Army. Additionally, fresh forces, albeit poorly equipped and relatively untrained, were committed to 5 Army, 16 Army and 30 Army in the form of six rifle divisions and five rifle brigades, leaving Zhukov with a mobile reserve of three tank divisions, three motorised rifle divisions, twelve cavalry divisions and fourteen tanks brigades, all of which were considerably under-strength. At this time the 80,000 troops of 10 Army, without tanks or heavy artillery, were completing their deployment in the Ryazan area east of Tula.

STAVKA had been planning a counter-offensive on the Moscow axis since early November but the plan only took its final form as the month drew to a close. The detailed planning was supervised by Shaposhnikov and Vasilevsky. In August Vasilevsky had been appointed Chief of the Operations Department of the General Staff, in which role he was effectively Shaposhnikov's deputy, and he had been promoted to the rank of lieutenant-general on 28 October. In its final form STAVKA's plan required a general offensive by Kalinin Front, Western Front and the right flank forces of Southwestern Front. The latter included 13 Army, 3 Army and an operational group commanded by Timoshenko's deputy Kostenko. This offensive was initially designed to squeeze Army Group Centre along its entire front, to tie down front line forces to prevent their redeployment, and to force Bock's forces back from Moscow. Yet as the offensive unfolded, it developed into a campaign to encircle and destroy Army Group Centre.

By 4 December the German offensive had clearly stalled and STAVKA issued orders for the counter-offensive to begin the next day, though in effect it had begun days earlier with the commitment of 1 Shock Army and 20 Army against III Pz Group. In the early hours of 5 December 31 Army attacked across the frozen Volga at Kalinin, and before noon the offensive was joined by 29 Army on 31 Army's right flank. Bock, realising that the seizure of Moscow was no longer attainable, but unaware of Soviet intentions, prepared plans for a withdrawal of Army Group Centre to more defensible positions. Later that afternoon 5 Army struck IX Corps' positions south of Istra. The next day, as 1 Shock Army and 20 Army (the latter by this time under See Map 9 the command of Lt-Gen A A Vlasov) attacked to the west from the Dmitrov area towards Klin and Solnechnogorsk, 30 Army attacked to the southwest from northwest of Rogachevo. Lelyushenko's forces achieved a breakthrough and advanced to the northeast of Klin. Since the loss of the communications hub at Klin would have left most of III Pz Group isolated east of the town, Reinhardt ordered his forces to pull back from their positions facing 1 Shock Army and 20 Army, and he diverted 1 Pz Div to defend the town. On 7 December, with 30 Army almost overrunning Schaal's headquarters north of Klin, and Reinhardt's forward forces having to abandon some of their heavy equipment, 16 Army struck Reinhardt's extreme right flank, and as III Pz Group pulled back, it began to expose IV Pz Group's left flank positions. Hoepner ordered a withdrawal of IV Pz Group, as a result of which he was peremptorily sacked by Hitler and replaced by Col-Gen Richard Ruoff, the long-standing commander of V Corps. On 8 December Lelyushenko's forces moving west to the north of Klin, cut the rail link to Kalinin. Bock ordered 10 Pz Div north from XL Pz Corps' area to assist Reinhardt, and he subordinated III Pz Group to IV Pz Group and hence, since IV Pz Group was subordinated to IV Army, Kluge became responsible for the entire front from south of Kalinin to north of Tula. With the transfer north of 10 Pz Div, IV Pz Group's already compromised defences were further weakened and Ruoff was compelled to continue the withdrawal to the Istra begun by Hoepner. Despite the growing threat to III Pz Group from 30 Army's advance northwest of Klin, Zhukov was frustrated by the relatively slow progress of the offensive, particularly that being made by 1 Shock Army. On 9 December he issued a directive to his army commanders ordering them to bypass German strong-points and to use combined-arms combat groups to strike as deeply as possible into Army Group Centre's rear areas, and he ordered V I Kuznetsov to cut the road southeast of Klin by 10 December.

In Konev's area the advance was also disappointingly slow. The offensive by 29 Army was being held by IX Army, though the offensive by 31 Army was somewhat more effective, pushing more than 10km into the German lines east of Kalinin. On Zhukov's left flank 10 Army attacked German positions in the Mikhailov area on 6 December, and the next day it took the town. Farther west Belov's corps was threatening the rear of 17 Pz Div in the Venev area, and 50 Army had managed to widen its supply corridor to the north. On the evening of 7 December Zhukov ordered Boldin to launch an offensive from Tula to the south in order to cut the escape route of II Pz Army to the west. Boldin attacked the next day but made little progress. With much of his army under threat of encirclement, on 8 December Guderian ordered his forces to withdraw from the east and the northeast of Tula, and his forces were able by 10 December to bring Golikov's army to a halt on the Shat and the Don. Boldin tried again on 11 December to break Guderian's lines to the south of Tula but with no greater success. However Belov's corps continued to drive deep into II Pz Army's positions south of Venev, and took Stalinogorsk on 11 December. Off Guderian's right wing, in II Army's area, 13 Army struck to the north of Elets, while the operational group under Kostenko struck to the northwest from the Kastornoe area. II Army, temporarily under the command of Schmidt, was unable to hold the Soviet attacks. Gorodniansky's forces took Elets on 9 December, and Kostenko broke through Schmidt's lines and advanced to the northwest, encircling XXXIV Corps west of Elets. At the same time 3 Army took Efremov and pushed back II Army's left flank. These advances allowed Timoshenko to introduce the reserve 61 Army, commanded by M M Popov, on Southwestern Front's right flank between 3 Army and Western Front's 10 Army. With II Army's left flank in disarray, Guderian's right flank was at risk, and an offensive by 49 Army to the southwest from the Tarusa area threatened to isolate Guderian's left flank at Tula. Remnants of XXXIV Corps' two infantry divisions were able to reach the main German line to the west, but they did so without most of their heavy equipment. On 14 December Brauchitsch subordinated II Army to II

Pz Army, and Guderian was authorised to withdraw farther west, a move that would expose the right flank of IV Army northwest of Tula.

On Kluge's left flank III Pz Group, defying the best efforts of 30 Army and 1 Shock Army, continued to hang onto Klin, but on 12 December 16 Army took Istra and 20 Army took Solnechnogorsk. With the bulk of III Pz Group escaping from the 'Klin bulge', Zhukov ordered Lelyushenko and V I Kuznetsov to encircle Klin by 13 December. Reinhardt managed to hold the town until late on 15 December but he was beginning to lose close control of his increasingly panicky forces. The next day Kalinin was taken by 31 Army and 29 Army, and 30 Army was returned to Kalinin Front's command.[6] With the loss of Kalinin, the right flank of IX Army began to pull back to the west. Meanwhile Rokossovsky and Vlasov continued to press IV Pz Group west of the Istra. As the retreat of Ruoff's forces became increasing disorganised, Zhukhov committed 33 Army and 43 Army to an offensive against IV Army.

On 16 December Bock formally requested permission to withdraw Army Group Centre to shorter and more easily defended positions to the west. When permission was refused, Bock, claiming ill-health, resigned on 18 December and was replaced by Kluge. General Ludwig Kubler temporarily assumed command of IV Army until January, when he was succeeded by General Gotthard Heinrici, the long-time commander of XLIII Corps. On 19 December Brauchitsch resigned and Hitler, issuing orders for Army Group Centre to cease any further withdrawals, assumed command of OKH. Guderian was next, dismissed on 25 December after continuing to insist on further withdrawals. He was replaced by Schmidt, Weichs resuming command of II Army, and one week later the new commander of II Pz Army was promoted to the rank of colonel-general.

Winter Offensive

By mid-December it was clear to STAVKA that the threat to Moscow had been eliminated and that Army Group Centre was no longer capable of effective offensive operations. With the capture of Elets, Klin and Kalinin, the Soviet General Staff began to consider the possibility of an advance through Orel to Bryansk in the south, linked to an advance west of Rzhev to Smolensk in the north, that could encircle the vast bulk of Army Group Centre. Stalin endorsed the idea, and he insisted on a general offensive across the entire front that would also relieve Leningrad, retake Kharkov and relieve Sevastopol. Zhukov opposed this wider offensive. He argued that the Red Army did not possess the resources to mount a powerful offensive across the entire front, and that Army Group North and Army Group South occupied generally favourable defensive positions. Instead, he suggested, reserves, particularly of armour, should be concentrated in the centre where Army Group Centre was still off-balance and where German morale was at its lowest. However Stalin, keen to bring the war to an early and successful conclusion, encouraged by the success of the Moscow counter-attack, and scenting a possible collapse of the *Ostheer*, was not persuaded to limit his immediate ambitions.

On 17 December Meretskov received his orders for an offensive to be mounted across the Volkhov, and he was assigned two of the reserve armies from the Moscow

---

6   By then 29 Army was under the command of Major-Gen V I Shvetsov after Masennikov was assigned to command the new 39 Army.

area, 59 Army under the command of Galanin, and a third incarnation of 26 Army still under the command of Sokolov. The next day Kurochkin, who had been in command of Northwestern Front since October when STAVKA had relinquished its direct control of Front operations, was issued with a directive requiring a broad offensive aimed at Kholm, Vitebsk and Smolensk. Northwestern Front still held Ostashkov on the deep left flank of Army Group Centre and geographically was ideally positioned to strike south into the army group's rear. For the offensive, Northwestern Front was to be heavily reinforced, reinforcement that included 60 Army from the Moscow defence zone. Kurochkin's only problems were a shortage of food, lack of fuel, an overloaded and totally inadequate supply system, and unsuitable terrain for an offensive on the scale required.

At the same time, in order to facilitate the strike towards Orel, Bryansk Front was reconstituted under the command of Cherevichenko, Malinovsky, who had been promoted to the rank of lieutenant-general in November, taking over command of Southern Front. The new Bryansk Front, incorporating 61 Army, 3 Army and 13 Army, did not become operational until 24 December at which time STAVKA reintroduced the Southwestern Direction command under Timoshenko to supervise Bryansk, Southwestern and Southern Fronts. Kostenko then assumed command of Southwestern Front, while at 3 Army Batov replaced Kreizer on 22 December, Lt-Gen V N Lvov assuming command of 51 Army after Batov's departure from the Taman Peninsula.

Timoskenko had proposed a major offensive in the Ukraine requiring substantial reinforcement of Southern and Southwestern Fronts. The required reinforcements were not available and the plans had to be scaled back. Nonetheless, Timoshenko was assigned 57 Army, one of the new armies raised in the Moscow area in the first half of December. His objectives were to seize Orel and Kursk with Bryansk Front and the right flank 40 Army and 21 Army of Southwestern Front, while on the right wing of Southern Front Malinovsky would strike for Pavlograd and river crossings at the Dnieper bend. The force deployment and senior commanders in the south-western theatre had changed somewhat since the recapture of Rostov. Kharitonov's 9 Army had been withdrawn into reserve. Tsyganov had been moved from the command of 38 Army to command 56 Army on Southern Front's left wing. North of 56 Army along the Mius was 18 Army under the command of Major-Gen F V Kamkov. On Kamkov's right was 12 Army under the command of Major-Gen K A Koroteev, and occupying Southern Front's right flank was Lopatin's 37 Army. Tying in with 37 Army was 6 Army on the left flank of Southwestern Front. After Malinovsky's departure from 6 Army Gorodniansky was transferred from 13 Army to 6 Army in January, and Major-Gen N P Pukhov took over at 13 Army. On 6 Army's right flank occupying the line east of Kharkov was 38 Army. After Tsyganov's departure from 38 Army, Major-Gen A G Maslov, 38 Army's Chief of Staff, assumed command. East of Oboyan was Gordov's 21 Army and on Southwestern Front's right flank facing Kursk was 40 Army under the command of Podlas.

In the Taman Peninsula the Transcaucasian Front under Lt-Gen D T Kozlov had assembled Lvov's 51 Army and Major-Gen A N Pervushin's 44 Army[7] for an invasion of the Crimea across the Kerch Straits.

---

7   44 Army was another of the new armies raised at the beginning of December.

For the forces of Bryansk Front, Western Front and Kalinin Front the great offensive being approved by STAVKA represented little more than a continuation of the counter-offensive begun during the first week of December on the Moscow axis. By 18 December the whole of Western Front was engaged in offensive action. Zhukov's central armies facing IV Army were making only slow progress, but on IV Army's flanks the retreat of the panzer groups and of the panzer army were threatening to degenerate into a rout. In the south all eyes were on Kaluga. OKH was determined it should be held, and STAVKA that it should be taken. In order to be able to approach Kaluga from the south, Boldin formed an operational group of infantry, cavalry and armour under the command of his deputy Major-Gen V S Popov for a deep strike into the gap between IV Army's right flank XLIII Corps and XLVII Corps of II Pz Army. The operational group entered Kaluga on 21 December to find it being fiercely defended by elements of Heinrici's XLIII Corps, and it took until 28 December for V S Popov to secure the town. Meanwhile the rest of 50 Army together with 49 Army on its right were struggling to push west to support the operational group. On Boldin's left, Golikov's 10 Army had crossed the Plava and was pushing towards Belev, while Belov's corps, reinforced with cavalry from 10 Army, was given orders to strike deep into the German rear near Sukhinichi and then turn north to Yukhnov behind IV Army's lines. To support Belov and protect the cavalry corps' left flank, Golikov was to take Sukhinichi.

On Zhukov's right, operational groups from 20 Army and 16 Army took Volokolamsk on 20 December, and five days later the right flank of Western Front and the left flank of Kalinin Front had reached the Kotlyaki – Ostaslevo line. Here the panzer groups had established some well-defended positions on the river line of the Lama-Ruza bringing the Soviet advance to a temporary halt, while on Konev's right IX Army was desperately defending the Volga bend positions. By 25 December STAVKA had formed three additional shock armies by redesignating three existing armies. In transit to Volkhov Front, 26 Army became 2 Shock Army; Lt-Gen M A Purkayev's 60 Army forming up between 34 Army and 27 Army of Northwestern Front became 3 Shock Army; and Berzarin's 27 Army south of Ostashkov, in the process of being heavily reinforced, became 4 Shock Army, command of which was given to Eremenko after his discharge from hospital. Berzarin then assumed command of 34 Army.

By 26 December Maslennikov's 39 Army, having moved into position between 22 Army and 29 Army north of Rhzev, was ready to spearhead Kalinin Front's right flank offensive. Maslennikov struck towards the west of Rzhev. His advance was not rapid, but it ground through Strauss's defences on the Volga bend and, with the whole of Kalinin Front committed to offensive action, IX Army was unable to redeploy forces from other sectors. With Soviet forces advancing to the west south of Kaluga and pushing south in the Rzhev area, Kluge began to recognise the potential strategic threat to Army Group Centre, where IV Army was still holding the line east of Mozhaisk. The dilemma for OKH was how to respond. To try to pull back out of the potential trap in the prevailing weather conditions, with transport and fuel in chronically short supply and with virtually every kilometre of the front under continuous attack, could prove to be disastrous. Yet the consequences of trying to defend what was rapidly becoming the Moscow salient, could be even worse. The decision was made by Hitler; every centimetre was to be contested.

At the southern extremity of the front elements of 51 Army from Transcaucasian Front began to land at Kerch on 26 December. In appalling weather conditions, and against determined German opposition, Soviet losses were high. The landing on the south of the peninsula was crushed but the Soviet lodgement in the north defied the efforts of the defending XLII Corps to destroy it. On 29 December 44 Army began landings at Feodosiya against weak Rumanian opposition. The landings at Feodosiya threatened XLII Corps' rear and, in a withdrawal that infuriated Hitler, the corps pulled back to the neck of the peninsula – the so-called Ak-Monai positions. This left the bulk of the Kerch Peninsula in Soviet hands and, crucially, the landings diverted part of Manstein's army from the siege of Sevastopol where, in the second half of December, the Soviet defences were under immense pressure and were beginning to crack. Yet the objective of the landings was not to relieve the pressure on Sevastopol, it was to take back the Crimea, and in this the operation was a failure, the exploitation of the landings being too slow and Manstein's reaction too fast and effective for Kozlov's forces to be able to break out from the Kerch Peninsula and Feodosiya. In mid-January Manstein, who had been promoted to the rank of colonel-general at the turn of the year, struck back. He took Feodosiya and threw the Soviet forces in the Crimea onto the defensive along the Ak-Monai positions. Pervushin was killed in the Feodosiya fighting and was replaced by Lt-Gen S I Chernyak.

By the end of the year German casualties on the Eastern Front had risen to more than 930,000, but the Red Army's losses were around five times as great, and included more than three-quarters of a million killed and missing with more than two and a quarter million taken prisoner. On the Moscow axis in particular, formations on both sides were often shadows of their former selves. By 25 December more than 100,000 cases of frostbite had been reported by Army Group Centre. Some of Kluge's battalions were reduced to less than 100 men, while Zhukov had divisions of just 2,000 personnel and tank brigades that could not muster the equivalent of a full strength tank company.

On 1 January 40 Army and 21 Army on Southwestern Front's right wing launched their offensive towards Kursk and Oboyan against Paulus's VI Army. By 3 January both Soviet armies were engaged in heavy fighting on the line of the Seim, and the next day 21 Army cut the Belgorod – Kursk road and began to invest Oboyan. However, by 5 January the progress of 21 Army had stalled after a succession of German counter-attacks, and five days later Paulus's forces, attacking the junction of the two armies north of Oboyan and simultaneously attacking 21 Army's positions south of the town, had begun to break into the rear of Gordov's assault groups. On 5 January the right flank of 38 Army attacked towards Belgorod, but Maslov mishandled the attack and gave Paulus adequate warning of what was being prepared. As a result 38 Army made little progress. On 7 January Bryansk Front's 61 Army, joined three days later by the rest of the Front, launched an offensive on the Orel axis, but it made even less progress than had been made by the right flank of the neighbouring Southwestern Front. During the second week of January Timoshenko's offensives north of Kharkov ground to a halt.

At the time that Bryansk Front began the offensive towards Orel, Northwestern Front opened its broad offensive with Morozov's 11 Army on the Front's right flank south of Lake Ilmen striking towards XVI Army's positions at Staraya Russa, its objective being to take the town and to then turn to the northwest, threatening the right flank of XVIII Army anchored on northern shore of the lake. Morozov's offensive was intended to be coordinated with the offensive by Volkhov Front and Leningrad Front, the overall objective of which was to destroy XVIII Army. Since only half of 2 Shock Army and 59 Army had arrived in theatre, Meretskov's offensive north of Lake Ilmen was launched prematurely. Yet Meretskov had been left with little choice. The start date for the offensive had been set by Stalin, and Mekhlis, one of Stalin's cronies who was despatched to various command headquarters to sniff out political disloyalty, was at Meretskov's side to berate him for tardiness and inefficiency. Volkhov Front's attacks were totally ineffective, and the offensive was abruptly halted. For Meretskov, its only benefit was the dismissal on 10 January of Sokolov, a wholly incompetent former NKVD commander. Klykov assumed command of 2 Shock Army, and Yakovlev took command of 52 Army. The main part of Northwestern Front's offensive began on 9 January when Kurochkin's two shock armies attacked west and southwest from the Ostashkov area across frozen lakes, 3 Shock Army towards Kholm, and 4 Shock Army towards Andreapol. Purkayev's forces made little initial progress but 4 Shock Army, despite heavy losses, quickly took Peno, breaking through the German lines towards Andreapol. Kurochkin diverted some of Eremenko's forces to 3 Shock Army and by 12 January Purkayev's forces began to make progress. Thereafter, XVI Army's entire front was ripped open by Kurochkin's offensive. All Busch could do was to try to hold the communication nodes in an effort to deny Kurochkin's forces the mobility to penetrate too deeply to the west.

At IX Army Strauss was having similar problems. The penetration of 4 Shock Army towards Toropets had exposed his left flank, and as 39 Army, supported on its left by 29 Army, continued to grind its way towards Rzhev, Konev launched his right flank 22 Army in an offensive from Selizharovo south towards Belyi. By the end of the second week of January Maslennikov's 39 Army had broken through IX Army's lines west of Rzhev, slicing off XXIII Corps from the rest of IX Army.

On 8 January Zhukov was instructed to launch three offensives by his Front's left, centre and right. The left flank was to strike northwest towards Vyazma, the centre was to outflank Mozhaisk from the south and the right flank, in cooperation with the left flank of Kalinin Front, was to drive on Gzhatsk and cut the Vyazma – Mozhaisk communication route. On the right, 20 Army, incorporating 2 Gds Cav Corps under Major-Gen I A Pliev, led the offensive, supported on its flanks by 1 Shock Army and 16 Army. At the same time 5 Army advanced towards Mozhaisk. On Zhukov's left flank, 50 Army, aided by the advances of 49 Army on its right, had been making good progress west of Kaluga, but 10 Army had hit strong German defences at Sukhinichi. Unable to take the town, Golikov's forces bypassed it and continued to the west. On 13 January, six days into Cherevichenko's abortive offensive towards Orel, 61 Army was subordinated from Bryansk Front to Zhukov's command, but M M Popov's forces were too far south to be of any immediate benefit to Zhukov's offensive.

On 15 January, and for the first time in the war, Hitler issued an order for a large-scale withdrawal. Army Group Centre, under the growing spectre of encirclement, was permitted to move its front opposite Moscow back to a line running north to south 130km west of the capital. This permitted a shortening of the front, thereby freeing up troops for the flanks. As part of this withdrawal Ruoff's forces, designated IV Pz Army on 1 January, were able to withdraw to new and shorter defence lines east of Gzhatsk.[8] Despite Zhukov's heavy losses in the course of the winter offensive, the progress of his right flank and central armies gave him cause for optimism; Medyn was taken by 43 Army on 14 January, Veriya by 33 Army on 19 January and Kondorovo by 49 Army the same day. Yet, despite 5 Army's capture of Mozhaisk on 20 January, Zhukov's optimism was shattered on 19 January with STAVKA's decision to withdraw 1 Shock Army from Western Front and to move it to the Staraya Russa area to support Kurochkin's offensive south of Lake Ilmen. On Zhukov's left flank Schmidt had organised an operational group to strike into the left flank of 10 Army from the Zhizdra area in order to re-establish contact with the surrounded German force at Sukhinichi. By 19 January this operational group had taken Lyudinovo, prompting Zhukov to transfer Rokossovsky's headquarters south to the Sukhinichi area where it would assume command of half of 10 Army's forces in order to try to restore the situation

On 15 January, the day that Hitler authorised the withdrawal of Army Group Centre's forces, Strauss was replaced as commander of IX Army by Model.[9] Two days later Hitler, angered at the Soviet breakthroughs against XVI Army, irritated by Leeb's insistence that XVI Army should pull back farther to the west, and still resentful of the loss in December of German positions east of the Volkhov, sacked Leeb. Kuechler was appointed to command Army Group North, and General Georg Lindemann, the commander of L Corps, replaced Kuechler at XVIII Army. On 16 January 4 Shock Army took Andreapol, and by 20 January it had reached Toropets where Eremenko's forces secured large stocks of German food and fuel, a seizure of supplies that greatly assisted the subsequent development of Eremenko's offensive to the south. Farther north, Busch hung on grimly to Staraya Russa and Kholm, but the westward advance of 11 Army and 3 Shock Army had left his army's II Corps, with its 100,000 personnel, dangerously exposed at Demyansk in the Valdai hills east of the Lovat.

Since the southerly advance of Vostrukov's 22 Army was parallel to that of 4 Shock Army, STAKVA took the decision on 19 January to transfer the two shock armies from Kurochkin's to Konev's command. Eremenko's forces were to cut Army Group Centre's main supply route through Vitebsk and Smolensk, and 3 Shock Army was to take Velikie Luki and continue west to the Vitebsk – Orsha area. Kurochkin understood the logic of the decision to transfer 4 Shock Army to Kalinin Front, but he argued unsuccessfully for the retention of 3 Shock Army by Northwestern Front. Morozov was able to cut the German supply route to Demyansk from Staraya Russa, and by 8 February Kurochkin had II Corps completely surrounded. In order to facilitate the destruction of the German forces in the Demyansk pocket, STAVKA decided to reinforce 34 Army, which was investing the eastern half of the pocket. At Kholm Purkayev had managed to encircle a force of some 5,000 German troops during the last week of January but was unable to take the town. Kuechler organised an airlift of supplies to the encircled German forces at Demyansk and Kholm, and this air supply system became sufficiently effective that all of II Corps' supply needs at Demyansk

---

8   Reinhardt's III Pz Group had been similarly redesignated as III Pz Army on 1 January, and Reinhardt had been promoted to the rank of colonel-general.

9   With Model's departure, command of XLI Pz Corps passed to the 12 Pz Div commander, the newly-promoted Lt-Gen Josef Harpe.

could be met. Over a seventy-two day period, more than a hundred flights per day brought in 60,000 tons of supplies and evacuated 35,000 wounded.

While Konev's newly strengthened right flank was being used for a deep penetration of Army Group Centre's rear, 39 Army, supported by 11 Cav Corps, was to break though west of Rzhev and link up with Zhukov's left flank at Vyazma, from which the destruction of Army Group Centre would almost certainly follow. Yet Zhukov's left flank was under considerable pressure. By 24 January Schmidt's relief force had broken through to Sukhinichi and had established a narrow but viable supply corridor. By the fourth week of January Zhukov's offensives were running out of steam. Only 33 Army, advancing to the southwest between Mozhaisk and Malolaroslavets, and Belov's corps advancing westwards north of Sukhinichi, were continuing to make significant progress. Efremov was ordered to continue west to Vyazma where he would join with both Belov, whose corps was approaching the town from the southeast, and Col N V Gorina's 11 Cav Corps from Kalinin Front moving on Vyazma from the north. The advances of Soviet forces into the flanks of Army Group Centre had left Vyazma as the key supply hub to Kluge's entire command, and it was a town that he was determined to hold.

Despite the best efforts of Shvetsov and Maslennikov to take Rzhev, and despite the deep Soviet penetration to the west of the town, IX Army hung on to Rzhev, to Sychevka and to the rail line south to Vyazma. On 22 January Model launched an offensive from Rzhev to the west into 29 Army's forces, and IX Army's encircled XXIII Corps in the Azarovo area attacked to the east. The next day XXIII Corps made contact with VI Corps near Rzhev, and it was then Konev who found his forces split in two, with 39 Army, 11 Cav Corps and much of 29 Army southwest of Rzhev cut off from the rest of Kalinin Front north of the Volga. In an increasingly confused situation, Konev ordered 11 Cav Corps to continue to move south towards Vyazma, and he organised a counter-attack to try to break the newly-formed XXIII Corps – VI Corps link. After this counter-attack failed, Konev had to arrange for the supply of Shvetsov's and Maslennikov's forces through the 22 Army zone to the west where Vostrukov's forces had reached, but were unable to take, Belyi. The offensives of Kalinin Front, like those of Western Front had run out of steam. Kalinin Front had just thirty-five tanks in an operational condition, and a typical rifle division in 4 Shock Army was operating with just 2,000 personnel, one-quarter of the strength with which it had begun the offensive.

In the south Timoshenko, frustrated with his failed offensives against II Army and VI Army on the Orel, Kursk, Oboyan and Belgorod axes, turned his attention to the left flank of XVII Army in the Izyum – Slavyansk area. Riabyshev's new 57 Army was inserted into this area between Southwestern Front's left flank 6 Army and Southern Front's right flank 37 Army, and three cavalry corps were made available to exploit any breakthrough on this axis. A breakthrough towards Lozova would simultaneously permit a strike north towards Kharkov west of the Donets, a potential crossing of the Dnieper at Dnepropetrovsk, and a strike south to the Sea of Azov to isolate I Pz Army. Timoshenko's renewed offensive came too late to take advantage of a temporary command crisis at Army Group South Headquarters. On 12 January Reichenau fell gravely ill and died five days later. His replacement was not appointed until 18 January when Bock, seemingly sufficiently recovered from his incapacitating

See Map 10

illness of a month earlier, took command. On that day 6 Army and 57 Army attacked to the west. Both armies made progress for several days but Gorodniansky's advance ground to a halt at Balakliya in the face of determined German resistance, though to the south of Balakliya 6 Army, with support from 6 Cav Corps, cut the Kharkov – Lozova road on 26 January and took Lozova deep in the German rear the next day. From Lozova, Gorodniansky turned his divisions north towards Kharkov, but further progress was blocked by determined German resistance using forces sent south from the Kharkov area. Riabyshev's army hit similar determined resistance from Hoth's forces at Slavyansk on 22 January and the advance stalled. To try to achieve a successful outcome Timoshenko moved 9 Army from Malinovsky's reserve to the area southeast of Slavyansk between 57 Army and 37 Army. Malinovsky's intention was to use 9 Army, supported by 1 Cav Corps and 5 Cav Corps, to break through to the southwest towards Krasnoarmeyskoye northwest of Stalino and deep behind the line of I Pz Army, but Hoth's furious counter-attacks in the Slavyansk area prevented Kharitonov from organising an offensive. On Kharitonov's left, attacks by 37 Army against Hoth's right flank were similarly held, though on Kharitonov's right, elements of 57 Army began to penetrate Hoth's defences at Kramatorsk 10km south of Slavyansk. In response Bock moved Mackensen's III Pz Corps from I Pz Army to the Krasnoarmeyskoye area and to Kramatorsk to block any further advance by Riabyshev's forces. With Timoshenko unable to break the German defences at Balakliya and Slavyansk, defences that constituted the shoulders of his penetration, he was unable, despite the introduction of 57 Army and 9 Army into the salient during February and March, to exploit the penetration beyond Lozova. The resultant 80-kilometre square salient into the German front became known as the Izyum bulge or the Barvenkovo salient. Losses on both sides were high. By the end of January XVII Army had become so battered that it was amalgamated with I Pz Army to form 'Army Group Kleist' and III Pz Corps was combined with other units north of Krasnoarmeyskoye to form the 'Mackensen Group'.

After Volkhov Front's 7 January offensive had stalled, Meretskov was given permission to reorganise his forces, but the permission was accompanied by continued harassment from Mekhlis, and with a demand from STAVKA that the offensive be renewed by 13 January. Meretskov, arguing that he needed more time, nonetheless renewed his offensive on the due date. Once again 4 Army made no progress, and was actually thrown onto the defensive by German attacks. Galanin's 59 Army farther south also failed to make any progress, but on Meretskov's left wing 2 Shock Army and 52 Army did make some progress. Klykov's forces reached the Novgorod – Chudovo road, but there ran into ferocious resistance from German units determined to keep open the communication and supply route. Farther south 52 Army's advance towards Novgorod began to slow and eventually stalled. Off Meretkov's right flank, Leningrad Front's 54 Army, which had coordinated an offensive south of Lake Ladoga with Meretskov's attacks, also failed to make any significant progress. On 24 January a breakthrough on a narrow sector of the German line south of Chudovo was achieved by 2 Shock Army. Meretskov, expecting substantial reinforcement of his Front, ordered 2 Shock Army, supported by Major-Gen N I Gusev's 13 Cav Corps, to push through the breach, and he ordered Galanin and Yakovlev to widen the breach from north and south. Kuechler's forces held on tenaciously to the shoulders of the breach, which was less than a kilometre wide, as Meretskov's forces made equally determined efforts to widen it.

Meanwhile, at Stalin's insistence, 2 Shock Army was to advance on Lyuban from the southeast, Galanin was to secure Chudovo, and 54 Army was to renew its offensive south of Lake Ladoga, break through Kuechler's line and advance on Lyuban from the northeast. By mid-February the breach in the German line through which 2 Shock Army was being supplied had been widened sufficiently to prevent the supply convoys being subjected to direct fire artillery attack. During the second half of February Stalin continued to insist on energetic action by 2 Shock Army and 54 Army to reach and take Lyuban, and he was continually frustrated by the slow progress being made. At the beginning of March he sent a delegation to Meretskov's headquarters, a delegation that included Vlasov, appointed as Meretskov's deputy. In mid-March Klykov fell ill and Vlasov assumed command of 2 Shock Army. On 19 March a German offensive against Vlasov's supply corridor was successful, and 2 Shock Army was cut off for a week until an operational group, moved south from 54 Army, was able to reopen the supply route. Thereafter Vlasov argued vociferously that 2 Shock Army was in too vulnerable a position and should be withdrawn, but Stalin continued to insist that the salient be held and Lyuban taken. Vlasov's problems were compounded when Khozin, who did not appreciate the dire predicament of 2 Shock Army, persuaded Stalin that the Leningrad siege could be more quickly lifted if Volkhov Front were disbanded and the bulk of its forces incorporated into Leningrad Front.

By early February Kluge was beginning to sense that the mortal threat to his command was fading. Fresh divisions from the west were beginning to make their presence felt, the key towns were still in German hands and the road and rail links to them were being kept open. In particular, the recently arrived LIX Corps Headquarters under the command of Lt-Gen Kurt von der Chevallerie had been assigned to organise the defence of the vulnerable Velizh – Velikie Luki sector, and III Pz Army Headquarters was moving west to coordinate the defence of the Vitebsk area. Despite LIX Corps' best efforts, Velizh was surrounded by 4 Shock Army on 29 January, but Eremenko's forces did not have the strength to take the town. In a continuing advance to the south, 4 Shock Army surrounded Demidov on 3 February, but was too weak to take the town or to seriously threaten Smolensk to the southeast. Farther south Rokossovsky had been able to take Sukinichi on 29 January but XXIV Pz Corps, which since 8 January had been under the command of the newly-promoted Lt-Gen Langermann, had prevented any subsequent rapid advance towards Zhizdra or Kirov. Govorov's advance towards Gzhatsk had stalled, as had the offensives by 43 Army, 49 Army and 50 Army towards Yukhnov. Rhzev and Belyi were still in German hands despite deep Soviet penetrations to the south. Crucially, these penetrations had been unable to cut the Vitebsk – Smolensk – Vyazma road and, despite Zhukov's and Konev's best efforts, Vyazma and the roads leading from it to the north and east remained in German hands. It was a similar story in the III Pz Army/XVI Army sector where Vitebsk, Velizh, and Staraya Russa remained beyond the reach of Kurochkin's and Konev's forces, while Kholm and Demyansk, though surrounded, continued to deny Northwestern Front freedom of movement to the west. Even the commitment of 1 Shock Army on the Staraya Russa axis in February failed to dent XVI Army's defences south of Lake Ilmen.

On 1 February, in order to try to better coordinate the offensives by Western Front and Kalinin Front, STAVKA reconstituted the Western Direction Command under Zhukov. Zhukov also retained his role as commander of Western Front, but Golikov was appointed as his deputy and V S Popov assumed command of 10 Army. Zhukov's top priority was Vyazma. Gorina's 11 Cav Corps had reached the town from the north on 26 January but had been too weak to either capture it off the march or to permanently interdict the road into it from Smolensk. On 25 January lead elements of Belov's corps, approaching Vyazma from the southwest, were cut off from their heavy equipment, support services and supplies by German counter-attacks. A similar fate befell much of 33 Army approaching Vyazma in two columns from the east when on 3 February IV Pz Army, attacking to the south, re-established contact with IV Army. Beginning on the night of 27 January and over a six-day period, more than two thousand men from 4 Abn Corps were dropped west of Vyazma to assist in taking the town. The paratroops were widely scattered and less than two thirds of those dropped, mainly from 8 Abn Bgd, were able to form up into a coherent combat unit. Despite the presence of many thousands of Soviet combat personnel to the north, east and south of Vyazma, they were unable to take what had become a heavily defended fortress town and, isolated as they were from their own sources of supply, were unable to cut the road and rail links into Vyazma. To break what was rapidly becoming a stalemate, Zhukov's new command was heavily reinforced, but Konev's reinforcement was almost entirely negated on 17 February when Model's forces surrounded elements of nine divisions of 29 Army southwest of Rzhev. Shvetsov's forces tried to break out to the south but only 6,000 men made it to 39 Army's lines. On the nights of 18 February and 19 February the bulk of 4 Abn Corps was dropped west of Yukhnov in order to establish a link between the Soviet armies east of Yukhnov and 33 Army east of Vyazma. Of the seven thousand men dropped only half were able to gather into organised combat units, and these were largely isolated between Yukhnov and Vyazma by German defences. During March the Soviet effort against Vyazma fizzled out. Much of 33 Army was lost, and Efremov committed suicide after the failure of a breakout attempt. Belov survived and began an epic escape that, months later, would bring him and a substantial portion of his corps back to Soviet lines. Nonetheless, at Stalin's insistence, the Soviet offensives on the central axis continued through March and into April, but they achieved little in terms of additional territorial gain. Indeed the pendulum had started to swing the other way. By mid-February the left flank of 3 Shock Army, which had reached Velikie Luki on 3 February in a deep penetration of the German lines, was being pushed back towards Toropets; by the end of February III Pz Army had re-established contact with the German garrisons at Velizh and Demidov.

By the end of February the Soviet forces in the Kerch Peninsula had been heavily reinforced in preparation for a breakout attempt. A new Front had been created on 28 January to directly command the two armies in the Kerch Peninsula, and Kozlov had been appointed as the Crimean Front commander. The build up to the offensive, which was scheduled for 27 February, was minutely observed by XI Army, to the extent that Manstein was able to accurately predict days in advance the date of the offensive, and was consequently able to take effective counter-measures. Kozlov's attack, inexpertly conducted, was broken up by effective German ground defence, artillery fire and aerial attacks. In March Mekhlis was sent to cast his inexpert eye over Kozlov's headquarters. Intimidated by Mekhlis's political connections, Kozlov was inclined to defer to Stalin's crony whenever there was a difference of opinion in operational decisions. In March and early April Kozlov and Mekhlis committed 51 Army and 44 Army to two further offensives against the German positions, which in terms of territory gained achieved virtually nothing. Yet, as in January and February, the presence of a large and aggressive Soviet force in the eastern Crimea prevented Manstein from being able to commit XI Army fully to the reduction of the Sevastopol garrison.

North of Lake Ilmen and south of Livny, the Soviet winter offensives achieved little other than deep and potentially vulnerable salients southeast of Lyuban and south of Kharkov. On the central axis the offensives had been far more successful. The *Ostheer* had been thrown back from the gates of Moscow, and Army Group Centre had come close to complete destruction. By April 1942 the result of the desperate and often confused fighting in the enormous sector between Lake Ilmen and Livny had left a highly convoluted frontline in which German forces continued to hold many of the key towns (Staraya Russa, Demyansk, Kholm, Vitebsk, Velizh, Belyi, Smolensk, Rzhev, Gzhatsk, Vyazma, Roslavl and Bryansk), and kept open most of the supply routes into them, while Red Army forces, at the end of their offensive capability, held vast tracts of land between the road networks deep in the rear of many of the German garrisons.

4

Pause for Breath

In a conflict that lasted nearly four years there were surprisingly few occasions when there was a general pause in offensive operations across the entire front. The period from early April to early May 1942 may be considered one such period. Both sides were exhausted, both needed to regroup and resupply, and the inevitable season of mud rendered offensive operation highly problematic. The Red Army had quite literally exhausted its offensive potential, while German casualties on the Eastern Front had risen to nearly 1.2 million.

The previous nine months had been truly remarkable. During that time the Second World War had been transformed from a largely western European conflict to a pan-European war and then, with the Japanese attack on Pearl Harbour on 7 December 1941 and Hitler's declaration of war against the United States four days later, to a genuinely global conflict.

In Poland, Norway, France and the Balkans the *Wehrmacht* had grown accustomed to the short victorious war. With due allowance for its tremendous scale, the invasion of the Soviet Union had been seen in similar light and the *Wehrmacht* considered that it had little new to learn other than how to exploit to the maximum the Red Army's rigid command system, inexperienced officer corps, predictable tactical deployment and the deficiencies in its mobility and logistic support. Hitler had been contemptuous of the combat capability of the Red Army and he considered the Soviet Union to be a fragile political entity on the verge of implosion. This opinion was summed up in his declaration, "We have only to kick in the door and the whole rotten structure will collapse."

The events of the summer and autumn had certainly confirmed the view that the war would be short. During the vast encirclements at Minsk, Smolensk, Uman, Kiev, Melitopol, Bryansk and Vyazma it seemed to German commanders that the collapse of the Red Army could only be weeks, perhaps days, away. In October Axis forces on the Eastern Front achieved a manpower superiority over the opposing Soviet forces of nearly two to one. That the Soviet Union could sustain the losses of resources, manpower and territory during the summer and autumn of 1941, and then achieve a strategic victory at the gates of Moscow at the turn of the year seemed to most to be little short of miraculous. Yet a host of practical factors made such a victory not only possible but perhaps inevitable. One of the key factors was the existence of the Soviet strategic reserve. Pre-war Soviet military planning had assumed that the army's manpower would need to be replaced every six months or so during the course of a major war. Consequently the Soviet Union had steadily acquired a pool of around fourteen million men with at least rudimentary military training. At the outbreak of war the mobilisation of this manpower resource swung into action. The result was the creation during the second half of 1941 of forty-six new armies based on hundreds of new divisions and brigades. Poorly trained, poorly equipped and under-strength these new formations may have been, but they were a tangible military asset and in a steady stream they became available for deployment. Little wonder that to the German commanders, fighting the Red Army seemed like fighting the mythical multi-headed Hydra, with new Soviet armies springing into existence as fast as the armies in the field could be cut down. On 11 August 1941 Halder admitted that, "… we have underestimated the Russian colossus … [their] divisions are not armed and equipped to our standards. But … if we smash a dozen of them the Russians just put up another dozen…" By the end of November 1941 the manpower superiority of Axis forces on the Eastern Front had ended and would never recur. This remarkable turnaround in force ratios owed much to Stalin's decision at the beginning of October to transfer substantial forces from the Far East to the west, and this in turn was the result of convincing evidence submitted at the end of September by Richard Sorge, a Soviet spy at the German embassy in Tokyo, that a Japanese attack on the Soviet Union would not take place before the spring of 1942.

On its own, military manpower could not have saved the Soviet Union. But by early 1941 the Red Army had at its disposal a raft of new military equipment with the potential to match anything in the *Wehrmacht*'s arsenal. The best of the new fighters, the Yak-1, proved capable of taking on the Me-109s, and the new Il-2 ground attack aircraft was to prove to be devastatingly effective in the battles ahead. German troops were to find the T34 medium tank and the KV1 heavy tank to be perhaps the worst surprises of the early months of the war. With each passing month the reliability of the T34s improved and the competence of the Soviet tank commanders in the use of these battle-winning weapons increased. In the summer of 1941 the Red Army also acquired a highly effective new anti-tank gun. This was the long-barrelled 57mm ZiS-2 that was easily capable of destroying any tank that the *Ostheer* could place on the battlefield. Unfortunately for Soviet forces the production costs of the weapon were high and production was discontinued at the end of November 1941 in the mistaken belief that the standard Soviet 45mm anti-tank gun was sufficient for current and future purposes. Soviet infantry also possessed some useful new weaponry. For close quarter and urban fighting the PPSh submachine gun was introduced in 1940 and, subject to ongoing development, was to remain in use throughout the war. It may have been outclassed by the equivalent German weapon, the MP40, but unlike the MP40 the PPSh was simple and cheap to manufacture and was subsequently produced in prodigious numbers. Another highly successful infantry weapon introduced in 1940 was the 120mm heavy mortar. This mortar was so effective that the Germans copied it almost exactly. In 1941 two different types of 14.5mm anti-tank rifle were introduced, the PTRS and the more common PTRD. These weapons, nearly half a million of which were manufactured during the war, were reasonably effective against light tanks and were a threat to the German medium tanks if they could score a hit in the sides or rear at short range. At the outbreak of the war Soviet artillery was also being upgraded, with the 76mm F-22 USV divisional gun, the 122mm M-30 divisional howitzer and the 152mm ML-20 corps gun-howitzer already in quantity production.

The continuing availability of these weapons depended entirely on the ability of Soviet industry to maintain their production, and the ruthlessly efficient transfer of military productive capacity from the vulnerable areas of the Ukraine and western Russia to the safety of the Volga and beyond, was another key factor in the survival of the Soviet Union. Despite its vicissitudes, during the second half of 1941 Soviet industry produced 4,177 tanks, a figure that exceeded the 3,796 tanks and self-propelled guns produced in Germany in the whole of that year. By the end of March 1942 Soviet tank production had been increased to nearly 2,000 machines per month, a rate of production that Germany would never match.

Another key factor in the survival of the Soviet Union in 1941 was the speed with which the Red Army adapted its structure in response to the realities of the conflict with the *Wehrmacht*. As early as 15 July, with the war just twenty-three days old, Zhukov issued the first of what would be a series of directives on the revised structure of Soviet units. Mechanised corps were disbanded, and motorised rifle divisions were converted to conventional rifle divisions. Tank divisions and subsequently the rifle divisions were reduced in size to around 10,000 personnel, though in the battle for Moscow a rifle division was typically half that size. Only a few of the new tank divisions were actually formed, new tank formations being based on the smaller tank brigade of nine tank companies, six of them composed of light tanks, and the size of a tank company, particularly the medium tank company, was standardised at ten tanks. This process was formalised in an order of 23 August 1941. Also, at the insistence of Voronov, the artillery support to rifle divisions was reduced to one artillery regiment, the other being withdrawn for use in 'strategic artillery' formations. Most of the higher level organisational changes in the Red Army were driven by the chronic shortage of experienced or qualified senior commanders. The shortage was due in part to Stalin's purges, but losses at the front and the rapid expansion of the Red Army as the hundreds of new divisions and brigades were created were major contributory factors. As a result, the Fronts needed to create formations more easily handled by inexperienced middle-rank commanders. This was achieved by steadily disbanding the rifle corps so that by the end of 1941only six of the original sixty-two remained and the armies, designated 'Rifle Armies', were reduced in size to five or six rifle divisions with appropriate tank brigade and strategic reserve artillery reinforcement as was required for a particular task. Below army level the lack of experienced or qualified commanders and the long lead times needed to create new rifle divisions led to the need to create smaller autonomous combat units. The solution, one that persisted through to 1943, was the rifle brigade. Initially a somewhat ad-hoc formation based on a rifle regiment with assigned artillery support, some 250 rifle brigades were raised in the first year of the war and by the summer of 1942 their structure had been formalised to four rifle battalions, an artillery battalion of twelve 76mm regimental guns, an antitank battalion of twelve 45mm anti-tank guns, a heavy mortar battalion of eight 120mm mortars, and a separate submachine gun company. With a little over 5,000 personnel, these brigades had become well balance 'half-divisions' having a substantial headquarters staff with signals, reconnaissance, engineering and transport companies.

In an effort to compensate for the almost total destruction of the Soviet tank park in the early months of the war, the Red Army saw a dramatic expansion of cavalry forces during this period. Based on a pared-down cavalry division structure of just 2,600 men these forces, used in combat as mobile light infantry, offered Soviet commanders a degree of operational mobility that was simply unavailable to them in the form of mechanised formations. The result of the suite of structural changes during the second half of 1941 was a Red Army in which the army and subordinate units could be more efficiently commanded by a smaller number of commanders obliged to work with inexperience headquarters staff.

Yet one retrograde decision was taken in July 1941 that to some degree undermined the positive structural changes within the Red Army. This was the decision to reintroduce dual command at army, divisional and even regimental level. Dual command was a system whereby a unit's senior political officer had the right to question the operational decisions of the unit commander. It had been concluded in 1940 that the resultant ambiguity in this command system had been a contributory factor to the Red Army's poor performance against the Finns in the Winter War of 1939/40, and the practice had subsequently been discontinued. Its reintroduction in July 1941 was due in large part to the disastrous performance of the frontier armies, and what was perceived in Moscow as a lack of fighting spirit by many unit commanders. Stalin was determined that henceforth the Party's influence would be fully brought to bear on the military command decisions. The result was the second-guessing of those command decisions by people with little military training and the reintroduction of ambiguity into the command structure. In addition, the organisational difficulties at senior command level, already burdened by a generally low standard of staff work and inefficient communication systems, were further exacerbated by the rapidity of change in senior command posts. In the first six months of the war Southern Front had four different commanders, as did Northwestern Front (including an 'interregnum' period of direct STAVKA control). In the same period Leningrad Front was created from Northern Front and had five different commanders, while Bryansk Front was created, disbanded and reformed. At army level the changes in command could be even more rapid. In the first fifteen weeks of the war 21 Army experience seven changes in command, and in an eight-week period 13 Army had five different commanders. The Red Army's performance on the battlefield was also inhibited by the insistence, through the chain of command, of strict obedience to orders. In a system where everything was to be controlled from the centre, displays of initiative by commanders at all levels were positively discouraged. As a result, and when combined with the inexperience of Soviet commanders, with few exceptions Soviet operational tactics were predictable and 'by the book', enabling German commanders to anticipate and effectively counter Soviet actions.

During the first period of the war, the Red Army was on a steep learning curve and the lessons were bought at high cost. Yet steadily through experience, by adopting and adapting the things that worked and discarding, irrespective of conventional wisdom, those that didn't, the effectiveness of Soviet combat units began to rise. To his credit, Stalin was prepared to learn from his own mistakes. After the appointment of a raft of politically loyal NKVD officers to senior combat command positions had proved to be generally disastrous, there evolved a more meritocratic system of promotion that rewarded the strategically perceptive and tactically effective, as a result of which the frequency of change at senior command level began to decline. The command abilities of Zhukov, Vatutin, Voronov and Vasilevsky, had been recognised from the start. Others such as Rokossovsky, Konev, Tolbukhin and Malinovsky, deemed competent for moderately senior command prior to the outbreak of hostilities, were to demonstrate an outstanding ability for command at the highest level. Others, Cherniakhovsky, Katukov, Grechko and Pliev among them, through their demonstrable ability on the battlefield, rose from relative pre-war obscurity to become outstanding senior commanders. There were many others, such as Major-Gen M T Romanov whose 172 Rifle Div conducted a skilful and determined defence of Mogilev in July 1941, whose potential could only be glimpsed before they were killed or taken prisoner in the early months of the war. Stalin himself gradually came to recognise that his senior generals often knew better than he what was required to win a campaign, and he increasingly came to trust their judgement over his own.

A considerable Soviet propaganda effort was expended in exhorting each Soviet soldier and civilian to maximum effort. Appeals to patriotism and the protection of family quickly replaced calls for the stoical defence of Bolshevism. The issuing of medals, awards and rewards became commonplace. Another innovation came on 18 September 1941 when Order No 308 was issued at Zhukov's suggestion in which 100 Rifle Div, 127 Rifle Div, 153 Rifle Div and 161 Rifle Div were, in recognition of their example in fighting German forces in the central sector at Elnia, designated as 'Guards' divisions, numbered 1 to 4. These were the first of the Red Army's Guards divisions, the personnel in them being given special pay and other preferences. In all, 121 Guards divisions were to be formed during the war, and the concept was gradually expanded to include tank brigades, rifle corps, tank corps, armies and tank armies. The 'Guards' designation was generally awarded only to formations that had demonstrated outstanding combat performance, but an exception was the Guards Artillery Division, a designation given to all rocket artillery divisions.

At senior command level, trends at OKW and OKH ran counter to those at STAVKA. Where Stalin began to appreciate the limitations of his military expertise, Hitler, from an initial position of mere arbiter of strategy, became increasingly involved in tactical decision-making. From his order of December 1941 for Army Group Centre to stand fast, and his decision to dismiss 'defeatist' commanders, he concluded that he above all had the wisdom and the will to force a final victory. From his decision that II Corps should hold fast at Demyansk, and the subsequent successful defence of the pocket, he concluded that large formations of encircled German troops could be adequately supplied by the *Luftwaffe* while continuing to pose a significant threat to the enemy rear.[1] After the resignation of Brauchitsch on 19 December 1941 Hitler assumed the post of Commander in Chief OKH thereby eliminating the army's last vestige of service independence. Thereafter he began to appoint politically loyal generals to senior command positions, and increasingly he began to micromanage combat operations. In doing so he undermined one of the strengths of the German army, the delegated authority of commanders on the battlefield to make independent command decisions and their ability to respond flexibly to changes in operational circumstances.

Having anticipated a conflict of around eight weeks duration, prior to 1942 there had been little planning by the German High Command for a prolonged conflict. Weapon development projects during 1941 had been scaled back or cancelled and virtually no preparation had been made for the possibility of the conflict continuing into the depths of a Russian winter. Yet having faced a larger, better-equipped and more resilient foe than it had anticipated, as the winter of 1941 approached OKH

---

1   On 26 April 1942 Busch managed to lift the siege of II Corps by punching a narrow but viable supply corridor through to the encircled corps. Nine days later the German garrison at Kholm was relieved after a siege lasting nearly 15 weeks.

found that it was facing an enemy whose morale was still unbroken, that was, unlike the *Ostheer*, fully equipped for winter fighting, and that was adapting its tactics in light of bitter experience. An example of evolving Soviet tactics was the clash that took place between Eberbach's 5 Pz Bgd and Katukov's 4 Tank Bgd southwest of Mtsensk in October 1941. Katukov concentrated his force and used advantages of surprise, terrain and armament range to good effect.[2] Clashes of this sort prompted the *Wehrmacht* to revive pre-war plans for the development of a heavy tank, and for the development of a new medium tank that could emulate the combat capability of the T34. Until such new weapons could be both developed and produced in quantity, the *Ostheer* would be left to fight using tanks designed in the 1930s.

Fortunately for Germany, in the PzKpfw Mk IV it had a machine that was capable of extensive development in its power train, its armament and its armour. During its development the Mk IV became the backbone of the panzer forces, and for a time gave the *Ostheer* a renewed qualitative edge. The Mk III was too small and too light for such major upgrading, but there remained an urgent requirement for thicker armour and an improved gun. The most immediate improvement to the Mk III and the Mk IV was a doubling of their armour protection through the fitting of face-hardened spaced plates, and the acceptance of a consequent reduction in their mobility. The Mk IV was up gunned through the replacement of its short-barrelled 7.5cm infantry support weapon with a highly effective 43-calibre variant of the new 7.5cm anti-tank gun. The Mk III was not capable of taking the 7.5cm anti-tank gun, but its armament was improved somewhat by the replacement of its 42-calibre 5cm gun with a variant of the long-barrelled (60-calibre) 5cm Pak 38 (L/60) anti-tank gun that was being issued to the infantry. The deficiencies of the infantry's standard 3.7cm anti-tank gun had been recognised since 1940. Though light and manoeuvrable, it was almost useless in dealing with the T34 and KV1 and was a factor in the rout of 112 Inf Div by part of 32 Tank Bgd supported by 239 Rifle Div southeast of Tula in November 1941. In response, the process, begun in 1940, of replacing the infantry's 3.7cm gun with the Pak 38 (L/60) was accelerated. Also available was a variant of the 7.5cm anti-tank gun developed for infantry use (the Pak 40). Although the 7.5cm was an effective weapon it was too heavy to be manoeuvred manually and had to be towed into position by motorised transport, severely limiting its operational flexibility. The highly effective 8.8cm dual-purpose anti-aircraft and anti-tank gun was even more unwieldy, and at 4.4 tonnes was nearly ten times the weight of the early 3.7cm gun. In 1940 the *Wehrmacht* had begun the development of the self-propelled gun, a turretless armoured fighting vehicle based on the chassis of a tank with a gun fitted to a fixed casement. Such weapons generally had a lower profile than a tank, were easier and cheaper to manufacture and, depending on their configuration, could be used as mobile indirect fire artillery, as direct fire infantry support weapons, or as 'tank-killers'. In the direct fire infantry support assault gun role, Germany developed in 1940 the StuG III based on the PzKpfw Mk III chassis and armed with the short-barrelled 7.5cm infantry support gun. In the same year the *Panzerjäger* I, the first 'tank-killer' self-propelled gun, was developed based on the PzKpfw Mk I tank chassis and armed with a 4.7cm Pak(t)

---

2   Later in the war Katukov was to command a tank army, and Eberbach was to command a panzer army.

gun. These weapons were the first of a range of increasingly powerful self-propelled guns developed by Germany during the course of the war.

The main weapons of the German artillery arm were developed in the early 1930s. At regimental level, two infantry support guns predominated – the short-barrelled 7.5cm leIG18 and the somewhat cumbersome 15cm sIG33. At divisional level, artillery support was based primarily on the 10.5cm sK18 field gun, the 10.5cm leFH18 howitzer and the 15cm sFH18 heavy howitzer. In the early period of the war these artillery pieces, used in conjunction with the German army's efficient and effective fire control system, proved to be eminently fit for purpose, and they were subject to little further development. The leFH18 was upgraded in 1941 to achieve a modest increase in range, and to improve the range of the sFH18, the ammunition for the gun was modified to provide a rocket propulsion element to the shell's propellant system. The German army had a range of larger calibre artillery pieces (15cm and above), and significant use was made of captured guns, but the mainstay of the artillery arm remained the regimental and divisional artillery weapons with which Germany went to war in 1939.

As a means of countering the improved armour protection of tanks, in conjunction with the introduction of faster and heavier anti-tank projectiles, considerable development went into the design of the projectiles. The first improvement from the simple solid shot was the addition of a softer metallic cap to prevent the break-up of the armour penetrating component on impact. Further improvements were achieved by the use of tungsten carbide in the main shot, and the streamlining of the shot to achieve higher muzzle velocities by the fitting of a ballistic cap to the impact cap. Such developments were pursued by both sides during the early period of the war and the result of this work had a considerable impact on force structure and tactics as the war progressed.

In the air, both sides strove to improve the performance of their aircraft, neither side gaining a distinct technological advantage. The Red Army took some time to recover from the devastating aircraft losses of the first few days of the war, but in a combat zone as large as the Eastern Front neither side would ever achieve true air superiority. All that could be achieved was local and often merely temporary advantage on a particular strategic axis.

By 1942 no amount of technical innovation could offer Germany a realistic prospect of winning the war, and it is difficult to envisage circumstance in which, from the *Ostheer*'s situation in the spring of 1942, it could have achieved a victory in the East; that is, to have forced the Soviet Union to capitulate. An issue that has generated considerable speculation is whether Germany could have achieved that victory if it had acted differently in 1941. It seems unlikely that a capitulation of the Soviet Union could have been achieved even then. In August 1941 Army Group Centre simply did not have the resources to continue to batter its way east along the Moscow axis, and any attempt to do so in September would have left it with elongated and increasingly vulnerable flanks. The clearing of the flanks, particularly the turn south by II Pz Group, was not only the path of least resistance, it was the sensible military option. By the end of August, when it appeared that the offensive against Southwestern Front was likely to reach a successful conclusion, German High Command had been faced with a decision about the further conduct of the war in 1941. It had three basic options. The first was to adopt a defensive posture after the Kiev operation using the panzer formations as a powerful mobile reserve, and to use all available infantry to secure Leningrad. This option was favoured by only the most cautious and disbelieving of *Wehrmacht* intelligence assessments of Red Army strength.[3] The second option, as articulated in Hitler's Directive of 30 July, was to use the combined power of Kleist's and Guderian's panzer groups to conduct deep penetrations into the eastern Ukraine to secure the Donbas region. The two panzer groups constituted a powerful mobile force in an area where the Red Army was deficient in both effective fighting units and prepared defences. It is possible that such an offensive could have been extended to close the Volga traffic at Stalingrad and to seize the Caucasian oil fields, securing in the autumn of 1941 much if not all of what the *Wehrmacht* spent most of 1942 trying to achieve. Hitler, with an eye to the broader economic issues, probably favoured this option during most of August. It may not have won the war, but it would have been Germany's best chance of securing an unequivocal strategic victory in 1941. The third option, strongly favoured by Halder, Bock, Guderian and Hoth, and the one finally chosen by Hitler, was to move on Moscow. Not only did this final German offensive of 1941 fail but, given what we now know, that failure was almost inevitable. Enormous effort had been expended by the Soviets in preparing the city for defence, and it was where Stalin, in defiance of Zhukov's advice, had placed the bulk of the Red Army's strategic reserve. In addition, the panzer forces needed for an assault on Moscow were in the wrong place in September 1941; II Pz Group was in the south and IV Pz Group, together with half of III Pz Group, was in the north, and it would take time to relocate the panzer forces to Army Group Centre. Despite the spectacular success of the opening phase of Operation Typhoon, the capture of Moscow was always going to be a two-stage operation.

Towards the end of November 1941 as the panzers inched their way forward to the Moscow suburbs, German expectations of an imminent Soviet collapse remained prevalent, but they had acquired an air of desperate belief. Hope was sustained by erroneous German military intelligence estimates of Red Army strength and combat capability. These suggested that the Red Army was played out; that one more push should bring Moscow within reach and Stalin to an accommodation. By that time, the problem for Army Group Centre was that it too was nearly played out. The furious, but wasteful and seemingly futile Soviet offensives at Velikie Luki, Gomel, Smolensk, Elnia and along the final approaches to Moscow had fatally sapped Army Group Centre's strength. The inability of the Germans to take Moscow at the end of November 1941 renders somewhat moot the questions of whether, had they taken the city, they could have held it through the winter, or of whether the capital's loss would have necessarily led to the collapse of the Soviet regime.

The Soviet counter-offensive of 5 December 1941 sent shock waves through the German military and political establishment. Within weeks it had become clear that, not only might this be a long war, but with the Red Army clawing its way into the deep flanks of Army Group Centre, and an Anglo-American military alliance about to be forged across the English Channel, it was a war that Germany might actually be at risk of losing. The German defeats at Tikhvin and Rostov could have been explained away as tactical adjustments prior to the onset of a winter pause; but the reverse at the gates of Moscow was an unambiguous strategic defeat for all to see. The Soviet victory had

---

3   Of which Stuelpnagel was one; his strategic 'timidity' being duly noted by OKH.

not only thrown the invaders back from the capital, it had exploded the myth of the unbeatable *Wehrmacht*, and that in turn was to have a profound psychological effect not only on the two main combatants, but also on political and military observers across the globe.

Hitler's disappointment that Operation Barbarossa had not ended with the capture of Moscow was matched by Stalin's disappointment that the Red Army's winter offensives had not achieved more. By the spring of 1942 the operational initiative was returning to the *Ostheer*, and Hitler had to decide where next to strike. The *Ostheer* was no longer capable of the multiple simultaneous strategic offensives that had characterised Operation Barbarossa. Its choices came down to one of two; a strike at Western Front in a renewed attempt to take Moscow, or a strike into southern Russia, to the Don Bend, the Caucasian oilfields and the lower Volga. Hitler chose the south, explaining to Paulus, "If I do not get the oil of Maikop and Grozny, then I must end this war."

During the spring and early summer of 1942 Army Group South was massively reinforced at the expense of both Army Group Centre and Army Group North. Bock received II Army and, for the all-important mobile operations, IV Pz Army, transferred to his left flank from Army Group Centre. At the end of May Hoth replaced Ruoff as commander of IV Pz Army and Ruoff assumed command of XVII Army. In I Pz Army and IV Pz Army Bock had the majority of the *Ostheer*'s panzer divisions, and of the 129 German divisions on the Eastern Front on the eve of the summer offensive, 54 were in Army Group South. To provide sufficient infantry for the forthcoming offensive the infantry divisions of Army Group North and Army Group Centre had been stripped of 'excess' manpower. A fully manned German infantry division at that time contained 17,734 personnel (a panzer division had a somewhat smaller authorised strength of 15,600). In the German army there had always been specialist infantry formations such as mountain divisions, and during the late 1930s Germany had experimented with other formations – divisions with a small panzer component, and *Jäger* ('hunter' or 'pursuit') divisions. From this period of experimentation it was concluded that divisions based on just six instead of the normal nine infantry battalions were viable combat formations.[4] Such divisions might contain three two-battalion regiments or two three-battalion regiments, and most of the infantry divisions of Army Group North and Army Group Centre were reduced to one or other of these configurations during the summer of 1942. Yet Kuechler's and Kluge's infantry divisions were still expected to defend the same length of front line. It was Bock's army group that felt the benefit of these changes, almost all of its infantry divisions retaining the nine-battalion structure. It was a similar story in the panzer divisions; those of Army Group South would have three tank battalions each while those in Army Group North and Army Group Centre would have only one. Even so it was recognised by OKH that German manpower in the south, particularly as the offensive developed and frontlines lengthened, might be insufficient for the objectives to be achieved. During the winter of 1941/42 Army Group South had lost most of its combat support from Germany's Axis allies. The Hungarian troops had been withdrawn at the end of November 1941,

---

4   The German light infantry divisions that participated in Operation Barbarossa were such six-battalion formations. One was redesignated 7 Mtn Div in the autumn of 1941, and the rest were redesignated *Jäger* divisions in July 1942.

and most of the Rumanian troops had returned to barracks over the winter.[5] After some diplomatic arm-twisting, Hitler obtained a commitment from the Hungarian government to supply a field army to Army Group South during the summer of 1942. The Rumanians agreed to increase their contribution back to two field armies, and Mussolini also promised an army. Not all of these Axis forces would be available for combat operations at the start the *Ostheer*'s summer offensive, but their availability later in the offensive had been factored into the OKH planning.

During the spring of 1942 Red Army personnel numbers in the Western theatre continued to rise, and by the summer of 1942 there were approximately three Red Army personnel for every two Axis personnel. In addition, Soviet tank production had increased to such an extent that at the end of March 1942 the Red Army could reintroduce the tank corps. Initially with an authorised strength of little more than 5,500 men with 20 heavy tanks, 40 medium tanks and 40 light tanks, the corps were to consist of two tank brigades and a genuinely motorised rifle brigade with more than 300 trucks. By the autumn of 1942 twenty-five such corps had been formed, many through the acquisition of formerly independent tank brigades. During the latter part of 1941 and early 1942 the Soviet tank brigade had undergone a number of organisational changes, largely reflecting changes in the Soviet tank park. By mid-1942 light tank production was based almost entirely on the newly developed T70 and on the T60, the latter being a lightly armed post-invasion rushed modification of the amphibious T40. At the end of June General Y N Fedorenko, head of Soviet tank forces, laid down the principles for the future operation of armoured forces. Tank corps were to be concentrated on strategic missions as directed by Front commanders and would not be used for head-on attacks unless heavily supported by aircraft and artillery. Instead they would aim for weak spots in German defensive positions and would be directed at strategic targets some 50km behind enemy lines. Logistic support would be properly organised and would be sufficient for five days of continuous operation. In their deployment the tank corps were to make maximum use of surprise and favourable ground. Artillery and support aviation were to coordinate their operations with the armour and infantry as closely as possible. These principles were hardly revolutionary but they had not previously been clearly articulated in Soviet doctrine. Unfortunately for Soviet commanders, only the T34 was suitable for the required deep and rapid exploitation of the breakthrough sector. The KV1 was too slow and of too limited a range for such a role and even the supposedly nimble T60 had difficulty maintaining contact with the medium tanks across country. In July 1942 the structure of the tank brigade was changed again to include 32 T34s and 21 light tanks. The KV1s were withdrawn from the tank brigades for use as infantry support (NPP) tanks, and Soviet weapons designers began work on the development of a new even heavier infantry support tank.

During 1942 new directives were issued by STAVKA on the conduct of operations at the tactical level; NPP tankers were to ensure that gaps of more than four hundred metres were not allowed to develop between them and the following infantry; tank-to-tank battles were to be avoided unless the terrain conditions and force ratios were highly favourable, with artillery being used preferentially to counter German tanks;

5   Only two Rumanian corps remained in the *Ostheer* during this time; a mountain corps with XI Army in the Crimea and VI Rum Corps within XVII Army.

infantry forces were to scout for, mark out and, if possible, destroy enemy antitank mines and obstacles; pockets of resistance bypassed in the initial advance were to be closed off and annihilated, not left to disrupt rear services. These were just some of the lessons learned at heavy cost by the Red Army.

The final organisational manifestation of Fedorenko's requirement for the concentration of armoured power was the tank army. On 25 May 1942 the State Defence Committee issued an order for tank armies to be formed, the first of which became operational just three weeks later. Initially based on two tank corps, an independent tank brigade and one or two rifle divisions, the structure of the tank army was to evolve during the course of the war. In September 1942 the Red Army also began to reintroduce tank regiments. These were small units, initially of less than 350 personnel, and unlike the tank brigade, the purpose of which was independent deep penetration of enemy positions, the tank regiment was designed for the direct support of infantry. The tank regiments introduced in September 1942 had around 40 light and medium tanks, but in October Guards heavy breakthrough tank regiments began to be formed based on twenty or so KV1 heavy tanks and with little more than 200 personnel.

While, during the spring of 1942, Hitler was preparing the *Ostheer*'s summer offensive, Stalin was not content to sit back and await events. He wanted to put the growing military strength of the Red Army to operational use and, while he accepted in principle the analysis of the General Staff that the Red Army should, at the strategic level, adopt a defensive posture during the summer of 1942, in practice he encouraged his generals to conduct localised spoiling attacks – so-called 'active defence' or 'partial offensives' – that cumulatively negated the 'strategic defensive' concept.

5

Stalingrad

During the first week of May 1942 improving ground conditions presented both the *Ostheer* and the Red Army with offensive opportunities. Hitler had already determined that the *Ostheer*'s strategic offensive for the summer would be directed into, and beyond, the great bend of the Don, but OKH had a number of lesser objectives to be urgently addressed. In the north, 2 Shock Army, mired in marsh and forest though it may have been, still represented a threat to Lyuban. In the south, the Izyum Bulge was a threat to Kharkov, and would have to be eliminated prior to the *Ostheer*'s main summer offensive. In the Crimea, Sevastopol still defied Manstein's XI Army, while in the Kerch Peninsula the threat to XI Army had increased with the introduction of a third Soviet army into Kozlov's command.

For STAVKA the offensive priority in May 1942 was Kharkov. In mid-March Timoshenko had proposed two offensives against Army Group South in order to encircle Kharkov and thereby forestall any planned German strike against Moscow from the southwest. These proposed offensives were to be from the Izyum Bulge south of Kharkov, and from bridgeheads across the northern Donets northeast of the city. Yet Timoshenko's ambition did not end with Kharkov; using a massively reinforced Southwestern Front, he proposed to develop the offensive into a wider campaign to retake the eastern Ukraine. Timoshenko was denied the reinforcements required for such a strategic effort, but even the planned operation to retake Kharkov, for which he did obtain STAVKA's approval, stretched the concept of 'active defence' beyond any reasonable limit. In addition, Zhukov was authorised to prepare offensive operations to retake Demyansk and Rzhev, and both Khozin and Kozlov were authorised to prepare 'partial offensives' to lift the siege of Leningrad and recover the Crimea.

In the event it was the *Ostheer* that struck first.

The Crimea

On the morning of 8 May three of Manstein's corps from XI Army struck the Soviet armies defending the neck of the Kerch Peninsula. The offensive did not come as a complete surprise to Kozlov and Mekhlis, who were effectively in joint command of Crimean Front, but they failed to make any adequate provision to meet the German attack. Major-Gen K S Kolganov's 47 Army, another of the new armies raised in December 1941, had been assigned to Crimean Front and positioned on the Front's right flank in the neck of the peninsula. With 51 Army in the centre and 44 Army on the left, the Front was a quarter of a million men strong with 3,500 guns and 350 tanks. Yet most of the combat forces were committed close to the frontline, leaving the Front with little operational flexibility. Kozlov expected the main German effort to be made in the north against 47 Army, but in fact Manstein struck with XXX Corps against 44 Army in the south, supported on its left flank by XLII Corps. Within hours Crimean Front's communication, command and control system, inadequate to begin with, collapsed almost completely. Chernyak's section of the front began to disintegrate, and Manstein's right hook, assisted by a sea-borne landing behind Chernyak's line, broke through and swung northeast towards the Sea of Azov. Kolganov, largely unaware of what was happening at the other end of the front, and unable to get much sense out of Front Headquarters, did not begin to pull his army back until it was too late. As Chernyak and Lvov began an increasingly chaotic retreat to the east, much of 47 Army became trapped with its back to the Sea of Azov. By 14 May Manstein's forces had reached Kerch, leaving Kozlov little choice but to begin to plan for a beachfront evacuation across the Kerch Strait. Yet the peninsula's evacuation, under skies dominated by the *Luftwaffe*, proved to be hardly less disastrous than had been its defence. By 20 May it was virtually all over. In just twelve days Crimean Front had lost virtually all its heavy equipment and more than 175,000 men, mainly as prisoners, though Lvov was one of the fatalities. Overseeing the debacle was the somewhat transient 'North Caucasian Direction', established during the fourth week of April under Budenny, and disbanded one month later. Crimean Front was also disbanded and a new North Caucasian Front was established under Budenny's command to defend the Taman Peninsula and the adjacent coastal areas from attack across the Kerch Strait. In addition, the Transcaucasian Military District between the Black Sea and the Caspian Sea was converted into an operational Front. For Soviet commanders everywhere the campaign's only redeeming feature was the official admonishment and subsequent demotion of Mekhlis.

With the elimination of any threat from the eastern Crimea, Manstein was free to turn his full attention to the continued resistance of the 100,000 Soviet defenders of Sevastopol. Hunkered down in their bunkers, tunnels and trenches around the city, Petrov's force, adequately supplied by the Black Sea Fleet, had defied XI Army for eight months. Manstein had brought in Germany's heaviest siege guns, a direct hit from which could blow apart a reinforced concrete bunker, and in early June he began a massive artillery and aerial bombardment of the Soviet defensive positions. Supplies from the surface ships of the Black Sea Fleet were interdicted, forcing the defenders to rely on submarines for resupply. Throughout June German and Rumanian troops steadily eliminated the Soviet defensive positions, particularly at the northern extremity of the defences at Severnaya Bay. At the end of June, with the defenders low on ammunition, STAVKA ordered the evacuation of key personnel, but the vast majority could not be evacuated. By 4 July the fighting was largely over, though many units, their situation entirely hopeless, did continue to resist well into July. For his success in the Crimea, Manstein was rewarded with a promotion to Field Marshal.

Kharkov

As Kozlov's forces were being driven back along the Kerch Peninsula, Timoshenko opened his carefully prepared offensive to retake Kharkov. Since the winter fighting, there had been numerous changes of command in the south. In mid-April Southwestern Direction had lost command responsibility for Bryansk Front. Timoshenko then assumed direct command of Southwestern Front but he also retained command of Southwestern Direction (Kostenko becoming deputy 'Direction' commander). During the previous month Golikov had been appointed to the command of Bryansk Front to which 40 Army had been transferred from Southwestern Front's right flank. A number of army commanders were also changed during this time. Timoshenko had acquired a new army, which was placed under the command of Riabyshev. Podlas replaced Riabyshev at 57 Army (by then firmly ensconced in the Izyum Bulge) and Lt-Gen M A Parsegov was appointed to replace Podlas at 40 Army. In addition, Moskalenko had replaced Maslov at 38 Army and Major-Gen A A Grechko replaced Koroteev at 12 Army.

The army that Timoshenko acquired was one of the new armies raised in December 1941. Designated 28 Army (the previous army with this designation having been lost in the Smolensk campaign), and released from the strategic reserve on 10 April, it was inserted into the line in the Volchansk area between 21 Army and 38 Army. In the Izyum Bulge, in addition to part of 38 Army, 6 Army, 57 Army and part of 9 Army, Timoskenko had created a powerful operational group under the command of Major-Gen L V Bobkin. Timoshenko's plan was simple enough; Riabyshev, supported by Gordov on his right and by Moskalenko on his left, was to strike to the southwest, and Gorodniansky, promoted in March to the rank of lieutenant-general, was to strike to the north. The result would be a wide encirclement of Kharkov and the elimination of German forces from the Donets area. The left flank of Gorodniansky's 6 Army would be secured by Bobkin in a strike towards Krasnograd.

Timoshenko's offensive into the flanks of VI Army opened on 12 May. In the south Gorodniansky achieved a breakthrough and Timoshenko committed 6 Cav Corps through the gap in the German lines. In the north Riabyshev and Gordov concentrated six rifle divisions and four tank brigades in a narrow 15km sector facing XVII Corps. Pounded by artillery and aerial attack XVII Corps' lines buckled but Timoshenko, with 3 Gds Cav Corps not yet fully assembled in the north, was unable to achieve an operational breakthrough. For several days Paulus struggled to contain the Soviet advance, and he achieved some success in the north where he was able to commit 3 Pz Div and 23 Pz Div in a counter-attack against the left flank of 28 Army and right flank of 38 Army. Nonetheless Riabyshev advanced to within 20km of Kharkov before his offensive began to stall in the face of a series of German hedgehog defences.

In April, Golikov, from reserves flooding into his command, had managed to create an additional army (a reconstituted 48 Army which became operational on 20 April). These reserves included four of the new tank corps, and on 23 April Golikov was ordered to prepare an offensive to encircle Orel. This was scheduled to begin at the same time as Timoshenko's offensive against Kharkov but Golikov was not ready in time and obtained STAVKA's permission for a delay of four days. On 16 May he was ordered to postpone his plans for Orel, divert the Front's combat aircraft to his left flank and to launch his left flank 40 Army into an immediate offensive against Kursk in an effort to support Timoshenko's stalling offensive farther south. In the event 40 Army's forces were too unprepared and too far to the north of Kharkov to have any effect on Timoshenko's situation.

At Army Group South Headquarters, Bock had been planning an offensive of his own. Using VI Army and 'Army Group Kleist', it was scheduled to begin on 19 May in the Izyum Bulge area. Consequently, Bock already had significant forces in position around the salient when Timoshenko's offensive opened. With Malinovsky's Southern Front relatively inactive and with Riabyshev's offensive confined to a fairly narrow sector, Bock was also able to release forces from other sectors of the front.

On 17 May, two days earlier than originally planned, Kleist attacked the 9 Army positions near the southern shoulder of the bulge in the Slavyansk area, and pushed Kharitonov's forces back nearly 20km, thereby exposing the left flank and rear of 57 Army. Malinovsky responded by diverting reserves including 5 Cav Corps to reinforce 9 Army, and Timoshenko requested reinforcements from STAVKA to hold the salient. Vasilevsky recommended that the offensive should be broken off and the armoured forces in the area (including 21 Tank Corps and 23 Tank Corps) that were waiting to exploit the southern penetration towards Kharkov, should be turned around and used against I Pz Army. But Vasilevsky who, due to Shaposhnikov's poor health had become acting Chief of the General Staff on 24 April, and who was promoted two days later to the rank of colonel-general, was overruled by Stalin who had been reassured by Timoshenko that the available defensive measures were adequate. Yet by the next day I Pz Army had torn a gap more than 60km wide in 9 Army's lines. On 19 May VI Army struck into the northern shoulder of the bulge from Balakliya and, with 6 Army, 57 Army and Bobkin's group in imminent danger of encirclement, Timoshenko ordered a halt to the offensive. Kostenko was sent to command the forces within the salient but he was unable to prevent the German jaws from closing on the pocket on 23 May. One week later, after furious but unsuccessful Soviet efforts to break out of the encirclement, the fighting in the Barvenkovo Pocket ended. Kostenko, Podlas and Bobkin were killed in the fighting and Gorodniansky committed suicide rather than risk capture. Less than one in ten of the troops in 6 and 57 Armies escaped. In 6 Army alone, with Group Bobkin, the losses were close to 150,000 personnel including most of the army's senior commanders, and the army also lost more than 450 tanks. At the end of June, 6 Army was disbanded for a second time and the remnants of 57 Army were withdrawn to the east. Timoshenko was criticised for poor co-ordination of the Fronts, failure to adequately secure the flanks of the salient and defective control of his forces.

During May, Soviet losses in the Crimea and the Kharkov area exceeded 450,000 personnel, of which a third of a million were killed or captured. These losses, which included more than a thousand tanks, would severely weaken the ability of the Soviet armies in the southern theatre to withstand the German strategic offensive that was then only weeks away.

Betrayal on the Volkhov

Soviet losses between 7 January and the end of April in the attempt to take Lyuban and relieve Leningrad had also been high. With Soviet casualties of more than 300,000, nearly one-third of them killed or missing, there had been little to show for the sacrifice. After Volkhov Front had been disbanded at the end of March, Khozin moved to command the 'Volkhov Operational Group', a subunit of Leningrad Front, and Govorov was moved from 5 Army to command the Front. In January, at the height of the Soviet winter offensive, the headquarters of 8 Army had been moved across Lake Ladoga and, under Major-Gen A V Sukhomlin, had assumed command of the right wing of 54 Army south of the lake in order to allow Fedyuninsky to concentrate on the Lyuban offensive. Hence, during the spring of 1942, six Soviet armies were arrayed between Lake Ladoga and Lake Ilmen facing part of XVIII Army. Throughout that time, Lindemann had held on tenaciously to the shoulders of 2 Shock Army's penetration, interdicting its supplies and constraining first Klykov's and then Vlasov's ability to mount an effective offensive against Lyuban from the southeast.

By the end of April it was clear that 2 Shock Army, low on supplies and at great risk of being cut off again, could serve no useful purpose in the marshes west of the Volkhov, and Khozin was ordered to organise the withdrawal of Vlasov's troops. This was something that Vlasov had been arguing for since March; by May, deep in the season of mud, mobility was severely impaired and Khozin was unable to coordinate his forces to achieve a break out of 2 Shock Army. At the end of May, Lindemann managed to close the supply corridor to 2 Shock Army for a second time. It had become apparent to Stalin that the decision to disband Volkhov Front had been a mistake and on 8 June Volkhov Front was reconstituted and Meretskov was reappointed to its command.[1] Galanin and Yakovlev had been attempting to break through to 2 Shock Army, and on 10 June, under the direction of Meretskov and Vasilevsky, they renewed their efforts. After a week of heavy fighting, the narrowest of corridors was punched through to Vlasov's positions. In scenes of near chaos, wounded troops were evacuated and a portion of Vlasov's force escaped before Lindemann closed the corridor yet again. By 23 June the perimeter of 2 Shock Army had shrunk to the point where all parts of Vlasov's command were at risk from German artillery fire. That night a final breakout attempt was made, Vlasov's troops securing two temporary escape routes. The next day Vlasov ordered his men to break up into small groups to escape as best they could. Vlasov was one of the many who did not make it back to Soviet lines.

Soviet losses in terms of dead and prisoners of war during the campaign to relieve 2 Shock Army exceeded 50,000. Vlasov felt that he and his men had been betrayed by incompetence at the highest levels of the Soviet command, and in particular by Stalin in his obdurate insistence during April that the offensive against Lyuban should continue after the vulnerability of 2 Shock Army's supply corridor had been amply demonstrated. Stalin, on the other hand, was not alone in feeling betrayed by Vlasov's subsequent cooperation with his German captors.

Operation Blue

The outlines of Germany's strategic offensive in the summer of 1942 had been set in a Directive issued by Hitler on 5 April, the primary objective of which was "... the final destruction of the Soviet Union's remaining human defensive strength." Specifically, Army Group South was to destroy the Soviet armies west of the Don in a huge pincer movement prior to securing the northern Caucasus region and Stalingrad. This would provide Germany with access to much of the region's oil wealth; would dissuade Turkey from entering the war on the side of the Allies, (and might bring Turkey into the Axis fold); would interdict the river traffic on the lower Volga; and may even have set the stage for cutting supplies to the Soviet Union through Persia (Iran). German preparations for the summer's strategic offensive had been meticulous, and, with the Crimea secure and the Barvenkovo salient eliminated, the essential preparatory work had been completed. By late June Army Group South had an overall strength of 74 divisions, 54 of which were German. A further 8 divisions were being formed or transferred from the west and these would constitute a strategic reserve.

---

1   During April and May, Meretskov had served as deputy commander of Western Front and as commander of 33 Army.

The divisions designated to spearhead the operation had an adequate complement of motor vehicles, though motor transport provision in other divisions was much less generous. In the air the offensive would be supported by IV Air Fleet, reinforced to a strength of 1,500 aircraft.

See
Map 11
The plan for Operation Blue, finalised during June, involved a strike east from Kursk by II Army and IV Pz Army to cross to the left bank of the Don and secure Voronezh. Subsequently IV Pz Army would advance down the right bank of the Don, leaving II Army and II Hun Army to use the river barrier to protect IV Pz Army's left flank from counter-attacks by Bryansk Front. At the same time VI Army would advance to the east from the Kharkov area to join IV Pz Army on the Don. The two armies would continue along the right bank of the river, VI Army continuing to protect the left flank of IV Pz Army, and at the Don Bend IV Pz Army would strike across the 60km gap between the Don and the Volga to take Stalingrad and isolate Southwestern Front from any retreat to the east. With Southwestern Front cut off from retreat, I Pz Army would advance down the right bank of the Donets into the rear of Southern Front, cross the river near its confluence with the Don, and advance on Maikop via Prletetarskaya. Off I Pz Army's right flank, XVII Army would take Rostov, cross the lower Don and secure the Kuban in conjunction with XI Army from Kerch crossing to the Taman Peninsula, while III Rum Army, initially positioned behind XVII Army, would be available for flank protection on the left. For this southern thrust VIII It Army would also subsequently become available as reserve. OKH considered that Army Group South's objectives were all easily achievable given the resources available to it.

A detailed order of battle for the *Ostheer* at the start of the offensive is given in Appendix VII. For Army Group South this may be summarised as follows:

Army Group South – Field Marshal Fedor von Bock
- II Army commanded by Weichs. II Army had direct command of LV Corps, but also had overall command responsibility for IV Pz Army and II Hun Army. II Army was positioned to the west of Livny
- IV Pz Army commanded by Hoth included XIII Corps, XXIV Pz Corps (commanded by Langermann) and XLVIII Pz Corps (commanded by Kempf). Hoth's forces were west of Tim.
- II Hun Army commanded by Lt-Gen Gusztáv Vitéz Jány included VII Corps and III Hun Corps. Jány's army was northeast of Oboyan.
- VI Army commanded by Paulus occupied the sector between the upper Donets and the Oskol north of Kupyansk, and included XXIX Corps, VIII Corps, XL Pz Corps (commanded by Stumme), and XVII Corps.
- I Pz Army commanded by Kleist included LI Corps, VI Rum Corps, XLIV Corps, XI Corps and III Pz Corps (commanded by Mackensen). Kleist's army occupied the Kupyansk – Kostiantynivka sector. (Within days of the start of the offensive General Walter von Seydlitz-Kurzbach's LI Corps would be transferred to VI Army).
- XVII Army commanded by Ruoff included LII Corps, Italian Expeditionary Corps, XLIX Mtn Corps and IV Corps. Ruoff's army occupied the front south along the Mius to the Sea of Azov.

- XI Army commanded by Manstein included LIV Corps, Rum Mtn Corps, XIV Pz Corps (commanded by Wietersheim), Rum Cav Corps, VII Rum Corps, XLII Mtn Corps and XXX Corps. At the end of June Manstein was still preoccupied with the final stages of the siege of Sevastopol, though XIV Pz Corps was in the process of being moved north out of the Crimea.

In reserve were three German infantry divisions, VI Hun Corps of four light divisions, and II It Corps of three divisions. Moving into theatre in the south during July were the Italian Alpine Corps of three Alpine divisions, VII Hun Corps of three light divisions, and III Rum Army of three cavalry divisions, three mountain divisions and three security divisions.

STAVKA had been expecting Hitler's summer offensive, and the Soviet General Staff's Military Intelligence Directorate had accurately predicted that it would be directed towards the Don Bend. Yet Stalin and most of the General Staff did not believe this assessment, convinced that the offensive would be from Kursk towards Voronezh or, more probably, from Orel towards Tula, with the objective of driving a deep hook through Bryansk Front and behind Western Front's left flank to attack Moscow from the southeast. The Western Direction command had been disbanded on 5 May, and Bryansk Front had previously been removed from the Southwestern Direction command. These organisational changes were to ensure that STAVKA had direct control over the Fronts that lay in the anticipated path of the German offensive. To meet this threat, half of the Red Army's strength was concentrated in the Northwestern, Kalinin, and Western Fronts, with only one-fifth allocated to Bryansk and Southwestern Fronts, and only one-tenth allocated to the Southern and Caucasian Fronts. Nine new reserve armies were also positioned on the Moscow axis, though some were still in the process of forming up. The first of the Red Army's 'tank armies', 5 Tank Army, was located north of Voronezh together with three tank corps.[2] These tank forces, though part of Bryansk Front, could only be committed to offensive operations with STAVKA's approval.

A detailed order of battle for the Red Army at the start of the offensive is given in Appendix VIII. For the Fronts on the southern axis this may be summarised as follows:

- Bryansk Front commanded by Golikov including Pukhov's 13 Army facing II Army, and Parsegov's 40 Army facing IV Pz Army and part of II Hun Army.
- Southwestern Front commanded by Timoshenko with Gordov's 21 Army facing part of II Hun Army and the left flank of VI Army, Riabyshev's 28 Army facing the centre of VI Army, Moskalenko's 38 Army facing the right flank of VI Army and the left flank of I Pz Army, and Lopatin's 9 Army facing the centre of I Pz Army.
- Southern Front commanded by Malinovsky with Major-Gen P M Kozlov's 37 Army facing the right flank of I Pz Army and the left flank of XVII Army, Grechko's 12 Army facing the left centre of XVII Army, Kamkov's 18 Army facing the right centre of XVII Army, and Tsyganov's 56 Army facing the right flank of XVII Army.

---

2   5 Tank Army became operational on 16 June under the command of Lizyukov and was roughly equivalent to a German panzer corps.

- North Caucasian Front commanded by Budenny with Major-Gen G P Kotov's 47 Army and Major-Gen N I Trufanov's 51 Army, both armies in the Taman Peninsula.
- Transcaucasian Front commanded by General I V Tyulenev with Lt-Gen A A Khryashchev's 44 Army and Major-Gen V F Sergatskov's 46 Army, both armies in the Caucasus region between the Black Sea and the Caspian Sea.

(On 27 June Southwestern Direction was abolished and Timoshenko was left with command responsibility only for Southwestern Front's armies).

On 19 June, a German light aircraft carrying a staff officer from 23 Pz Div made a forced landing on the wrong side of the frontline. The officer, contrary to regulations, was carrying plans for part of Operation Blue as they related to XL Pz Corps. Hitler was furious and blamed Stumme, replacing him several weeks later with Schweppenburg. The plans were found by Soviet forces and were passed quickly up the chain of command. Yet Stalin was suspicious of their content, believing them to be a deliberate deception. This belief was strengthened when on 22 June, the anticipated start date for the offensive, nothing happened. On 26 June Golikov was ordered to revive his plans for an offensive, in conjunction with Western Front, to take Orel; but less than 48 hours later, with the ink barely dry on the final plan for the strike against Orel, Bryansk Front Headquarters began to receive disquieting news from its left flank armies.

At 06:00 on 28 June a carefully coordinated deluge of fire from artillery, aircraft, tanks and motorised infantry hit 40 Army east of Kursk. The attacks also hit the left flank of 13 Army. Pukhov's forces withstood the onslaught reasonably well but XLVIII Pz Corps broke through 40 Army's lines at the junction with 13 Army and XXIV Pz Corps broke through in the centre. Racing east towards the Kshen, XXIV Pz Corps crashed into 40 Army Headquarters on 30 June and, though Parsegov and most of his staff escaped, army headquarters lost contact with Golikov and with its subordinate units. Meanwhile, through the gap that had been the right flank of 40 Army, Kempf's forces raced towards Voronezh.

Golikov responded by obtaining STAVKA approval to move 16 Tank Corps to the Kshen south of Livny, and he requested permission to pull back the left wing of 40 Army still facing II Hun Army southwest of Tim. This was refused but STAVKA released 17 Tank Corps (commanded by Feklenko) to Golikov, moving it to Kastornoe where Parsegov was to try to re-establish his headquarters, and STAVKA moved 1 Tank Corps (commanded by Katukov – promoted in November 1941 to major-general) to cover 13 Army in the Livny area. In addition, STAVKA transferred 4 Tank Corps (commanded by Lt-Gen V A Mishulin) and 24 Tank Corps (commanded by Major-Gen V M Badanov) from Southwestern Front to Bryansk Front. Yet these additional assets were of little immediate benefit to Golikov. The tank corps from Southwestern Front would take time to arrive, and Golikov was unable to establish any direct communication with either Mishulin or Badanov, while Feklenko's corps, arriving at Kastornoe, was low on fuel. Golikov's problems were further compounded when Stalin suggested that the operation of the tank forces should be coordinated through

Fedorenko, who had arrived at Kastornoe at the end of June without any staff and with access only to a rudimentary communications net.

On 30 June VI Army launched its offensive against Southwestern Front east of Kharkov. Stumme's panzer corps broke through on the left flank of 21 Army striking northeast towards Novy Oskol. By 2 July XLVIII Pz Corps was driving Parsegov, together with 4 Tank Corps, 24 Tank Corps and a severely mauled 17 Tank Corps, back towards Voronezh and XXIV Pz Corps had turned to the southeast towards Stary Oskol. With both Langermann and Stumme striking for the Oskol from northwest and southwest respectively, the left wing of 40 Army and the bulk of 21 Army were at risk of encirclement. Stalin's counter-attacking instincts notwithstanding, Vasilevsky, as Chief of the General Staff, did much to ensure that the Red Army did not repeat the strategic mistakes of 1941. On 1 July the threatened forces were given permission to withdraw.

The next day Golikov was advised that two of the strategic reserve armies were to be made operational and assigned to Bryansk Front. These armies (one, the second formation of 60 Army, and the other a third incarnation of 6 Army) were to be deployed north and south of Voronezh. By 4 July, elements of Hoth's army had crossed the Don. With a German assault on Voronezh imminent, STAVKA assigned M M Popov to the command of 40 Army, and it committed 5 Tank Army to an offensive against IV Pz Army's forces southwest of Voronezh. On 5 July, as 5 Tank Army's attacks began, XLVIII Pz Corps reached the western outskirts of the city and VI Army, having reached Ostrogozhsk, turned south. Lizyukov failed to concentrate the powerful armoured force at his disposal. His attacks failed to have any significant impact on the German offensive, and over the subsequent two weeks Lizyukov was to lose more than half of his army's 640 tanks. By 6 July, though Kempf's forces, reinforced with 16 Mot Div, were fighting their way through Voronezh, it was becoming apparent to STAVKA that significant elements of IV Pz Army and VI Army had turned to the southeast, and that Moscow was not the *Ostheer*'s strategic target. Just the day before, on 5 July, the left flank of Zhukov's Western Front had launched a 'spoiling attack' against German positions around Bolkhov north of Orel in anticipation of a major German offensive towards Moscow.

With the realisation that he had been wrong-footed by the German offensive, Stalin recognised that the military resources, so carefully husbanded in the Moscow area, would have to be moved to the south. This would take time, and a successful German offensive that had begun on 2 July in the Rzhev area to eliminate a 39 Army salient between Belyi and Olenino (Operation Seydlitz) was a constraining factor. In the south Stalin set the General Staff two immediate priorities – to avoid a large-scale encirclement of Southwestern Front and to hold Voronezh. Elsewhere he ordered that offensives should be mounted against the Rzhev salient and on the Volkhov.[3]

For the defence of Voronezh, STAVKA began hurried preparations for the formation of a new Front using the left flank forces of Bryansk Front. Vatutin, who had spent most of the war as chief of staff at Northwestern Front, was given command of the new Voronezh Front and Golikov, deemed to have done a poor job of defending the approaches to the city, was assigned as Vatutin's deputy. The creation of the new

---

3   These offensives, which could not be mounted until later in July, achieved little in terms of territorial gain, though they did tie down German forces in the centre and north.

Front and the deployment of 18 Tank Corps to theatre came too late to save Voronezh from German occupation, but Vatutin had the resources to prevent any significant expansion of the German bridgeheads on the left bank of the Don. These resources included the new 6 Army (commanded by Kharitonov) and 60 Army (commanded by Major-Gen I D Cherniakhovsky), both of which became operational on 9 July. After Golikov's departure from Bryansk Front Headquarters, Rokossovsky replaced him, assuming his first Front command on 14 July.

By the beginning of the second week of July, Operation Blue appeared to be going according to plan and Hitler was immensely satisfied with the progress that had been made. There had been fierce Soviet resistance in Voronezh, and the Soviet forces in the Livny area had stood their ground effectively, but the tank battles to the west and southwest of Voronezh had followed a reassuringly familiar pattern. What excited Hitler most were the events south of the Voronezh axis where the Soviet armies appeared to be melting away. One explanation that OKH had to consider was that the forces of Southwestern Front were pulling back to avoid encirclement; but to Hitler an entirely credible explanation was that after a year of horrendous losses, and faced with a well-planned and well-resourced German offensive, Red Army morale had collapsed. On the Oskol, the jaws of two panzer corps had snapped shut on very little. The bulk of 21 Army had escaped to the east in good time. Whether it had done so in good order or as part of a disorganised rout, it was difficult for OKH to discern. On 10 July Hitler decided to make some radical changes to the operation. Paulus would continue to the southeast down the right bank of the Don into the Don Bend as planned, but he would do so without Hoth's panzer army in the van. Kleist's panzer army would strike to the northeast from south of Izyum to meet IV Pz Army which, under orders issued the day before, was preparing to move south. Having encircled and destroyed Southwestern Front in the Rossosh – Chertkovo – Valuki area, the two panzer armies would turn to the southeast and drive in parallel towards the lower Don. No conceivable Soviet reserve force would be able to prevent both panzer armies from crossing the river, and Southern Front would be trapped west of the Donets between the panzer armies and XVII Army. With two panzer armies across the lower Don, and with two Soviet Fronts destroyed, a range of exciting operational possibilities for the Germans could open up – the Caucasus, the entire Soviet Black Sea coast, the Caspian Sea and the lower Volga might all be brought under Axis control.

OKH decided that such a complex operation would be too much for one Army Group Headquarters to manage, and consequently Army Group South was divided into two. The northern group, designated Army Group B and commanded by Bock, would initially include II Army, II Hun Army, VI Army and IV Pz Army. The southern group – Army Group A – included I Pz Army, XVII Army and XI Army. Army Group A was placed under the command of Field Marshal Wilhelm von List.

During the second week of July it was not only the attention of the German High Command that had shifted south from the Voronezh axis. The movement of IV Pz Army and VI Army down the right bank of the Don clearly threatened the rear of Southwestern Front, and the problems of the Soviet southern axis were compounded when, on 10 July, III Pz Corps from I Pz Army struck 37 Army south of Slavyansk, and XVII Army struck 56 Army's positions on the Mius. The concept of trading space for time had been anathema to Soviet military doctrine; the idea of trading Soviet space for time, doubly so. Less than a year earlier, any Soviet commander advocating such a strategy would, at the very least, have found his military career to be in severe jeopardy – the appellation of traitor was easily acquired in the Soviet Union. Yet at the end of the first week of July 1942 that is precisely what STAVKA, after much anguish and debate, set out to do. Timoshenko began the withdrawal of his Front towards the Don on the night of 7 July, and the right flank 37 Army of Southern Front was also authorised to begin a withdrawal. It was the movement of these armies, often skilfully covered by the use of rearguard units, which caused the optimistic excitement at Hitler's headquarters. Yet as Hoth's and Kleist's forces advanced towards Markivka to the northwest of Chertkovo, the great haul of prisoners continued to elude Army Group South.

Escaping the attempted encirclements by the German panzer armies came at a price for Southwestern Front. By 12 July Timoshenko's command was close to disintegration. Riabyshev, Moskalenko and the recently promoted Lt-Gen Lopatin were beginning to lose control of their armies as their forward divisions continued to fall back to the east and southeast, desperate to keep one step ahead of their German pursuers. Only 21 Army under Gordov's uncompromising control retained its cohesion. On 12 July STAVKA released three more armies from the strategic reserve and created a new Stalingrad Front under Timoshenko's command with all forces on the Stalingrad axis subordinated to him. At the same time Southwestern Front was disbanded. The newly released armies from the strategic reserve were designated 62 Army, 63 Army and 64 Army to be commanded by Major-Gen V I Kolpakchy, V I Kuznetsov and Gordov respectively. At 21 Army Major-Gen A I Danilov, the army's chief of staff, assumed command.

Bock had been less than delighted by the new command arrangements for Army Group South and by the changes in strategy. He wanted to deal decisively with the newly-created Voronezh Front before it became a serious threat to his army group's rapidly extending left flank, but he was denied permission to delay the advance down the Don. Bock also took issue with OKH's orders to divert the whole of IV Pz Army away from the Don towards Chertkovo, and he objected to Hitler's proposal to transfer IV Pz Army from Army Group B to List's command. On 13 July Bock was sacked and replaced by Weichs, General Hans von Salmuth, a former commander of XXX Corps, assuming command of II Army. To take account of Army Group B's concerns over its left flank, VIII It Army, in the process of being formed from the three Italian corps either already in theatre or in the process of arriving, would be moved north to the right flank of II Hun Army, which was itself moving forward to the Don south of Voronezh.

Malinovsky was tasked with holding Millerovo east of the Donets. Deep in what had been Southern Front's rear, its loss would compromise Malinovsky's ability to defend the left bank of the lower Donets, but he had few resources available to defend the town. By 15 July IV Pz Army had reached Millerovo, and two days later parts of 9 Army and 38 Army, having escaped encirclement at Markivka, became encircled in the Millerovo area. Facing little further organised resistance, Hoth's panzers set off on a 150km dash to the south towards the Don upriver from its confluence with the Donets, and I Pz Army moved south farther to the west. On 18 July XVII Army took Voroshilovgrad from Malinovsky's forces, forces that were already falling back from their defences on the Mius towards the Donets and the lower Don.

During the weeks that followed the formation of Stalingrad Front, there were numerous changes in force structure as both sides adjusted to an increasingly fluid and often confused situation. Paulus found the mobility of his army being constrained as resources were diverted south to overcome 56 Army's defence of Rostov. When German forces west of the city found their mobility impeded by the limited transport infrastructure, substantial forces were diverted to the north. In the shuffling of forces, the headquarters of XIV Pz Corps and LII Corps from XI Army were transferred to I Pz Army, and XIV Pz Corps was then transferred to VI Army. Meanwhile Paulus had seen XL Pz Corps transferred to I Pz Army, had lost the command of XXIX Corps, and was subsequently to gain command of General Karl Strecker's XI Corps from I Pz Army. Hoth's army, having seen XIII Corps diverted to II Army, acquired VI Rum Corps from I Pz Army and IV Corps from XVII Army. On the Soviet side there were numerous command changes as STAVKA struggled to move reserves south and to pull frontline units back to the east in order to establish a viable defence line based on the Don and the Chir.

Meanwhile Hitler, determined to direct the operations of Army Group A and Army Group B personally, moved his operational headquarters to Vinnitsa in the western Ukraine on 16 July. With the fall of Rostov on 23 July after furious street fighting, Hitler, still immensely satisfied with the progress being made and convinced that the Red Army south of Voronezh was in a state of collapse, issued another Directive for the campaign that greatly expanded its scope. Army Group A, in addition to taking Maikop, was also to take the other Caucasian oilfields hundreds of kilometres farther to the southeast at Grozny and along the Caspian, possibly as far south as Baku. List was also to take the Black Sea port of Batumi 600 kilometres south of Rostov near the Turkish border, the last homeport for the Soviet Black Sea Fleet. In his Directive, Hitler also for the first time gave Paulus specific instructions to take Stalingrad, after which VI Army was to advance down the Volga to the Caspian Sea at Astrakhan. With a successful breakthrough to the Kuban from the lower Don seeming to be inevitable, there was no longer a role for XI Army in the south. Manstein, his army headquarters and the heavy siege guns, were to be transferred north for another attempt to take Leningrad, and many of XI Army's formations were redistributed among the armies of Army Group A and Army Group B. The planned offensive across the Kerch Strait was scaled down and the forces involved were to be subordinated to XVII Army. Halder and List objected strongly to this widening of the operational objectives, arguing that 'Army Group South' had the resources to secure the lower Volga or the Caucasus but not both. To such pessimism and timidity, Hitler took great exception.

On 21 July XIV Pz Corps established a viable bridgehead on the left bank of the Chir. Although fuel shortages and determined resistance from advance formations of 62 Army and 64 Army prevented its immediate exploitation, after the disaster at Barvenkovo in May and the virtual disintegration of Southwestern Front during July Stalin had lost patience with Timoshenko. Gordov was promoted to the rank of lieutenant-general and on 22 July he replaced Timoshenko as commander of Stalingrad Front. Lt-Gen V I Chuikov took command of 64 Army. By this time 63 Army, reinforced with 22 Tank Corps, 23 Tank Corps and 3 Gds Cav Corps, was

See Map 12

beginning to secure the line on the left bank of the Don from Pavlovsk south to Serafimovich. Farther south, 62 Army, 13 Tank Corps and 64 Army had taken up defensive positions along the Chir and on the Tsimla south of Chernishkovsky. On 63 Army's left flank, 21 Army, still in the process of retreating, would defend the Don from Serafimovich to Kletskaya. The remnants of 28 Army and 38 Army were also being absorbed into the defensive arrangements of Stalingrad Front.

On 23 July, as Vasilevsky in his role of STAVKA representative to Stalingrad Front was arriving at Gordov's headquarters, elements of VI Army broke through on 62 Army's right flank between the Chir and the Don and encircled two of Kolpakchy's divisions. A German breakthrough across the upper Chir into the Don Bend would threaten both 62 Army and 64 Army with encirclement, and Vasilevsky ordered preparations for a counter-attack to restore the situation. On 25 July 64 Army came under pressure on both flanks from LI Corps and XIV Pz Corps. The next day the pressure increased forcing 64 Army back from its positions on the Tsimla to the right bank of the Don at its confluence with the Chir, and Chuikov was required to intervene personally to restore order among his troops who were on the verge of panic after hearing rumours of a German breakthrough against 62 Army. Moving into the bend of the Don from the east was 28 Tank Corps from the STAVKA reserve and this corps was combined with 13 Tank Corps and residual forces from 38 Army to form 1 Tank Army under the command of Moskalenko's army headquarters. The determined resistance of Stalingrad Front on the Chir inflicted heavy casualties on Paulus's right flank. Much to Hitler's annoyance it had also stalled the German advance into the Don Bend. Farther south, IV Pz Army had reached the lower Don near Tsimlyansk on 19 July, and in its subsequent crossing of the river had encountered little resistance from the scattered forces of 37 Army. It was clear that I Pz Army would also encounter little resistance in its crossing of the Don downriver near its confluence with the Donets as Malinovsky's armies pulled back south of the river in some disorder. Malinovsky moved 18 Army to 56 Army's left flank to defend the Sea of Azov coastline south of the Don estuary. The Don estuary and the left bank of the Don in the Rostov area was defended by 56 Army (then under the command of Major-Gen A I Ryzhov), with 12 Army on its right covering the river from Olginskoy to the Manych. Into the gap between Southern Front and Stalingrad Front, 51 Army was being hurriedly transferred from North Caucasian Front to the Kotelnikovo sector of the Don.

List's response to Hitler's Directive of 23 July was to plan for XVII Army to strike through 56 Army towards Krasnodar, I Pz Army to strike through 12 Army towards Maikop and IV Pz Army to strike towards Voroshilovsk. By 26 July the breakout across the lower Don was progressing well. In the XVII Army area the elite *Grossdeutschland* Mot Div, transferred from Voronezh, took Bataysk south of Rostov on 27 July. But List's plans were then thrown into some confusion by another change of tack from Hitler. Since VI Army's advance into the Don Bend was clearly stalling against increased Soviet resistance, Hitler decided to divert IV Pz Army from its advance to the south and turn it to the northeast for an advance up the left bank of the Don to outflank the Soviet positions on the right bank of the river in the Don Bend. Meanwhile XXIV Pz Corps would be transferred from IV Pz Army to the right flank of VI Army's command to assist in the breaking of the Soviet defences on the lower Chir.

During the last week of July the fighting in the Don Bend intensified. By 25 July Paulus had reached the Don in the Golubinsk area 10km north of Kalach-on-Don. With the disbandment of 38 Army, Moskalenko's tank army became operational on 26 July and was thrown into an offensive westward to relieve the two surrounded divisions on 62 Army's right flank. Under almost constant air attack 1 Tank Army ground its way north from Kalach-on-Don in the direction of Verkhe-Buzinovka and into the right flank of the German penetration as the two encircled divisions of 62 Army attempted to break out to the east. The next day 21 Army attacked across the Don from the Serafimovich – Kletskaya sector to break into the rear of the German forces attacking the right flank of 62 Army. At the end of July the headquarters of the recently disbanded 28 Army, then under the command of Major-Gen V D Kriuchenkin, was used to form 4 Tank Army, comprised primarily of 22 Tank Corps and 23 Tank Corps which were in the process of moving south across the Don from the 63 Army sector. Kriuchenkin's forces crossed the Don from its eastern extremity at Kachalinskaya to attack due west for an attempted link-up with 1 Tank Army but Gordov had to divert 23 Tank Corps from 4 Tank Army to stiffen 64 Army south of Kalach. By the beginning of August, Gordov's counter-offensive in the Don Bend had clearly stalled and had failed to push Paulus back from the river. Yet Paulus, low on fuel and ammunition, did not have the resources to eliminate the large Soviet bridgeheads on the right bank of the Don at Serafimovich, Kletskaya, Kremenskaya, Kachalinskaya and Kalach.

Farther south, Southern Front was being pushed back from the lower Don, and on 28 July STAVKA took the decision to disband Malinovsky's Front and to assign its forces to North Caucasian Front. Budenny's Front was to be divided into two operational groups; a 'Coastal Group' under Cherevichenko to include 47 Army, 18 Army and 56 Army, and a 'Don Group' under Malinovsky to include 51 Army, 37 Army and 12 Army. At the same time Stalin ordered the 'Not One Step Back' order. This order prohibited any withdrawal of Red Army personnel without specific orders and it established penal combat units to which those deemed to be cowards, panic-mongers and traitors who had escaped summary execution would be sent. These penal units were to be assigned the most dangerous missions, often of a suicidal nature, and blocking detachments in the rear would ensure that personnel in the penal units did not deviate from their mission. Yet command restructuring and the issuing of 'stand fast' orders could not alter the fact that the Soviet armies in the south were in general retreat. On 29 July I Pz Army took Proletarsk 50km south of the Don and the next day crossed the Manych near Salsk. During the first half of August, Army Group A advanced deep into the Kalmyk Steppe, along the Manych and towards the Black Sea coast. For the panzer and motorised troops of List's command the war acquired a strange new reality. Advancing kilometre after kilometre, day after day over flat and often featureless terrain, there was hardly an enemy soldier to be seen. Progress was constrained almost entirely by mechanical breakdown and the availability of fuel supplies. On 5 August Voroshilovsk was taken; by 6 August the Kuban had been reached at Armavir; by 9 August Maikop had been reached, though the wellheads had been destroyed; by 12 August the left flank of I Pz Army had taken Elitsa and XVII Army was approaching Krasnodar.

At the end of July IV Pz Army was transferred back to the command of Army Group B. Hoth's forces, advancing to the northeast, ran into 51 Army southwest of Kotelnikovo, but 51 Army was unable to offer an effective defence of the Kotelnikovo area, and Hoth's forces broke through, advancing towards the Askay and driving 51 Army to the east.[4] The threat that this advance posed to Stalingrad Front's defence of the Don Bend was clear, and both STAVKA and Gordov were forced to make some hurried command changes. Using the left flank forces of 64 Army, and shuffling reserves still arriving from the north, Gordov set up an operational group under Chuikov's command to defend the Askay in an attempt to block any further advance by IV Pz Army up the left bank of the Don. Major-Gen M S Shumilov, known to Gordov as a competent deputy commander of 21 Army, was assigned as the new commander of 64 Army. Gordov also dismissed Kolpakchy, replacing him at 62 Army with Lopatin, whose 9 Army had been almost entirely lost in the retreat from the Donets.[5] STAVKA assigned 51 Army to Stalingrad Front and began to assemble airborne troops in the Moscow area into the first of the 'Guards' armies under Golikov's command in preparation for their dispatch to Stalingrad Front. At virtually the same time STAVKA took the decision to divide Gordov's command. The northern group of armies would retain the name Stalingrad Front and the southern grouping would be designated Southeastern Front. Eremenko, who was still recovering from wounds sustained in the spring when he was in command of 4 Shock Army, was assigned to command Southeastern Front. The boundary between the Fronts was to run east from Kalach-on-Don and along the Tsaritsa to the Volga. Yet the Tsaritsa was a river that ran through the centre of Stalingrad. This boundary decision was taken on the assumption that VI Army could be held to the right bank of the Don and that any threat to the Volga river traffic and to Stalingrad itself would come from Hoth's forces in the south. Yet Eremenko was not the only commander who considered it perverse to have the defence of a city divided between two commands when that city was clearly a strategic German target. Gordov's problems were further compounded when, on 5 August, VIII It Army under the command of General Italo Gariboldi moved into position on the right flank of II Hun Army to defend the right bank of the middle Don and to assume command of an Italian corps that was already in position on the Don west of Serafimovich. This released two of VI Army's corps from flank protection duties, making them available to Paulus for use in the Don Bend. By 7 August Paulus had the resources to mount a major new offensive against Soviet forces in the Don Bend. This offensive achieved a breakthrough into the right flank of Lopatin's new command and the next day, refused permission by Gordov to pull back to the Don, 50,000 Soviet troops from 62 Army had been encircled west of the river. Despite having seen XXIV Pz Corps transferred from his command to II Hun Army, on 15 August Paulus launched a powerful attack against 4 Tank Army north of Kalach. Within days VI Army had closed up to the river along almost its entire length, leaving Stalingrad Front with just two relatively

---

4   At that time 51 Army was under the command of Major-Gen T K Kolomiyets – command of this army changed between Trufanov and Kolomiyets several more times over the subsequent twelve months.

5   9 Army was placed under the command of Major-Gen F A Parkhomenko and continued to withdraw to the southeast, accumulating reinforcements as it did so.

small bridgeheads on the right bank of the Don Bend; one at Serafimovich and the other at Kremenskaya.

Eremenko arrived in Stalingrad on 4 August. That day IV Pz Army forced a crossing of the Askay but Hoth was unable to break completely through Chuikov's defences. Two days later Eremenko's new Front came into being when 1 Tank Army, in existence for less than two weeks, was disbanded and its headquarters was used to establish the Southeastern Front Headquarters. In addition to 64 Army, Chuikov's operational group and 51 Army, Eremenko was also to receive 57 Army, which, under the command of Major-Gen F I Tolbukhin, had been rested, reinforced and re-equipped after the disasters of the Barvenkovo pocket. Tolbukhin's army was in the process of moving up to the front south of the Volga in the area of Lake Sarpa. Farther south 51 Army was pulling back to the east towards Lake Barmantsak and the northern fringes of the Kalmyk Steppe. On 9 August Stalin decided to reorganise the command structure on the Stalingrad axis. Eremenko, in addition to being commander of Southeastern Front was also to assume command of Stalingrad Front. Gordov would be Eremenko's deputy at Stalingrad Front and Golikov would become deputy commander of Southeastern Front. At 1 Gds Army, Moskalenko would take over from Golikov. On the southern approaches to Stalingrad, Chuikov and Shumilov were being pushed back by Hoth's forces but there did not seem to be any imminent risk of a German breakthrough. Eremenko was more concerned about the Stalingrad Front sector where there was every indication that, having secured the right bank of the Don, Paulus would launch an attack across the river.

The Caucasus

Responsibility for the defence of the approaches to the Caucasus fell to Tyulenev's Transcaucasian Front. Tyulenev, in consultation with STAVKA, decided to try to stop I Pz Army on the Terek and to do so, after the disbandment of the Don Group on 10 August, he formed an operational group designated the Northern Group of Transcaucasian Front. Maslennikov, one of the few remaining NKVD generals that Stalin still considered competent for frontline command, was transferred from 39 Army in the Rhzev area to command this new operational group. It consisted of 44 Army, which had been under the command of Petrov since the beginning of August, Parkhomenko's 9 Army, and, from 11 August, the remnants of P M Kozlov's 37 Army.[6] Tyulenev, in addition to trying to deal with the approaching German panzer forces, was also burdened with a bewildering series of staff changes at his Front headquarters and, in particular, with the presence, as STAVKA representative in the Caucasus, of Lavrenty Beria, head of the NKVD. Beria not only interfered in Tyulenev's command decisions but also pursued an agenda of his own, using the considerable number of NKVD troops in the region to round up and deport tens of thousands of civilians, mainly Chechens and Ingushi, who it was thought might be tempted to render tacit support to the advancing German forces. In the process, Beria virtually assumed command of Sergatskov's 46 Army, which had been charged with defending the passes through the mountains.

---

6   Grechko's 12 Army had already been transferred to the Coastal Group of North Caucasian Front, and the forces of 24 Army had been dispersed between 12 Army and 37 Army.

Kleist's panzers had covered nearly a thousand kilometres in a little over six weeks when, on 25 August, they reached and took Mozdok on the left bank of the Terek. Another 100km would take them to Grozny. Yet the strength of the panzer force had been severely depleted by mechanical failure during the long advance. The breakdown rate of vehicles of all types had come to greatly exceed the repair capacity of the forward workshops, and the combat capability of the German infantry divisions declined at the end of an increasingly long and tenuous supply line. It took Kleist until 2 September to establish a viable bridgehead on the right bank of the Terek, by which time a new 58 Army, formed around the still extant headquarters of Khomenko's 24 Army, was in position to support the Northern Group. By mid-September Maslennikov's left flank had begun to buckle but I Pz Army was unable to achieve a breakthrough. On 6 October III Pz Corps took Malgobek on the Terek, but throughout October Kleist was only able to make slow progress. The front eventually stabilised at the beginning of November some 80km northwest of Grozny, on the approaches to Orjonikidze in the foothills of the Caucasus, and at Nalchik.

In the North Caucasian Front area during the first half of August, Ryzhov's depleted 56 Army command was pushed back from Krasnodar south across the Kuban towards the Black Sea, but by the middle of the month the front had stabilised somewhat 50km north of Tuapse. Meanwhile, to the southeast, XLIX Mtn Corps fought its way through the foothills of the Caucasus, and by 22 August the Swastika flag was flying from the top of Mount Elbrus, the tallest peak in the range. Six days later Sergatskov was replaced at 46 Army by Lt-Gen K N Leselidze after German forces had come close to breaking through the mountain range at the Marukh Pass north of Sokhumi. Budenny pulled 47 Army out of the Taman peninsula to defend the port of Novorossiysk. By the beginning of September Novorossiysk was being attacked by Ruoff's forces, and STAVKA had become alarmed at the prospect of a breakthrough down the Black Sea coast through Tuapse and Sochi and across the Georgian border to Sokhumi. Not only would this put the port of Batumi and the Black Sea Fleet at risk but it would also allow XVII Army to turn to the southeast and march through Georgia towards the Caspian Sea, thereby outflanking the potentially formidable mountain defences of the Caucasus. This threat, caused by the loss of Krasnodar and the presence of German troops in Novorossiysk, rendered Budenny's Front command somewhat superfluous, and North Caucasian Front was disbanded at the beginning of September. Its forces were incorporated into Transcaucasian Front as an operational group designated the Black Sea Group. Some days later, as 47 Army was being pushed back out of Novorossiysk, Petrov was appointed as the operational group commander. Petrov did much to ensure that 47 Army continued to hold an industrial sector at the eastern extremity of the town, and also the eastern section of the wide bay leading into Novorossiysk. In so doing, he limited the port's value to XVII Army. Petrov also strengthened the group's right flank, helping to ensure that XVII Army's offensives north of Tuapse made little progress. On 18 September Grechko's 12 Army was disbanded. Its forces were incorporated into 18 Army and Grechko was appointed to replace Kotov as commander of 47 Army.

It was not only STAVKA that was alarmed by the progress of Army Group A towards the Caucasus. Stalin's western allies were also alarmed at the prospect of a German breakthrough into Persia. Their concern was such that the British government, despite its military difficulties in North Africa and the Far East, offered to provide troops for the defence of the Caucasus. The offer was rejected by Stalin. Lt-Gen P I Bodin, Chief of the Operations Department of the General Staff and a man who knew Stalin's mind, told Tyulenev, " ... the Allies are trying to take advantage of our difficult position and obtain our consent to the despatch of British troops into Transcaucasia .... it is our duty to take all measures to repel the enemy's attack, wear them out and defeat them. Hitler's hopes and the desires of the Allies must be buried ..."

Hitler's hopes and his expectations had expanded somewhat during the rapid advance of Army Group A to the south. The autumn of 1942 marked the high-water mark of German military success. Its forces were in occupation from the Caucasus to the Atlantic; from the Arctic to Egypt. In the Atlantic, U-Boats were sinking Allied shipping at a far greater rate than new tonnage could be launched. In North Africa British forces were on the defensive just 100km from the Nile. By the end of August little had happened to dissuade Hitler from the view that the Red Army was finished. On 9 September Hitler sacked List, accusing him of excessive caution and blaming him for the slow-down in the rate of advance of Army Group A. From his headquarters at Vinnitsa, Hitler assumed direct operational command of Army Group A. Next to go was Halder, dismissed by Hitler on 22 September with the words, "We need National Socialist ardour now, not professional ability."

Hitler had already planned that, after the capture of Stalingrad, panzer forces would strike north up the Volga into central Russia taking Moscow from both west and east. Meanwhile, in plans that were subsequently formalised into 'Plan Orient', German forces would also strike through the Caucasus into Persia to join Rommel's forces, which, after breaking the British positions at El Alemein, would cross the Sinai into Jordan and Iraq. After securing the oil resources of the Persian Gulf, the German armies would then link up with the Japanese in India. This was as close as Hitler came to the oft-quoted parody of his megalomania – 'Today Europe – tomorrow, the world!'

At the end of September, Ruoff, his offensives into the western Caucasus and down the Black Sea coast having stalled, reorganised his forces in an effort to break through the Black Sea Group's defences north of Tuapse. This offensive made progress at the time when 'Plan Orient' was being drafted, and XVII Army came close to surrounding much of 18 Army. After Kamkov's forces had been pushed back to the last ridgeline on the approaches to Tuapse, Petrov moved Grechko to the command of 18 Army, Kamkov taking over at 47 Army. Petrov and Grechko stabilised the Soviet line north of Tuapse and then organised an offensive of their own that drove Ruoff's forces back to the Pshish – a success for which Petrov was rewarded by promotion to the rank of lieutenant-general. By late October, with the onset of winter conditions, it was clear that the Soviet defences in the Caucasus and along the Terek would hold.

The Volga

On 18 August Paulus began a series of attempts to establish a bridgehead on the left bank of the Don Bend. Three days later two small bridgeheads had been established and into the larger of these, near Vertiachy, Paulus directed XIV Pz Corps. By 23 August Wietersheim had expanded the bridgehead and was ready to break out across the 60km of steppe to the Volga north of Stalingrad. On that day the *Luftwaffe* launched a massive aerial bombardment of the city that killed thousands of civilians, incinerate the homes of thousands more and destroyed much of the city's infrastructure. With Hube's 16 Pz Div in the van, Wietersheim's corps broke out of the bridgehead and, against virtually no opposition, reached the Volga in less than 24 hours. Lacking the strength to hold open a corridor between the Don and the Volga, Wietersheim drew his forces into a defensive perimeter anchored on the Volga and began to interdict the Volga river traffic. On 24 August Paulus, his army on the right bank of the Don Bend under heavy attack from Soviet forces in the bridgeheads at Serafimovich and Kremenskaya, and actually yielding ground against 21 Army and 63 Army west of Serafimovich, was unable to spare forces to extend a supply corridor to Wietersheim's corps.

Stalin was furious with the course of events on the left bank of the Don. After initially approving the withdrawal of 62 Army and 64 Army to Stalingrad, he was persuaded by a report from Lopatin that the German presence on the Volga could be eliminated. On 26 August Lopatin launched his attack on XIV Corps. The attack failed, but Wieterheim's command was badly shaken and Wietersheim reported that his corps could not withstand another attack on that scale. Yet Lopatin did not have the resources for repeat performance. Attacks continued over the next two days but on a lesser scale and XIV Pz Corps survived them. On 26 August Zhukov was appointed Deputy Supreme Commander of the Red Army, and the next day was told by Stalin that he was to be sent to Stalingrad to supervise the operations of the two Fronts. By then two more of the Soviet Union's reserve armies were being activated for deployment to the Stalingrad axis; these armies were designated 66 Army and the fourth formation of 24 Army. On 2 September, four days after Zhukov arrived in theatre, Paulus managed to secure a corridor from the Don to XIV Pz Corps, and the next day his forces made contact with IV Pz Army west of Stalingrad near Pitomnik. The corridor to XIV Pz Corps isolated 62 Army from the rest of Stalingrad Front and Lopatin's army came under Southeastern Front's command. For several days previously, both Paulus and Hoth had reported a diminution in Soviet resistance as 62 Army and 64 Army pulled back towards Stalingrad to avoid the threat of being cut off west of the city by Hoth's advance to the north. On 3 September on the northern flank of VI Army's penetration to the Volga, Moskalenko's newly arrived 1 Gds Army launched an attack to break through to 62 Army, but the attack, hastily organised, made little progress. On 5 September Moskalenko tried again supported by the newly arrived 24 Army commanded by the demoted though somewhat rehabilitated Major-Gen D T Kozlov. Once again no significant progress was made, though the attacks did divert much of VI Army's strength to the north away from Stalingrad, and Stalin ordered that these attacks, supported by the arrival of Malinovsky's 66 Army, should be continued.

Stalingrad

In 1925 the city of Tsaritsyn on the Volga was renamed Stalingrad, and subsequently work began to transform it into a model Soviet city. New factories were built northwards along the Volga as the city underwent a period of industrial expansion, and apartment blocks constructed from concrete and steel replaced many of the older stone and wooden buildings in the residential districts to the south. By the end of the 1930s the residents had come to enjoy ample leisure facilities; parks, theatres and restaurants. Including the outlying northern districts of Rynok and Spartakova, Stalingrad stretched some

30km along the right bank of the Volga towards the Volga bend. The city was narrow, few of its buildings being more than 5km from the Volga. West of the city centre and just 6km from the Volga was the city's airport. Between the airport and the city was Stalingrad's main topographical feature, Mamayev Hill. This hill dominates the city and its possession would represent a significant advantage to attacker and defender alike. Visible from Mamayev Hill, and stretching away to the north, were the city's industrial complexes – the Red October Factory, the *Barrikady* Factory and the Tractor Factory, the latter largely given over to the production of tanks. A few kilometres south of Mamayev Hill and north of the Tsaritsa were the administrative centre of the city, the main railway station and the ferry terminal linking the city with the east bank of the Volga. South of the Tsaritsa lay the residential districts; wooden houses to the west that had been largely burned out by the bombing, and modern apartment blocks closer to the Volga. Dominating the residential district was an enormous grain silo. Built of thick concrete, it resembled a mediaeval keep, and like its mediaeval forebear it was to prove to be largely impervious to the destructive power of the contemporary ordnance.

On 25 August a state of siege was declared in the city and authorisation was given for the evacuation of the civilian population. Yet the evacuation order came late and the evacuation of wounded troops took priority over civilians. Consequently when the fighting inside the city began there were still many thousands of civilians trapped on the right bank of the Volga.

By 2 September the objectives of Operation Blue had been achieved; German forces had a secure stranglehold on the Volga river traffic and the bombing of Astrakhan that had begun early in August had left much of the port facilities in ruins, while in the south the Maikop oilfields were firmly in German hands. There was no strategic reason for Stalingrad to be taken other than to eliminate it as a potential bridgehead over the Volga from which a Soviet counter-attack could be launched, and it is possible that, had it retained its pre-Revolutionary name, Hitler may have been content simply to besiege it, neutralising its industrial capacity through aerial and artillery bombardment. Such a strategy would have left Paulus with stronger flanks and a mobile reserve.

Wietersheim, having witness as early as 24 August the Soviet determination to defend the city, certainly had no enthusiasm for an urban conflict and he made clear his opposition to the use of panzer forces in street fighting. For his objections he was dismissed on 28 August and replaced by Hube. Initial indications early in September suggested than a German assault on the city would be successful. By 10 September XLVIII Pz Corps had reached the Volga near its bend between Stalingrad and Krasnoarmeisk, and had isolated 62 Army from 64 Army. Once isolated within the city, 62 Army could only be supplied from the left bank of the Volga, and initially the bulk of that supply came through the ferry terminal's central landing stage a kilometre or so north of the Tsaritsa's confluence with the Volga. With 62 Army's perimeter shrinking by the hour, Chuikov was appointed to replace Lopatin as army commander, and the next day Eremenko received permission to withdraw his Front headquarters from Stalingrad to the left bank of the Volga. On 12 September Zhukov reported to Stalin that repeated attempts to break through to 62 Army from the north had failed and, though the attacks would continue, all available forces had been committed and a breakthrough was unlikely without substantial reinforcement. Zhukov and Vasilevsky then began to draft the outline of a plan to attack weaker

German positions farther west as part of an encirclement of VI Army launched from the Serafimovich bridgehead.

On 13 September as Zhukov and Vasilevsky were preparing to discuss their counter-offensive proposals with Stalin, Paulus and Hoth launched a coordinated offensive against 62 Army. The attack made some progress and drove Chuikov's headquarters off Mamayev Hill and into a tunnel complex built into the ravine of the Tsaritsa riverbed. The next day as Chuikov tried to counter-attack, the German offensive intensified. Panzer and infantry forces took the crest of Mamayev Hill, reached the main railway station and advanced down the Tsaritsa to within a kilometre of Chuikov's relocated headquarters. To defend the central landing stage, Chuikov committed the last of his reserves and sent urgent requests to Eremenko for reinforcements. That night much of 13 Gds Rifle Div under the command of Major-Gen A I Rodimtsev crossed in small boats. The division landed, somewhat dispersed, in the midst of a veritable inferno and at dawn, unable to form up into a cohesive unit, it was committed piecemeal to the defence of the central landing stage and to assist in the retaking of Mamayev Hill. By 15 September German troops had been pushed back from the central landing stage enabling more Soviet reinforcement to arrive from the left bank of the Volga, and the next day Soviet forces retook the crest of Mamayev Hill. Losses on both sides were high. Only a day or two after landing, Rodimtsev was counting the casualties in his division in the thousands. In the south of the city, a few dozen Soviet marines defending the grain silo held out for three days against sustained bombardment, engendering in the attacking German troops a mixture of frustration, bewilderment and grudging admiration.

Chuikov ordered his troops to engage in close combat with the Germans in order to constrain the German use of artillery and air strikes against them. He organised his frontline forces into small, specialized combat teams for seizing, securing and holding objectives that could be as small as a single building. The main weapons were the submachine gun and the grenade, though extensive use was also made of flamethrowers and sniper rifles. The frontline often ran through the middle of buildings, the demolition of which offered few advantages to an attacker since rubble offered almost as effective a defensive feature as an intact building. The fighting even extended underground to cellars, tunnels and the sewers. Combat in Stalingrad was brutal, uncompromising and unrelenting. The constant fear of imminent death and an incessant assault on the senses from pulverising detonations, flares, smoke, putrefaction, alarms and the cries of the wounded left few opportunities for rest or sleep. In such circumstances the combat capability of even the most highly trained and motivated soldiers declined rapidly. What set Stalingrad apart from innumerable other urban battles on the Eastern Front was not necessarily its ferocity, but its scale and its duration.

On 17 September the air temperature in the city fell sharply, an indication to everyone that the summer was over. The next day 66 Army, 24 Army and 1 Gds Army, all having been substantially reinforced, attacked the left flank of XIV Pz Corps in a renewed attempt to break through to 62 Army. Suffering heavy losses on the open steppe against accurate artillery fire and air attack, the Soviet armies made little progress. They tried again on 19 September as Chuikov launched an offensive of his own towards the north. Neither effort made a significant dent in the German defences.

The attritional nature of the fighting in Stalingrad sucked in reinforcements on both sides. Paulus could only obtain reinforcements in the city by weakening his flanks. On 16 September Paulus had acquired XLVIII Pz Corps from Hoth in order to assist in trying to clear Soviet forces from the southern part of the city. Chuikov, having been forced out of his headquarters again, this time by the advance of German troops down the Tsaritsa, was faced with the difficulty of moving reinforcements and supplies across a river that was increasingly under German observation and subject to directed artillery fire. Chuikov's problems were compounded on 23 September when German troops reached the Volga below the central landing stage, cutting off the southern wing of 62 Army from the rest of his command, and forcing him to switch the landing points for his reinforcements and supplies to less vulnerable though less effective locations farther north. The fighting continued almost unabated throughout the rest of September, during which the isolated southern wing of 62 Army south of the Tsaritsa was pushed back over the Volga. On 27 September, one day after the Swastika flag was raised symbolically over the government building in Stalingrad's Red Square, Paulus launched another major effort against 62 Army, this time north of Mamayev Hill. By the end of September Soviet forces had been pushed back from the summit of Mamayev Hill, and Chuikov was left in control of just 30 square kilometres of the city north of the city centre where he had to fend off repeated attacks against the Red October and *Barrikady* factory complexes. Massed Soviet artillery regiments on the left bank of the river were available to break up German attempts to concentrate troops in any particular locality in preparation for an attack, but they could not prevent German forces at the beginning of October from edging into the fringes of the Tractor Factory from the north. On 5 October militia units raised from factory workers, units that had been fighting independently, were brought under Chuikov's command. At the end of September XLVIII Pz Corps, the bulk of its forces having already been absorbed into Seydlitz's LI Corps, was returned to IV Pz Army.

While the fighting in the city of Stalingrad preoccupied Paulus and Chuikov, there had been a great deal of peripheral activity along the Don and the Volga. After attempts to relieve Stalingrad from the north had failed, at the end of September and the beginning of October STAVKA tried to break through to Chuikov with an offensive by Eremenko's 64 Army, 57 Army and 51 Army south of the city.[7] In terms of closing the gap to 62 Army, Eremenko's offensive was no more successful than those in the north, but 57 Army and 51 Army were able to advance against Rumanian forces in IV Pz Army to reach the defiles between lakes Sarpa, Tsatsa and Barmantsak south of the Volga bend. In fact the Rumanian forces were almost routed by these attacks and Hoth, whose command at that time included four Rumanian divisions, formally expressed to OKH his concern about their reliability and suggested that, as a matter of operational policy, a German division should be available as a backstop to every four Rumanian divisions deployed at the front.

On 28 September STAVKA decided to reconfigure the two Fronts involved in the Stalingrad battles. Southeastern Front was renamed Stalingrad Front and the former

---

7   Eremenko also had available a third incarnation of 28 Army which had been formed from reserves on 9 September and which was based on the headquarters of the former Stalingrad Military District. This army, placed under Gerasimenko's command, was deployed on the left flank of 51 Army to cover the approaches to Astrakhan.

Stalingrad Front was renamed Don Front, to be commanded by Rokossovsky.[8] It was also decided, in preparation for a wider counter-offensive, to divide Don Front into two parts, the left wing west of Kletskaya, incorporating 63 Army and 21 Army, to be placed under the command of Vatutin and designated Southwestern Front.[9] As these arrangements were being made, 1 Gds Army's forces were assigned to 24 Army, the Guards army headquarters was withdrawn into reserve, 4 Tank Army was introduced into the line on the right of 24 Army in the Kachalinskaya area, while at 24 Army D T Kozlov was replaced by Galanin. STAVKA also took the decision to use the newly withdrawn Guards army headquarters as the basis for Vatutin's new Front headquarters. The creation of Vatutin's new command was carried out in secret to prevent Weichs and OKH from being able to discern STAVKA's intentions.

By early October those intentions had been largely decided. Encouraged by the success of 57 Army and 51 Army, after an inspection of the Lake Sarpa area Vasilevsky had concluded that a sizable mechanised force could be secretly assembled behind the recently captured defiles, and that a successful armoured breakthrough against the Rumanian defenders was entirely feasible. On the extreme left flank of VI Army Zhukov, after a separate inspection of Soviet positions on the right bank of the Don, had concluded that a breakout from the bridgehead at Serafimovich and from a smaller bridgehead at Kletskaya was also feasible. A double offensive from north and south into the deep flanks of VI Army could surround Paulus, cut him off from his sources of supply west of the Don, and force VI Army into a general withdrawal. Such a manoeuvre, it was speculated, may even hold the possibility of trapping part of VI Army in the city and forcing its surrender. The planning for this counter-offensive, given the codename Operation Uranus, would continue throughout October and into November as the forces necessary for its implementation were assembled. In the meantime Chuikov, unaware of the wider strategy, was to be provided with sufficient reinforcements to hold at least part of Stalingrad and keep the bulk of VI Army locked in place in continued efforts to secure its capture.

That capture had become an obsession for Hitler, who prompted Paulus repeatedly to redouble his efforts. To help provide VI Army with the means to drive 62 Army from the city, at the end of September OKH began to move Dumitrescu's III Rum Army into position on the Don to relieve German divisions on VI Army's left flank. In the process, the headquarters of XVII Corps, which had been commanding the German divisions on the Serafimovich sector of the Don front, was withdrawn to Army Group reserve. Hitler, OKH and Army Group B were fully aware of the risks to VI Army's flanks, but Hitler remained convinced that the Red Army was fully committed on the Volga, and that any meaningful Soviet offensive would take place on the Moscow axis. This view was supported, and not without good reason, by German military intelligence assessments of Red Army activity and force deployment around Rzhev and opposite the II Pz Army sector north of Voronezh.

On 14 October, after several days of relative calm, Paulus launched another major effort to take the factory district and eliminate 62 Army, opening with a massive air and artillery bombardment. He had acquired Lt-Gen Ferdinand Heim's 14 Pz Div from IV Pz Army (leaving Hoth with just two motorised infantry divisions, two

8   Lt-Gen M A Reiter took command of Bryansk Front after Rokossovsky's departure.
9   Golikov was to be appointed to command Voronezh Front after Vatutin's departure.

German infantry divisions and four Rumanian infantry divisions), had committed all his reserves and had pulled in another infantry division from his flank. By the evening of 15 October, 14 Pz Div had broken through the Tractor Factory complex to reach the Volga. Approximately 1,500 Soviet troops were cut off to the north of this penetration and on 16 October German troops began to penetrate the northern fringes of the *Barrikady* Factory complex. Chuikov, struggling to communicate with both Eremenko and with subordinate units from a headquarters that was under constant attack, requested permission to withdraw his headquarters to the left bank of the Volga, but his request was refused. Over the following week the fighting continued unabated. The forces cut off in the north, though reinforced from the east bank, were squeezed into an area of eight square kilometres in Rynok and Spartakova, while the main body of 62 Army was left holding a 10km-long bridgehead on the right bank of the Volga that was less than a kilometre deep. During the fourth week of October 64 Army in the south and 66 Army in the north, the latter supported by 24 Army on its right flank, once again attempted to break through to the city and once again made little progress. Yet by 29 October, after two weeks of possibly the most intense fighting of the entire battle inside the city, the German attacks on Chuikov's ragged perimeter dissipated. Paulus did not have the resources to mount another offensive on the scale of 14 October. Sporadic German attacks continued but they were highly targeted and had a minimal impact. On 8 November Hitler, in a speech to the Party faithful, stated that he wanted to avoid another Verdun, and he declared, "I wanted to capture [Stalingrad] and … we are quite content, we have as good as got it."

In fact Paulus was to make a final effort to push 62 Army back from its Stalingrad bridgehead. Temperatures in the area had been falling below freezing and on 9 November they dropped sharply. Ice floes in considerable numbers had begun to appear on the Volga. They made navigation increasingly hazardous and threatened Chuikov's already tenuous reinforcement and supply links with the left bank. In the early hours of 11 November battle groups from six German divisions launched an offensive against Chuikov's positions and reached the Volga on a front of nearly half a kilometre, splitting off Soviet forces in the Red October factory complex from those in the *Barrikady* complex farther north. This final German offensive left 62 Army split into three parts.

Uranus

The manpower shortages that had been a significant factor in VI Army's failure to secure Stalingrad were endemic to the entire *Ostheer*. By the late autumn of 1942 OKH estimated that the *Ostheer*, having suffered more than 1.5 million casualties since the start of the Russian campaign, was some 20 percent below authorised strength, and there was no obvious way to make up in its entirety the 800,000 shortfall in personnel. OKW had 65 divisions deployed in theatres other than the Eastern Front but this was considered to be the minimum necessary to meet Germany's operational requirements in those theatres. One significant source of under-utilised manpower was the *Luftwaffe*, and Hitler ordered the release of 200,000 *Luftwaffe* personnel for ground combat operations. Yet Goering, reluctant to relinquish any control over an air force that had become a personal fiefdom, was unwilling to release those men for absorption into the army. He insisted that they be formed into twenty *Luftwaffe* field divisions and four *Luftwaffe* field corps headquarters, and that they continue to be commanded by *Luftwaffe* officers. These divisions, though small in comparison with a standard German infantry division – comparable to a regular army 'light' division, were adequately equipped, but the officers and men were not adequately trained for ground combat. Armies to which such divisions were assigned were often ordered to use them only for defensive operations. Including the Axis personnel in Finland and north-eastern Norway, Axis combat forces on the Eastern Front numbered 3.5 million at the beginning of November 1942, of which fully one million were allied troops, predominantly Finns, Rumanians, Hungarians and Italians. Facing this Axis force, and despite having suffered 1.9 million casualties since the start of Operation Blue (more than half of which were men killed, missing or taken prisoner), the Red Army had nearly 6.1 million personnel deployed.

A series of Soviet offensives on the Moscow and Leningrad axes during the late summer, though of only marginal success in terms of territory recovered, did succeed in tying down the forces of Army Group North and Army Group Centre, and even diverted some reinforcements to these commands that might otherwise have gone to Army Group B. Towards the end of August Manstein assumed command of the front facing Leningrad with XI Army Headquarters, two corps headquarters and four infantry divisions, together with the siege guns brought north from Sevastopol. On 4 September, while preparing an operational plan to take Leningrad, Manstein was diverted to deal with a threatened breakthrough by Leningrad Front eastwards along the shore of Lake Ladoga. This task was not completed until mid-October, by which time the planned offensive against the city had been postponed. On 22 September during the fighting south of Lake Ladoga in the Mga area, a trial batch of four of the new Mk VI Tiger tanks was used for the first time in offensive action. The heavy tanks proved to be difficult to manoeuvre in the swampy ground and the outcome was not considered to have been a success.

Col-Gen Kurt Zeitzler, who had been appointed to the post of Chief of Staff at OKH after Halder's dismissal, had been able to use the prestige of his new appointment to resolve one anomaly in the German command structure – the interference in OKH policy decisions by OKW, and specifically by Jodl. There had been times in the early stages of the war when OKH had found it useful to obtain Jodl's support for a particular strategic proposal, but more often than not his second-guessing of OKH strategy on the Eastern Front had proved to be an unmitigated nuisance. Zeitzler obtained Hitler's approval for OKH alone to be responsible for operational policy on the Eastern Front and for Zeitzler, not Jodl, to present the regular situation reports to Hitler as they related to the *Ostheer*. In consequence the *Führer* Directives, issued through OKW, would no longer apply to the Eastern Front. Instead Hitler would issue Operational Orders in relation to the *Ostheer*, and those Operational Orders would be issued through OKH. The trade-off for Jodl was that OKW would decide strategy for all other theatres without reference to OKH. The first of Hitler's Operational Orders was issued on 14 October, requiring Axis forces on the Eastern Front, excluding Army Group A and VI Army, to prepare to assume a rigid defensive posture for the winter.

During October the Soviet armies to the north and south of Stalingrad kept up their attacks on the right flank of Army Group B. The objective of these attacks was primarily to relieve the pressure on 62 Army but also to try to secure more advantageous positions from which to launch the counter-offensive. In this effort Southwestern Front had been particularly successful, enlarging its bridgehead at Serafimovich west along the right bank of the Don to create a lodgement 50km long and up to 20km deep. Dumitrescu repeatedly requested reinforcements to eliminate this dangerous Soviet bridgehead but Weichs did not have the forces to spare for such an operation. No less than seventeen German divisions were committed to VI Army in its attempts to take the city and fend off the Soviet attacks on its flanks.

Meanwhile Vatutin and Eremenko received substantial reinforcements for the

See
Map 13

coming offensive. Vatutin's primary reinforcement was 5 Tank Army commanded by Lt-Gen P L Romanenko, which was deployed in the Serafimovich bridgehead between 63 Army and 21 Army.[10] Romanenko's army included six rifle divisions, 1 Tank Corps, Major-Gen A G Rodin's 26 Tank Corps and 8 Cav Corps. At the beginning of November Danilov was replaced as commander of 21 Army by Major-Gen I M Chistyakov, and 21 Army was reinforced with Major-Gen A G Kravchenko's 4 Tank Corps and Pliev's 3 Gds Cav Corps. On Southwestern Front's right flank 63 Army, which was redesignated as the second formation of 1 Gds Army on 5 November, received less substantial reinforcement since, after the introduction of 5 Tank Army into the Serafimovich bridgehead, 1 Gds Army was left facing VIII It Army, and consequently the Guards army was to play only a subsidiary role in the offensive. The three armies of Don Front also received less reinforcement since their role in the coming offensive was primarily to tie down the left flank of VI Army (XI Corps, VIII Corps and the left flank of XIV Pz Corps) from east of Kletskaya to the Volga. From west to east Rokossovsky had 4 Tank Army (redesignated 65 Army on 22 October after Batov had assumed command from Kriuchenkin), Galanin's 24 Army, to which 16 Tank Corps was assigned, and 66 Army. The command of 66 Army had also changed, Major-Gen A S Zhadov having taken over after Malinovsky had been transferred to Voronezh Front as Golikov's deputy. To the south, Eremenko's reinforcement included 4 Cav Corps, 13 Tank Corps and the first of the new mechanised corps to see action. The mechanised corps were more powerful formations than the tank corps; they included slightly more tanks but more importantly, incorporated within their component mechanised brigades a better balance of forces, particularly with regard to motorised infantry, to seize and hold objectives deep in the German rear. Major-Gen V T Volsky's 4 Mech Corps and 4 Cav Corps were assigned to the right flank of Trufanov's 51 Army south of Lake Sarpa facing VI Rum Corps. Tolbukhin's 57 Army, reduced to two rifle divisions, two tank brigades and 13 Tank Corps, was concentrated on a narrow sector southwest of the Volga bend facing the junction of IV Pz Army's IV Corps and VI Rum Corps, while Shumilov's 64 Army faced IV Corps.

Operation Uranus was scheduled to begin on 9 November but delays in getting the necessary reinforcements into position resulted in a ten-day postponement. During this time, despite Soviet attempts at concealment, Army Group B became aware of the presence of elements of 5 Tank Army southwest of Serafimovich. Orders had already been issued for the transfer of 6 Pz Div and two infantry divisions from Western Europe to the Army Group B area, but they would not arrive until the end of November. From IV Pz Army Weichs withdrew the headquarters of XLVIII Pz Corps

---

10   The first formation of 5 Tank Army had been disbanded in mid-July, a second formation being activated in early September.

(commanded by Heim after the end of October) in order to form a mobile reserve between the Don and the Chir. To this reserve he assigned the under-strength 22 Pz Div from VIII It Army, and 1 Rum Pz Div from III Rum Army. Superficially Heim's command, with more than 160 tanks, appeared to be a reasonably strong formation, yet three-quarters of the tanks were in the Rumanian panzer division, a division that had never seen action and which was equipped primarily with pre-war Czech light tanks mounting 37mm guns. After the transfer of XLVIII Pz Corps Headquarters from IV Pz Army, Hoth was left with two German infantry divisions operating on his left flank as part of IV Corps; 29 Mot Div as reserve; and 16 Mot Div operating against 28 Army in the featureless depths of the Kalmyk Steppe on his right flank. The rest of his command was composed of five Rumanian infantry divisions and two Rumanian cavalry divisions. These forces, with the exception of 16 Mot Div, were placed under IV Rum Army Headquarters commanded by General Constantin Constantinescu-Claps. Constantinescu was subordinated to IV Pz Army, but Hoth only retained direct command of 16 Mot Div.

By mid-November the Red Army had achieved a manpower superiority on the Stalingrad axis of roughly 2:1. In addition to the 13 rifle divisions of 62 Army inside Stalingrad and the nine mobile corps of Southwestern, Don and Stalingrad Fronts, Vatutin, Rokossovsky and Eremenko also had 53 rifle divisions (each typically of around 6,000 men), nine tank brigades and ten other independent and specialist brigades.

The Soviet offensive opened on the morning of 19 November with an attack through freezing fog by 5 Tank Army and 21 Army against III Rum Army. Dumitrescu's army had more than 150,000 Rumanian and more than 11,000 German troops organised into eight infantry and two cavalry divisions. On Chistyakov's left, Batov's 65 Army attacked VI Army's XI Corps but made little progress; and against Romanenko's right flank, 7 Rum Inf Div held its ground; but in the long central sector between Bolshoy and Kletskaya, after the commitment at noon of the Soviet mobile forces, the resistance of the Rumanian divisions, inadequately supplied with anti-tank guns, began to collapse. Only 6 Rum Inf Div on the right flank of 21 Army's offensive fought back effectively. By mid-afternoon Vatutin's five mobile corps were pouring through Dumitrescu's shattered central defences. For several crucial hours Weichs had little clear idea of what was happening. Communications with the forward units of III Rum Army had broken down and the appalling weather conditions made aerial reconnaissance difficult. Late in the day Weichs ordered Paulus to move Hube's XIV Pz Corps Headquarters, together with the three panzer divisions on the Volga, to support XI Corps on the right bank of the Don in the Verkhne-Buzinovka area. Responsibility for the defence of the entire sector of the front between the Don and the Volga was delegated to General Walter Heitz's VIII Corps. Yet the real danger to VI Army lay not in the small bend of the Don but farther to the west out of the Serafimovich bridgehead, and OKH ordered Heim to stop Romanenko's advance. Heim tried unsuccessfully to coordinate his two panzer divisions. During the night the Rumanian panzer division collided with 26 Tank Corps and, during the course of the next morning, suffered heavy losses. Rodin's advance was delayed but not stopped, and his tanks began to turn to the southeast, towards Ostrov and Kalach-on-Don. On Rodin's right, 1 Tank Corps clashed with the few dozen tanks of 22 Pz Div and over the next two days pushed the panzer division back south towards the

Chir. On Rodin's left, Kravchenko's corps turned to the southeast in parallel with 26 Tank Corps' advance to the Don, while on Kravchenko's left, Pliev moved east into the left flank of XI Corps.

On 20 November Eremenko's armies attacked. Constantinescu's Rumanian divisions in VI Rum Corps were routed almost immediately, and IV Corps' right flank 20 Rum Inf Div, with inadequate anti-tank defences, was overwhelmed by 13 Tank Corps. With the centre of IV Rum Army collapsing, Hoth was left with just 29 Mot Div to try to hold the Soviet mobile formations to the east and southeast of Buzinovka. Volsky's advance fell behind schedule during the afternoon and evening of 20 November but, after continuing to move forward through the night, 4 Mech Corps reached the area of Abganerovo at dawn. From there, deep behind IV Pz Army's front, Volsky could move northwest towards Buzinovka, while 4 Cav Corps could move west and southwest towards the Don and the Askay.

It was not until 21 November that Weichs and OKH realised the full implications of the Soviet offensives. Later that day elements of 4 Tank Corps reached the Don in the Golubinsk area where, nearly four months earlier, VI Army's panzers had first reached the river after breaking through 62 Army's defences. Weichs realised that powerful Soviet mechanised columns were also advancing from the northwest and the southeast towards Kalach, the arterial supply route to VI Army across the Don. West of the Don Bend there were few German combat forces, and the rear services personnel in the area, under conditions of wild rumour and increasing panic, began to flee, many of them east across the Don to the apparent safety of the VI Army area. Hitler was furious at the way the situation was unfolding and heaped the blame on Heim for the inability of XLVIII Pz Corps to stop 5 Tank Army.[11] Kalach was taken by 26 Tank Corps on the morning of 22 November, and Rodin's forces made immediate preparations for a crossing of the river later that evening. Volsky's advance continued through 21 November and by noon of 22 November he had taken Sovietsky, some 10km northwest of Buzinovka. With his limited resources, all Hoth could do was use 29 Mot Div to try to prevent 13 Tank Corps from linking up with 4 Mech Corps. Describing VI Rum Corps as 'fleeing remnants', Hoth felt constrained in his ability to manoeuvre the two Rumanian cavalry divisions that constituted VII Rum Corps because he believed that any planned retreat would rapidly turn into uncontrolled flight. In the early afternoon of 23 November advanced units from 26 Tank Corps and 4 Mech Corps met near Sovietsky. STAVKA believed that it had surrounded up to 90,000 Axis personnel. In fact the true figure was more than three times that number; it included the whole of VI Army together with General Erwin Jaenecke's IV Corps; and it included both 29 Mot Div from IV Pz Army and the right flank division from III Rum Army. Of the twenty-two Axis divisions surrounded, twenty were German. In addition a further five Rumanian divisions had been trapped between Verkhe Fomikhinsky and Raspopinskaya by the parallel advance of 26 Tank Corps and 4 Tank Corps.

---

11   Heim was subsequently arrested for this failure.

6

The End of the Beginning

The meeting of Southwestern Front and Stalingrad Front at Sovietsky on 23 November 1942 represented neither the end of Operation Uranus nor the end of the Battle of Stalingrad. Nor did it represent a point at which the Red Army turned an endless series of defeats into an endless series of victories. The Red Army had achieved notable successes prior to November 1942 and within weeks thereafter it was to suffer two serious defeats. Yet 23 November 1942 does represent a turning point in the war. On that date Germany's aspirations to inflict a military defeat on the Soviet Union were finally dashed, and on that date the Red Army demonstrated that it had acquired the necessary resources and the expertise to conduct a deep penetration offensive and bring it to a successful conclusion. Thereafter the weakness of Germany relative to the Soviet Union, weakness in terms of frontline manpower and in terms of the production of the machinery of war, became increasingly evident.

The Cauldron

Having surrounded the German forces in Stalingrad, STAVKA had two immediate priorities; firstly to maintain and constrict the cordon around the encircled forces in order to compel their surrender, and secondly to expand to the maximum possible extent the gap between the surrounded forces and the rest of Army Group B in order to prevent the two groups from re-establishing direct contact. For the latter task 5 Tank Army was turned to the west to push the Axis forces back to the Chir, and 51 Army was turned to the southwest to drive IV Pz Army back beyond the Askay. For the elimination of the encircled German forces, STAVKA deployed seven armies. The three armies of Rokossovsky's Don Front continued to press VI Army from the north. On the eastern sector VI Army faced 62 Army within the city and 64 Army farther south. Completing the encirclement 57 Army occupied the southern flank and Southwestern Front's 21 Army turned to the east to attack VI Army's positions in the Don Bend. Stalin, with no appreciation of the true size of the surrounded German force, expected its immediate elimination. He had other plans for the forty-seven Soviet rifle divisions, four tank corps and nine independent tank brigades that formed the Stalingrad cordon, and he wanted the issue to be resolved in days, not weeks.

See Map 13

On 20 November, before OKH had understood either the magnitude or intent of the Soviet offensive, Hitler decided to detach the armies on the Stalingrad axis from Army Group B. Manstein and his XI Army Headquarters, then in the process of moving into the Velikie Luki – Nevel area on the left flank of Army Group Centre, were to return to the south to assume command of Army Group B's right wing, which would be designated Army Group Don. Weichs and Army Group B would be left with II Army, II Hun Army and VIII It Army. On 22 November Hitler, his hands full with the unfolding disaster at Stalingrad, relinquished direct personal command of Army Group A. He turned command of the army group over to Kleist, and Mackensen was appointed to the command of I Pz Army. On 23 November General Karl-Adolf Hollidt's XVII Corps Headquarters, which had been withdrawn from VI Army into army group reserve at the end of September, was provided with one of the two German infantry divisions in VIII It Army and was combined with XLVIII Pz Corps and the remnants of III Rum Army to form an operational group in order to defend the Chir.

When Manstein arrived in theatre he was to find the forces that would constitute his new army group in a parlous state. Hoth's command at IV Pz Army consisted of 16 Mot Div, the headquarters of IV Rum Army, two Rumanian cavalry divisions and the four routed infantry divisions of VI Rum Corps. Manstein's most potent force, the twenty-two divisions of VI Army, was surrounded. (All forces within the encirclement were subordinated to VI Army on 23 November). On his left flank Manstein had Hollidt's force, which included the badly mauled XLVIII Pz Corps incorporating 6,000 Rumanian troops that the panzer corps had managed to extricate from the Soviet encirclement of III Rum Army's centre. Most of the Rumanian troops on the Chir were from a few remnant divisions that had been on the left flank of III Rum Army at the time of the Soviet offensive. Nominally Dumitrescu's army comprised four infantry divisions and the remnants of a cavalry division, all organised into two corps, but in reality within Group Hollidt III Rum Army had become almost a virtual army, with a headquarters increasingly staffed by Germans, and a front held by scratch German formations. Understandably the arrival of the reinforcement divisions from Western Europe, and in particular Major-Gen Erhard Raus's 6 Pz Div with its full complement of modern tanks and self-propelled guns, was eagerly anticipated.

After the encirclement of VI Army Zeitzler, Weichs, Manstein, Paulus and the VI Army senior staff all assumed that a breakout of the encircled forces to the southwest would be ordered. Escape south had been blocked by the advance of 13 Tank Corps to Tsybenko and by the manning of the west bank of the Chervlenaya, but Soviet forces in the direction of the Askay were widely dispersed and without any coherent defence lines. There was also a considerable degree of reticence about the advance of 51 Army down the left bank of the Don against virtually no opposition. However, since any breakout attempt by VI Army was likely to be in the direction of the Askay, and hence into the rear of 51 Army's advance, Trufanov's caution may have been understandable. Within the encirclement, in what had become known as 'the cauldron', Seydlitz, in anticipation of the breakout, ordered LI Corps to pull out of Rynok and to begin destroying stores and equipment that could not be easily moved. Yet Hitler had other plans. A considerable amount of his personal prestige was involved in the German presence on the Volga, and he had been advised by Goering that VI Army's supply needs could be met by the *Luftwaffe*. Goering gave that assurance despite having been advised by his own staff that less than half of VI Army's stated needs could be met by an airlift. Hitler accepted Goering's assurance; it was what he wanted to hear, and during the spring of that year he had witnessed the undiminished combat capability of II Corps after it had been surrounded at Demyansk. Hitler was also mindful of the positive benefits of his 'stand fast' order after the Soviet counter-offensive on the Moscow axis during the previous winter.

"I will not leave the Volga", he told Zeitzler. It was one of Hitler's 'irrevocable decisions', which he rationalised with the argument that if the German positions on the Volga were abandoned in 1942, they would have to be retaken at even greater cost in 1943. No amount of reasoned argument from Zeitzler's staff and the theatre commanders on the immediate dangers of such a strategy, and the fallacy of the assumptions on which it was based, would dissuade Hitler from his decision. Stalingrad would have to be relieved by an offensive from the west. On 24 November Hitler ordered IV Pz Army to stop the Red Army north of Kotelnikovo in order to provide a jumping off point for a relief operation to Stalingrad from the southwest, and two days later he ordered Manstein to use XLVIII Pz Corps to maintain a bridgehead near the confluence of the Chir and Don to provide a secondary jumping off point for a relief effort from the west. Manstein was under no illusion about the prospects for such an offensive but the attempt would have to be made.

Within the encirclement a bemused Paulus had to come to terms with Hitler's decision that there would be no breakout from the Volga. Yet morale within VI Army remained generally high. Hitler and Goering had assured the army that it would receive what it needed and Manstein was preparing a relief effort. Paulus was ordered to concentrate his panzer forces in the south-western sector of the encirclement in order to be in a position to meet and assist the relief effort from Kotelnikovo. This required the relocation of XIV Pz Corps from the Don Bend, which would have left XI Corps in an untenable position on the river's right bank. Consequently XI Corps was pulled back to the east bank of the Don, a redeployment that was completed by 26 November. Over the subsequent few days VI Army continued to pull back some 15km east of the Don to create a tighter defensive perimeter enclosing little more than a thousand square kilometres. By the beginning of December, on the eve of a concerted effort by the encircling Soviet armies to break into VI Army's defensive positions, Paulus had positioned the four divisions of IV Corps to cover the southern sector of the cordon with the three divisions of XIV Pz Corps on its right. The four divisions of XI Corps covered the western sector, the three divisions of VIII Corps faced the bulk of 66 Army in the north, and the six divisions of LI Corps continued to defend the Volga sector and the city. The remaining two divisions were held back as army reserves. The divisions of VI Army withstood the Soviet offensives of the first week of December reasonably well. The German forces gave ground in places but the Soviet armies suffered heavy casualties and it became clear to STAVKA that this was an operation that would not be over in days. During the first few weeks of the encirclement Paulus tried repeatedly to make Hitler understand that VI Army's position was untenable. Not only was the *Luftwaffe* failing to provide the hundreds of tons of supplies each day that were required to meet VI Army's most basic requirements, but the steady attrition of the army's irreplaceable vehicles was eroding its mobility. By the third week of December VI Army no longer had the vehicles and fuel, nor even the fodder for the horses, to effect a successful breakout across the frozen steppe to the German positions beyond the Askay. Everything depended on the relief effort being prepared by Manstein.

Winter Storm

Army Group Don became operational on 27 November at which time XI Army was formally disbanded. Army Group Don was responsible for 550km of front south from Vechenskaya to the Chir, along the Chir to its confluence with the Don, along the Don to Kotelnikovo and then farther south to the Sal and the Manych. As reserves began to arrive from the west and from other sectors of the front in the Caucasus, Voronezh and Orel, Manstein was able to strengthen Group Hollidt. Hollidt used two German infantry divisions to stiffen III Rum Army, and XVII Corps acquired first a mountain division and a *Luftwaffe* field division, and in early December another infantry division and 17 Pz Div. On the lower Chir, XLVIII Pz Corps was subsequently reinforced with 11 Pz Div. The southern wing of Manstein's command was composed of the newly-formed Group Hoth, which included 16 Mot Div in the Elitsa area, an unreliable but virtually unopposed IV Rum Army facing east along the upper Sal, and LVII Pz Corps in the Kotelnikovo area. Kirchner's LVII Pz Corps had been returned to frontline operations as part of XVII Army in August, and at the end of November the corps headquarters was moved east to the Don where Kirchner was allocated an initially under-strength 23 Pz Div, together with 6 Pz Div, which was in the process of arriving from France. With these forces and the promise of another panzer division and several more infantry divisions, Manstein began to plan the relief of Stalingrad, an offensive that was to begin during the second week of December.

After several delays the Stalingrad relief effort, codenamed Winter Storm, began on 12 December. Manstein had originally planned that LVII Pz Corps would advance up the left bank of the Don from Kotelnikovo while XLVIII Pz Corps advanced up the right bank toward Kalach from its positions at the confluence of the Don and the Chir. However, 5 Tank Army, reinforced with divisions diverted from 21 Army and 65 Army at Stalingrad, launched an offensive on 30 November against Group Hollidt's positions on the Chir, with the objective of reaching a line to the southeast of Morozovsk and depriving the Germans of their remaining bridge over the Don at Verkhne-Chirskaya. This offensive made little overall progress but the pressure exerted on Hollidt's forces was such that Manstein was required to divert much of XLVIII Pz Corps to defensive action west of Oblivskaya. Consequently when Manstein's offensive began, it consisted of just two panzer divisions striking to the northeast from Kotelnikovo. In the course of the delay preparatory to the offensive, 23 Pz Div had been heavily reinforced from its initial complement of just 30 operational tanks, and the reinforcement included a company of Mk VI Tiger tanks. Yet STAVKA had not been idle either. On 10 December, after the failure of 5 Tank Army's offensive on the Chir, another of the Soviet reserve armies had been made operational and introduced between 5 Tank Army and 51 Army. Designated 5 Shock Army under the command of M M Popov, it comprised five rifle divisions and Major-Gen P A Rotmistrov's 7 Tank Corps. In addition 4 Mech Corps and 3 Gds Cav Corps were assigned to Popov's command from 51 Army and 21 Army respectively, while 51 Army received 13 Tank Corps from 57 Army. It had been intended that 5 Shock Army would support a renewed offensive against German positions on the lower Chir, but events on Popov's left flank led to a revised mission plan.

The initial brunt of Operation Winter Storm was taken by 126 Rifle Div and 302 Rifle Div of 51 Army. By the end of the first day the panzer divisions had reached Nebykovo and the Aksay. Initially 13 Tank Corps and later 4 Mech Corps from 5 Shock Army were introduced to try to stem the German advance. A three-day tank battle commenced on 14 December north of the Askay involving 4 Mech Corps, 13 Tank Corps and 7 Tank Corps, the latter attacking the German bridgehead over the Don at Nizhne-Chirskaya. The day after Operation Winter Storm began, Stalin authorised the deployment of another new formation, 2 Gds Army. Initially under the command of Kreizer, this powerful reserve, formed by an order of 23 October from another of the reserve armies, was originally intended for use in an offensive towards Rostov. It was then decided to deploy it to the Stalingrad area to assist in reducing the Stalingrad pocket. Consisting of 1 Gds Rifle Corps and 13 Gds Rifle Corps each of three divisions, and 2 Gds Mech Corps of three mechanised brigades, it was placed under the command of Malinovsky (Kreizer becoming Malinovsky's deputy). Diverted to the Myshkova and becoming operational on 15 December, by 17 December Malinovsky was able to deploy 2 Gds Army's mechanised corps and two of its rifle divisions south of the river line. On 15 December 17 Pz Div joined LVII Pz Corps, but Kirchner's forces remained stalled between the Askay and the Myshkova. On 18 December 4 Cav Corps from 51 Army, and 4 Mech Corps from 5 Shock Army together with one of Popov's rifle divisions, were subordinated to 2 Gds Army, and 4 Mech Corps was redesignated 3 Gds Mech Corps. The next day LVII Pz Corps achieved something of a breakthrough, reaching the Myshkova near Gromoslavka some 50km from VI Army's perimeter. Yet the rest of 2 Gds Army had already begun to de-train along the Myshkova, and LVII Pz Corps could advance no further. By the end of the third week of December Manstein had to report that Kirchner would be unable to break through to VI Army. Operation Winter Storm had failed and on the Volga VI Army would have to fight on alone.

Mars

On 26 September 1942, the day that formal approval was given by STAVKA for Operation Uranus, approval was also given for a major offensive against Army Group Centre's Rzhev salient. This operation was given the codename Mars.

For Stalin and Zhukov the Rzhev salient was unfinished business left over from the fighting of the previous winter. The frontline in this region resembled a letter 'S' laid on its back, and German forces held most of the towns on the periphery of the loops. From Velikie Luki the front ran east of Nevel, north of Velizh, west of Belyi, northwest of Olenino, northeast of Rzhev, east of Sychevka, and in the III Pz Army sector it ran east of Gzhatsk and east of Vyazma. The Rzhev salient, occupying the eastern loop of the 'S', was approximately 150km square, stretching from Belyi north to Olenino, east to Rzhev and south to Sychevka, and it left German forces just 200km from Moscow. The left flank armies of Kalinin Front overhung the salient from the north and west in the western loop of the 'S' in what was known as the Toropets bulge. Several offensives by both sides during the summer and into the autumn of 1942 had not significantly changed the strategic situation from that which pertained in March. In July, Model had driven 39 Army from the upper Luchesa and in doing so IX Army had regained possession of the Belyi – Olenino road. In August, 29 Army, 31 Army and 20 Army had retaken Zubtsov, and had pushed IX Army on the eastern face of the Rzhev salient, back to the Vazuza. In the final week of September Lt-Gen Lelyushenko's 30 Army had broken into Rzhev and had come close to taking the city before being repelled by the defending VI Corps. The cost to the Soviets had been high. In the Luchesa fighting much of 39 Army had been surrounded and subsequently lost, and in the Red Army offensive operations around the north and east of the salient from 30 July to the end of September, the Soviets had suffered more than 200,000 casualties.

See Map 14

Operation Mars was to be conducted by the right wing of Western Front, and by the bulk of Kalinin Front. There had been numerous command and organisational changes in Western Front and Kalinin Front during the summer and early autumn. After Zhukov's appointment as Deputy Supreme Commander, Konev had taken command of Western Front and Purkeyev had taken command of Kalinin Front. After Purkayev's departure from 3 Shock Army, Lt-Gen K N Galitsky took over as the shock army's commander. During the autumn Western Front had acquired 30 Army, 29 Army and 31 Army from the left flank of Kalinin Front. On Western Front's right flank, 30 Army occupied the frontline opposite Rzhev. In early November Lelyushenko was transferred from 30 Army to the command of 1 Gds Army, and Major-Gen V I Vostruhov was appointed to the command of 30 Army in his place. On 30 Army's left was Major-Gen V S Polenov's 31 Army and farther south, northeast of Sychevka, was Major-Gen N I Kiriukhin's 20 Army. On the left of 20 Army was Khozin's 29 Army. Occupying the northern face of the salient was Major-Gen A I Zygin's 39 Army on Kalinin Front's left flank. Farther south, facing the defences of Belyi, was Major-Gen F G Tarasov's 41 Army.[1] Between 41 Army and 39 Army was Iushkevich's 22 Army.

The plan for Operation Mars was complex. It required 20 Army and 31 Army, supported by 29 Army, to attack German defences along the Osuga and Vazuza rivers northeast of Sychevka. Facing the formidable defences of Rzhev, 30 Army was not expected to achieve more than tying down the German defenders to prevent their redeployment elsewhere in the salient. A cavalry-mechanized group of 6 Tank Corps and 2 Gds Cav Corps would be available to exploit any breakthrough in the 20 Army sector with the objective of securing Sychevka. In the 20 Army rear, two more tank corps were available for subsequent exploitation to the south. Meanwhile Kalinin Front was to conduct its main attack both south of Belyi with 41 Army supported by 1 Mech Corps, and along the Luchesa north of Belyi with 22 Army supported by 3 Mech Corps. At the same time 39 Army at the northern extremity of the salient would launch a secondary offensive southward across the Molodoi Tud towards Olenino, while Kalinin Front's 3 Shock Army would attack westwards to take Velikie Luki at the western extremity of Kalinin Front's lines. An additional mechanised force, 2 Mech Corps, was deployed between Velikie Luki and Belyi. Once German defences had been penetrated in 41 Army's sector, 1 Mech Corps would exploit to the east. With the mechanised corps attacking eastward from the Belyi area, the cavalry-mechanised group from the 20 Army sector would be able to attack the Rzhev defences from the south to link up with the mechanised forces from the 41 Army sector. Additionally, 22 Army/3 Mech Corps would advance eastward up the Luchesa valley to break through the German defences, from where it would be in a position to turn both south and north to assist 41 Army in the capture of Belyi and to encircle German forces at Olenino in conjunction with 39 Army's offensive.

Four of IX Army's five corps were located within the salient and, in thoroughly familiar terrain, they had been improving their defensive positions for months. Model deployed XXVII Corps with seven infantry division along the north-eastern face of the salient in the Rzhev – Zubtsov sector. General Arnim's XXXIX Pz Corps was positioned along the Osuga and Vazuza on the eastern face of the salient to cover the Sychevka sector. Arnim had one panzer division and two infantry divisions in

---

1   41 Army was a new army that became operational in May 1942.

the frontline, and two divisions, one of them a panzer division, in reserve. On the western face of the salient General Harpe's XLI Pz Corps had two infantry divisions in forward defence and in reserve had a panzer division and a motorised division. To the north and northwest Model deployed XXIII Corps, which included five infantry divisions, one of which was motorised. On Model's left wing in the Demidov area facing 43 Army and part of 4 Shock Army was his VI Corps, the left flank of which was anchored on Velizh. In addition Kluge had deployed three panzer divisions of the army group reserve in the vicinity of the salient. The Red Army's summer attacks against the Rzhev salient had not finally concluded until early October, but it was clear to German military intelligence that that a major offensive against Rzhev would be renewed after the autumn rains, and Model had been expecting it to begin since the end of October. On the extreme left flank of Army Group Centre, facing the two shock armies in the Toropets bulge, LIX Corps, commanded by General Kurt von der Chevallerie, was assigned directly to Army Group Centre. With only five divisions to cover 160km of front, Chevallerie had to rely for defence on a series of strong points, of which Velikie Luki on his left flank was key. In November Chevallerie had reason to believe that his sector of the front would be reinforced by the arrival of Manstein's XI Army Headquarters and additional divisions in preparation for an offensive against the bulge, but this expectation was dashed on 20 November when Manstein and his army headquarters were diverted to the Don. Chevallerie's only reinforcement was the initially weak II *Luftwaffen Feldkorps* with two *Luftwaffe* field divisions that were inserted into the line on the right flank of LIX Corps west of Velizh.

The commencement of Operation Mars was subject to numerous delays. It had originally been scheduled to begin at the end of October, a week or so in advance of the scheduled start of Operation Uranus. In fact, primarily because Zhukov needed the ground to be sufficiently frozen to provide unrestricted manoeuvre to his mechanised forces, it did not commence until after the start of the Stalingrad offensive. Operation Mars opened on the morning of 25 November with concentrated artillery strikes in the main breakthrough sectors. The effectiveness of the artillery fire was compromised on the eastern face of the salient by heavy snowfalls that restricted visibility. In the 31 Army sector and the right flank of 20 Army the subsequent ground attacks quickly stalled. One of left flank divisions of 20 Army was more successful and established a bridgehead across the Vazuza. Into this bridgehead Kiriukhin moved a rifle division from his reserve, and at the end of the day, despite the fact that German troops still held numerous strong points within the bridgehead and the perimeter was being fiercely defended, Konev decided that the bridgehead was large enough to commit 6 Tank Corps and 2 Gds Cav Corps together with a reserve rifle corps to exploit the breakthrough. The next day, as Col P M Arman struggled under heavy and accurate German artillery fire to get his tank corps across the Vazuza, Arnim decided to commit his reserved panzer division to the elimination of the bridgehead.

On the other side of the salient the Soviet offensive was initially more successful. South of Belyi, Tarasov's forces, supported by Major-Gen M D Solomatin's 1 Mech Corps, broke through Harpe's defences and on 26 November the whole of Solomatin's corps was committed to the breach, subsequently advancing 30km through deep snow into heavily forested terrain that was virtually devoid of roads. Farther north 22 Army, supported by Katukov's 3 Mech Corps, broke through the German defences at the junction of XLI Pz Corps and XXIII Corps, and pushed the German defenders back up the Luchesa valley towards the road north from Belyi to Olenino. At the northern extremity of the salient the offensive by 39 Army, though it was able in places to force back XXIII Corps, never achieved a breakthrough and was unable to reach its objective, the Olenino to Rzhev road. Farther west Galitsky's forces also gained ground and, by 28 November, 3 Shock Army had encircled Velikie Luki from north and south trapping 7,000 German defenders within the town. Hitler refused permission for the surrounded troops to break out and instead ordered that they be supplied by air, and that a relief effort be mounted. For a few days at the end of November some of Galitsky's troops also cut the Leningrad – Vitebsk railway south of Novosokolniki, one of Army Group North's key supply routes. OKH responded by diverting divisions from Army Group North, and Chevallerie's command was upgraded to an operational group. The railway through Novosokolniki was cleared and preparations were made to relieve both Velikie Luki and two regimental-sized battle groups cut off to the southwest of the town.

On the eastern face of the salient Zhukov and Konev insisted that 31 Army and the right flank of 20 Army continue to assault the German defences in order to prevent Arnim from diverting resources to the south to attack the mobile Soviet forces in the Vazuza bridgehead. Polenov and Kiriukhin complied with their orders, but the cost in terms of the lives of their men was enormous. On 27 November the combined forces of 6 Tank Corps and 2 Gds Cav Corps broke out from the bridgehead to cross the road from Sychevka to Rzhev, but in the process the cavalry forces suffered heavy losses. During the course of 28 November German counter-attacks along the road isolated the bulk of the cavalry-mechanised group from the Vazuza bridgehead. On 30 November the isolated forces were ordered to break out to the east and to re-establish contact with 20 Army. This they did on 1 December but not until they had suffered further heavy losses. Konev decided to reinforce 20 Army with 5 Tank Corps and to try once again to achieve a breakout from the bridgehead. By then the situation on the western face of the salient had begun to develop unfavourably for Kalinin Front.

In the Luchesa valley sector Iushkevich's and Katukov's forces, after being weakened by heavy losses, were unable to reach the Belyi – Olenino road. After strenuous efforts on both sides, the battle in the Luchesa valley degenerated into a positional stalemate and the front began to stabilise. In the 41 Army sector Tarasov, instead of concentrating on expanding the area of his breakthrough and isolating Belyi, allowed himself to be drawn into a battle for the town. Harpe organised the defence of Belyi and began to organise a counter-offensive. By the beginning of December Solomatin was on the defensive and a week later a mechanised brigade northeast of Belyi had been cut off and destroyed. By 10 December, after several days of intense combat and using the reserve panzer divisions from Army Group Centre, Harpe was able to surround most of 1 Mech Corps and much of 41 Army southeast of Belyi. The surrounded forces were placed under Solomatin's command and ordered to break out, but they were unable to do so and Tarasov did not have the resources to break into the encirclement.

On 11 December Zhukov, having reinforced 29 Army, re-equipped 6 Tank Corps, and reinforced 20 Army with 5 Tank Corps and divisions from 31 Army, ordered a renewed offence against Sychevka. He also transferred divisions from 30 Army to 39

Army and ordered Zygin to redouble his efforts on the northern face of the salient. The renewed offensive, launched into the teeth of well prepared German defences, made little progress at enormous cost. By mid-December Operation Mars was largely over. On the night of 15/16 December Solomatin ordered his forces to abandon their equipment and to try to break out in small groups. Only around one-third of his force reached 41 Army's lines.

In the immediate aftermath of the fighting IX Army Headquarters reported that, though the Soviets had planned the offensive well, they failed to exploit tactical opportunities as they arose and resorted to repeated senseless attacks on well-defended positions. Only on the Velikie Luki sector did the Soviet forces achieve some success, though it was at a high price. For a time in the battles around Novosokolniki at the beginning of the second week of December Galitsky's forces had the town enveloped on three sides, but by the middle of the month incessant German counter-attacks had pushed 3 Shock Army back. Yet, though Galitsky was unable to take Novosokolniki, he was able to thwart a determined German effort to relieve the garrison at Velikie Luki in the second half of December.

There has been much speculation about a further Soviet offensive plan, codenamed Jupiter, that had been prepared to build on the anticipated success of Mars. It is suggested that simultaneous strikes would have been made against III Pz Army in the Vyazma area, the strikes coming due west from Western Front's central sector and southeast from the newly captured region between Belyi and Sychevka. There is little evidence of detailed planning for such an operation but it would have uncharacteristic of Zhukov not to have had a follow-up plan to exploit any success to the full, and the two armies in the Western Front zone south of the 29 Army sector were heavily reinforced with armour (three independent tank corps and a tank army) at the time of Operation Mars.

Subsequent official Soviet histories of the war portrayed the fighting at Velikie Luki and around the Rzhev salient in November and December 1942 not as a coordinated offensive, but rather as a disparate set of diversionary operations to tie down German forces in Army Group Centre in order to prevent their redeployment to the Stalingrad axis where they might have compromised the success of Operation Uranus. This may have been the effect of Operation Mars but it was not the primary intent. The two operations, Mars and Uranus, were complementary but each had a specific strategic objective. The primary objective of Operation Mars was to eliminate the Belyi – Rzhev – Sychevka salient by encircling and destroying IX Army. The simultaneity of Uranus and Mars was designed to prevent OKH from switching reserves between the two axes in a manner that would allow it to deal with the Soviet offensives sequentially. Operation Mars was on the same scale as Operation Uranus. The seven armies around the salient, together with 3 Shock Army facing Velikie Luki and the Front reserves in the 20 Army sector, deployed 53 rifle divisions, 20 independent rifle brigades, 16 independent tank brigades, two motorised rifle brigades, three independent mechanised brigades, three mechanised corps, three tank corps and a cavalry corps. The number of tanks lost in combat in Operation Mars, some 1,700, exceeded by several hundred the total number of tanks initially committed in Operation Uranus. The Soviet personnel losses in Operation Mars were considerably higher than those in Operation Uranus. Red Army casualties in the Stalingrad offensive operations from 19 November 1942 to

2 February 1943 were less than 500,000. In the offensive operations against the Rzhev salient in the relatively brief period from 24 November to 16 December the casualties numbered more than 750,000, and to these should be added the more than 100,000 casualties in the Velikie Luki sector between 24 November 1942 and 20 January 1943. Approximately one-third of the Soviet casualties represent personnel killed or missing. Casualties in IX Army were approximately 40,000. The tangible gains achieved for such a disproportionate rate of loss were some 80 square kilometres of territory on the eastern edge of the salient, the securing of the heavily fortified Urdom area in the 39 Army sector together with part of the Karskaya area in the 22 Army sector, and an advance of some 20km by 3 Shock Army to surround Velikie Luki. Measured in those terms Operation Mars represented a considerable strategic offensive effort by the Red Army, and a not inconsiderable defeat.

Saturn

Prior to the commencement of Operation Uranus, STAVKA had planned a supplementary offensive with the codename Saturn. This was to be an ambitious operation involving a powerful strike through the Don defences of VIII It Army upriver from Vechenskaya, on to the west of Millerovo, across the middle Donets, and finally to Rostov. This offensive would be combined with a simultaneous offensive by Transcaucasian Front's Black Sea Group towards Krasnodar and the Taman Peninsula. To support the offensive towards the Donets, a strike would also be made across the lower Chir and down the right bank of the Don towards Rostov. A successful outcome to these offensives would isolate the entire southern wing of the *Ostheer* east of the Sea of Azov, a disaster from which it would be unlikely to recover. Yet as Operation Uranus progressed, it became apparent that the resources necessary for the proposed Operation Saturn would not be available. Not only were seven Soviet armies inextricably committed to the reduction of the unexpectedly resistant Stalingrad cauldron, but the main strike force of the proposed offensive, 2 Gds Army and subsequently 6 Mech Corps, had been diverted to the other side of the Don Bend to contain Operation Winter Storm. Additionally 5 Tank Army's offensive against Group Hollidt on the lower Chir was being checked. In consequence STAVKA had to scale down the proposed offensive to something less ambitious and more achievable. The result was Operation Little Saturn, in which the initial strike across the Don would be from the same location as previously planned but passing to the east of Millerovo to outflank Group Hollidt's defences on the Chir. A retreat of Axis forces from the Chir would disrupt the Stalingrad relief effort, would increase the physical isolation of VI Army, and would permit the Red Army to return to the Donets from where it could plan the recovery of Kharkov, Rostov and the Donbas.

In preparation for the offensive, 1 Gds Army had been heavily reinforced during the second half of November and the first half of December. It had been expanded into an operational group under the command of V I Kuznetsov as its boundary with 5 Tank Army on its left had been extended to include the upper Chir. As the operational group was further reinforced with five rifle divisions, three tank corps, a mechanised corps, six independent tank regiments and sixteen artillery/mortar regiments, it was split into two armies. The right wing under Kuznetsov retained the

1 Gds Army designation, and the left wing, under the command of Lelyushenko, was designated 3 Gds Army.

In its final form, Little Saturn was to be conducted across 300km of the front by the left flank 6 Army of Golikov's Voronezh Front and by the two Guards armies of Southwestern Front, supported on the left flank by 5 Tank Army. The offensive, for which Major-Gen F M Kharitinov's 6 Army had also been reinforced with several rifle divisions and a tank corps, would involve more than 400,000 Red Army troops with more than a thousand tanks. Despite having been scaled down from the initial ambitions of Saturn, it is a measure of the growing capacity of the Red Army at this time that such a well-resourced offensive could be mounted at a time when strenuous efforts were being made to reduce the Stalingrad perimeter, Operation Winter Storm was being ground to a halt, and Operation Mars had barely concluded. See Map 13

The boundary between Army Group B and Army Group Don was at Vechenskaya, and so the impending Soviet offensive would fall on the right flank of Army Group B and the left flank of Army Group Don. On his right flank Weichs had VIII It Army holding a stretch of front along the Don from north of Pavlovsk downriver to Vechenskaya. Gariboldi's army included one German and ten Italian divisions organised into four corps. Along the middle Chir Hollidt's primary defence against 3 Gds Army was III Rum Army.

Operation Little Saturn opened on 16 December. Thick fog across much of the battlefield restricted the accuracy of the Soviet artillery bombardment and led to the cancellation of the planned air attacks. The first day of the offensive did not go well for Vatutin with advances of a few kilometres at best, but it was resumed the next day. Aggressive Soviet reconnaissance in the days prior to the opening of the offensive, particularly against II It Corps' positions in the area east of Novaya Kalitva, had alerted Axis commanders to the imminence of an attack, and elements of three German reinforcement divisions had arrived in the Novaya Kalitva – Boguchar area by 17 December. Kuznetsov's 1 Gds Army attacked Gariboldi's Don positions at four separate locations, but the main effort, and the main success, was on the army's right wing from its bridgehead over the Don at Verkhniy Mamon in a small loop of the Don 20km upriver from Boguchar. It was here that Kuznetsov had concentrated his mechanised forces. Off 1 Gds Army's right flank, 6 Army, operating east of Novaya Kalitva from shallow bridgeheads on the right bank of the Don, also began to break through II It Corps' defences on 17 December. By the next day, though Axis forces held onto Novaya Kalitva and Boguchar, resistance in the 60km gap between them had crumbled. At the other end of the front, by end of 18 December 3 Gds Army had punched a 20km gap in the lines of the defending III Rum Army on the upper Chir, and had committed its mechanised corps to the breakout. By 19 December most Axis forces between Novaya Kalitva and the upper Chir were in general retreat. North of 3 Gds Army's breakthrough, I Rum Corps retreated to the southwest. Gariboldi's right flank XXIX Corps of three Italian divisions under a German corps headquarters began to withdraw in the general direction of Millerovo, while its neighbour to the left, XXXV It Corps, pulled back to the southwest towards Markivka on the upper Derkul. On 19 December Major-Gen P P Poluboyarov's 17 Tank Corps of 6 Army took Kantemirovka less than 20km from the Ukrainian border, and that evening 6 Army was transferred to Vatutin's command. Vatutin was at that time given permission to expand the operation into a general pursuit to the southeast from the breakthrough area west of Boguchar. On the left flank Major-Gen B S Bakharov's 18 Tank Corps advanced down the right bank of the Don, rolling up remaining Italian defensive positions along the river and seizing the key town of Meshkovskaya, which it held against determined Axis counter-attacks. On the right of 18 Tank Corps, Major-Gen P P Pavlov's 25 Tank Corps pushed down the road from Boguchar towards Degtevo, while on Pavlov's right Badanov's 24 Tank Corps struck south towards Chertkovo. At the same time 17 Tank Corps was turned south into the eastern fringes of the Ukraine in order to be able to attack Millerovo from the northwest.

For the third time in less than a month the *Ostheer* had witnessed the collapse of vital flanking positions held by its Axis allies. The fleeing Italian divisions finally attempted to form a new defensive line along the Donets to the south of Millerovo, which they began to occupy at the end of December. Only the Italian Alpine Corps, which had not been attacked, was still in position on the Don north of Novaya Kalitva. The general contempt with which many German officers regarded Rumanian forces, and the Rumanian officer corps in particular, was possibly exceeded by their contempt for the Italian military. When, during the course of Operation Little Saturn, a colleague of the Italian Foreign Minister enquired informally of a senior OKW officer whether the Italian army had suffered heavy losses, he was told, "No losses at all; they are running away."

OKH moved the headquarters of XXIV Pz Corps to the area west of Kantemirovka to coordinate German forces between Novaya Kalitva and the upper Derkul, and as the crisis developed it moved General Maximilian Fretter-Pico's XXX Corps Headquarters south from Army Group North's reserves in order to create Army Detachment Fretter-Pico on 23 December. Fretter-Pico was initially given overall command of Axis forces between Novaya Kalitva and Millerovo, that is, between the right flank of the Alpine Corps and the left flank of Group Hollidt. Available to Fretter-Pico were disparate Axis forces in the area including two German infantry divisions southwest of Novaya Kalitva, another German infantry division with the under-strength 27 Pz Div west of Kantemirovka, and 19 Pz Div, only recently withdrawn from the fighting at Belyi, moving into defensive positions along the Derkul. With these Fretter-Pico, under the command of Army Group B, was also expected to relieve Axis forces that had been surrounded at Chertkovo and in the village of Gartmashevka northwest of Chertkovo.

As Army Detachment Fretter-Pico was being established, Manstein, in the process of withdrawing 11 Pz Div from XLVIII Pz Corps' positions on the lower Chir and moving 3 Mtn Div to Millerovo, advised Hitler that some of Kirchner's forces, particularly 6 Pz Div, would have to be diverted from the stalled IV Pz Army offensive on the Mishkova to stabilise Army Group Don's disintegrating left flank. On 24 December as 25 Tank Corps together with Major-Gen I N Russiyanov's 1 Gds Mech Corps from 3 Gds Army approached Morozovsk, Badanov's corps, redesignated 2 Gds Tank Corps on 26 December, took Tatsinskaya farther west. Morozovsk and Tatsinskaya were not only major German air bases and supply depots being used to supply VI Army, but they lay astride the main rail and road route supplying the right wing of Group Hollidt on the lower Chir. Hollidt responded effectively. He assigned 6 Pz Div to XLVIII Pz Corps which, since the beginning of December, had been under the command of General Otto von Knobelsdorff, and Knobelsdorff used elements of 6 Pz Div and 11 Pz Div to surround 24 Tank Corps and block the approach to Morozovsk. After five days Badanov, having destroyed most of the German infrastructure at Tatsinskaya, was forced to break out to the east where he was assisted by 25 Tank Corps diverted for the purpose from the Morozovsk area.

By the end of December the offensive was drawing to a close against increasing Axis opposition, but it had secured a large area of territory on the right bank of the Don, and had diverted German reserves, including two panzer divisions, from the Stalingrad relief effort. Following the breakthrough on the Don, 1 Gds Army and 6 Army wheeled to the west, where German forces had formed a defensive line running south from Ivanovka, a village 5km south of Novaya Kalitva, to the lower Derkul. In the Ivanovka area XXIV Pz Corps assumed the defensive burden, leaving Fretter-Pico with responsibility for the sector from Kantemirovka to Millerovo. Between the Derkul and the Kalitva German forces hung on to Millerovo, preventing any further Soviet advance to the south, while east of the Kalitva 3 Gds Army overhung Army Group Don's left flank and, in fierce fighting that went on into January, continued to threaten Morozovsk.

Death of an Army
On 24 December Eremenko, recognising that Operation Winter Storm had stalled and that some German units were being withdrawn from the Myshkova for use against Southwestern Front, launched a counter-offensive against Hoth's group. Reinforced by 7 Tank Corps and Major-Gen S I Bogdanov's 6 Mech Corps, 2 Gds Army attacked across the Myshkova against Hoth's left hitting the weakened LVII Pz Corps, which by this time had been reduced to a couple of dozen operational tanks. By 25 December, 7 Tank Corps had crossed the Askay to seize Generalovsky. Straddling the Don along the lower Chir and the lower Myshkova, 5 Shock Army maintained pressure on the junction between Group Hollidt and Group Hoth, and on 26 December it was transferred from Stalingrad Front's command to Southwestern Front. On Malinovsky's left, 51 Army attacked Rumanian positions east of the Sal, and, as a result, on 27 December VII Rum Corps on the eastern flank of LVII Pz Corps began a disorganised retreat that left Kirchner's corps stranded as 3 Gds Mech Corps and 13 Tank Corps began a wide encirclement of Kotelnikovo from the southeast. On 28 December Malinovsky, his forces securely across the Askay and his left flank pressing on towards Kotelnikovo, launched 2 Gds Mech Corps across the Don from south of the Askay to begin the process of clearing the west bank of the Don in the Tormosin area south of Oblivskaya. With the support of an offensive by 5 Shock Army north of Oblivskaya, this process was completed by the end of the month, and farther south German forces had been cleared from Kotelnikovo by 29 December.

On 26 December Paulus formally reported the self-evident fact that VI Army no longer possessed the mobility to break out from the cauldron, and it steadily became clear that Manstein's loss of Kotelnikovo and Tormosin represented the end of any prospect of relief from the west. Yet, quoting Hitler's assurances, in his New Year message to his troops Paulus restated his confidence in VI Army's eventual relief. Meanwhile Hitler continued to devise unrealistic plans for a new relief effort to be mounted sometime in February, before which VI Army's continued resistance would serve to tie down Soviet forces that would otherwise be deployed elsewhere against the

Ostheer. Continued resistance at Stalingrad might have been a more realistic long-term prospect if VI Army had been receiving the promised supplies. The airlift of food, fuel and ammunition continued to fall far short of VI Army's minimum requirements for combat operations, and consequently the army's quartermaster had to dig deep into his heavily depleted stocks. The *Luftwaffe* simply did not have the necessary transport aircraft for the enterprise, and resort to the use of bombers as transports made little practical difference. Additionally, the *Luftwaffe* at this stage of the war was under exceptional strain, fighting a genuine two-front war in Russia and North Africa, with 400 aircraft having been diverted from Russia to the Mediterranean by the end of November. German aircraft losses on the supply runs to the cauldron steadily increased into the hundreds as the balance of air power in the region shifted. Nonetheless for the troops on the ground the airlift maintained the illusion that VI Army was an integral part of a coherent strategy, and morale in VI Army at the end of the year remained generally quite high. Supplies, however meagre, were arriving, as were the eagerly awaited letters from home, and on the return flights non-essential personnel and many of the wounded were being evacuated. The evacuations, together with the ferocity of the Soviet offensive against the cauldron in the first half of December and the subsequent attritional nature of the fighting, had reduced the personnel strength of VI Army to around 150,000 by the first week of 1943. On 5 January the air temperature, which throughout November and December had been fluctuating between sharp frosts and partial thaws, fell precipitously.

At the beginning of January STAVKA restructured its forces in the region. On the western sector of the Stalingrad cordon, 21 Army had been transferred to Don Front in early December after XI Corps had pulled back east of the Don, and subsequently, on 1 January 1943, 62 Army, 64 Army and 57 Army were transferred from Stalingrad Front to Don Front. Rokossovsky, supported by Voronov as STAVKA representative, would be responsible for the destruction of VI Army, and Eremenko's forces, renamed Southern Front, would advance along the Don and the Sal towards Rostov with 2 Gds Army and 51 Army.

Stalin's continued impatience for the recapture of Stalingrad was relayed to Voronov and Rokossovsky in no uncertain terms. After several delays and the rejection by Paulus of Red Army truce envoys sent to discuss terms for VI Army's surrender, a renewed offensive against the cauldron (Operation Ring), concentrating against the relatively poorly defended southern and western sectors, was begun on 10 January with a thunderous one-hour artillery barrage. The attacks by 24 Army and 66 Army against the centre and right of Heitz's VIII Corps and against Strecker's XI Corps, both holding well-defended positions on the northern boundary of the cauldron, made little progress. In the city, 62 Army maintained the pressure on LI Corps to prevent the redeployment of Seydlitz's troops to more vulnerable sectors of the front. Attacks by 64 Army against Jaenecke's IV Corps in the south, though for a time threatening a breakthrough in one sector, achieved little in terms of territorial gain. However in the west and northwest 21 Army and 65 Army broke through against XIV Pz Corps and the left wing of VIII Corps, and over the next few days ground their way east towards the main German airbase at Pitomnik. Despite desperate German defensive action, Pitomnik, some 25km west of the city, fell on 16 January leaving VI Army with just the airbase at Gumrak and the small airfield on the western outskirts of the city.

After a week of intense fighting, the area of the cauldron had been halved, but in the process Don Front had suffered heavy casualties, and thereafter the intensity of the fighting had declined. On 20 January, after few days of relative calm, Rokossovsky was ready to renew the offensive and 65 Army broke through towards Gumrak, bringing the airbase under heavy artillery fire. On 22 January Gumrak fell to Batov's forces.

During the second half of January the morale of VI Army declined rapidly. Prior to the loss of Pitomnik, the troops, despite being perpetually hungry and having their defences compromised by lack of ammunition, had retained a degree of optimism. After the loss of the two airbases it became increasingly apparent that VI Army was doomed. Conditions within the cauldron became desperate, and desertions of German troops increased. On occasions whole battalions, or the remnants of what had been whole battalions, surrendered. From the south, west and north VI Army was pushed back into the city. On 26 January Mamayev Hill was taken by 62 Army, and VI Army was cut in two when forces from Chistyakov's 21 Army reached troops of Rodimtsev's Guards division between Mamayev Hill and the Red October factory complex. Paulus and his headquarters staff found themselves in the smaller, southern, enclave. Over the following days this enclave continued to shrink until, by 30 January, very little was left in German hands. That day Paulus was promoted to the rank of Field Marshal. Hitler approved the promotion in the expectation that, as a Field Marshal, Paulus would never surrender his command or allow himself to be taken prisoner. He was wrong; on 31 January Paulus surrendered himself and what little remained of his command. In the northern pocket around the Red October complex Strecker and the remnants of his XI Corps held out for a further two days.

Some 290,000 Axis personnel were surrounded at Stalingrad on 23 November. Of those it is estimated that 13,000 were Rumanian or Italian and that around 25,000 were Soviet volunteer auxiliaries – men who for a variety of reasons had chosen to fight for the Axis cause. Some 25,000 personnel, many of whom were seriously wounded, were flown out of the cauldron before the airstrips were rendered unusable. Only around 91,000 Axis personnel, including 22 German generals, were left alive in the Stalingrad area at the beginning of February 1943, and of those only 5,000 were ever to see their homes again. Of the quarter of a million German military personnel surrounded at Stalingrad, ninety percent were either killed or taken prisoner. This was a grievous loss to an *Ostheer* that had already been seriously under-strength. The loss of military equipment was also enormous, perhaps the equivalent of six months of German military industrial production. Soviet claims after the war were that in the Stalingrad offensive they captured or destroyed 3,500 tanks and self-propelled guns, over 12,000 artillery pieces and mortars, and 75,000 vehicles.

The Start of the Long Road Back
On the side of the victors, in addition to the general jubilation, Stalin was generous with the dispensation of awards, medals and promotions. Five of the armies involved in Operation Ring were subsequently awarded 'Guards' status. Voronov, Rokossovsky, Chistyakov, Galanin, Zhadov, Malinovsky, Shumilov, Tolbukhin, Rotmistrov, Volsky, Kharitonov and Rodin were all promoted at the end of 1942 or during the early weeks of 1943. Zhukov, already deputy commander of the Red Army, was promoted

to Marshal of the Soviet Union. Vatutin, whose star was on the rise, was promoted twice, to Colonel-General in the first half of December and again to Army General two months later. In recognition of his pivotal pole in the planning and coordination of Operations Uranus and Little Saturn, Vasilevsky was also promoted twice, to Army General in mid-January and to Marshal of the Soviet Union a month later.

Yet during the dying days of 1942 the attention of both STAVKA and OKH had shifted from the somewhat static drama on the Volga to the complex and fluid situation around the Donets and the lower Don, a situation replete with threat and opportunity. An advance by Eremenko's forces to Rostov, or a breakthrough across the Donets towards Taganrog or Mariupol by Southwestern Front, would put Army Group A at risk. Of these, the most immediate threat to Kleist's command lay in the direct approach to Rostov from the east, where Eremenko's armies were advancing towards Kotelnikovo. In response Hitler issued Operational Order 2. Army Group A was to pull back its left flank in stages to Salsk where it would tie in with IV Pz Army. Hoth would be permitted to pull back his left flank along the left bank of the Don as far as Tsymlyanskaya, and Hollidt, his left flank still at considerable risk, could pull back from the Chir to the line Tsymlyanskaya – Morozovsk. On 28 December, with VII Rum Corps in increasingly chaotic retreat east of the Sal, Manstein informed Hitler that to protect the left flank of Army Group A, he would have to turn IV Pz Army to the east, south of the Sal, and he gave Kirchner permission to withdraw to the Sal from his increasingly exposed position at Kotelnikovo. This withdrawal left a gap between the Sal and the Don that Eremenko's forces could exploit to advance on Rostov. Hitler ordered that 7 Pz Div, badly needed by Manstein on the frontline, was to be held at Rostov to prepare the city's defences.

While Hitler was grudgingly approving limited and inevitable withdrawals, Stalin was preparing a major expansion of offensive operations. For weeks Leningrad Front and Volkhov Front had been planning, and intensively training for, an offensive to lift the siege of Leningrad. By the end of 1942 STAVKA had completed planning for a major offensive designed to destroy Army Group B in an attack towards Kursk and Kharkov. Additionally, to take maximum advantage of the loss of German morale after the encirclement of VI Army and to maximise the territorial gain before the onset of the spring thaw that would bring a six-week suspension of operations, plans were laid for another offensive to trap Army Group A in the Caucasus by means of an offensive towards Rostov involving the four southern Fronts (Voronezh, Southwestern, Southern and Transcaucasian).

As early as 22 December, when it had become apparent that Operation Little Saturn would be successful and that Operation Winter Storm would fail, Golikov had attended a STAVKA session in Moscow to discuss operational plans for a second strike on the middle reaches of the Don aimed at II Hun Army and the remains of VIII It Army between Kantemirovka and Voronezh as a prelude to the liberation of Kursk and Kharkov. Golikov learned that his mission was to destroy the Hungarian and Italian armies in the Ostrogozhsk – Rossosh line (the offensive was named the Ostrogozhsk-Rossosh operation), and that his offensive towards Kharkov was to be complemented by a renewed offensive by Southwestern Front. As early as September 1942 Voronezh Front had acquired Lt-Gen N E Chibisov's 38 Army[2] from the left flank

---

2   This second formation of 38 Army was formed from one of the reserve armies and was assigned to Bryansk Front in early August 1942.

of Reiter's Bryansk Front to support Cherniakhovsky's 60 Army in the Voronezh area, but the impending offensive would primarily involve 40 Army, which by January 1943 was under Moskalenko's command and incorporated 4 Tank Corps. Voronezh Front would also have the second formation of 3 Tank Army, which became operational at the beginning of January and was positioned on Golikov's left flank. This new tank army was commanded by Lt-Gen P S Rybalko, and it included 12 Tank Corps, 15 Tank Corps and four rifle divisions. As Front reserve, Golikov had Major-Gen P M Zykov's 18 Rifle Corps. This corps would subsequently be used as the core of a new army, designated 69 Army, to be commanded by Lt-Gen M I Kazakov. Kazakov's army would come to incorporate many barely trained, poorly equipped conscripts from the recently liberated territories, and would not be made operational until early February, that is, until several weeks after the offensive had commenced. Farther south, in a renewed offensive to demolish the remnants of III Rum Army, Vatutin was to advance west of the Derkul to establish himself on the Aydar in the Starobelsk area, and from there to strike south towards Mariupol. For this task Southwestern Front would be further reinforced with mechanised forces.

While Voronezh Front and Southwestern Front with their fifty-four rifle divisions and ten tank corps, together with a number of independent rifle and tank brigades, ski troops and cavalry, were to bear the main weight of the impending offensive, Southern and Transcaucasian Fronts were also to participate. After taking Kotelnikovo, Eremenko's Southern Front, in a continuation of its ongoing operations, was directed to strike at Shakhty in order to outflank Rostov from the north and at the same time advance across the Manych from Proletarsk towards Tikhoretsk into the rear of I Pz Army. For the attack towards Shakhy, 5 Shock Army would be transferred from the command of Southwestern Front to Southern Front. At the southern extremity of the front, Petrov's Black Sea Group of Tyulenev's Transcaucasian Front was ordered to prepare a strike north through Kransnodar to link up with Eremenko's forces at Tikhoretsk, while the Front's Northern Group under Maslennikov was given the more modest task of maintaining pressure on I Pz Army on the Terek.

On 8 January Leningrad and Volkhov Fronts began Operation Spark, an offensive designed to break the blockade of Leningrad. The siege of Leningrad had proved to be a terrible ordeal for the civilian population, the first winter particularly so. Within a few months of the start of the siege, Leningrad had degenerated from a relatively prosperous fully functioning city to an urban fortress subject to continuous bombardment in which public transport ceased to operate, the water supply failed and, during a particularly severe winter, food and fuel became desperately short. Through the carefully regulated food distribution system the ration had been repeatedly cut. The city had been systematically stripped of anything edible or combustible, and the city authorities had gone to extraordinary lengths to find alternative sources of food. Stocks of industrial starches, fats and greases had been processed for utilisation in foodstuffs, and bread had been bulked with sawdust. The privations had been at their most acute during the period in which the waters of Lake Ladoga had begun to freeze sufficiently to restrict boat traffic, but before they had frozen sufficiently to carry vehicle traffic. The very old, the very young and the infirm had been the first to succumb to the direct and indirect effects of malnutrition and hypothermia, and the death toll rose into the hundreds of thousands. Bodies lay in the streets uncollected and in the cemeteries unburied. Yet by the summer of 1942, though the supply situation remained critical, the city had survived the worst and conditions for the civil population began to improve somewhat. Hundreds of thousands of the city's inhabitants had been evacuated across Lake Ladoga, thereby reducing the supply needs of the city and, despite the presence of enemy gunboats on the lake, the supply system into Leningrad had become more effective. A fuel pipeline, laid across the lake bed, provided the armies of Govorov's Leningrad Front with greater mobility, but the breaking of the blockade by the re-establishment of a land-link with the Russian interior remained a priority. In October 1942 an attempt to do precisely that had failed, though it had diverted Manstein's XI Army from its preparations for a final assault on the city. By December Manstein and XI Army had gone. Nonetheless the defences constructed by Lindemann's XVIII Army in the Schlusselburg corridor, the neck of German-held territory between Mga and Lake Ladoga, were formidable. The Soviet forces deployed at the beginning of 1943 for the direct defence of the city were largely unchanged from the end of 1941. Defending the northern approaches from the Finns was 23 Army, 42 Army defended the approach from the west and 55 Army defended the southern sector of the perimeter. After XVIII Army's forces had reached the Gulf of Finland west of Leningrad at the end of September 1941, 8 Army had been cut off from Leningrad along the coastal strip around Oranienbaum between Sosnovy Bor and Petrodvorets. In January 1942 the headquarters of 8 Army had been moved to the eastern side of the Schlusselburg corridor, and the forces defending the Oranienbaum salient had been designated as an operational group under Leningrad Front. In October 1942 the forces on the Neva defending Leningrad from the east along the western face of the Schlusselburg corridor, were upgraded from an operational group to the newly designated 67 Army. This army, under the command of Major-Gen M P Dukhanov, would be responsible for the western sector of the Operation Spark offensive. On the eastern face of the Schlusselburg corridor, Lt-Gen V Z Romanovsky's 2 Shock Army was in position south of Lake Ladoga. North of the Mga to Volkhov railway, the right flank divisions of Lt-Gen F N Starikov's 8 Army would play a supporting role on Romanovsky's left. In April 1942 Leningrad Front had relinquished command of the last of its forces east of the Schlusselburg corridor and Meretskov's Volkhov Front became responsible for all forces south of Lake Ladoga. Hence responsibility for the coordination of operations on the eastern sector of the corridor fell to Meretskov. Operation Spark was not a large-scale offensive by Soviet standards. It involved less than a score of rifle divisions but its careful planning and the intensive preparatory training of the assault troops led to rapid success. Attacking across the frozen Neva into XXVI Corps' defences, 67 Army broke through at several points south of Schlusselburg. Romanovsky's forces were equally successful, breaking through the German defences northeast of Sinyavino and striking to the west. Within six days, and despite ferocious German resistance, XXVI Corps had been cleared from the northern section of the corridor, and had been pushed back to new positions facing north on either side of Sinyavino. Lindemann rushed reinforcements to the area to prevent any exploitation of the Soviet offensive farther south towards Mga, and the German defences at Sinyavino held against determined Soviet attacks throughout the second half of January. Despite the Soviet failure to exploit the initial success of the offensive, the main objective had been achieved; Schlusselburg and the area along the lakeshore, though still within range of German artillery fire, were securely in Soviet hands. In February a rail link between Leningrad and the Russian interior through the newly liberated territory was completed, and thereafter, though the city itself remained under artillery fire from the southwest, the worst of the siege was over.

The most southerly part of STAVKA's strategic offensive opened on 1 January with an attack by 51 Army from Gluboky towards the Manych west of Proletarsk, while 2 Gds Army on its right flank continued its attack directly towards Rostov. At the same time, Gerasimenko's 28 Army advanced from Elitsa down the Manych towards Proletarsk. At the start of the offensive German forces in the Caucasus numbered more than three-quarters of a million.[3] In the face of the Soviet offensive in the Caucasus and the direct threat to Rostov, the latitude given to Kleist in Operational Order 2 was clearly inadequate to deal with the threat to his deep left flank, and Kleist responded by concentrating on holding the shoulders of Army Group A's positions and withdrawing his centre from the potential pocket. The retreat from the Terek began on 3 January, and from the passes of the main Caucasus range, two days later, though formal approval from OKH (Hitler) for I Pz Army to pull back to Rostov was not given until 24 January. Faced with the sudden withdrawal of I Pz Army from its forward positions around Mozdok and Nalchik, Maslennikov's Northern Group of Transcaucasian Front was presented with an opportunity to disrupt Mackensen's withdrawal. Deploying 4 Gds Cav Corps, 5 Gds Cav Corps, 44 Army, 58 Army, 9 Army and 37 Army, forces which between them included seven tank brigades, Maslennikov had the resources to overwhelm the German retreat, but he and his army commanders bungled the pursuit from the southeast. The advance of 58 Army (by then under the command of Major-Gen K S Melnik, Khomenko having been appointed to the command of 44 Army) was so slow that its forces found themselves, by default, as part of Maslennikov's second echelon. Consequently the long withdrawal of I Pz Army towards Voroshilovsk and Armavir was able to proceed relatively untroubled.

Petrov's Black Sea Group of Transcaucasian Front deployed 47 Army, 56 Army, 18 Army and 46 Army for its offensive against XVII Army. This offensive, conducted in appalling weather conditions, began on 11 January with a diversionary attack by Petrov's right flank 46 Army towards Maikop. This attack accelerated German plans for a withdrawal, and German forces facing the adjacent 18 Army also began to withdraw. The main attack by 56 Army and 47 Army did not begin until 16 January, several days later than originally planned. At 56 Army Grechko had been appointed as commander to conduct the offensive north through Krasnodar towards Tikhoretsk, with Bataysk as his ultimate objective. On the left flank Kamkov's 47 Army launched an offensive to the northwest in order to retake Novorossiysk.

The Soviet attack across the Chir in the closing days of 1942 had pushed the right flank of Group Hollidt to the west of Tormosin. In attempting to comply with Operational Order 2, Hollidt's forces, technically 'Army Group Hollidt' after 27 December when III Rum Army's two corps were withdrawn and replaced with XXIX Corps (four Italian and three Rumanian divisions) and Corps Mieth[4], began

---

3   I Pz Army had five divisions, two independent regiments and sixteen independent battalions, and XVII Army had seventeen divisions, five independent regiments and twelve independent battalions.

4   Lt-Gen Friedrich Mieth's newly-formed corps, initially based on a German infantry division and a *Luftwaffe* field division, was, in July 1943, designated as the IV Corps, the second time this

a withdrawal that developed into an unintended though prolonged 140km retreat to the Donets. On Hollidt's left, Fretter-Pico's forces were assigned to Army Group Don, and Fretter-Pico acquired command responsibility for the remains of VIII It Army and III Rum Army. During the course of Hollidt's withdrawal Fretter-Pico had to commit the newly available 4 Pz Div on 4 January to strengthen the disintegrating 304 Inf Div, a division that was supposed to be linking with and protecting Hollidt's left flank, but which was under attack from two Soviet tank corps driving for the Donets. The next day Hollidt, under considerable Soviet pressure and under the threat of being outflanked, was finally forced to give up the Morozovsk air base.

On the direct approach to Rostov 3 Gds Tank Corps had pushed patrols along the southern bank of the Don to within 30km of the city by 7 January. Hitler expected that a battalion of twenty Tiger tanks in the Rostov area would be capable of defeating the Soviet tank corps, but the performance of the new tanks fell far below expectation. In the second week of January, as I Pz Army, pulling back towards Rostov, closed the gap between Army Group A and Army Group Don, Hitler allowed IV Pz Army to move back to a line facing north on the Manych canal.

By 11 January 2 Gds Army and 51 Army had reached the Manych between its confluence with the Don and Proletarsk. Within 2 Gds Army was a powerful mobile group of 3 Gds Tank Corps, 2 Mech Corps, 6 Mech Corps and 98 Rifle Div under the overall command of Rotmistrov, which on 17 January was ordered to cross to the south bank of the Manych and to go for Bataysk and Rostov. These attacks, fiercely resisted by IV Pz Army using reinforcements drawn from Group Hollidt, prompted an acceleration of the withdrawal of I Pz Army in order to ensure that its left flank could link up with the right flank of IV Pz Army at Salsk. Mackensen's retreat from the north Caucasus region was as rapid as had been his advance five months earlier. By mid-January his forces had withdrawn to Pyatigorsk; a week later they were abandoning Cherkessk, Nevinnomyssk and Voroshilovsk; by 24 January Armavir was in Soviet hands, and, farther north, 28 Army had advanced 50km west of Salsk.

On 23 January, with the prospects for the Soviet encirclement of twenty-four Axis divisions east of the Sea of Azov diminishing rapidly, Eremenko was urged to greater effort in his attempt to take Bataysk. At the same time, with 47 Army's offensive against Novorossiysk stalled and 56 Army struggling on the approaches to Kransnodar, Petrov was also urged to greater effort to take Novorossiysk and to secure the Taman Peninsula. Yet these objectives remained beyond the Red Army's immediate reach. Mackensen's forces continued to pull back towards Rostov, and XVII Army conducted a steady withdrawal of its left and centre towards the Sea of Azov. On 24 January, after mobile units of the Northern Group had linked up with Southern Front's 28 Army, a separate North Caucasian Front, based on the Northern Group's forces, was established under Maslennikov's command. Maslennikov's Front was given several objectives; its right flank was to support Southern Front's offensive against Bataysk, its left flank (37 Army) was to support Petrov's efforts against Krasnodar, and in the centre 9 Army, which had been commanded by Major-Gen V V Glagolev since the end of August 1942, was to strike at Timashevsk on XVII Army's left flank north of Krasnodar. By early February, after an advance by Maslennikov's right flank forces from Tikhoretsk down the Soskya to the Sea of Azov near Yeysk, the *Ostheer*'s frontline in the south

---

formation had existed, the original IV Corps having been destroyed at Stalingrad.

had been split in two. Elements of I Pz Army that had been south of the Soskya were later subordinated to XVII Army, the latter having become isolated in the Taman Peninsula and the Kuban. Ruoff's defences on his right flank remained stubbornly anchored on Novorossiysk, containing within a small bridgehead a Soviet sea-borne landing designed to outflank the port. Father north, though Soviet forces had taken the oilfields of the Maikop area by the end of January, their advance stalled on the approaches to Krasnodar. By 5 February both the Black Sea Group and the bulk of Maslennikov's forces were left with the same objective – investment of the 400,000 personnel of Army Group A, including two panzer divisions, in the Taman Peninsula and the Kuban. Consequently North Caucasian Front's right flank (44 Army and most of Maslennikov's mobile forces, the latter having been grouped together as a cavalry/mechanised group under Lt-Gen N I Kirichenko), was transferred to Southern Front, and the Black Sea Group came under the operational control of North Caucasian Front. Maslennikov then had the sole task of retaking the Taman Peninsula, and with all seven armies he renewed his offensive on 9 February. Kamkov continued to try to batter his way through Ruoff's defences in the mountain ridges north of Novorossiysk, while 56 Army and 18 Army attacked Krasnodar. In the centre 37 Army and 46 Army attacked in the Korenevsk area, and on the right flank 58 Army and 9 Army attacked towards Varenikovskaya. In the first few days some progress was made and Krasnodar was taken on 12 February. Yet Petrov was unable to take Novorossiysk, investment of which was prolonged and unsuccessful. During the second half of February and through March, though Maslennikov's forces took Troitskaya and advanced down the Kuban river, the offensive eventually stagnated, and on 16 March the Black Sea Group Headquarters was disbanded. By April Maslennikov's efforts had failed to the point that XVII Army had been able to assume the initiative.

The main part of STAVKA's strategic offensive in the south, that of Southwestern Front and Voronezh Front, was co-ordinated by Zhukov and Vasilevsky, and was planned to begin on 14 January with Golikov's forces attacking Army Group B over the upper Don. Golikov's initial objective was to clear German forces from the Liski – Kantemirovka section of the Voronezh – Millerovo railway in order to ease Vatutin's chronic supply problems. By the beginning of 1943 Army Group B, despite the losses on its southern wing during Operation Little Saturn, still appeared to be a powerful force. On its left flank the eleven infantry divisions of the newly-promoted Col-Gen Salmuth's II Army occupied a line from north of Livny to the Don north of Voronezh, the city of Voronezh itself, and down the Don for some twenty-five kilometres. Occupying the next eighty kilometres of the Don defences were the ten Hungarian divisions of Jány's II Hun Army. Along the final thirty kilometres of the Don front in the Rossosh sector as far south as Novaya Kalitva, was the Italian Alpine Corps. West of the Don, in the Ivanovka area between Novaya Kalitva and Kantemirovka, XXIV Pz Corps had established a degree of stability, but farther south, between Kantemirovka and Millerovo, Fretter-Pico struggled to form a cohesive frontline.

On 12 January Moskalenko began a reconnaissance in strength from his Don positions in the area north of Liski. STAVKA's plan was that 40 Army in the north would strike towards Alekseyevka to link up with 3 Tank Army striking to the northwest from the Ivanovka area. The Soviet offensive came as no surprise to Weichs; since mid-December he had been watching a build-up of Soviet forces along the upper

See Map 15

Don, and he had had weeks to prepare his defences. Yet on 13 January in the face of 40 Army's aggressive reconnaissance action, 7 Hun Light Div began an unexpected and chaotic retreat that prompted Moskalenko to begin his offensive a day early. On 14 January, as the left flank of II Hun Army began to disintegrate, Rybalko began his offensive from the Ivanovka – Kantemirovka area aimed due west towards Belgorod and Kharkov. Rybalko achieved a rapid breakthrough and Major-Gen V A Koptsov's 15 Tank Corps overran the headquarters of XXIV Pz Corps. With the Red Army pushing behind Jány's positions from the south, the centre and right of II Hun Army, together with the defences of the Italian Alpine Corps, disintegrated. By the evening of 18 January Golikov's encircling forces met. On 19 January Soviet cavalry routed 5 It Inf Div, and by that time the Soviets estimated that they had killed 56,000 Axis troops and taken a similar number prisoner with thirteen divisions including 1,700 tanks surrounded. From their forward positions west of Alekseyevka, Golikov's forces could thrust northwest towards Kursk, and north towards Kastornoe in order to encircle the 125,000 personnel of II Army west of Voronezh. This 'Voronezh-Kastornoe' operation, proposed by Vasilevky on 18 January, was to commence on 24 January to take advantage of the precarious position of II Army's deep salient between Bryansk Front and the left wing of Voronezh Front.

The spectacular success of Voronezh Front during the third week of January was not being matched by Vatutin, who was only slowly pushing Fretter-Pico back towards the Donets. On 20 January Vatutin proposed to STAVKA a revised seven-day operation by Southwestern Front to cut off and destroy Army Group Don in the Donbas region. This plan, Operation Leap (or Gallop), was approved by STAVKA, but in the meantime Vatutin was directed to maintain the pressure against Fretter-Pico and the left flank of Group Hollidt. Southwestern Front, which had been conducting offensive operations since 19 November, had for weeks been operating at the end of a barely adequate supply line through Kalach-on-Don. Vatutin required until 29 January to redeploy his forces and to acquire, through the recently available rail link from Voronezh, the necessary supplies for the new offensive. It is a measure of how thinly stretched were Vatutin's forces that the Axis troops surrounded at Chertkovo, their numbers having been swollen by the arrival of thousands of Italians fleeing south and west from the Don, were able to hold out until mid-January before breaking out through attenuated Soviet lines in a desperate thirty-kilometre trek to German-held positions in the Belovodsk area. Farther south Fretter-Pico's forces, after successfully extricating 14,000 surrounded troops from Millerovo, and despite the pressure being applied by Southwestern Front, were able to cross in good order to the right bank of the Donets north and east of Voroshilovgrad. Elements of 1 Gds Army managed a limited crossing of the Donets near Voroshilovgrad on 23 January and took Starobelsk on the Aydar the next day, but otherwise the German defences on the approaches to the lower Donets held up reasonably well.

For Operation Leap, Vatutin would have Kharitinov's 6 Army (incorporating Pavlov's 25 Tank Corps), V I Kuznetsov's 1 Gds Army, Lelyushenko's 3 Gds Army and M M Popov's 5 Tank Army.[5] In preparation for the impending operation, Vatutin consolidated the bulk of his mechanised forces into a powerful 'Front Mobile Group'.

5   At the end of December M M Popov had replaced Romanenko at 5 Tank Army and Lt-Gen V D Tsvetayev replaced Popov at 5 Shock Army.

This formation, which included 4 Gds Tank Corps (formerly 17 Tank Corps), 18 Tank Corps, 3 Tank Corps, 10 Tank Corps, three rifle divisions and two independent tank brigades, was placed under Popov's command, and Rotmistrov was appointed to command 5 Tank Army. At full establishment the Front Mobile Group would have been equivalent to a German panzer army in terms of tank strength, but when the offensive began it had a total of just 137 tanks.

Although during the final week of January Army Group Don appeared to be containing the pressure exerted by Southwestern Front and Southern Front, farther north the situation for German forces facing Voronezh Front was far more serious. After the collapse of II Hun Army, Golikov appeared to have a free run west towards Kharkov and northwest towards Kursk, while II Army was left with an open flank on its right and a front that bent back in the north leaving it vulnerable to encirclement. The Soviet encirclement effort against II Army, not entirely unexpected by Weichs or Salmuth, began on 24 January with an attack north by 40 Army towards Kastornoe. That evening II Army began to pull back from Voronezh and from its Don defences but the move came too late. The Soviet offensive was joined by 60 Army and 38 Army, and, later, by Pukhov's 13 Army of Bryansk Front attacking from the north of the salient in the Livny area. Voronezh was retaken on 26 January, and on the morning of 28 January forces from the two Fronts met at Kastornoe encircling two of II Army's three corps. With II Army largely encircled and facing destruction, Hitler replaced Salmuth on 3 February, appointing General Walter Weiss, commander of XXVII Corps, to pull II Army's irons from the fire.

The Soviet offensives of January 1943 had sliced Army Group B away from Army Group Don, and had destroyed Army Group B as an effective command. By the end of the month II Hun Army and VIII It Army, including the Italian Alpine Corps, had been eliminated from the Axis order of battle, and Soviet forces had advanced 140km on a 240km front taking around 87,000 prisoners. Despite the disappointing performance of Southern Front in not seizing Rostov, the performance of Voronezh Front in the second half of January had been spectacular, and Golikov's left flank was still advancing west, closing up to the Oskol. In a little over two months since 19 November the Red Army had crushed the four armies of Germany's allies in Russia, had dealt serious blows to two German armies and, in addition, had completely destroyed what had once been Germany's most powerful field army. As a result, STAVKA's ambitions became positively expansive as Stalin once again began to think in terms of an overwhelming series of offensives from the Baltic to the Black Sea that would bring the war to a rapid conclusion. The offensives in the south by Voronezh Front, Southwestern Front and Southern Front were perceived as a pursuit to the Dnieper, and the isolation against the north shore of the Sea of Azov of all German forces in the south. In the centre, forces released from Stalingrad would be used for an offensive towards Smolensk that, in conjunction with an offensive by Kalinin and Western Fronts, would aim to encircle and destroy Army Group Centre. Meanwhile Northwestern Front would be required to destroy the German forces in the Demyansk area in order to facilitate the passage of powerful mobile forces into the rear of Army Group North. For the offensives in the centre and north, additional mechanised forces would be required. On 15 January a new tank army, designated 2 Tank Army and commanded by Romanenko, became operational and was assigned to Bryansk Front. Less than two weeks later approval was granted for the formation of another tank army. Designated 1 Tank Army and based on the headquarters of 29 Army (which army was formally disbanded on 2 February), the new tank army became operational on 7 February and was assigned to Northwestern Front. Katukov, who had been promoted to the rank of lieutenant-general less than a month earlier, was appointed to command 1 Tank Army.

Yet, as had been the case a year earlier, Stalin's ambition exceeded the capacity of the Red Army to deliver. As Operations Spark and Mars had shown, Army Group North and Army Group Centre occupied powerful defensive positions, while on the Donets sector the considerable Axis losses suffered during the Soviet Chir and Don offensives of December and January had been predominantly of non-German personnel.

Sting in the Tail
On 27 January Hitler ordered the transfer from Army Group A to Army Group Don of I Pz Army Headquarters together with two corps headquarters, a panzer division, an infantry division and two security divisions, though the latter, being manned by older men, and deficient in artillery and motorised transport, were not suitable for front line action. On this date Hitler also promised Manstein that an offensive would be launched not later than 12 February by two SS divisions in the Kharkov area. The SS divisions had been moving to the area as part of Hitler's plans, formulated after the failure of Operation Winter Storm, to mount a renewed offensive in 1943 to relieve VI Army. The plans for a renewed Stalingrad relief effort may have been overwhelmed by subsequent events, but the SS divisions, in the form of the SS Pz Corps under SS General Paul Hausser, were becoming available by the end of January. Hausser's corps, widely distrusted by the *Ostheer*'s regular officers, included 1 SS Pz Gdr Div (*Leibstandarte*), 2 SS Pz Gdr Div (*Das Reich*) and, by mid-February, 3 SS Pz Gdr Div (*Totenkopf*). Since each of the SS panzer grenadier divisions had a full regiment of panzers, they were panzer divisions in all but name.

Vatutin's Operation Leap commenced on 29 January and the next day Popov's Front Mobile Group, introduced between 6 Army and 1 Gds Army, struck from its positions on the left bank of the Donets north of Lysychansk. Popov's objective was Krasnoarmyeskoye and ultimately the Sea of Azov at Mariupol, but first he would have to cross the Donets and take Slavyansk some 10km south of the river. As Vatutin's offensive gathered pace, Mackensen's I Pz Army Headquarters was preparing to take command of the forces of Army Detachment Fretter-Pico (the Slavyansk – Voroshilovgrad sector of the front), though its primary reinforcement in the form of 3 Pz Div and 11 Pz Div was stuck in deep snow near Rostov. Responding to Vatutin's unfolding offensive, Manstein's strategic priority was to prevent his command from becoming isolated east of the Dnieper, and the most immediate threat came from Popov's mechanised forces in the Slavyansk area. Manstein moved 7 Pz Div, his most powerful and immediately available reserve, to Slavyansk. Although 7 Pz Div was quickly surrounded, the defence of Slavyansk completely disrupted the timetable for Operation Leap, which had anticipated that Popov's Group would reach Mariupol by 5 February. Yet by that date Popov and Kuznetsov were still snarled up in the Slavyansk area, and Vatutin was forced to move the axis of his advance along the line of least resistance farther west towards Barvenkovo. On Popov's right, 6 Army took Izyum on 5 February. Farther downriver 3 Gds Army had established viable bridgeheads across the Donets north of Voroshilovgrad by the end of January, and on 2 February Lelyushenko's forces crossed the Donets east of Voroshilovgrad.

Also on 2 February Golikov's left flank armies attacked to the southwest in the first phase of a hurriedly prepared operation codenamed Star, the objective of which was to capture Kursk and the Kharkov industrial area. To meet this attack, the scattered units from what had been Army Group B's southern wing, together with the recently redeployed *Grossdeutschland* Mot Div in the Belgorod – Volchansk area and Hausser's SS divisions in the Kharkov area, were subordinated to the newly-formed Army Detachment Lanz. This formation, part of Army Group B, was commanded by General Hubert Lanz, and was charged with the defence of Kharkov and the protection of the left wing of Army Group Don. Aiming to outflank Kharkov from the south and southwest, 3 Tank Army reached the Donets in the Pechengi – Chuguyev sector south of Kharkov on 4 February but was held to the left bank by 1 SS Pz Gdr Div. On 5 February the newly-formed 69 Army struck for Kharkov through Volchansk, and on Kazakov's right, 40 Army, redeploying rapidly after the Kastornoe operation, aimed for the Belgorod area. Meanwhile, on Moskalenko's right, 60 Army advanced towards Kursk, the town falling to Cherniakhovsky's forces on 8 February. In its rear 60 Army left surrounded portions of II Army fighting in encirclement or breaking out across the Tim to the northwest.

While 7 Pz Div in Slavyansk held off Vatutin's forces, elements of 3 Pz Div arriving from Rostov forced through a relief column from the southeast and re-established contact with the town. Mackensen, fighting in territory thoroughly familiar to him from the battles of 1942, moved his XL Pz Corps and III Pz Corps headquarters into the area. Although German forces were pushed back from Barvenkovo on 9 February and from Lozova the next day, General Sigfrid Henrici's XL Pz Corps was able to prevent any rapid Soviet exploitation south from the Barvenkovo – Slavyansk area and, coordinating their actions from north and south, 7 Pz Div and 11 Pz Div were able to push back the defences of Poluboyarov's 4 Gds Tank Corps and the associated 3 Tank Corps from the Krivoy Torets valley in the Druzhkivka – Kramatorsk area 20km south of Slavyansk.

When, by 6 February, the scale of the Soviet offensive and the damage done to Army Group B was made apparent to Hitler, Manstein obtained permission to trade space for time, but only after having convinced Hitler that the diverging Soviet thrusts (towards Kursk and Kharkov), and their weakening supply situation, would create a favourable opportunity for a devastating counterstrike using the relatively undamaged German forces in the area. Hitler gave Army Group Don permission to pull back to the Mius, and two days later Group Hollidt, having barely completed its withdrawal from the Chir to the lower Donets, began a further withdrawal 160km to its rear, while on Hollidt's right IV Pz Army joined the retreat, pulling back first to Rostov and then along the Gulf of Taganrog.

On 8 February *Grossdeutschland* Mot Div, operating on the SS Corps' left flank, was driven from Belgorod and fell back behind the Donets, but in the Pechengi – Chuguyev sector 1 SS Pz Gdr Div continued to hold 3 Tank Army to the left bank of the river until 10 February, by which time Kharkov had been largely surrounded from the north and west. On 11 February the bulk of the SS Pz Corps (*Leibstandarte* supported by

Grossdeutschland) attacked south from Merefa to try to re-establish a link between Army Group B and the tenuous left flank of Army Group Don in the Pavlograd area. This attack made good progress, but two days later the weakened left flank of Hausser's corps was forced back to the outskirts of Kharkov. On 13 February Army Group Don was redesignated Army Group South and Manstein assumed responsibility for Army Detachment Lanz. At the same time Army Group B Headquarters was withdrawn from theatre and the remnants of II Army were transferred to the command of Army Group Centre. By 14 February Hausser's panzers had advanced 50km to the south from Merefa but during the advance, through what was effectively a gap between the left flank of Voronezh Front and the right flank of Southwestern Front, had made little contact with Soviet forces. Meanwhile in Kharkov, with the city on the verge of being completely surrounded, Hausser authorised a withdrawal that was completed by 16 February. This withdrawal, made in defiance of orders, cost Lanz his job and his replacement on 20 February by Kempf, while Hausser escaped with little more than a reprimand.

During the second week of February Vatutin and Golikov assumed, and reported to STAVKA and the General Staff, that German forces were withdrawing towards the Dnieper. Aerial reconnaissance and other intelligence information was interpreted accordingly, failing to note the concentration of German armour on the flanks of the deepest Soviet penetration, while the continuing stubborn German defence of Slavyansk was interpreted as a delaying action to cover the withdrawal to the Dnieper. The assumptions made about German intentions prompted STAVKA, the Soviet General Staff and the Front commanders to act incautiously with armies that were outrunning their logistical support. On 8 February, aware that Manstein's right wing on the lower Don and the lower Donets had begun preparations to pull back to the west, STAVKA ordered Vatutin to block the apparent German withdrawal to the Dnieper. Vatutin was also ordered to secure Dnepropetrovsk and Zaporozhye as quickly as possible after he had taken Lozova. Accordingly Vatutin directed Kharitinov towards Krasnograd. Kuznetsov was given the task of securing Slavyansk and then moving on Artemovsk, while at the same time turning his right flank west towards Zaporozhe. Popov's main objective was to take Krasnoarmeyskoye, and he acted quickly. On 11 February 3 Tank Corps was left at Kramatorsk to continue the defence of the town against 7 Pz Div and 11 Pz Div, while 4 Gds Tank Corps conducted a rapid advance deep behind German lines to take Krasnoarmeyskoye later that day.

The sudden appearance of a Soviet tank corps in the Krasnoarmeyskoye area came as a surprise to Mackensen, but he was already in the process of deploying Knobelsdorff's XLVIII Pz Corps with two panzer divisions southwest of the town, and Poluboyarov, his corps already low on fuel, found himself cut off from contact with Soviet forces to the north, contact that was not fully restored for several days. By 16 February no German forces remained on the Donets and 3 Gds Army, after nearly two weeks of ferocious street fighting, had taken Voroshilovgrad. Meanwhile, far to the west, 6 Army and the right wing of 1Gds Army had advanced beyond Lozova towards Holubivka and Pavlograd. On Manstein's other flank Rostov had been abandoned by IV Pz Army on 14 February, and Southern Front (once again under the command of Malinovsky after 2 February), was pursuing Manstein's right wing towards the Mius. By 18 February Group Hollidt and IV Pz Army had moved into the Mius river defensive positions, the same positions occupied by Army Group South more than a year earlier. This line was penetrated briefly by 3 Gds Mech Corps, but a sudden thaw prevented the corps from receiving necessary reinforcement, and it was pushed back to the east bank of the river.

Manstein's counter-offensive against Southwestern Front and Voronezh Front (known in Germany as the Donets Campaign or Manstein's Counterstrike) began on 19 February, and over the subsequent weeks Manstein and his subordinates were to engage in the sort of warfare at which they excelled – employing concentrated mechanised forces that had freedom of manoeuvre over an open battlefield. Manstein was assisted by a briefly resurgent *Luftwaffe* that was able to provide ample air cover, ground support and aerial reconnaissance in the eastern Ukraine. See Map 16

By 18 February Soviet armour had taken Pavlograd, and was just 55km from Zaporozhe with no German force in position to oppose it, and there existed a 175km gap between the right flank of Army Detachment Kempf and the left flank of I Pz Army. The next day the headquarters of IV Pz Army arrived in Dnepropetrovsk, the IV Pz Army forces on the Mius having been transferred to Group Hollidt. Hoth took command of the SS Pz Corps from Army Detachment Kempf. He also took command of Knobelsdorff's XLVIII Pz Corps deployed west of Krasnoarmeyskoye, and subsequently of Kirchner's LVII Pz Corps Headquarters arriving from the Mius. Manstein's counter-offensive involved using Hausser's corps in the area around Krasnograd and, from the area around Krasnoarmeyskoye, XLVIII Pz Corps together with I Pz Army's XL Pz Corps to snip off the head of the advancing Soviet columns driving towards the Dnieper. As the offensive developed, it would involve other forces on the flanks of the initial offensive, together with reserves arriving from Western Europe and the Crimea.[6] The German forces gathered to open the Donets offensive included seven panzer divisions, 5 SS Pz Gdr Div *Wiking* (an understrength SS division that was, in effect, a motorised division), and four infantry divisions.

The initial strike of the counter-offensive was launched while Hoth was still establishing his army headquarters at Dnepropetrovsk. On 19 February 2 SS Pz Gdr Div, having been pulled out of Kharkov just four days earlier, was quickly off the mark, advancing rapidly south from Krasnograd to reached Novomoskovsk near Dnepropetrovsk the next day. The main attack began on 20 February with XLVIII Pz Corps (6 Pz Div and 17 Pz Div) striking north from 40km west of Krasnoarmyeskoye towards Pavlograd. This attack cut the supply lines of 25 Tank Corps, which had reach the Dnieper 18km north of Zaporozhe, and it hit the flank of 1 Gds Army. On 21 February *Das Reich* turned east from Novomoskovsk towards Pavlograd, which it reached later that day. As it advanced, *Das Reich* drove Soviet forces north of the Samara and into the path of 3 SS Pz Gdr Div, which had begun to advance east between the Samara and the Orel on 23 February to strike the right flank of 6 Army southeast of Krasnograd. Meanwhile, in the XL Pz Corps sector, Mackensen had withdrawn 7 Pz Div from Slavyansk and had used it in conjunction with 9 Pz Div and 5 SS Pz Gdr Div to surround much of Popov's force north of Krasnoarmeyskoye.

---

6   On 12 February seven divisions were authorised for transfer to Manstein from the west, and on 19 February Hitler ordered Kleist to evacuate as many men as possible from the Taman Peninsula for transfer to Army Group South. By 27 February 50,000 personnel had been airlifted out of the peninsula, and by 6 March the number had risen to 100,000.

Manstein's offensive took Vatutin completely by surprise and it was not until 23 February that Vatutin began to issue orders for a withdrawal of forces that by then had become surrounded.[7] On 23 February III Pz Corps (11 Pz Div, 3 Pz Div and 19 Pz Div) from the Slavyansk area joined XL Pz Corps in a thrust to the northeast. Manstein then ordered I and IV Pz Armies to destroy Popov's mobile group south of the Pavlograd – Barvenkovo railway, though Popov was able to extricate much of his force to the Barvenkovo area. Only on 25 February did Vatutin admit the true state of affairs to STAVKA, by which time the right wing and centre of his Front had been shattered and was in full retreat. On 25 February Manstein issued orders for a continuation of the offensive in a thrust into the left flank of Voronezh Front. Hoth's forces would head north towards Kharkov in an offensive that would be joined by 1 SS Pz Gdr Div from north of Kransnograd, while I Pz Army was to retake Izyum and close off the Donets crossings. By 27 February Lozova had been retaken and the panzer armies were pushing Vatutin's right wing back towards the Donets. In the last days of February the offensive was reinforced with the *Grossdeutschland* Mot Div, which held an attempt by Golikov's two left flank armies to act against the left flank of Hoth's panzer forces attacking 6 Army.[8] By the evening of 28 February XL Pz Corps, striking to the north, reached the Donets west of Izyum. The transfer of an already weakened 3 Tank Army from Golikov's left flank to Southwestern Front on 28 February in order to mount a more coordinated attack on Hoth's left flank achieved little, and by 4 March, having crashed into IV Pz Army south of Kharkov, 3 Tank Army had been effectively eliminated as a mechanised strike force. Meanwhile 6 Army and 1 Gds Army were falling back on the Donets between Andreyevka and Krasny. By 6 March, I Pz Army had closed to the Donets along most of its front, though several Soviet bridgeheads on the right bank remained, and 3 Gds Army retained possession of Voroshilovgrad. Two days later 3 Tank Army was driven from its defensive positions south and west of Merefa, thereby exposing the left flank of 69 Army southwest of Bogodukov, and easing the path of the German panzer formations in their advance north towards Kharkov.

The German offensive by this time was winding down, some panzer divisions having already been transferred to other areas. Temperatures were rising and a thaw had begun to impede the mobility of the German mechanised forces. Yet Manstein decided to push the advance further to encircle Kharkov from the west and north. This was achieved by 9 March and Manstein, unwilling to storm the city, considered this to be mission accomplished. Yet Hausser still had unfinished business in Kharkov. On 11 March, again acting in defiance of orders, he sent two divisions from his corps into the city from the west and north. After several days of ferocious street fighting, Kharkov was retaken yet again on 15 March. With the loss of Kharkov, Golikov pulled his forces back to the left bank of the Donets. Taking advantage of the sudden absence of Soviet resistance on the right bank of the river, Hausser's forces raced north along the railway line from Kharkov to take Belgorod off the march on 18 March, this despite the reinforcement of the depleted rifle divisions of 69 Army with 3 Tank Corps and 2 Gds Tank Corps, the latter with 170 tanks. The capture of Belgorod was the final

---

7   25 Tank Corps tried to break out to the northeast, but most of the corps was lost and on 15 March Pavlov was taken prisoner.

8   Golikov had issued the necessary orders on his own initiative on 21 February.

act of the Manstein Counterstrike. The campaign had achieved a remarkable reversal of fortune for the *Ostheer*'s southern wing; a sector of the front that had suffered a devastating series of reverses since mid-November. Yet the German February/March counter-offensive, which established Manstein as Germany's pre-eminent strategist, was to prove to be the last definitively successful large-scale German offensive of the war.

Hitler's approval on 6 February for the withdrawal of Army Group South to the Mius was not the only concession he made to the overstretched *Ostheer* in the aftermath of the Stalingrad disaster. On the same day he yielded to lobbying from Zeitzler and Kluge, and agreed in principle to the abandonment of the Rzhev salient. The reasoning behind this decision lay in a concession he had made to Army Group North a week earlier. On 31 January he had succumbed to arguments by Kuechler and Zeitzler that II Corps' eleven divisions, committed to the defence of the Demyansk pocket, could be more usefully employed elsewhere, and he had approved the withdrawal of II Corps from the pocket. With that decision taken, there could no longer be any prospect of eliminating the Toropets bulge, the huge Soviet salient between Rzhev and Demyansk, and consequently little purpose to the continued defence of Rzhev. An additional factor in the Rzhev decision was the progressive weakening of IX Army within the salient as its forces were withdrawn during January to deal with crises in other sectors of the front. This process would inevitably continue through February as the *Ostheer* struggled to deal with the massive rent in its frontline between Livny and Voroshilovgrad, and further withdrawals from IX Army would leave its line too attenuated for successful defence against another Soviet offensive. The other *raison d'être* for the presence of German forces at Rzhev and Gzhatsk, a renewed offensive against Moscow, even Hitler had to acknowledge was no longer valid.

The approval for withdrawals from Demyansk and Rzhev came after Hitler had finally given approval in mid-January for a breakout by the garrison at what had come to be described as a miniature Stalingrad at Velikie Luki. After a renewed effort by Chevallerie had come close but ultimately failed to break through to the town, the remnants of the garrison were authorised to attempt to break out towards the relief column. Only 176 survivors from the original 7,000 strong garrison reached German lines. On 20 January the headquarters of III Pz Army was moved from the Vyazma area to take command of the Group von der Chevallerie forces west of Velikie Luki, and to establish a more coherent defensive line on Army Group Centre's left flank in the Velikie Luki – Nevel – Velizh sector of the front. With limited resources Reinhardt restored some semblance of order to the German lines, pulling back the frontline in places to release forces for a rationalisation of the defences. He then set about trying to subdue the considerable partisan forces, particularly those to the northeast of Vitebsk, which had been operating with virtual impunity against German rear services.

As Reinhardt rationalised the frontline west of Velikie Luki, Kuechler and Busch began to plan the withdrawal of II Corps from Demyansk to positions on the Lovat. These plans were well advanced when, on 15 February, Timoshenko, in command of Northwestern Front since October 1942, launched an offensive against the salient. To Stalin's fury this offensive, codenamed Polar Star, was botched. Despite having been in position for months, the Soviet commanders had little understanding of the German dispositions, and the forces assigned to cutting the Ramushevko corridor between the salient and the Lovat did not begin their part of the offensive until 23

February. By then it was too late. The leisurely four-week long German withdrawal from the salient began on 20 February, and the careful advanced planning ensured that the Ramushevko corridor was well-defended throughout. The withdrawal of IX Army from the Rzhev salient (Operation Bueffel) did not received final approval until 27 February. The operation began on 1 March and was completed by 24 March. In the process, Rzhev was retaken by Soviet forces on 3 March and Vyazma nine days later. The withdrawal reduced Kluge's frontline by more than 350km, it released sixteen divisions for use in other areas and it allowed Army Group Centre to occupy a carefully prepared fortified line between Velizh and Kirov. For his successful extraction of IX Army from the salient, Model was promoted in April to the rank of colonel-general.

During the first week of February STAVKA was at long last able to release for deployment elsewhere the 34 rifle divisions and 10 independent rifle and tank brigades that had been involved in the final subjugation of VI Army. In mid-February Don Front was disbanded and Rokossovsky's headquarters was transferred north to the Voronezh – Livny area as the headquarters of the newly-created Central Front that was to support an offensive against Army Group Centre that had already begun.

After the collapse of II Army in the last week of January, and the subsequent advance of Voronezh Front's 60 Army towards Kursk, II Pz Army found itself in a deepening salient around Orel, and Schmidt was required to constantly extend his right flank to the west to maintain a frontline and so prevent a strike to the north by 60 Army. On 12 February Pukhov's 13 Army, on the left flank of Reiter's Bryansk Front, was diverted from mopping up operations at Voronezh to attack II Pz Army's positions south of Orel. In this offensive Pukhov was joined on his right flank by 48 Army. Romanenko took command of 48 Army for this offensive, Rodin replacing Romanenko at 2 Tank Army. In conjunction with these attacks on II Pz Army's right flank, Lt-Gen I K Bagramyan's 16 Army attacked Schmidt's left. Skilful German resistance and heavy rainfall meant that by 24 February the offensive had made little progress. Across the entire front both sides were aware that the impending biannual season of mud would soon bring an end to offensive operations.

When Rokossovsky's headquarters arrived in the Livny area it was assigned 2 Tank Army, and was inserted into the sector south of Orel between Voronezh Front and Bryansk Front. Rokossovsky's task was to strike to the west, deep behind II Pz Army's right flank and, from northwest of Lgov, to turn north towards Roslavl, thereby encircling II Pz Army and much of IV Army. Racing north from the Stalingrad area to join Central Front were Batov's 65 Army and Chistyakov's 21 Army. Also assigned to Central Front was the newly-raised 70 Army. This new army, the creation of which was authorised on 14 October 1942, was formed on 5 February 1943 and became operational in the middle of that month. It was commanded by the young and inexperienced Lt-Gen G F Tarasov, and its six rifle divisions were predominantly manned by former NKVD frontier guards. Rokossovsky's offensive was scheduled to commence on 15 February but did not open until ten days later. Even then, most of Rokossovsky's divisions were still in transit from the south. The offensive was led by 2 Tank Army and 65 Army, it being planned that 21 Army and 70 Army would join the offensive before the end of the month. Reiter was relieved of responsibility for the capture of Bryansk, and ordered to concentrate on Orel and the destruction of the flank formations of II Pz Army. Batov's forces, their right flank protected by 13 Army, made

Colour Maps

1. Barbarossa – Outline Plan for the Initial Phase (June-July 1941)

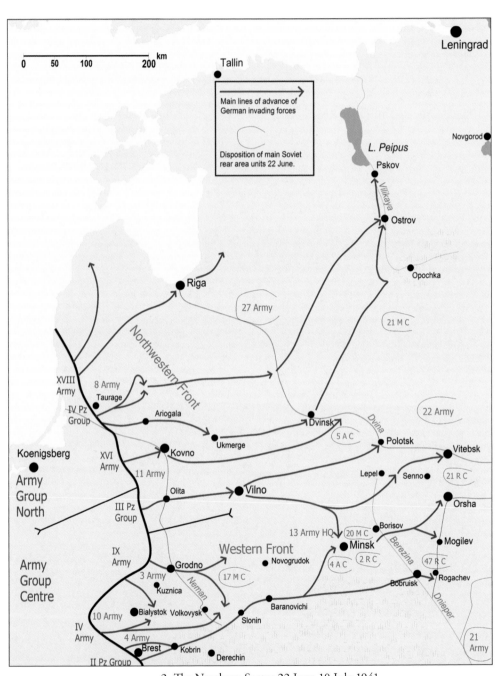

2. The Northern Sector 22 June-10 July 1941

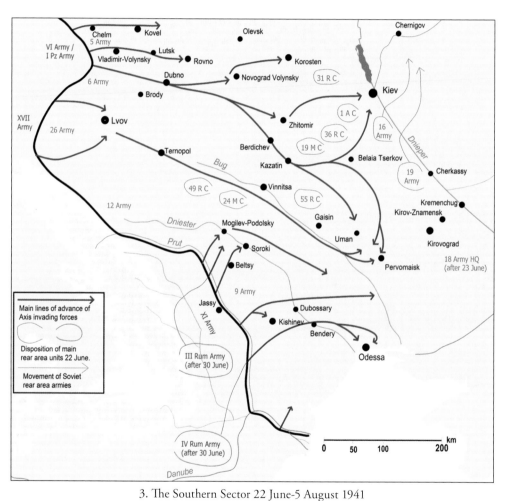

Chernigov

Chelm
Kovel
Olevsk

VI Army /
I Pz Army
Lutsk
Vladimir-Volynsky
Rovno
Korosten

5 Army

6 Army
Dubno
Novograd Volynsky
31 R C
Kiev

Brody

XVII
Army
Lvov
1 A C

26 Army
Zhitomir
16
Army

Ternopol
Berdichev
36 R C

Bug
Kazatin
19 M C
Belaia Tserkov
19
Army
Cherkassy

49 R C
Vinnitsa
55 R C

12 Army
24 M C
Kremenchug
Kirov-Znamensk

Dniester
Mogilev-Podolsky
Gaisin
Kirovograd

Prut
Soroki
Uman

Beltsy

9 Army
Pervomaisk
18 Army HQ
(after 23 June)

Jassy
Dubossary

XI Army
Kishinev

Bendery

III Rum Army
(after 30 June)
Odessa

IV Rum Army
(after 30 June)

Danube

Dnieper

Main lines of advance of
Axis invading forces

Disposition of main
rear area units 22 June.

Movement of Soviet
rear area armies

km
0   50   100   200

3. The Southern Sector 22 June-5 August 1941

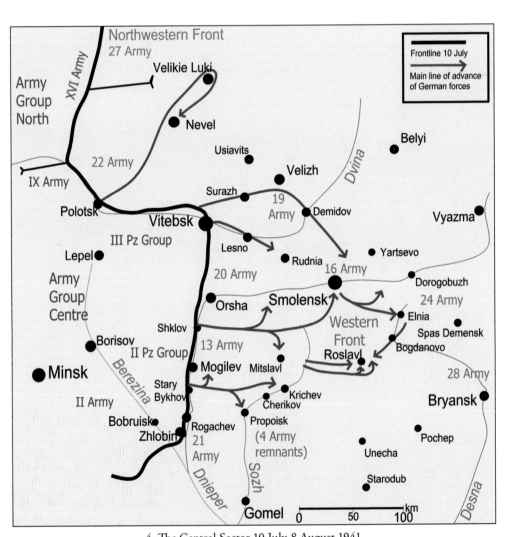

4. The Central Sector 10 July-8 August 1941

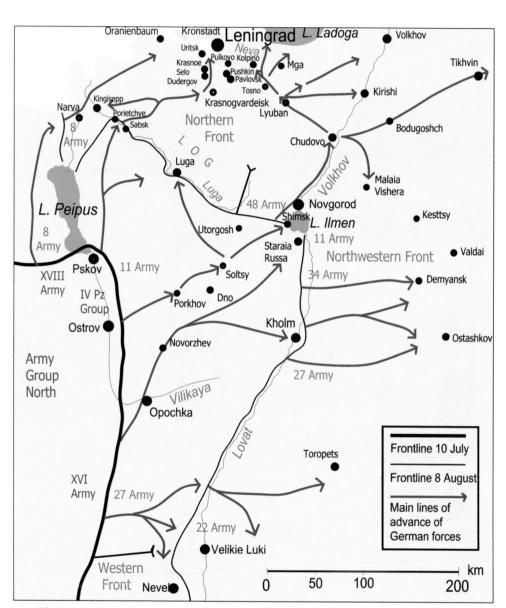

5. The Leningrad Axis: Approach to the German High Water Mark 10 July-9 November 1941

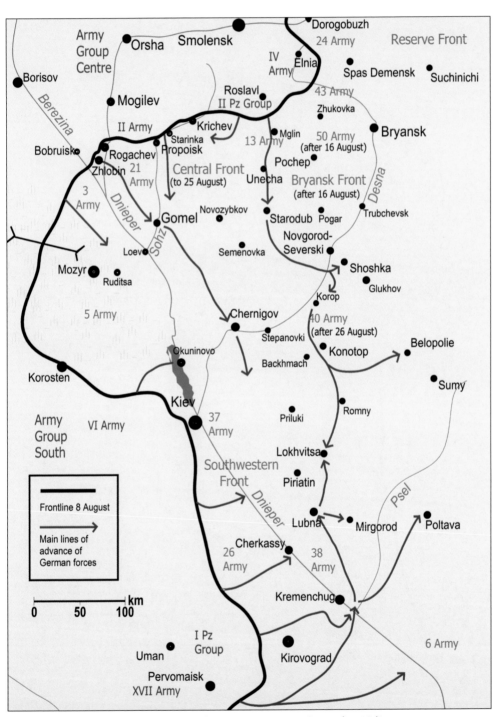

6. The Kiev Encirclement: 8 August-21 September 1941

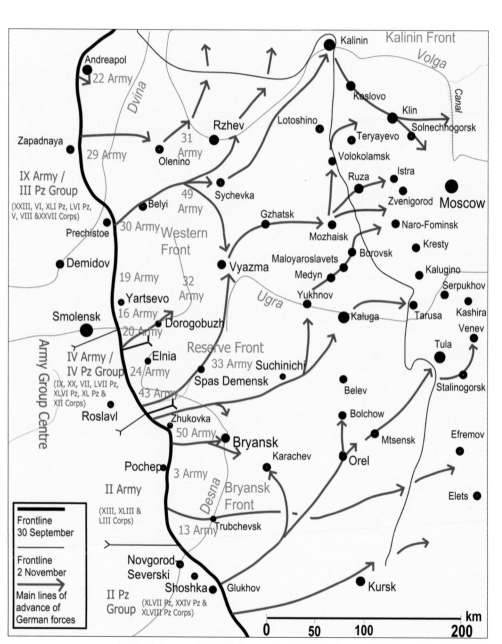

Andreapol
22 Army
Zapadnaya
29 Army
IX Army /
III Pz Group
(XXIII, VI, XLI Pz, LVI Pz,
V, VIII &XXVII Corps)
Prechistoe
30 Army
Demidov
19 Army
Yartsevo
16 Army
Smolensk
20 Army
Army Group Centre
IV Army /
IV Pz Group
(IX, XX, VII, LVII Pz,
XLVI Pz, XL Pz &
XII Corps)
Roslavl
Elnia
24 Army
43 Army
Zhukovka
50 Army
Pochep
II Army
(XIII, XLIII &
LIII Corps)
Novgorod-
Severski
Shoshka
II Pz
Group
(XLVII Pz, XXIV Pz &
XLVIII Pz Corps)

Dvina
Olenino
31 Army
Rzhev
49 Army
Sychevka
Belyi
32 Army
Western Front
Vyazma
Dorogobuzh
Reserve Front
33 Army Suchinichi
Spas Demensk
Bryansk
Karachev
3 Army
Desna
Bryansk Front
13 Army Trubchevsk
Glukhov

Kalinin
Kalinin Front
Volga
Koslovo
Klin
Solnechnogorsk
Lotoshino
Teryayevo
Volokolamsk
Ruza
Istra
Gzhatsk
Zvenigorod
Moscow
Mozhaisk
Naro-Fominsk
Maloyaroslavets
Borovsk
Kresty
Medyn
Kalugino
Ugra
Yukhnov
Serpukhov
Kaluga
Tarusa
Kashira
Venev
Tula
Belev
Stalinogorsk
Bolchow
Mtsensk
Efremov
Orel
Elets
Kursk

Canal

Frontline
30 September

Frontline
2 November

Main lines of
advance of
German forces

km
0   50   100   200

7. The Moscow Axis: 30 September-5 December 1941

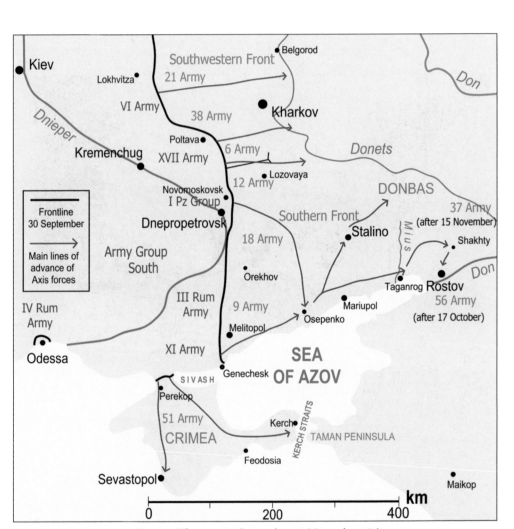

8. Eastern Ukraine: 30 September–21 November 1941

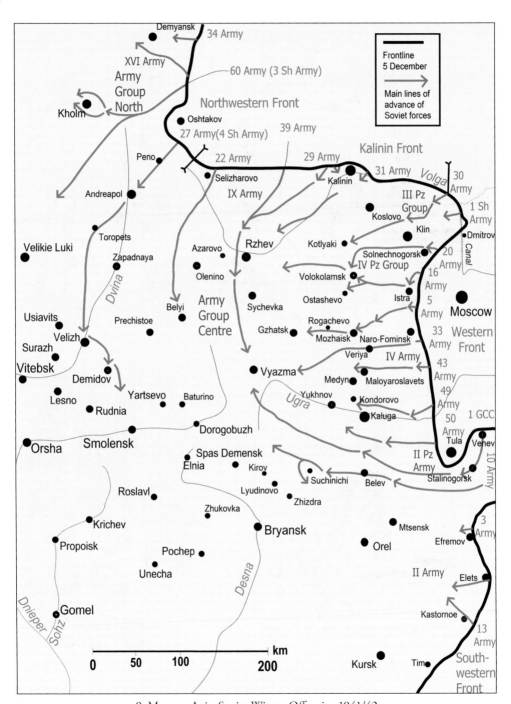

9. Moscow Axis: Soviet Winter Offensive 1941/42

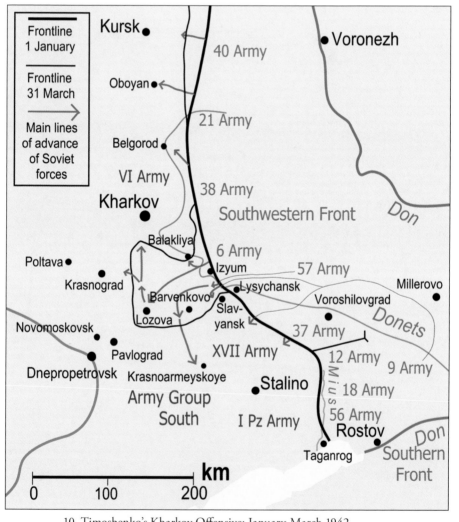

Frontline
1 January

Frontline
31 March

Main lines
of advance
of Soviet
forces

Kursk

Voronezh

40 Army

Oboyan

21 Army

Belgorod

VI Army

38 Army

Kharkov

Southwestern Front

Don

Balakliya

6 Army

Poltava

Izyum

57 Army

Millerovo

Krasnograd

Barvenkovo

Lysychansk

Voroshilovgrad

Donets

Lozova

Slav-
yansk

Novomoskovsk

37 Army

XVII Army

12 Army

9 Army

Dnepropetrovsk

Pavlograd

Krasnoarmeyskoye

Stalino

18 Army

Army Group
South

I Pz Army

56 Army

Rostov

Taganrog

Don

Southern
Front

km

0   100   200

10. Timoshenko's Kharkov Offensive: January-March 1942

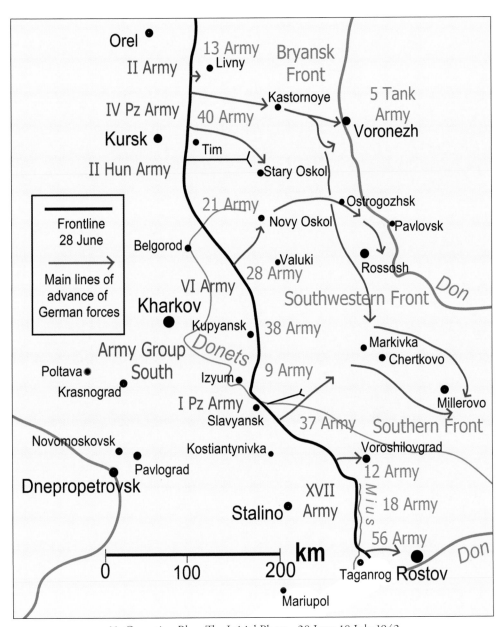

11. Operation Blue: The Initial Phase - 28 June-18 July 1942

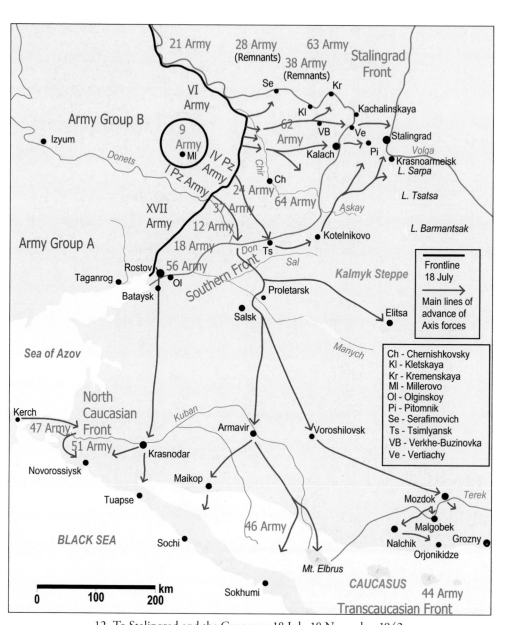

21 Army   28 Army   63 Army
(Remnants)
38 Army   **Stalingrad**
(Remnants)   **Front**

VI Army

Army Group B

9 Army

Izyum

Donets

Ml

IV Pz Army

I Pz Army

Chir

62 Army

Se

Kl

VB

Kalach

Kr

Kachalinskaya

Ve

Stalingrad

Pi

Volga

Krasnoarmeisk

L. Sarpa

L. Tsatsa

L. Barmantsak

Ch

24 Army

XVII Army

37 Army

12 Army

64 Army

Askay

Kotelnikovo

Army Group A

18 Army

56 Army

Don

Ts

Sal

Rostov

Taganrog

Ol

Batatysk

Southern Front

Proletarsk

Salsk

Kalmyk Steppe

Elitsa

Manych

Sea of Azov

Kerch

47 Army

North Caucasian Front

51 Army

Novorossiysk

Kuban

Krasnodar

Armavir

Voroshilovsk

Maikop

Tuapse

Mozdok

Terek

BLACK SEA

Sochi

46 Army

Malgobek

Nalchik

Grozny

Orjonikidze

Mt. Elbrus

CAUCASUS

44 Army

Sokhumi

Transcaucasian Front

Frontline
18 July

Main lines of
advance of
Axis forces

Ch - Chernishkovsky
Kl - Kletskaya
Kr - Kremenskaya
Ml - Millerovo
Ol - Olginskoy
Pi - Pitomnik
Se - Serafimovich
Ts - Tsimlyansk
VB - Verkhe-Buzinovka
Ve - Vertiachy

km
0   100   200

12. To Stalingrad and the Caucasus: 18 July–18 November 1942

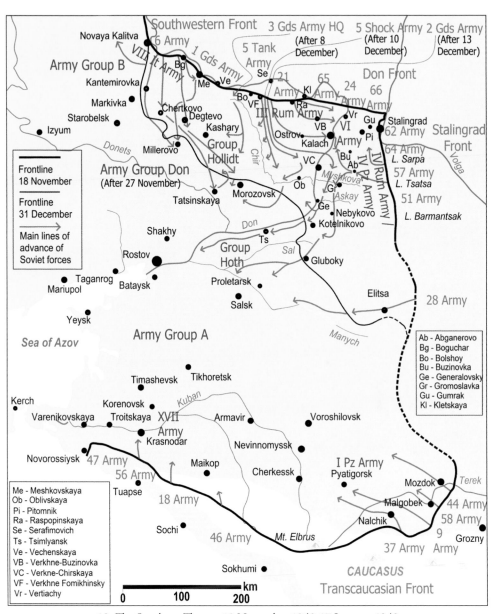

13. The Southern Theatre 18 November 1942-17 January 1943

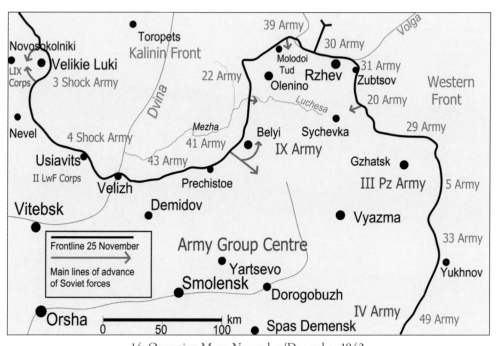

14. Operation Mars: November/December 1942

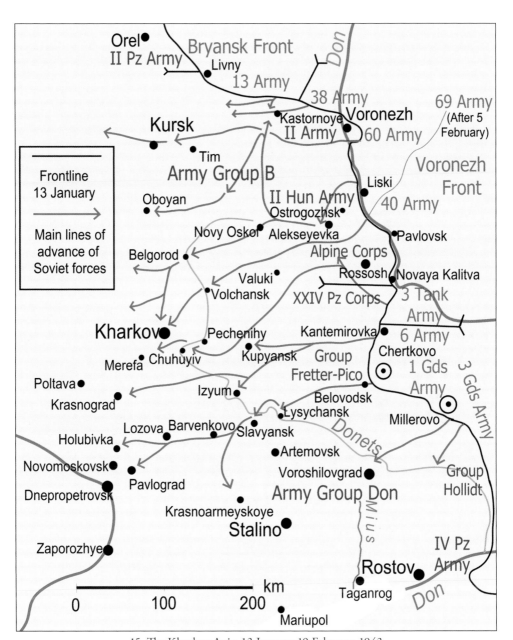

15. The Kharkov Axis: 13 January-19 February 1943

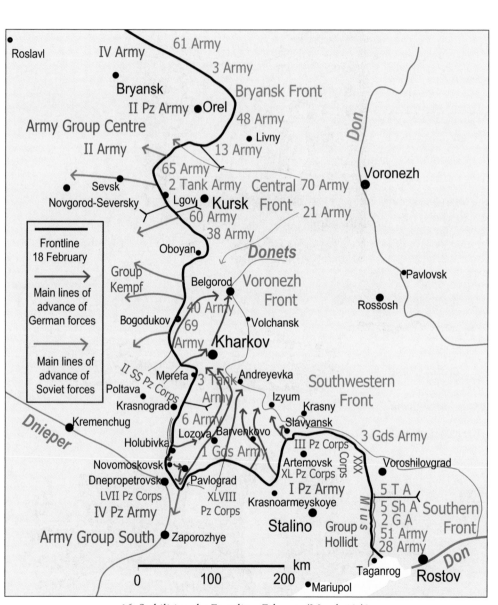

Roslavl
IV Army
61 Army
3 Army
Bryansk
Bryansk Front
II Pz Army ●Orel
48 Army
Army Group Centre
●Livny
II Army
13 Army
65 Army
Voronezh
Sevsk
2 Tank Army
Central 70 Army
Novgorod-Seversky
Lgov Kursk
Front
60 Army
21 Army
38 Army
Oboyan
Donets
Group
Kempf
Belgorod
Voronezh
Front
●Pavlovsk
40 Army
Bogodukov
69
●Volchansk
Rossosh
Army
Kharkov
II SS Pz Corps
Merefa ● 3 Tank
Andreyevka
Southwestern
Poltava
Army
Izyum
Front
Krasnograd
Krasny
Slavyansk
Kremenchug
6 Army
Lozova Barvenkovo
3 Gds Army
Holubivka
III Pz Corps
Novomoskovsk
1 Gds Army
XL Pz Corps
Voroshilovgrad
Dnepropetrovsk
Artemovsk
LVII Pz Corps
Pavlograd
I Pz Army
5 T A
IV Pz Army
XLVIII
Krasnoarmeyskoye
5 Sh A Southern
Pz Corps
2 G A Front
Army Group South ●Zaporozhye
Stalino Group
51 Army
Hollidt
28 Army
km
Rostov
0   100   200
Taganrog
Don
●Mariupol

Dnieper

Don

Minus

XXX Corps

Frontline
18 February

Main lines of
advance of
German forces

Main lines of
advance of
Soviet forces

16. Stabilising the Frontline: February/March 1943

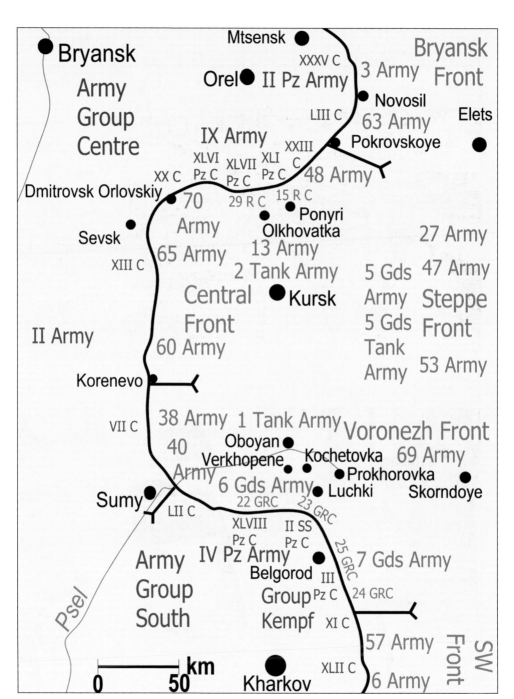

17. Operation Citadel: Disposition of Forces 4 July 1943

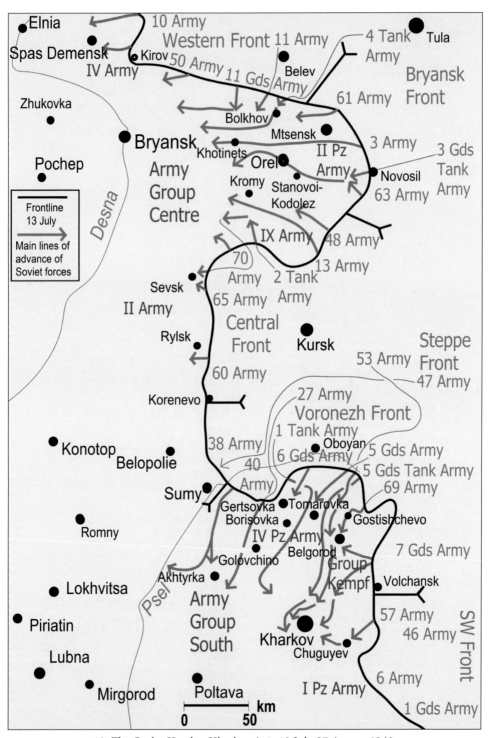

18. The Orel – Kursk – Kharkov Axis 13 July-27 August 1943

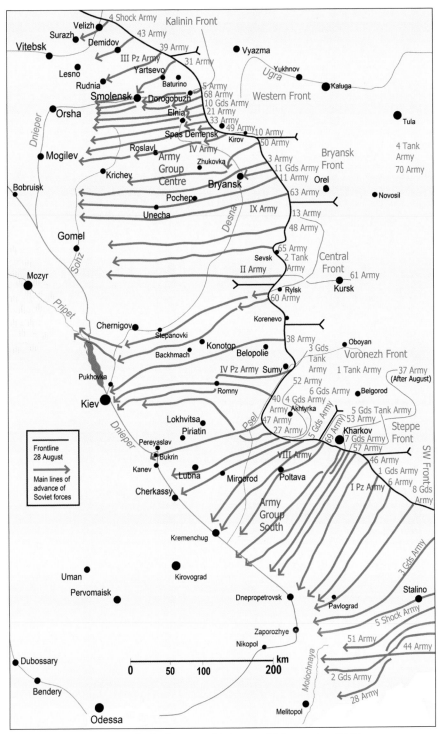

19. Towards the Dnieper: 28 August–30 September 1943

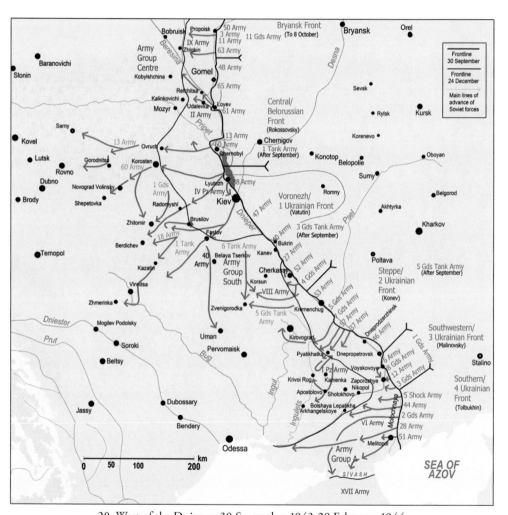

20. West of the Dnieper: 30 September 1943-28 February 1944

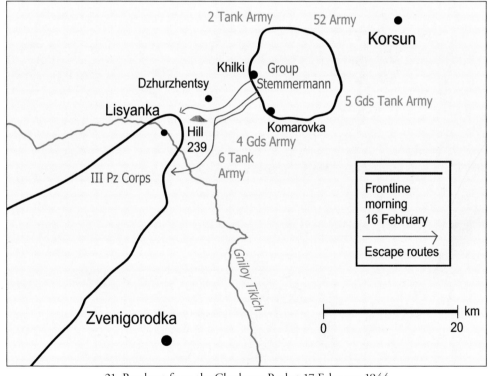

2 Tank Army   52 Army   Korsun

Khilki   Group Stemmermann

Dzhurzhentsy

Lisyanka   5 Gds Tank Army

Hill 239   Komarovka

4 Gds Army

6 Tank Army

III Pz Corps

Gniloy Tikich

Zvenigorodka

Frontline
morning
16 February

Escape routes

km

0   20

21. Breakout from the Cherkassy Pocket 17 February 1944

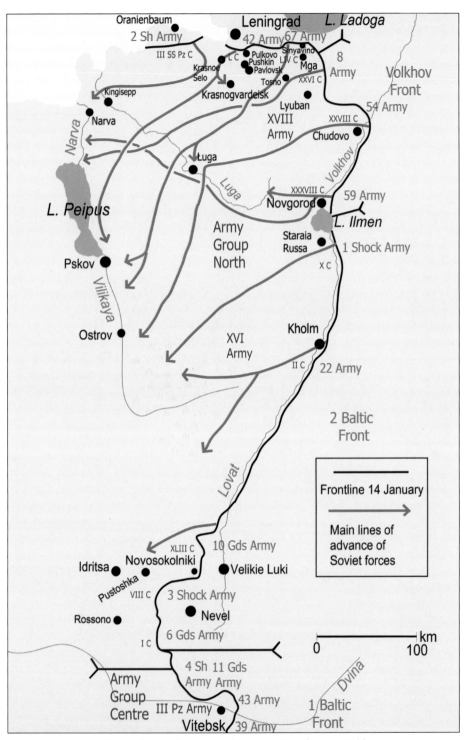

22. To the Panther Line: 14 January–28 February 1944

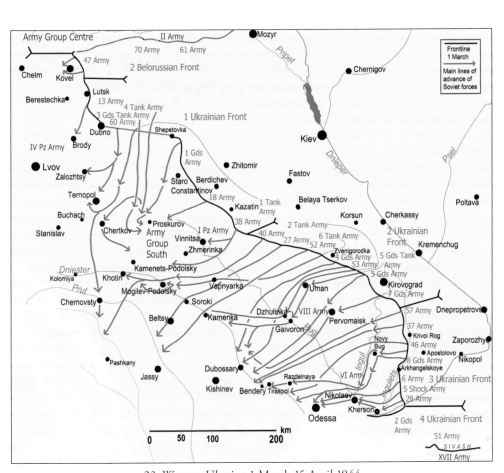

23. Western Ukraine 1 March–15 April 1944

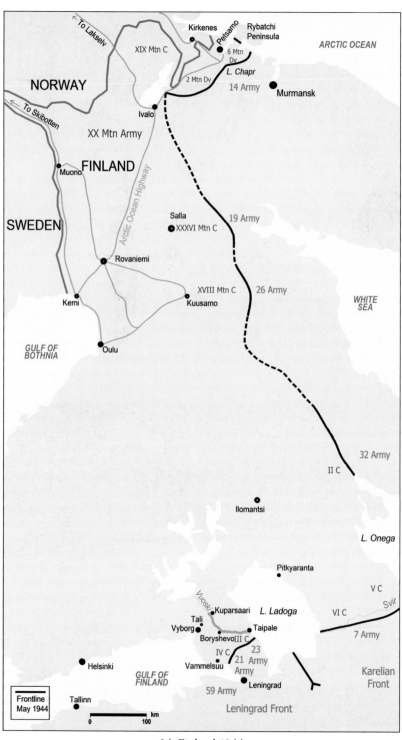

To Lakselv
Kirkenes
Petsamo
Rybatchi
Peninsula
ARCTIC OCEAN
XIX Mtn C
6 Mtn
Dv
2 Mtn Dv
L. Chapr
NORWAY
14 Army
Murmansk
To Skibotten
Ivalo
XX Mtn Army
FINLAND
Muono
19 Army
SWEDEN
Salla
XXXVI Mtn C
Rovaniemi
XVIII Mtn C
26 Army
WHITE
SEA
Kemi
Kuusamo
Arctic Ocean Highway
GULF OF
BOTHNIA
Oulu
32 Army
II C
Ilomantsi
L. Onega
Pitkyaranta
V C
Svir
Vuoksi
Kuparsaari
L. Ladoga
VI C
Tali
Vyborg
Taipale
7 Army
Boryshevo III C
IV C
23
21 Army
Army
Helsinki
Vammelsuu
Karelian
Front
GULF OF
FINLAND
59 Army
Leningrad
Frontline
May 1944
Tallinn
km
0   100
Leningrad Front

24. Finland 1944

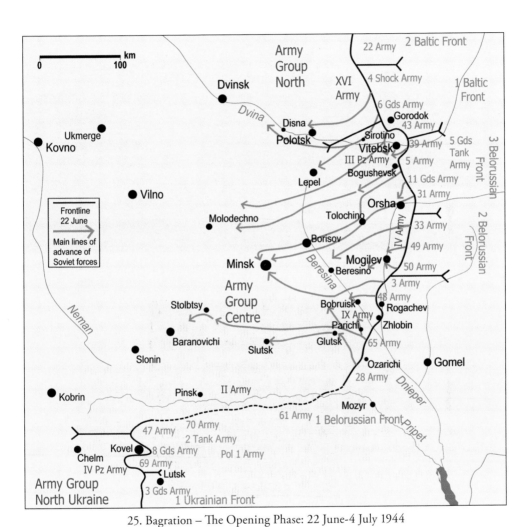

25. Bagration – The Opening Phase: 22 June-4 July 1944

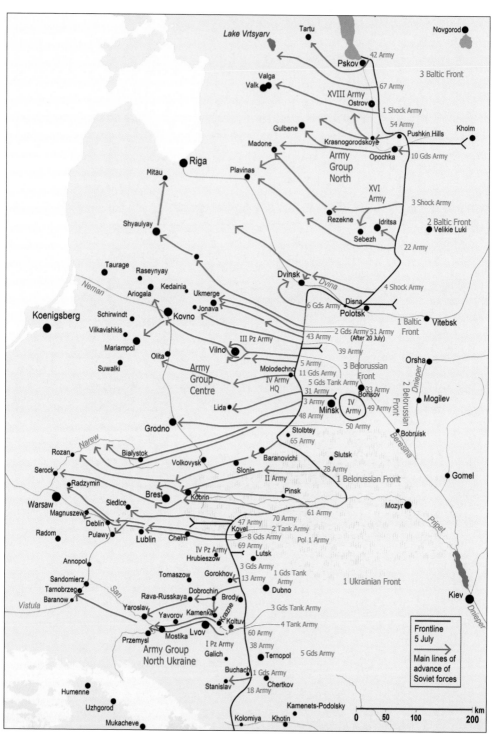

26. Northern and Central Sectors 5 July–13 September 1944

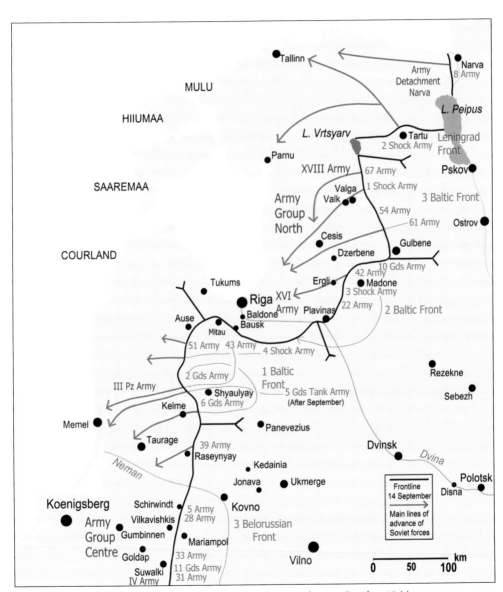

MULU

HIIUMAA

SAAREMAA

COURLAND

Tallinn

Army
Detachment
Narva

Narva
8 Army

L. Peipus

L. Vrtsyarv

Tartu
2 Shock Army

Leningrad
Front

Parnu

XVIII Army

67 Army

1 Shock Army

Valga
Valk

54 Army

61 Army

Pskov

3 Baltic Front

Ostrov

Army
Group
North

Cesis

Dzerbene

Gulbene

10 Gds Army

42 Army

Ergli

Madone
3 Shock Army

Tukums

Riga XVI
Baldone Army Plavinas
Bausk

22 Army

2 Baltic Front

Ause

Mitau

51 Army 43 Army

4 Shock Army

2 Gds Army

1 Baltic
Front

III Pz Army

Shyaulyay
6 Gds Army

5 Gds Tank Army
(After September)

Rezekne

Sebezh

Memel

Kelme

Taurage

Panevezius

Dvinsk

Dvina

Polotsk

39 Army
Raseynyay

Kedainia

Neman

Jonava

Ukmerge

Disna

Koenigsberg

Schirwindt
Vilkavishkis

Army
Group
Gumbinnen
Centre
Goldap

Suwalki
IV Army

5 Army
28 Army

Kovno

3 Belorussian
Front

Mariampol

33 Army

11 Gds Army
31 Army

Vilno

Frontline
14 September

Main lines of
advance of
Soviet forces

km

0   50   100

27. To the Courland Peninsula: 14 September–31 October 1944

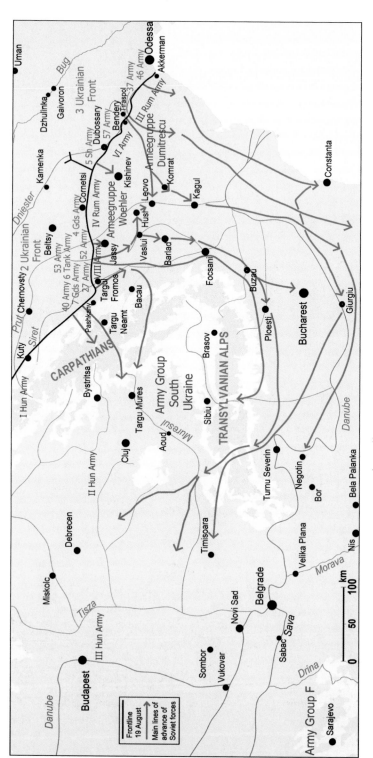

28. Into the Balkans: 19 August–28 September 1944

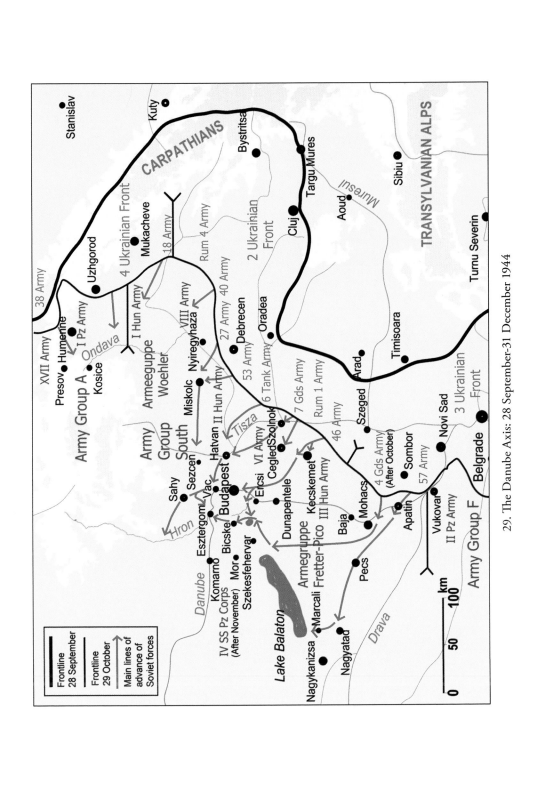

29. The Danube Axis: 28 September–31 December 1944

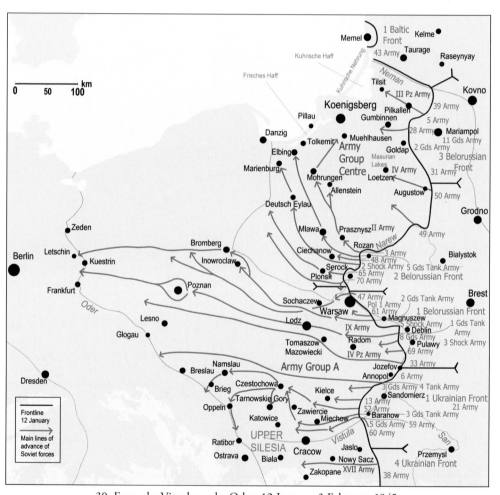

30. From the Vistula to the Oder: 12 January-3 February 1945

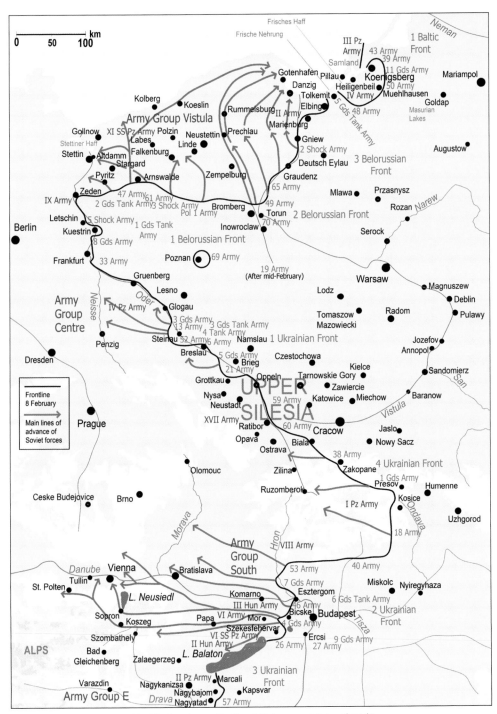

31. Closing in on Berlin: 8 February–16 April 1945

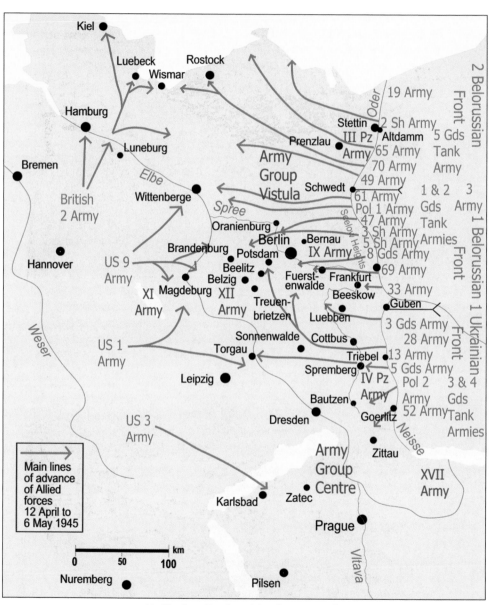

Kiel

Luebeck
Wismar   Rostock

Hamburg

Bremen   Luneburg

British   Wittenberge
2 Army

Hannover

US 9
Army   Brandenburg
                        Potsdam
                Beelitz
         XI Magdeburg   Belzig
         Army   XII
                   Army Treuen-
                         brietzen

US 1   Sonnenwalde
Army   Torgau

         Leipzig

US 3
Army
                        Dresden
                Karlsbad   Zatec

Main lines
of advance
of Allied
forces
12 April to
6 May 1945

                Prague

0   50   100 km

Nuremberg   Pilsen

Oder
19 Army
Stettin   2 Sh Army Altdamm 5 Gds
III Pz   65 Army   Tank
Prenzlau Army   70 Army   Army
          Schwedt 49 Army
                  61 Army   1 & 2   3
                  Pol 1 Army Gds   Army
          Oranienburg 47 Army Tank
                  3 Sh Army Armies
   Berlin   Bernau 5 Sh Army
            IX Army 8 Gds Army
         Fuerst-   69 Army
         enwalde Frankfurt
                Beeskow   33 Army
                          Guben
         Luebben
                Cottbus   3 Gds Army
                           28 Army
                Triebel   13 Army
         Spremberg   5 Gds Army
                  IV Pz   Pol 2   3 & 4
                  Army   Army   Gds
          Bautzen   52 Army Tank
                  Goerlitz   Armies
         Army
         Group   Zittau
         Centre   XVII
                           Army

2 Belorussian Front
1 Belorussian Front
1 Ukrainian Front
Seelow Heights
Elbe
Spree
Weser
Neisse
Vltava

32. The Last Battle: 16 April-5 May 1945

good initial progress against weak opposition, advancing deep into the German rear. Rodin's forces, which included two tank corps and Major-Gen V V Kriukov's 2 Gds Cav Corps, rapidly exploited this breach, advancing through Sevsk towards Novgorod-Seversky. By 1 March Rokossovsky had achieved significant success, enveloping the flanks of II Pz Army to the north and II Army to the south.[9] By this time 70 Army had joined the offensive on Batov's right to threaten a further advance on Orel and Bryansk. However, 21 Army, which it had been expected would be available to develop the offensive towards Orel, had not yet reached the battlefield, nor had either 62 Army or 64 Army, both of which had been assigned to Rokossovsky from his former Don Front. With a supporting rifle group, 2 Gds Cav Corps had reached the Desna north of Novgorod-Seversky by 7 March, but this was the high-water mark of Rokossovsky's offensive, which ground to a halt in the face of increasing German opposition from divisions that had been withdrawn from the Rzhev – Vyazma salient. Additionally, on 13 March as 21 Army became available, it was diverted to the south to support Voronezh Front in stemming the advance by IV Pz Army, which was on the verge of taking Kharkov and threatening to move farther north to Belgorod. On 12 March Reiter's Bryansk Front was disbanded; 61 Army being assigned to Western Front, and the rest of its forces coming under Rokossovsky's command. Yet this restructuring could not prevent Kriukov from being pushed back from Novgorod-Seversky to the east bank of the Sev. Chistyakov's army, having deployed south of Kursk, was given the multiple tasks of cutting the Oboyan road; of covering the approaches to Kursk; of covering Katukov's 1 Tank Army (which, having been hurriedly withdrawn at the beginning of March from Operation Polar Star, was concentrating southeast of Kursk); and of joining with Katukov in crushing any northward German advance from Belgorod. By 20 March Chistyakov's army had successfully occupied the line assigned to it; Voronezh Front's 69 Army had pulled back over the Donets; Katukov had concentrated his tank army near Oboyan; and 64 Army was also moving up to the Donets to secure the southern approaches to Kursk. By 21 March Central Front's offensive had stalled and STAVKA became concerned about a possible counter-offensive by II Pz Army from Orel towards Tula that would hit the boundary of Central Front and Western Front. Consequently Bryansk Front was reformed, again under Reiter's command, on the Orel – Tula axis.[10] No German offensive towards Tula was launched and by 26 March the frontline had stabilised south of Orel around the large Kursk salient and, south from Belgorod, along the Donets/Mius river lines. By the end of March the spring thaw was underway bringing an end to further offensive action across virtually the entire front.

Tipping Point
The cessation of major offensive action at the end of March 1943 lasted longer than either OKH or STAVKA expected, and the period from April to July 1943 marks a suitable delineation of the four-year conflict into two halves. This delineation is not only chronological. The first half of the conflict, unlike the second, was characterised

---

9   By the beginning of March II Army, though reduced to two corps, had several divisions in reserve
      and had recovered most of its strength.

10   This new Front was at first designated Kursk Front, then on 25 March it was renamed Orel Front
      before being renamed Bryansk Front three days later.

by successful German summer offensives and by Soviet winter counter-offensives that regained some, if not all, of the lost territory from the summer. To some extent the first half of the conflict was a war between equals; the Soviet Union and the Red Army had the advantage of size, an advantage largely negated by German technical and tactical superiority. The *Ostheer* began the conflict with a spectacular strategic success, and in March 1943 demonstrated to the Red Army that it was still a force to be reckoned with. Yet at some time between the commencement of Operation Uranus and the dying effort of STAVKA's overly ambitious Roslavl offensive, there occurred a tipping point in the conflict; a point at which the balance of military power shifted definitively to the Red Army. It is questionable whether Germany could ever have brought the Soviet Union to the point of capitulation, but during the winter of 1942/43, despite the failures of Operations Mars and Polar Star, despite the Soviet defeat in the Donets Campaign, and despite the failure of Rokossovsky's Roslavl offensive, the Soviet Union and its Red Army finally acquired the necessary combination of organisational balance, military expertise and military/industrial capacity that would enable it to destroy the *Ostheer*.

7

Deceptive Calm

During the early spring of 1943 Manstein was hopeful, despite the onset of the season of mud and the appearance of 21 Army and 1 Tank Army south of Kursk, that he would be able to develop the Belgorod offensive farther north to eliminate the threatening Kursk salient occupied by Voronezh Front and Central Front. Hitler was of a similar mind, and as early as 13 March he had issued Operational Order 5, requiring Manstein to assemble north of Kharkov by the middle of April a powerful mechanised force for an offensive north towards Kursk. This offensive would begin as soon as ground conditions permitted and would be coordinated with a strike south from Orel by a reinforced II Pz Army. The combined offensive was given the codename Citadel. On 15 April Hitler issued Operational Order 6, requiring that Citadel be prepared for commencement at short notice at any time after the end of April, the northern component of which was to be coordinated by IX Army. By May the Soviet defences in the salient were becoming well consolidated, and on 3 May Hitler conferred with his generals as to whether a delay in the offensive would be to the greater benefit of the *Ostheer* or the Soviets. Manstein, Kluge and Zeitzler objected to a delay, but Hitler decided on a postponement to June in order to enable more of Germany's new heavy armoured fighting vehicles to be deployed, and for more detailed preparations to be made. Few then realised that the necessary preparation would take until July.

By the late spring of 1943, as the *Ostheer* prepared for its third summer offensive on the Eastern Front, there was a widespread belief in Germany that events would unfold in a similar manner to the two preceding years and that, if another disaster on the scale of Stalingrad could be avoided, Russia might be driven by sheer exhaustion to negotiate a peace. Yet the military situation in the summer of 1943 was radically different to 1941 or even 1942. The success of the German Donets operation, and the toehold that German forces still held in the Taman Peninsula, could not mitigate the disasters that had befallen the *Ostheer* in the preceding months. The Soviet offensives that had begun in November 1942 had wiped one German and four satellite armies from the Axis order of battle. Germany's efforts against the Soviet Union had been largely abandoned by its southern European allies, for whom fighting in the depths of Russia, hundreds of kilometres beyond their borders, had lost any attraction. At the end of February the remaining Italian troops in Russia were withdrawn, the Italians having suffered 185,000 casualties including 20,000 fatalities and 64,000 taken prisoner. Most of the remaining Hungarian forces in Russia, having suffered 140,000 casualties, were withdrawn to home territory before the end of May. The Rumanians had lost 250,000 personnel killed, missing and wounded since the commencement of Operation Uranus. From a peak of 650,000 in the late summer of 1942, by the summer of 1943 Germany's allies in the south had reduced their manpower contribution to 150,000. The Hungarians retained a reserve corps of three light divisions, and most of the rest were Rumanians. On the northern flank the Finns seemed to have reconciled themselves to a modest territorial ambition, and it is probable that in 1943 they would have accepted Soviet terms based on a return to the 1939 borders. By 1 March 1943 *Ostheer* strength was estimated to be 470,000 short of requirements and greater efforts were demanded of Nazi administrators to find new sources of manpower. One policy that was not pursued in Germany until quite late in the war was the mobilisation of women to serve in the war industries. Nazi creed required women to produce and raise Aryan children; their role was domestic, not industrial. Men were diverted from industry to serve in the armed forces, but their places were taken by prisoners of war and by slave labourers from the occupied territories. Greater demands were placed on the *Luftwaffe* and *Kriegsmarine* to release additional personnel for frontline duty. Men were taken from the anti-aircraft defences of the Reich to be replaced by Hitler Youth members, some as young as fifteen. As a result of these efforts, and the diversion of forces from other theatres, during February and March 1943 German manpower in the *Ostheer* increased by half million, and had increased by a further 700,000 by mid-July.

The Red Army that the *Ostheer* faced in 1943 was a transformed entity from the Red Army of 1941. Perhaps its greatest internal success came on 9 October 1942 when the institution of the military commissar was abolished. The political officers became *zampolits* – an abbreviation of commander's deputy for political work. They lost their separate ranking system, and over the subsequent six months were sent for assessment and subsequent appointment to standard military ranks within the army. Though still able to report on the political reliability and revolutionary zeal of their unit commanders, their role became one of educator, advisor and propagandist for the Party, and they concerned themselves primarily with the general welfare, education and morale of the troops. Freed from the dual command system, unit commanders were once again able to take operational decisions without reference to their unit's political officer. The recognition by the Party of the increased status of the Red Army and its commanders was symbolised by the adoption early in 1943 of new uniforms for officers. The old system of discrete triangles, cubes, rectangles and stars as symbols of rank on the collars of otherwise undistinguished uniforms was replaced by a system of shoulder boards. By the end of the war uniforms for senior officers, particularly the 'parade' uniforms, had grown more ostentatious, and included flamboyant sleeve badges and cap badges with 'gold leaf'. During the first half of 1943 the word 'officer', by that time shorn of its Tsarists associations with elitist arrogance, incompetence and arbitrary cruelty, began to replace 'commander' as the general term for personnel of senior rank, and in July the term 'officer' was formally introduced into the Soviet military structure.

The increased competence and professionalism of the Soviet officer class was reflected in the army's battlefield performance, which in turn was a reflection of improved organisation and staff work. By 1943 there was little new for the Red Army to learn in terms of defensive operations, but the requirements for effective offensive operations were still being formulated. In this regard Soviet high command recognised the need to adequately address three issues; the concentration of sufficient forces and firepower on a narrow breakthrough sector, the development and consolidation of the tactical breakthrough sector to prevent it being subsequently sealed off, and the maintenance of the operational exploitation of the breakthrough to an appropriate depth. For the first two of these, shock armies or combined-arms armies were to be used, and tank corps, mechanised corps or tank armies would be deployed for the exploitation phase. Experience had already demonstrated a host of practical problems associated with offensive operations; tanks churning up roads and bridges making them impassable for support units and artillery; the need for improved signalling procedures among tank crews in order for them to be able to hold their course during an attack; it had shown that rifle divisions needed at least a tank battalion for infantry support work, and that tank units needed the ability to operate for at least 24 hours on their own. By this time it had become standard practice to equip the armies preparing for offensive operations with sufficient supplies for ten days of operations and for an advance of around 100km.

By 1943 the Red Army had settled on most of the senior commanders who would see it through to victory. Govorov, Meretskov, Konev, Rokossovsky and Malinovsky would remain as Front commanders to the end of the war, while Zhukov, Vasilevsky and Voronov would continue to coordinate multi-Front offensives as STAVKA representatives in the field. The loss of Kharkov cost Golikov his job at Voronezh Front. A General Staff investigation of the Manstein Counterstrike reported that Golikov had been less than candid with STAVKA in his reports from the frontline. Vatutin took over at Voronezh Front, Malinovsky took over at Southwestern Front, and Tolbukhin was appointed to command Southern Front. Soon afterwards both Malinovsky and Tolbukhin were further promoted and, though they were radically different personalities, they developed a highly effective working relationship throughout the rest of the war. Success on the battlefield also earned Rokossovsky a further promotion, his second in little over three months, this time to Army General. After the failure of Operation Polar Star, Timoshenko was removed from frontline command, Konev taking over at Northwestern Front. With Konev's departure from Western Front, the Front's chief of staff, Col-Gen V D Sokolovsky, took command, and in March Eremenko was appointed to command Kalinin Front. At the General Staff Headquarters Stalin had dismissed a series of generals from the post of Chief of the Operations Directorate during 1941 and 1942. The individual in that post reported regularly to Stalin on the operational situation at the front, and Stalin was constantly dissatisfied with either the quality of the reports or the personality of the person presenting them.[1] In December 1942 Lt-Gen A I Antonov, former chief of staff at Transcaucasian Front, was appointed as Chief of the Operations Directorate. Antonov was a man who could meet Stalin's exacting standards, and in April 1943 he was promoted to the rank of colonel-general and appointed Deputy Chief of the General Staff. In that role, and as a result of the continued prolonged absences of Vasilevsky from Moscow, Antonov became the *de facto* Chief of the General Staff. In April 1942 Lt-Gen A A Novikov became Commander in Chief of the Red Air Force, the VVS, a post he was to retain to the end of the war. Not all of Novikov's predecessors had survived Stalin's disapproval of their performance, but under Novikov the performance of the Red Air Force steadily improved. Novikov was able to translate the theory of air power and combat methods into more effective practice. Using the increased numbers and improved performance of Soviet aircraft, he organised the different types of aircraft (bomber, ground attack

---

1   Vasilevsky, as Chief of the General Staff, was unable to report to Stalin routinely since he was usually absent from Moscow.

and fighter) into separate aviation divisions within the air armies and air corps. Most aircraft assets still resided with the Front commanders, but they were concentrated into air armies, typically one to each Front, the practice of dispersing the aviation effort among individual field army commanders having been long since abandoned. A significant number of aircraft remained with the air defence command and, though the Soviet Union did not have a true strategic bomber force, there was a separate long-range bomber command, the ADD, which was subordinated directly to STAVKA.

After eighteen months of war the Red Army considered that it had identified the optimum structure for its core unit – the rifle division. At the end of 1942 a definitive organisational arrangement was issued for a rifle division of around 9,500 personnel, of whom more than 800 would be required for headquarters staff and divisional services (reconnaissance, signals, engineering etc.). The combat power of the rifle division lay in its three rifle regiments, but at divisional level there was also a field artillery regiment (twenty 76mm divisional cannon and twelve 122mm howitzers), an anti-tank battalion (twelve 45mm anti-tank guns), and a training battalion of 400 men. The rifle regiment of 2,500 personnel, ten percent of whom were required for the regimental headquarters and services (reconnaissance, signals, transport etc), had a traditional 'triangular' or 'tripod' structure at the base of which was a platoon of forty men with six light machine guns. Three platoons, together with a mortar platoon of two light (50mm) mortars, a machine gun squad with a single medium machine gun, and a medical squad formed a rifle company. Three rifle companies formed a rifle battalion, but at battalion level there were a number of supporting units. These included a mortar company of nine medium (82mm) mortars, an anti-tank gun platoon with two 45mm anti-tank guns, an anti-tank rifle platoon with nine 14.5mm anti-tank rifles, and a small machine gun company of nine medium machine guns. Battalion headquarters, which also commanded a signals platoon, a medical platoon and a transport platoon, included just four officers. Three battalions formed a rifle regiment, which also had a submachine gun company (100 men), an anti-tank rifle company of twenty-seven 14.5mm anti-tank rifles, and an anti-tank gun battery of six 45mm anti-tank guns, an infantry gun battery of four 76mm regimental guns, and a mortar battery of seven heavy (120mm) mortars. The Guards rifle divisions had a similar structure but with slightly greater firepower in the divisional artillery regiment, the regimental mortar battery, the battalion's machine gun company and the rifle company's machine gun squad.

Yet having defined its optimum divisional structure, the Red Army discovered that, as the war progressed and losses continued to mount, there were insufficient personnel available to fully man the Soviet Union's five hundred divisions. In offensive operations from November 1942 to March 1943 the Red Army suffered more than two million casualties. Reluctant to disband divisions in order to release personnel for other units, STAVKA opted for the only other alternative, to reduce divisional manpower. The first step was taken in August 1943 with a 15% reduction in the authorised platoon size to 34 men (and with a halving of the number of light machine guns to three). In addition, at company level the light mortar platoon was eliminated and at battalion level the machine gun and mortar companies were each reduced in size by one-third. These and other changes at regimental level reduced the authorised size of the rifle regiment to a little over 2,000 personnel, and reduced divisional size to around 8,000.

Even this modest size was not generally achieved; the typical divisional strength during the summer of 1943 being around 7,000 personnel, and in Central Front divisions averaged only 5,500.

During 1942 the rifle corps began to reappear, not generally as an intermediate command between divisional and army headquarters, but as an intermediate command between rifle brigade and army. Typically these rifle corps contained three rifle brigades. During 1943 these corps commands began to resume their traditional role within the army structure, the direct command of several divisions.

It was, however, in the armoured forces that the most radical changes took place. To the tank brigade was added an anti-aircraft battery of four 37mm anti-aircraft guns and four heavy machine guns. The tank corps was also strengthened by the addition of a third tank brigade, a mortar regiment (with thirty-six 120mm mortars) and an assault gun regiment with twenty-five assault guns. In comparison with Germany, the Soviet Union had been slow to adopt the self-propelled gun concept, preferring to concentrate its military/industrial effort on the production of tanks. Yet the effectiveness of the German StuG III assault gun had been undeniable, and during the second half of 1942 approval was given for the production of two Soviet equivalents. One was the SU-76M based on a modified T70 chassis and mounting a ZiS-3 76mm gun. Thin-skinned and open-topped, the SU-76 was unaffectionately nicknamed the 'bitch'. The other was the SU-122 based on a fully enclosed T34 chassis and mounting a 122mm M-30 divisional howitzer. Production of both weapons commenced at the end of 1942 and, during the following year, they became available in significant numbers. The SU-76 may have been unpopular but it was cheap to manufacture, and during the second half of 1943 production of the T70 was discontinued in order to allow the tank's chassis to be manufactured exclusively for the assault gun role. During the course of the war more than 12,600 SU-76s were produced. In the first half of 1943 a third assault gun began to appear in significant numbers. This was the SU-152, based on a KV1 chassis and mounting a 152mm howitzer. This popular weapon, nicknamed the 'beast killer' or 'animal hunter', could destroy the new German heavy tank, the PzKpfw VI Tiger. A variant of the SU-122, the SU-85 mounting a modified 85mm anti-aircraft gun, was also produced in the second half of 1943 for the 'tank destroyer' role. More than 4,000 Soviet self-propelled guns were produced in 1943, and during 1944 this figure would be trebled.

During the course of 1943 the tank corps continued to grow in size through the introduction of more anti-aircraft units and an expansion of the assault gun provision to three regiments. By the end of the year the tank corps had an authorised strength of 12,000 personnel and more than 250 armoured fighting vehicles. This increase in size also reflected the further development of the constituent tank brigades which, by the end of 1943, had dispensed with their light tank component and were based on three tank battalions each of twenty-one T34s. The weakness of the tank corps lay in its limited ability to hold an objective once seized. The tank corps only had one motorised rifle brigade of three motorised rifle battalions. The brigade was adequately provided with reconnaissance, artillery, anti-aircraft, anti-tank and mortar units, but it was spread thinly between the three tank brigades, each of which only had one small submachine gun battalion of 500 men as embedded infantry support. By contrast the mechanised corps had three mechanised brigades, comparable to the motorised rifle brigades but with the inclusion in each of a tank regiment. From the beginning, the mechanised corps of more than 15,000 personnel, 200 tanks, 50 heavy mortars, 36 anti-tank guns, 36 field guns and 8 *Katyusha* (BM-13) rocket launchers, had been a well-balance force for offensive operations. Changes in the mechanised corps through 1943 were less dramatic than those in the tank corps; the tank regiments in eight mechanised corps were upgraded to tank brigades and most corps received three regiments of self-propelled guns.

The tank armies, the cutting edge of Soviet strategic offensives, increasingly came to be based on two tank corps and a mechanised corps. Another successful Soviet offensive formation that developed from the crucible of experience was the cavalry-mechanised group, typically consisting of a cavalry corps and a mechanised corps. In these groups the cavalry acted as mobile light infantry capable of maintaining contact with rapidly advancing mechanised formations and capable of penetrating deep behind enemy lines with minimal supply needs. With the development of the tank army and the cavalry-mechanised group as the Red Army's primary offensive arm, the significance of the shock army declined. At the same time the rifle armies developed from mere assemblages of a handful of rifle divisions into more balanced formations as the Soviet tank park grew and the artillery arm began to recover from the horrendous losses of 1941. With tank brigades and heavy artillery regiments assigned to the rifle armies on a more permanent basis, these armies were designated 'combined-arms armies', and the distinction between them and the shock armies declined in significance.

Changes to the Soviet artillery arm were predominantly organisational, as most of the weapons development effort went into new guns for the armoured fighting vehicles. The most significant change in terms of weaponry was the development and mass production of the ZiS-3 divisional gun. The 76mm divisional guns, the F-22 and its replacement, the F-22USV, had been in quantity production in the years preceding the German invasion, but they were costly to manufacture and the F-22 was a cumbersome field weapon. At the end of 1941 a new divisional gun, the 76mm ZiS-3 was developed. Based on the carriage of the ill-fated 57mm ZiS-2 anti-tank gun, the ZiS-3 had a low profile, was relatively inexpensive to manufacture and could double as a reasonably effective anti-tank gun. During 1942 production of the F-22USV ceased and the ZiS-3, produced in the tens of thousands during the course of the rest of the war, became the standard Soviet 76mm divisional gun. During 1943 the ZiS-3 began to replace the 45mm anti-tank gun in many independent anti-tank divisions and brigades, and by the end of the year it had begun to be issued to the anti-tank battalions of the rifle divisions. Production of the excellent ZiS-2 gun, suspended in 1941, was resumed in 1943, but output did not peak until near the end of the war. Of the larger calibre weapons the only significant new development was the 152mm D-1 howitzer, production of which began at a modest rate in 1943. The D-1 was a replacement for the adequate but expensive M-10 howitzer, production of which ceased at the outbreak of war.

In November 1942 the Red Army began to form artillery divisions that by the end of the year would be based on three howitzer regiments (each of twenty M-30 122mm howitzers), two gun regiments (each of eighteen 122mm A-19 guns or 152mm ML-20 gun-howitzers), three anti-tank regiments (each of twenty-four 76mm guns) and four mortar regiments (each of twenty 120mm heavy mortars). These artillery divisions were strategic assets assigned to Front commands to provide fire superiority over the main penetration axes during major offensive operations. Most of these divisions, redesignated 'breakthrough artillery divisions', underwent expansion during 1943 to include thirty-two 152mm howitzers, twenty-four 203mm B-4 howitzers, an additional twenty-four 122mm howitzers and, eventually, thirty-six *Katyusha* rocket launcher systems. A few 'heavy gun artillery divisions' containing a gross of ML-20 gun-howitzers were also formed.

The Soviet Union was considerably aided in its Great Patriotic War by the Lend-Lease programme. In terms of weaponry, the predominant contributions were tanks and aircraft. In all more than 12,000 American and British tanks were supplied to the Red Army, equivalent to some six months of Soviet domestic tank production. Yet they seem to have been little appreciated. The British Matilda infantry support tanks were criticised for their inadequate armament, and the American Stuart light tanks for their inadequate armour. The American Lee M3 medium tank, the 'grave for seven brothers', was particularly disliked. Only the British Valentine light tank, widely used for reconnaissance purposes after termination of production of the T70, seems to have been favourably regarded. The Churchill and Sherman tanks were officially considered to be inferior to their Soviet equivalents, though of the Red Army's elite Guards mechanised corps, fully one-third were extensively equipped with Shermans, as was one of the Guards tank corps.

More than 18,000 military aircraft were supplied from Britain and America, equivalent to nine months of the Soviet Union's average wartime aircraft production. The aircraft supplied included the A-20 attack bomber, the Hawker Hurricane, the P-40, the P-39 and the P-63 fighters. Most numerous were the P-39 Airacobra and its derivative the P-63 Kingcobra. The P-39 was outperformed at high and medium altitudes by other American fighters, and was not widely adopted by the USAAF, but at low altitudes it proved to be an effective fighter. Since the primary role of the Soviet Air Force was tactical support to ground operations, most aerial combat on the Eastern Front took place at low altitudes, and Soviet pilots found the P-39 to be a valuable asset. The P-63, developed by the Bell Aircraft Corporation to address the deficiencies of the P-39, was primarily used by the Soviet Air Force as a ground attack aircraft.

Yet the major strategic benefit to the Soviet Union of the Lend-Lease programme lay less in the weapons systems supplied than in basic raw materials, food and transport equipment. In a country almost entirely dependent on rail transport, the Soviet Union produced less than a hundred locomotives during the entire war, but it received nearly two thousand locomotives from America. Two-thirds of the Red Army's trucks were supplied through the Lend-Lease programme. The Soviet Union received 300,000 tons of explosives, 40,000 field radios, 400 radar systems, 400,000 machine tools and millions of tons of foodstuffs, steel, aluminium and chemicals. For Soviet troops on the frontlines, many wrapped in British-made greatcoats, the words 'Spam' and 'Studebaker' became part of the military lexicon.

The main Soviet criticism of the Lend-Lease programme was that its benefits came too late to make a crucial difference. Most of the supplies arrived in 1943 and 1944, and too little arrived in the desperate days of 1941 and 1942. There is some merit in this argument as, for example, of the total number of aircraft supplied to the Soviet Union, less than ten percent had been delivered by the beginning of November 1942.

Yet it is possible that the limited amount of material supplied before 1943 did make a crucial difference to the conflict up to that point, and it is unlikely that the Soviet victories of 1943 and 1944 could have been achieved on the scale they were without the direct and indirect military benefits of Lend-Lease.

Stalin was, to say the least, dismayed when he was formally advised early in June 1943 that there would be no Allied invasion of Western Europe that year. His constant complaint during the first three years of the war was that the Soviet Union was bearing almost the entire burden of the war alone. His frustration may have been understandable, but during 1943 this complaint became less credible. In the Pacific the Japanese were increasingly on the defensive, leaving Stalin with few concerns about a Siberian incursion from the Japanese army in Manchuria. The Mediterranean had become a largely Allied lake, further constraining any possible threat to the Soviet Union's southern border from Turkey. In the closing phase of the fighting in North Africa, irrecoverable Axis losses exceeded 200,000 personnel and included almost the entire German V Pz Army. The strategic air offensive against Germany was having a considerable impact on the German transport infrastructure and on key industrial sectors, particularly gasoline production. It was also having an adverse effect on both civilian and military morale. After 1942 most of Germany's aircraft, and most of its aircraft losses, were in the West.[2] The impending threat of an Allied invasion of Europe, and occupation duties in the occupied territories, kept around one-third of Germany's divisions away from the Red Army. In central and southern Norway alone, some 400,000 German troops were held ready to defend against what Hitler perceived as a likely attempt by the western Allies to deprive Germany of the mineral resources of Scandinavia; and from North Africa the Allies could potentially launch an invasion of southern Europe anywhere from Sardinia to Crete.

Hitler made his strategic priorities clear in a Directive on 3 November 1943, though his general strategy had been decided months earlier after the loss of North Africa, and the *Kriegsmarine*'s defeat in the Battle of the Atlantic. Germany would concentrate on defeating the inevitable Anglo-American invasion. Only once the invasion forces had been comprehensively destroyed would the entire resources of the Reich be directed towards the defeat of Bolshevism. Until then, the role of the *Ostheer* would be to ensure that the Red Army was kept as far as possible from Germany's borders. Stalino, Kharkov, Orel, Smolensk, Novgorod and Mga were all firmly in German hands, and seemed to most Germans to be at a sufficiently safe distance that the ebb and flow of battle would have a negligible direct impact on the homeland. The casualty trains flowing in from the east, and the enemy bombers flying in from the west, made it abundantly clear to the German people that difficult days lay ahead and that an outright German victory was no longer likely, but few Germans imagined that the Reich would emerge from the conflict without some tangible benefit from the years of military effort, and from the spectacular victories of 1939, 1940 and 1941.

As in the Red Army, during 1943 the *Ostheer* adapted its organisational structure somewhat to reflect the realities of a prolonged conflict with a powerful and resourceful enemy. In the panzer divisions the authorised number of tanks in the panzer regiment remained at 200, but the reality was that in most divisions the number of tanks was

---

2   After the summer of 1943 three-quarters of German aircraft losses and 85% of day-fighter losses occurred in the West, a balance of loss that continued through 1944.

closer to 100. Increasingly, the motorised divisions were assigned armoured fighting vehicles, often tanks but also self-propelled guns, and in June 1943 the divisions became known as panzer grenadier divisions.

The term panzer grenadier was not adopted until 1942. Infantry in panzer divisions from 1939 onwards were known as *Schützen* troops.[3] In 1942, in a historical reference to the army of Frederick the Great, Hitler renamed infantry regiments as grenadier regiments. Thereafter the *Schützen* regiments and the soldiers in them began to be redesignated as panzer grenadiers, as did infantry units and troops in the motorised divisions. The *Waffen SS* also created several panzer grenadier divisions by the same methods, or by creating new divisions from scratch later in the war. A number of panzer grenadier divisions in both the army and the SS were upgraded to panzer divisions as the war progressed. The panzer grenadier divisions were organized as combined arms formations, usually with six battalions of truck-mounted infantry (organized into either two or three regiments), a battalion of tanks, and a standard division's complement of artillery, reconnaissance, engineers, anti-tank, anti-aircraft and other support units. All these support elements would also be mechanized in a panzer grenadier division, with the weapons of the artillery, anti-tank and anti-aircraft units being generally towed by trucks. A few elite units might have a second battalion of armoured fighting vehicles together with armoured personnel carriers for some of their infantry formations.[4] Organisationally a panzer grenadier division had one less tank battalion than a panzer division, but two more infantry battalions, and thus was almost as strong as a panzer division, especially on the defensive.

The distinction between panzer corps and army corps, and between panzer army and field army, had been largely eroded by the summer of 1943. By then five of the *Ostheer*'s panzer corps were without any panzer divisions, and neither II Pz Army nor III Pz Army had any panzer corps or panzer divisions in their order of battle.

In the autumn of 1943 the reduction of German infantry divisions to six battalions (based on three regiments) was formally adopted as the standard divisional structure. Additionally the manning level of a rifle company was significantly reduced by a 25% cut in the number of squads per platoon. These changes, which largely reflected the reality of divisional structure already pertaining, reduced the authorised strength of infantry divisions to around 13,000. Divisional, regimental and battalion support elements remained largely unchanged from the beginning of the war, though their scale reflected the reduced unit sizes. (In 1944 further modest changes in divisional structure reduced the authorised strength of German infantry divisions to 12,350 personnel).

The success of the SS Panzer Corps in the Manstein Counterstrike, a success achieved against the expectations of most regular army officers, was a contributory factor to a doubling of the number of *Waffen SS* divisions during the course of 1943. Eight *Waffen SS* divisions had been raised before the end of 1942 including two mountain divisions and a cavalry division. A further three *Waffen SS* divisions were raised in early 1943, two panzer divisions and a panzer grenadier division, enabling the SS to form

---

3   The term *Schützen* was originally used in the sense of light infantry, similar to *Jäger*.

4   Of 226 panzer grenadier battalions in the whole of the German Army, *Luftwaffe* and *Waffen SS* in September 1943, only 26 were equipped with armoured half tracks, the rest being equipped with trucks.

additional corps headquarters, and in June the *Waffen SS* corps serving in Army Group South was redesignated II SS Pz Corps. Membership of the SS depended primarily on a demonstrably 'pure Aryan' genealogy and a commitment to Nazi ideology. Such criteria were not confined to ethnic Germans, and Himmler saw his SS fiefdom as a genuinely pan-European entity. Consequently, several of the new *Waffen SS* divisions raised before the end of 1943 were from non-German personnel; Norwegians, Croats and Latvians. Thereafter the supply of enthusiastic healthy young Aryans began to dry up. The SS continued to expand, a total of thirty-eight *Waffen SS* divisions being raised before the end of the war, but after 1943 only three further *Waffen SS* divisions of ethnic Germans were raised. For the rest, entry criteria were drastically modified resulting in the eventual creation of twenty-five non-German *Waffen SS* divisions, some even composed of Russians, Ukrainians and Balkan Moslems. These new divisions were sometimes lavishly equipped, at the expense of regular army units. As the war progressed Hitler's preference was to use newly manufactured weapons to equip new divisions rather than to re-equip existing divisions. Consequently the combat effectiveness of many experienced frontline divisions declined as their equipment base was depleted.

After the realisation in 1941 that the war against the Soviet Union might be more protracted than originally assumed, Germany took a series of measures to place its economy on a firmer war footing and to revive a raft of weapon development projects that had previously been thought unnecessary. By 1943 those measures had begun to have a tangible impact on the frontline. German production of armoured fighting vehicles, which had been little more than 4,000 in 1942, increased to nearly 13,700 in 1943 and, despite the vicissitudes of the Allied bombing campaign, would rise to nearly 19,000 in 1944. Although these figures compare unfavourably with Soviet production rates of armoured fighting vehicles (2,000 per month in 1943 and 2,500 per month in 1944), the rate of loss of German armoured fighting vehicles on the Eastern Front was generally less than a third of Soviet losses. The Soviets had standardised ruthlessly on the production of the T34 tank, but by 1943 the T34 had become increasingly vulnerable to German anti-tank weaponry, and its 76mm gun had become less effective against the latest German armoured fighting vehicles. In the PzKpfw IVG and particularly in the PzKpfw IVH, production of which began in April 1943, Germany had regained the qualitative advantage in tank production. The PzKpfw VI Tiger, only 650 of which were produced in 1943, was virtually invulnerable to the T34 at distances of more than a few hundred metres. The latest German tank, the PzKpfw V Panther, which had been modelled on the T34, was a far superior weapon system. Introduced in the spring of 1943, the Panther was initially plagued with teething problems, and the great majority of the 1,850 machines produced in 1943 were delivered in the second half of the year; yet its impact served to strengthen the Soviet realisation that continued mass production of the 1941 model T34 would not be sufficient to compensate for its increasing inferiority. So great were the Soviet tank losses in 1943 that, despite the impressive production rate of T34s, the Red Army's tank park grew only slightly over the course of that year. It was clear that the Soviet Union needed a medium tank with thicker armour and a more powerful gun. Since a more powerful gun could not be fitted to the existing T34 turret, it was concluded that a redesign of the T34 would be required. Yet the result of this redesign, a better-armoured T34 with an 85mm gun and an enlarged crew of five, would not appear on the battlefield until the spring of 1944. In the meantime, the Red Army would have to operate with the existing T34, for which a shortage of trained tank crews, rather a shortage of machines, was to prove to be the main constraining factor in Soviet armoured operations in the closing months of 1943.

Much of the dramatic increase in the German production of armoured fighting vehicles after 1942 was due to the increasing emphasis on the production of the relatively uncomplicated self-propelled guns in preference to tanks. Building on the success of the StuG III assault gun, of which more than 9,400 were produced during the war, the Germans also produced more than 1,200 StuH 42s (a StuG III with a 10.5cm howitzer – the official designation of which was the *Sturmhaubitze 42*, Sd.Kfz 142/2) and, commencing in November 1943, a production run of more than 1,100 StuG IVs based on a PzKpfw IV chassis and mounting a 7.5cm gun. From May 1943 Germany also began to produce the *Sturmpanzer* IV mounting a 15cm gun, but only a few hundred were manufactured before the end of the war. In the tank destroyer role Germany produced no less than ten different weapon systems. During the middle period of the war the most common was the *Marder* III, based on the PzKpfw 38(t) tank chassis and mounting either a 7.5cm Pak 40 anti-tank gun or a captured Soviet F-22 divisional gun adapted for the anti-tank role. From 1942 to 1944 some 1,500 *Marder* IIIs were produced. In April 1944 production was switched to the *Hetzer*, essentially a reconfigured *Marder* III with a lower profile and an improved 7.5cm gun, and from August 1944 Germany also began to produce the *Jagdpanzer* IV. Based on the PzKpfw IV chassis, the *Jagdpanzer* IV initially mounted the same gun as the *Hetzer* but was later fitted with the long-barrelled 7.5cm Pak 42L/70. More than 2,500 *Hetzer*s and some 1,000 *Jagdpanzer* IVs were produced in the last year of the war. Germany also produced around one thousand 'tank killers' based on the 8.8cm Pak 43 or the 12.8cm Pak 44 guns during the later period of the war. The first and most numerous was the *Nashorn*. This armoured fighting vehicle was based on a new chassis that used components from the PzKpfw III and the PzKpfw IV, and it mounted an 8.8cm gun. Production began in early 1943 and more than 470 were produced. For success in the forthcoming German summer offensive, Hitler in the spring of 1943 placed a great deal of faith in the *Panzerjäger* Tiger (P). Based on a prototype PzKpfw VI chassis, the *Panzerjäger* Tiger (P), known initially as the Ferdinand but after subsequent modification renamed the *Elefant*, mounted a long-barrelled 8.8cm gun. In fact the production run of this weapon was short, only 90 being produced in 1943. More successful was the *Jagdpanther*: based on the PzKpfw V chassis and mounting the latest of the long-barrelled 88s, nearly 400 were produced from 1944 to the end of the war. The monstrous *Jagdtiger*, based on the Tiger II chassis and mounting the 12.8cm anti-tank gun, was produced late in the war in similar numbers to the earlier Ferdinand. Self-propelled artillery was produced in smaller numbers than the assault guns or 'tank killers'. The *Wespe* was the most common weapon in the middle period of the war. Based on the PzKpfw II chassis, the *Wespe* mounted the standard German 10.5cm howitzer, and 662 were produced between 1942 and 1944. Using the same composite chassis as the *Nashorn*, the *Hummel*, mounting the standard German 15cm howitzer, appeared in mid 1943, and 713 were produced before the end of the war. Between April 1943 and September 1944 several hundred *Grille* self-propelled artillery guns were produced based on the PzKpfw 38(t) chassis and mounting a 15cm infantry gun. Recognising the effectiveness of the Soviet *Katyusha* rocket artillery, the Germans subsequently produced their own versions mounted on their half-track vehicles. These weapons systems were the *Panzerwerfer* (15cm rockets) and the *Wurfrahmen* (30cm rockets).

The story of German aircraft production in the middle period of the war mirrored somewhat that of armoured fighting vehicle production. In 1943 Germany produced 20,600 aircraft, a substantial increase on the less than 13,000 produced in 1942, and production would increase to more than 35,000 in 1944. In the early period of the war on the Eastern Front the *Luftwaffe*'s bomber force was based primarily on the Heinkel He 111 and Junkers Ju 88 twin-engined medium bombers, though by the end of 1942 the He 111 was being progressively replaced by the recently developed Dornier Do 217. By 1942 German aeronautical engineers had largely perfected the Me 109 fighter, annual production of which doubled to 6,000 in 1943 and doubled again in 1944, and they had adapted the excellent new Fw 190 fighter to the ground attack role. Also during 1943 the number of Ju 87 'Stuka' dive bombers produced was nearly 1,700, double the figure for 1942, and the aircraft were modified for the anti-tank role. Yet with the *Luftwaffe* fighting a genuinely two-front war, its rate of aircraft loss exceeded German aircraft production rates and, where aircraft were available for combat missions, sortie numbers were increasingly constrained by fuel shortages.

For the Red Air Force the situation was very different. Despite losing 22,500 aircraft in 1943, Soviet aircraft production exceeded the losses by a significant margin, leaving the Red Air Force some 50% stronger in terms of combat aircraft numbers at the end of that year than at the beginning. Thereafter, though Soviet aircraft losses increased to more than 2,000 per month, a loss rate that compared unfavourably with the German loss rate on the Eastern Front of 800 aircraft per month, the rate of Soviet production increased still faster. The principal aircraft of the Soviet Air Force during the war were the Ilyushin Il-2 *Shturmovik* ground-attack 'flying tank', the Yak fighter in its many variants, and the La-5/La-7 developments of the LaGG-3 fighter. Each produced in the tens of thousands, they accounted for the majority of Soviet wartime aircraft production. By 1943 the *Shturmovik*, despite being highly vulnerable to German fighters, had become the scourge of German mechanised forces in the east. In addition, the Yak and Lavochkin fighters in their later variants had become the equal of the German fighters. In the tactical bomber role the Pe-2 was the mainstay of the Soviet war effort, more than 11,000 of the numerous variants being built. The excellent Tu-2 tactical/medium bomber did not appear in significant numbers until the spring of 1944, and the pre-war DB-3, subsequently developed into the Il-4, was the predominant aircraft used by the Red Air Force for the medium bomber role, with nearly 7,000 being built.

Perhaps the development that had the greatest impact on the nature of the conflict in the later stages of the war was not a new armoured fighting vehicle or a new aircraft, but the exploitation of a curiosity observed during the late nineteenth century in the effect of certain explosive charges. The phenomenon, known as the Munroe effect, arises from the fact that, during an explosion, energy is directed away from the surface of the explosive material. If that surface happens to be a concave void, the blast energy will be focussed, concentrated into a localised area, to produce in that area a jet of plasma moving at many times the speed of sound. The plasma produced by such 'shaped charges', particularly when the concave surface is lined with a metal foil such as copper, can penetrate steel to a depth two or three times the diameter of the initial shaped charge. By 1943 this effect was being put to practical use on the battlefield to destroy armoured fighting vehicles. Known as shaped charge or HEAT (high explosive anti-tank) munitions, they differed fundamentally from previous anti-tank munitions. Until 1943 stand-off destruction of tanks had depended almost entirely on providing solid projectiles with the maximum possible kinetic energy in order that they be able penetrate the depth of armour. Since kinetic energy is a function of mass and velocity, the trend had been towards increasing the weight and the muzzle velocities of the projectiles. The final manifestation of this approach was the discarding sabot round. Armour penetration for a given mass of shot is maximised by concentrating the force of the impact in as small an area as possible and by maximising the impact velocity. The discarding sabot helps to achieve both these objectives by using a standard anti-tank gun to fire a small diameter 'metal arrow' projectile encased in a lightweight sheath or 'sabot'. The consequent low mass of the round raises the muzzle velocity of the projectile, and the sabot is designed to fall away from the central projectile after leaving the muzzle of the gun. In HEAT munitions the kinetic energy of the round is not a relevant factor. Of greatest significance is the diameter of the shaped charge relative to depth of armour to be penetrated. By 1943 a range of methods of delivering HEAT munitions to their intended targets were being developed. One typical application was the provision of HEAT rounds to standard wide-bore low velocity artillery pieces such as infantry guns or assault guns, to provide them with a hitherto unavailable anti-tank capability. One drawback with this application was that HEAT rounds do not work effectively if the round is spinning, and if an artillery round is not spinning, accuracy is rapidly lost over distances of more than a few hundred metres. In the West it was quickly realised that if HEAT munitions could be married to a lightweight mortar device or recoilless gun, then platoon sized infantry units could be provided with a potent stand-off anti-tank weapon for close support.[5] While the Western Allies developed the Bazooka and the PIAT, the Soviet Union decided to continue to use the increasingly ineffective 14.5mm PTRD anti-tank rifle. This was not an entirely perverse decision since HEAT rounds could be made to detonate prematurely and ineffectually by the fitting of a spacer plate on the outside of a tank hull. The most widespread use of the recoilless gun HEAT round concept was in the German army, where in 1943 the *Panzerfaust*, a single-use disposable recoilless weapon fitted with a HEAT round, began to appear in prodigious numbers. In 1943 Germany also developed the *Raketenpanzerbüchse*, more commonly known as the *Panzerschreck*. This weapon, nicknamed the 'stove pipe', fired an 8.8cm rocket-propelled, fin-stabilized HEAT round. Armed with such weapons a single infantryman could destroy the most heavily armoured tank from a significant distance, and their presence, particularly in urban environments, had a profound effect on the relative confidence of infantry platoons and tank crews when facing each other on the battlefield.

5   A recoilless gun is one without a breech – essentially a hollow tube – in which the momentum of the projectile that would be experienced as recoil in a breech gun is largely balanced by the blast of the explosive's combustion gasses from the rear of the barrel. Also, since the barrel is not required to contain the enormous pressures of the explosive's combustion gasses, the barrel can be made relatively thin and hence relatively light.

After the frenetic events of the winter of 1942/43, the season of mud cast an eerie calm over most of the Eastern Front. Continuing through May and into June, it was however a deceptive calm. On both sides preparations proceeded apace for the next round of operations. By the summer of 1943 the *Ostheer* held a frontline that ran from the south-western suburbs of Leningrad east to the northeast of Mga, then south to Lake Ilmen east of Novgorod. From the southern shore of the lake the frontline ran east of Staraya Russa, east of Kholm, west of Velikie Luki, east of Nevel and southeast from Velizh to Kirov. South of Kirov a long serpentine section of front included the German held Orel salient pushing deep into the Soviet lines, and the Soviet held Kursk salient pushing deep into the *Ostheer*'s lines. From Kirov the frontline ran east to Lyudinovo and on to the northeast of Mtsensk from where it turned south to Novosil and on to Pokrovskoye (the boundary between Bryansk Front and Central Front). From Pokrovskoye the frontline then ran southwest before turning west some 10km north of Ponyri and Olkhovatka and on to Dmitrovsk Orlovskiy. From there the frontline turned south, running east of Sevsk, to Korenevo and east of Sumy. From Sumy the frontline ran east to the north of Belgorod, then south and southeast along the Donets for three hundred kilometres to the west of Voroshilovgrad and then south along the Mius to the Sea of Azov east of Taganrog.

Along this enormous frontline the focus of attention for both sides was the Kursk salient, a tempting target for the traditional German *Blitzkrieg* encirclement offensive, and seen by the *Ostheer* as unfinished business from the fighting of the early spring. Yet by the summer the entire nature of the proposed Citadel offensive had changed. Instead of an offensive to catch the Red Army off balance and restore the frontline south of Orel, it was building to a slugging match between well-rested and well-prepared opponents, where the potential prize for Germany was the envelopment and destruction of Central Front and Voronezh Front, and the renewed creation of a viable threat to Moscow. The presence of twenty German mechanised divisions around the Kursk salient from early April made it obvious to STAVKA that the Orel – Kursk – Belgorod area was of major strategic significance to the German High Command. A German offensive was expected as soon as ground conditions would permit, and Stalin had to be repeatedly persuaded by his generals throughout April, May and June not to initiate a pre-emptive strike against the Germans in this area, but to assume the defensive until the momentum of the German offensive had been absorbed. Stalin, mindful of the failed defensive operations of the summers of 1941 and 1942, remained uncertain, and before long two-fifths of the Red Army's rifle formations and all its tank armies were concentrated in the vicinity of the salient. In terms of artillery, the salient was reinforced with 10,000 guns and mortars including ninety-two heavy artillery regiments, 6,000 anti-tank guns and 920 *Katyusha* batteries. Even outside the salient, the armies were amply provided with artillery, 16 Army in particular receiving more than twice its normal allocation of guns and howitzers. In the air the Soviets committed 2,000 fighters, 800 ground attack aircraft and 700 bombers. Aerial reconnaissance, information from partisans and prisoners, information from the British Ultra code-breaking project, and the monitoring of German radio traffic all gave the Soviets a detailed picture of German preparations and intentions. The delay in the German offensive meant that the Red Army was able to establish eight defence lines echeloned to a depth of 160km with more than 3,000 mines per kilometre on the critical sectors and chessboard-style anti-tank resistance points. Yet Stalin, having been persuaded of the case for a defensive posture in the face of German preparations at Kursk, insisted on a comprehensive counter-offensive strategy for implementation once the German offensive had been defeated. By the early summer this strategy had been prepared and much of the preliminary work for its implementation had been completed.

Among the many changes in the Red Army during the spring and early summer of 1943 was the creation of seven new Guards armies and two Guards tank armies. At the beginning of May, 24 Army, 66 Army, 21 Army, 64 Army, 62 Army, 30 Army and 16 Army were redesignated 4 Gds Army, 5 Gds Army, 6 Gds Army, 7 Gds Army, 8 Gds Army, 10 Gds Army and 11 Gds Army respectively, though for security reasons these changes of designation were not made public until July. In April 1943 Rybalko's 3 Tank Army was redesignated as a field army, the second formation of 57 Army.[6] Subsequently a new tank army designated 3 Gds Tank Army, and also commanded by Rybalko, was formed. In February 1943 the first of the Guards tank armies, designated 5 Gds Tank Army had been formed. This Guards tank army, though it did not become operational until July, existed simultaneously with 5 Tank Army for a time until the latter was withdrawn from operational service on 20 April and subsequently disbanded.[7]

On 13 March 1943 STAVKA created a Reserve Front that was subsequently redesignated Steppe Military District and then Steppe Front, and, as the largest operational reserve ever fielded by the Red Army, it was positioned east of Kursk. In June Konev was appointed to its command, Kurochkin resuming command at Northwestern Front after Konev departure. Also in June M M Popov replaced Reiter as commander of Bryansk Front.

In the *Ostheer* the senior command and organisational changes that took place during the spring and early summer of 1943 were on a far more modest scale. Hitler had been determined to try to expunge the humiliation of VI Army's surrender at Stalingrad by forming a new VI Army, and on 6 March he did just that by renaming Group Hollidt.[8] Hollidt's command was not unworthy of the 'army' designation; it consisted of thirteen combat divisions and two security divisions, and it included four corps headquarters. On 10 April Schmidt, openly critical of Hitler's operational decisions on the Eastern Front, was dismissed and replaced at II Pz Army by General Heinrich Cloessner.

One sector of the frontline that had not been quiet during the spring of 1943 was the Taman Peninsula. In March, with little progress being made against Kleist's defences, Koroteev was appointed to replace Glagolev at 9 Army and Leselidze was appointed to the command of 18 Army. By late April 1943 Maslennikov's forces had been rationalised to 9 Army operating on the right flank of North Caucasian Front along the Shaporsky axis, P M Kozlov's 37 Army operating on the Kievskoye axis, Grechko's 56 Army on the Krymskaya axis and 18 Army continuing to invest Novorossiysk.[9] A renewed Soviet offensive with fifteen divisions and thirty brigades was launched on 29 April across the entire Taman front, but significant progress

---

6   The first formation of 57 Army had been redesignated 68 Army at the end of January that year.

7   Rotmistrov was appointed to command 5 Guards Tank Army and Lt-Gen I T Shlemin replaced Rotmistrov at 5 Tank Army prior to its disbandment.

8   Since 23 January the official designation of Hollidt's command had been Army Detachment Hollidt.

9   46 Army and 47 Army had been withdrawn to High Command reserve and the four divisions of 58 Army were part of the Front reserve.

was only made in the 56 Army sector where Grechko's forces had taken Krymskaya by 4 May. Yet no further progress could be made against Kleist's fall-back defensive position, the so-called 'Blue Line' from Kievskoye to Neberjayevskaya. By mid-May the offensive against XVII Army's eleven forward divisions was called off. The failure cost Maslennikov his command and he was replaced by Petrov, but STAVKA recognised that a successful offensive against the Blue Line would take months to prepare and could not be expected before the late summer. In the relatively quiet interim Jaenecke, who had been flown out of the Stalingrad cauldron before the final surrender, replaced the 60 year old Ruoff at XVII Army on 25 June.

8

The Beginning of the End

By early July 1943 the *Ostheer* had been strengthened to more than 3.5 million personnel with 194 combat divisions of which only fourteen divisions were non-German. Although twelve of the German divisions were the somewhat unreliable *Luftwaffe* field divisions, sixteen were panzer divisions, six were panzer grenadier divisions and five were SS panzer grenadier divisions. Additionally the *Ostheer* contained more than thirty independent self-propelled gun battalions, an independent 'tank destroyer' regiment and two independent panzer brigades equipped with the latest tanks and self-propelled guns. Also facing the Red Army were nearly half a million Finnish and German troops in Karelia and the Arctic. A summary of the *Ostheer* order of battle at the commencement of Operation Citadel is given in Appendix IX.

At this time XVIII Army occupied the frontline from the Baltic to Lake Ilmen, and XVI Army occupied the sector from Lake Ilmen to north of Velikie Luki. During the late spring of 1943 Model's IX Army Headquarters was moved from the sector northeast of Smolensk to be inserted between II Pz Army and II Army south of Orel, leaving III Pz Army and IV Army to cover the frontline from Velikie Luki to Kirov. The northern and western faces of the Orel salient were covered by II Pz Army, and IX Army covered the southern face of the Orel salient that was also the northern face of the Kursk salient. On Army Group Centre's right flank, II Army covered the western face of the Kursk salient to the east of Sumy. The sector from the east of Sumy to west of Belgorod was covered by IV Pz Army, and Kempf's group covered the Belgorod sector south along the Donets. The main sector of the Donets from Kharkov to the Mius was occupied by I Pz Army, and VI Army occupied the sector along the Mius to the Sea of Azov. A summary of the German order of battle around the Kursk salient in early July 1943 is given below:

See Map 17

- IX Army commanded by Col-Gen Walter Model. Model's powerful army included; General Johannes Friessner's XXIII Corps with 383 and 216 Inf Divs, 78 Assault Div and part of 36 Inf Div; General Ferdinand Schaal's XLI Pz Corps with 86 and 292 Inf Divs and 18 Pz Div; Lt-Gen Joachim Lemelsen's XLVII Pz Corps with 21 Pz Bgd, 6 Inf Div and 20, 9 and 2 Pz Divs; General Hans Zorn's XLVI Pz Corps with 31, 7, 258 and 102 Inf Divs; and XX Corps commanded by General Rudolf Freiherr von Roman with 72, 45, 137 and 251 Inf Divs. In reserve Model had 299 Inf Div and part of 36 Inf Div, and in his operational area as part of Kluge's army group reserve was an operational group commanded by Lt-Gen Hans-Karl von Esebeck that included 10 Pz Gdr Div and 12 Pz Div.
- II Army commanded by General Walter Weiss. Anticipated to be in a largely defensive role during the battle, II Army included General Friedrich Siebert's

XIII Corps with 82, 340, 377 and 327 Inf Divs; and General Ernst-Eberhard Hell's VII Corps with 26 Inf Div, part of 323 Inf Div, 75, 68 and 88 Inf Divs.

- IV Pz Army commanded by Col-Gen Hermann Hoth. Hoth's army included LII Corps commanded by General Eugen Ott with 57, 255 and 332 Inf Divs; General Otto von Knobelsdorff's XLVIII Pz Corps with 3 Pz Div, 11 Pz Div, most of 167 Inf Div, *Grossdeutschland* Pz Gdr Div and 10 Pz Bgd; and SS General Paul Hausser's II SS Pz Corps with 1 SS Pz Gdr Div (*Leibstandarte*), 2 SS Pz Gdr Div (*Das Reich*), 3 SS Pz Gdr Div (*Totenkopf*) and part of 167 Inf Div.

- General Hermann Kempf's powerful group (Army Detachment Kempf) was a full field army in all but name. It comprised III Pz Corps commanded by General Hermann Breith with 6, 7 and 19 Pz Divs, and 168 Inf Div; XI Corps commanded by General Erhard Raus with 320 and 106 Inf Divs; and Lt-Gen Anton Dostler's XLII Corps with 161, 282, and 39 Inf Divs.

In the north IX Army and II Army were part of Kluge's Army Group Centre, while IV Pz Army and Army Detachment Kempf were part of Manstein's Army Group South.

The Axis forces between the Barents Sea and the Black Sea faced some 6.9 million Soviet personnel. South of the Karelian Isthmus Leningrad Front and Volkhov Front faced XVIII Army; Northwestern Front faced XVI Army; Kalinin Front and Western Front faced III Pz Army, IV Army and the left flank of II Pz Army; Bryansk Front faced II Pz Army; Central Front faced IX Army and the left wing of II Army; Voronezh Front faced the right wing of II Army, IV Pz Army and Army Detachment Kempf; Southwestern Front faced I Pz Army and Southern Front faced VI Army. A summary of the order of battle of Soviet forces facing the *Ostheer* at the beginning of July 1943 is given in Appendix X. Below is a summary of the Red Army order of battle around the Kursk salient at that time.

- The left wing of Col-Gen V D Sokolovsky's Western Front included Lt-Gen I V Boldin's 50 Army of seven rifle divisions and a tank brigade, and Lt-Gen I K Bagramyan's 11 Gds Army. Bagramyan's army included twelve rifle divisions, most of them Guards divisions organised into three Guards rifle corps. Bagramian also had four tank brigades and his army was heavily reinforced with artillery (3,000 guns and heavy mortars) including four artillery divisions from the strategic reserve. In reserve Sokolovsky had Lt-Gen K P Trubnikov's 10 Gds Army of six rifle divisions. Additionally as part of his Front reserve Sokolovsky had two tank corps, four tank brigades, a rifle division and a rifle brigade. In the Rzhev area Sokolovsky also had 20 Army as part of his Front reserve but 20 Army was without any operational divisions or mobile units.

- Col-Gen M M Popov's Bryansk Front included Lt-Gen P A Belov's 61 Army of eight rifle divisions and a tank brigade, the six rifle divisions of Lt-Gen A V Gorbatov's 3 Army, and the seven rifle divisions of Lt-Gen V I Kolpakchy's 63 Army. Three of Belov's divisions were Guards divisions organised under 9 Gds Rifle Corps. Popov's Front reserve included 1 Gds Tank Corps, 25 Rifle Corps of three rifle divisions, and four tank regiments.

- Col-Gen K K Rokossovsky's Central Front had on its right wing the seven rifle divisions and three tank regiments of Lt-Gen P I Romanenko's 48 Army. On Romanenko's left was Lt-Gen N P Pukhov's powerful 13 Army. Pukhov's nine rifle divisions and three airborne divisions were organised into 17 Gds Rifle Corps, 18 Gds Rifle Corps, 29 Rifle Corps and 15 Rifle Corps. Pukhov also had a cavalry corps, a tank brigade and five tank regiments, and his army was heavily reinforced with artillery. On Pukhov's left were the eight rifle divisions, one tank brigade and three tank regiments of Lt-Gen I V Galanin's 70 Army. On Galanin's left was Lt-Gen P I Batov's 65 Army and on the left wing of Central Front was Lt-Gen I D Cherniakhovsky's 60 Army. Between them Cherniakhovsky and Batov had fourteen rifle divisions, four rifle brigades, a tank brigade and four tank regiments, and to assist with the command and control of the infantry they also had four rifle corps headquarters. In reserve near Fatezh Rokossovsky had Lt-Gen A G Rodin's 2 Tank Army with 16 Tank Corps, 3 Gds Tank Corps and a tank brigade, and as Front reserve he also had 9 Tank Corps and 19 Tank Corps.
- General N F Vatutin's Voronezh Front had the six rifle divisions and two tank brigades of Lt-Gen N E Chibisov's 38 Army on its right flank, and Lt-Gen K S Moskalenko's 40 Army with seven rifle divisions, a tank brigade and two tank regiments was on Chibisov's left. The main strength of Voronezh Front was on its left wing with Lt-Gen I M Chistyakov's 6 Gds Army and Lt-Gen M S Shumilov's 7 Gds Army. The rifle divisions of these armies were predominantly Guards units and the armies were organised almost identically. Each had six rifle divisions in two rifle corps with a seventh rifle division and tank support under army headquarters command. Chistyakov had 22 Gds Rifle Corps and 23 Gds Rifle Corps with two tank brigades and two tank regiments, and Shumilov had 24 Gds Rifle Corps and 25 Gds Rifle Corps with a tank brigade and three tank regiments. In reserve behind the Guards armies Vatutin had Lt-Gen M E Katukov's 1 Tank Army (31 Tank Corps, 6 Tank Corps and 3 Mech Corps), and the five rifle divisions of Lt-Gen V D Kriuchenkin's 69 Army. As Front reserve Vatutin had 2 Gds Tank Corps, 5 Gds Tank Corps and the three Guards rifle divisions of 35 Gds Rifle Corps.
- On the right flank of General Malinovsky's Southwestern Front was Lt-Gen N A Gagen's 57 Army. Gagen had eight rifle divisions and two tank brigades. Three of his rifle divisions were Guards divisions within 27 Gds Rifle Corps.
- Col-Gen I S Konev's Reserve Front included Lt-Gen A S Zhadov's 5 Gds Army (five rifle divisions, two airborne divisions and 10 Tank Corps); Lt-Gen S G Trofimenko's 27 Army (six rifle divisions, a tank brigade and a tank regiment); Major-Gen A I Ryzhov's 47 Army (six rifle divisions); Lt-Gen I M Managorov's 53 Army (seven rifle divisions and two tank regiments); and Lt-Gen P A Rotmistrov's 5 Gds Tank Army (5 Gds Mech Corps, 29 Tank Corps and subsequently 18 Tank Corps). In addition Konev had 4 Gds Tank Corps, 3 Gds Mech Corps, 1 Mech Corps, 2 Mech Corps and three Guards cavalry corps. Also included in Konev's order of battle at the beginning of July was 4 Gds Army, but this army only became operational for four days in mid-July before being withdrawn into the strategic reserve.

In addition to Reserve Front, STAVKA had further significant reserves available northeast of Orel. Those reserves included Major-Gen E P Zhuravlev's 68 Army, Lt-Gen I I Fedyuninsky's 11 Army, Lt-Gen V M Badanov's 4 Tank Army, and, still forming up, Lt-Gen P S Rybalko's 3 Gds Tank Army. Consequently the Red Army was well prepared to face the anticipated German offensive. Although the *Ostheer* had achieved parity with the Red Army in armoured fighting vehicles in the Kursk area (in excess of 3,000 vehicles on each side), the Germans were outnumbered more than two to one in men and guns.

Hitler and OKH were aware that the delays to the start of Operation Citadel, delays upon which Hitler had insisted in order to increase the number of Tigers, Panthers and Ferdinands in the Kursk area, were enabling the Soviets to construct ever more formidable defences. As late as mid-June Hitler had doubts as to whether to proceed with the operation at all. What he most certainly did not want was to see the *Ostheer* bled white in an effort to grind its way through to Kursk. Success would depend on a rapid breakthrough of the Soviet defences and the subsequent speedy encirclement of Soviet forces within the salient. In his final authorisation for the offensive to proceed, Hitler cited its effects on morale and on world opinion, in particular the opinion of wavering allies and potentially belligerent neutrals, as the prime reasons for the operation. Many in OKH and in the *Ostheer* also had reservations about the operation but they were aware that without it a substantial part of the *Ostheer*'s mechanised strength would almost certainly be withdrawn for deployment to other theatres.

Citadel

Germany's last strategic offensive in the east began at dawn on 5 July 1943. Rokossovsky had anticipated that the main German blow against his Front would come on the right, along the Orel-Kursk axis through Ponyri. This sector was defended by 13 Army which had 29 Rifle Corps and 15 Rifle Corps forward, each with two divisions as first echelon and one division as second echelon. Pukhov's army had been reinforced with 4 Artillery Breakthrough Corps with its 700 heavy guns and howitzers. In the Voronezh Front sector Vatutin anticipated three probable axes of attack on his centre and left, a 100km sector defended by 6 Gds Army (Oboyan area) and 7 Gds Army to its left. So confident was STAVKA that it had discerned OKH's intentions, that on 4 July both 6 Gds Army and 7 Gds Army began a massive artillery barrage to disrupt German troop movements and final preparations, and in the early hours of the following morning 13 Army did likewise.

Model's main effort towards Olkhovatka and later Ponyri was centred on XLVII Pz Corps with XLI Pz Corps and XLVI Pz Corps on the flanks, and XXIII Corps in reserve. Lemelsen's corps hit the junction of 29 Rifle Corps' 15 Rifle Div and 81 Rifle Div, and during the first day penetrated 6km into the Soviet defences. By noon Rokossovsky had allowed Pukhov to move up 17 Gds Rifle Corps, and he decided to counter-attack in the Olkhovatka area the next day with 2 Tank Army.[1] In addition, 18 Gds Rifle Corps was deployed to the northeast of Ponyri to prevent a widening of the German breakthrough on the flank.

---

1   3 Gds Tank Corps was deployed to the south of Ponyri, 16 Tank Corps to the northwest of Olkhovatka and 19 Tank Corps, committed to 2 Tank Army, was to the west of Olkhovatka.

In the south the weight of Hoth's offensive on the first day was in the Oboyan direction through Cherkasskoe, just five kilometres north of XLVIII Pz Corps' frontline positions. Hoth's operational plan was for XLVIII Pz Corps and II SS Pz Corps to make parallel thrusts with the main attack in each corps to be made by a single division. *Grossdeutschland* Div, reinforced with the 200 Panthers of 10 Pz Bgd spearheaded the XLVIII Pz Corps attack supported by 3 Pz Div and 11 Pz Div on its flanks. Hausser's main attack was with 1 SS Pz Gdr Div on the left of his line, supported by 2 SS Pz Gdr Div and 3 SS Pz Gdr Div to the right. Hauser had fewer tanks than Knobelsdorff but Hausser had the support of the greater part of the 1,200 aircraft that the *Luftwaffe* had managed to concentrate in the Kursk area in preparation for the offensive.

In the XLVIII Pz Corps sector, though Knobelsdorff had concentrated his corps' main effort in the centre, it was here that success was least apparent. *Grossdeutschland* Div supported by 11 Pz Div on its right hit 6 Gds Army's 67 Gds Rifle Div, a division that had been reinforced with two anti-tank regiments. Despite the overwhelming force brought to bear on a narrow front, Hoth found Knobelsdorff's progress to be disappointingly slow. Cherkasskoe, scheduled to be taken by mid-morning, was not secured until late in the day. On the XLVIII Pz Corps' sector 3 Pz Div had the greatest success, driving back 71 Gds Rifle Div more than 5km. Yet having committed virtually all his forces in the opening hours, Knobelsdorff had little by way of reinforcement with which to exploit the relative success on his corps' left flank. Hausser's attack fell primarily on 6 Gds Army's 52 Gds Rifle Div, a division that had been reinforced with anti-tank artillery and a tank regiment. Although in comparison with XLVIII Pz Corps, progress by the SS divisions was good, Bykovka more than 10km beyond the start line being taken by the end of the first day, this was still less than half the depth of penetration that had been anticipated by Hoth, and the Soviets' second defence line had not been breached.

During the afternoon of 5 July, with 67 Gds Rifle Div disintegrating in the face of the furious attacks of XLVIII Pz Corps, Vatutin ordered 1 Tank Army to move 6 Tank Corps and 3 Mech Corps to cover Oboyan and to prepare for a counter-attack towards Tomarovka, some 25km northwest of Belgorod, at dawn the next day. In addition 2 Gds Tank Corps and 5 Gds Tank Corps were to concentrate east of Luchki to attack in the direction of Belgorod, and in the evening 35 Gds Rifle Corps was used to reinforce 7 Gds Army which was struggling to hold Army Detachment Kempf to the right bank of the Donets. Kempf had been required to break out of three small bridgeheads held by German forces on the left bank of the Donets in the Belgorod area, and his 7 Pz Div was to force a crossing of the river farther south. Once established on the left bank, Kempf was to strike to the northeast toward Skordnoye in order to protect Hausser's right flank. Kempf's attacks out of the bridgeheads stalled but 7 Pz Div established a deep and viable bridgehead which, during the afternoon, Kempf began to reinforce with 6 Pz Div. Yet the failure of Breith's corps to break out of the northern bridgeheads meant that Voronezh Front retained a deep wedge between IV Pz Army and Army Detachment Kempf, and consequently Hausser's right flank was unprotected.

On the evening of 5 July STAVKA approved the transfer of 27 Army from Steppe Front to Vatutin's command as the battered 67 Gds Rifle Div was withdrawn to the rear. In the north on the morning of 6 July the counter-attack by 2 Tank Army (together with an offensive by the three right flank rifle divisions of 13 Army) was thrown back and Model's offensive, reinforced with 2 Pz Div and 9 Pz Div, ground slowly forward to the west of Ponyri. Rokossovsky was obliged to take two tank regiments from 65 Army and a rifle division from 60 Army to reinforce 13 Army. By the end of 6 July German forces had progressed only a few kilometres further but Model still had reserves in 18 Pz Div and 4 Pz Div approaching the battlefield, and additional reserves in Group Esebeck south of Orel.

On the morning of 6 July Katukov persuaded Vatutin to defer the planned counter-attack and to put 1 Tank Army in a defensive posture with the tanks dug in. By the end of 6 July the Germans were deep into the defensive zones of 6 Gds Army and 7 Gds Army, and Vatutin had been promised further reinforcements including 10 Tank Corps, the newly introduced 2 Tank Corps, and, over Konev's protests, 5 Gds Tank Army from Steppe Front. The fighting in the south continued uninterrupted through the night of 6/7 July and by dawn Hausser's Corps was beyond Luchki, northwest of which Katukov and Chistyakov moved in artillery, tank units and the remnants of 67 Gds Rifle Div in order to block the German advance. During 7 July the front held by 51 Gds Rifle Div of Chistyakov's second echelon was shattered and late in the evening 40 Army was ordered to transfer a rifle division and all its artillery to the 6 Gds Army / 1 Tank Army command in order to try to hold the German advance towards Oboyan. In the north on the morning of 7 July, 9 Pz Div and 18 Pz Div attacked towards Olkhovatka, 2 Pz Div and 20 Pz Div attacked farther west towards Samodurovka, and a powerful assault group attacked towards Ponyri. The main German thrust, subsequently reinforced by 4 Pz Div, was developing towards the Olkhovatka heights. Up to 300 German tanks broke through to Kashara and Samodurovka, and farther east the Ponyri railway junction changed hands several times. On the morning of 8 July, in a coordinated effort, 9 Pz Div, 18 Pz Div, 2 Pz Div and 4 Pz Div together with 6 Inf Div renewed their attack along the Ponyri – Samodurovka – Olkhovatka sector, but the attack on the Olkhovatka heights stalled. Model was dismayed to find such a heavily defended position so far behind the original frontline. He spent the whole of 9 July preparing for a renewed attack on the heights but the attacks, conducted on 10 July and 11 July, failed to achieve a breakthrough.

In the south, during the late morning of 8 July, five-hundred of Hoth's tanks attacked along a 6km sector towards Oboyan, smashing the junction between 1 Tank Army's 3 Mech Corps and 31 Tank Corps. With Hoth's forces advancing to the north, Katukov was reinforced with 10 Tank Corps and other tank and artillery regiments, and Vatutin was given command of 5 Gds Army from Steppe Front. Hoth concentrated the panzer divisions of the two panzer corps (less 2 SS Pz Gdr Div), with four infantry divisions covering the flanks, into the Verkhopene – Kochetovka sector with orders to blast a way through to Oboyan. On 9 July, with German tanks approaching 6 Gds Army's headquarters at Kochetovka, Chistyakov was forced to withdraw his main headquarters to 1 Tank Army's area leaving his chief of staff, Major-Gen V A Penkovsky, at Kochetovka with a forward battle headquarters to maintain contact with the rifle divisions. By the evening Chistyakov had established a new defensive area for 6 Gds Army but German forces were within 20km of Oboyan. In order to speed up the advance, Hoth decided to switch the axis of his main effort from due north towards

Oboyan to the northeast in order to gain the high ground around Prokhorovka, from which he could outflank Oboyan from the east and open the road to Kursk.

By 9 July, despite 7 Gds Army having been reinforced on its right flank by 69 Army, Army Detachment Kempf had pushed a deep bulge into the Soviet line in its drive north towards Prokhorovka. Having been formally subordinated to Vatutin's command, 5 Gds Tank Army was being deployed northwest of Prokhorovka. Meanwhile 27 Army with 4 Gds Tank Corps was deployed to Kursk, 53 Army with 4 Mech Corps was deployed to the southeast of the city, and 5 Gds Army reinforced with 2 Tank Corps and 2 Gds Tank Corps was being moved under cover of darkness to positions on the Psel between Oboyan and Prokhorovka with orders to be fully deployed by 11 July. Despite the fact that throughout 10 July Hoth continued a concerted drive north towards Oboyan, Vatutin was aware of the change of operational axis of IV Pz Army. Recognising that to find the forces to mount the simultaneous efforts against Oboyan and Prokhorovka, Hoth had been obliged to weaken his flanks, Vatutin obtained permission from STAVKA to attack in a series of concentric blows from east, north and west into IV Pz Army's penetration of his frontline. Early on the morning of 11 July Breith's three panzer divisions, together with three infantry divisions, attacked north towards Prokhorovka, and a few hours later XLVIII Pz Corps attacked towards Oboyan. At 09:30 the three SS divisions began the main effort northeast to Prokhorovka. The relatively good progress the Germans had made in the south compared to the north was ascribed by STAVKA to Vatutin having spread his forces too thinly over too great a distance. STAVKA's nervousness over the situation in Vatutin's sector is reflected in the fact that by 11 July the responsibility for the defence of Prokhorovka had been assumed by Zhukov and Vasilevsky.

The First Soviet Summer Offensive

The contrast between Vatutin's problems at Oboyan/Prokhorovka and the situation on the northern face of the Kursk salient could not have been greater, for on 11 July, having concluded that IX Army's offensive had been contained, STAVKA authorised reinforced reconnaissance battalions from Bryansk Front and the left flank of Western Front to begin to probe II Pz Army's defences along the Orel bulge. The Soviet attacks were recognised by Army Group Centre as preparations for a major offensive and they had an immediate effect, diverting resources from IX Army to II Pz Army. In fact the impending offensive against Orel was the start of a rolling series of Soviet offensives across the entire Eastern Front that were to continue unabated for the next nine months. At dawn on 12 July, after a two-hour artillery bombardment, the Soviet offensive began and, for all practical purposes, the *Ostheer*'s actions after that date represented an unsuccessful twenty-two months long exercise in damage limitation. The next day Hitler placed II Pz Army under IX Army's (i.e. Model's) command. Bagramyan's powerful 11 Gds Army, attacking almost due south towards Khotinets made surprisingly good progress against II Pz Army's defence but no mobile exploitation force was available to support Bagramyan's success. Orders were issued for 4 Tank Army to move to the area but this would take time. Along other sectors of the Orel salient the Soviet attacks were less successful, coordination between infantry and artillery often being poorly managed, and the artillery bombardments proving to be poorly targeted. The offensive was accompanied by a well-planned partisan offensive that was expected to starve Army Group Centre of supplies and inhibit its ability to manoeuvre, yet, though very destructive, the partisan efforts were less effective than STAVKA had hoped.

Meanwhile in the south, 12 July was to be the climactic day for Manstein's efforts to make Operation Citadel a success. By dawn of that day, with 6 Pz Div and 7 Pz Div of III Pz Corps 12km south of the SS divisions moving on Prokhorovka from the west, 5 Gds Tank Army together with as much of 5 Gds Army as was available off the march, was committed to the offensive at Prokhorovka. Rotmistrov's instructions to his men were simple; "Forward, forward!" (Rotmistrov had told his tank crews to close to less than 500 metres). However the counter-offensive from 5 Gds Tank Army had been anticipated and Hausser had put II SS Pz Corps onto the defensive that morning. By the end of the day Rotmistrov's four tank corps reported the loss of 340 tanks from a total of 654 operational armoured fighting vehicles (29 Tank Corps lost nearly three-quarters of its tanks) prompting Stalin to ask of Rotmistrov: "Tell me, idiot, how you lost your army"; and there were credible reports that Stalin intended to prosecute Rotmistrov for the events of 12 July. Certainly the T34s had to close with the Tigers in order to be able to fight them on anything like equal terms and two-fifths of Rotmistrov's tanks were the light T70s. On a score of occasions desperate Soviet tank commanders were reduced to ramming the German armoured fighting vehicles. The result was a tactical defeat for the Soviets with a far greater number of Soviet tanks destroyed, but a strategic defeat for Germany since Army Group South's forces had been held all along their line of advance and their prospects of achieving the objectives of Citadel, the encirclement and destruction of Voronezh Front and Central Front, were disappearing. Although fierce fighting was to continue around Prokhorovka for several more days, and although by 13 July a sizable Soviet force had become trapped between the right flank of II SS Pz Corps and the left flank of III Pz Corps, Hitler, citing primarily the Allied invasion of Sicily on 10 July, but also because of the opening of the Soviet offensive against Orel and what appeared to be an impending Soviet offensive in the Donbas, began to divert resources from the Citadel offensive. In particular XXIV Pz Corps, which had been in transit from I Pz Army to support IV Pz Army, was returned to the I Pz Army sector. In addition, Hitler made clear his intention to transfer Hausser's corps to Italy as soon as the situation on the Eastern Front could be stabilised.

See Map 18 By 14 July, Western Front had been reinforced with 11 Army, and 11 Gds Army had penetrated 15km into II Pz Army's lines in the north. On the same day, the right flank armies of Central Front joined in the offensive against the Orel salient by attacking to the north, 2 Tank Army penetrating towards Kromy. Two days later, as Kluge was struggling to contain the Soviet advances into the Orel salient and Manstein began to pull his left flank back to the pre-Citadel positions, STAVKA issued orders for Konev's Steppe Front to become operational, which it did late on 18 July. Having relinquished three armies to Voronezh Front, Konev only had 53 Army and 47 Army remaining but he was assigned 7 Gds Army and 69 Army from Voronezh Front, and he assumed responsibility for the section of front opposite Army Detachment Kempf to the east of Belgorod. To add to OKH's woes, on 17 July a sixteen-day offensive was opened by Tolbukhin's Southern Front against VI Army along the Mius line. The offensive, conducted in conjunction with Southwestern Front attacking across the Donets southeast of Izyum, was ultimately unsuccessful but it did cause Army Group South to divert panzer divisions away from the Belgorod area to the Donbas during the second half of July.

In the Orel salient 11 Gds Army's advance was, by 17 July, slowing against stiffening German resistance, and 4 Tank Army had still not arrived. By the next day Bagramyan's offensive had stalled just 20km from Khotinets. On 19 July Rybalko's 3 Gds Tank Army, assigned to Bryansk Front, was committed to support the stalled westerly offensives of 3 Army and 63 Army by attacking from Novosil towards Kromy via Stanovoi-Kodolez, an offensive that STAVKA thought would also assist Central Front's northerly offensive. In fact 3 Gds Tank Army (essentially 12 Tank Corps, 15 Tank Corps and 2 Mech Corps) quickly ran into stiff opposition from German armoured forces and stalled. On 20 July Rybalko was turned 180 degrees to attack northeast in order to assist 3 Army in crossing the Oka. The tank army was then, under Stalin's direct order, turned back to the southwest and again assigned the task of taking Stanovoi-Kodolez, this time by 22 July. After several days assaulting well defended positions, 3 Gds Tank Army, by then a much weakened force, was withdrawn into reserve and reassigned to Central Front. Badanov's 4 Tank Army (11 Tank Corps, 30 Tank Corps and 6 Gds Mech Corps) was not in position to support Bagramyan until 26 July. By then four panzer divisions were in position in the Orel salient to repel any armoured advance, and Badanov's five-hundred brand new tanks, ordered by STAVKA to attack Bolkhov instead of driving into the German rear through Khotinets, suffered heavy losses and made little progress. At this point 11 Gds Army, 11 Army, 4 Tank Army and an operational group under Kriukov came under the command of Bryansk Front as 3 Army and 63 Army were ordered to increase their efforts to take Orel from the east. However, as a result of 4 Tank Army's efforts, a considerable German force had been placed under threat of encirclement in the Bolkhov area, and German forces began to pull out of the Bolkhov pocket, pursued closely by 61 Army. In fact the Bolkhov withdrawal became part of a wider withdrawal of German forces from the Orel salient after Kluge was informed by Hitler on 26 July that Army Group Centre would be required to release around a dozen divisions for deployment elsewhere. This could only be done by reducing the frontline and this in turn meant a withdrawal of IX Army / II Pz Army to the incomplete defences of the Hagen Line, which ran north to south just 20km east of Bryansk from Kirov to the north-western tip of the Kursk salient. Model's withdrawal from the Orel Salient began on 1 August, Orel was taken by Soviet forces on 5 August and by 17 August the last German forces had retired into the Hagen defences. By then IX Army had formally taken over the II Pz Army positions, and the headquarters of II Pz Army was withdrawn and subsequently deployed to the Balkans for the defence of the eastern Adriatic against a possible landing by the Western Allies. For Bryansk Front, the rapidly shortening frontline that resulted from the German retreat to the Hagen Line meant the withdrawal of 61 Army from the Orel sector in mid-August and its subsequent redeployment to the Ukraine. At the same time, on the German side of the frontline, XLVII Pz Corps was transferred to the Ukraine from IX Army.

In the Belgorod area the Germans had returned to their Citadel start line by 23 July and Steppe Front occupied the line from Volchansk to north of Tomarovka. There the Soviet forces paused for eleven days for resupply and reinforcement. After elaborate Soviet deception plans and the diversion of German armoured forces, including II SS Pz Corps and III Pz Corps, from the Belgorod area to the Donbas region to deal with Tolbukhin's offensive, an offensive by Voronezh Front and Steppe Front (the Belgorod-Kharkov Operation) commenced on 3 August towards Belgorod. This offensive completely wrong-footed Manstein who had approved the diversion of the panzer forces to the south on the assumption that Voronezh and Steppe Fronts were incapable of immediate further offensive action after the events of the first half of July. He had expected a Soviet offensive against Kharkov, but not until later in August. That offensive, using 5 Gds Army, 6 Gds Army and 53 Army together with 48 Rifle Corps of 69 Army, was launched along a sector of just 30km from Gertsovka to the northern Donets east of Gostishchevo. It was coordinated by Zhukov and avoided the failings of the offensive against the Orel salient – unsophisticated artillery bombardment and ineffective deployment of armoured forces on the wrong axis at the wrong time. Katukov's and Rotmistrov's two tank armies were to be concentrated in the area of 5 Gds Army, would operate in dense formations of up to 70 tanks per kilometre, and would be configured for rapid breakthrough in considerable depth. The artillery was similarly concentrated to bring more than 200 guns per kilometre onto the main penetration axes in order to create a barrage curtain across the first German defence line, a barrage curtain stretching back more than a kilometre. This was not the 'routine stuff' about which Zhukov had made bitter complaint during the Orel offensive. The August offensive demonstrated the growing power and sophistication of Soviet offensive action with each attacking rifle division having so much artillery support that it had specialised multi-battalion artillery groups to support the attacking infantry regiments and additional heavy artillery to bombard rear assembly areas to disrupt rear area defence. Zhukov aimed the main weight of the offensive at the junction of IV Pz Army's two remaining corps and at the junction of IV Pz Army and Army Detachment Kempf in what was to become a hallmark Soviet offensive practice – launching offensives where possible at the junctions of major German formations where a coordinated enemy response would prove more difficult to organise. By the end of the first day the defending 167 Inf Div on the right flank of LII Corps northeast of Tomorovka was largely shattered. Manstein reacted quickly, deploying 6 Pz Div the next day to try to close the breach, but a 12km gap in the German lines remained open. Nonetheless it took the early commitment of elements of 1 Tank Army and 5 Gds Tank Army to achieve the final penetration of the German lines. It had been intended that these forces would be held back to exploit the penetration in an advance to the north and northwest of Kharkov, and, as a result, the exploitation phase did not get fully underway until 6 August, though 20km to the east 7 Gds Army and 69 Army supported by 1 Mech Corps had encircled several thousand German troops in Belgorod by 5 August. Supporting the main offensive on the right, 40 Army and 27 Army attacked from the south-western corner of the Kursk salient in the direction of Akhtyrka (an advance that threatened the encirclement of five German divisions between Borisovka and Golovchino) and Steppe Front's 7 Gds Army, operating with 69 Army, after clearing Belgorod was tasked with advancing along the Donets towards Kharkov. Meanwhile, in a thrust farther south, 57 Army had crossed the Donets and had taken Chuguyev. Hitler cancelled the transfer of 2 SS Pz Gdr Div and 3 SS Pz Gdr Div out of theatre and these SS divisions together with 3 Pz Div were assigned to III

Pz Corps.[2] As further reinforcement Manstein received 7 Pz Div which had previously been withdrawn to OKH reserve. He also received three divisions from Army Group A, and *Grossdeutschland* Div, returned to him after a brief transfer to Army Group Centre, was deployed to the Akhtyrka area. Yet given the scale of the Soviet offensive this was inadequate reinforcement. To expand its room for manoeuvre, IV Pz Army assumed responsibility for 60km of frontline and the four associated divisions of VII Corps on the right flank of II Army, but there was little that Hoth could do to close the widening gap between his own right flank and the left flank of Kempf's group. By 8 August that gap was 60km wide. Konev was assigned 57 Army from the right flank of Southwestern Front and he was also assigned 5 Gds Tank Army, the latter operating within the area of 53 Army moving on Kharkov from the northwest.[3]

A thrust south of Bogodukov, some 30km northwest of Kharkov, on 11 August by 1 Tank Army and part of 6 Gds Army was held by a German counter-attack from 2 SS Pz Gdr Div, 3 SS Pz Gdr Div and 5 SS Pz Gdr Div (*Wiking*) that lasted until 17 August. However, the commitment of the SS divisions to this counter-offensive meant that they were unavailable for the defence of Kharkov, and on 12 August Kempf proposed to abandon the city. This proposal was categorically rejected by Hitler, to which Kempf retorted that the threatened encirclement of Kharkov from the north and east would result in another Stalingrad. Two days later on 14 August, as Konev's forces were battling their way into Kharkov's suburbs, Kempf was relieved of command. He was replaced on 16 August by General Otto Woehler, the former commander of I Corps, and the next day the army detachment was redesignated VIII Army. The counter-attack by the SS divisions northwest of Kharkov, and a build up of German forces farther west near Akhtyrka prompted Vatutin to commit his four right flank armies, reinforced with three tank corps, to further offensive effort in order to counter the German moves. Pressure on Army Group South increased on 13 August when Southwestern Front launched a major offensive into the Donbas, and five days later Southern Front launch another offensive against the Mius river line. On 18 August Vatutin launched a concentrated attack on XLVIII Pz Corps' 57 Inf Div, which was holding a section of line midway between Akhtyrka and Sumy. Within two days 57 Inf Div had been reduced to the status of a regimental-sized battlegroup, and a 15km gap had been opened in the centre of IV Pz Army's front. A little of Manstein's gloom was lifted on 18 August when *Grossdeutschland* Div and 7 Pz Div, operating under IV Pz Army's command, broke out of a bridgehead at Akhtyrka and by 20 August had established contact with 3 SS Pz Gdr Div in VIII Army's zone. Despite the fact that by 20 August Vatutin's right flank had passed to the north of Akhtyrka, penetrating some 30km farther to the west and threatening the German defence of the town, the linking of IV Pz Army with VIII Army had eliminated the immediate potential threat to Poltava (and consequently to Army Group A and the right flank of Army Group South).

Yet the threat to VIII Army's grip on Kharkov remained. Steppe Front continued to close in on the city and by 22 August the Front's 5 Gds Tank Army and 53 Army were west and southwest of Kharkov, while 7 Gds Army and 57 Army were to the

---

2   Hausser's headquarters and 1 SS Pz Gdr Div were already in transit to Italy.

3   47 Army was transferred from Steppe Front to the right flank of Voronezh Front for deployment between 38 Army and 40 Army.

east and southeast. Woehler, like Kempf before him, formally requested permission to abandon the Soviet Union's 'fourth city'. This time Hitler acquiesced and on 22 August German forces began to withdraw. Kharkov had changed hands for the fourth and final time, and a delighted Stalin rewarded Konev with a promotion. Meanwhile Hoth was attempting to deal with the Soviet breakthrough in the centre of his front that could again threaten Poltava, this time from farther west. As a result of this breakthrough, German forces began to pull back from Akhtyrka, concerned about a potential envelopment on their left flank. This withdrawal released forces that by 25 August had allowed Hoth to assemble two divisions for a counter-attack into the gap. The counter-attack was successful and by 27 August IV Pz Army had managed to establish a continuous front while maintaining its link with VIII Army.

On 26 August Central Front launched an offensive against II Army in the direction of Sevsk. Although Sevsk was taken on the first day, the offensive quickly stalled and 2 Tank Army suffered heavy losses when Weiss counter-attacked using reserves drawn from IX Army.[4] However, while the Soviet offensive at Sevsk was being held, a supporting attack farther south by Central Front's 60 Army broke through II Army's lines near Rylsk, slicing off Siebert's XIII Corps from the rest of II Army. Reinforcing success, Rokossovsky shifted his main effort to his left flank, and 38 Army was removed temporarily from Voronezh Front's command to be placed at Rokossovsky's disposal. With XIII Corps isolated south of this breakthrough, and with Rokossovsky diverting 13 Army from farther north into the breach, Siebert was given permission to bend his line back southwest of Rylsk. For the *Ostheer* the effect of this change in direction of Rokossovsky's offensive was to move the burden of defence from the right flank of Army Group Centre to the left flank of Army Group South. Kluge found the easing of the burden on his right flank to be entirely welcome, for on 28 August Western Front renewed an offensive against his centre that had begun three weeks earlier. On 7 August Sokolovsky launched Operation Suvorov, an assault to be supported six days later by the left flank of Kalinin Front, with the objective of ejecting German forces, predominantly III Pz Army, IV Army and elements of II Pz Army that had not at that time been incorporated into IX Army, from the Smolensk and Bryansk regions. This first phase of Operation Suvorov made little progress, and although Spas Demensk was taken on 13 August, by the third week of August the offensive had petered out. Eremenko renewed his efforts against the boundary of III Pz Army and IV Army on 23 August with no better result. Using 10 Gds Army and a new formation of 21 Army, by 28 August Sokolovsky had realigned the axis of his offensive west towards Elnia rather than southwest towards Roslavl, and his forces took Elnia three days later. Dorogobuzh fell to Western Front at the beginning of September, but Sokolovsky then came up against a well-defended German line and was forced to halt again to prepare for a renewed offensive in mid-September. By 3 September the pressure against Army Group Centre had eased somewhat and II Army, in the process of being further reinforced with XXXV Corps from Model's command, was able to begin a relatively untroubled withdrawal to the Desna. However this withdrawal and Rokossovsky's continuing offensive against IV Pz Army, to which XIII Corps had been

---

4   XX Corps had been assigned to II Army in the first half of August, and at the end of the month LVI Pz Corps Headquarters, having been transferred from IV Army to IX Army in the second half of August, was redeployed to II Army.

assigned, resulted in an 80km gap between Army Group Centre and Army Group South as Central Front reached the Desna on a broad front.

In the north STAVKA found the progress of its operations to be disappointing. Towards the end of July Leningrad and Volkhov Fronts had begun an offensive against Army Group North's positions around Mga. On 23 August Govorov and Meretskov ended this largely fruitless offensive, one that never seriously threatened Army Group North, and which was seen by Kuechler as primarily an attempted to tie down German forces in the north.

Despite the considerable successes of the summer, Stalin's ambitions were much wider, almost excessively so, and after the offensive in the Orel – Kharkov sector, STAVKA planned a phased autumn/winter offensive along the entire Eastern Front. Stalin had reason to be confident. The Red Army was beginning to master the art of balancing the actions of a series of Fronts; creating local superiority, preventing the Germans from either redeploying effectively or taking full advantage of areas of Soviet weakness; employing successful tactical solutions to breaking deep and strongly fortified defensive lines; supplying armies effectively during large scale advances; and matching objectives with the resources necessary for their achievement.

The situation in the south seemed particularly rich with opportunity. Not only was there an enormous gap between Kluge's and Manstein's army groups, but Soviet forces were on the Desna. A strike south from west of Akhtyrka through Poltava could carry the Red Army across the Dnieper north of its great bend between Kremenchug and Dnepropetrovsk. From there continued penetration to the south could isolate the bulk of Army Group South and the whole of Army Group A in the Crimea and around the Sea of Azov.

The Eastern Rampart

On 11 August 1943 OKH issued orders for the construction of a strategic defensive line, the Eastern Rampart or East Wall, which stretched from the Narva, along Lake Peipus, east of the key towns of Pskov, Vitebsk and Orsha and to the Sozh at Propoisk. From there the defence line ran down the Sozh east of Gomel and across to the Desna at Chernigov, down the Desna to the Dnieper, along the middle Dnieper to Zaporozhe and along the Molochnaya to the Sea of Azov at Melitopol. The Eastern Rampart also included the Kerch Peninsula. Hitler had been reluctant to sanction its construction because an eastern defence line was, by definition, acknowledgement that Germany was strategically on the defensive in the east. In addition, Hitler was concerned that once this defence line was complete it would be seen by the *Ostheer's* troops and its generals as a boundary beyond which it was unnecessary to engage in major defensive battles with the Red Army. Yet the eruption of Soviet offensives along See Map 19 almost the entire frontline from Mga to Taganrog had left OKH with little option but to create a precautionary strategic backstop line. At Hitler's insistence the term 'Eastern Rampart' was not widely used. The line in the Army Group North and Army Group Centre zones was given the codename Panther; farther south its codename was Wotan. At the end of August 1943 Army Group South and Army Group A could muster 52 infantry divisions and 16 panzer or panzer grenadier divisions, forces that including the five divisions transferred from IX Army. Farther north Army Group Centre had 57 infantry divisions, 7 panzer divisions and 3 panzer grenadier divisions; though in reality more than a dozen of these divisions were little more than battlegroups. More than half of Army Group Centre's divisions were in well-entrenched positions, but Kluge had little confidence that his forces would be able to withstand a concerted Soviet autumn offensive.

If the pressure against Army Group Centre was diminishing at the end of August, that against Army Group South was growing. An offensive by Southern Front at the end of that month had succeeded in shattering the Mius river line defences and Taganrog was taken. On 2 September Lelyushenko's 3 Gds Army of Southwestern Front forced the Donets between Izyum and Voroshilovgrad, and four days later Lt-Gen Russiyanov's 1 Gds Mech Corps, amply supported by rifle divisions, broke through the I Pz Army / VI Army boundary.

During August Vatutin saw several significant changes to his Front's order of battle; Lt-Gen Koroteev's 52 Army and 4 Gds Army were released from High Command reserve and assigned to Voronezh Front, and at the end of the month 70 Army was withdrawn to High Command reserve, Galanin being reassigned from 70 Army to command 4 Gds Army. On 4 September Voronezh Front joined Rokossovsky's offensive against Manstein's left wing, launching a powerful attack with its right flank on a broad front between the Psel and the Vorskla using 52 Army and several tank and mechanised corps. To support this offensive 3 Gds Tank Army was in the process of being transferred to Vatutin from Central Front. By the end of the first week of September the left flank of Central Front and the right flank of Voronezh Front had pushed on towards Konotop and Romny. Hitler responded by promising Manstein four infantry divisions for the defence of the Dnieper, and four more divisions, two of them panzer divisions, from Army Group Centre to close the gap between II Army and IV Pz Army. However, of the divisions from Army Group Centre, three were to come from II Army and, with the crossing of the Desna south of Novgorod-Seversky by Central Front's 65 Army on 9 September, II Army could not spare them.

The advance of Rokossovsky's and Vatutin's forces to Konotop and Romny prompted STAVKA to consider the strategic possibilities that could be derived from a major Soviet breakthrough to the Dnieper. These included the complete splitting of Army Group South from Army Group Centre, the liberation of Kiev, and the encirclement of Army Group South by a sweep south to the Bug. Stalin's confidence was boosted by Tolbukhin's success in the south, where STAVKA had begun to withdraw forces from Malinovsky's command in order to reinforce Southern Front. On the night of 6 September Stalin issued revised orders for the Fronts and a realignment of the Fronts' boundaries. The left flank of Central Front, in the process of being reinforced with Belov's 61 Army, would attack towards Chernigov, and the Front's right flank would attack towards Gomel; Voronezh Front, by this time reinforced with 3 Gds Tank Army and 1 Gds Cav Corps, would strike towards the Bukrin bend of the Dnieper in order to outflank Kiev from the south; and Steppe Front would aim for Kremenchug. Konev's command was being reinforced with three armies; Lt-Gen M N Sharokhin's 37 Army, which had been withdrawn from North Caucasian Front into High Command reserve in July; Zhadov's 5 Gds Army from Voronezh Front; and Glagolev's 46 Army from Southwestern Front. At the same time 5 Gds Tank Army was withdrawn from Steppe Front and taken into High Command reserve.

On 7 September the previous day's breakthrough of 1 Gds Mech Corps on the I Pz Army / VI Army boundary was reinforced by 23 Tank Corps in a race to the west that by the next day had taken the two corps close to Pavlograd. Also on 8 September, Tsvetaev's 5 Shock Army of Southern Front took Stalino, prompting Hitler to agree to the abandonment of the Donets basin and the withdrawal of I Pz Army and VI Army to the Wotan Line. Mackensen and Hollidt bought themselves some freedom of manoeuvre in this withdrawal when, on 12 September, retreating rapidly to the west, they re-established contact and in the process surrounded 1 Gds Mech Corps and 23 Tank Corps near Pavlograd. Only part of the surrounded force was able to break out to Soviet lines two days later and, thereafter, the German retreat to the west slowed. As a result VI Army was able to hold the insubstantial Molochnaya river line, thereby keeping open the overland communication links with the Crimea.

On 9/10 September the newly-promoted Col-Gen I E Petrov launched a well-prepared offensive by the three armies of North Caucasian Front against the thirteen divisions of Jaenecke's XVII Army in the Taman Peninsula. As Major-Gen A A Grechkin's 9 Army and Lt-Gen A A Grechko's 56 Army attacked the German Blue Line defences directly from the east, Leselidze's 18 Army, in conjunction with the Black Sea Fleet supporting amphibious landings behind the Blue Line positions, made a final attempt to take Novorossiysk. The port fell on 16 September and Leselidze immediately moved his forces out to the northwest, to the Neberjayevsky Pass some 10km inland, thereby compromising Jaenecke's ability to defend the Blue Line. The decision to abandon the Blue Line had in fact been taken before the Soviet offensive began. Through most of August Kleist had been lobbying for a withdrawal of XVII Army to the Crimea, and authorisation was given by Hitler on 3 September, nearly a week before Petrov began his attacks. Hence the Soviet offensive only served to accelerate a process that would have been completed anyway. In the second half of September Jaenecke began a measured withdrawal, first to Taman and then across the Kerch Strait to the Crimea where Kleist had a further eight divisions in the Crimea Operational Group. By 9 October the last German troops had left the Taman Peninsula and Petrov was rewarded with a second promotion to the rank of Army General.

By mid-September the frontline in the Ukraine was in a state of flux in which the Soviet advance to the Dnieper was being constrained more by the Red Army's shortage of transport than by enemy action. In the southern Ukraine VI Army, its centre anchored on Melitopol, was transferred to Army Group A on 15 September.[5] The transfer of VI Army was at Kleist's request since he suspected that Manstein might move forces north from VI Army to where they were certainly desperately needed, and thereby risk the isolation of Army Group A in the Crimea should Hollidt be driven back across the Nogay Steppe to the lower Dnieper. On Manstein's left flank, IV Pz Army was on the point of collapse, having been split into three separate groups with 60 Army enlarging its bridgeheads on the right bank of the Desna while 61 Army and 7 Gds Cav Corps pushed forward between 13 Army and 65 Army. During the second week of September Hoth had received Chevallerie's LIX Corps Headquarters, transferred to IV Pz Army from III Pz Army to assume command of the forces on Hoth's left flank, and on 12 September Hoth had assumed command of all units south of the Desna, a change that gave him command of II Army's 8 Pz Div. Since II Army

---

5   Less VI Army's left flank corps which went to I Pz Army.

could not spare any more of the divisions promised by Hitler to Army Group South from Army Group Centre,[6] Kluge had been obliged to take two divisions from IV Army for transfer to Manstein, a move that weakened the Smolensk defences where a Soviet offensive was expected at any time. Kluge knew that IV Army would have to retreat when this offensive started, and with the retreat of II Army already underway, IX Army would be exposed on both flanks.[7] On 14 September the renewed offensive by Western Front and Kalinin Front against Army Group Centre opened with the left flank of Western Front aiming for the upper Desna and Roslavl, the centre for Smolensk, and the right, in cooperation with Kalinin Front, the Yartsevo area.

In the Ukraine 61 Army, 7 Gds Cav Corps and 13 Army had, by 15 September, reached Nezhin, more than 50km west of Konotop, and the right flank of Voronezh Front had outflanked Poltava and had pushed more than half a dozen German divisions towards the Dnieper near Kanev. At this point Rokossovsky wanted to turn 60 Army south into the flank of these divisions, a move that might possibly cut off the further retreat to the west of up to a dozen German divisions. However Zhukov, perhaps with an eye to the larger prize of the encirclement of the whole of Army Group South, insisted on a continued drive to the west since, by mid-September, there was clearly a general German withdrawal to the Wotan Line. This German withdrawal had been authorised by Hitler, to whom the threat presented by the Soviet advances had been made abundantly clear. Yet Hitler gave the withdrawal order with great reluctance, and it was done for the sole purpose of stopping the Red Army once and for all on the Eastern Rampart.

On the night of 14 September, after the magnitude of the developing offensive against Army Group Centre had been gauged, Kluge, with OKH's approval, gave II Army permission to fall back west of the Desna and he ordered Model to begin the withdrawal of the centre of IX Army. By 16 September Lt-Gen V S Popov's 10 Army from Western Front was across the upper Desna, and farther north Yartsevo had fallen to Soviet forces after fierce fighting. On 17 September, with Army Group Centre conducting its planned and measured withdrawal to the Eastern Rampart, 11 Gds Army of Bryansk Front took Bryansk and M M Popov was ordered to move his Front's forces forward to the Sozh no later than 3 October in order to be able strike into the flank of Army Group Centre. On 19 September Army Group North took command of XLIII Corps on Kluge's left flank, thereby acquiring three additional divisions but also 80km of additional front containing the Novosokolniki and Nevel communication hubs. Towards the end of the month it was becoming clear to OKH that a major Soviet offensive in the vicinity of the new Army Group North – Army Group Centre boundary some 20km southeast of Nevel was in preparation.

Meanwhile, in the Ukraine, Hoth had been given permission to break contact with VIII Army, to pull back to the west, and to position IV Pz Army east of Kiev. By 18 September Hoth had pulled his forces back far enough to establish some cohesion within his army. The withdrawal order was also issued to VIII Army and came as a huge relief to Woehler. Since the beginning of September VIII Army had been attenuated

---

6   II Army was committing two security divisions and a Hungarian division, none of which were considered to be effective combat units, to the defence of its extending right flank.

7   A Soviet cavalry corps had by that time penetrated IX Army's left flank and had taken Zhukovka, thereby cutting the Bryansk – Roslavl railway.

to the point where it could no longer maintain a continuous front. This was despite the fact that rear service units had been stripped of manpower to man the frontline; only 'sole surviving sons' and 'fathers of large families' were left in VIII Army's rear echelon positions – categories designated by Hitler as exempt from frontline duty. The threadbare condition of IV Pz Army and VIII Army was something that Manstein's shuffling of corps commands between the two armies during September could not mitigate. The next problem for Manstein was getting his army group, which covered a 600km front, back across the Dnieper using the five available crossings at Kiev, Kanev, Cherkassy, Kremenchug and Dnepropetrovsk. Hitler also insisted that I Pz Army should adequately secure the Zaporozhe bridgehead east of the Dnieper bend in order to protect VI Army's left flank and the Nikopol mineral mines.[8]

In Army Group Centre's area Kluge's measured withdrawal was disrupted by the loss to Kalinin Front of Demidov on III Pz Army's right flank, and by the threat of disintegration of IV Pz Army's front, which had the potential to allow an advance by Central Front behind II Army's flank towards Gomel. Hence by the last week in September the withdrawal to the Panther Line had degenerated into something of a scramble. If it was a scramble along Army Group Centre's front, in Manstein's area the withdrawal had become little more than a race with the Red Army to the Dnieper. Soviet commanders at every level were exhorted by threats and inducements to get their troops to, and across, the river without delay. On 19 September lead elements of Rokossovsky's forces crossed the Dnieper at its confluence with the Pripet. Between 19 September and 23 September the lead elements of Vatutin's forces reached the Dnieper north and south of Kiev and established a bridgehead at the bend of the Dnieper at Bukrin. On 21 September Rokossovsky moved Cherniakhovsky's 60 Army farther north from its bridgeheads over the Desna, and Vatutin directed 38 Army farther north in order to force the Desna at Pukhovka. From Pukhovka, Chibisov was tasked with establishing a bridgehead across the Dnieper north of Kiev by 27 September from where, in cooperation with Moskalenko's 40 Army, he would be required to encircle Kiev.

The first Soviet forces to cross the Dnieper south of Kiev were from 40 Army and from Rybalko's 3 Gds Tank Army on 22 September (having advanced more than 150km in four days), and by 24 September a viable bridgehead some 15km wide had been established 80km southeast of Kiev at Bukrin. This was just one of forty improvised crossings that had been made by 26 September, most of which were south of the city, though 40 Army also had a small bridgehead north of Kiev, and by the end of the month Central Front's bridgehead at the confluence of the Dnieper and Pripet had been extended 25km west on both sides of the Pripet. The Bukrin crossing was supported by an improvised airborne assault by two airborne brigades on the night of 23 September but due to poor preparation (aircraft with insufficient fuel, inability to transport anti-tank equipment, and inadequate radio communication equipment) and a series of operational blunders in which troops were dropped in a widely dispersed pattern and even on the wrong side of the river, the airborne assault ended in unmitigated failure. By 24 September Shumilov's 7 Gds Army and Sharokhin's 37 Army from Steppe Front had begun crossing the Dnieper south of Kremenchug, and on 28 September this fortress town was taken by two of Konev's other armies,

8   VI Army had withdrawn behind the Eastern Rampart by 20 September.

Zhadov's 5 Gds Army[9] and Managorov's 53 Army. The forces of Southwestern Front reached the Dnieper on 26 September when detachments of Lt-Gen I T Shlemin's 6 Army seized two small bridgeheads south of Dnepropetrovsk. Between 27 and 29 September Voronezh Front's 38 Army seized two small bridgeheads north of Kiev in the Svaromya – Lutezh area that were subsequently linked to form a single lodgement 15km long and 10km deep. Such had been the speed of the Soviet drive to the Dnieper that the Germans had been unable to destroy or transport to the west much of the industrial infrastructure of the eastern Ukraine. Although by the end of the month Manstein's forces were across the river, they were struggling to establish a coherent front against the numerous Soviet bridgeheads on the west bank. Manstein had lost the opportunity to stop the Red Army on what should have been a formidable defence line, and Hitler was incensed at the speed and apparent ease with which the Red Army had breached the Eastern Rampart in the south.

At the beginning of October Army Group Centre, despite the transfer of forces to other fronts, was still the largest of the army groups in the east. It comprised 42 infantry divisions, eight panzer and panzer grenadier divisions and four *Luftwaffe* field divisions. However, as had been the case a month earlier, of Kluge's forces twelve infantry and four panzer 'divisions' were actually only regimental-sized battlegroups. Army Group Centre moved its last units into the Eastern Rampart positions on 2 October at which time a lull fell over most of the Eastern Front. It was a lull that was to last for no more than a few days, for on 29 September STAVKA had issued a directive requiring Voronezh Front to cooperate with the left wing of Central Front in taking Kiev and driving beyond the Ukrainian capital to reach Fastov and Belaya Tserkov and, subsequently, to attain the line Berdichev – Zhmerinka – Mogilev-Podolsky. Meanwhile, in the sector from Gomel to Vitebsk, Army Group Centre was to be attacked from the north by Kalinin Front, from the east by Western Front and from the south by Central Front. Although the Soviet offensives on the central axis had been less spectacularly successful than the offensives in the Ukraine, by the end of September Kalinin, Western and Bryansk Fronts had cleared up to the Eastern Rampart and, in recapturing Bryansk, Roslavl and Smolensk, had pinned significant German forces (up to sixteen divisions) in the central sector that were consequently unable to assist German forces in the south. Also, having been pushed back to the Pripet Marshes, the *Ostheer* lost the ability to easily transfer forces between the southern and central sectors.

The Soviet Autumn Offensives

The offensive that Kluge had been expecting from Kalinin Front on his left flank opened on 6 October when, after a diversionary attack by Eremenko's two left flank armies against the centre of III Pz Army, Galitsky's 3 Shock Army attacked the left flank division of III Pz Army, and Major-Gen V I Shvetsov's 4 Shock Army hit III Pz Army farther south in the Usvyaty area. Within hours of the opening of Eremenko's offensive Reinhardt's left flank division, a *Luftwaffe* field division, collapsed completely, and a Soviet mobile Guards rifle division with tank support turned northwest behind Army Group North's newly extended right flank to take Nevel during the afternoon. Hitler was infuriated at the loss of Nevel with its not inconsiderable fortifications, and

---

9   Zhadov's army was transferred from Voronezh Front to Steppe Front in September

he blamed the staff of XLIII Corps for incompetent handling of their resources. By 8 October a 25km gap had opened between Army Group North and Army Group Centre, but the next day Eremenko, unnerved by the ease and extent of the breakthrough, called a temporary halt. In the resultant pause the two army groups re-established contact and brought in reserves to stabilise the front. On Kluge's other flank II Army, having failed in early October to eliminate the large Central Front bridgehead over the Dnieper north of Chernobyl, had managed by 11 October to restore contact with Army Group South northwest of Chernobyl on the south side of the Pripet. Kluge was concerned about II Army, it had its back to the Pripet Marshes and, in addition to being vulnerable at its junction with Army Group South, was also vulnerable on its other flank where Central Front held bridgeheads on the west bank of the Sozh north and south of the Gomel communications hub. However, it was in the central area of II Army's front that Rokossovsky was planning to strike. On 15 October two of Rokossovsky's armies, 65 Army and 61 Army, attacked a 30km sector of the front around Loyev south of the confluence of the Sozh and Dnieper. The offensive made good progress and was joined by 48 Army attacking across the lower Sozh. By 20 October Rokossovsky's forces held a bridgehead over the Dnieper 100km long and 16km deep north of its confluence with the Pripet, favourable positions from which to launch a subsequent advance into southern Belorussia. Yet over the next two days Rokossovsky's forces were unable to advance much further towards Retchitsa, and on 22 October Rokossovsky abandoned this offensive and began to switch his forces to IX Army's sector of the front.[10] On 27 October Kluge was injured in a car accident and did not return to active service until July 1944 in France. His replacement at Army Group Centre was Busch from XVI Army, appointed on 29 October, his command at XVI Army being assumed by General Christian Hansen, the long-standing former commander of X Corps.

See Map 20

In the south Tolbukhin had been given the task of breaking VI Army's defence of the Molochnaya river line and closing up to the lower Dnieper, a key to which was I Pz Army's bridgehead at Zaporozhe in Southwestern Front's area. Southern Front's offensive opened on 9 October and was coordinated with an offensive by Southwestern Front. By mid-October Southern Front had breached the Molochnaya river fortifications and Lt-Gen I G Kreizer's 51 Army had reached Melitopol on 12 October. By the second week in October Malinovsky had breached the Dnieper defences north of Zaporozhe, and using Chuikov's 8 Gds Army, Danilov's 12 Army and Lelyushenko's 3 Gds Army together with the re-equipped 1 Gds Mech Corps and 23 Tank Corps, broke into the bridgehead itself, thereby exposing the left flank of VI Army. Manstein had already informed OKH that he intended to withdraw from the bridgehead and Hitler asked Kleist if Army Group A had sufficient forces to assume the defence of the Zaporozhe bridgehead from Army Group South. But Kleist was already fully committed defending the Melitopol area against Tolbukhin's offensive, and when 1 Gds Mech Corps and 23 Tank Corps reached the outskirts of Zaporozhe late on 13 October, Manstein ordered Mackensen to withdraw to the right bank of the river the next day. Farther north, from a bridgehead over the Dnieper midway between Kremenchug and Dnepropetrovsk, Konev's forces struck the left flank of I

---

10   STAVKA's instructions were for Rokossovsky to take Minsk with attacks through Zhlobin and Bobruisk.

Pz Army on 15 October. For this breakout Konev had concentrated 37 Army, 7 Gds Army and Gagen's 57 Army together with 5 Gds Tank Army recently released from High Command reserve, and he was in the process of transferring 5 Gds Army to the breakthrough from further upriver. The breakout was successful and Rotmistrov's tanks were committed on the afternoon of the first day.

During October STAVKA undertook a major restructuring and redesignation of the Fronts. On 8 October Bryansk Front was disbanded, the bulk of its forces being transferred to Central Front, and one week later Baltic Front was established on the Idritsa line of advance under the command of M M Popov.[11] On 20 October Kalinin Front was renamed 1 Baltic Front and the recently formed Baltic Front was renamed 2 Baltic Front.[12] Also on 20 October Central Front was renamed Belorussian Front; Voronezh Front was renamed 1 Ukrainian Front; Steppe Front was renamed 2 Ukrainian Front; Southwestern Front was renamed 3 Ukrainian Front; and Southern Front was renamed 4 Ukrainian Front.

By 18 October, three days after Konev began his breakout from his Dnieper bridgehead, the left flank of I Pz Army was in tatters and Pyatikhatka, some 50km west of the Dnieper, was in Soviet hands. Mackensen, expecting Konev to turn either right towards VIII Army's right flank at Kremenchug or left towards the centre of I Pz Army at Dnepropetrovsk, began to assemble a force of four panzer divisions for a counter-attack. Two of those divisions, 3 SS Pz Gdr Div (*Totenkopf*) and 11 Pz Div, were from VIII Army, and the other two, 14 Pz Div and 24 Pz Div, were in transit from Europe. In addition, on 20 October OKW released 384 Inf Div, 1 Pz Div, 25 Pz Div and 1 SS Pz Div for transfer to OKH command in the east.[13] In fact, contrary to Mackensen's expectations, Konev's forces did not turn but continued to the southwest threatening to isolate the whole of Manstein's right wing and Kleist's Army Group A east of the Ingulets. By 23 October Rotmistrov's tanks, in the van of Konev's advance, were on the outskirts of the communications hub and supply depot of Krivoi Rog, but they were unable to successfully storm the town off the march. By then I Pz Army was at risk of closer encirclement in the Dnieper bend after 3 Ukrainian Front's 8 Gds Army broke out of a small bridgehead on the Dnieper at Voyskovoye, and on 25 October General Hans Hube, who had taken over from Mackensen at 1 Pz Army two days earlier, was forced to abandon Dnepropetrovsk and subsequently Dneprodzerzhinsk to Malinovsky's forces.[14] Despite his problems in the Dnieper bend, Manstein was able to hold Konev's forces at Krivoi Rog, and on 24 October he transferred XL Pz Corps Headquarters from I Pz Army to the right flank of VIII Army with instructions to use 14 Pz Div and 24 Pz Div together with 3 SS Pz Gdr Div to counter-attack the right flank of 2 Ukrainian Front's penetration towards Krivoi Rog. (Henrici had fallen ill at the beginning of October and he was replaced as commander of XL Pz

---

11   The new Front was based on the headquarters staff of 58 Army, the army being disbanded at that time.

12   Popov had been assigned 11 Gds Army from his former Bryansk Front command and 6 Gds Army from High Command reserve, and he also acquired 22 Army from Kurochkin's Northwestern Front leaving the recently promoted Col-Gen Kurochkin with just nine rifle divisions in 1 Shock Army and 34 Army. On 20 November the depleted Northwestern Front was disbanded.

13   The 1 SS Pz Div was 1 SS Pz Gdr Div (*Leibstandarte*) refitted as a full panzer division.

14   Hube had been flown out of the Stalingrad cauldron in the second half of January 1943 and spent most of that year in Sicily and Italy.

Corps by General Ferdinand Schoerner, a committed Nazi known for his energy and determination as a corps commander in the Arctic).

Farther south, after twelve days of savage street fighting, Kreizer was finally able to clear Melitopol of German forces on 24 October. The loss of Melitopol split VI Army in two. South of the Soviet penetration were two German and two Rumanian divisions, the latter rapidly losing morale. When an attempt on 27 October by 13 Pz Div to close the breach from the north failed, and when three days later VI Army's southern wing was smashed by a new offensive from 51 Army and 28 Army, the northern wing began to fall back across the featureless Nogay Steppe towards Nikopol while the four divisions in the south abandoned any significant attempt at defence and retired to the lower Dnieper. By the beginning of November, 4 Ukrainian Front had reached the Perekop Isthmus into the Crimea, thereby isolating XVII Army in the peninsula, and Tolbukhin had secured bridgeheads on the southern shore of the Sivash. Hollidt was able to maintain a bridgehead on the left bank of the Dnieper at Nikopol but after the loss of overland contact with the Crimea, VI Army returned to Manstein's command. Thereafter, I Pz Army assumed responsibility for the Nikopol bridgehead, VI Army being responsible only for the defence of the lower Dnieper.

As early as 18 October Kleist had requested an evacuation of the Crimea because forces were being constantly withdrawn from the peninsula to strengthen VI Army. Marshal Ion Antonescu, the Rumainian leader, also wanted the peninsula to be abandoned but Hitler refused, citing the bombing and sea-borne invasion risk to the Rumanian oil fields as reasons to defend the Crimea. On 26 October as Soviet forces advanced west from Melitopol, Kleist authorised XVII Army to abandon the Crimea but this order was immediately countermanded by Hitler. By that time XVII Army was left with just one German and seven unreliable Rumanian divisions, and Jaenecke, contrary to orders, continued to prepare for an evacuation of the peninsula until threatened with dismissal by Kleist. During the first ten days of November North Caucasian Front's 18 Army, in an audacious amphibious assault with 56 Army, secured a small beachhead on the Kerch Peninsula northeast of Kerch, which it held against determined efforts by XVII Army to repel it.[15]

Manstein's counter-attack with XL Pz Corps against the right flank of Konev's deep penetration towards Krivoi Rog began on 27 October, and by 30 October Schoerner had forced 2 Ukrainian Front back around 30km, badly mauling two mechanised corps and nine rifle divisions in the process. After this success Hitler intended to transfer XL Pz Corps back to I Pz Army and, with the three panzer divisions released by OKW on 20 October, to use them in an offensive across the Nogay Steppe from the Nikopol bridgehead to re-establish contact with the Crimea.

Throughout October VIII Army had resisted strenuous efforts by Vatutin to break out of the Bukrin bridgehead, prompting STAVKA to change its plans. After a carefully disguised redeployment of forces that included the transfer of 3 Gds Tank Army from Bukrin north to Lutezh, Vatutin, on 1 November, launched a diversionary

---

15 On 20 November North Caucasian Front was reorganised into the Independent Black Sea Army under Petrov. Petrov's army was based on 56 Army, and 18 Army was withdrawn into High Command reserve.

offensive by 40 Army and 27 Army in the Bukrin bridgehead.[16] On 3 November the main offensive from the Lutezh bridgehead began, and Vatutin achieved a rapid breakout by 38 Army, 60 Army and 3 Gds Tank Army together with 1 Gds Cav Corps and Lt-Gen A G Kravchenko's 5 Gds Tank Corps. This breakout was achieved with the support of a massive concentration of artillery, some 300 guns per kilometre – an artillery concentration for which the defending VII Corps on the southern sector of the bridgehead was entirely unprepared. By 5 November IV Pz Army's front around Lutezh had collapsed, and that evening 38 Army and 5 Gds Tank Corps had reached Kiev. By the next day, with Soviet forces in complete control of the city, it was clear to Manstein that the Soviet offensive would continue to the southwest, potentially outflanking the entire Dnieper front in the Ukraine. He deployed 25 Pz Div, arriving from the west, to the Fastov area and was promised that the other two panzer divisions, still in transit from the west to the Nikopol area, would be diverted north. However, Manstein's proposal to also redeploy XL Pz Corps from I Pz Army to the Kiev area was refused; Hitler wanted the proposed offensive from I Pz Army's Nikopol bridgehead to go ahead as planned. By 8 November Manstein had concluded that I Pz Army did not have the strength to conduct the Nikopol offensive without reinforcement and the next day instructed Hube to plan the operation only on the basis of more forces becoming available, which they never did.

In fact during the first half of November Manstein's attention was almost exclusively focused on his left flank where IV Pz Army, having recently taken command of XXIV Pz Corps from the left flank of VIII Army, had been split into three parts that were beginning to be pushed in divergent directions. During the ten days after Vatutin had secured Kiev, 1 Ukrainian Front advanced to the northwest and to the west, but its main advance was, as Manstein had anticipated, to the southwest. As a result, IV Pz Army's LIX Corps on the left was being pushed northwest by 60 Army towards Korosten; Hoth's centre (XIII Corps, VII Corps and XLII Corps) was being pushed west towards Zhitomir; and General Walther Nehring's heavily reinforced XXIV Pz Corps on the right flank, still holding part of the Dnieper front, was having to bend its left flank as a barrier to Soviet forces moving south from Kiev. It was here that 3 Gds Tank Army took Fastov on 6/7 November.

General Arthur Hauffe had taken over command of XIII Corps from Siebert in September, and General Franz Mattenklott assumed command of XLII Corps in early October, but in fact during the final three months of 1943 Hauffe, Mattenklott and Dostler were shuffled around different commands by the panzer army headquarters, partly in response to prolonged leave taken by Hell during this time but primarily in response to the often chaotic and occasionally desperate disposition of the army's forces. What Hoth needed most was the promised reinforcement. After the loss of Fastov, General Heinrich Eberbach's XLVIII Pz Corps Headquarters was assigned to IV Pz Army from VIII Army to defend the Fastov area using the three panzer divisions that were still in the process of arriving from the west.[17] On 12 November Eberbach, his divisions still not fully assembled, was ordered to attack the left flank of 38 Army,

---

16   In late October, as part of the redeployment, Lt-Gen F F Zhmachenko assumed command of 40 Army and Moskalenko replaced Chibisov at 38 Army. By that time 13 Army and 60 Army had been transferred to the command of 1 Ukrainian Front.

17   XLVIII Pz Corps had been assigned to VIII Army from IV Pz Army in the first half of September.

which at that time was about to take Zhitomir. This offensive made little progress and Moskalenko's forces took the town later that day. However on 14 November, 25 Pz Div having been replaced by the more experienced 7 Pz Div from XXIV Pz Corps, and Eberbach having been replaced by General Hermann Balck, XLVIII Pz Corps tried again. This time it made more progress and Vatutin's advance beyond Zhitomir slowed. In Korosten Chevallerie wanted to pull LIX Corps back to the west but Hitler insisted that the town continue to be defended, and in consequence much of Chevallerie's corps became surrounded. Despite hurried arrangements to supply the surrounded forces by air, the defence of Korosten was ultimately unsuccessful and the town was taken by 60 Army on 17 November. The next day 13 Army took Ovruch. Yet despite IV Pz Army's acute problems, Vatutin's dispersion of effort in pushing back IV Pz Army in different directions had its dangers, and 1 Ukrainian Front was ordered to go over to the defensive on its left and centre, and to continue the advance only with 13 Army and 60 Army.

The over-extension of 1 Ukrainian Front became clear on 19 November when XIII Corps, then still under the command of Hauffe, together with Balck's XLVIII Pz Corps, retook Zhitomir, and by 23 November 1 SS Pz Div had pushed east to Brusilov. On 24 November Chevallerie's LIX Corps retook Korosten. Hence by the final week of November IV Pz Army had restored a degree of stability to its frontline and in retaking Zhitomir and Korosten had re-established the rail link with Army Group Centre. Hoth then went on extended leave and was replaced by Col-Gen Raus.[18] Subsequently XLVIII Pz Corps, with 1 Pz Div and 1 SS Pz Div, was moved farther north between LIX Corps and XIII Corps, and XLII Corps Headquarters, assigned two panzer divisions and three panzer grenadier divisions, assumed responsibility for XLVIII Pz Corps' former positions between XIII Corps and VII Corps west of Fastov.

If the second half of November had brought some relief to IV Pz Army, the same could not be said for the rest of Manstein's command. On 13 November Konev's 2 Ukrainian Front began to expand a bridgehead it had secured north of Cherkassy. On 20 November Hube reported that constant pressure against the Nikopol bridgehead had attenuated his infantry strength to an unacceptable level. Six days later he warned that without reinforcements, I Pz Army would have to give up the bridgehead. In fact I Pz Army and VIII Army received little by way of reinforcement and the Soviet Fronts continued the attritional warfare into the middle of December at which time Cherkassy was lost after a link up between 52 Army and 4 Gds Army.

In IV Pz Army's sector XLVIII Pz Corps was ordered to begin an offensive eastward from north of Zhitomir on 6 December (by which time the soft ground had frozen) and to reach Radomyshl, from where it was to turn northeast into the flank of 60 Army in order to relieve the pressure on LIX Corps at Korosten. After making initially good progress, the corps ran into increasingly stiff opposition from Soviet forces that were preparing another offensive of their own towards Zhitomir, and by 21 December, after having secured Radomyshl and re-established contact with LIX Corps, Balck went over to the defensive.

---

18   In December Hitler ordered that Hoth was not to return to IV Pz Army or be given any other command. The *Ostheer* was to be committed to static defence, and the mobile defence, of which Hoth was a master practitioner and which, in Hitler's view, had cost Germany vast tracts of territory in Russia and the Ukraine, would no longer be tolerated.

Hansen's first order of business after arriving at XVI Army Headquarters at the end of October was dealing with the creation by the Soviets of 2 Baltic Front north of Velikie Luki, and the strengthening of the Soviet forces in the Nevel bulge through the introduction of 4 Shock Army. On 28 October the two shock armies began to attack the left flank of III Pz Army, and by 2 November had achieved a breakthrough. Assigned to 2 Baltic Front, Chibisov's 3 Shock Army turned north behind Hansen's right flank and 4 Shock Army advanced to the southwest. In addition, Popov began to introduce forces from 6 Gds Army and 11 Gds Army into the gap between the two German army groups. On 4 November Hitler ordered Kuechler and Busch to organise immediate counter-attacks from north and south of the breakthrough zone to close the gap. With both shoulders of the breakthrough zone holding reasonably well, Army Group Centre launched a two-division attack on 8 November that by the end of the day had penetrated 8km into the Soviet lines. The complementary Army Group North attack did not begin until two days later. It proved to be an ad-hoc affair by half a dozen battalions that ran into stiff opposition and made little progress. Kuechler at that time was more concerned with signs of an impending offensive from Leningrad Front than with events near Nevel. Meanwhile Eremenko and Popov continued to push their armies forward. In the north they were within 15km of the railway line running west from Novosokolniki in the vicinity of Pustoshka, while in the south they were between Dretun and Gorodok northwest of Vitebsk. On 20 November Bagramyan assumed command of 1 Baltic Front from Eremenko and the next day 11 Gds Army, which had been transferred to 1 Baltic Front's command, pushed back the penetration into the breakthrough corridor that had been achieved by III Pz Army two weeks earlier. Also during the third week of November, 4 Shock Army began to turn east into the rear of III Pz Army, thereby threatening Vitebsk. By 23 November 4 Shock Army was within 5km of Gorodok but rising temperatures during the last week of November and the consequent thawing of the frozen ground, began to slow the Soviet movements. During this time on the other side of the 80km Dvina-Dnieper land bridge from Vitebsk to Orsha, Western Front had been making furious attempts to take Orsha, but had been beaten off by IV Army. On 13 December, 11 Gds Army, by then under the command of Galitsky, attacked the northern flank of III Pz Army and by 15 December came close to encircling two divisions. The next day the northernmost division was encircled, and over the subsequent six days Reinhardt ordered the encircled division to break out (which it did at a cost of 2,000 troops and all its heavy equipment), and he pulled his left flank back to an arc 30km north of the formidable defences of Vitebsk. All prospect of the *Ostheer* closing the gap between the two army groups was gone and in theory Bagramyan had an open route to the west. But with so much resource having gone into the offensives in the Ukraine, logistically his options were limited. On 23 December 11 Gds Army and 4 Shock Army, supported by 39 Army and 43 Army to the east, attacked the Vitebsk perimeter. Over the subsequent five days Busch provided Reinhardt with an additional four divisions (two of them from Army Group North) and, though III Pz Army was pushed back, a further six weeks of effort by Bagramyan failed to secure Vitebsk. Since Kuechler was unable to retake Nevel, on 27 December he was given permission to shorten his line in the Nevel area by withdrawing from the vicinity of the town and pulling back closer to the Pustoshka – Novosokolniki railway. This withdrawal eliminated a potential flank threat from Soviet forces near Pustoshka, and enabled Kuechler to free troops for the defence of the western face of the Nevel bulge, a bulge that was held east of Rossono and south of Pustoshka.

By 7 November the ragged condition of II Army and what appeared to be the imminent collapse of IV Pz Army on Army Group South's left flank had caused Busch sufficient concern to request (unsuccessfully) that Army Group Centre's right flank be taken back from the Chernobyl area. Three days later Belorussian Front tried again to break out from the Loyev bridgehead and after two days had achieved significant penetration of II Army's lines. At the same time Pukhov's 13 Army on the right flank of 1 Ukrainian Front struck to the north into II Army's weakly defended right flank west of Chernobyl. Weiss was denied permission to move relatively inactive forces from the Chernobyl sector to where they were desperately needed – his disintegrating centre and his exposed right flank, but he was able to pass responsibility for the Gomel area, together with the command of the defending XXXV Corps, to IX Army. On 13 November Rokossovsky's forces, with Belov's 65 Army in the van, had reached Retchitsa, and II Army was split in two. In the north Weiss's priorities were to stop Rokossovsky from crossing back to the left bank of the Dnieper from Rechitsa (from where Soviet forces could threaten Gomel from the west), and to hold the continuing north-westerly drive of Belorussian Front on the lower Beresina. In the south Weiss's priorities were to hold Udalevka, the southern shoulder of Rokossovsky's penetration, and to somehow prevent Rokossovsky from moving west to take II Army's key supply base at Kalinkovichi some 50km to the west. On 18 November Weiss used two divisions to attempt to close the gap in his lines, but the attack made little headway. By 20 November Chernobyl had been retaken by 1 Ukrainian Front, and forward detachments of Belorussian Front were only 30km east of Kalinkovichi. Weiss used the two divisions from his failed counter-attack to screen the town to the east but the bulk of his forces, at Hitler's insistence, were still in their original positions on the Dnieper. The next day Belorussian Front took Udalevka and began a move to the southwest, a move that threatened II Army's right flank, prompting Hitler on 22 November to give permission for a limited withdrawal by II Army. At the same time responsibility for the defence of both the left bank of the Dnieper opposite Retchitsa and the left bank of the Berezina near its confluence with the Dnieper was passed to IX Army. By the fourth week in November Rokossovsky had regrouped his forces sufficiently to conduct an offensive by Gorbatov's 3 Army and Boldin's 50 Army into the centre of IX Army south of Propoisk, and he followed this up the next day with a thrust into the new junction of IX Army and II Army south of the Beresina. By 13 November, after Soviet forces had cut the Kalinkovichi – Gomel railway west of Retchitsa, Gomel had ceased to be of any tactical value to the Germans. On 23 November Hitler sanctioned the beginning of a withdrawal from the city, a withdrawal that took three days to complete. By 25 November Belorussian Front was across the Eastern Rampart on the Sozh to a depth of 30km over a breadth of 80km. During the next week, such was the speed of Belorussian Front's advance that Busch's attempts to contain it came to nothing. By 30 November, Belorussian Front had reached the Dnieper west of Propoisk, though farther south II Army had established a front east of Kalinkovichi. By 4 December IX Army had withdrawn behind the Dnieper and had freed up forces for a possible counter-attack. A combined offensive by II Army

See Map 20

and IX Army to re-establish a continuous front between them began on 20 December. This offensive, codenamed Operation Nikolaus, included 16 Pz Div, newly arrived from Italy. By 22 December the spearheads met at Kobylshchina, and turned east to cross the upper Ipa and to try to clear the Zhlobin to Kalinkovichi railway line. This continued offensive eventually stalled short of its objective and on 26 December Busch terminated the operation. For the first time in nearly three months II Army and IX Army held an almost continuous front, but there still existed a 100km gap between Army Group Centre and Army Group South in the depths of the southern Pripet Marshes, and the Red Army held a 160km stretch of the west bank of the Dnieper northwest of Kiev that offered favourable positions for a further advance into southern Belorussia.

The Soviet Winter Offensives

By 24 December, with Axis forces in the Crimea isolated, the front from south to north ran along the lower Dnieper (with the German bridgehead opposite Nikopol still in place). North of Zaporozhe the Red Army held a deep bridgehead on the west bank of the Dnieper from which further significant offensive operations could be launched. This bridgehead stretched to the northwest as far as Kanev. The Germans still held a section the Eastern Rampart around Kanev but the front then ran west to the east of Zhitomir, Korosten, Mozyr, and Zhlobin. Along this section of the front Vatutin's 1 Ukrainian Front held a salient that stretched from a point north of the German bridgehead on the east bank of the Dnieper at Kanev to the border with Belorussia where it linked with Belorussian Front. From north of Zhlobin Western Front and 1 Baltic Front joined Belorussian Front in facing Army Group Centre in a line that ran to the east of Orsha and Vitebsk. From Vitebsk the front ran northwest to Dretun and then north towards Pustoshka. It then ran south of the Pustoshko – Novosokolniki railway line. From Novosokolniki 2 Baltic Front faced XVI Army north to Staraya Russa along the Lovat to Lake Ilmen. North of the lake from Novgorod, the front ran east of Chudovo to Mga, (Volkhov Front holding a small bridgehead on the west bank of the Volkhov), then south of Leningrad to the Gulf of Finland. Along this section of the line Volkhov Front and Leningrad Front faced XVIII Army. Leningrad Front's 23 Army faced Finnish forces in the Karelian Isthmus. A stagnant front ran from the south-eastern shore of Lake Ladoga along the Svir to Lake Onega, north to Belomorsk and then to the Barents Sea west of Murmansk.

Towards the end of 1943 the *Ostheer* was again experiencing severe manpower shortages with many divisions operating considerably below the already downgraded authorised strength. In addition to the losses experienced during July and August, leaving the *Ostheer*'s regular army manpower at less than 2.5 million for the first time, in the last four months of the year the *Ostheer*'s dead and missing amounted to a further quarter of a million, and the sources of replacement manpower were drying up. With draft orders failing substantially to produce the anticipated number of recruits, on 5 December OKW issued an order (Basic Order 22) requiring one million combat troops to be found from rear echelon personnel. Fitness standards were lowered and no able-bodied men under thirty were to remain in rear area assignments. The quality of the troops was also falling, with fewer divisions being classified as able to stand

and fight in a crisis situation. Many German-speaking recruits drafted from outside the Reich were stating openly that they had no intention of fighting.

The blood-letting of the second half of 1943 may have cost the *Ostheer* dear, but the Red Army paid a terrible price for its victories. During that time the Red Army suffered more than 5 million casualties, by far the highest six-monthly casualty rate of the entire war. Of those casualties, nearly 1.4 million were irrecoverable losses (killed, fatally wounded and missing). A significant proportion of these Red Army losses occurred in operations that yielded little in terms of Soviet territorial gain, and could at best have been said to have tied down German forces to prevent their redeployment. In 1943 Western Front alone suffered more than 940,000 casualties, during which time its only significant operational success was in August/September – Operation Suvorov, an operation that accounted for around one-third of the Front's total losses for that year. Yet in the areas where the Red Army did advance, a significant pool of additional manpower became available. This was the male civilian population of conscription age that had been living in German occupied Soviet territory. Such had been the rate of the Red Army's advance that the Germans had had insufficient time to move much of this manpower resource to the west. The new Red Army recruits were often thrown into battle with the bare minimum of training and equipment, but they helped to swell the depleted army ranks and, like most soldiers on the Eastern Front, they learned quickly.

In the closing weeks of 1943 STAVKA rationalised its force deployment somewhat. Eight army commands were disbanded including 68 Army, 12 Army, 44 Army, 9 Army, 56 Army and 11 Army. Also disbanded were 67 Army and 4 Army, though 55 Army was subsequently renamed 67 Army (55 Army disappearing from the Red Army order of battle), and 34 Army was renamed 4 Army (34 Army disappearing from the Red Army order of battle). Additionally 63 Army was disbanded in mid-February 1944.

STAVKA, maintaining the strategic initiative into 1944, decided that during its winter campaign of 1943/44 it would launch an offensive along the entire front from the Baltic to the Black Sea but that the chief effort would be on the flanks, and particularly in the south where the four Ukrainian Fronts had 177 divisions, each with a typical strength of 5,000 men. Western and 1 Baltic Fronts, despite a relative lack of reinforcement, were expected to conduct offensives to destroy Army Group Centre's forces in the Orsha – Vitebsk area and to advance to the Ula, while Rokossovsky was expected to advance on Minsk via Bobruisk. As had become usual in major strategic actions, the activities of the Fronts were co-ordinated by Zhukov and Vasilevsky, whose strategic objective in the Ukraine was to crush Army Group South between the Dnieper and the Dniester. The key Soviet Front was 1 Ukrainian Front which overhung the German forces to the southeast. Early in December Zhukov and Vatutin submitted a plan for further offensive operations by 1 Ukrainian Front that required the retaking of Korosten on the right wing, the capture of Belya Tserkva south of Fastov on the left, and the main blow in the centre to destroy German forces in the Berdichev – Kazatin area south of Zhitomir, with subsequent exploitation towards Vinnitsa.

Vatutin's Last Offensive

Vatutin's objectives, as finally articulated by STAVKA, were to strike west towards Lutsk while developing his main offensive southwest towards Vinnitsa and Mogilev-

Podolsky. Operations began on 24 December 1943 against the twenty-three divisions of IV Pz Army. Raus had seven panzer and panzer grenadier divisions in IV Pz Army but his forces were overwhelmed by 1 Ukrainian Front, which by December had been reinforced with Katukov's 1 Tank Army, Grechko's 1 Gds Army, Leselidze's 18 Army, two tank corps and a considerable quantity of artillery. By the evening of the first day the two tank armies were committed. The next day, having achieved a breakthrough against IV Pz Army's XLII Corps, 1 Tank Army turned to the southwest towards the railway junction of Kazatin and the road junction of Berdichev. Raus moved Balck's XLVIII Pz Corps from south of Korosten to attack the right flank of the Soviet penetration. In response Vatutin committed Pukhov's 13 Army, Cherniakhovsky's 60 Army and 1 Gds Army on his Front's right wing, supported by Rybalko's 3 Gds Tank Army, to attack Chevallerie's LIX Corps and XIII Corps (at that time under the command of Dostler) in the area around, and to the south of, Korosten. Vatutin also committed Zhmachenko's 40 Army on his Front's left wing to an offensive south of Fastov. By 28 December Soviet forces had reached Kazatin, and two days later LIX Corps on IV Pz Army's left flank was in full retreat, opening up a gap between it and XIII Corps on its right. On 29 December Cherniakhovsky's forces took Korosten and outflanked Zhitomir from the northwest, while 1 Gds Army moved in from the east. Additionally Zhmachenko's 40 Army had forced a 75km gap between the right flank of Mattenklott's XLII Corps and the left flank of Hell's VII Corps. The two right flank corps of IV Pz Army (VII Corps and XXIV Pz Corps) held a stationary front from the Fastov – Belaya Tserkov railway line east to the Dnieper and down the river to Kanev where it tied in with VIII Army.

Although the inadequacy of Hitler's static defence policy had become apparent after the first day of Vatutin's renewed offensive, it was not until the end of the year that OKH ordered radical measures to contain the Soviet breakthrough. Nehring's XXIV Pz Corps Headquarters assumed responsibility for XLII Corps' sector of the front, with XLII Corps Headquarters assuming command of XXIV Pz Corps' sector. More importantly OKH approved Manstein's decision to move Hube's I Pz Army Headquarters to Uman to take command of VII Corps and the relocated XLII Corps, and III Pz Corps Headquarters was removed from the Kirovograd sector of VIII Army's front to join I Pz Army, it being planned that the corps' 16 Pz Div and 17 Pz Div would follow later. III Pz Corps was also to be reinforced with a panzer grenadier division and a light division from Army Group A. Breith was to assemble III Pz Corps east of Vinnitsa to act as Hube's strike force. Similarly, to act as IV Pz Army's strike force, Raus was provided with General Hans Gollnick's XLVI Pz Corps Headquarters and three divisions (one of them a panzer division) from the other army groups.

On 31 December Vatutin's forces took Zhitomir, and Berdichev was taken six days later. Vatutin's offensive against IV Pz Army, in addition to breaking Manstein's left wing to three separate parts, had also put Army Group South's right flank, still far to the east on the lower Dnieper, at increased risk of encirclement. Yet Hitler refused to sanction any withdrawal from the Dnieper bend. With LIX Corps pushed back to Gorodnitsa by 3 January, and with the gap between XXIV Pz Corps and VII Corps still open, Vatutin began to develop his offensive to envelop Raus's three central corps. On 4 January Dostler reported that XIII Corps was on the verge of disintegration with divisional frontline strength down to a few hundred men. (The following day

Dostler was reassigned and command of XIII Corps was returned to Hauffe). Farther south VII Corps had been pushed away from Belaya Tserkov and stood facing west, its back to XLII Corps. On IV Pz Army's other flank, in order to avoid being pushed into the Pripet Marshes west of the Slutch, LIX Corps, after 4 January, was forced to pull back farther to the southwest into territory that, until 1939, had been part of eastern Poland. In doing so it widened the gap between Army Group South and Army Group Centre to more than 150km. Chevallerie was ordered to use the main part of LIX Corps' strength (two infantry divisions) to pull back along the Shepetovka road (where it was followed by 60 Army), and the rest of its force, designated 'Corps Detachment C', together with a security division, to pull back along the Rovno road (where it was followed by 13 Army). Since in the fringes of the Pripet Marshes roads were particularly important to the manoeuvre of large forces, German possession of Shepetovka and Rovno would limit any potential Soviet offensive in this area. On 14 January Manstein ordered Hauffe's XIII Corps Headquarters to move to Rovno to take command of 'Corps Detachment C' and the security division, but after 7 January the gap between the two army groups was widened further when Belorussian Front pushed back II Army from Kalinkovichi to the Ipa.

On 1 Ukrainian Front's other flank, with III Pz Corps still not assembled, on 6 January Vatutin began to shift the weight of his offensive south to take advantage of the yawning gap between IV Pz Army and I Pz Army. To meet this penetration by 1 Tank Army and 40 Army, Manstein prepared to employ III Pz Corps and XLVI Pz Corps to strike west and east respectively to attack the flanks of Vatutin's southerly advance towards Vinnitsa. Part of Manstein's plan included the withdrawal of VII Corps and XLII Corps south to the Ross, but Hitler refused to sanction such a withdrawal. Breith set up a weak screening force to try to block the Soviet advance but 40 Army continued south to the east of the screening force and 1 Tank Army exploited the gap between III Pz Corps and XLVI Pz Corps east of Vinnitsa on Breith's left flank. By 10 January Zhmachenko's army had reached the outskirts of Uman, and 1 Tank Army, from southeast of Vinnitsa, had turned part of its force west to approach Zhmerinka from the east. After two days of heavy fighting III Pz Corps and XLVI Pz Corps managed to bring Katukov's advance to a halt. By then Vatutin's armies were outrunning their supplies, and German counter-measures had managed to stabilise the front along the Goryn and to the east of Rovno, Shepetovka and Vinnitsa. On 15 January, as a temporary halt was being called to 1 Ukrainian Front's offensive, Manstein and Hube engineered a counter-attack against 40 Army's penetration to Uman. III Pz Corps' two panzer divisions, having dealt with 1 Tank Army's threat to the corps' left flank, were transferred to the right flank to attack to the east from north of Uman. This attack was conducted in conjunction with VII Corps, which had extended its left flank to the south and then to the west in an attempt to meet III Pz Corps. At the same time XLVI Pz Corps was reinforced and transferred to I Pz Army's command to enable Hube to coordinate the ejection of 1 Tank Army from the Vinnitsa area. Two days later III Pz Corps had made steady progress to the east and was only a few kilometres from making contact with Hell's VII Corps, leaving 40 Army in an untenable position in Uman. On 24 January, XLVI Pz Corps attacked from the Vinnitsa area into the right flank of 1 Tank Army and the next day, Uman securely back under German control, III Pz Corps switched direction again and attacked to the west to hit the left flank of

1 Tank Army from the east. The attack on 1 Tank Army was anticipated by Vatutin and made only slow progress. Vatutin was provided with additional reinforcements including Lt-Gen S I Bogdanov's 2 Tank Army,[19] 47 Army (at that time under the command of Lt-Gen Polenov and comprising just three divisions) and 5 Mech Corps. On 20 January 5 Mech Corps was combined with Kravchenko's 5 Gds Tank Corps to create 6 Tank Army under Kravchenko's command. This left Vatutin in command of an immensely powerful Front of eight field armies and four tank armies.

On 27 January, with 60 Army advancing on Shepetovka from Novograd Volinsky, 13 Army attacked the Sarny area with the aim of enveloping Rovno and Lutsk from the west. By the end of the month Soviet cavalry and partisans were operating almost at will to the west of Rovno, reaching beyond Lutsk towards Kovel. On 2 February XIII Corps, its position in Rovno having become untenable, abandoned the town and, to screen the approach to Lvov more than 100km to the southwest, pulled back to Dubno along the Lvov road. This left the Soviet cavalry divisions farther north free to take Lutsk and close in on Kovel. Soviet cavalry were also ranging west of Dubno, and on 9 February Manstein reinforced XIII Corps with an infantry division and began to assemble 7 Pz Div and 8 Pz Div under XLVIII Pz Corps Headquarters for an offensive northwards towards Lutsk and Kovel. Two days later Vatutin's main force had reached the line Lutsk – Shepetovka. For more than a week IV Pz Army's left flank was close to disintegration. The counter-attack by XLVIII Pz Corps did not begin until 22 February but went well, reaching Lutsk by 27 February and Kovel by the end of the month. This closed the gap between Army Group South and Army Group Centre but there remained a 50km gap between XIII Corps at Dubno and LIX Corps south of Shepetovka.

On 29 February Vatutin was mortally wounded in an attack on his vehicle by Ukrainian nationalist partisans, and Zhukov, who had been coordinating the actions of 1 Ukrainian Front and 2 Ukrainian Front, assumed direct command of the former.

The Cherkassy Pocket

Manstein's problems in January and February 1944 were not confined to his left wing. At the beginning of 1944 VIII Army's front stretched from Kanev, along the Dnieper for 30km and then south 30km east of Kirovograd where it linked with VI Army in the section of front that Hollidt had acquired from I Pz Army. Woehler faced 2 Ukrainian Front, and by 2 January he had successfully closed off a breakthrough by Konev's forces 25km north of Kirovograd. Three days later, on 5 January, Woehler had to contend with a more powerful blow from 2 Ukrainian Front near the VIII Army / VI Army boundary, an offensive that broke through Woehler's lines and then turned north threatening the encirclement of Lt-Gen Nikolaus von Vormann's XLVII Pz Corps in Kirovograd. Manstein reacted quickly, giving Woehler the left flank corps of VI Army and the two panzer divisions that had been designated to join III Pz Corps at Uman. On 8 January Konev's forces took Kirovograd but by 10 January, despite the presence of 1 Ukrainian Front's forces deep behind his left flank near Uman, Woehler had managed to regain some balance on his right, having extricated XLVII Pz Corps from possible encirclement and having brought Konev's advance to a halt some 15km west of Kirovograd. Although Manstein, Hube and Woehler all

---

19   Rodin, the previous commander of 2 Tank Army, had been injured earlier in the year.

requested that the forces on the Dnieper in the Kanev area be pulled back, Hitler refused to authorise the withdrawal.

The section of front that had been bequeathed to VI Army after the move of I Pz Army Headquarters to Uman was an unenviable one, consisting of a deep salient into Soviet held territory from the upper Ingulets southeast to a point some 30km east of Nikopol on the right bank of the Dnieper near the southern extremity of the Dnieper bend. This was the easternmost extremity of the *Ostheer*'s front. From there the front turned back to the southwest, crossed to the left bank of the Dnieper into the Nikopol bridgehead, ran parallel to the river on its left bank to a point downriver from Bolshaya Lepatikha and then along the river to its estuary. From the northern tip of the Nikopol bridgehead to the Dnieper estuary VI Army was faced by 4 Ukrainian Front, and on the north-eastern face of the salient by 3 Ukrainian Front. After Schoerner's success at Krivoi Rog in October, he had been appointed to command the *Ostheer*'s three most south-easterly corps, two holding the Nikopol bridgehead, and the other on the right bank of Dnieper east of Nikopol. This was an area to which Hitler attached great significance and he wanted its defence in the hands of someone who would not be tempted to withdraw under pressure.

On 10 January Malinovsky, taking advantage of falling temperatures and hardening ground, launch an offensive against XXX Corps down the railway line from Dnepropetrovsk towards Apostolovo on the west bank of the Buzuluk. Initial coordination between the Soviet infantry and armour was poor; the tanks moved ahead of infantry support and suffered heavy losses from two reserve panzer divisions that Hollidt rushed to the area. Yet Malinovsky kept up the offensive and over the subsequent few days sheer weight of numbers pushed Fretter-Pico's XXX Corps back 8km, at which point Tolbukhin launched an attack into the centre of the Nikopol bridgehead. Hollidt managed to hold Tolbukhin's attack and brought Malinovsky's offensive to a halt, but he was unable to push back Malinovsky's advance, which had reached perilously close to the Krivoi Rog – Nikopol road. Having achieved a temporary degree of stability, during the second half of January Hollidt's position was to worsen as several of his divisions were siphoned off to Army Group A and to VIII Army.

By then Woehler was in acute difficulty. On 24 January a reconnaissance in force by Konev's troops between Cherkassy and Kirovograd hit a weakly-held sector of VIII Army's front and penetrated it in a number of places. The next day Konev developed these penetrations into a full-scale offensive by Ryzhov's 4 Gds Army prompting Woehler to submit another urgent appeal to OKH for the troops on the Dnieper in the Kanev area, by then in a deep salient, to be withdrawn. Again the withdrawal request was refused. On 25/26 January Konev's offensive, proceeding more slowly than STAVKA had anticipated, was joined by 1 Ukrainian Front in a co-ordinated effort to cut off the Kanev salient between them by striking towards Zvenigorodka. On 26 January, with I Pz Army's resources fully stretched, Soviet mechanised forces from 6 Tank Army penetrated the VII Corps – XLII Corps boundary and advanced rapidly to the south. Despite the fact that the spring thaws began early in 1944 and that before the end of January the snows were melting and the going was difficult, on 28 January spearheads from 6 Tank Army met forces from 4 Gds Army at Shpola 70km southwest of Kanev encircling some 55,000 troops of I Pz Army's XLII Corps and VIII Army's and XI Corps. At the same time Rotmistrov pushed his armour west to meet 6 Tank Army at Zvenigorodka thereby securing the outer ring of the encirclement. On the same day the tips of XLVI Pz Corps and III Pz Corps met at Oratov some 80km east of Vinnitsa, snipping off 1 Tank Army's penetration to the south while netting more than 5,000 prisoners and destroying more than 700 Soviet tanks and self-propelled guns.

The most senior officer among the surrounded German troops from XLII Corps was Lt-Gen Theobald Lieb who commanded 'Corps Detachment B', a divisional-sized unit that had been formed some months earlier from 112 Inf Div and the remnants of two other infantry divisions. Lieb was outranked by General Wilhelm Stemmermann, the commander of XI Corps, who was given overall command of the surrounded force: designated Operational Group Stemmermann, it was placed under VIII Army's operational control. Soviet expectations with regard to the encirclement were high, it being assumed that the bulk of VIII Army had been surrounded, and, sensing another Stalingrad in the making, Konev gave Stalin his personal assurance that no Germans would escape. Stemmermann's group comprised six under-strength divisions including 5 SS Pz Gdr Div (*Wiking*), but not the dozen or so divisions that Konev and STAVKA had initially assumed. Yet, long after the true situation was known, Soviet accounts of the battle continued to exaggerate the size of the surrounded force, the intensity of the fighting and the scale of the German losses.

Manstein immediately set about preparing a counter-attack and he organised an air supply to Stemmermann's force in what had become known as the Cherkassy Pocket, though the pocket was actually west of Cherkassy and was centred on the town of Korsun Shevchenkovsky. At the beginning of the year the encircled corps had moved most of their food stocks to Korsun in anticipation of a withdrawal to the south, and so the air supply effort was able to concentrate on delivering ammunition and fuel. Manstein transferred 14 Pz Div from VI Army to VIII Army, and he ordered I Pz Army to begin moving III Pz Corps to the east for the counter-attack. At the same time, Woehler was ordered to move XLVII Pz Corps to VIII Army's left flank, and to coordinate its attack with that of III Pz Corps farther north. What Manstein envisaged at this stage was simply an attempt to relieve the surrounded forces but Hitler had ambitions of developing the attack into a major offensive to retake Kiev.

The relief effort began on 4 February, by which time the air lift was in operation, subsequently delivering a daily average of eighty tonnes of fuel and ammunition into the pocket. Ground conditions for both sides were difficult, the fighting taking place in appalling weather and thick mud. By 6 February XLVII Pz Corps, with 11 Pz Div in the van, had made virtually no progress, and though III Pz Corps had managed to advance, it was still more than 30km from the south-western corner of the pocket. That evening Hitler approved a breakout by the encircled forces. As III Pz Corps, with two heavy panzer regiments in the van, battled its way to the east, Stemmermann began to shrink the pocket's perimeter from the north and east. On 11 February III Pz Corps occupied the southern portion of the small town of Lisyanka, the northern end of which crossed the Gniloy Tikich. Yet it took another two days for the corps to push forces to the north bank of the river to secure the northern end of the town. By 15 February, the limited forces that III Pz Corps could support north of the river had not even reached Dzhurzhentsy, which lay just a few kilometres northeast of Lisyanka. The exhausted relief forces could advance no further and ahead of them lay

See
Map 21

the fiercely defended 'Hill 239'. Meanwhile Group Stemmermann had been attacking to the southwest, taking the villages of Novo-Buda, Komarovka and Khilki just 7km from III Pz Corps' positions. By 16 February the pocket had shrunk to a diameter of less than 10km and the encircled forces numbered less than 50,000, more than 4,000 wounded having been flown out of the pocket before the loss of the airfield at Korsun on 12 February. The breakout of the remaining troops was scheduled for the night of 16/17 February, to be undertaken by three columns and a rearguard. Lieb was appointed to lead the breakout, Stemmermann remaining behind with the rearguard of 6,500 men – all that was left of 57 Inf Div and 88 Inf Div.

After the loss on 16 February of Komarovka on the south-western extremity of the pocket, hurried last-minute reorganisation was required to enable the southern and central columns to begin from the same area. In the darkness and confusion the Soviet forces did not initially understand what was happening, and in the early hours of 17 February the advance battalions of the breakout effort from the northern and central columns began to reach III Pz Corps' lines. The route of the southern column, which included the SS troops, took it close to Hill 239, an impregnable obstacle. After encountering resistance, the southern column began to shift to the south in order to bypass the hill and, as a result, ran into difficult terrain that took it to the swollen Gniloy Tikich south of III Pz Corps' bridgehead over the river. By dawn, as the rearguard was beginning its withdrawal and the bulk of Group Stemmermann was strung out between the pocket and III Pz Corps' positions, Konev had realised what was happening and, mindful of his pledge to Stalin, unleashed a deluge of fire on the escaping columns. It was a deluge of fire that, among many others, took the life of Stemmermann. The difficult terrain and ground conditions meant that most of the German heavy equipment and motorised wheeled vehicles had to be abandoned. Only tracked vehicles and horse-drawn wagons could be expected to traverse the escape route. The difficult ground conditions inhibited Soviet force manoeuvre to at least the same extent as it did the Germans, but available Soviet armour was ordered to attack the escaping units, cut them into isolated groups and then destroy them piecemeal. Caught on foot and in the open with few anti-tank guns, many German units were attacked by tanks and cavalry, and massacred. As the morning progressed, increasingly effective Soviet resistance ensured that more of the units from the escape columns were diverted from proximity to the relief force outside Lisyanka towards the south, finding themselves on the east bank of the Gniloy Tikich and more than a kilometre from the German relief force beyond the opposite bank. Although the river was less than 20m wide, it was fast-flowing, and all equipment, including hand weapons, had to be abandoned in order to try to swim across. Many drowned in the attempt. In many units cohesion and military discipline broke down completely in what became a desperate scramble for personal survival. To the exhausted but disciplined soldiers of III Pz Corps, the abysmal psychological condition of the well-fed, well-clad survivors of Group Stemmermann came as a shock. Of the 45,000 troops that made the escape attempt some 36,000 reached German lines, but few of them were fit for immediate return to active service. Most had to be returned to central Europe for an extended period of recuperation before they could again be considered combat ready.

Apostolovo and Krivoi Rog

On 30 January Malinovsky struck again at the XXX Corps section of the front west of the Buzuluk. Over the preceding two weeks forces had been moved north from 4 Ukrainian Front to Malinovsky's command, and the assaulting Soviet armies, 46 Army and 8 Gds Army, were provided with ample air support and support from mechanised forces. Fretter-Pico responded with highly effective use of his artillery which broke up the Soviet infantry attacks and rendered the Soviet advances on the first day relatively insignificant. The next day Malinovsky tried again and XXX Corps, while still maintaining a continuous front, was pushed back 4km. The following day, 1 February, as Hollidt struggled to get reinforcements to Fretter-Pico, XXX Corps' line broke and Malinovsky's forces pushed into a 10km wide gap west of the Buzuluk.

See
Map
20

Over the subsequent days XXX Corps' cohesion began to disintegrate as increasingly isolated and disparate groups tried to make their way west to the Kamanka and the relative safety of LVII Pz Corps' positions around Krivoi Rog.

In order to prevent Manstein from transferring too much of VI Army's resources to the north (and under the pretext of limiting Manstein's work-load) Hitler, on 1 February, transferred VI Army back to to command of Army Group A. By 2 February, with both sides trying to manoeuvre through deep mud, Chuikov's 8 Gds Army took Sholokhovo, and a mechanised corps secured a bridgehead over the Komenka as two of Hollidt's weak reserve panzer divisions, 23 Pz Div and 9 Pz Div, attempted to counter-attack the flank of the penetration. Early that evening OKH authorised a withdrawal of Schoerner's three corps to the Apostolovo area, though Hitler still wanted to maintain a small bridgehead over the Dnieper at Bolshaya Lepatikha. Unless frozen, the ground of the Dnieper flood plain around Nikopol is almost impassable, and the winter of 1943/44 was unusually mild. The only good road in the region stretched back northwest from Nikopol through Sholokhovo and Kamenka to Krivoi Rog. The only railway ran west from the Nikopol area to Apostolovo from where it split to run northwest and southwest. The withdrawal of XVII Corps from its salient towards the Dnieper bend east of Nikopol went surprising smoothly, as did the withdrawal of IV Corps from the northern part of the Nikopol bridgehead on the river's left bank, though most of the heavy equipment and motorised wheeled vehicles had to be abandoned. Despite the fact that on 4 February forward units of 8 Gds Army reached Apostolovo, during 4 February and 5 February Schoerner was able to use the railway line running west from Nikopol to move his divisions to the Buzuluk where they could set up screening positions south of Sholokhovo. Meanwhile Lt-Gen Glagolev's 46 Army was attempting to move west of Apostolovo in order to outflank Krivoi Rog from the south, while 8 Gds Army continued to the south and southwest in an effort to encircle the Schoerner's entire force.

Hollidt proposed a counter-offensive to retake the Apostolovo area using both Schoerner's forces on the Buzuluk and divisions withdrawn from XXIX Corps in the southern part of the Nikopol bridgehead around Bolshaya Lepatikha, and on 6 February Kleist approved the withdrawal of XXIX Corps from the left bank of the Dnieper. On 8 February, with all German troops from the northern part of the Nikopol bridgehead back on the right bank of the Dnieper, IV Corps began an offensive west towards Apostolovo while XVII Corps protected its rear. Two days later 9 Pz Div and part of 24 Pz Div began a separate attack north towards Apostolovo from the

XXIX Corps sector on the right bank of the Dnieper. By the next day the German effort against Apostolovo had clearly stalled and Hollidt had to acknowledge that the town was firmly in Soviet hands. The panzer divisions were ordered to push east, and IV Corps to push south, in order to establish contact around the southern fringe of the Soviet penetration. By 12 February Kleist was able to report that VI Army had a more or less continuous front, though the last gap southwest of Apostolovo was not closed until a week later.

Malinovsky, in sending 8 Gds Army to the southwest from Apostolovo instead of southeast had missed an opportunity to isolate IV Corps and XVII Corps east of the Buzuluk. Yet VI Army's front was weak and highly vulnerable to another concerted Soviet offensive from the Apostolovo area – either to the southwest towards the Dnieper estuary, or to the northwest towards Krivoi Rog. The renewed Soviet offensive was not long in coming. On 21 February Soviet forces broke into Krivoi Rog, which Kleist gave up without a fight in order to avoid costly street battles. By the end of February no German forces remained in the vicinity of the Dnieper bend and, with VI Army being pushed back to the line of the Ingulets, 4 Ukrainian Front was free to turn its attention to the Crimea. Kleist strongly advocated a withdrawal of Army Group A to the Bug, something that Manstein had previously advocated for VI Army, but Hitler would do nothing more than acknowledging the inevitable, agreeing to VI Army retiring behind the Ingulets as far south as Arkhangelskoye. With Konev's forces gathering in strength on the VIII Army – VI Army boundary south of Kirovograd, Manstein transferred the right flank corps of VIII Army to Kleist, though no Soviet offensive in this area subsequently developed.

Leningrad to the Panther Line

By January 1944 Army Group North's front between the Gulf of Finland and the Volkhov had come to resemble the trench-line battlefields of the Great War's Western Front. During the autumn of 1943 Kuechler had been obliged to give up several infantry divisions, and by way of replacement he had received mainly SS units recently raised in the Baltic States. Additionally, in less critical areas of his front, Kuechler had several notoriously unreliable *Luftwaffe* field divisions. At the turn of the year Army Group North's situation deteriorated further when, during the week ending 4 January 1944, Kuechler was obliged to transfer three of his best divisions to Army Group South to assist Manstein in the management of his disintegrating left flank. It had been Hitler's intention to transfer just one division from Kuechler's command, and to then pull Army Group North back to the Eastern Rampart during January 1944. However, at the end of December 1943 Lindemann expressed confidence in the ability of XVIII Army to hold its positions around Leningrad and along the Volkhov, prompting Hitler, when he learned of the comments, to reconsider both the manning needs of Army Group North and the necessity of withdrawal.

Army Group North had been expecting an offensive in the Leningrad area since November, and had noted a significant increase in shipping activity between Leningrad and Oranienbaum, but in the absence of information about a significant increase in Soviet reserves in the area, the assumption was that it would follow the format of earlier offensives and could be relatively easily contained. In any case, plans for a withdrawal to the Eastern Rampart were well advanced and it was assumed that

See
Map
22

this would be ordered in the event of Army Group North encountering any serious difficulty from a Soviet offensive. XVIII Army's front was a long arc from the coast west of Oranienbaum to north of Mga, to the Volkhov northeast of Chudovo, and south to Novgorod on the north shore of Lake Ilmen. Its order of battle was not dissimilar to that of the preceding summer (see Appendix IX). Lindemann had lost I Corps to XVI Army, and III SS Pz Corps, deployed on the army's left wing along the eastern half of the Oranienbaum salient, had replaced *III Luftwaffen Feldkorps*. On 10 January XVIII Army reported an infantry combat strength of 58,000 men. XVI Army held the line from the southern shore of Lake Ilmen to Kholm and to Novosokolniki. In addition, Hansen's army was responsible for around two-thirds of the Nevel bulge. As previously described, since the summer of 1943, in addition to acquiring I Corps from XVIII Army, XVI Army had also acquired XLIII Corps from the left flank of III Pz Army.

Army Group North was faced by Govorov's Leningrad Front of 33 rifle divisions, Meretskov's Volkhov Front of 22 rifle divisions, and, south of Lake Ilmen, by M M Popov's 2 Baltic Front of 45 rifle divisions. All the Red Army's tank armies were in the south, and all the independent tank and mechanised corps were committed to the southern or central axes. In the north, mechanised support was based on four independent tank brigades and less than a dozen independent tank regiments attached to each Front. Nonetheless, Soviet tank strength greatly exceeded German tank strength in the region. The order of battle of Leningrad and Volkhov Fronts was also similar to that of the previous summer (see Appendix X). On 25 November 1943 Volkhov Front had seen its 4 Army disbanded and towards the end of 1943 Leningrad Front had seen its 67 Army and 55 Army amalgamated into a new 67 Army on its left flank north of Mga. During November and December 1943, as 42 Army maintained the central defence of Leningrad, 2 Shock Army had been covertly deployed to the Oranienbaum salient. The salient had remained largely unchanged since September 1941 when XVIII Army had reached the coast west of Leningrad, isolating Soviet forces along a narrow coastal strip on either side of Oranienbaum. Since then the salient had been supplied from Leningrad with the assistance of the Baltic Sea Fleet, and for more than two years neither side had had the resources to change the *status quo* of the salient's perimeter. STAVKA planned an offensive for mid-January 1944, the primary objectives of which were for Volkhov Front to advance to the Luga, and for Leningrad Front to advance to Kingisepp in order to envelop XVIII Army. To minimise German suspicions, no new armies were introduced into the order of battle, but the existing armies were surreptitiously strengthened. Important command changes were also made at the end of 1943. Fedyuninsky was appointed to command 2 Shock Army and Maslennikov, who had been promoted to the rank of colonel-general earlier in the year, was appointed to command 42 Army.

At dawn on 14 January Fedyuninsky's army launched its attack out of the Oranienbaum salient towards Ropsha, a village 12km west of Krasnoe Selo. The attack involved artillery support densities of 140 guns per kilometre, and it hit a *Luftwaffe* field division of SS General Felix Steiner's III SS Pz Corps. The *Luftwaffe* division began to crumble almost immediately and Lindemann was obliged to commit his only significant reserve, 61 Inf Div, to stabilise the defence. The next day 3,000 guns and mortars firing 1,000 rounds per minute for more than an hour and a half heralded an attack by 42 Army on L Corps' positions on the Pulkovo Heights south of Leningrad. This attack was also aimed at Ropsha, the intention being to surround and destroy the left wing of XVIII Army in the Peterhof area, but General Wilhelm Wegener's L Corps responded quickly and the corps' artillery broke up the initial attacks. By the end of the day, in accordance with STAVKA's timetable, Lt-Gen V P Sviridov's 67 Army, together with the whole of Volkhov Front from east of Mga to Lake Ilmen, had joined the offensive against XVIII Army; Volkhov Front's main effort being 59 Army's attempt to take Novgorod.

On 16 January, with no new Soviet units seeming to have been committed, Kuechler was optimistic that the offensive could be contained. However during the course of the next day the situation between Oranienbaum and Leningrad deteriorated and by 18 January Lindemann reported that the III SS Pz Corps and L Corps fronts in that area were collapsing. In the afternoon spearheads from 42 Army reached Krasnoe Selo, and Kuechler sought Hitler's permission to pull back two divisions on the coast north of Krasnoye Selo to prevent them being cut off. Unable to obtain an affirmative response Kuechler, late in the evening, issued the withdrawal order on his own authority, a decision grudgingly endorsed by Hitler, but it came too late and only elements of the divisions were able to effect an escaped. After days of gruelling combat, during which Soviet forces sustained heavy casualties, and after the commitment of the second echelons of 2 Shock Army and 42 Army, on the evening of 19 January advanced units of the two armies met in the vicinity of Russko-Vysotsky some 8km southwest of Krasnoye Selo. At the other end of Lindemann's front, on 19 January five battalions of General Kurt Herzog's XXXVIII Corps were all but encircled in Novgorod by Lt-Gen I T Korovnikov's 59 Army, and Hitler's authorisation for their withdrawal was only issued in the early hours of the following morning. At that time Hitler also, though with great reluctance, gave permission for XVIII Army to pull XXVI Corps back from Mga and to straighten its line along the Leningrad – Chudovo highway in conjunction with General Herbert Loch's XXVIII Corps at Chudovo. This fall-back line, known as the *Rollbahn*, had been prepared for just such a contingency in order to release combat units for deployment elsewhere. On 21 January, by which time it had become apparent to Kuechler that the Soviet armies had ample reserves, 42 Army attacked towards the key communications hub of Krasnogvardeisk. The next day Lindemann reported that the town could not be held unless he gave up Pushkin and Pavlovsk farther north in order to release forces for Krasnogvardeisk's defence. Hitler, having already authorised, albeit belatedly, a withdrawal from the coast west of Leningrad, a withdrawal from Mga, and a withdrawal from Novgorod, was insistent that there be no further withdrawals, nor would he sanction any steps preparatory to a withdrawal to the Eastern Rampart. On 23 January Lindemann, on his own authority, issued the order to evacuate Pushkin and Pavlovsk, advising OKH that if it wished to countermand the evacuation order it would have to do so by appointing a new commanding officer for XVIII Army. The next day Soviet forces reached the outskirts of Krasnogvardeisk in the north, and in the south reached the bend of the Luga southeast of the town of Luga. Kuechler was faced with a gaping hole in the centre of his front between XVIII Army and XVI Army, and the impending loss of Krasnogvardeisk would compromise Lindemann's ability to supply his divisions farther east. Consequently Kuechler requested permission to withdraw to the Luga, but this was refused. Along the entire front and despite, to Govorov's fury, the employment by forward Soviet commanders of linear assault tactics, often undertaken by unsupported infantry, towards the end of January the resistance of XVIII Army began to crumble. By 29 January XVIII Army's infantry combat strength had been reduced to just 17,000 men, and Lindemann had been obliged to strip LIV Corps and XXVI Corps of their combat units for employment by other corps or by army headquarters directly.[20] Only on 30 January did Hitler approve a withdrawal to the Luga, by which time Soviet forces had reached the Luga in its lower reaches and had forced crossings in several places. Meanwhile 59 Army had pushed XXXVIII Corps back 80km from Novgorod, and 8 Army, together with 54 Army, had pushed Lindemann's centre back from the main Moscow – Leningrad railway running through Chudovo, Lyuban and Tosno. This represented the final lifting of the epic siege of Leningrad, which was officially declared free on 26 February, though the effective date of the lifting of the siege was 26 January when the Moscow – Leningrad railway line was cleared.

At the end of January Hitler, dissatisfied with Army Group North's handling of operations north of Lake Ilmen, sacked Kuechler and, to replace him, recalled Model from extended leave.[21] By this time XVIII Army's front had been pushed back almost to the Narva in the north. South and east of the Narva, Lindemann was left with scatterings of isolated units holding parts of previous frontline positions. Model was able to take advantage of the latitude Hitler occasionally gave to new commanders and authorised Lindemann to take his front back to a shorter line to the north and east of Luga. Using forces freed by this move, together with two reserve divisions from the west and south, Model proposed that Lindemann should plan an advance down the Luga towards Narva. By 2 February, Fedyuninsky's 2 Shock Army, having taken Kingisepp, had secured a small bridgehead over the Narva south of Narva city, though the Soviets were unable to take the town itself.

The Panther Line positions in the northern half of the Army Group North sector were naturally strong, based on the Narva and Lake Peipus. During the first week of Model's command of Army Group North, the new army group commander was more concerned with events in the XVI Army sector, where the Eastern Rampart did not posses the inherent advantages of the XVIII Army sector and where 2 Baltic Front had advanced to the south of Staraya Russa and to the west of Novosokolniki. By 6 February, 12 Pz Div, one of the two reinforcement divisions supplied to Army Group North, had closed the gap between XVIII Army and XVI Army, and was subsequently moved north to Pskov. Over the next four days Model tried to organise the proposed counter-attack downriver from Luga, but constant Soviet pressure on XVIII Army prevented the necessary consolidation of forces. By 11 February the key component of this counter-attack, 58 Inf Div, the second of Army Group North's two reinforcement divisions, had been split in two and surrounded. It was subsequently able to fight

20   On 27 January General Otto Sponheimer's LIV Corps Headquarters, which had been on XVIII Army's left flank, was withdrawn to Narva to organise force deployment at the northern extremity of the Panther Line.

21   Hitler had intended to use Model to replace Manstein, and so Model's appointment to Army Group North was something of a reprieve for the Army Group South commander – someone Hitler considered to have advocated tactical withdrawal once too often. Harpe, who after the command of XLI Pz Corps had served as acting commander of IX Army on several occasions during Model's absences, was formally appointed to the command of IX Army.

its way out but lost one-third of its manpower and all of its heavy equipment in the process. That evening Model gave up plans for the counter-attack and he authorised Lindemann to pull XVIII Army back to the Panther Line positions. The next day, 12 February, 67 Army took Luga but the anticipated bag of German prisoners was not taken because Model had been able to pull his forces back in time and was consequently able to begin preparations for the defence of Pskov. On that day Leningrad Front expanded its bridgehead over the Narva south of Narva city, and it established a new bridgehead farther north. This was achieved in the face of determined resistance from LIV Corps and III SS Pz Corps, combined under the command of Sponheimer. Two days later, on 14 February, Soviet ski troops reached the western shore of Lake Peipus, and the German security division in that area reported that its Estonian troops were deserting. This convinced Model that the entire army group should be withdrawn behind the Eastern Rampart, a withdrawal that had been approved in principle by Hitler the day before. Model moved 12 Pz Div to the lakeshore area to expel the Soviet ski troops, and he set a deadline of 1 March for completion of the withdrawal to the Panther Line positions.

In the north, the battles around Narva during the third week of February degenerated into a stalemate and Govorov had already begun to extend his left flank south towards Pskov, advocating that for the sake of unity of control on the Pskov line of advance, Volkhov Front should be disbanded and that the whole Pskov sector should be handed over to him.[22] STAVKA concurred and on 15 February Volkhov Front was disbanded, Meretskov being reassigned to the command of Karelian Front. XVI Army had already begun the process of pulling back from the south of Lake Ilmen to the Panther Line positions between Pskov and Ostrov when, in mid-February, 67 Army began to advance to the southwest from Luga to Pskov. Consequently 67 Army's advance did not seriously threaten XVI Army's left flank. In XVI Army's hurried and extended withdrawal of more than 150km, Hansen allowed 2 Baltic Front to advance unopposed; though in a failure of tactical intelligence Lt-Gen G P Korotkov and his staff at 1 Shock Army did not realise that XVI Army had pulled out of Staraya Russa until two days later.

With Bagramyan having little success in the Vitebsk area despite two months of continuous attacks, STAVKA decided to use some of his resources to reinforce 2 Baltic Front, and a somewhat rehabilitated Marshal Timoshenko was sent as STAVKA representative to coordinate the operations of the two Baltic Fronts. On 19 February the attacks against III Pz Army's Vitebsk defences ceased. Subsequent German aerial reconnaissance reported large-scale movement of Soviet forces north from the Vitebsk area, and the reports prompted Model to speculate about a Soviet offensive from the Nevel bulge, either south of Idritsa towards Dvinsk or north behind Army Group North's flank.

On 24 February General Johannes Friessner, the former commander of XXIII Corps, was assigned to command the forces in the Narva area. Designated Army Detachment Narva, these forces were based on III SS Pz Corps, and were reinforced with an infantry division that had been transferred from Norway.

---

22   Govorov, like M M Popov, had been promoted twice in 1943 and was no longer out-ranked by Meretskov.

Friessner was able to successfully thwart further efforts by Govorov to exploit the Soviet penetration of the Panther Line in the Narva area, and by the end of February the front had stabilised along much of the Panther Line from Lake Peipus to Vitebsk. Despite the breaches of the line between Narva and Lake Peipus and north of Nevel, the key towns of Narva, Pskov and Ostrov remained in German hands. Yet STAVKA was far from finished with its offensive plans. During the closing days of February Govorov made strenuous efforts to take Pskov, and at the beginning of March, 2 Baltic Front attacked VIII Corps with two armies north of Pustoshka, and it attacked X Corps with two armies south of the town. Costly and protracted though these offensives were, the German lines held. At the same time Soviet offensives were launched out of the Narva bridgehead, south of Pskov, and, still farther south, in the Idritsa sector. The lack of progress in these attacks prompted a request to STAVKA by Front commands that, prior to another offensive being undertaken, divisions be brought up to a strength of at least five thousand men. The offensives were renewed in April but with no better result, after which the spring rains brought an effective end to the Soviet campaign in the north.

9

Return to the Stalin Line

The rolling series of Soviet offensives that had begun on 12 July 1943 did not end in the spring of 1944. Over the Eastern Front as a whole there was no meaningful delineation between the Red Army's winter and spring campaigns. Operational pauses occurred at various points along the Eastern Front during this time, but there was never a general pause. In the Ukraine and southern Belorussia, a series of offensives drew to a close at the end of February 1944, but at that time the offensive against Army Group North had not concluded. When the northern offensive drew to a close, new offensives were underway in the south. Having grasped the strategic initiative in July 1943, STAVKA was determined not to lose it.

There was in fact little for STAVKA to fear. Hitler had settled on a strategy of strategic defence in the East until the Anglo-American invasion of Western Europe, expected in the spring of 1944, could be dealt a fatal blow. German intelligence could not know the detail of what had been discussed at the Tehran Conference at the end of November 1943, but it could be sure that coordination of strategy between the Eastern and Western theatres would have been high on the agenda. Among the German General Staff there were few who still believed in ultimate German victory against what was increasingly being called the United Nations. Yet most accepted that Hitler's strategy was the only route by which Nazi Germany might be able to achieve a favourable peace settlement, for if the Western Allies could be neutralised, a deal might then be struck with Russia. Failure of Hitler's strategy was the nightmare scenario – a successful Allied invasion of Western Europe resulting in a war on two fronts with millions of well-equipped United Nations personnel firmly established in mainland Europe just a few hundred kilometres from Germany's western border. With this prospect in mind, plots against Hitler's life intensified, for many of Germany's senior military and political figures saw Hitler, rather than lack of success on the battlefield, as the main obstacle to a peace settlement.

Plots against Hitler's life were not new. Prior to 1944 the one that came closest to success was that hatched by a group that included General Henning von Tresckow, chief of staff at Army Group Centre. During a visit by Hitler to Army Group Centre in March 1943, Tresckow arranged for one of the visiting party to deliver a gift of brandy to an old friend back in Germany. The 'gift' was in fact a disguised bomb, designed to detonate once Hitler's plane was airborne on the return journey. The bomb failed to detonate and was subsequently recovered by the conspirators without the plot being uncovered. Subsequent attempts to kill Hitler using suicide bombers at scheduled venues were frustrated by Hitler's habit of constantly changing his schedule. The final plot, that orchestrated by Claus Schenk Count von Stauffenberg, a staff officer at Hitler's headquarters, required Stauffenberg to carry a time-bomb in a briefcase into one of Hitler's regular military conferences. Stauffenburg's first attempt, on 26 December

1943, was frustrated by Hitler's sudden decision to cancel the conference. It was not to be Stauffenburg's last attempt.

In stark contrast, Stalin's position could not have been more secure. With the liberation of each major city came national celebration and formal gun salutes in Moscow. Increasingly, after the spring of 1943, the Soviet media began to associate the growing list of Red Army victories with the military strategy and personal direction of Marshal Stalin. (Stalin assumed the rank of Marshal of the Soviet Union in January 1943). Although, contrary to implications made in that same media, Stalin never visited the frontline, he was generous with awards and promotions for those carrying the burden at the front.

Perhaps the most honoured commander in this period was Konev; promoted to Army General in August 1943 after the capture of Kharkov, he was further promoted to Marshal of the Soviet Union in February 1944 after the fighting around the Cherkassy pocket. Rotmistrov also received two promotions during this time, the second of which was to the newly-created rank of Marshal of Armoured Forces. As previously noted, the Front commanders Govorov and M M Popov were promoted to the rank of Army General; so too were Tolbukhin, Sokolovsky, Eremenko and Bagramyan. Other senior promotions included Grechko, Leslidze, Kurochkin, Chuikov, Shumilov, Gordov, Rybalko, Moskalenko, Cherniakhovsky, Glagolev, Gusev, Tsvetaev and Bogdanov, all promoted to the rank of Colonel-General.

Uncertain Allies
The first full negotiating session of the Tehran Conference was held on 28 November 1943, and the conference lasted a further three days. The main Soviet agenda item was the Second Front; in particular, a commitment from Roosevelt and Churchill on its timing and location. Before the end of the conference it was agreed that the main Allied effort would be directed towards a landing in north-western France before June 1944, with a supplementary landing in southern France soon afterwards. Stalin was immensely satisfied with this commitment, though he still considered that it came at least one year too late. The main agenda item raised by Roosevelt was the issue of Soviet involvement in the war against Japan once the war in Europe had been concluded. On this the Western Allies received an agreement in principle that Stalin would declare war on Japan once Hitler had been defeated. Roosevelt, Churchill, and Stalin also agreed that the Axis powers should be presented with a single option for concluding the war, unconditional surrender, and that no negotiations on any other terms would be conducted. The exception was to be Finland, where Stalin recognised the desire of Britain and America that Finland should not be occupied, and that a negotiated solution to the conflict should be sought based on a return to the 1940 border. It was also agreed that, once defeated, Germany would be divided into occupation zones to be controlled by the Soviet Union, Britain and the US. Perhaps the most difficult issue on the agenda was the future territorial boundary of Poland. Poland was the issue on which Britain had gone to war in 1939, and in London Churchill harboured the Polish Government in Exile, a body reluctant to consider any change to the country's borders. The German discovery near Smolensk the previous spring of the bodies of thousands of Polish army officers taken prisoner by the Soviets in 1939 had already

strained relations between Stalin and his Western Allies.[1] Negotiating from a position of weakness with regard to the unfolding of events in Eastern Europe, Roosevelt and Churchill agreed to consider the Soviet demand that Poland be moved to the west, its eastern border being along the so-called 'Curzon Line' which had been the approximate dividing line between Soviet and German forces in the autumn of 1939, and its western border being along the Oder and Neisse rivers in Germany. Considering the ideological differences and inherent distrust between the parties, the Tehran Conference proved to be a remarkably productive meeting.

Hitler's ideological differences with his allies were not particularly profound, and most of his allies viewed with alarm the advance of the Red Army towards their borders. Yet their responses, based on pure national self-interest, were varied; from a stiffening of the will to resist, to a desire to seek a negotiated settlement. Depending on the individual circumstances, Hitler countered with either military support, threats, the withholding of vital supplies, or plans for political/military intervention.

Perhaps the greatest blow to Hitler's Axis coalition was the collapse of Mussolini's regime in September 1943. Militarily Mussolini's Italy had proved be of limited value to Germany, but among his allies, Mussolini had been Hitler's staunchest political supporter. The collapse of the Fascist regime, and with it the Italian military machine, had left Germany to fight alone against the Anglo-American advance through Italy. By the winter of 1943/44 Germany had been obliged to commit more than a dozen of its best divisions in Italy, and by the late spring of 1944 this had increased to 22 divisions.

On 10 March 1944 Franco informed Hitler that the Spanish division on the Eastern Front, the 250 Inf Div or 'Blue Division', which was fighting with Army Group North, was to be withdrawn. This was more of a political than a military blow to the German war effort, though the combat capability of the Spanish division had been well regarded. Far more serious was the news that, since 12 February 1944, the Finns had been conducting secret negotiations with the Soviets on an armistice agreement. Since the autumn of 1941, when the Soviet/Finnish frontline had settled to a kind of passive belligerence along frontiers that Finland felt it could defend and which STAVKA felt to be of insufficiently high priority to attack, there had been a growing weight of opinion in Finland for a negotiated settlement with Russia. After the defeat in January 1944 of Army Group North at Mga, Leningrad and along the Volkhov, proposals within Finnish government circles to explore armistice terms were accepted by the leadership as a pragmatic response to military reality. After learning of the armistice talks Hitler responded by drastically reducing the supply of arms and ammunition to the Finns; a dangerous gambit since it reduced the capacity of the Finns to resist a possible Soviet attack should the armistice negotiations fail. On 17 March 1944 the Finns did reject the Soviet terms as too onerous, and they rejected revised terms one month later.

In March 1944 some of Rumania's best troops were deployed along its northern border to defend against a possible attack by Hungary. Rumania's two eastern armies, IV

---

1   In 1940 Stalin had ordered the murder of 22,000 Polish officers, of which a significant portion had been buried in a mass grave in the Katyn woods near Smolensk. After their discovery Stalin vehemently denied responsibility, blamed the Nazis, and after the area had been retaken by the Red Army in the autumn of that year, attempted to fabricate evidence implicating the Germans in the massacre. Churchill and Roosevelt had little doubt that Stalin was responsible but found it expedient to accept Stalin's denial.

Army and III Army were deployed in garrison duties in south-western Ukraine behind the German VIII Army and VI Army respectively. Antonescu, while disagreeing with much of Hitler's strategy, particularly with regard to the Crimea, remained loyal to the Axis, and in the Crimea there were seven Rumanian divisions deployed as part of the German XVII Army. Yet Antonescu presided over an increasingly dispirited country that was manifestly unwilling to endure the kind of sacrifice necessary to defend itself effectively against the Red Army. Rumania's entry into the war had been primarily to redress pre-war territorial losses, particularly in Bessarabia. Few Rumanians had ever had much interest in territory east of the Dniester, and the mauling inflicted on Rumania's forces in the Volga and Don battles a year earlier had done much to sap the nation's will to fight.

Conversely, the mood in Hungary grew more belligerent the closer the Red Army drew towards Hungary's borders. An unwilling participant in the war from the start, Hungary had never done more than the minimum necessary to pacify Hitler's demands. In the autumn of 1943 Hitler had become so concerned about possible Hungarian defection from the Axis that he had directed the Operations Staff of OKW to prepare a plan for the military occupation of the country. By the end of February 1944 Hitler was on the verge of putting the plan into effect, but the subsequent diversion of the requisite forces to the frontline in the western Ukraine, together with a combination of credible threats and substantial concessions from Admiral Miklos Horthy, the Hungarian Regent, persuaded him to defer the invasion order. However, on 19 March several SS divisions entered the country in a largely bloodless 'invasion'. Many in Hungary welcomed the intervention, an intervention that resulted in the formation of a more overtly pro-German and anti-Semitic Hungarian administration.

The Western Ukraine

See Map 23 At the beginning of March 1944 German forces in the Ukraine still held positions on the Dnieper, but those positions only covered the final 100km of the river to its estuary. From the Dnieper, the German front ran back to the northwest for approximately 700km to Lutsk and Kovel south of the Pripet Marshes. In the south of the Ukraine German forces could fall back on the Bug and the Dniester river barriers, but overhanging everything was the Soviet penetration to the west of Rovno that could potentially enable any further Soviet offensive from this area, to the south and southwest, to bypass the river barriers and trap the whole of Army Group South and Army Group A east of the Carpathians. This threat, emanating from the potential collapse of his left wing, had been a constant theme of Manstein's tenureship of Army Group South for more than a year. Of prime importance east of the Carpathians was the Odessa railway. This rail line, the main supply route for Army Group South and Army Group A, ran from Lvov to Odessa via Tarnapol, Proskurov and Zhmerinka. There was a secondary rail line to Odessa running east of the Carpathians from Lvov to Stanislav to Chernovtsy to Jassy, but protection of the main line was one of Manstein's key objectives.

Although at the beginning of March Army Group South possessed a more cohesive frontline than for many weeks previously, there was still a gaping hole between XIII Corps at Dubno and LIX Corps at Shepetovka; and the army group's left flank remained Manstein's greatest concern. To address this Manstein, having already given the threatened right flank corps of VIII Army to VI Army, shuffled his forces somewhat. He assigned VII Corps on I Pz Army's right flank to VIII Army, and assigned LIX Corps, the right flank corps of IV Pz Army, to I Pz Army. This left I Pz Army with responsibility for the Shepetovka area, but IV Pz Army remained responsible for the gap to the west of that area and for the rest of the front north to Kovel. In addition to shuffling army boundaries northwards, Manstein also assigned III Pz Corps to the Proskurov area in I Pz Army's rear, though it would be later in the month before it could get there, and he assigned two panzer divisions and three infantry divisions arriving from the west as reinforcement for IV Pz Army.

When the heaviest of the fighting in the Ukraine concluded at the end of February, Manstein might have been forgiven for thinking that he would have a few weeks to recover his balance, possibly longer if the spring rains set in with a vengeance. Yet during the preceding weeks Soviet forces had demonstrated that they could continue to conduct offensive operations through rain and deep mud, making effective use of the light, single-horse peasant *panje* wagon; and with all six Soviet tank armies still facing Army Group South, Manstein was to be given just a few days grace before he would be obliged to face a particularly difficult four weeks.

STAVKA had decided as early as 18 February to continue through March its offensive campaign on the southern axis, with the objective, once again, of destroying the *Ostheer*'s right wing. On 17 February STAVKA created 2 Belorussian Front. Placed under Kurochkin's command, this new Front, which became operational on 24 February, was positioned to cover the frontline facing II Army through the western and central Pripet Marshes on 1 Ukrainian Front's right wing. This left Rokossovsky, whose forces were designated 1 Belorussian Front, free to concentrate on IX Army along the direct route to Minsk from the east and southeast.

Kurochkin had 16 rifle divisions, 6 cavalry divisions and a tank brigade organised into Belov's 61 Army (formerly part of Belorussian Front), Polenov's 47 Army (from 1 Ukrainian Front), and 70 Army (from STAVKA Reserve and under Ryzhov's command). Kurochkin was to build on earlier Soviet success in the Kovel and Lutsk areas by attacking Kovel, with Brest as the ultimate objective. Facing Kurochkin was Weiss's II Army, the right flank of which had been extended west through the Pripet Marshes in order to maintain contact with Army Group South, thereby leaving much of II Army facing south. With just three infantry divisions, two brigades, the divisional-sized 'Corps Detachment E' and a security division, Weiss had to cover hundreds of kilometres of frontline. Yet much of this frontline ran through virtually impenetrable tracts of marsh. In the centre and on the west of this line Weiss based his defences on Pinsk and on Kovel.

At the beginning of March Zhukov had 55 rifle divisions in Pukhov's 13 Army, Cherniakhovsky's 60 Army, Grechko's 1 Gds Army, Lt-Gen E P Zhuravlev's 18 Army and Moskalenko's 38 Army.[2] Additionally, Zhukov had Rybalko's 3 Gds Tank Army in reserve behind 60 Army, Katukov's 1 Tank Army in reserve behind 38 Army, and, as Front reserve, he had Badanov's 4 Tank Army. Zhukov's frontline stretched from south of Kovel to east of Vinnitsa, and much of it, particularly in the Dubno – Shepetovka sector, faced south. The objective set for 1 Ukrainian Front was to attack from Rovno

---

2   Zhuravlev was appointed to the command of 18 Army after Leselidze was hospitalised with a fatal illness in February 1944.

south to Chertkov in order to compromise any German attempts to make a stand on the Bug. If possible, it was to advance further to Chernovtsy in order to similarly compromise any stand on the Dniester or Prut river lines. Opposing Zhukov were the two panzer armies that between them had ten infantry divisions, seven panzer divisions, three panzer grenadier divisions, 'Corps Detachment C', an artillery division and a security division. Additional divisions were moving east towards the IV Pz Army sector, but some of these had been earmarked for the occupation of Hungary.

At the beginning of March Konev's 2 Ukrainian Front was, of comparable size to 1 Ukrainian Front. It comprised 51 rifle divisions within Zhmachenko's 40 Army (from 1 Ukrainian Front), Trofimenko's 27 Army, Koroteev's 52 Army, Lt-Gen I K Smirnov's 4 Gds Army, Managorov's 53 Army, Zhadov's 5 Gds Army and Shumilov's 7 Gds Army. In addition, Konev had Bogdanov's 2 Tank Army (transferred from 1 Ukrainian Front) in reserve behind 40 Army; Kravchenko's 6 Tank Army (also transferred from 1 Ukrainian Front) in reserve behind 52 Army; and Rotmistrov's 5 Gds Tank Army in reserve behind 5 Gds Army. Konev's task was to attack out of the Zvenigorodka area towards Uman and, ultimately, Jassy. Facing Konev was Woehler's VIII Army with seven infantry divisions, six panzer divisions, two panzer grenadier divisions and a mountain division.

Malinovsky's 3 Ukrainian Front comprised 56 rifle divisions, 2 mechanised corps, a tank corps and a cavalry corps of three cavalry divisions. These forces were organised into Gagan's 57 Army (transferred from 2 Ukrainian Front), Sharokhin's 37 Army, Glagolev's 46 Army, Chuikov's 8 Gds Army, Shlemin's 6 Army, Tsvetaev's 5 Shock Army (transferred from 4 Ukrainian Front), and Lt-Gen Grechkin's 28 Army (also transferred from 4 Ukrainian Front). Malinovsky's main strike force was a cavalry-mechanised group under the command of Lt-Gen I E Pliev, a group that was composed of the Front's cavalry corps and one of its mechanised corps. Malinovsky faced the main part of Hollidt's powerful VI Army with its 26 divisions and 8 corps headquarters. The six divisions that constituted the right flank of VI Army still held the right bank of the lower Dnieper and faced part of 4 Ukrainian Front, but Tobukhin was preoccupied with preparations for an offensive into the Crimea against XVII Army, and Hollidt was aware that the main danger emanated from Malinovsky's forces on his centre and left. Here STAVKA set Malinovsky the task of expanding his bridgeheads over the Ingulets, forcing the lower Bug and advancing to Odessa.

The first attack of STAVKA's spring offensive came from 1 Ukrainian Front. On 4 March Cherniakhovsky's 60 Army struck the junction of IV Pz Army and I Pz Army in the gap in the German lines between Dubno and Shepetovka, and quickly broke through. Zhukov committed 4 Tank Army and 3 Gds Tank Army into the gap, 3 Gds Tank Army breaking out to the south. East of Shepetovka 1 Gds Army broke through I Pz Army's lines and also pushed south. The next day 13 Army attacked IV Pz Army's positions north of Dubno, striking southwest towards Brody. In the Shepetovka area LIX Corps, outflanked on both sides, fell back to the south. By 6 March the tank armies had penetrated 40km into the German lines, with Shepetovka and the rail line to Tarnapol providing the main axis of advance. By this time the gap between the two panzer armies was 150km wide from Ostrog to the Slutch, and LIX Corps was isolated at Staro Constantinov. North of the railway between Proskurov and Tarnapol, Manstein was able to assemble elements of 1 SS Pz Div and 7 Pz Div (the latter with no operational tanks) under Balck's XLVIII Pz Corps Headquarters. He also tried to speed up the redeployment of III Pz Corps to the Proskurov area, and to detrain west of Ternapol two of the new infantry divisions arriving to reinforce IV Pz Army. By 10 March these redeployments, together with the extraction of LIX Corps from Staro Constantinov to the south, enabled Raus to launch ferocious counter-attacks that stalled Zhukov's offensive along the Proskurov – Tarnapol axis and which, to a large extent, placed 1 Ukrainian Front on the defensive in this area. They also left German forces in control of both Proskurov and Tarnapol, though XLVIII Pz Corps was ultimately unable to hold its line to the north of the railway.

On 8 March Hitler announced, in *Führer* Order 11, the creation of a new defensive designation, the *Festung* (fortress or fortified area). This was to be a locality with a designated garrison under the command of an officer having the status of a corps commander. The significance of the corps commander status was that the officer concerned would be authorised to order executions. Additionally, the *Festung* commander would be answerable only to the army group headquarters, and would be charged with ensuring that the garrison under his command would neither retreat nor surrender. The purpose of the *Festung* was to deny the Red Army access to vital communication hubs in order to inhibit their forward mobility after an operational breakthrough. In the Army Group South zone Vinnitsa, Pervomaysk, Kovel, Brody, Proskurov and Tarnapol were designated as *Festungen*.

On 5 March Konev's 2 Ukrainian Front opened an offensive with 5 Gds Army against VIII Army east of Uman. Zhadov achieved a rapid breakthrough, prompting the early commitment of 5 Gds Tank Army. Two days later, with Rotmistrov exploiting the breakthrough just 40km from Uman, and with the other two tank armies available to further exploit the breach, Konev launched another offensive with 7 Gds Army at the VIII Army – VI Army boundary on his left flank west of Kirovograd. On 9 March Soviet forces took Uman, seizing large stocks of supplies and equipment at what had been a major German depot, and compromising Woehler's ability to make a stand on the Bug. Late on 11 March advance elements of 16 Tank Corps and 29 Tank Corps, from 2 Tank Army and 5 Gds Tank Army respectively, established bridgeheads over the upper Bug at Dzhulinka and Gaivoron. On Woehler's left flank, Hell's VII Corps, attempting to defend the Gaivoron area, disintegrated under the subsequent Soviet pressure. Its depleted divisions pulled back in a disorganised state towards the Bug, losing all contact with I Pz Army's right flank. Consequently Soviet mechanised forces were able to advance west into the gap virtually unopposed, and on 12 March they cut the main Lvov – Odessa railway.

Farther south on 6 March, 3 Ukrainian Front opened an offensive against VI Army's front on the Ingulets south of Krivoi Rog, denting VI Army's lines to a depth of 8km. Despite the early commitment by Hollidt of his two reserve divisions to try to blunt Malinovsky's offensive, on 7 March Pliev's forces broke out, reaching Novy Bug that night, and taking the town, just 10km east of the Ingul, the next day. Hitler had forbidden any withdrawals but Hollidt was in no doubt that withdrawal was the only way to save his army. To avoid an incriminating paper trail, VI Army Headquarters began to withdraw its bulging left flank through the process of issuing verbal orders only. On 8 March Kleist informed OKH that if VI Army continued to try to fight east of the Bug, it would be destroyed. At that time Malinovsky's forces at Novy Bug could have struck south to Nikolaev trapping the southern half of VI Army, or they could have struck west to get across the Bug ahead of VI Army. As at Apostolovo in February, Malinovsky split his forces in an attempt to do two things at once, and again achieved neither.

On 12 March, his left flank in tatters, Woehler's main concern was that 2 Ukrainian Front would turn south between the Bug and the Dniester in order to trap VIII Army and VI Army. His army had been reduced to four panzer divisions, four infantry divisions and a handful of battle groups, and Konev even had sufficient additional forces to cross the Dniester and turn south down the valley of the Prut to encircle VIII Army and VI Army even farther west. In fact STAVKA was in the process of redirecting the Fronts in a manner that would take the pressure off VIII Army somewhat after mid-March, but at the expense of increased pressure for Hube. On 11 March Malinovsky was ordered to speed the pursuit of German forces in order to cut them off from the lower reaches of the Bug, and thereafter to head for the Prut and ultimately the Danube. The next day STAVKA confirmed that Zhukov's objective remained Chernovtsy in order to cut off I Pz Army from retreat to the west and to cut the communication links between German forces in Poland and those in the Ukraine. Zhukov's forces were to advance in two directions, on Lvov and on Chernovtsy via Khotin. Zhukov's left flank armies were to take Vinnitsa and Zhmerinka and then, in conjunction with 4 Tank Army, to move on Kamenets-Podolsky, while on the right flank 13 Army was to reach the Berestechka – Brody – Zalozhtsy line. In the centre Katukov's 1 Tank Army would strike for Chertkov and then Chernovtsy. Konev's forces were also to advance in two thrusts, one to Mogilev-Podolsky and one to Kishinev. The southerly drive of 2 Ukrainian Front down both banks of the Dniester was aimed at the line of retreat of VI Army, VIII Army and III Rum Army, the objective being to trap them between 2 Ukrainian Front and 3 Ukrainian Front. In the north, Konev's objective was to cooperate with 1 Ukrainian Front in encircling I Pz Army. Meanwhile Kurochkin's 2 Belorussian Front was to attack towards Kovel on 17 March.

By 12 March an attempt by Hollidt to pinch off the Soviet penetration of his lines by retaking Novy Bug had failed, and subsequently VI Army found itself in a race with Soviet forces to get to the lower reaches of the Bug. Malinovsky was presented with an opportunity to encircle seven German divisions in an area between the Ingulets and the Ingul some 40km north of Kherson. However, after 12 March the southerly advance of 8 Gds Army from Novy Bug to Nikolaev slowed and, though Pliev's group set out from Novy Bug on a deep outflanking drive, only three of Hollidt's divisions were encircled. The encirclement was not tight and the surrounded German divisions were able to break through Chuikov's lines to reach the Ingul by mid-March. On 13 March Grechkin's 28 Army of 3 Ukrainian Front took Kherson, thereby clearing the last stretch of the Dnieper of German troops, and leaving Tolbukhin free to turn his attention entirely to the task of retaking the Crimea.

By 15 March Vapnyarka, a major rail junction on the main Odessa rail line, had been taken by 16 Tank Corps. Additionally Zhukov had launched an offensive father north with his left flank 38 Army that had split off the right flank corps of I Pz Army (Gollnick's XLVI Pz Corps) from the rest of Hube's command. Moskalenko's forces plunged into the gap so created, driving towards Vinnitsa. Gollnick tried to move his corps to the south to cover the Dniester crossings at Mogilev-Podolsky and Yampol, some 5km north of Soroki. Yet, in moving south, the corps ran into Kravchenko's 6 Tank Army, which was racing west after crossing the Bug, and in consequence XLVI Pz Corps was pushed to the west ahead of the tank army. The Dniester was reached east of Soroki by 29 Tank Corps on 17 March, and two days later 5 Mech Corps, from 6 Tank Army, cleared Mogilev-Podolsky of German forces. Hence by 19 March Kravchenko had split the German front running from Mogilev-Podolsky to Soroki and, though engineers from one of VII Corps' divisions had destroyed the Dniester bridge at Mogilev-Podolsky, 5 Mech Corps began a major crossing of the river the next day.[3] As 5 Mech Corps was crossing the Dniester, Vinnitsa was taken by Moskalenko's forces, but by that time elements of 38 Army were past Zhmerinka and heading southwest, unopposed in the gap between XLVI Pz Corps and the rest of I Pz Army. By 22 March Konev's forces had reached the Dniester in strength between Kamenka and Mogilev-Podolsky, and were in the process of building numerous bridges in order to facilitate a continuation of the offensive to a considerably greater depth.

By 21 March Hollidt had secured a solid front on the Bug but on this date, unwell and out of favour with Hitler after the withdrawal of VI Army's left flank from the Ingulets, he learned that he was to be dismissed from command of VI Army as soon as a replacement could be found.[4] On 24 March Hollidt travelled to Woehler's headquarters where the two commanders agreed that their armies must pull back to the Dniester and that, if necessary, they would act without army group or OKH approval. The next day reconnaissance units of 2 Ukrainian Front reached Beltsy 80km west of the Dniester in Bessarabia and deep behind VIII Army's front. Woehler desperately needed the support of IV Rum Army but he found its command staff reluctant to defend the upper Prut, though they were willing to defend the 'Strunga Line' from Jassy west towards the Carpathians. On 26 March, as 27 Army and 52 Army reached the Prut along a 60km stretch of the river north of Jassy, Kleist informed OKH that he had taken command of VIII Army from Army Group South and, without OKH approval, he issued orders for a general withdrawal to the Dniester. The next day Hitler reluctantly acquiesced to this, but only on condition that Army Group A held a bridgehead along the Black Sea from Tiraspol to Odessa. In the course of VI Army's withdrawal, Nikolaev fell to Soviet forces on 28 March.

On Manstein's left flank, furious counter-attacks against 1 Ukrainian Front by III Pz Corps, LIX Corps, XLVIII Pz Corps and the infantry divisions arriving at Ternopol from the west (the third division arrived on 12 March), had kept Soviet forces away from Ternopol and Proskurov, and on 16 March Raus estimated that he would be able to retake the lost section of railway line between the two towns within a few days. However, after 12 March, with the cutting of the railway line to Odessa by Konev's forces farther south, the strategic significance of the Ternopol – Proskurov section of railway had declined significantly. Yet the strategic significance of a deep Soviet penetration to the south of Ternopol towards Chernovtsy remained. On Raus's left flank, 13 Army pushed German forces out of Lutsk and Dubno on 16 March, and *Festung* Kovel was surrounded. To relieve Kovel, Manstein took some of the forces recuperating after their escape from the Cherkassy pocket (including the

---

3   The bridge at Yampol had been destroyed by the same German division on 17 March.

4   General Maximilian de Angelis, the commander of XLIV Corps, took command of VI Army on 8 April.

SS *Wiking* Div) and organised them into a strike force that was ultimately successful in re-establishing contact with the town.

By 21 March Zhukov had reorganised his forces on the Ternopol – Proskurov sector, and was ready to renew his offensive effort against IV Pz Army. In overwhelming force, 1 Ukrainian Front broke through the German lines between Ternopol and Proskurov, carrying 1 SS Pz Div (*Leibstandarte*), 7 Pz Div and 68 Inf Div southwards with them. Turning to the east, 3 Gds Tank Army and 1 Gds Army advanced on Proskurov, and 1 Tank Army turned west to encircle the German garrison at *Festung* Ternopol. Two days later, continuing to the south, forward Soviet mechanised forces from 4 Tank Army (by that time commanded by Lelyushenko) reached Chertkov, severing I Pz Army's supply line railway from Stanislav to Proskurov. With Zhukov's forces pushing south from Chertkov, and Konev's forces pushing west from one of its bridgehead over the Dniester south of Mogilev-Podolsky, I Pz Army was under threat of encirclement. Since 1 SS Pz Div, 7 Pz Div and 68 Inf Div had become detached from IV Pz Army, and were being pushed into I Pz Army's zone, Manstein assigned them to Hube's command, ordering him to anchor his right flank on the Dniester and to prepare to pull back his left flank in order to release forces for the retaking of Chertkov. However, it was not until the early hours of 26 March that Hitler gave permission for a withdrawal I Pz Army from the Proskurov area, by which time 4 Tank Army had turned to the east and was approaching Kamenets-Podolsky deep in I Pz Army's rear. Meanwhile, part of 40 Army from 2 Ukrainian Front was advancing on the Dniester northwest of Mogilev-Podolsky beyond which lay Khotin and the prospect of encircling most of I Pz Army east of the Prut. The force at risk of encirclement comprised twenty divisions, half of them panzer or motorised divisions. Hitler reluctantly agreed to release to Manstein from OKW reserve Hausser's II SS Pz Corps with its two infantry divisions and the newly-raised 9 SS Pz Div and 10 SS Pz Div. Manstein ordered Hube to break out to the west, effectively moving his army along the north bank of the Dniester; attacking to the west while withdrawing from the north and east. This would mean crossing the Zbruch and Seret rivers (which flowed north to south into the Dniester) across the line of advance of 3 Gds Tank Army and 4 Tank Army; but the only alternative, the one preferred by Hube, was to move south across the Dniester east of Khotin where Soviet forces were weaker but where the river was more than a kilometre wide. By 28 March, with 40 Army having reached Khotin, the encirclement of I Pz Army to the north of Kamenets-Podolsky was complete. Though surrounded by 3 Gds Tank Army, 4 Tank Army, 1 Gds Army, 18 Army, 38 Army and elements of 40 Army, a 15km gap existed between 4 Tank Army, which was down to 60 tanks, and 1 Gds Army. Zhukov expected any attempted breakout by 1 Pz Army to be to the south across the Dniester and into Rumania, and his forces, in the process of deploying to meet that eventuality, were caught off-balance by Hube's breakout to the west. By 29 March Hube had secured two bridgeheads across the Zbruch, but was not receiving enough supplies by air for I Pz Army to fight its way through a Soviet defence of the Seret. At the end of March a blizzard began that was to last three days, inhibiting ground movement but during which II SS Pz Corps began to detrain and air supply could continue largely unhindered. On 2 April I Pz Army attacked west across the Seret near Chertkov. By 4 April Hube's forces had fought off two Soviet tank corps that had been brought south during the clearing weather, and I Pz Army continued to push west through Chertkov. The next day II SS Pz Corps launched an attack eastwards from IV Pz Army's lines to the west of Buchach, hitting Cherniakhovsky's 60 Army which was holding the outer ring. The deployment of Hausser's corps had gone undetected by Soviet intelligence, and Cherniakhovsky was taken by surprise at the power of the German attack. On 6 April II SS Pz Corps and I Pz Army met at Buchach. By 10 April the whole of I Pz Army was west of the Seret and the threat of encirclement had passed.[5]

Manstein may have successfully orchestrated the escape of I Pz Army from encirclement, but he was unable to prevent Zhukov from securing Chernovtsy on the secondary rail line to Odessa on 29 March. This put Army Group A, thereafter dependent on the unreliable Rumanian railway system for supply, in an impossible position, and served to confirm the correctness of Kleist's order issued on 26 March for a general retreat of Army Group A to the lower Dniester.

During the last week of March, with Soviet forces approaching the Hungarian border, Hungary began to mobilise additional forces and positioned its VII Corps on the upper Prut, keeping its VIII Corps in position behind Army Group Centre. By the end of the month VII Corps had been joined by the newly-raised VI Corps to form I Hun Army under the command of Col-Gen Geza Lakatos. On 30 March OKW released one of its divisions in Hungary, 1 Mtn Div, to Army Group South for the defence of the Tartar Pass. This transfer was strongly resisted by Jodl who, two weeks later, argued that of the 131 divisions in OKW theatres – that is, not in the OKH theatre – only 41 were suitably equipped for employment on the Eastern Front, and 32 of those were already engaged in Italy and Finland.

Hitler was infuriated at the loss of the western Ukraine, and at midnight on 30 March Manstein and Kleist were relieved of their commands, to be replaced by the newly-promoted Field Marshal Model and Col-Gen Schoerner. On 5 April Army Group South was redesignated Army Group North Ukraine, and Army Group A was redesignated Army Group South Ukraine. By this time, with I Pz Army still in the process of trying to break out across the Seret, and with VI Army still in the process of pulling back from the Bug, Soviet forces reached the Carpathians to the west of Kolomiya and Chernovtsy. On 3 April the German bridgehead on the left bank of the Dniester to Odessa, upon which Hitler had insisted when approving the withdrawal of VI Army, was cut in two south of Razdelnaya, and in the process 3 Ukrainian Front surrounded several German and Rumanian divisions in the Razdelnaya area. In scenes of near total chaos VI Army troops tried to fall back across the Dniester. Odessa, the main supply base for the Crimea, was abandoned by Axis forces, and fell to 8 Gds Army, 5 Shock Army and 6 Army on 10 April. By then the Red Army's offensives in the western Ukraine had largely run out of steam. In the second week of April German mechanised forces stopped a Soviet advance west of Jassy, and VIII Army, together with IV Rum Army, was able to form a line from Dubosarry on the Dniester to Jassy to Pashkany and north along the Carpathians to link in with the right flank of Army Group North Ukraine. On the lower Dniester the last German forces had pulled back to the right bank of the river by 14 April, but VI Army had been unable to prevent Malinovsky from establishing several bridgeheads over the river,

---

5   Ten days later, having saved his army from disaster, Hube was killed in a plane crash and was replaced by Chevallerie.

one south of Tiraspol and the others north of Bendery. On 11 April an attempt by 9 SS Pz Div to relieve the Ternopol garrison began but made only slow progress. On the night of 15 April the remnants of the surrounded German force in the town tried to break out but only 53 men of the original 4,000-strong garrison reached German lines, and the town was finally secured by 1 Ukrainian Front on 17 April. Zhukov's forces subsequently made some determined efforts to cross the upper Seret, but were stopped by spirited defensive actions from VII Hun Corps. By the end of April the front had stabilised from Kovel, to Brody, to Tarnopol, to Buchach, to Kolomya, to Pashkany, to Tirgu Frumos, to Dubossary and down the lower Dniester.

The Soviet spring offensive in the Ukraine had been an astounding success, and had inflicted enormous damage on the *Ostheer*. To maintain credible defences on several sections of the front, an increasingly threadbare *Ostheer* had to rely on 'corps detachments' – divisional-sized groupings of depleted divisions, the first of which had been formed in November 1943 – and had to rely on security divisions to man frontline positions. Another organisational innovation widely employed by OKH after the Soviet spring offensive of 1944 was the *Armeegruppe* – a combat force intermediate in size between an army group (*Heeresgruppe*) and an army. This organisational device was designed to improve the reliability and combat capability of the Rumanian divisions on the *Ostheer*'s right wing, divisions that Army Group South Ukraine needed in order to create a credible frontline. Each *Armeegruppe* consisted of a German army and a Rumanian army, the overall command of which came under one of the two army headquarters.

Despite the Soviet successes, in the spring of 1944 the Red Army once again paid a heavy price in casualties. The various operations from 24 December 1943 to 17 April 1944 by the Ukrainian Fronts to recover the western Ukraine generated more than 1.1 million Soviet casualties, around a quarter of them irrecoverable losses.

The Crimea

By the spring of 1944, despite the attenuation of German forces along the length of the Eastern Front, Hitler had increased the strength of the German garrison in the Crimea from one to five divisions. Jaenecke's XVII Army, bottled up in the Crimea for more than five months, also included seven Rumanian divisions. Tolbukhin's planning for the Crimean campaign had been prolonged and meticulous. For the offensive he had eighteen rifle divisions and a tank corps in Lt-Gen Zakharov's 2 Gds Army and Kreizer's 51 Army. The Guards army was positioned on the Front's right wing facing German forces in the Perikop Isthmus, and Kreizer's army faced Rumanian troops farther east across the Sivash. For weeks Soviet engineers had secretly been constructing causeways across the Sivash, work that had gone undetected by the Rumanian defenders. By the second week of April Tolbukhin was ready to launch the attack, an attack that was coordinated with the twelve rifle divisions of Eremenko's Independent Coastal Army, formerly the Independent Black Sea Army, in the Kerch Peninsula.[6]

On 8 April the assault by 4 Ukrainian Front in the Perikop Isthmus and across the Sivash began. The assault across the isthmus by 2 Gds Army was held by the

6   The Coastal Army had been under Eremenko's command since February after an operation in January by Petrov to expand the Soviet positions on the Kerch Peninsula had failed to make significant progress.

German defenders, but 51 Army successfully crossed the Sivash over the partially submerged causeways and pushed the Rumanian defenders back. By 9 April, 10 Rum Inf Div, defending the key section of the Sivash, began to disintegrate and at the same time Eremenko's forces attacked out of the Kerch bridgehead. By the next day XVII Army was in general retreat to the Gneisenau Line, an arc of some 70km radius from Sevastopol, and encompassing Simferopol; and preparations were being made by Jaenecke for the evacuation by air and sea of non-essential personnel from Sevastopol to Constanta in Rumania. On 11 April Kreizer's forces took Dzhankoy in a breakthrough that threatened the Axis withdrawal from Kerch towards Sevastopol. Many Axis units could not retreat fast enough and were captured. By 12 April Soviet forces had breached the Gneisenau Line in several places, and three days later the Independent Coastal Army advancing from Kerch was incorporated into 4 Ukrainian Front. Having seen the Gneisenau Line defences compromised, Jaenecke authorised a continuation of the withdrawal to the main Sevastopol defences, which were fully occupied by 16 April. On 18 April XVII Army, in the process of evacuating some 40,000 non-essential personnel, reported that it had suffered over 30,000 casualties, and that of the more than 120,000 troops remaining under command, the 46,000 Rumanians were unfit for combat and only one-third of the German troops could be counted as combat-effective. In consequence XVII Army estimated its combat strength at just five regimental-sized battle groups. Nonetheless Hitler insisted, in order to quell any possible belligerency from Turkey, that the city should be held until the anticipated Anglo-American invasion of Western Europe had been defeated. Sevastopol's defences were formidable, and Tolbukhin was unable to take the city off the march. Instead, he was obliged to pause in order to prepare a coordinated assault. On 28 April Jaenecke was replaced as commander of XVII Army by General Karl Allmendinger who, as one of XVII Army's corps commanders, was a man Hitler believed could more enthusiastically conduct the defence.

By early May Tolbukhin was ready to launch his assault on the city. In a feint against the Axis defences, Soviet forces struck to the north on 5 May, and launched the main assault near Balaklava two days later. Late in the day on 7 May Soviet forces reached the Sapun Heights overlooking the city, and the next day Hitler authorised a general evacuation. After four days of bitter fighting, Sevastopol fell late on 9 May. By noon on 12 May the remaining 25,000 German troops in the Crimea, concentrated into the Kherson Spit, had surrendered. Total Axis losses were 96,700, two-thirds of them German, and the irrecoverable losses were 57,500, over half of them German, and with the majority taken prisoner. The Axis losses included several thousand men drowned at sea when two evacuation ships were torpedoed by Soviet submarines. Unusually for a Soviet offensive operation, Red Army losses were lower than those of the Axis. Tolbukhin's total casualties were a little under 85,000 with irrecoverable losses of less than 18,000. When the fighting was over 4 Ukrainian Front Headquarters and XVII Army Headquarters were rendered temporarily redundant. The Coastal Army resumed its independent status in defence of the Crimea, while 2 Gds Army and 51 Army were withdrawn into STAVKA reserve.

Preparations for the Final Soviet Summer Offensive

In the seventeen months to mid-April 1944 the Red Army had advanced along the southern axis, from the Terek to the Prut, a distance of 1,600km. In the same period on the central axis it had only advanced from the upper Don to the upper Dnieper, a distance of just 600km. The disproportionate advances between the two axes had produced an extended frontline in Belorussia stretching laterally east to west through the Pripet Marshes; 1 Ukrainian Front was within striking distance of Lvov in the west, while 1 Belorussian Front's right wing lay hundreds of kilometres farther east at Zhlobin. It was an anomalous situation that, from its appearance on the situation maps, became known as the Belorussian balcony. On 5 April Kurochkin's 2 Belorussian Front, in existence for less than two months, was disbanded, its forces and its 500km of frontline being incorporated back into 1 Belorussian Front.[7] Most of the territorial gain on the central axis through 1943 and into 1944 had been achieved on the southern wing; more centrally Western Front had only advanced 300km from Vyazma towards Orsha, and most of this advance had been achieved in the late summer of 1943. In the period from mid-October 1943 to the end of March 1944, Sokolovsky conducted eleven unsuccessful offensive operations on the Orsha, Vitebsk and Bogushev axes, and during that time his Front incurred nearly a third of a million combat casualties. It was a performance for which Sokolovsky was severely criticised, and it resulted in his dismissal as Western Front commander in mid-April 1944. Sokolovsky's surprise replacement was Cherniakhovsky, the young but highly successful commander of 60 Army.

In their consideration of the options for the summer offensive, STAVKA was aware that the cross-channel invasion of Western Europe was scheduled for the second half of May. Irrespective of whether the invasion proved to be a success, it seemed reasonable to assume that in early June the *Ostheer* would be compelled to function on its own resources, denied the opportunity to call on reinforcements from the west. Having taken the decision in principle to direct the Red Army's summer offensive along the central axis, in the second half of April STAVKA began a major restructuring of the Belorussian and Baltic Fronts. In the north a new Front, designated 3 Baltic Front, was formed based on the staff of 20 Army, (20 Army being disbanded). This new Front, placed under the command of the methodical Maslennikov, was effectively a recreation of Volkhov Front since the enlarged Leningrad Front had been found, during the previous two months, to be too unwieldy and to be attempting to achieve too many objectives simultaneously. (The new Front incorporated 42 Army, 67 Army and 54 Army from Leningrad Front, and 1 Shock Army from 2 Baltic Front). At roughly the same time, and for much the same reasons, Western Front was disbanded and divided into two new Fronts. Western Front's headquarters staff at Krasnoye, Cherniakhovsky still in command, was designated 3 Belorussian Front and was assigned command responsibility for the northern sector of the former Front west of Smolensk. The southern sector of what had been Western Front east of Mogilev was placed under the command of Petrov. Utilising the headquarters staff of the recently disbanded 10 Army, Petrov's new command, designated the second formation of 2 Belorussian Front, set up its headquarters at Mstislavl. Petrov had the misfortune to have Mekhlis,

---

7   On his right flank Rokossovsky simultaneously relinquished his 50 Army and 10 Army to Western Front.

somewhat rehabilitated into Stalin's inner circle, on his army's military council. Another senior command change made in the final week of April was the replacement of M M Popov at 2 Baltic Front by Eremenko. In May Zhukov relinquished command of 1 Ukrainian Front in order to coordinate the upcoming central axis offensive. Konev replaced Zhukov at 1 Ukrainian Front, Malinovsky moved to the command of 2 Ukrainian Front, and Tolbukhin replaced Malinovsky at 3 Ukrainian Front.

On 22 May a two-day conference began in Moscow to debate the details of what had been entitled Operation Bagration. A key component of the operation was a strategic deception plan to convince OKH that the Red Army's summer offensive would be directed from the Ukraine. This was not a particularly difficult sell. Soviet pre-war planning for an invasion of Eastern Europe had envisaged that the main offensive would emanate from the Ukraine, and, given the strategic situation in the early summer of 1944, an offensive by 1 Ukrainian Front into Galicia, in a strike to the northwest down the Vistula, made perfect strategic sense. Such an offensive could use the river to protect an expanding left flank as far as Warsaw, and might then reach the Baltic some 250km farther north to isolate the bulk of the *Ostheer* from direct overland contact with the Fatherland. To aid the deception plan, four of the Soviet tank armies were kept in the south, and efforts were made to disguise the movement of 5 Gds Tank Army, and subsequently 2 Tank Army, to the central axis. Additionally, 3 Ukrainian Front and 3 Baltic Front were required to generate signals traffic and operational manoeuvres indicative of preparations for a major offensive, while in the active operational areas on the central axis deployments were made covertly and at night. Although the initial phase of the offensive would be directed against Army Group Centre north of the Pripet, plans were also laid for a subsequent expansion of the offensive to the flanks. This second phase, to be directed against Army Group North and Army Group North Ukraine, would commence some weeks after the initial phase, as soon as the heavy artillery regiments, required for the destruction of the German forward defences in Belorussia, could be relocated.

The operational plan was complete by the end of May and was based on simultaneous strikes at the flanks of Army Group Centre at Vitebsk and Bobruisk to envelop and destroy the German forces in these centres, and simultaneously to attack and destroy German forces in Mogilev. Attacks would be mounted on narrow fronts where high concentrations of artillery would be employed, and where infantry would be committed in densely packed formations. Air support would be used initially to suppress German artillery. Armour would be committed only after a breakthrough had been achieved and would advance without regard to the flanks. It had become axiomatic in Soviet offensives that where the mechanised forces succeeded, the offensive as a whole succeeded, and where the mechanised forces failed to achieve an operational breakthrough, the offensive failed. The planning for Bagration reflected not only the culmination of such operational experience in conducting offensive operations, but also the need to conserve the now limited manpower resource in a Red Army whose four-hundred and eighty divisions could not be maintained at anywhere near authorised strength. Massed frontal assaults were not only increasingly rare, they tended to be associated with command failure. The Red Army's Field Regulations for 1944 reflected these changes, and represented a remarkable transformation in approach from equivalent pre-war documents. From a pre-war situation where initiative was actively discouraged, the 1944 Regulations stated, "The readiness to take responsibility on oneself for a daring action and to carry it to a conclusion in a persistent manner is the basis for action of all commanders in battle". Yet increased operational sophistication notwithstanding, it remained the case that Soviet combat units directly involved in an offensive could generally expect to suffer more than 20% casualties in the achievement of their objectives.

STAVKA decided that, for Operation Bagration, Vasilevsky would coordinate the actions of 1 Baltic Front and 3 Belorussian Front, while Zhukov would coordinate the two other Belorussian Fronts. The initial breakthrough was to be followed by the envelopment of Minsk from both northwest and southwest, and the isolation and destruction of Army Group Centre. The role of 1 Baltic Front would be to cooperate with 3 Belorussian Front in destroying German forces in the Vitebsk – Lepel area, and to then to force the Dvina in an advance to the Lepel – Chasniki area. Meanwhile 3 Belorussian Front would cooperate with both 1 Baltic Front and 2 Belorussian Front in the destruction of German forces at Vitebsk and at Orsha (in the latter case by attacking along the Minsk highway to Borisov), and to then advance to, and across, the Berezina. Early in June Petrov fell foul of Mekhlis's venom when Mekhlis complained to Stalin of purported deficiencies in Petrov's command ability. As a result, there was a late change in command at 2 Belorussian Front when Petrov, subsequently demoted, was replaced by the newly-promoted Col-Gen G F Zakharov. Zakharov's task would be to take Mogilev and then advance to the Berezina. Rokossovsky was to concentrate four armies on his right flank south of Rogachev in preparation for a strike at Bobruisk, the objective being to envelop the town from both sides of the Berezina and to surround the German forces there, with the ultimate objective of Minsk.[8] Subsequently Rokossovsky would be required to develop his offensive to include his centre and left flank in support of a general advance beyond Minsk towards the Vistula. The planning contributions of the Front commanders notwithstanding, it was STAVKA and the Soviet General Staff who decided not only the strategy for the offensive but also the tactical details of the operational planning. This Zakharov discovered for himself in early June when he tried to change the jumping off point for his Front's main advance. Yet the detailed tactical planning was only undertaken to achieve a breakthrough of the main German defence line – to a depth of some 60km. Thereafter there were few detailed plans, only requirements for general lines of advance to a further depth of 150km. This was a departure from previous STAVKA practice, and was the result of a decision to delegate to the Front commanders a considerable degree of responsibility for development of the offensive after the initial phase in order to be able to exploit to the maximum operational opportunities as they arose.

A participant in the second phase of the operation by 1 Belorussian Front's left wing would be the newly-raised Polish 1 Army. British-equipped Polish troops had been fighting in the Mediterranean theatre since 1941, and a Polish armoured division had been raised in England to participate in the invasion of Western Europe. Most of the Polish volunteers in these units were former prisoners of the Red Army from the 1939 conflict, who Stalin had permitted to travel to the Middle East via Persia. On 9 May 1943 the Soviet government made public a decision that had been taken some time earlier, to establish a formation of Polish combat troops to operate as an

8   Rogachev itself had been taken by Rokossovsky's forces at the end of March.

integral part of the Red Army. Stalin was determined to maintain absolute control over this force, which grew to corps size. Soviet officers were appointed to the some of the most senior command posts, and a significant number of the more junior officers were Russians masquerading as Poles. Issued with false identities and claiming to be from towns and regions of eastern Poland devastated by the war, these impostors were usually identifiable from their unusual accents and inability or reluctance to discuss their hometowns or regions. Building on the Polish corps, Polish 1 Army had grown to four divisions with 80,000 personnel by June 1944.

Facing the four Soviet Fronts preparing for Bagration were III Pz Army, IV Army, IX Army and II Army of Army Group Centre, together with parts of XVI Army and IV Pz Army of the flanking army groups. As a result of both the success of the Soviet deception strategy and poor German military intelligence at the front, OKH failed completely to anticipate where the Soviet summer offensive would fall. On 12 May its assessment of Soviet intentions was that the main Soviet effort would be south of the Carpathians into Rumania, and, recognising the potential attraction to STAVKA of an offensive down the Vistula with the consequent possibility of isolating Army Group Centre and Army Group North, OKH anticipated an additional substantial offensive into Galicia from the Kovel – Ternopol area aimed at Lublin and possibly Warsaw. In the same assessment no significant offensive action against Army Group Centre or Army Group North was expected. Early in May Busch had begun to reinforce its right flank corps (General Friedrich Hossbach's LVI Pz Corps) and on 10 May Zeitzler suggested using Hossbach's corps as the nucleus of a reserve army that would be available to strike at Soviet concentrations east of Lvov. On 20 May Hitler, at Model's request, transferred the heavily-reinforced LVI Pz Corps to Army Group North Ukraine for use by Model in an offensive south of Kovel. As a result, Army Group Centre lost around half of its armour to Army Group North Ukraine, but Model only became responsible for around one-twentieth of Busch's front. Though Busch was concerned to recover LVI Pz Corps to his own command as soon as possible, he saw his role primarily as that of transmitting Hitler's instructions down the chain of command to his subordinates and of exercising his professional abilities in the completion of those instructions.

The second half of May saw several senior command changes in the *Ostheer*. On 18 May Raus replaced Chevallerie as commander of I Pz Army, Col-Gen Josef Harpe took command of IV Pz Army, and General Hans Jordan, the former commander of VI Corps, took over from Harpe as commander of IX Army. In May Heinrici, who had commanded IV Army with distinction for nearly two and a half years, and who had done so much to thwart Sokolovsky's efforts to break through to Orsha, contracted hepatitis and was hospitalised. On 4 June command of IV Army passed to General Kurt von Tippelskirch, the former commander of the army's XII Corps.

Meanwhile the Soviet build-up for Bagration proceeded apace. The four Fronts were heavily reinforced. With 24,000 guns and heavy mortars, 2,300 *Katyushas*, 2,700 tanks, 1,350 self-propelled guns and 6,000 aircraft, the Soviet forces assembling for the offensive had a considerable superiority over Army Group Centre in the machinery of war, and the 800,000 personnel of Army Group Centre would be outnumbered three to one. In addition, 2 Gds Army and 51 Army were in the process of being transferred from the Crimea, to be concentrated east of Smolensk and southeast of

Gomel respectively. At the end of May Jordan reported an increase in Soviet forces north of Rogachev, but the activity was assessed by German military intelligence to be a deception.

In its initial planning, STAVKA had hoped to commence the Belorussian operation in the first half of June, but the sheer scale of the offensive, and the logistical problems associated its preparation, meant that the target date had to be put back to some time in the third week of June. Before then STAVKA had some unfinished business farther north.

The Karelian Isthmus

After the failure of the Finnish armistice negotiations in April 1944, STAVKA planned a summer offensive by Leningrad Front against Finnish forces in the Karelian Isthmus. For this purpose the headquarters of 21 Army, in STAVKA reserve since the autumn of 1943, was assigned to the isthmus. Placed under the command of Lt-Gen D N Gusev, 21 Army incorporated Leningrad Front's rapidly expanding reserves, and was deployed on the left wing of the Karelian Isthmus in preparation for an offensive towards Vyborg. The long-standing 23 Army under the command of Lt-Gen A I Cherepanov, which had been defending the Soviet positions in the isthmus since 1941, was heavily reinforced and was concentrated in the eastern sector of the isthmus positions. In eastern Karelia, between Lake Ladoga and Lake Onega, was 7 Army commanded by Lt-Gen A N Krutikov, and north of Lake Onega was 32 Army commanded by Gorolenko. These two armies, part of Meretskov's Karelian Front, were also reinforced from STAVKA reserve.

Opposing the Soviet armies were Finnish IV Corps (General T Laatikainen) and Finnish III Corps (General H Siilasvuo) in the Karelian Isthmus, Finnish VI and V Corps on the Svir, and Finnish II Corps north of Lake Onega. The Finnish army had no effective anti-tank weapons, and its forces had never been on the receiving end of the Red Army's updated assault tactics.

The Soviet offensive was opened by 21 Army on 9 June along most of IV Corps' front with a massive artillery barrage that included 1,000 *Katyushas* and 175 guns of the Baltic Fleet, most of them of a calibre greater than 125mm. Such was the intensity of the barrage that it was reportedly heard in Helsinki. At dawn the next day, after a further artillery bombardment, and supported by nearly 500 tanks and more than 500 bombers and ground attack aircraft, 21 Army launched its ground offensive. On IV Corps' western flank the positions of its 10 Inf Div at Valkeasaari were penetrated to a depth of 10km north of the coastal railway line. Some 16km behind the frontline positions, the Finns had constructed a second defence line from Vammelsuu to south of Taipale on the southern bank of the Vuoski. This second defence line roughly followed the old Soviet-Finnish border. By the end of 10 June it was clear to Finnish High Command that 10 Inf Div was disintegrating and that the second line could not be held without reinforcement. Consequently Marshal Carl Gustav Mannerheim, the Finnish Armed Forces Commander in Chief, ordered in a reserve division and transferred a regiment from the adjacent III Corps. In addition the Finnish armoured division was ordered to move forward from its positions near Vyborg.

On 11 June the offensive was joined by 23 Army in attacks against III Corps, heavy artillery following closely in the wake of the infantry. Laatikainen and Siilasvuo

See Map 24

were ordered to fall back to the second defence line, a withdrawal that was completed by the next day (12 June). Also on 12 June Mannerheim initiated the transfer of a division and a brigade from eastern Karelia, and he also called on Germany for military assistance. On 13 June the Finnish second line was attacked and the next day, as Soviet heavy artillery was brought to bear, Leningrad Front switched the axis of its attack and broke through again, this time penetrating the line in the centre of IV Corps' positions. By 15 June the entire western half of IV Corps' positions on the second line had been destroyed and Soviet forces were pushing towards Vyborg. On 16 June Mannerheim ordered the retreat of IV Corps and III Corps to the third defensive line from Vyborg to Kuparsaari and along the northern bank of the Vuoski to Taipale, and he ordered the transfer to the isthmus of more forces from eastern Karelia. Much of this third defensive line lay behind formidable natural defences, but the defences had only been under construction for six months and were not complete. The decision to transfer forces from eastern Karelia to the isthmus left the defences of VI Corps and V Corps untenable, and so Mannerheim also issued orders for a withdrawal from the Svir to a line running north from Pitkyaranta. On 18 June Finnish forces began to pull out of their bridgehead over the Svir, a withdrawal that came the day before an offensive by 7 Army was scheduled to begin. The main attack by 7 Army began on 21 June making rapid progress into the abandoned Finnish lines. Although the Finns along the Svir escaped the destructive effects of a Soviet offensive against their lines, they were constantly harassed in their subsequent retreat towards the northern end of Lake Ladoga.

Meanwhile the retreat of IV Corps and III Corps to the third Finnish defensive line in the Karelian Isthmus was still in progress. On 20 June, Vyborg, Finland's second city, was abandoned by Finnish forces, to be secured by the left flank of 21 Army late that evening. By then IV Corps was in the line between Vyborg and the Vuoski, while III Corps had pulled back north of the river (maintaining a bridgehead on the south bank near Vuosalmi). This was the line where the Soviet offensive of 1939 had been stopped. With the capture of Vyborg and the abandonment by Finnish forces of most of eastern Karelia, much of the Soviet territorial demand made as part of the armistice negotiations had been, or was in the process of being, secured by military action. Consequently, on 21 June the Finns re-opened armistice contacts with Moscow, but while the negotiations were being conducted the fighting continued.

On 13 June, recognising the strategic advantages to Germany of preventing a Finnish collapse, Hitler lifted the German arms embargo, and six days later the Finns received nine thousand single-shot disposable anti-tank grenade launchers (the *Panzerfaust*). On 22 June they received further German aid in the form of five thousand anti-tank rocket launchers (the *Panzerschreck*), and the next day a German self-propelled gun brigade arrived in theatre to provide direct support at the frontline. The Germans also provided air support, but the price for this military aid was a series of inter-governmental discussions between Germany and Finland on closer cooperation, and a subsequent declaration by Finland that it would not hold further armistice negotiations with the Soviet government.

On 21 June, in an expansion of its offensive, STAVKA ordered Korovnikov's 59 Army from the Narva front to cross the Gulf of Finland, while 21 Army was to break the Finnish lines at Tali and link up with 59 Army. Meanwhile 23 Army was to force the Vuoksi north of Boryshevo, and advance to Lake Ladoga to trap III Corps against the western shore of the lake. Gusev's attack on Tali went in on 25 June, breaking through the Finnish lines to a depth of 4km. By this time the Finns had deployed the supplies and reinforcements from Germany, but in four days of desperate fighting, though they managed to contain the Soviet penetration, they were unable to eliminate it. However, Soviet losses in the isthmus had been high and after three weeks of continuous offensive action the Soviet advance began to falter. After a further week of fighting along the Finnish fall-back positions at Tali, and after an unsuccessful attempt over several days in early July to break through the Finnish defences north of Vyborg, the offensive by 21 Army had petered out by 6 July.

Korovnikov commenced his offensive on 1 July and began to attack the mainland on 7 July but was unable to secure a firm foothold. His attack was met by the German 122 Inf Div, which had arrived in theatre on 28 June to support the Finnish defences. Cherepanov attacked III Corps' bridgehead on the Vuoski north of Boryshevo on 4 July. By 9 July the Finnish bridgehead had been eliminated and 23 Army crossed the Vuoski to establish its own bridgehead north of the river. By 15 July, though Cherepanov's bridgehead over the Vuoski had been made secure, 23 Army's offensive had also petered out. In eastern Karelia the Finns had reached their fallback line by 7 July. Farther north II Corps pulled back from 32 Army to the 1940 border, reaching its stop line east of Ilomantsi by 28 July.

A combination of difficult terrain, fierce Finnish resistance and high Soviet losses had left the Soviet armies weakened and exhausted. In eastern Karelia by 28 July the Finns had managed to stabilise their front from the northern end of Lake Ladoga north to the stop line east of Ilomantsi. STAVKA was aware that if the offensives against the Finns were to be continued, its forces would need to be rested and reinforced. At this stage in the war, with the Finns again discussing armistice terms, STAVKA had higher priorities, for by then its summer offensive in Belorussia was well under way. From mid-July the best Soviet units were withdrawn for deployment to other fronts and, though a further month of inconclusive fighting lay ahead in eastern Karelia (the Svir-Petrozavodsk Operation which officially ended on 29 August), the key battles had been fought by 11 July.

Mannerheim became the Finnish President on 4 August. Three weeks later further contact was made with Moscow, and Soviet armistice terms were accepted on 2 September to come into effect on 4 September. On 19 September a provisional peace treaty was signed in which Finland was spared military occupation but had to make unpalatable territorial concessions and incurred onerous reparations liabilities.

Bagration

A summary of the *Ostheer*'s order of battle at the time of Operation Bagration is given in Appendix XI. A summary of the order of battle of Field Marshal Ernst Busch's Army Group Centre is given below:

- III Pz Army commanded by Col-Gen Georg-Hans Reinhardt.
  The panzer army included; General Rolf Wuthmann's IX Corps with 252 Inf Div and Corps Detachment 'D'; General Friedrich Gollwitzer's LIII Corps with 246 Inf Div, 4 LwF Div, 6 LwF Div and 206 Inf Div; and General Georg

Pfeiffer's VI Corps with 197 Inf Div, 299 Inf Div and 256 Inf Div. In reserve Reinhardt had 95 Inf Div and three security divisions.

- IV Army commanded by General Kurt von Tippelskirch.
  The army included General Paul Voelckers' XXVII Corps with 260 Inf Div, 25 Pz Gdr Div, 78 Assault Div and part of 55 Inf Div; General Robert Martinek's XXXIX Pz Corps with 337 Inf Div, 12 Inf Div, 31 Inf Div and 110 Inf Div; Lt-Gen Vincenz Mueller's XII Corps with 18 Pz Gdr Div, 267 Inf Div and part of 57 Inf Div. Tippelskirch's reserve consisted of a single security division.
- IX Army commanded by General Hans Jordan.
  Jordan's army included Lt-Gen Kurt-Juerger von Luetzow's XXXV Corps with 383 Inf Div, 45 Inf Div, 6 Inf Div, 296 Inf Div, 134 Inf Div and part of 129 Inf Div; General Hellmuth Weidling's XLI Pz Corps with 36 Inf Div, 35 Inf Div and part of 129 Inf Div; and General Frielich Herrlein's LV Corps with part of 292 Inf Div and 102 Inf Div.
- II Army commanded by Col-Gen Walter Weiss.
  The army included General Otto Tiemann's XXIII Corps with 7 Inf Div, 203 Security Div and a panzer grenadier brigade; General Gustav Hoehne's VIII Corps with 211 Inf Div and 5 Light Div; and General Rudolf von Roman's XX Corps with Corps Detachment 'E' and a cavalry brigade. In reserve Weiss had two Hungarian 'reserve' divisions, a Hungarian cavalry division, and a cavalry brigade.
- In addition Busch had 14 Inf Div and 707 Inf Div as his Army Group Reserve.

A summary of the order of battle of the Red Army ground forces facing the *Ostheer* at the end of June 1944 is given in Appendix XII. A summary of the forces primarily involved at the commencement of the operation is given below:

- 1 Baltic Front commanded by General I K Bagramyan.
  Bagramyan's Front included Lt-Gen P F Malyshev's 4 Shock Army (4 rifle divisions); Lt-Gen I M Chistyakov's 6 Gds Army (9 rifle divisions and 2 artillery divisions); and Lt-Gen A P Beloborodov's 43 Army (7 rifle divisions and a tank corps).
- 3 Belorussian Front commanded by Col-Gen I D Cherniakhovsky.
  Cherniakhovsky's Front included Lt-Gen I I Lyudnikov's 39 Army (7 rifle divisions and a tank brigade); Lt-Gen N I Krylov's 5 Army (9 rifle divisions, 2 tank brigades and an artillery division); Lt-Gen K N Galitsky's 11 Gds Army (9 rifle divisions, a tank corps and a mortar division); and Lt-Gen V V Glagolev's 31 Army (8 rifle divisions and a tank brigade). In reserve Cherniakhovsky had Marshal Rotmistrov's 5 Gds Tank Army (a tank corps, a mechanised corps and a cavalry corps).
- 2 Belorussian Front commanded by Col-Gen G F Zakharov.
  Zakharov's Front included Lt-Gen V D Kryuchenkin's 33 Army (3 rifle divisions): Lt-Gen I T Grishin's 49 Army (11 rifle divisions and 2 tank brigades); and Lt-Gen I V Boldin's 50 Army (8 rifle divisions).

- 1 Belorussian Front commanded by General K K Rokossovsky.
  Rokossovsky's powerful Front included Lt-Gen A V Gorbatov's 3 Army (13 rifle divisions, a tank corps and a mortar division); Lt-Gen P L Romanenko's 48 Army (9 rifle divisions and an artillery division); Lt-Gen P I Batov's 65 Army (8 rifle divisions, a tank corps, a mechanised corps and an artillery division); Lt-Gen A A Luchinsky's 28 Army (9 rifle divisions and 2 artillery divisions); Lt-Gen P A Belov's 61 Army (6 rifle divisions); Lt-Gen V S Popov's 70 Army (4 rifle divisions); Lt-Gen N I Gusev's 47 Army (10 rifle divisions and a tank brigade); and Lt-Gen V I Kolpachki's 69 Army (9 rifle divisions). As reserve Rokossovsky also had Brigadier-General Zygmunt Berling's Polish 1 Army (4 rifle divisions and a tank brigade); a cavalry-mechanised group under Lt-Gen V V Kriukov (comprising a tank corps and a cavalry corps); and a separate cavalry corps. Moving into theatre on Rokossovsky's left wing were Col-Gen V I Chuikov's 8 Gds Army (9 rifle divisions) and 2 Tank Army (2 tank corps and an independent tank brigade) commanded by the newly-promoted Col-Gen S I Bogdanov. Also moving into Rokossovsky's positions on his right and centre were a further three tank corps, a mechanised corps and another cavalry corps. From these, another cavalry-mechanised group would be formed under the command of Lt-Gen I A Pliev.
- In addition STAVKA was moving Lt-Gen I G Kreizer's 51 Army and Lt-Gen P G Chanchibadze's 2 Gds Army into theatre on the central axis from the Crimea.

See Map 25 By June 1944 the frontline north of Kovel ran through the middle of the marshes south of the Pripet to its confluence with the Ptich, and from there it ran northeast to Zhlobin on the right bank of the Dnieper. North of Zhlobin, which was still in German hands, Rokossovsky's forces held a significant bridgehead on the right bank of the Dnieper between Rogachev and Stary Bykhov. From there the front crossed to the left bank of the Dnieper and ran some 50km to the east of Mogilev, east of Orsha and on to the east of Vitebsk. From Vitebsk, with an accommodation for the loss of Nevel, it roughly followed the line of the Eastern Rampart north through Lake Peipus to Narva.

Rokossovsky's forces held by far the longest section of this frontline, from south of Kovel, where they faced the extreme left flank of IV Pz Army, through the entire length of the Pripet Marshes to the Dnieper south of Zhlobin. Along this sector of the front they faced II Army and IX Army. Rokossovsky's forces also faced IX Army on the Dnieper east of Zhlobin, and they were responsible for the length of the bridgehead over the Dnieper north of Zhlobin where they faced the extreme right flank of IV Army. Consequently 1 Belorussian Front, with more than a million personnel, was by far the most powerful of the four Fronts deployed for the operation. Zakharov's forces covered some 150km along the Mogilev sector facing the bulk of IV Army east of the Dnieper. Cherniakhovsky's forces faced the left flank of IV Army and the southern half of III Pz Army south of the Dvina from east of Orsha to northeast of Vitebsk. Bagramyan's forces, facing the northern half of III Pz Army and the extreme right flank of XVI Army, held some 150km of frontline north of the Dvina in a concave arc from the north of Vitebsk. At their closest point, Bagramyan's forces were only 30km from Polotsk.

Operation Bagration was scheduled to begin on 19 June but continued transport difficulties in transferring the necessary forces and supplies to the combat zone resulted in a further delay of several days. Hence it was mere coincidence that the Soviet summer offensive opened on 22 June, three years to the day after the commencement of Operation Barbarossa. The offensive, which began in 1 Baltic Front's area and developed southwards over the subsequent two days, achieved the strategic surprise for which STAVKA had hoped. While Army Group Centre counted just three mechanised divisions in its order of battle, OKH had deployed eighteen German mechanised divisions south of Kovel, where Model and Schoerner also had a Hungarian and a Rumanian panzer division. The distribution of tactical air support was similarly disproportionate. OKH may have been badly wrong-footed by the Soviet offensive, but not everyone on the German frontline was surprised. On 22 June Jordan, complaining bitterly about OKH's policy of rigid defence, wrote in the IX Army war diary, "The army [IX Army] has felt bound to point out repeatedly that it considers the massing of [enemy] strength on its front to constitute the preparation for this year's main Soviet offensive, which will have as its objective the reconquest of Belorussia."

As Jordan was writing, Soviet forces began to probe Army Groups Centre's lines at numerous points, and events north of Vitebsk were already beginning to unfold in accordance with STAVKA's plan. Bagramyan's opening attack hit a 20km sector of III Pz Army's lines southwest of Gorodok; a sector held by an overextended IX Corps. Reinhardt had been oblivious to the presence of Chistyakov's army along his front, and in any case had expected any offensive by 1 Baltic Front to develop west towards Polotsk on the extreme right flank of XVI Army. Consequently he had allocated Wuthmann little by way of reserves, and was forced to commit his army's reserve division almost immediately. Additionally OKH released a reserve division from Army Group North's zone near Polotsk. Despite this, Sirotino fell on 23 June to the guardsmen of 23 Gds Rifle Corps from 6 Gds Army where, on his left flank, Chistyakov had the support of the right flank divisions of 43 Army (1 Rifle Corps). Having broken through Wuthmann's lines, Bagramyan committed 43 Army's mechanised reserve (1 Tank Corps) on 23 June to exploit the breakthrough, racing for the Dvina, which it reached the next day. At noon on 24 June, 6 Gds Army began crossing the Dvina deep behind III Pz Army's left flank.

A rapid breakthrough was also achieved by 39 Army on 3 Belorussian Front's northern flank, where Lyudnikov's forces attacked on a 15km section of front southeast of Vitebsk against the left flank of III Pz Army's VI Corps. Farther south, at the junction of VI Corps' 299 Inf Div and 256 Inf Div, the German defences collapsed in the face of a devastating attack by 5 Army. Over the next twenty-four hours the left wing of Pfeiffer's corps disintegrated as 197 Inf Div and 299 Inf Div were overwhelmed by the force of Cherniakhovsky's right wing offensive.

On 23 June the left flank forces of 3 Belorussian Front and the right flank of 2 Belorussian Front began an offensive towards Orsha, Borisov and Mogilev, leaving IV Army's front near collapse by the end of the day. Although IV Army survived the attacks against its frontline, largely because the preliminary Soviet bombardment had been bungled, by 24 June Cherniakhovsky's left flank forces had reached Senno, some 50km southwest of Vitebsk, and had begun to turn south behind the flank of IV Army. As a result of the relatively poor progress on his left flank, Cherniakhovsky was compelled to commit 5 Gds Tank Army on the Bogushevsk axis in 5 Army's zone, rather than through 11 Gds Army's zone as had been planned. Rotmistrov's army was reinforced with an additional tank corps, but the mechanised corps and the cavalry corps were withdrawn to create a temporary cavalry-mechanised group, initially led by the cavalry corps commander Lt-Gen N S Oslikovsky, and subsequently by the mechanised corps commander Lt-Gen V T Obukhov. Since, by 25 June, 5 Army had taken Bogushevsk, Oslikovsky's group was ordered to exploit this penetration.

The breakthroughs north and south of Vitebsk placed LIII Corps, in the centre of III Pz Army's lines, at risk of encirclement. Vitebsk had been partially surrounded by Soviet forces since the end of 1943, and Busch could see no way of closing III Pz Army's front without either giving up Vitebsk with its formidable defences or obtaining substantial reserves from OKH. On 24 June, totally committed to Hitler's policy of static defence, and refusing IV Army permission to withdraw from the east bank of the Dnieper, Busch nonetheless obtained Hitler's permission to withdraw most of Gollwitzer's divisions from the Vitebsk area. (At Hitler's specific instruction 206 Inf Div was to remain behind to continue the defence of the city). Gollwitzer had already moved 4 LwF Div to the southwest in an effort to keep open an escape route, but the withdrawal order from OKH came too late. Under Vasilevsky's supervision, the left flank of 39 Army (5 Gds Rifle Corps) had been cooperating with 43 Army's central corps (60 Rifle Corps) in an encirclement operation around Vitebsk. By the afternoon of 25 June the two rifle corps had linked up southwest of the city, trapping the bulk of Gollwitzer's corps, some 38,000 German troops. Over the next two days LIII Corps was split into three sections and destroyed; on the evening of 25 June the bulk of 4 LwF Div was isolated from the rest of Gollwitzer's command, and the next day 246 Inf Div and 6 LwF Div, trying to pull back to the southwest, were cut off from contact with 206 Inf Div in the city. By the evening of 26 June the defences of 206 Inf Div in Vitebsk were crumbling and Gollwitzer, in defiance of OKH orders, authorised the division to withdraw. Reinhardt's command had been shattered. All that was left was a weakened IX Corps pulling back towards Polotsk, and the right flank of VI Corps attempting to make a stand in the Bogushevsk area. In between was a gaping hole where LIII Corps and the left flank of VI Corps should have been. By 27 June some 30,000 troops from LIII Corps had been killed or captured, and though 8,000 men, mainly from 4 LwF Div, broke out through the encirclement, most were subsequently surrounded and killed in their efforts to reach German lines.

Yet by then, the rupture of III Pz Army's line was not Busch's most serious problem. On 24 June the right flank armies of 1 Belorussian Front began their offensive against IX Army; 3 Army and 48 Army striking to the west from the Rogachev area against XXXV Corps, as 65 Army and 28 Army struck to the north against XLI Pz Corps from the Ozarichi area between the Berezina and the Ptich. Jordan's main concern was XXXV Corps, and he committed the OKH reserve division (20 Pz Div), which was in the process of arriving from the south, to the east bank of the Berezina against 48 Army. By the next day it was clear that of the four armies committed by Rokossovsky, 65 Army and 28 Army west of the Berezina were making the better progress, and that Rokossovsky's objective was Bobruisk. Jordan, following Tippelskirch's lead from the day before, asked for permission to withdraw from the trap being formed west of Zhlobin, but this was also refused by Busch. Against orders, Tippelskirch began to pull IV Army back, considering it to be the only way he could hold his army together. By the end of 25 June it was becoming apparent to OKH that Army Group Centre's situation was growing desperate: Reinhardt's forward front had been shattered and, with the centre of III Pz Army surrounded, Reinhardt was attempting to form a front on the Dvina and Ulla rivers, committing his unreliable security divisions to frontline defence; IV Army could only hold its front together by retreating (it had taken command of the remnants of VI Corps, which were being pushed south into IV Army's area); and the bulk of IX Army was in imminent danger of being encircled by a pincer movement on Bobruisk from the east and the south. In response Hitler ordered that two divisions be transferred from Army Group North to support Army Group Centre. On 26 June Zakharov, having closed up to the Dnieper, used a mobile group to force the river near Dobreika, and he organised assault groups from 49 Army and 50 Army to prepare to take Mogilev. At the same time, farther north, 5 Gds Tank Army reached Tolochino, cutting IV Army's escape route to the west of Orsha. Tippelskirch responded by ordering his army back behind the Dnieper, Orsha being taken by 11 Gds Army and 31 Army the next day. Yet with 3 Belorussian Front and 1 Belorussian Front closing in behind its flanks, any further retreat by IV Army would involve the crossing of a single road bridge over the Berezina at Beresino.

Unlike Tippelskirch, Jordan reluctantly obeyed Busch's orders not to retreat. Those orders stood throughout 26 June, during which time Zhlobin was outflanked from the west, and 28 Army and 65 Army took Parichi and pressed on to the Ptich at Glutsk. Hitler accepted, late on 26 June, that a new defensive line should be formed on the Berezina, but this was not relayed to Busch until the following night, and it was not until 28 June that Tippelskirch received definitive orders from Busch to get IV Army back behind the Berezina. By then it was too late. On 27 June STAVKA's plan for the opening phase of the offensive came to fruition when 1 Belorussian Front enveloped Bobruisk trapping 70,000 of Jordan's men in, and east of, the town. Jordan's headquarters were outside the pocket, but his remaining corps (LV Corps) was subordinated to II Army. This left IX Army with 12 Pz Div, which was in the process of arriving via Minsk from Army Group North. All Jordan could do was prepare to set up his headquarters at Marina Gorka 50km southeast of Minsk on the railway line to Bobruisk in order to try to hold the approaches to Minsk from the southeast and thereby maintain an escape route for IV Army. It was not a burden that Jordan was required to carry for long; that same day he was replaced by the newly-promoted General Nikolaus von Vormann.

On 28 June Mogilev fell to Zakharov's forces after two days of savage fighting in which Soviet assault formations suffered heavy casualties. Thereafter, 2 Belorussian Front's role became somewhat secondary, pushing IV Army back towards the Berezina, while more dramatic events were taking place to the north and the south.

Despite the uncomfortably high Soviet casualty rates, STAVKA was delighted with the results of the initial phase of the offensive, and prepared new objectives for the Front commanders. In the north Bagramyan was to strike for Polotsk. Farther south Cherniakhovsky and Rokossovsky were to strike beyond Minsk, enveloping the Belorussian capital from north and south, and seizing the towns of Molodechno and

Baranovichi, possession of which would cut the escape route of German forces from Belorussia and would allow further exploitation towards Vilno and Białystok. As part of this process, Pliev's cavalry-mechanised group would exploit the breakthrough in the Bobruisk area to strike west towards Slutsk.

By 28 June, with STAVKA on the verge of achieving its long-held ambition of the total destruction of Army Group Centre, OKH finally acknowledged that the Soviet offensive in Belorussia was no diversionary effort. Yet it still believed that an even more powerful blow against Army Group North Ukraine was imminent. Hitler decided that Model should, effective from 29 June, take command of Army Group Centre.[9] Model had certainly inherited a desperate situation. In the Bobruisk area tens of thousands of encircled troops from IX Army were attempting to break out to the west, but otherwise IX Army had ceased to exist. Furthermore, IV Army's situation was growing increasingly dangerous; the bridge at Beresino was being bombed, Pfeiffer and Martinek had been killed, 3 Belorussian Front had reached Borisov on the Berezina north of Beresino, and Pliev's cavalry-mechanised group had reached Slutsk. By 30 June the bridge at Beresino had come under Soviet artillery fire, while the bulk of IV Army was still on the left bank of the Berezina, streaming back to the increasingly chaotic choke point at Beresino.

Model proposed to OKH that Army Group North should shorten its lines by withdrawing its right flank in order to release divisions for deployment to Army Group Centre. This proposal was dismissed by Hitler, but he did order II Army to pull back its exposed left flank east of the Slutch in order to release forces for the defence of the approaches to Baranovichi. On 1 July Vormann directed a regiment of 12 Pz Div at Marina Gorka to open a corridor from the west through 65 Army's lines, enabling around 10,000 of the remnants of IX Army's forces that had been escaping along the railway line from Bobruisk, to reach Marina Gorka.

West of Minsk lay the largely impenetrable Nalibocka forest. The only escape routes from Minsk were the road and rail lines running southwest to Brest through Stolbtsy and Baranovichi, and the railway and road northwest to Vilno through Molodechno. By 2 July most of IV Army was across the Berezina but 5 Gds Tank Army was approaching Minsk from the direction of Borisov, and Rokossovsky's forces had reached Bobovnya some 25km southeast of Stolbtsy. Tippelskirch and his army headquarters were sent from Beresino to Molodechno to try to organise the defence of an area that was being threatened by advance elements of Obukhov's cavalry-mechanised group. Farther south Vormann directed 12 Pz Div to Stolbtsy after attempts to organise stragglers into a defence of the town had failed. On 2 July units from 5 Gds Tank Army entered Minsk from the north and northwest to find the ruined city defended by a scattering of German troops. The next day elements of 31 Army joined Rotmistrov's forces in the city, and later that day they linked up with elements of 1 Gds Tank Corps and 3 Army arriving in the city from the south. This link-up between 3 Belorussian Front and 1 Belorussian Front trapped 105,000 German troops of IV Army east of the Belorussian capital.

Renewed efforts by Vormann on 3 July to take Stolbtsy failed. With Rokossovsky's forces pushing on towards Baranovichi, Vormann had to direct his resources farther

---

9   Model retained nominal command of Army Group North Ukraine but effective command passed
     to Harpe, and Harpe's duties at IV Pz Army were assumed by Nehring.

west and, as a result, the German troops within the encirclement were left to their fate. In fact IX Army Headquarters was so short of staff and communications equipment that it was taken out of frontline operations entirely, and responsibility for the defence of Baranovichi was given to II Army. Vormann's troops west of Stolbtsy were able to find an escape route farther south across the upper Neman, where up to 15,000 men were able to reach the relative safety of Western Belorussia. Farther north a few stragglers from IV Army subsequently escaped through the Nalibocka forest, but the great bulk of Army Group Centre was lost to Soviet prison camps. The last German forces in the Minsk pocket surrendered on 11 July, and by then Army Group Centre had suffered losses well in excess of 300,000 personnel, the great majority of them irrecoverable losses of dead, missing and prisoners.

Six days later, on 17 July, tens of thousands of German troops captured in the opening phase of Operation Bagration were paraded through Moscow. Lt-Gen Siegfried von Westphal, a senior staff officer based in the West wrote, "The end draws near … Only scattered remnants of thirty divisions escaped death and Soviet captivity."

For the *Ostheer* the events of the preceding few weeks had been a disaster on a scale greater than Stalingrad; and, as at Stalingrad, STAVKA was both prepared to reward its successful generals (Rokossovsky, Cherniakhovsky, Galitsky, Chistyakov, Batov, Krylov, Glagolev and Boldin were all promoted) and was determined to take full advantage of the *Ostheer's* woes.

The Baltic Gap

In the final week of June, when it was clear that Operation Bagration was unfolding successfully, STAVKA began to put the finishing touches to plans for an expansion of the offensive farther north. Since late 1943 STAVKA had been drawn to the potential for an offensive down the Dvina along the Polotsk – Dvinsk axis to reach the Baltic near Riga, and so cut off Army Group North. Yet the ferocious German resistance at Vitebsk, and the month-long fighting necessary to take Gorodok at the end of 1943, was proof that such an offensive would require considerable preparation. In plans developed in the late spring of 1944, the attention of the Soviet General Staff began to be drawn to central Lithuania as a prime objective for 1 Belorussian Front in a subsequent phase of operations should the initial phase of Operation Bagration prove successful. From central Lithuania, a strike could be made north to the Gulf of Riga, or west to Memel, either of which would isolate Army Group North. An advance from Vitebsk to central Lithuania, a distance of 350km, would require considerable flank support, a task that would be assigned to 1 Baltic Front in an advance along the Dvina to Dvinsk in south-eastern Latvia. Additionally Army Group North would be attacked at multiple points by 2 Baltic Front, 3 Baltic Front and Leningrad Front.

When Operation Bagration opened on 22 June, Lindemann, who had succeeded Model as Army Group North commander at the end of March, ordered 290 Inf Div from Hansen's left flank, and 24 Inf Div from the XVI Army reserve, to the army's right flank near Polotsk (see Appendix XI). The next day XVIII Army faced attacks along a wide front, but mainly against 121 Inf Div on its right flank. On 24 June the Soviet attacks shifted south against 205 Inf Div and 83 Inf Div near the right flank of XVI Army. By then 1 Baltic Front had broken through III Pz Army's left flank, and 24 Inf Div, in the process of moving into position east of Polotsk, lost contact with friendly forces on both its flanks. The next day Hitler declared Polotsk a *Festung* and appointed General Carl Hilpert, the commander of I Corps, as the *Festung*'s commandant. He also ordered the transfer of 212 Inf Div from XVIII Army to Army Group Centre, and Lindemann lost his army group reserve (12 Pz Div) to Busch. By 26 June IX Corps, on III Pz Army's left flank, was being pushed back to the west, and had lost contact with the right flank of XVI Army east of Polotsk. Over the following days this gap, which became known as the Baltic Gap, grew wider as 6 Gds Army advanced westwards south of the Dvina and III Pz Army continued to fall back towards the Lithuanian border. Since Reinhardt did not have the resources to close the gap, the task was delegated to Lindemann, and on 28 June he sent a battle group south to try to re-establish contact with III Pz Army. He also transferred two divisions from Army Detachment Narva to XVI Army's extreme right flank. Three days later Hitler ordered Lindemann to launch an offensive from the Polotsk area to close the still-growing Baltic Gap, but Lindemann, under growing pressure in the Polotsk area, did not have the resources to comply. On 2 July he sent some scratch units to attack 6 Gds Army west of Polotsk but later that day, his right wing completely outflanked, he authorised the evacuation of the *Festung*. The next day Lindemann's decision to abandon Polotsk was approved by OKH but only in order to free up forces for an offensive towards III Pz Army, and Lindemann was given unequivocal orders to counter-attack to the west from the Polotsk area. Loyal Nazi though he was, Lindemann refused, and on 4 July, the day that Polotsk was abandoned to 6 Gds Army and 4 Shock Army, he was replaced at Army Group North by General Johannes Friessner.[10]

Freissner placed General Paul Laux and Laux's II Corps Headquarters in command of three infantry divisions on the right flank of XVI Army, and on 4 July launched them in a counter-attack west of Disna against 6 Gds Army. Chistyakov responded quickly and II Corps' attack made little progress. The next day 4 Shock Army attacked XVI Army's forces north of the Dvina, severely limiting Hansen's freedom of manoeuvre. On 6 July, with 6 Gds Army still pushing westwards south of the Dvina towards Dvinsk, and 4 Shock Army attacking westwards north of the river, Friessner ordered his right flank to pull back to Latvia, but this order was countermanded by Hitler. Not only was Army Group North to stand firm, but XVI Army was to lose two more divisions to Army Group Centre. On the Soviet side of the frontline Bagramyan was to give up his right flank 4 Shock Army operating north of the Dvina to 2 Baltic Front. The two Fronts were to cooperate in an offensive against Dvinsk, but Bagramian had not yet acquired 39 Army from the right flank of 3 Belorussian Front, part of STAVKA's arrangement to shift the axis of 1 Baltic Front's advance farther to the south.

---

10   With Freissner's departure, General Anton Grasser, the commander of XXVI Corps was appointed to command Army Detachment Narva.

10

Out of Russia

After the astounding success of the first phase of Operation Bagration and the encirclement of IV Army east of Minsk, STAVKA set its sights on Vilno, Kovno, Białystok, Brest, Lublin and Warsaw; and farther north, on Riga. OKH was frantically moving reserves from the west and from other army groups to stem the tide along a 400km sector of front that was being defended by just eight divisions, but in the process it weakened Army Group North Ukraine and Army Group North in areas that were about to experience the second phase of the Soviet summer offensive.

On 7 July, in response to the disasters in Belorussia and the failure of German forces to eject the Western Allies from Normandy, Hitler ordered the formation of fifteen new grenadier divisions and ten panzer brigades. To man these units the army would be required to use all the replacement allocation for the Eastern Front for July and August, and would have to secure nearly 50,000 personnel from hospital releases; command and support staff would come from the survivors of previously decimated divisions. See Map 26

On 3 July Obukhov's cavalry-mechanised group began the fight for Molodechno against German forces coalescing around IV Army Headquarters, and at the same time Pliev's cavalry-mechanised group fought along the approaches to Baranovichi. Within three days 3 Belorussian Front's forces in the Molodechno area had achieved a considerable degree of freedom of movement northwest towards Vilno and southwest towards Lida, and 5 Gds Tank Army on the right wing of 3 Belorussian Front had begun an advance towards Vilno. At the same time, though II Army had managed to slow Rokossovsky's drive towards Baranovichi, 1 Belorussian Front continued to advance. By 8 July Baranovichi and Lida were in Soviet hands and 3 Belorussian Front was racing for the Neman on a broad front between Kovno and Grodno. After having advanced more than 300km in 16 days, the forward units of 3 Belorussian Front were beginning to outrun their supplies and, though 5 Gds Tank Army had the 15,000 German defenders of Vilno securely surrounded by 9 July, Cherniakhovsky's overall advance was beginning to slow. Rotmistrov was also learning that tank operations conducted in the forests and marshes of Belorussia were radically different to those conducted on the open plains of the Ukraine. His army's losses had begun to mount, and the vicious fighting in support of 5 Army and Obukhov's 3 Gds Mech Corps against the surrounded German garrison in Vilno further depleted his pool of armoured fighting vehicles. The fighting in Vilno concluded on 13 July with a further 7,000 German prisoners filing into Soviet prison camps, but by 16 July the operational strength of 5 Gds Tank Army had declined to the point where it had to be withdrawn for refitting.

In 1 Baltic Front's sector 43 Army had, by 9 July, crossed the Lithuanian border to cut both the Dvinsk – Vilno railway and, still farther west, the Dvinsk – Kovno road. By that time 39 Army had been made available to 1 Baltic Front for the continued drive west towards Kovno, Jonava and Kedainia, and Bagramyan directed part of 43 Army, with 1 Tank Corps, to turn northeast along the Kovno – Dvinsk road into the rear of German forces that were holding up the advance of 6 Gds Army.[1] Bagramyan ordered the rest of 43 Army to veer north towards Panevezius, a move that kept the flanks of III Pz Army and XVI Army apart, and which maintained the existence of the Baltic Gap. STAVKA was concerned to prevent a general withdrawal of Army Group North from the Baltic region with the escape of a huge potential prize. Consequently, on 13 July, it ordered some regrouping to strengthen 3 Belorussian Front, where units from 11 Gds Army had crossed the Neman in the Olita area, and were holding a substantial bridgehead against repeated German counter-attacks. The assignment of 39 Army, operating north of Vilno, to 1 Baltic Front was reversed, and Lyudnikov's forces reverted to 3 Belorussian Front's command. Additionally 1 Baltic Front was relieved of responsibility for the Kovno axis, STAVKA having made the decision to reinforced Bagramyan with 51 Army and 2 Gds Army from the Crimea in order to facilitate a strike directly towards Shyaulyay through the Baltic Gap, with the ultimate objective of Riga. At the same time 2 Belorussian Front, having completed the elimination of German forces in central Belorussia, had taken command of Oslikovsky's 3 Gds Cav Corps, which was involved in fighting for Grodno, and the Front was moving into position along the Neman between 1 Belorussian Front and 3 Belorussian Front.

Despite the presence of Soviet spearheads closing on Dvinsk, Kovno, Grodno, Białystok and Kobrin, and despite the loss on 15 July of Olita on the left bank of the Neman, by mid-July Model was beginning to regain some cohesion in his force deployments in the Army Group Centre zone. He had received some reinforcements, enabling III Pz Army to establish a front to Kovno and along the Neman to Olita, and IV Army was deployed along the southern reaches of the river as far as Grodno. At the same time II Army, its right flank still firmly linked with IV Pz Army north of Kovel, was pulling its centre and left flank back from Pinsk and Baranovichi to the east of Brest and Białystok, and the staff of IX Army Headquarters were given responsibility both for finding and organising the stragglers that were still drifting west and for fortifying the East Prussian frontier.

If Model felt that the situation in the Army Group Centre zone was stabilising by mid-July, he was aware by then that the situation in the Army Group North Ukraine zone was about to get a great deal worse. The OKH assessments in the early summer, that the main Soviet summer offensive would be directed through Galicia, had not been without foundation. Konev's 1 Ukrainian Front was being heavily reinforced and at the end of June IV Pz Army had been given permission to straighten its line somewhat by giving up Kovel, and in early July it was allowed to continue this process by abandoning a bulge in its right flank around Torchin. Army Group North Ukraine was expecting an offensive towards Lvov, and by 12 July Harpe, having concluded that the offensive was imminent, pulled his forces back from their forward positions.

Konev had an immensely powerful force of more than a million men at his disposal, comprising sixty-four rifle divisions, ten tank and mechanised corps (most of them in three tank armies), and two cavalry corps. Konev was faced by thirty-four infantry divisions, five panzer divisions and a motorised division; 900,000 men

---

1   Chistyakov's forces had by that time become splayed out along a 160km front and were no longer making rapid progress.

with 900 tanks and self-propelled guns in an area suited to defence. The objectives that Konev set were for the northern armies (Gordov's 3 Gds Army and Pukhov's 13 Army) to strike towards Rava-Russkaya from west of Lutsk, and for the central armies (Kurochkin's 60 Army and Moskalenko's 38 Army) to strike from west of Ternapol towards Lvov with the objective of trapping German forces west of Brody and splitting Army Group North Ukraine into two parts; one pushed back to Polesia, and the other to the Carpathians. To support the offensive, Grechko's 1 Gds Army and Zhuravlev's 18 Army on the left wing of 1 Ukrainian Front would strike west and northwest from Chertkov and Kolomiya towards Galich and Stanislav respectively. The objective was to bring 1 Ukrainian Front onto a line from Hrubieszow to Tomaszow to Yavorov to Galich. Stalin had wanted a single thrust, arguing that a double thrust from one Front was a dilution of effort and risked failure in both objectives. Konev continued to argue for a double thrust and Stalin finally acceded, remarking to Konev, "Very well, go ahead ... on your own responsibility". OKH was clearly expecting the Lvov offensive, but Konev did everything possible to conceal the strike towards Rava-Russkaya.

On 6 July STAVKA issued a special directive highlighting errors in Soviet operations in Belorussia, deficiencies that Konev's forces, among others, would be expected to avoid. The errors included moving staff headquarters and command posts before adequate communication links had been established at the new location; ineffectual use of radio communication; and use of first echelon forces for secondary tasks.

On the evening of 12 July Soviet reconnaissance detected the German withdrawal from frontline positions in anticipation of an imminent Soviet artillery barrage, and so Konev decided on the immediate commitment of 3 Gds Army and 13 Army. Konev's offensive, launched a day earlier than planned, was initially disappointing. By the end of 13 July Gorokhov had been taken, but IV Pz Army launched counter-attacks from its second line. After three days Konev's offensives had made little progress, though small penetrations had been made at several points in the German line. On 16 July Konev committed Katukov's 1 Gds Tank Army against the right flank of IV Pz Army.[2] By 17 July this northern thrust had broken through towards Rava-Russkaya despite fierce counter-attacks from the panzer divisions of XLVI Pz Corps (16 Pz Div and 17 Pz Div – assigned from reserves after the commencement of Operation Bagration). Later that day Katukov's forces crossed the Bug at Dobrochin, the first Soviet troops to enter Poland. By 18 July Katukov's thrust had pushed 20 Pz Gdr Div (newly assigned to IV Pz Army from the reserves) beyond the Bug, and Konev's forces occupied Kamenka and Krasne, cutting off German formations in Brody from their retreat routes to the west.

The opening attack from 1 Ukrainian Front's central sector on the afternoon of 14 July got off to a poor start. By 16 July a narrow corridor south of Koltuv (the Koltuv corridor) had been opened in the German line, into which Konev decided to commit Rybalko's 3 Gds Tank Army. Rybalko, hoping to widen the corridor and break out to Lvov, met determined resistance from III Pz Corps (1 Pz Div and 8 Pz Div) on I Pz Army's left flank. This resistance forced Konev to commit Col-Gen Lelyushenko's 4 Tank Army to the corridor on 17 July. The commitment of both tank

---

2   1 Tank Army had been awarded 'Guards' status on 24 April 1944 shortly after Katukov had been promoted to the rank of colonel-general.

armies into such a narrow corridor carried considerable risks for 1 Ukrainian Front since it involved the possible isolation of the bulk of its mechanised force. However by 18 July forward units of 3 Gds Tank Army had reached Krasne, linking up with the northern thrust forces of a mobile group based on Lt-Gen V K Baranov's 1 Gds Cav Corps, and trapping six German divisions, including the whole of Hauffe's XIII Corps, west of Brody. Meanwhile determined attempts by Breith's III Pz Corps to pinch off the Koltuv corridor were ultimately unsuccessful.

With the right flank armies of 1 Belorussian Front west of Pinsk by mid-July, Rokossovsky was able to utilise his left flank armies (led by N I Gusev's 47 Army and Chuikov's 8 Gds Army) for a further offensive, which began on 17 July, in a double drive for Siedlce and Lublin. This offensive against II Army increased substantially the pressure on the Army Group Centre – Army Group North Ukraine junction, pressure that had already been exerted by 1 Ukrainian Front. From his reserves on his left flank Rokossovsky had created another cavalry-mechanised group from a cavalry corps and a tank corps, the group being placed under the command of Lt-Gen V V Kriukov. By 20 July, 8 Gds Army had reached the western Bug and was approaching Chelm, at which point Bogdanov's 2 Tank Army was committed on the Lublin axis, and Kriukov's group exploited northwest towards Siedlce to threaten the rear of German forces in Brest and Białystok.

On 20 July the long-planned bomb plot against Hitler was carried out using a briefcase bomb planted under a table where Hitler was conducting one of his regular military conferences. Hitler survived, and the associated attempted coup was quickly crushed, but since the plotters included many members of the General Staff, Hitler's distrust of his generals increased still further. One of Hitler's first acts after the assassination attempt was to appoint Guderian, a general who was above suspicion, as acting Chief of Staff at OKH. Since, in the immediate aftermath of the attempted coup, Hitler was somewhat preoccupied with events in Berlin, Guderian, exuding confidence and National Socialist zeal, had for a few days a considerable degree of freedom in operational decision-making.

Harpe's difficulties in facing Konev's offensive were made worse by a general retreat of II Army towards Brest, which compromised Army Group North Ukraine's left flank. In addition, Soviet tanks had reached Rava-Russkaya by 18 July and were also to the north and east of Lvov. Nehring reported that, in order to hold his army together, he would need to pull back behind the San. The Brody pocket was eliminated on 22 July, only around 5,000 of the 30,000 German troops originally surrounded being able to break out to the safety of I Pz Army's main lines. Meanwhile Konev's westward offensive continued. Yaroslav was taken by 1 Gds Tank Army on 23 July, a move that threatened the German defence of Lvov. This threat was increased when, on 24 July, Mostika came under attack; yet as early as 22 July Soviet forces had reached the centre of Lvov.

In the 1 Belorussian Front sector on 22 July, as the right flank of II Army was beginning to occupy the Brest defences, 2 Tank Army passed through Chelm, and by the end of that day was approaching the Vistula west of Lublin. During the course of this advance Bogdanov was wounded, and command of 2 Tank Army was transferred to the army's chief of staff Major-Gen A I Radzievsky. On 23 July, 2 Tank Army reached Lublin, bypassed the 900 strong *Festung* Lublin garrison, and continued to the northwest.

Model fully expected that Konev, supported by Rokossovsky's left flank, would strike from Lvov across the San, past Lublin to Warsaw. From there Soviet forces could encircle II Army and strike north into the rear of Army Group Centre. Model proposed a general withdrawal to the Vistula – San line but Guderian, promising reinforcements and declaring, "We must take the offensive everywhere", issued a directive on 24 July demanding firm defences, counter-attacks and an end to retreats. Part of Model's response was to return IX Army Headquarters to frontline operation in the Warsaw area to defend the approaches to the Vistula from Siedlce south to Puławy (though initially Vormann had command of just one division).

By 23 July Army Group North Ukraine had been split in two by 1 Ukrainian Front's advance to the San north of Przemyśl. IV Pz Army was falling back to the Vistula and I Pz Army, with I Hun Army, was being pushed southwest to the Carpathians. On 24 July Badanov's 4 Tank Army crossed the San between Przemyśl and Yaroslav. STAVKA then set Konev the task of developing his offensive in a north-westerly direction in order to force the Vistula upriver from its confluence with the San and to secure a bridgehead in the Sandomierz area. The left wing of the Front was to seize the passes over the Carpathians leading to Humenné, Uzhgorod and Mukacheve, a consequence of which was that 1 Ukrainian Front was beginning to operate in two diverging directions. In response to these developments, and in order to forestall Soviet intentions, OKH transferred two and a half divisions from other areas to be placed under XVII Army Headquarters, and to be inserted between IV Pz Army and I Pz Army east of Cracow.

The battle for Lvov eventually involved 60 Army, much of 4 Tank Army and part of 3 Gds Tank Army, and fighting continued until 27 July. By then the capture of Stanislav by 1 Gds Army on 26 July, and the capture of Przemyśl the same day by 3 Gds Tank Army with support from 1 Gds Tank Army, rendered the continued German defence of Lvov untenable, and I Pz Army began to abandon its remaining positions in the city. Konev's mechanised forces on the west bank of the San raced past the right flank of IV Pz Army and, by the evening of 29 July, a bridgehead had been established by 3 Gds Tank Army over the Vistula south of Tarnobrzeg; a bridgehead that was held against repeated German counter-attacks. By the next day two more bridgeheads had been taken by Rybalko's forces north and south of Annopol in conjunction with a cavalry-mechanised group commanded by Lt-Gen S V Sokolov, but these proved to be too small to be effectively enlarged. However, on 31 July lead elements of 1 Gds Tank Army and 13 Army crossed the Vistula along an undefended section of the river near Baranow, and established a viable bridgehead 12 km wide and 8 km deep. Over subsequent weeks this bridgehead was, despite furious German efforts against it, steadily expanded.[3] In order to allow him to concentrate on developing the crossing at Baranow into what was to become the Sandomierz bridgehead (Sandomierz was captured on 18 August), at the end of July Konev suggested that his left flank armies on the 'Carpathian axis' should come under independent command, and by the beginning of August the staff of 4 Ukrainian Front had been transferred from the

---

3   Partly as a result of his failure to eliminate this bridgehead, on 5 August Nehring was replaced as commander of IV Pz Army, exchanging roles with Balck at XLVIII Pz Corps.

Crimea to the Stanislav area. Given the task of clearing the Borislav area, 4 Ukrainian Front was reformed on 5 August under the command of Petrov. Konev relinquished command of 1 Gds Army and 18 Army to Petrov together with 3 Mtn Rifle Corps later in the month.

Through the efforts of 65 Army, 70 Army and 28 Army, 1 Belorussian Front had reached Brest by 28 July. An attempt by 70 Army and 28 Army to envelop Brest from south and north to encircle German forces in the city failed after the defenders pulled back in good time. After crossing the Bug, 47 Army turned northwest towards Siedlce in order to try to cut off the escape of German forces retreating west from Brest, but it took five days of fighting before Kriukov's group and elements of 47 Army could secure the town on 31 July. By 25 July, 2 Tank Army had reached the Vistula at Deblin and Puławy but was unable to cross off the march. Radzievsky turned two tank corps north, and on 31 July they reached Radzymin only 20km from Warsaw. On 1 August elements of 8 Gds Army crossed the Vistula northwest of Magnuszew and began to establish a viable bridgehead.

With three Soviet bridgeheads across the Vistula south of the Polish capital, and with Soviet tanks within 20km of the city, the people of Warsaw sensed that their long ordeal under German occupation was about to end.

Into the Baltic States

On 9 July Hansen, who had been unable to close the Baltic Gap, and who had made no secret of his dissatisfaction with Hitler's refusal to permit a withdrawal of XVI Army into Latvia, was replaced at XVI Army by Laux. A highly competent commander Laux may have been, but he was no more successful than Hansen in holding to the east against 2 Baltic Front, and at the same time closing the Baltic Gap to the west. On 10 July Eremenko's 2 Baltic Front opened an offensive into the left flank and centre of XVI Army's lines on the Idritsa axis, and Laux found himself preoccupied with the task of preventing a Soviet breakthrough to Rezekne. Two days later, as the lines of XVI Army's X Corps and VI SS Corps began to disintegrate, Friessner reported that German positions south of Ostrov could not be maintained. He urged Hitler to pull Army Group North back from Estonia and northern Latvia, asking to be relieved of command if OKH insisted on defending positions north of Riga. Hitler would have none of it, confident that Model would soon have the resources to close the Baltic Gap. Although averting a disaster on the scale that had befallen the armies of Army Group Centre, Laux was only able to hold XVI Army together through a process of steady withdrawal into Latvia; Opochka being taken by 10 Gds Army on 15 July, and Sebezh falling to 3 Shock Army two days later. On 15 July Eremenko's offensive was joined by 3 Baltic Front. STAVKA had concluded that a frontal attack against XVIII Army's entrenched defences at Pskov and Ostrov would be unlikely to succeed, and so 3 Baltic Front's offensive was launched farther south, and Maslennikov's two left flank armies – General N D Zakhvatayev's 1 Shock Army, which had been transferred from 2 Baltic Front to 3 Baltic Front in early July, and Lt-Gen S V Roginsky's 54 Army – were to be used for the opening phase of the offensive. The initial attack hit Wegener's L Corps, which had been transferred from XVI Army to the right flank of XVIII Army, and two days later the main attack came from a bridgehead over the Velikaya at Strezhnev north of Pushkin Hills, attacking Herzog's XXXVIII Corps.

The forward defences of Herzog's corps crumbled rapidly and by midnight of 17 July Roginsky's forces had secured Krasnogorodskoye, thereby denying XVIII Army the opportunity to make a stand on the Sinaya. The next day Roginsky turned part of 54 Army north to outflank Ostrov, as rest of his army continued west to the Lzha. Friessner reported to OKH that Army Group North had suffered 50,000 casualties since 22 June, and that only seven fully combat effective divisions remained in XVIII Army and XVI Army. Hitler nonetheless continued to demand counter-attacks, and insisted that Army Detachment Narva be stripped bare to provide the necessary forces.

By the end of 19 July, 3 Baltic Front was across the Velikaya at all points south of Ostrov, and 54 Army had crossed the Lzha into Latvia. The next day Soviet forces broke through at the boundary of XXXVIII Corps and Gollnick's XXVIII Corps. Thereafter Gollnick's defence of Pskov became untenable, and both he and Herzog ordered their forces to pull back. Since Hitler was at that time preoccupied with the aftermath of the bomb plot, these orders were not countermanded by OKH. On 21 July, with both XVI Army and XVIII Army in general retreat, Friessner reported to Guderian that unless Army Group North was pulled back south of the Dvina, it would disintegrate. On 23 July, notwithstanding his promotion on that day to the rank of colonel-general, Friessner was deemed 'unable to cope with organising the defence of the Baltic States'. Guderian was confident that Schoerner would be able to turn the situation around, and Friessner was required to exchange roles with Schoerner at Army Group South Ukraine. After Pskov fell to Maslennikov's forces on 23 July, STAVKA directed 3 Baltic Front towards Valga, a key junction connecting northern Latvia with Riga, and by the end of the month Maslennikov had reached the line of German defences stretching from the southern end of Lake Peipus to Gulbene.

Farther south, with 10 Gds Army advancing steadily towards Rezekne during the final week of July, Eremenko was able to direct his full attention to his left flank and the cooperation with 1 Baltic Front in the capture of Dvinsk, where 6 Gds Army's advance towards the city from the south had bogged down in difficult terrain. Chistyakov's offensive towards Dvinsk was called off on 25 July because by then 4 Shock Army, advancing westwards north of the Dvina with the support of 5 Tank Corps, was moving into position to attack the city from the north. On 27 July, the day that 10 Gds Army took Rezekne, Malyshev's forces took Dvinsk. Meanwhile, on 2 Baltic Front's right flank, Eremenko's forces had pushed on 80km across the Luban plain to take Madone on 20 July, but were halted from further advance by the defensive bastion of Plavinas. Throughout the whole of August, 2 Baltic Front was only able to push a further 20km towards Riga.

On the Leningrad Front sector, a Soviet offensive against the Narva line opened on 25 July, and Narva was taken the next day; but the offensive thereafter made little forward progress against heavy German resistance in good defensive terrain.

By 18 July OKH had become aware, through the monitoring of Soviet radio traffic, that an offensive into the Baltic Gap was imminent. Model advised Hitler that he did not have the strength to assist Army Group North in resisting the Soviet efforts. In fact Reinhardt, with his left flank northeast of Ukmerge, and under constant Soviet pressure, actually wanted to pull his left flank back to better protect Kovno. Zeitzler urged Hitler to abandon Estonia and northern Latvia, and pull Army Group North back to the Dvina. When Hitler rejected this proposal Zeitzler tendered his resignation.

Hitler, having already rejected Friessner's resignation six days earlier, insisted that Zeitzler remain in his post, and he issued an order forbidding officers to voluntarily relinquish their commands.

Bagramyan's offensive into the Baltic Gap against Shyaulyay with 51 Army and 2 Gds Army, the latter operating on 1 Baltic Front's left flank, began on the day of the assassination attempt against Hitler. By 22 July Panevezius had been taken by 51 Army, and two days later Ukmerge was taken, securing 51 Army's left flank as it continued to advance to the west. On 27 July, 51 Army, with 3 Gds Mech Corps, took Shyaulyay, after which Bagramyan secured permission to use 51 Army and 3 Gds Mech Corps for an advance north to the Gulf of Riga. At the same time 43 Army and 6 Gds Army would push on to the Dvina, covering Riga on the right flank. On 29 July, 3 Gds Mech Corps and 51 Army reached Mitau where intense street fighting irrupted, prompting Bagramyan to subordinate 3 Gds Mech Corps to Kreizer's command. The next day, with the fighting for Mitau unresolved, forward units of 3 Gds Mech Corps (Col S D Kremer's 8 Gds Mech Bgd) reached the Gulf of Riga, and achieved STAVKA's ambition of isolating Army Group North from overland contact with Germany. Thereafter STAVKA assigned Vasilevsky the task of coordinating the operations of the Fronts in Lithuania and the Riga area.

As Model and Reinhardt were attempting to coordinate a response to the breakthrough of 51 Army to Mitau on III Pz Army's left flank, Cherniakhovsky launched a powerful attack on Reinhardt's right flank on the Neman south of Kovno. By 30 July III Pz Army's defences on the Neman were beginning to collapse and Wuthmann's IX Corps in Kovno was in danger of encirclement by 5 Army's advances to the southwest and west of the city. Since Kovno was the lynchpin of German defences in Lithuania covering the approaches to East Prussia, Model refused Reinhardt permission to withdraw. In direct contravention of his orders, in the early hours of 31 July Reinhardt authorised a withdrawal of Wuthmann's forces from Kovno to the relative safety of the Nevayazha, some 15km to the west. By 1 August Kovno was in Soviet hands, Krylov's forces had begun to push IX Corps to the northwest, and Reinhardt's right flank had collapsed, leaving 2 Gds Tank Corps from Cherniakhovsky's reserve free to race for Mariampol and the East Prussian border. But it was the isolation of Army Group North east of Riga, the so-called 'breach in the *Wehrmacht*', that caused the greatest consternation at OKH, and elicited the most coordinated German response. A hastily prepared assault by Army Group North on the eastern face of 1 Baltic Front's salient to the Gulf of Riga in the first half of August was been beaten off by 51 Army, and resulted in Bagramyan being reassigned 4 Shock Army back from 2 Baltic Front for the defence of Shyaulyay against attacks from the east. As a result, OKH began to plan a more organised German counter-attack against the salient from the west.

By the beginning of August the Soviet offensives from Estonia to Galicia had run out of steam, or were beginning to do so. Bagramyan was unable to expand his grip on the Gulf of Riga coastline, Cherniakhovsky was unable to exploit the success he had achieved on the Neman, and Rokossovsky was struggling to secure the territory east of Warsaw. By 3 August, after the southern half of III Pz Army had pulled back to the East Prussian border defences, Model could claim a continuous front from Puławy all the way north to Shyaulyay. During the second week of August the *Hermann Goering* Pz Div and 19 Pz Div were successfully containing Rokossovsky's

Magnuszew bridgehead, and Model received several reinforcement divisions including the *Grossdeutschland* Pz Gdr Div from Army Group South Ukraine.

On 10 August, 3 Baltic Front launched offensives against XVIII Army's positions south of Lake Peipus and north of the Dvina (between Dvinsk and Riga). Soviet attacks against XVIII Army had been relentless for weeks, attenuating Schoerner's reserves, and on the first day of the renewed offensives, 3 Baltic Front broke through in both places. Schoerner demanded draconian measures from his subordinates, and on 12 August received news from Hitler that a relief effort – Operation Doppelkopf – from Army Group Centre would be mounted on 16 August in order to end Army Group North's isolation from the Reich. This offensive by III Pz Army was undertaken by six panzer divisions and the equivalent of a few infantry divisions grouped around two corps headquarters (General Sigfrid Henrici's XL Pz Corps and General Dietrich von Saucken's XXXIX Pz Corps) striking towards Mitau and Shyaulyay to reach the Mitau – Shyaulyay road. The two corps were able to push back 1 Baltic Front more than 15km. Saucken re-established a corridor along the coast to Army Group North on 20 August, but the attempt by Henrici to retake Shyaulyay from 2 Gds Army had, by 20 August, failed against skilful defence and substantial reinforcement of Chanchibadze's forces from Bagramyan's reserves. Those reserves included the still under-strength 5 Gds Tank Army (by this time under the command of Solomatin) and 1 Tank Corps. The fighting continued until the end of the month before it subsided, but the corridor between Army Group North and the Reich was never widened to more than 30km. Despite the continued precariousness of Army Group North's position, Hitler refused, for political reasons relating to Finland's continue participation in the war, requests for Army Group North to be withdrawn from Estonia and Latvia.

On the day that Army Group Centre's relief effort to Riga began, Model was ordered west to take command of Army Group B in France. Reinhardt took command of Army Group Centre, and the newly-promoted Col-Gen Erhard Raus replaced him at III Pz Army. On this day also, three Soviet armies from 3 Belorussian Front attacked III Pz Army's right flank, taking Vilkavishkis and, on 17 August, reaching the East Prussian border some 15km northwest of the town. Having reached the Raseynyay – Suwalki line, 3 Belorussian Front was poised to invade East Prussia, thereby threatening to cut off Army Group North yet again. In fact only one Soviet platoon managed to cross onto German soil, and this was subsequently wiped out. Nevertheless, over the next two days 3 Belorussian Front came close to breaking into East Prussia. Yet Cherniakhovsky's forces were unable to penetrate the formidable East Prussian defences in any significant strength, and subsequently, with the aid of *Grossdeutschland* Div, Army Group Centre was able to retake Vilkavishkis.

Farther north 3 Baltic Front breached the Lake Peipus – Gulbene line and, after a protracted advance by 67 Army through difficult terrain, took Tartu on 25 August, reaching the 'Vaalga Line' along Lake Vrtsyarv and the upper Gauya river. However a parallel advance by 1 Shock Army towards the bastion of Valk was held.

The Warsaw Uprising

In the closing days of July 1944 the westward advance of Rokossovsky's 1 Belorussian Front seemed unstoppable. In five weeks Rokossovsky's forces had advanced from the Dnieper to the Vistula, a distance, at its greatest extent, of nearly 600km. Although

Radzievsky had been frustrated in his attempt on 26 July to get 2 Tank Army's forces across the Vistula at Deblin and Puławy, he had every expectation when he turned two tank corps north along the right bank of the river, that they would be able to force a crossing closer to Warsaw. The capture of Warsaw seemed both inevitable and imminent, and a Soviet radio broadcast from Belorussia encouraged the city's population to expel the German occupiers.

Yet all was not as it seemed. The risk to Warsaw had been recognised by Model before Guderian issued his unrealistic directive about solid fronts and counter-attacks on 24 July, and it was this threat that prompted the dispatch of IX Army Headquarters with the powerful *Hermann Goering* Pz Div to form a screening line from Siedlce to the south. Vormann was promised additional divisions to be routed through Warsaw where the Germans knew that a civil uprising was a distinct possibility. Hence when Radzievsky's tank corps reached Otwock and Radzymin less than 20km from Warsaw on 31 July, they found the German defences in the area stiffening. This stiffening was achieved, not just by forces arriving from the west, but by elements of II Army falling back from Brest north of Siedlce. Warsaw had never been a strategic objective in STAVKA's planning for its summer offensive, and Rokossovsky's forces had largely outrun their supplies, so that by the end of July they were no longer in a position to mount an immediate offensive to take a well-defended city on the far side of a significant river barrier. Not all of this was understood by the leaders of the Polish 'Home Army' when they launched a civil uprising in the capital on 1 August. The uprising was expected to last just a few days prior to the arrival of Red Army forces in the city, and the timing of its launch had been set with that in mind. The 'Home Army' was affiliated to the London-based Polish Government in Exile, which, despite Churchill's incessant urging, had been unable to come to an agreement with Stalin over Poland's post-war borders. Hence the uprising had, in addition to the earnest desire of the one million Warsaw residents to oust their occupiers, a broader political dimension. The liberation of the city jointly by the Red Army and the Home Army would enhance the credibility of the Polish Government in Exile, and possibly strengthen its negotiating position with the Soviets. Conversely, it was not in Stalin's interests to see the Home Army claiming the credit for the liberation of the capital; those interests would be better serve if the Red Army alone could claim the credit for the liberation of the city.

At the beginning of August Radzievsky reported that at least three panzer divisions, part of XXXIX Pz Corps, were on the eastern fringes of the city, and that his forces could advance no further. By 2 August, 1 Belorussian Front had established two bridgeheads over the Vistula south of Warsaw (at Magnuszew and Puławy) but Rokossovsky was unable to secure the territory east of Warsaw through which II Army was still retreating. Consequently, 3 Tank Corps was in danger of encirclement from German forces retreating from the east, and it was pushed back from Radzymin and Wolomin 16km north and northwest of the city, while on Radzievsky's flank, some 37km east-southeast of Warsaw, 8 Gds Tank Corps was engaged in heavy fighting with the *Hermann Goering* Div. By 5 August, 2 Tank Army had been reduced to 31 operational armoured fighting vehicles, and was withdrawn from the front, its place being taken by 47 Army. At the same time 1 Belorussian Front's left flank forces were fully committed on the Vistula at Magnuszew, where initially 8 Gds Army had to defend the bridgehead against 19 Pz Div, 25 Pz Div and the *Hermann Goering* Pz Div until Polish 1 Army, 69 Army and a tank corps from 2 Tank Army could be committed to its expansion. Consequently Rokossovsky's centre and right were ordered onto the defensive, and two of his right flank armies were withdrawn into STAVKA reserve. The reality of the Red Army's problems along the Vistula only became apparent to the Polish leadership after the uprising had begun, and by then it was too late to do anything but continue the fight. Although the Home Army in the city had some 20,000 combatants with a further 20,000 active supporters, weapons and ammunition were in short supply. Within the first two days the Home Army had secured around half the city, but German units held on to many key strongpoints, and by 4 August the insurgent held areas comprised half a dozen isolated sectors, the largest of which was the city centre. However, the uprising in the Praga district on the right bank of the Vistula failed because of the overwhelming size of the German forces in that area, and thereafter the uprising was confined to districts on the left bank of the river.

By 3 August Himmler had assumed responsibility for suppressing the uprising. He dispatched relief formations to Warsaw consisting of SS and police units from Poznan, together with two paramilitary formations, the Dirlewanger Brigade and the Kaminski Brigade. These brigades were little more than anarchic brigand bands, but they were under Himmler's patronage and he could rely on them to carry out his orders to massacre the city's population and to level Warsaw as an example for the rest of Europe. Also joining the German forces in the city were units from the *Hermann Goering* Pz Div. Showing little regard for the fate of civilians caught up in the fighting, by 5 August German forces had begun mass executions of civilians in the captured districts.

In response to urgent requests from the Home Army and from the Polish Government in Exile, the Western Allies began preparations for an airlift of supplies to the insurgents. Stalin, however, refused to allow the supply aircraft to cross into Soviet airspace for landing and refuelling.[4] The Allied resupply effort had to be mounted from Italy, and the long return flights, which began on 7 August, could carry only limited tonnage and were highly vulnerable to German interdiction. By this means the Home Army in the city received little more than 100 tons of supplies throughout the entire uprising.

During the second week of the uprising German forces began to direct their main effort against the Old Town district north of the city centre in an offensive that was to continue unabated throughout the month. Its objective was to isolate the insurgents there and to push them away from a key bridge over the Vistula. After mid-August siege guns, incendiary rockets and remote-controlled vehicle mines began to be employed by German forces; weapons that, under skies dominated by the *Luftwaffe*, began to make a critical difference to German progress on the ground. By early September, despite a renewed attempt by 47 Army and the southern wing of 70 Army to break into the city, the Home Army's resistance in the Old Town had been crushed and its fighters had been pushed back from proximity to the river.

On 11 September Rokossovsky's forces resumed their offensive towards Warsaw, and Soviet aircraft began to challenge the *Luftwaffe*'s dominance of the city's airspace. German forces steadily lost control of Praga, pushed back to left bank of the Vistula.

---

4   This despite the fact that for months American bombers on deep penetration bombing missions into Eastern Europe had been landing and refuelling at Poltava in the Ukraine.

On 16 September the retreating German forces blew the remaining bridges into Warsaw from the east. This withdrawal, which included forces from 19 Pz Div, increased the strength of German forces available for deployment against the Home Army. Meanwhile 47 Army was relieved on the right bank of the river by Polish 1 Army. Over three days, commencing 13 September, troops from Berling's army attempted to cross the Vistula to make contact with the insurgents, but the inexperienced Polish troops were ultimately unsuccessful.[5]

By 29 September the Home Army perimeter had been reduced to a few city blocks, and three days later the fighting ceased. Approximately 200,000 of the city's population had been killed, and a further 55,000 were subsequently sent to concentration camps. Most of Warsaw's remaining population were expelled from the city as the Germans began to systematically strip the capital of anything of value. Much of the city was then put to the torch and significant civic buildings were blown up in an effort to fulfil Himmler's ambition to eradicate the Polish capital from the map.

From the Centre to the Flanks
With Model's departure from the Eastern Front on 16 August, Harpe assumed formal command of Army Group North Ukraine, and with the departure of Raus from I Pz Army to take command of III Pz Army from Reinhardt, Heinrici was placed in command of I Pz Army. Towards the end of the third week in August, the Eastern Front began to stabilise. North of Warsaw, Rokossovsky's forces pushed II Army back behind the Narew, and in early September took two bridgeheads over the river at Serock and Różan. Army Group North was left in control of the coastal areas of Estonia, Latvia and Lithuania from Gulbene to north of Mitau. Army Group Centre held the line from west of Mitau to west of Shaulyay to Schirwindt on the East Prussian border, then east of the Masurian lakes to northwest of Białystok, along the Narew and the Vistula as far as the area of Deblin. South of Deblin was the responsibility of Army Group North Ukraine, which covered the upper Vistula and the Sandomierz bridgehead, from where the front tracked southeast to the Carpathians, following the mountains forward of the Slovak and Hungarian borders to the Rumanian border. The northern half of the Carpathian line was held by I Pz Army (opposed by 1 Gds Army of 4 Ukrainian Front), and the southern half was held by I Hun Army (under command of Lt-Gen Bela Miklos) and was opposed by 18 Army. I Pz Army and I Hun Army were combined on 18 August (after Raus had left I Pz Army) under the command of Heinrici as *Armeegruppe* Heinrici. The remainder of the line to the Black Sea was held by Friessner's Army Group South Ukraine.

The offensives that had carried the Soviet armies on the central axis to the Vistula, the Narew and the East Prussian border in the course of the summer campaign had, from the Soviet perspective, been immensely successful. In particular, the establishment of five viable bridgeheads over the Polish river barriers augured well for the further continuation of the drive towards 'the beast's lair' come the winter. Yet by the end of August Soviet forces on the central axis had become highly attenuated and badly in need of rest and reinforcement. Consequently the five Fronts from 1 Baltic Front

---

5   In crossing the Vistula Berling acted without Front or STAVKA authorisation and was subsequently sacked.

to 1 Ukrainian Front were ordered temporarily onto the defensive, and STAVKA's attention was drawn to the possibilities of exploitation on the flanks, north and south.

For the *Ostheer* the Soviet summer offensive had been nothing short of a disaster. Losses had been around 450,000 men; eighteen divisions had been wiped out and another fifty had lost over half their strength. The territorial losses had also been immense, and the basis of Hitler's incessant objection to retreat – that eventually there would be nowhere to retreat to – was being increasingly understood. The Red Army stood on the Reich's border in East Prussia, and in Poland it was only 500km from Berlin. In the West, where during the summer of 1944 German manpower and territorial losses had been comparable to those in the East, Hitler's grand strategy had fallen apart as German forces abandoned France and pulled back towards the Siegfried Line or 'West Wall' along the Franco-German border.

In their consideration of their options for the autumn of 1944, the Soviet General Staff were primarily concerned with the development of an offensive on the southern axis along the Danube and into the Balkans. Yet in the north the task of retaking the Baltic States remained incomplete, and the newly-agreed armistice terms with Finland left the status of German troops in northern Finland more than a little uncertain.

The Courland Peninsula

At the beginning of September 1944 Army Group North and III Pz Army of Army Group Centre occupied what amounted to a deep serpentine beachhead approximately 130km wide that followed the Baltic coast from west of the Narva to south of the Neman. It was an unenviable position from which to try to conduct a protracted strategic defence. During the last week of August Loch, who had succeeded Lindemann as commander of XVIII Army at the end of March, had thwarted determined attempts by 3 Baltic Front to break through XVIII Army's lines, but had lost Tartu on 25 August. (One week later Loch was replaced by General Ehrenfried Boege, the former commander of XLIII Corps). Army Detachment Narva had been pushed back from See Map 27 the Narva, but Steiner's III SS Pz Corps still held a front from the north-eastern tip of Lake Peipus to the coast. From approximately half way down the western shoreline of Lake Peipus, II Corps' frontline ran west, north of Tartu, to the northern tip of Lake Vrtsyarv from where the rest of XVIII Army occupied the frontline south to the east of Valga and on to the northeast of Madone. XVI Army held a rough arc around Riga from west of Madone, across the Dvina half way between Dvinsk and Riga, to Bauske and on to the north of Mitau. Raus's III Pz Army held the line from west of Mitau to west of Shaulyay to Schirwindt on the East Prussian border. The armistice agreement between Finland and the Soviet Union had undermined the political imperative of German retention of the two northern Baltic States. Yet Hitler, citing the Navy's need to maintain the Baltic Sea as a training area, and believing that Stalin was seeking a peace deal, insisted that territory in the Baltic States be held. Soviet preparations for a renewed offensive were deliberate and obvious, and Schoerner was determined not to try to defend Estonia and northern Latvia. Instead, and in the absence of orders to withdraw Army Group North from the Baltic States entirely, he intended to withdraw to two defensive belts forming arcs 100km and 80km from Riga between the Gulf of Riga and the Dvina.

The Soviet offensive in the north by the three Baltic Fronts and Leningrad Front was resumed on 14 September 1944. The Soviets had 125 divisions, seven mechanised corps and seven other large groups (900,000 men, 17,500 guns and mortars, 3,000 tanks and 2,600 aircraft); the Germans had around 550,000 men with a further 50,000 Soviet auxiliaries of doubtful combat capability – 49 infantry divisions and 7 mechanised divisions. A partial regrouping of Soviet forces had been carried out in the eastern Baltic in preparation for this offensive. The Tartu area had been assigned to Leningrad Front, and the Front's 2 Shock Army was moved into position there. Govorov was to attack north from the Tartu area in an attempt to isolate Army Detachment Narva. Maslennikov's 3 Baltic Front had been assigned 61 Army from STAVKA reserve together with 10 Tank Corps, and was to penetrate German defences on two sectors to the south of Lake Vrtsyarv with a follow-up in the direction of Cesis and Riga. Eremenko's 2 Baltic Front was to threaten the German grouping in the Madone area along the northern bank of the Dvina towards Riga and, with part of its forces, towards Dzerbene. Bagramyan's 1 Baltic Front was to strike at Riga from the south with 43 Army and 4 Shock Army, and was to prevent any westward withdrawal of German forces. At the same time 1 Baltic Front's left wing, while protecting itself from German forces in the Memel area, was to advance to the coast in the Tukums area to cut off German forces from Courland.

A weakness of the offensive plan was that around three-quarters of the available forces were committed to the breakthrough sectors, leaving the secondary sectors with few forces for offensive action, and so leaving the Germans reasonably free to redeploy their forces as required to meet the main threat. In addition, 2 Baltic Front and 3 Baltic Front had undertaken little reconnaissance and were unaware of the strength of the German defences. Consequently, during the first three days of the offensive, these two Fronts and Leningrad Front were able to advance only a few kilometres beyond the frontlines at Tartu, Valga and Ergli. In the Bauske area an attack by 43 Army penetrated the German defences to a depth of 6km on the first day, and during the second day reached to within 40km of Riga. On 16 September a reinforced left flank corps from III Pz Army attacked east from the Ause area towards Bauske to restore the situation there, and the resultant penetration of Soviet lines over the next two days thwarted any Soviet move on Tukums and slowed the breakthrough by 43 Army, which, supported by 3 Gds Mech Corps, had advanced to within 25km of Riga. Bagramyan's offensive from Mitau to the coast west of Riga was running out of steam. On 19 September a Soviet spearhead passed Baldone and reached to with 16km of Riga, but the Soviet offensive could get no further. However, the dispatches Schoerner was receiving from the front farther north were far less encouraging. On 17 September Govorov's forces broke through General Wilhelm Hasse's II Corps defences near Tartu, and Boege reported to Schoerner that XVIII Army could not maintain its hold on the southern end of Lake Vrtsyarv. It was time for Schoerner to put his withdrawal plans into effect. He ordered III SS Pz Corps to pull back nearly 200km from the Narva to Parnu, and he ordered II Corps to swing its line back through 180 degrees from Lake Vrtsyarv to the Gulf of Riga. The next day III Pz Army was transferred to Army Group North, and Hitler gave permission for Schoerner to pull back to the Riga defensive line in the north, while using the divisions so released to attack 1 Baltic Front in the south in order to eliminate the salient towards Riga.

The withdrawal of German forces from the Narva area coincided with the offensive by the right flank of Leningrad Front. This offensive began on 17 September, and resulted in a relatively disorganised German retreat, which in turn meant that, though no German units were surrounded, some German forces had to retreat to the Courland Peninsula via the Baltic Islands of Mulu, Hiiumaa and Saaremaa. Tallinn was taken by Fedyuninsky's 2 Shock Army on 22 September, and Parnu two days later. Farther south progress by 3 Baltic Front and 2 Baltic Front was effectively controlled by XVIII Army as it retreated, the fortress of Valk falling to 3 Baltic Front on 19 September, while 2 Baltic Front was unable to take Plavinas. On 22 September Eremenko did achieve a breakthrough against X Corps west of Madone, but he failed to exploit it successfully and the penetration was contained by 11 SS Pz Gdr Div (*Nordland*), which had been redeployed from the flank. On 24 September, faced with increasing resistance by Army Group North and by the well-prepared defences around Riga, STAVKA decided to switch the axis of the offensive and to launch a concerted attack at the beginning of October into the junction of Army Group North and Army Group Centre towards the coast at Memel. Consequently, positions south of Riga were vacated by 1 Baltic Front, and were taken over by 3 Shock Army of 2 Baltic Front. STAVKA then reinforced 1 Baltic Front, and five armies of an assault group, together with 1 Tank Corp, 19 Tank Corps, 3 Mech Corps and Kreizer's 51 Army as second echelon, were concentrated under its command in the Shyaulyay area for a strike westwards towards Memel. The armies comprising the assault group were Beloborodov's 43 Army, Chanchibadze's 2 Gds Army, Malyshev's 4 Shock Army, Chistyakov's 6 Gds Army and 5 Gds Tank Army, the latter, since mid-August, being commanded by Volsky. Chistyakov was to strike to the northwest and Beloborodov was to strike to the west and southwest. As these armies diverged, 51 Army would be moved in to fill the gap, and Volsky would strike due west. A secondary strike would be made by 2 Gds Army on an 8km breakthrough sector towards the Dubysa aimed at Kelme and a link up with Lyudnikov's 39 Army on the Neman. It was expected that this secondary strike would encircle German forces east of Taurage and protect the left flank of the main offensive. Bagramyan's offensive would also be aided by a supporting offensive by 3 Belorussian Front towards Koenigsberg.

On 25 September Hilpert, who had assumed command of XVI Army after the death of Laux earlier in the month, reported that 1 Baltic Front's spearhead forces near Riga had been cut off and destroyed, and two days later he reported heavy Soviet road traffic moving away from XVI Army's positions and heading to the southwest. At the end of the month III Pz Army identified 4 Shock Army in its area and by 2 October OKH was aware that a Soviet offensive from the Shyaulyay area was in preparation, but the assumption was that such an offensive could not be launched before mid-October.

In fact the offensive opened on 5 October with a massive 90-minute artillery barrage west of Shyaulyay in the late morning. Where the flanks of 6 Gds Army and 43 Army met along a 15km breakthrough sector in front of the Venta, Bagramyan had concentrated nearly half of his available 60 divisions, and they quickly broke through the German lines to a depth of 8km. Farther south 2 Gds Army made a less impressive dent in the German defences before 39 Army opened its complementary offensive. The next day 5 Gds Tank Army was committed.

Fully aware of the potential consequences of the Soviet offensive, Army Group North began to withdraw divisions from the northwest of Riga during the evening of 6 October, allowing 2 Baltic Front and 3 Baltic Front to push forward into the vacated positions the next day. Later on 7 October III Pz Army's front broke open. Schoerner proposed giving up Riga, defending the Courland Peninsula and mounting a counter-attack against 1 Baltic Front, but on 8 October both 43 Army and 5 Gds Tank Army reached the German defences on the approach to Memel, and two days later they reached the coast north and south of the city. Isolated within Memel was Gollnick's XXVIII Corps, but it could be supplied by sea, and was subsequently able to hold out until January. Also on 10 October III Pz Army was transferred back to Army Group Centre, and the next day Hitler approved the withdrawal from Riga.[6]

On 13 October Soviet forces finally took the Latvian capital but by then 33 divisions of Army Group North had successfully withdrawn into the Courland Peninsula. The rest of Army Group North retreated to East Prussia, and only three German divisions were lost in the course of the autumn fighting in the Baltic States.

The task of eliminating the Courland pocket fell to 1 Baltic Front and 2 Baltic Front. Four armies from 1 Baltic Front (51 Army, 4 Shock Army, 6 Gds Army and 5 Gds Tank Army) were turned north to the Courland Peninsula on 10 October. On 16 October 3 Baltic Front was disbanded; three of its armies were assigned to 2 Baltic Front, Leningrad Front and 1 Baltic Front, and the fourth army, 54 Army, was disbanded. The forces of 1 Baltic Front were then joined by four armies of 2 Baltic Front (1 Shock Army, 3 Shock Army, 42 Army and 22 Army) in an offensive to eliminate Army Group North. Yet these not inconsiderable forces proved unable to dislodge the Germans from well-prepared defences during the second half of October, and STAVKA had to be content with blockading the two German armies of Army Group North.[7] The German forces in the Courland Peninsula, like the forces in Memel, were not completely isolated since they could be supplied by the German Baltic Fleet. In fact forces were transferred back and forth between Germany and the peninsula until the end of the war, and the German defences in the Courland Peninsula were to withstand five further Soviet offensives, the last of which ran from 17 March to 3 April 1945.

On 16 October three Soviet armies from 3 Belorussian Front (Krylov's 5 Army, Galitsky's 11 Gds Army and, for exploitation, Luchinsky's 28 Army[8] with 2 Gds Tank Corps), broke into East Prussia through IV Army's defences between Schirwindt and the Rominter Heide, a heavily forested area east of Goldap. This offensive was supported on the flanks by 31 Army and 39 Army. In three days Cherniakhovsky's forces had taken Goldap, the first German city in the east to fall, and, after penetrating well-prepared and fiercely defended German defence lines, they were threatening Gumbinnen on the direct route to Koenigsberg. To contain the Soviet advance towards Gumbinnen, OKH ordered Reinhardt to take the northern flank of III Pz Army back across the Neman, and to use the armour thereby freed to drive the Soviets from East Prussia. This effectively ended any prospect of a counter-attack against the Soviet penetration

---

6   In reality only one corps was transferred back to Army Group Centre with III Pz Army since XXVIII Corps was cut off in Memel and III Pz Army's other corps was cut off in the Courland Peninsula.

7   Bagramyan's forces in the Courland Peninsula were joined at the beginning of November by 2 Gds Army from the Neman front – only 43 Army from 1 Baltic Front being left on the Neman.

8   After a month as part of STAVKA reserve, 28 Army was returned to operational service with 3 Belorussian Front on 13 October.

to Memel, but German counter-attacks against Soviet forces in East Prussia held Cherniakhovsky's advance towards Gumbinnen and retook Goldap. Yet Reinhardt was unable to drive the Soviets completely from East Prussia. At the end of October Cherniakhovsky's offensive was called off. On 4 November 2 Belorussian and 3 Belorussian Fronts were formally ordered to go onto the defensive, and a similar order was issued to the right wing of 1 Belorussian Front a few days later. In the pause during November and December Reinhardt was able to strengthen his defences.

Arctic Warfare

German forces in central and northern Finland and in north-eastern Norway were deployed in three corps as part of Col-Gen Lothar Rendulic's XX Mtn Army.[9] In the far north, west of the Litsa, in positions it had held for three years, and facing Karelian Front's 14 Army, was General Ferdinand Jodl's XIX Mtn Corps. This corps of 53,000 men included 210 Inf Div, Divisional Group van der Hoop, 6 Mtn Div and 2 Mtn Div, and its primary task was to protect the Kolosyoki nickel mines in the Petsamo area. Only the two mountain divisions could be considered as fully operational combat divisions; 210 Inf Div consisted mainly of 'fortress' battalions defending the coastline west of Kirkenes, and Hoop's group was based around a *Luftwaffe* field regiment with the task of defending the neck of the Rybatchy Peninsula as flank protection for 6 Mtn Div. The north-eastern extremity of the frontline ran from the eastern bank of the Litsa estuary west towards Lake Chapr. This section of the line was held by 6 Mtn Div, and off its right flank, extending to the southwest from Lake Chapr, 2 Mtn Div held an extended line towards Ivalo. Two hundred kilometres to the south, Lt-Gen Emil Vogel's XXXVI Mtn Corps, straddling the railway line east of Salla, faced Karelian Front's 19 Army. Vogel's corps consisted of 167 Inf Div and 163 Inf Div. South of the Arctic Circle General Friedrich Hochbaum's XVIII Mtn Corps (6 SS Mtn Div and 7 Mtn Div) occupied a short front between Lake Pyra, Lake Top and Ukhta, and faced Karelian Front's 26 Army. No continuous front existed between the corps positions, the area being covered only by occasional patrols.

See Map 24

On 4 September 1944 an armistice agreement between Finland and the Soviet Union came into effect and on 19 September the Finns signed a provisional peace treaty. This had been anticipated by Germany, and plans were in hand (Operation Birke) to redeploy XX Mtn Army's forces to ensure the continued protection of both the Kolosyoki nickel mines and German occupied north-eastern Norway. On 6 September the plan was put into effect. Since this operation began as the winter was approaching, Rendulic was determined to conduct it at a deliberate pace, the first phase of which was to pull back the two southern corps to the 1940 Finnish border. Thereafter the plan was to pull the corps back to Kemi at the northern end of the Gulf of Bothnia, and then north to the road and rail hub at Rovaniemi. From there the Army's centre and right flank would withdraw to defensive positions well to the south of Ivalo and Skibotten; positions deep within Finnish territory. There were few roads in northern Finland, and those that existed largely dictated the axes of any potential military operation, particularly in winter. A road ran north from Rovaniemi to Ivalo (the Arctic Ocean Highway) from where it split, the Arctic Ocean Highway leg continuing to Kirkenes while a north-western leg ran to Lakselv. A road ran for 250km along the Finnish side

9   Dietl had been killed in a plane crash on 23 June 1944.

of the Swedish border north from Kemi to Muonio. A road also ran to Muonio from Rovaniemi. From Muonio a half-completed road continued north along the Swedish border to the area of Skibotten. Finally a road ran west through north-eastern Norway from Petsamo to Kirkenes and through the coastal communities of Tana, Lakselv, Billefiord, Alta and on to Skibotten – a distance of more than 500km. However the Kirkenes to Lakselv section of this road was normally impassable during the winter.

The first three weeks of the operation were relatively untroubled but on 28 September sporadic fighting broke out between German and Finnish forces. This continued until 8 October by which time German forces had withdrawn north of Rovaniemi. Once German forces were north of the Arctic Circle, Finnish forces followed but did not attack again. During this time OKW had been reviewing the necessity of maintaining XX Mtn Army in north-eastern Norway. Having been assured that Germany's stockpile of nickel was adequate for the foreseeable future, Hitler, on 3 October, approved the withdrawal of XX Mtn Army to the 'Lyngen Position', a short defence line that ran from the Barents Sea coast to the Swedish border just east of the Muonio to Skibotten road.

In early September 1944 Meretskov ordered his northern armies to begin preparations for a campaign against XX Mtn Army, operations that would have the objective of turning its flanks. The pivotal role would be played by Lt-Gen V I Shcherbakov's 14 Army in the far north, and Shcherbakov's army was increased in strength from two rifle divisions, two brigades and a few supporting artillery regiments to six rifle divisions, five brigades, more than a dozen artillery and mortar regiments, a tank regiment and a tank brigade (97,000 troops organised into five corps). Farther south Lt-Gen G K Kozlov's 19 Army and Lt-Gen L S Skvirsky's 26 Army with a total of nine divisions would play a secondary role.

On 7 October, while XIX Corps was in the process of evacuating its substantial stockpiles of equipment, 14 Army attacked. The offensive was opened by 131 Rifle Corps and 99 Rifle Corps and was directed at 2 Mtn Div's positions east and southeast of Lake Chapr. Unable to hold its forwards lines, the centre and left of 2 Mtn Div fell back 10km across the Titovka. Two days later the three brigades of 126 Light Rifle Corps attacked 2 Mtn Div's right flank. In danger of being cut off, 6 Mtn Div was pulled back and Jodl was assigned reinforcements from XXXVI Mtn Corps, elements of which were already moving north up the Arctic Ocean Highway. On 10 October Shcherbakov mounted a sea-borne landing to the west of Divisional Group van der Hoop's positions on the neck of the Rybatchy Peninsula. Since this threatened the left flank of the divisional group, Hoop was ordered to withdraw towards Petsamo. On the same day 6 Mtn Div's retreat route to Petsamo was cut by forces of 131 Rifle Corps, and 126 Light Rifle Corps cut the Arctic Ocean Highway 20km southwest of Petsamo. The bulk of Jodl's corps was in danger of being surrounded but by 12 October Divisional Group van der Hoop and 6 Mtn Div had secured an escape route to Petsamo. The next day 2 Mtn Div tried to dislodge 126 Light Rifle Corps from the Arctic Ocean Highway in an attack from the north. It was supported by two regiments of 163 Inf Div moving up from Ivalo attacking 126 Light Rifle Corps from the south, but the attacks could not break through Shcherbakov's stranglehold on the Arctic Ocean Highway. In fact forces from 126 Light Rifle Corps pushed to the north and cut the road west from Petsamo, isolating 2 Mtn Div, 6 Mtn and Divisional Group van der Hoop. On 14 October, as Soviet forces west of Petsamo stopped to regroup, Jodl's forces began to fight their way out, pulling back from their toehold in Russia by 15 October. By 18 October they had succeeded in breaking out but 2 Mtn Div was so depleted it had to be withdrawn from combat, its remaining operational units being merged with 163 Inf Div, which had been temporarily placed under Jodl's command. On that date 14 Army resumed its offensive, attacking 163 Inf Div with four of its five corps. As 163 Inf Div pulled back south down the Arctic Ocean Highway, narrowly avoiding being cut off by 127 Light Rifle Corps, 6 Mtn Div was tasked with defending the southern approaches to Kirkenes. These defences were attacked by 131 Rifle Corps, which threatened to cut XIX Mtn Corps' withdrawal route yet again. Jodl was forced to accelerate his withdrawal, abandoning around 90,000 tonnes of supplies in the process. By 24 October all German forces had withdrawn from east of Kirkenes. In late October two divisions from the Army of Norway were moved into positions between Skibotten and Lakselv to assist XX Mtn Army in its withdrawal, but the Soviet pursuit of XIX Mtn Corps ended, and on 29 October Soviet forces in the area went over to the defensive. By the end of October XVIII Mtn Corps had pulled out of Muonio in a relatively leisurely withdrawal to Skibotten, and on 3 November the rearguard of XXXVI Mtn Corps withdrew from Ivalo along the road to Lakselv. The successful withdrawal of XX Mtn Army was considerably assisted by relatively mild weather, which allowed the Kirkenes to Lakselv road to be kept open, and by the fact that during this time both the Soviet Union and the Western Allies were fully committed in other theatres.

The Southern Flank

When Friessner arrived at the headquarters of Army Group South Ukraine during the final week of July 1944 he found a sector of the Eastern Front that had been relatively quiet for more than three months. The frontline ran from Kuty, across the Siret, north of Târgu Frumos, north of Jassy, across the Prut and on to Cornetsi northwest of Kishinev. From there the frontline crossed to the Dniester northeast of Kishinev, and ran down the river to its estuary and the Black Sea. See Map 28

Army Group South Ukraine did not have enough German combat formations to maintain an effective defence across the entire front. Consequently the army group was obliged to make extensive use of Rumanian divisions, formations in which German troops had little confidence. In an effort to try to maximise the combat effectiveness of the army group as a whole, the army group command tried to ensure that the most vulnerable sectors were defended by German units and that, where possible, Rumanian formations were buttressed on either flank by German units – a process termed 'corseting'. By the second half of August this required the integration of 22 Rumanian divisions (including the Rumanian panzer division) and four Rumanian mountain brigades into the army group structure. At the highest level this process involved the use of the *Armeegruppe*. *Armeegruppe* Woehler (VIII Army and VI Rum Army) occupied the left wing of the front from Koty to Cornetsi, and *Armeegruppe* Dumitrescu (VI Army and III Rum Army) occupied the right wing. Within *Armeegruppe* Woehler 16 Rumanian divisions and four mountain brigades were integrated down to and below corps level with six German divisions. German divisions were deployed in strongly fortified positions in the Siret valley, north of Târgu Frumos and also north of Jassy.

Off the left flank of Army Group South Ukraine, holding the frontline along the Carpathians to the Slovak border as part of the newly-formed *Armeegruppe* Heinrici, was I Hun Army of Army Group North Ukraine. The right flank of *Armeegruppe* Woehler's positions tied in with VI Army, the latter occupying a sector of the front that crossed to the Dniester northeast of Kishinev and followed the river to the approximate centre of a Soviet bridgehead below Tiraspol. There VI Army's XXX Corps tied in with the left flank of Dumitrescu's III Rum Army which held the outer flank of the Eastern Front along the Dniester to its estuary and the Black Sea. (On 18 July General Maximilian Fretter-Pico left his long-standing command of XXX Corps to replace de Angelis as commander of VI Army). Within *Armeegruppe* Dumitrescu there was considerably less corseting, and of VI Army's 16 divisions only one was Rumanian. Conversely only one of III Rum Army's seven divisions was German, though this division was part of a German corps (XXIX Corps) that included two Rumanian divisions on the left flank of III Rum Army.

Army Group South Ukraine had been weakened by the transfer north of most of its mechanised divisions during the Red Army's summer offensives in Belorussia and the Baltic States. Yet Friessner still had 600,000 troops under his immediate command, with another fifty to sixty thousand personnel in the form of *Luftwaffe,* SS and police units. Another army, I Rum Army (four divisions) was entirely under Rumanian command and was being used to guard against possible Hungarian aggression across Rumania's northern border with Hungary into southern Transylvania. Soviet manpower superiority over the Axis forces on the Army Group South Ukraine sector was not overwhelming, but in terms of armoured fighting vehicles and aircraft, Friessner was heavily outnumbered.

After Turkey broke off diplomatic relations with Germany on 2 August, Friessner grew concerned about the possible political reaction in Rumania. Antonsescu's loyalty to the Axis cause was not seriously doubted, but as a political leader his authority was being rapidly eroded. As events were to show, what Friessner and Army Group South Ukraine's staff should have been more concerned with was the reliability of the Rumanian troop that defended two-fifths of the army group's frontline. On 16 August Woehler reported that an attack west of Jassy by 2 Ukrainian Front appeared to be imminent but that, from his conversations with Rumanian commanders, the Rumanian troops were confident and determined. Friessner was further comforted by a German military intelligence report advising that Soviet attacks against Army Group South Ukraine would be localised, and that no general offensive was to be expected.

Facing Army Group South Ukraine were Malinovsky's 2 Ukrainian Front and Tolbukhin's 3 Ukrainian Front; Malinovsky facing *Armeegruppe* Woehler and Tolbukhin facing *Armeegruppe* Dumitrescu. Malinovsky's forces on the upper Siret and the upper Prut overhung the centre and right of Army Group South Ukraine, so that a southward advance down either river valley would threaten VI Army with encirclement. By the late summer, though 2 Ukrainian Front's ranks had been swelled by a quarter of a million largely untrained new recruits from the liberated western Ukraine, the Soviet order of battle on the southern axis had not changed significantly since the end of June (see Appendix XII). Malinovsky had also acquired two additional cavalry corps, and Kravchenko, newly-promoted to the rank of colonel-general, had acquired an additional tank corps from Malinovsky's reserves for his 6 Tank Army. Tolbukhin had received a smaller number of the new Ukrainian recruits but 3 Ukrainian Front had been strengthened by an additional mechanised corps.

The objectives of the autumn campaign by the two Ukrainian Fronts were the destruction of Army Group South Ukraine and the subsequent seizure of the Balkans. It was one of the first operations to make significant use of the new Stalin (IS-2) heavy tanks, which were specifically designed for infantry support. Timoshenko co-ordinated the activities of the Fronts for STAVKA. The opening offensive by 2 Ukrainian Front was to be composed of a powerful strike between Pashkany and Jassy by Trofimenko's 27 Army, Koroteev's 52 Army, Managarov's 53 Army, Kravchenko's 6 Tank Army, Shumilov's 7 Gds Army and a cavalry mechanised group under the command of Major-Gen S I Gorshkov. This main offensive would be supported on the right flank by a strike from Zhmachenko's 40 Army into the Carpathians towards Cluj. Tolbukhin's offensive was to open with a strike by Gagen's 57 Army, Sharokhin's 37 Army and most of Shlemin's 46 Army from a Soviet bridgehead over the Dniester in a loop of the river south of Tiraspol. This was an area of marshland that seemed wholly unsuitable for the launching of a major offensive, and Army Group South Ukraine expected any attack from 3 Ukrainian Front to come from a smaller but more suitable bridgehead over the Dniester that Tolbukhin's forces had held north of Bendery. The deployment of Tolbukin's strike force in the Tiraspol bridgehead was conducted in the greatest secrecy and its scale went undetected by German intelligence.

The initial Soviet objective for the offensive (the Jassy-Kishinev Operation) would be the encirclement of VI Army in the Kishinev area. This was to be followed by a strike for the Focșani gap leading to Bucharest and Ploesti. Rather than attack down the narrow Siret valley, Malinovsky chose to mount the main attack northwest of Jassy on the Jassy – Vaslui – Bârlad – Focșani axis, with a secondary strike down the Prut valley on the left flank of VI Army. Tolbukhin's main offensive was directed at Huși on the west bank of the Prut, where a link up with Malinovsky's forces was anticipated. In addition, 46 Army, supported by one of the mechanised corps, would strike to the southwest in order to trap III Rum Army north of the Danube estuary. In order to support this latter move, several divisions of 46 Army commanded by Lt-Gen A N Bakhtin would, two days after the main offensive began, be used in a night-time amphibious assault on the west bank of the Dniester estuary at Akkerman.

The offensive began on 20 August. Several of the defending Rumanian divisions were on the verge of collapse before the opening barrage had been concluded, and two Rumanian divisions defending Jassy, facing a Soviet artillery density of 250 guns per kilometre in the key breakthrough sectors, abandoned their positions without a fight. Consequently Jassy was reached by 52 Army in the afternoon of the first day, and fell 24 hours later after heavy fighting with elements of two German divisions. By nightfall of 20 August, 6 Tank Army and 27 Army, with orders to clear the Mara heights, were breaking out to the south. On their right, 7 Gds Army and Gorshkov's cavalry-mechanised group were poised for a thrust south along the Siret to clear 6 Tank Army's flank. Tolbukhin's opening attack south of Tiraspol by 37 Army struck the boundary of VI Army and III Rum Army where Sharokhin had concentrated nearly 250 guns and mortars per kilometre of front. The right flank of Lt-Gen Georg Postel's XXX Corps was hit the hardest and within hours Fretter-Pico committed his only significant reserve (13 Pz Div) in a counter-attack. The Rumanian mountain division on the left flank of General Anton Reichard's XXIX Corps, tying in with the right flank of XXX Corps, was hit less heavily but nonetheless began to disintegrate. By the end of the first day it was in full retreat, taking the neighbouring Rumanian infantry division on its right with it. XXX Corps managed to hold the right shoulder of 37 Army's attack with a stout defence of the heights south of Bendery, though by 22 August 13 Pz Div was a spent force. However, in the XXIX Corps sector resistance had largely evaporated as the remnants of the corps pulled back to the west, leaving 37 Army and 57 Army, together with the Front's two mechanised corps, 4 Gds Mech Corps and 7 Mech Corps, to break clear of the Tiraspol bridgehead.

Army Group South Ukraine had nothing with which to stop Tolbukhin's breakout to the west and south. In fact it was not until the early hours of 21 August that Friessner began to realise the scale of the offensive that was being unleashed against him. Even then, he was hopeful that in the *Armeegruppe* Woehler sector, defensive positions on the Mara heights could be held. (The Mara heights positions were part of the Trajan Line defences that ran from Târgu Frumos south of Jassy and west to Kishinev). As the day progressed, however, the reality of what his army group was facing became clearer; the 30km gap that had opened up between VI Army and III Rum Army was bad enough, but Woehler was reporting that five of his Rumanian divisions had disintegrated, and that Malinovsky had extended his offensive west to the Târgu Frumos area where Soviet mechanised forces had penetrated the Trajan position. With Soviet forces advancing down the west bank of the Prut,[10] Friessner, on 21 August, ordered VI Army to pull back across the river before the Soviets could close the crossings. On 22 August 6 Tank Army, after striking down the Bârlad valley, was closing on Vaslui and heading for Huşi.

Over the next two days, with most Rumanian forces refusing to fight, the plight of VI Army grew increasingly desperate as Tolbukhin's forces on its right flank moved largely unopposed west from the Tiraspol breakout, and behind its left flank Malinovsky's forces continued to the south behind the Prut. By 23 August III Rum Corps of III Rum Army was isolated north of the Danube estuary; 2 Ukrainian Front had reached Huşi and Bârlad; and Tolbukhin's forces, advancing west, had passed Komrat, and were approaching the Prut from the east. On this day, in recognition of the disastrous military situation, the King of Rumania placed Antonescu under arrest and announced that the country had accepted the Allied armistice terms. All Rumanian forces still in action against the Red Army were ordered to lay down their arms. For the staff of Army Group South Ukraine this turned the disaster unfolding on the battlefield into a chaotic catastrophe. With VI Army largely surrounded, and Friessner's two Rumanian armies no longer in action, the *Ostheer*'s right flank, which since the beginning of the war had been anchored on the Black Sea, had disappeared. In fact from the right flank positions of 3 Mtn Div west of Târgu Neamţ, the *Ostheer* had no recognisable front in any direction except to the north. On 24 August, with 5 Shock Army from 3 Ukrainian Front's right wing in possession of Kishinev, Friessner's fortunes reached their nadir when armoured forces of 2 Ukrainian Front and 3 Ukrainian Front linked up at Leovo to complete the inner ring around VI Army. Most of VI Army was still east of the Prut, and Fretter-Pico, with his headquarters staff, was in Focşani outside the encirclement and in only intermittent radio contact with

---

10   52 Army had already turned east and was heading for Huşi.

his five subordinate corps.[11] Within the encirclement eighteen German divisions were being forced into two pockets on either side of the Prut inside the Jassy – Kishinev – Huşi triangle. Surrounded German forces had escaped encirclement in the past, and Friessner ordered a breakout to the west, past Bacău. However VI Army was not in a strong position to achieve the breakout, and Friessner could do little from outside the encirclement to support it.

The next day Rumania declared war on Germany, and on 26 August, with 2 Ukrainian Front approaching the lower Siret, 3 Ukrainian Front took Kagul to complete the outer ring around VI Army. While Malinovsky and Tolbukhin were left to deal with this sizable German force (which formed into three columns in an attempt to break out to Huşi), Malinovsky was also required to reach the eastern Carpathians on his right flank and drive through the Focşani gap along his centre. On 27 August Malinovsky's forces took Focşani and, though Fretter-Pico's VI Army Headquarters was still in being, that headquarters, and the rear echelon troops gathered around it, were forced to fall back towards Buzau. Two days later, as Tolbukhin's forces took Constanta, 25,000 German troops from VI Army broke out of the inner encirclement west of Huşi. By then the German lines, such as they were, lay far to the west, and few of VI Army's troops were to get that far. Some German troops drifted to the south in an effort to reach Bulgaria, though those that made it to the border were disarmed and interned by the Bulgarian authorities.

By the beginning of September OKH had formally acknowledged the loss of VI Army's five corps headquarters and seventeen German infantry divisions. The ten days of the Soviet Jassy-Kishinev Operation from 20 August to 29 August was, in terms of its military outcome, on a scale comparable to Stalingrad, and it would be followed by a four-months long pursuit operation that would take Soviet forces to the gates of Budapest. The Soviet victory in the Jassy-Kishinev Operation owed much to the meticulous planning that went into its preparation, the professionalism and *élan* with which it was conducted, and the care that the Soviets took in deceiving German intelligence over what was being planned. Yet the scale of the Soviet victory also owed much to the clear reluctance of many Rumanian formations to offer any meaningful resistance to the Red Army, thereby leaving VI Army's German divisions completely exposed on both flanks.

Pursuit through the Mountains

On 25 August Friessner advised OKH that Army Group South Ukraine would need to pull back to the protection of the mountains of central Rumania. Four days later, after the loss of VI Army and the defection of Rumania, OKH authorised Friessner to establish a front along the Carpathians and the spine of the Transylvanian Alps, and to tie in on his right flank with the Southeast Theatre Command (Yugoslavia and Greece) at the Iron Gate near Turnu Severin. By then Army Group South Ukraine had just four full divisions; three had been on VIII Army's left flank, and had escape the full force of the Soviet offensive, and one had been in the process of returning to theatre. Friessner had nothing with which to stop a rapid Soviet thrust into the eastern Transylvanian Alps through the Turnu Roşu and Predal passes south of Sibiu and Brasov respectively, and the more westerly Vulcan Pass was beyond his reach.

---

11   VIII Army's IV Corps had been caught in the encirclement and was assigned to VI Army.

Woehler, retreating from the Siret to the Carpathians, reported that VIII Army had barely enough troops left to organise blocking detachments in the Oitoz Pass (east of Târgu Mureş) and in the other passes to the north. Farther south, 2 Ukrainian Front kept pressing to the west, taking Ploesti on 30 August and entering Bucharest the next day. With the loss of the Ploesti oilfields Germany lost access to a substantial source of crude oil.[12] Consequently, after the loss of the Ploesti fields, Germany's dependence on the extraction of petroleum products from coal increased, and the *Wehrmacht*'s already acute shortages of petroleum grew steadily worse.

On the battlefield Friessner's only immediately available source of additional forces was Hungary. By August 1944 the Hungarian mobilisation had enabled two reserve armies to be created; a reconstituted II Hun Army of seven divisions and three brigades under the command of Lt-Gen Lajos Veress von Dalnoki, and a further nine under-strength and under-equipped divisions manned by the new recruits and recalled reservists of the newly-created III Hun Army under the command of Lt-Gen József Vitéz Heszlényi. On 23 August the Hungarian High Command activated II Hun Army and in early September, after it had been deployed to northern Transylvania, subordinated it to Army Group South Ukraine. On 5 September Friessner moved one of Dalnoki's corps south from Cluj towards the Turnu Roşu Pass. The Hungarians made good progress against weak opposition from Rumanian forces that had crossed into southern Transylvania at the end of August, prompting the Rumanians to ask for Soviet help. Malinovsky's vanguard force, 6 Tank Army, had been advancing west, south of the mountains, and by 5 September forwards units of Kravchenko's army had reached Turnu Severin. STAVKA had to decide whether Kravchenko should continue to the west across the Danube towards Belgrade, or turn to the north to prevent the Hungarians from seizing the mountain passes. Axis forces, once they had become entrenched in the Carpathians and the Transylvanian Alps, could present a formidable barrier to the further development of Soviet offensives in the south, and on 6 September Kravchenko's army began to turn north, to cross the mountains through the Vulcan and Turnu Roşu passes. By then, since Soviet forces were through the Predal Pass and had penetrated into the Oitoz Pass, Friessner began to prepare for the withdrawal of VIII Army and VI Army to the Muresul.[13] On 7 September, when it became clear that II Hun Army would be unable to close the Turnu Roşu Pass, and that one of 6 Tank Army's corps was heading for the Vulcan Pass, Friessner issued the order to withdraw.

On 2 September Tolbukhin's forces reached the Bulgarian border at Giurgiu on the Danube, and three days later the Soviet Union declared war on Bulgaria.[14] Three days after that, on 8 September, 3 Ukrainian Front crossed the Bulgarian border. No resistance was offered by Bulgarian forces and the next day, after a change of government in Sofia, the Soviet 'war' with Bulgaria was over and Tolbukhin saw 5 Shock Army withdrawn into STAVKA reserve.[15] The new Bulgarian government declared war on

---

12 Rumanian crude oil production had declined significantly after 1943 as a result of the bombing campaign by the Western Allies, but most of the deficit to that point had been met from development of the small Hungarian and Austrian fields.

13 Fretter-Pico's headquarters and service area troops had successfully pulled out of the Bazaul valley, and had taken command of LVII Pz Corps, formerly part of IV Rum Army, from VIII Army's right flank.

14 Bulgaria had only been at war with the Western Allies.

15 At the same time 4 Gds Army was withdrawn from 2 Ukrainian Front into STAVKA reserve.

Germany and made its 450,000 troops available to Tolbukhin on 17 September. For Friessner, the diversion of 3 Ukrainian Front into Bulgaria had the benefit of diverting Tolbukhin's attention from the plight of Army Group South Ukraine. On 15 September VIII Army and VI Army reached the Muresul in time to prepare a defence against Malinovsky's forces, which had been slowed down by the difficult conditions in the mountain passes. At this time, in order to stiffen Hungarian morale in facing the Red Army, II Hun Army was merged with VI Army to form *Armeegruppe* Fretter-Pico.[16]

In mid-September STAVKA decided to try to encircle Army Group South Ukraine with 3 Ukrainian Front, 2 Ukrainian Front, 4 Ukrainian Front and the left flank of 1 Ukrainian Front. Tolbukhin was ordered to move 4 Gds Mech Corps to Yambol in south-eastern Bulgaria, less than 50km from the Turkish border. At the same time 37 Army was deployed to the area north of Yambol, while 57 Army was to move to the Yugoslav frontier in the Negotin area. The southerly deployment was to cover the left flank against German, and possibly, Turkish action, while 57 Army would cooperate with 2 Ukrainian Front in an offensive against Belgrade. Malinovsky's Front was effectively divided in two, with the right flank (40 Army, 7 Gds Army and Gorshkov's group) in the eastern Carpathians on the line Bystritsa – Cluj – Aoud – Sibiu, and the left flank (27 Army, 53 Army and 6 Tank Army) advancing into the Transylvanian Alps. Although 52 Army was taken into STAVKA reserve, STAVKA gave Malinovsky 46 Army from 3 Ukrainian Front and a cavalry-mechanised group commanded by Pliev that had been formed from 7 Mech Corps and Pliev's 4 Gds Cav Corps. Malinovsky was ordered to strike towards Debrecen, the Tisza and Miskolc. Meanwhile 4 Ukrainian Front would push through the Dukla Pass north of Humenné in eastern Slovakia to complete the encirclement of the Germans behind the Carpathians. However, it would take time to organise such an offensive. On 8 September a heavily reinforced 38 Army on Konev's left flank[17] had attempted to break into Slovakia through the Dukla and Łupków passes in an offensive that was conceived as being coordinated with a 'Slovak uprising', an uprising that proved to be poorly organised and ultimately unsuccessful. Moskalenko had faced difficult terrain, well defended by the recently formed XI SS Corps of XVII Army and XXIV Pz Corps from I Pz Army. On 9 September 4 Ukrainian Front's 1 Gds Army began a supporting offensive to break into the German defences at Sanok, but this offensive also made little progress.

The Balkans

The turn of 6 Tank Army north through the Transylvanian Alps at the end of the first week of September came as a huge relief to Maximillian von Weichs. After Army Group B had been withdrawn from the Eastern Front in 1943, Weichs had subsequently been promoted to the rank of Field Marshal and had been appointed simultaneously to the command of the Southeast Theatre (Army Group F and Army Group E) and to the direct command of Army Group F (Yugoslavia). To oversee the coastal defences on the Adriatic, at risk from an attack by the Western Allies in Sicily,

---

16   On 17 September Fretter-Pico had reported that the Hungarians were in a catastrophic state, one mountain brigade having simply abandoned its positions.

17   At this time 38 Army included 52 Rifle Corps, 67 Rifle Corps, 101 Rifle Corps, 25 Tank Corps, 1 Gds Cav Corps and the Czechoslovak 1 Corps.

II Pz Army Headquarters had been transferred to the south-eastern theatre after the failure of Operation Citadel. In Albania, Greece and the Aegean Islands, Col-Gen Alexander Loehr was in command of Army Group E. Weichs's command, comprising 31 divisions and 7 German fortress brigades with a total theoretical combat strength of around 600,000 men, had been configured to perform only two missions: to defend the Balkan coast and islands, and to combat partisan activity. Events on the Eastern Front had been of no direct concern to the Southeast Theatre Command. This began to change in August when Turkey broke off relations with Germany, and the Bulgarian Government felt encouraged to re-establish consular relations with the Soviet Union, subsequently restricting German movements in the country. Of Weichs's 31 divisions only 15 were German, the mobility and combat capability of which were low, and 7 divisions were Bulgarian. With the defeat of Army Group South Ukraine in late August, and Bulgaria's defection in early September, a 600km front from the Hungarian border to the Aegean had suddenly opened up which Weichs was required to defend. The most immediate danger was in the south where a line from Thessalonica to Skopje to Niš had to be held in order for Army Group E to be able to escape north.

By the second week of September Weichs had neutralised and disarmed the Bulgarian forces within his command, and had set up a weak front along the eastern border of Yugoslavia and across the Danube west of the Iron Gate where he detected the first signs of a Soviet build-up. On 21 September a small British force landed on the Peloponnesus, and on 22 September Bulgaria declared general mobilisation, while 3 Ukrainian Front crossed the Danube into the bend west of Turnu Severin. Yet even by then Weichs, mindful of Hitler's determination to hold the chromium mines of northern Greece, had not taken the final decision to evacuate Greece entirely. On 25 September he committed 1 Mtn Div, under the command of Lt-Gen Walter Stettner Ritter von Grabenhofen, to eject Tolbukhin's forces from the bend of the Danube, but two days later he learned that Soviet forces from the left flank of 2 Ukrainian Front were advancing west between Timişoara and the Danube. By 29 September Weichs had concluded that a Soviet effort to take Belgrade was in the making, and on 3 October the order was issued for the evacuation of Greece, Albania and Macedonia, the evacuation to begin not later than 10 October. On 1 October elements of 57 Army began to cross the Bulgarian border into Yugoslavia along sectors that Stettner had been obliged to weaken in order to retake the Danube bend. On 4 October forward elements of 57 Army made contact with Yugoslav partisans near the Morava. Confident that within days Gagen would have much of his army on the river, Tolbukhin began the transfer of 4 Gds Mech Corps from southern Bulgaria to exploit this breakthrough, and he ordered Bulgarian 2 Army to begin an attack towards Niš. On 5 October, with Soviet forces in the process of taking Pancevo, just 16km downriver from Belgrade, Weichs moved his headquarters from Belgrade to Vukovar, and proposed to OKW that II Pz Army be converted into a fully operational army capable of tactical manoeuvre.

Tolbukhin's drive towards Belgrade was weakened at this time by the transfer of 46 Army north to 2 Ukrainian Front, but 4 Gds Mech Corps on 8 October, having bypassed Bor without being detected by German forces, appeared on the Morava 80km behind the front, and cut the southern rail link into Belgrade. The next day Bulgarian 1 Army began an offensive past Bela Palanka towards Niš, as strong Yugoslav partisan forces pushed deep into Serbia southwest of Belgrade and west of Niš. On 10 October, with the fall of Niš and Belgrade seeming imminent, the evacuation of Loehr's army group from Greece began. To deal with the Soviet forces on the Morava, Weichs stripped the Belgrade defences to create a task group, the equivalent of an operational division, to strike east to the mouth of the Morava, link up with 1 Mtn Div, and then for the combined force to move up the Morava. By 12 October this force had reached up the Morava to Velika Plana but by then 57 Army and the mechanised corps were across the river, and by the next day Soviet armour was just 10km south of the capital. This left Stettner's composite force trapped in the Morava valley. Weichs ordered that Belgrade be held until Stettner could fight his way north to the city but on 14 October Soviet and partisan forces entered Belgrade. Fighting in the city continued for five days, Weichs anticipating that Stettner's force would be able to fight its way west to the Sava and into the city, but Stettner was unable break through, and Belgrade was abandoned by German forces on 19 October. Over subsequent days less than 10,000 of the encircled men, carrying only hand weapons, reached the German lines across the Sava at Šabac. By 20 October all Loehr's escape routes north, with the exception of the Skopje to Sarajevo route, had been cut.[18] With an agreement between Stalin and Churchill that Soviet forces would not advance into Bosnia or Croatia, Tolbukhin was instructed on 18 October to move one rifle corps to the northern bank of the Danube and into the Samobor – Novi Sad area to cover the left flank of 2 Ukrainian Front, another of his rifle corps having already made contact with 46 Army.

In late October Weichs was in a desperate position but his problems suddenly eased when 57 Army was diverted north to assist with the drive into Hungary, thereby effectively ending Soviet advances in the Balkans. On 2 November Loehr was able to stop the latest of several Soviet attempts to advance on Kraljevo, a key point on the Skopje to Sarajevo route, and several days later Loehr stopped a Bulgarian advance at Skopje, thereby ensuring that his railway escape route was kept open long enough to get his troops to Sarajevo, and hence north to Hungary. By the time the evacuation was complete, only 30,000 German troops from Army Group E had been left behind, isolated on the Greek islands after having been unable to procure the necessary transport to the mainland. The frontline in the Balkans had by then stabilised from the Hungarian border along the Danube to Vukovar, across to the mouth of the Drina and then south down the Drina. This line was to hold until the end of the war.

---

18   Niš had been taken by Bulgarian forces on 15 October.

11

Berlin

By the end of 1944 most Germans had come to recognise what most of the German General Staff had suspected since the spring of 1943, that Germany was on the path to defeat and ruin. Germany's infrastructure was being bombed relentlessly after the Western Allies had achieved almost total air superiority over German airspace; Soviet troops were firmly ensconced along the East Prussian border; and in the West the ancient German city of Aachen, seat of power of Charlemagne and the early Holy Roman Empire, was firmly in American hands. Most Germans were also aware that the Allies were serious in their demand for unconditional German surrender as the only terms on which hostilities could be brought to an end. What the longer-term consequences of unconditional surrender might be were the subject of much speculation. The decision of the Allies to divide the Reich into occupation zones after Germany's defeat was widely known, and it was a common assumption among Germans that, after being held responsible for initiating two World Wars in less than thirty years, Germany would be subjected to a new and even more draconian Versailles Treaty – that it would, in effect, be de-industrialised and returned to a horse-powered agricultural economy. Some speculated on whether even bicycle manufacture would be proscribed. The fear of what occupation might bring added to the sense of national humiliation as the prospect of defeat drew closer, and accounted for much of the fanatical resistance shown by many Germans who would not have considered themselves to be enthusiastic Nazis. The sense of fear was greatest in the East, fear that was stoked by Goebbels' propaganda machine with its lurid accounts of rapacious Asiatic hordes preparing to descend on Aryan towns and villages.

Many Germans drew hope and comfort from propaganda stories of secret new miracle weapons, of which the V2 rocket was just the latest manifestation. The reality was that by late 1944 German industry, ever inventive and surprisingly resilient despite the aerial bombardment to which it had been subjected, did not have the capacity to produce enough of the new weapons – jet aircraft, rocket aircraft, ballistic missiles and King Tiger tanks – to affect the outcome of the war. Hitler, whose health was declining and whose thinking was beginning to become detached from an increasingly unpleasant reality, also placed great store in new weapons systems, some of which were barely beyond the design stage. At the strategic level, he anticipated that the new weapons, together with the German people's fanatical resistance, would prolong the war to the extent that Germany's enemies, no longer fighting for national survival, would baulk at the continuing loss of blood and treasure, and would seek an accommodation acceptable to Germany. Also, as the war the progressed, there remained the tantalising prospect that the improbable alliance between the people's dictatorship of communist Russia and the liberal democracies of the capitalist West would start to unravel to Germany's advantage. Many Germans also drew some comfort from the fact that, on the central axis, the Red Army appeared to have been stopped on the Vistula, and that the advance of the Western Allies had been severely disrupted by the German Ardennes offensive. Yet, as the winter of 1944/45 progressed, these comforts proved to be short-lived.

By the end of 1944 the *Wehrmacht* was, superficially at least, still an impressively powerful military machine with more than six million personnel under arms. In reality it was becoming somewhat skeletal, its ranks increasingly filled with semi-invalids, reluctant foreigners and the elderly. In Norway there were still 400,000 troops defending Germany's 'northern flank' and its mineral interests in Sweden against a threat that would never materialise. Some of Germany's best remaining divisions were in northern Italy holding back the Western Allies from the Po Valley and a possible link-up with Soviet forces in Yugoslavia. On the Western Front, attritional warfare on the approaches to the Rhine was steadily weakening the German defence to a thin veneer that was increasingly liable to shatter. By then 100 German divisions were tied down in Western Europe and Italy, and 17 were in Norway and Denmark. On the Eastern Front, where the soldiers of the *Ostheer* were outnumbered three to one, of the 143 German divisions left to face the Red Army, 30 were bottled up against the Baltic in the Courland Peninsula, and a further 10 were in the Balkans under OKW command as part of Army Group F. In a renewed attempt to address Germany's military manpower shortages, conscription requirements were further relaxed, personnel were seconded from the navy, and industry was further stripped of manpower thereby increasing Germany's dependence on slave labour still further. A new type of division had been formed – the *Volksgrenadier* ('people's grenadier') division. Often based on the remnants of existing infantry divisions and configured primarily for defence, the *Volksgrenadier* division, though somewhat smaller than a fully manned German infantry division of the time, generally had a higher proportion of submachine guns and close support artillery. The combat capability of the *Volksgrenadier* divisions varied hugely; some, based on veteran infantry divisions, were effective formations while others, newly-formed from poorly trained and unsuitable conscripts, proved to be highly unreliable. Additionally, in common with many German combat formations of the time, the *Volksgrenadier* divisions often operated well below authorised strength.

Among the Soviet General Staff it was considered axiomatic that the Red Army's victories of the summer of 1944 had determined the outcome of the war. The final defeat of Nazi Germany by a Red Army that was viewed as superior in numbers, equipment, and tactical skill, was considered to be predestined. As had become routine practice in the Red Army, sweeping victories brought a spate of promotions in their wake. At Front command level there had been promotions for Govorov, Malinovsky, Tolbukhin, Meretskov and Maslennikov, while at army command level Volsky, Pukhov and Trofimenko were promoted. Karelian Front was disbanded in November, Meretskov being sent to the Far East to begin preparations for the invasion of Manchuria.

After the pause in offensive operations by the Red Army on the central axis in the autumn of 1944, STAVKA began preparations for what was expected to be the final offensive against Germany. Those preparations would take many weeks to complete. Meanwhile, on the southern axis, STAVKA's attention had focussed on the Hungarian capital.

Into Hungary

During the third week of September 1944 6 Gds Tank Army[1] and 27 Army, pushing deeper into Transylvania, attempted to take Cluj, but were held by German forces. This failure prompted Malinovsky to begin to move his main force, including 6 Gds Tank Army, west to the Oradea – Arad area, where II Hun Army, on Friessner's right flank, had given up Arad without a fight on 21 September. At that time the front stretched along the northern and central Carpathians, across the southern Carpathians to Târgu Mureş, south of Cluj and Oradea, west of Arad and Timişoara, and southeast to the Bulgarian border. By 25 September elements of 6 Gds Tank Army were closing on Oradea, which they took the next day, but lost on 28 September to a German counter-attack. Friessner fully expected a renewed effort from Malinovsky in the Oradea area; either a strike west towards Budapest, or north towards eastern Slovakia, the latter to encircle VIII Army and *Armeegruppe* Heinrici along the Carpathians. In response OKH began to assemble a panzer force in the Debrecen area, though this was not expected to be fully available until 10 October. After the loss of Arad, III Hun Army, partially activated on 10 September and fully activated two weeks later, was deployed to the Arad area as part of *Armeegruppe* Fretter-Pico, and II Hun Army was temporarily moved east to be placed under Woehler's command as part of a new *Armeegruppe* Woehler. During the course of this re-deployment Army Group South Ukraine was redesignated Army Group South, and Army Group North Ukraine was redesignated Army Group A.

From Malinovsky, STAVKA wanted three separate thrusts; one by 46 Army, 53 Army and Pliev's cavalry-mechanised group from Arad to Budapest; one by 6 Gds Tank Army from Oradea to Debrecen and Miskolc; and a third by 27 Army, Gorshkov's cavalry-mechanised group and Rumanian 4 Army from the area of Cluj to Debrecen.[2] The ultimate objective of these offensives, made in conjunction with 4 Ukrainian Front's offensive through the Carpathians towards Uzhgorod, was the encirclement of Army Group South and *Armeegruppe* Heinrici. Petrov's Front, with the continued support of 38 Army off its right flank, had been making only slow progress but, after the withdrawal of a panzer division from the northern Carpathians, the rate of 4 Ukrainian Front's advance quickened somewhat and the Dukla Pass was secured by Moskalenko on 6 October.

Malinovsky's forces were operating on a wide front and the poor state of the Rumanian railway system severely constrained their rate of supply. Consequently 2 Ukrainian Front's autumn campaign was limited to a rolling sequence of relatively small-scale offensives. The opening offensive, a renewed attack by 6 Gds Tank Army from Oradea towards Debrecen on 6 October, was stopped by German forces, but farther south III Hun Army disintegrated in the face of a Soviet offensive by 53 Army and Pliev's cavalry-mechanised group from the Arad area. As the remnants of III Hun Army pulled back in disarray into Hungary and towards the dubious security of the Tisza between Szolnok and Szeged, Pliev's group was diverted to the northeast in order to outflank German forces defending the Oradea area. This diversion of mechanised forces unhinged the German defence of Oradea but it also ended the immediate threat

---

1   6 Tank Army had been awarded Guards status on 12 September.

2   Malinovsky by this time had two Rumanian armies under his command – Fourth and First – some twenty divisions indifferently equipped.

See Map 29

to Budapest. By the evening of 8 October Soviet forces were west of Debrecen, less than 200km from Petrov's forces breaking out from the Dukla Pass, and, in defiance of Hitler's orders, Friessner authorised Woehler to pull back from Cluj and the upper Muresul. On 10 October Friessner was able to use two recently-arrived panzer divisions, one from the Budapest area and the other at Debrecen, to counter-attack the Soviet penetration in the Debrecen area. The panzer divisions, attacking from east and west, cut off three Soviet corps. Three days of confused tank battles raged before the Soviet forces could break free on 14 October.

On 15 October Horthy announced in a radio broadcast that Hungary had accepted an armistice with the Soviet Union. However, Horthy's political support had been declining and he retained the confidence of neither the parliament nor his cabinet, both of which were inclined to continue the fight. The next day Horthy was replaced as head of state, but his departure left the Hungarian military deeply divided: whole units deserted to the Soviets, as did the Hungarian armed forces chief of staff. By this time Woehler had taken command of I Hun Army, and *Armeegruppe* Woehler's front resembled an arc, the centre of which was 120km east of Nyíregyháza. On 20 October Pliev's and Gorshkov's cavalry-mechanised groups struck north from the Debrecen area towards Nyíregyháza, threatening the deep right flank of *Armeegruppe* Woehler, and taking Nyíregyháza two days later. Friessner's instinct was to pull *Armeegruppe* Woehler back farther to the northwest but his chief of staff, Major-Gen Helmuth von Grolman, persuaded him to respond by turning some of his forces west to attack between Debrecen and Nyíregyháza, while a panzer force already in place between Nyíregyháza and the Tisza struck east. The manoeuvre succeeded and by 23 October, for the second time in two weeks, three of Malinovsky's corps had been cut off. German forces already pulling back from the Muresul added to the pressure on the encircled Soviet forces in the Nyíregyháza area. On 29 October the survivors from three defeated Soviet corps abandoned their vehicles and heavy weapons and fled south, leaving Army Group South with a continuous front for the first time in eight weeks. From the mouth of the Drava, where Friessner's forces tied in with Army Group F, the front ran north to Kecskemét, to the Tisza below Szolnok, along the middle Tisza and then east of the Tisza around Nyíregyháza. Meanwhile, farther north, after weeks of gruelling fighting, which had the limited benefit of preventing the redeployment of German forces to other areas, 4 Ukrainian Front took Mukacheve on 26 October and Uzhgorod the next day, bringing to an end its Carpathian – Uzhgorod operations. Petrov's forces moved up to the Starina – Sobrante – Cop line to share a boundary with 2 Ukrainian Front on the Tisza, but they failed to achieve a breakthrough, and the northern arm of the Soviet strategic pincer against Army Group South was contained by XXIV Pz Corps of I Pz Army and, west of the Dukla Pass, by XI SS Corps of XVII Army. In November 38 Army, on the left flank of 1 Ukrainian Front, was transferred to 4 Ukrainian Front after Moskalenko's offensive operations came to an end on 28 October.

Friessner's continuous front was to last little more than 24 hours. Malinovsky had prepared a detailed plan for the capture of Budapest in an offensive to commence on 2 November, but under direct orders from Stalin, he was obliged to begin the attack prematurely, throwing 46 Army supported by 23 Rifle Corps and 2 Mech Corps, into the attack on 29 October. Initially this attack went well, with an advance of 30km on the first day against Fretter-Pico's positions east of Kecskemét. Most of III Hun Army offered only token resistance, many of its personnel having deserted and returned home. Shortly thereafter II Hun Army was redeployed back to *Armeegruppe* Fretter-Pico to cover the right bank of the Danube on Army Group South's right flank. Kecskemét was taken on 1 November and Malinovsky received 4 Gds Mech Corps to support the advance towards the Hungarian capital. By 3 November the lead Soviet units from 4 Gds Mech Corps had reached the outer defences of Budapest southeast of the city, but by then those defences had been reinforced by German units. Shlemin was supported on his right flank by 7 Gds Army, which, by 4 November had crossed the Tisza and had taken Szolnok and Cegled. Yet, despite Malinovsky's frantic urging, 46 Army was unable to force its way into the city and on 6 November, his army low on ammunition and with the threat of a German counter-attack on his right flank, Shlemin pulled his forces back several kilometres to the south. He tried again on 10 November but, during a savage sixteen-day long battle with the German defenders, the nature of which was to characterise the subsequent fighting for the Hungarian capital, Shlemin's forces were once again unable to break through the city's outer defences. Malinovsky, in consultation with STAVKA, had already begun to prepare an alternative plan to take the capital – encirclement and siege. On 11 November Shumilov's 7 Gds Army began an advance northwards towards Hatvan against the left flank of *Armeegruppe* Fretter-Pico, as 53 Army and 27 Army advanced from the middle Tisza against the right flank of *Armeegruppe* Woehler towards Miskolc. By 16 November both towns had been reached but after days of fierce fighting, though Hatvan was taken, Miskolc remained in German hands. Throughout the last days of November, 2 Ukrainian Front fought its way to the north of Budapest but was eventually halted in the Matta hills northeast of the city. Farther north it was not until the end of November that 4 Ukrainian Front had reached the Ondava river line where the frontline stabilised through December.

On 7 November, 3 Ukrainian Front secured a small bridgehead over the Danube near Apatin. This was near the southern extremity of Army Group South's right flank, the boundary with Army Group F being at the confluence of the Danube and Drava. Three days later the Army Group F boundary was moved north to Baja, giving Weichs responsibility for what was seen as a potential threat to the left flank of his army group. On 11 November Tolbukhin's forces took another small bridgehead at Batina, 25km north of Apatin, but the forces in these bridgeheads were no longer confronted by II Hun Army; they faced II Pz Army. By then Tolbukhin was completing the regrouping of his Front in the Banat in preparation for a strike into Hungary from the southeast. On 22 November Zakharov's 4 Gds Army, assigned to 3 Ukrainian Front from STAVKA reserve on 3 November, broke out of the Batina bridgehead, and 57 Army broke out of the Apatin bridgehead. By 26 November they had taken Mohács and, as 57 Army began to move west towards Pécs, 4 Gds Army moved northwest towards the northern tip of Lake Balaton.[3] Pécs fell to Soviet forces on 29 November, but when, two days later, it became clear to OKH that Tolbukhin's main effort was being directed north of the Drava, rather than west towards Zagreb, II Pz Army was transferred from Army Group F to Army Group South, and Friessner was instructed to use it

---

3   To guard against possible Turkish intervention, 37 Army remained in Bulgaria and was removed from 3 Ukrainian Front's command, to be given independent army status.

to defend the area between Lake Balaton and the Drava southwest of Nagykanizsa. This area contained one of the few remaining sources of crude oil left to Germany. As 4 Gds Army drove north between Lake Balaton and the Danube, II Hun Army disintegrated and Friessner was forced to fill the gap by moving German units from other sectors, the transfer of a panzer division from the Miskolc area leading to the loss of that town on 4 December.

On 5 December Malinovsky launched a powerful strike towards Vac in the bend of the Danube to the north of Budapest. For this attack he used 7 Gds Army supported by 6 Gds Tank Army and Pliev's group to strike at the junction of VI Army and VIII Army from northwest of Hatvan. At the same time, on the right of this attack, 53 Army struck at Sezcen, and in the south 46 Army struck for the river island of Csepel in an effort to outflank Budapest from the southwest. By 8 December the combined forces of 7 Gds Army and 6 Gds Tank Army had broken through VI Army's defences in the Hatvan area to reach Vac, and in the south 46 Army had, despite heavy losses, taken Ercsi. Also on that day 57 Army had reached the southern edge of Lake Balaton. By 9 December Shlemin's 46 Army had reached the area of Lake Velence west of Ercsi between Lake Balaton and Budapest, linking up with 4 Gds Army on 3 Ukrainian Front's right flank. Friessner received reinforcements to attack Soviet forces in the Székesfehérvár area between Lake Velence and Lake Balaton, but between Lake Velence and Budapest Fretter-Pico had only the equivalent of a regimental-sized battle group. Ground conditions in this area were appalling, much of the land being under water, and Tolbukhin acted cautiously. On 12 December 46 Army was transferred back to 3 Ukrainian Front, its place in the line being taken by 18 Gds Rifle Corps from Malinovsky's reserve. Tolbukhin was charged with completing the task of outflanking Budapest from the southwest by attacking towards Bicske, to reach the Danube in the area of Esztergom, while Malinovsky's right flank armies, 40 Army, 27 Army and Rumanian 4 Army, were to strike north and northwest into Czechoslovakia in coordination with 4 Ukrainian Front. Tolbukhin then had 30 rifle divisions and four mobile corps, leaving Malinovsky with 28 rifle divisions and six mechanised, tank and cavalry corps together with 15 Rumanian divisions.

From Vac, 2 Ukrainian Front turned north towards Šahy. Although Friessner removed a panzer division from the defence of Budapest in order to defend Šahy, the town was taken by Malinovsky's forces on 14 December. There 6 Gds Tank Army remained for six days until 20 December, by which time Friessner had assembled sufficient forces to prevent a Soviet move west across the Danube, though he could not prevent Malinovsky's forces from advancing northwest towards the Hron. At the same time Tolbukhin launched an offensive on both sides of Lake Velence. By 22 December it had become clear to Friessner that Tolbukhin's objective was Esztergom, and that the two Soviet Fronts were attempting the close encirclement of Budapest. Later that day Friessner learned that he was to be replaced as commander of Army Group South by Woehler (command of VIII Army passing to General Hans Kreysing by 28 December), and that Balck was to take command of VI Army effective from 23 December. By that time 4 Gds Army had taken Biscske and had cut the railway running west out of Budapest. General Karl Pfeffer-Wildenbruch, commander of IX SS Mtn Corps, was placed in command of the Budapest garrison, which consisted of four German divisions, two Hungarian divisions and various smaller units – some 70,000 troops, nearly half of which were German.

On 26 December Tolbukhin's forces took Esztergom and linked up with 2 Ukrainian Front. The massive six-day offensive by the two Fronts had succeeded in its objective of encircling Budapest. For Hitler, the subsequent defence of the Hungarian capital came to hold enormous political and military significance, the outcome of the battle there seeming to him to presage the outcome of the war as a whole. Consequently he refused to contemplate a breakout by the garrison and instead, believing that STAVKA was equally focussed on the city, set about preparing for its relief.

Into the Reich

Soviet attacks in November and December on the East Prussian frontier and in Hungary had played on Hitler's sensitivities in these areas. As a result, 28 divisions were concentrated in East Prussia and 30 German divisions, one-third of which were panzer or panzer-grenadier divisions, were deployed in Hungary. These were the areas where OKH expected the Soviet winter offensive to be directed, and Hitler was confident that a strengthened Army Group South would be able to defeat the Red Army's left wing in Hungary, relieve the Budapest garrison and restore the front on the Danube. To assist in this process, in addition to eight Hungarian divisions that were still in frontline positions, the headquarters of IV SS Pz Corps from Army Group A's Warsaw sector and two SS panzer divisions from Army Group Centre would be redeployed to Hungary. If necessary, forces would even be diverted from the Ardennes offensive to restore the situation in Hungary. On the central axis 30 German divisions were left to defend the *Ostheer*'s positions in Poland. Those divisions were from II Army on the right flank of Army Group Centre, and from IX Army, IV Pz Army and XVII Army of Army Group A's left flank and centre. In addition Harpe had four panzer and two panzer grenadier divisions as part of his army group reserve to support the frontline divisions from north of Warsaw, along the middle reaches of the Vistula and along I Pz Army's positions in eastern Slovakia.

Detailed planning by STAVKA and the Soviet General Staff for a winter offensive in Poland evolved from the late autumn of 1944 as the situation at the front stabilised and the options for further exploitation became clearer. Yet the basic concept for the offensive had been determined by early November. Key to the initial phase of the offensive were five bridgeheads that had been established by Soviet forces over the Narew and Vistula. Two of those, across the Narew north of Warsaw, were at Różan and Serock. Over the Vistula south of Warsaw was the bridgehead of Magnuszew. Farther south, west of Lublin, was the bridgehead at Puławy, and still farther south, in the 1 Ukrainian Front zone, was the substantial bridgehead of Sandomierz, which by January was 75km long and 65km deep. The final STAVKA plans were certainly ambitious – the envelopment and destruction of German forces in Poland and East Prussia; high-speed exploitation across the eastern frontiers of the Reich; bouncing the Oder; enveloping Berlin; and further exploitation to the Elbe and beyond – all to be achieved in two phases in little more than six weeks after the commencement of operations. By early 1945 the preparations were well advanced and the concentration of Soviet forces on the central axis was nearing completion. That concentration of force was enormous. At the beginning of January the four central Fronts (1 Ukrainian Front

See Map 30

The Eastern Front 1941-45: A Photo Essay

Tens of thousands of photographs relating to the Eastern Front 1941-45 exist. This selection is not intended to be comprehensive, but to present, by means of a photo essay, some of the key aspects of this campaign using images that are either previously unpublished or encountered less often amongst the pages of other books.

German Commanders

Fedor von Bock   Hermann Hoth   Ewald von Kleist   Erich von Manstein

Soviet Commanders

I S Konev   K K Rokossovsky   A M Vasilevsky   G K Zhukov

(All images on this page from the collection of David M. Glantz)

A knocked-out Soviet OT-26 flamethrower tank, Russia, 1941. (Marek Tuszyński)

A dead Soviet soldier, Russia, 1941. (Marek Tuszyński)

Germans inspecting Soviet aircraft, Russia, 1941. The plane in the foreground is
a Yakovlev UT-1, the one to the rear a Polikarpov I-16. (Marek Tuszyński)

Russia 1941 – a destroyed Soviet Mikoyan-Gurevich MiG-3 fighter. (Marek Tuszyński)

Soviet prisoners, Russia, 1941. Note the youth of many of the soldiers. (Marek Tuszyński)

Destroyed Soviet and German aircraft, Russia 1941. In the foreground is a Soviet Polikarpov UTI-4, a two seater training version of the I-16 Soviet fighter. To the rear is a German aircraft, a Henschel Hs 126. (Marek Tuszyński)

German tankers struggle to free their tank from the clutching
mud after rain, autumn 1941 (Lev Lopukhovsky)

Winter landscape: a German Junkers Ju 52 transport plane in white winter
camouflage colours prepares to take off in the snow after the onset of the
Russian winter 1941/42. (Imperial War Museum COL 353)

Soviet troops dressed in snow suits counter-attack against German soldiers in December 1941. (Imperial War Museum RUS 1206)

The pilot, gunner and bombardier of a Soviet Pe-2 crew receive their mission, Kalinin Front, early 1942. (Svetlana Gerasimova)

Two dust-covered German despatch riders relax with cigarettes by their Zundapp motorbike after delivering a despatch on the Eastern Front, 1942. (Imperial War Museum COL 161)

German despatch riders dig out their Zundapp motorbike which is bogged down in mud on the Eastern Front, Spring 1942. (Imperial War Museum COL 167)

Marines of the Soviet Northern Fleet manning trenches on the forward edge
of their defensive line, 1942. (Imperial War Museum RUS 3592)

German tanks pause in their advance to Stalingrad having successfully destroyed
several Russian tanks, smoke from which can be seen rising on the right of
the photograph, September 1942. (Imperial War Museum HU 5163)

A pall of smoke hangs over Stalingrad as German infantry move into the outskirts of the city, September 1942. (Imperial War Museum HU 5152)

A German signpost in Stalingrad. The text reads: "Entry into the city forbidden. Sightseers endanger not only their own lives but also the lives of their comrades". Autumn 1942. (Imperial War Museum HU 5175)

Soviet soldiers fire on a German-held block of flats in Stalingrad, Autumn 1942. (Imperial War Museum RUS 3699)

Advancing elements of the Soviet 158th Rifle Division, Kalinin Front west of Rzhev, November 1942. (Svetlana Gerasimova)

A graveyard of armor between the German and Soviet positions in the northeastern part of Rzhev, early 1943. (Svetlana Gerasimova)

Soviet T-60 light tanks and ski infantry move into attack the enemy across snow-covered terrain during the Winter Offensive of 1942-43. Unlike the German troops, the Red Army was well equipped to withstand the severe Russian winter and trained to use the conditions to their advantage. (Imperial War Museum RUS 1656)

A long column of German prisoners, poorly clad against the Russian winter, marches through Stalingrad after Field Marshal Paulus's surrender, January 1943. (Imperial War Museum MISC 60748)

German units withdrawing from the city of Rzhev, March 1943. (Svetlana Gerasimova)

Waffen-SS infantry streetfighting in Kharkov, March 1943. (Cody Images)

Armoured vehicles belonging to 1 SS Pz Div *Leibstandarte Adolf Hitler* assembled for the Battle of Kursk, summer 1943. (Cody Images)

Otto Baum and Karl Ullrich, officers from 3 SS Pz Div *Totenkopf*, Kursk, July 1943. (Cody Images)

Soviet infantry on the move, summer 1943. (Cody Images)

A Hungarian soldier preparing to fire an 81mm mortar, 1943. (Cody Images)

Finnish officers visit German defensive positions south of Lake Ladoga, 1943. (Cody Images)

Soviet Cossack horsemen crossing a river, Spring 1944. (Imperial War Museum RUS 4229)

A German 8.8cm flak gun in the anti-tank role, northern Russia, February 1944. (Cody Images)

A German SdKfz 251/10 Ausf C half-track, equipped with a 3.7cm Pak anti-tank gun, passes wrecked Soviet vehicles, February 1944. (Cody Images)

Soviet marines in Sevastopol, the Crimea, May 1944. (Cody Images)

Rumanian mountain troops marching to the front, south of Jassy, May 1944. (Cody Images)

The Karelian Isthmus 1944 - Finnish troops with a 7.5cm Pak 40 anti-tank gun. (Cody Images)

50,000 German prisoners captured at Vitebsk, Minsk, and Bobruisk during Operation Bagration are marched through Moscow, 17 July 1944. In a symbolic gesture, the streets were hosed down after they had passed. (Cody Images)

A youthful member of the Polish Home Army during the
Warsaw Uprising, August 1944. (Marek Tuszyński)

Soviet infantry from 1 Baltic Front 1944 forcing the Venta River
north-west of Shyaulyay, October 1944. (Cody Images)

Soviet BM-13 Katyusha rocket launchers fire against German positions in the winter of 1944/45. Vehicles are modified Studebaker US6 trucks. (Cody Images)

A Soviet Lend-Lease M4A2 Sherman tank in eastern Germany, 1945. (Cody Images)

The marketplace of the Old Town, Warsaw, 1945, showing the effects of
the Warsaw Uprising and subsequent actions. (Marek Tuszyński)

Troops from the Soviet-sponsored Polish LWP/Army parade through
liberated Warsaw, 19 January 1945. (Marek Tuszyński)

A Soviet T-34/85 tank moves cautiously through a German town
in the closing stages of the war, 1945. (Cody Images)

Civilians trudge through a devastated Berlin, 1945. Red Army troops
with Studebaker US6 trucks can also be seen. (Cody Images)

Red Army soldiers approach Berlin's Reichstag, May, 1945. (Cody Images)

and the three Belorussian Fronts) had 254 rifle divisions, eighteen tank corps and six mechanised corps. By comparison the three southern Fronts had 89 rifle divisions, three tank corps and five mechanised corps; and the three northern Fronts had 93 rifle divisions, a mechanised corps and a tank corps. Vasilevsky remained responsible for the coordination of the Baltic operations, but the huge scale of the proposed offensive on the central axis meant that coordination of the Fronts would be managed by STAVKA and the General Staff directly. Zhukov took command of 1 Belorussian Front from Rokossovsky, and Rokossovsky took command of 2 Belorussian Front from Zakharov, Zakharov being assigned to the command of 4 Gds Army prior to its deployment to 3 Ukrainian Front from STAVKA reserve.

Facing Cherniakhovsky, Rokossovsky, Zhukov and Konev were Reinhardt's Army Group Centre and most of Harpe's Army Group A. The ten divisions of Raus's III Pz Army covered the northern sector in East Prussia, and the fifteen divisions of General Friedrich Hossbach's IV Army occupied the frontline from southwest of Mariampol, east of the Masurian lakes, to the upper Narew.[4] On Hossbach's right the ten divisions of Weiss's II Army occupied the Narew sector to the southern end of the Serock bridgehead. As army group reserve, Reinhardt had three panzer divisions. From the right flank of II Army the seven divisions and two brigades of Army Group A's IX Army, commanded by General Smilo Freiherr von Luettwitz, held the frontline south to cover the Warsaw area and the Vistula as far as the area of Deblin.[5] South of Deblin was the responsibility of General Fritz-Hubert Graeser's IV Pz Army, its seven divisions holding the Vistula line from the Deblin area to the southern end of the Sandomierz bridgehead.[6] From the Sandomierz bridgehead, the front tracked southeast towards the Carpathians, and this sector was held by the six divisions of General Karl-Friedrich Schulz's XVII Army.[7]

Opposing the German armies on the central axis were 35 Soviet armies, five of them tank armies. The right flank sector, covering the final 90km of the Neman from the village of Sudagi to the Baltic coast, was held by Beloborodov's 43 Army of 1 Baltic Front. Offensive operations south of the Neman and along the East Prussian border defences as far as Augustow were the responsibility of Cherniakhovsky's 3 Belorussian Front. Cherniakhovsky's command included Lyudnikov's 39 Army, Krylov's 5 Army, Luchinsky's 28 Army, Chanchibadze's 2 Gds Army and 31 Army commanded from December 1944 by Lt-Gen P G Shafranov. In reserve Cherniakhovsky had Galitsky's 11 Gds Army and two tank corps.

Rokossovsky's 2 Belorussian Front was deployed along the Narew north of its confluence with the Vistula. It included Boldin's 50 Army, Grishin's 49 Army, Gorbatov's 3 Army, N I Gusev's 48 Army, Fedyuninsky's 2 Shock Army, Batov's 65 Army and V S Popov's 70 Army. In reserve Rokossovsky had two tank corps, a mechanised corps, Volsky's 5 Gds Tank Army and a cavalry corps.

---

4   Tippelskirch had been replaced at IV Army by Hossbach in July 1944.
5   Vormann had been replaced at IX Army by Luettwitz in September 1944 and IX Army had been transferred from the command of Army Group Centre to Army Group A in November.
6   On 21 September 1944 command of IV Pz Army changed for the last time, Graeser assuming command from Balck.
7   Each of the *Ostheer's* new army commanders on the central axis, Schulz, Luettwitz, Graeser and Hossbach, had all been commanders of panzer corps.

Zhukov's 1 Belorussian Front was deployed along the Vistula to Jozefov with the bridgeheads at Magnuszew and Puławy. It included Major-Gen F I Perkhorovich's 47 Army, Lt-Gen S G Poplawski's Polish 1 Army, Belov's 61 Army, Berzarin's 5 Shock Army, Chuikov's 8 Gds Army, Kolpakchi's 69 Army with a subordinated tank corps, and Tsvetaev's 33 Army. In reserve Zhukov had V I Kuznetsov's 3 Shock Army, a tank corps, two cavalry corps, Katukov's 1 Gds Tank Army and 2 Gds Tank Army.[8]

Konev's 1 Ukrainian Front was deployed in the sector from Jozefov to Jasło, a sector that included the Sandomierz bridgehead. Konev's command included Lt-Gen V A Gluzdovsky's 6 Army, Gordov's 3 Gds Army with a subordinated tank corps, Pukhov's 13 Army, Koroteev's 52 Army, Zhadov's 5 Gds Army and Kurochkin's 60 Army. In reserve Konev had D N Gusev's 21 Army, Korovnikov's 59 Army, two tank corps, a mechanised corps, Rybalko's 3 Gds Tank Army, Lelyushenko's 4 Tank Army, and a cavalry corps.

STAVKA's plan envisaged 2 Belorussian Front striking out of the Narew bridgeheads to the Gulf of Danzig, thereby cutting off Army Group Centre from overland contact with the rest of Germany. This, together with a strike into the deep right flank of IV Army in the Allenstein area in conjunction with an offensive into East Prussia by 3 Belorussian Front, would destroy Reinhardt's forces. Thereafter, in the second phase of operations, Rokossovsky would advance along the Baltic coast through eastern Pomerania, providing flank protection to 1 Belorussian Front in its advance through central Poland. Zhukov's forces would break out from their Vistula bridgeheads and strike for Poznan. In its second phase of operations 1 Belorussian Front would strike for Berlin and the Elbe beyond. Konev would break out the Sandomierz bridgehead and strike for Breslau and, in the second phase of operations, would strike for the Elbe in the Dresden area. As 1 Ukrainian Front advanced, its left flank would lengthen, and so a simultaneous and complementary offensive was planned by 4 Ukrainian Front and the right flank of 2 Ukrainian Front to clear the right flank of Army Group A from southern Poland and Slovakia. In particular, Moskalenko's 38 Army on the right flank of 4 Ukrainian Front would strike west through southern Poland south of Cracow towards the Czech border and Ostrava, as 60 Army on 1 Ukrainian Front's left flank took Cracow from the northeast. Meanwhile pressure on German forces in Hungary and the Balkans would be maintained by 2 Ukrainian and 3 Ukrainian Fronts, their ultimate objective being Vienna.

The offensive required an enormous preparatory logistical effort in order to sustain a largely continuous advance from the Vistula to the Elbe. Coordination of air support with ground operations was carefully planned, and, as had become normal in the opening phase of such operations, the artillery concentration in the breakthrough sectors was overwhelming. STAVKA's planning had assumed that operations would commence on 20 January but, in order to meet a request from Churchill for the Red Army to ease the pressure on the Western Allies after the Ardennes offensive, the start date was brought forward to 12 January. Although initial operations were planned in great detail, further objectives were provided in outlined only in order to enable the ground forces to respond flexibly to changing circumstances. By the second week of January the four central Fronts, with 43 Army on the Baltic flank, numbered 3.38

---

8   2 Tank Army had been awarded Guards status in November 1944 and Bogdanov returned to its command in January 1945.

million personnel in 258 rifle divisions, eighteen tank corps, six mechanised corps, four cavalry corps, an airborne division and twenty-two independent brigades of armoured fighting vehicles.

By comparison the entire *Ostheer* from Courland to the Balkans only numbered a little over 2.3 million personnel, and that included some 100,000 Hungarians still in the fight; the centre and left wing of Army Group A – IX Army, IV Pz Army and XVII Army numbered just 400,000. In December German military intelligence presented OKH with an assessment of Red Army strength and intentions on the central axis that proved to be reasonably accurate, but the assessment was dismissed by Hitler as a work of lunacy. German tactical intelligence on Soviet units near the frontline was generally reliable, but at the strategic level, threat assessments had, on occasions, proved to be disastrously inaccurate. Hence when Guderian proposed, based on the military intelligence assessment of Soviet strategy on the central axis, that German forces should withdraw to shorter lines, Hitler dismissed the proposal out of hand. After the German intelligence failures prior to Bagration and the Jassy-Kishinev operation, Hitler's scepticism may have been understandable. Yet the consequence was that Army Group A and the right flank of Army Group Centre were ill-prepared to meet a major Soviet offensive. Army Group A's best fortified positions were the forward ones on the Vistula line, and its broader defensive strategy envisaged that a series of defensive belts between the Vistula and the Oder would be occupied, if required, by advancing reserves and by forces retreating from farther east. It was a strategy that assumed there would be an adequate supply of advancing reserves and that events would unfold in a manner that permitted forces from farther east to retreat. Given the state of the *Wehrmacht* in 1945, and the effectiveness of the Red Army's offensive tactics as displayed in the Bagration and Jassy-Kishinev operations, those assumptions were to prove to be more than a little optimistic.

The offensive from 1 Ukrainian Front began at 05:00 on 12 January in a breakout from its Sandomierz bridgehead. The initial offensive did not rely on mere brute force. Deception plans convinced IV Pz Army that any breakout effort would be made on the Soviet left flank by 60 Army towards Cracow. After taking the first defence line and eliminating key strongpoints in strict accordance with the 1944 Field Regulations, a second artillery barrage, lasting 107 minutes, commenced at 10:00 employing up to 300 guns per kilometre. At 11:17 Soviet infantry began to move into gaps left in the line by the artillery barrage, prompting the German defenders to emerge from their bunkers to occupy the firing positions of the second defence line. At this the Soviet riflemen laid down, and the artillery barrage switched to these firing positions. The end of the fixed artillery barrage was signalled by a volley of rocket artillery, after which the infantry and support tanks advanced behind a rolling barrage. The German defences were almost completely broken by noon of the first day, enabling the two tank armies to be committed to exploit the breakthrough two hours later. By the end of the day the gap in the German lines was 35km wide and 18km deep. The strength and speed of the advance meant that German reserves were thrown in piecemeal and with little effect. From the reserves, Nehring's XXIV Pz Corps tried to make a stand at Kielce, but the town was captured on 15 January after being invested from the east, south and west. Its capture meant that the right flank of 1 Ukrainian Front was secure and that there was little to prevent the Front advancing towards Breslau. On the left wing of 1 Ukrainian Front, 60 Army, subsequently supported by 59 Army and 4 Gds Tank Corps moving into the widening gap between 60 Army and 5 Gds Army, advanced along the north bank of the Vistula towards Cracow, cutting XVII Army off from the rest of Army Group A.

Zhukov's offensive against IX Army opened on 14 January creating large gaps in the German defences along the Magnuszew and Puławy bridgeheads. Zhukov's primary objective was a broad advance south of the Vistula to the Poznan – Bromberg line, from where a turn to the left would be made for a strike to the Oder. The boundary between the advancing 1 Belorussian and 1 Ukrainian Fronts was set in a straight line west-northwest from Jozefov to half way between Poznan and Leszno, from where it projected due west. In the Magnuszew bridgehead, just 25km long and 12km deep, Zhukov had packed in half of the Front's rifle divisions and 70% of its armour and artillery, creating an artillery gun density of 250 tubes per kilometre in the penetration sector. A reconnaissance in depth by 22 reinforced rifle battalions and 25 other rifle companies after a massive 25 minute artillery barrage so unhinged the German defences and was so successful, that the subsequent planned 70 minute barrage was cancelled (except in 61 Army's sector), and German forward positions were in Soviet hands by late morning. The secondary offensive from the Puławy bridgehead was to be conducted along the Radom – Łódź axis by 33 Army and 69 Army supported by two tank corps and a cavalry corps. As in the south, German reserves, committed piecemeal, were unable to halt the advance of 1 Belorussian Front. On the afternoon of 15 January the Front's right wing, which included 47 Army, also went over to the offensive, crossing the Vistula north of Warsaw. The next day, in cooperation with the left flank units of 2 Belorussian Front, 47 Army's movement along the south bank of the Vistula threatened German forces in the Warsaw area with a deep outflanking movement from the north. By the evening of 17 January the bulk of 2 Gds Tank Army had reached the vicinity of Sochaczew from the southeast, threatening the main German escape route from the Polish capital; 61 Army was advancing on the city from the south; 47 Army north of the city was still advancing west; while earlier in the day Polish 1 Army had begun to attack the city from the north and northwest. That evening Warsaw was in Soviet hands, and over the next few days German forces west of the city were encircled and mopped up. Army Group A had virtually disintegrated and, after the loss of Warsaw, Harpe was sacked, to be replaced by Schoerner. At the same time Luettwitz was dismissed from IX Army and was replaced by General Theodor Busse, formerly the commander of XVIII Army's I Corps. Meanwhile 1 Gds Tank Army had passed north of Radom, and the threat of encirclement of German forces, including the reserve XLII Corps, developed southeast of the town as 1 Belorussian Front advanced rapidly towards Tomaszów Mazowiecki, and 1 Ukrainian Front advanced towards Częstochowa. German attempts to escape this encirclement failed and most of XLII Corps was lost.

On 13 January III Pz Army was hit south of the Neman in the fortified lines between Pilkallen and Goldap by 3 Belorussian Front. Cherniakhovsky's objective was to attack along the Koenigsberg axis, with 39 Army, 5 Army and 28 Army making the initial breakthrough north of Gumbinnen; he was then to split III Pz Army off from the rest of Army Group Centre and also to envelop IV Army among and west of the

Masurian lakes. However, 3 Belorussian Front met fierce resistance, sustaining heavy casualties and making little progress in the first days of the offensive.

On 14 January 2 Belorussian Front attacked II Army out of the Serock and Różan bridgeheads (the Narew itself being a significant obstacle at that time of year). Rokossovsky's primary objective was Marienburg and the coast. The main attack was launched by 3 Army, 48 Army and 2 Shock Army from the Różan bridgehead, employing a gun density of 220 tubes per kilometre firing for most of the day, with a second attack from the more southerly Serock bridgehead using 65 Army and 70 Army to break out to the west. On 15 January 2 Belorussian Front succeeded in pushing back II Army and, using 8 Mech Corps, 8 Gds Tank Corps and 1 Gds Tank Corps for the exploitation, by the next day 48 Army with 8 Mech Corps took Ciechanów. Rokossovsky reinforced this success by committing 5 Gds Tank Army to the Ciechanów axis on 17 January. Although by then II Army was strained to breaking point, Hitler refused to allow IV Army to retreat. Since, in the opening Soviet attacks, Army Group Centre had been less damaged than Army Group A, Hitler had withdrawn Pz Corps *Grossdeutschland* which, with its two panzer divisions, had formed the heart of Reinhardt's reserves, and moved them to Army Group A, where the corps soon found itself defending Łódź. The next day, inadequately reinforced, II Army's front snapped, opening a gap on both sides of the Mława, and Soviet forces took Przasnysz. On the right and centre of II Army, XXIII Corps and XXVII Corps were pushed to the west, and II Army's left flank XX Corps together with IV Army (to which XX Corps was subsequently subordinated) were pushed north into southern East Prussia. With a tank corps in support, 65 Army and 70 Army pushed out of the Serock bridgehead to the west providing flanking cover north of the Vistula and, since Army Group A's flank had broken away south of the Vistula, it faced little opposition; Modlin, at the confluence of the Narew and Vistula, was taken by 70 Army on 18 January, and 65 Army took Płońsk. With the fall of Mława on 19 January, and with lead elements of 5 Gds Tank Army in the town, 2 Belorussian Front was in position to strike northwest, deep into German-held territory. However, on 20 January Rokossovsky was ordered to turn the armies that had broken out from the Różan bridgehead, including 5 Gds Tank Army, north and northeast towards the Vistula Lagoon (between Elbing and Koenigsberg) in order to assist 3 Belorussian Front in the isolation of German forces in East Prussia. This left Rokossovsky with just his two left flank armies from the Serock bridgehead to clear the lower Vistula and to cover the right flank of 1 Belorussian Front in its drive for the Oder. This in turn forced Zhukov, in order to protect his extended right flank, to commit 61 Army, 47 Army, Polish 1 Army, 2 Cav Corps and his reserve 3 Shock Army to face northwards.

South of the Vistula, 8 Gds Army took Łódź on 17 January, and still farther south 38 Army on 4 Ukrainian Front's right flank began an offensive towards Nowy Sacz via Jasło on 16 January. Attacks towards Cracow by 59 Army and 60 Army along the north bank of the Vistula, and towards Nowy Sacz by 38 Army, led to the deep outflanking of XVII Army on both sides, and on 16 January XVII Army began to withdraw towards the south of Cracow.

On 17 January both Zhukov and Konev were authorised to undertake a rapid advance to the Oder. Konev was also ordered to take Cracow and Breslau and to use his reserve armies to outflank the Silesian coalfields from the north.[9] On that day the reserve 21 Army was deployed in the Miechów area for an attack on XVII Army west towards Zawiercie and then Tarnowskie Góry north of the Katowice industrial area. By 18 January Cracow was under threat of encirclement by 60 Army, 59 Army and 4 Gds Tank Corps, having been outflanked far to the north by 3 Gds Tank Army and 5 Gds Army. German forces in Cracow abandoned the city on 19 January. In fact by 18 January German forces had no effective frontline between Radom and Kielce.

During the second half of January a high speed pursuit of German forces developed in front of 1 Belorussian and 1 Ukrainian Fronts that was akin to the German 'Blitzkrieg' offensives of 1940/41. The major Soviet combined arms formations moved by forced marches in columns, with mobile pursuit detachments in the van. When counter-attacks on the flanks developed, or when large German groups were left in the rear, separate units and formations were given the assignment of eliminating them, rejoining the major formations later. In this period much of the fighting was done by the leading detachments of the mobile columns, but did not involve them in fighting for strongpoints, these being bypassed, leaving light screening forces to cover them. With Soviet forces emerging on the lines of communication of large retreating groups or of reserves covering strong points, the German forces thereby threatened with encirclement were left with little choice but to retreat, and so give up their defensive positions without a fight. Soviet air superiority assisted in this form of mobile strike in depth, just as the *Luftwaffe* had done in 1940/41. The vast superiority of the Soviets in terms of manpower, armour and artillery contributed greatly to the success of the Soviet offensive.

Between 19 January and 3 February elements of 23 divisions and over 200 independent battalions were moved by the Germans from other sectors to face 1 Belorussian Front, and IX Army was effectively doubled in strength. Nonetheless the Soviet advance remained rapid during the third week of January. On 21 January Inowroclaw was taken by 2 Gds Tank Army's 12 Gds Tank Corps, and two days later Bromberg was captured by its 9 Gds Tank Corps. By 25 January a German force of 60,000 had been surrounded at Poznan, the reduction of which was assigned to 8 Gds Army, 69 Army and elements of 1 Gds Tank Army.

In the centre of his Front, Konev's drive to Breslau resulted in his lead elements crossing into Germany on 19 January, and 52 Army crossed the German frontier at Namslau the next day. For the task of outflanking the Silesian coalfields, Konev used 21 Army (reinforced with a tank corps and a cavalry corps) to invest the area from the northeast and north, 59 Army and 4 Gds Tank Corps would attack towards Katowice, and 60 Army would move in from the south. By 20 January, 21 Army, supported by 1 Gds Cav Corps, had bypassed German forces in Silesia from the north, and on 23 January its right wing reached the Oder near Oppeln, while the left flank reached Tarnowskie Góry and Beuthen (midway between Tarnowskie Góry and Katowice). By 22 January elements of 4 Tank Army and 5 Gds Army had reached the Oder at several points; 4 Tank Army farthest north between Breslau and Glogau. By late on 25 January, 1 Ukrainian Front had seized several bridgeheads over the Oder on either side of Breslau. Pukhov and Gordov found their final push to the Oder to be particularly

---

9   Stalin had issued specific instructions that damage to the Silesian industrial infrastructure was to be kept to a minimum.

difficult against fierce resistance from the remnants of XXIV Pz Corps and XLII Corps. While 3 Gds Tank Army, 3 Gds Army, 13 Army and 52 Army were reaching the Oder, 59 Army and 60 Army, on the left flank, lagged behind. To threaten German forces in the industrial area with encirclement, and so force a retreat, Konev turned 3 Gds Tank Army and 1 Gds Cav Corps, which had reached Oppeln, southeast into the German rear and down the east bank of the Oder towards Ratibor; at the same time 21 Army ceased its outflanking move to the northwest and attacked the German forces directly, moving east towards Katowice. This caused a rapid retreat of German forces from the area, easing the advance of the Front's left flank. With 4 Ukrainian Front advancing west to the south of Katowice, by 29 January the whole Silesian industrial area was abandoned by the Germans, and less than one-third of the 100,000 German defenders escaped to the southwest. By 30 January Konev's forces had established two large bridgeheads over the Oder, one near Steinau between Breslau and Glogau, and the other between Breslau and Oppeln. The latter, south of Brieg, was subsequently expanded to a lodgement 80km wide and 25km deep. Meanwhile the left wing of 1 Ukrainian Front had reached the Oder, and 15km north of the Czech border had secured bridgeheads on the west bank. Co-operating closely with 1 Ukrainian Front, 4 Ukrainian Front reached the Biała – Zakopane line by the end of January, inflicting heavy losses on XVII Army and I Pz Army, and tying down forces that might have been transferred north.

Cherniakhovsky, having failed to break through on a broad front in the first few days of 3 Belorussian Front's offensive, began to shift his forces north to concentrate 30km south of the Neman. On 18 January they took Pilkallen and, with the commitment of 11 Gds Army and 1 Tank Corps to the offensive, III Pz Army's front broke open between the Neman and Pregel (Pregolia) rivers, with III Pz Army forced to withdraw its front away from the Prussian border; Tilsit being taken the next day (19 January). On 21 January Rokossovsky's offensive picked up speed, 2 Shock Army reaching Deutsch Eylau, and 3 Gds Cav Corps, supported by 48 Army, turning north to Allenstein (taken on 23 January) in a drive that could potentially push the whole of Army Group Centre away from the coast and into an encirclement in East Prussia. IV Army was being pushed into near encirclement 200km from the coast. Its situation might have been worse if Boldin had not failed to detect the withdrawal of German forces from the Augustow Canal until two days later, an error that cost him his command, and his replacement at 50 Army by his Chief of Staff, Lt-Gen F P Ozerov. On 23 January Mohrungen was taken by 10 Tank Corps, and by nightfall 2 Belorussian Front had cut all the roads and railways crossing the Vistula except the coastal road through Elbing. After dark on that day 5 Gds Tank Army's leading tank detachment from 29 Tank Corps approached the city and, finding that the defences had not been alerted, rolled through the main streets. By daylight, when the next wave of Soviet tanks arrived, the Germans had recovered enough to fight them off and force them to detour east around the city, but the lead detachment had reached the coast near Tolkemit, isolating IV Army and III Pz Army, together with six infantry divisions and two motorised divisions of II Army, in East Prussia. II Army held Elbing but elsewhere was being forced back to the west bank of the Vistula. III Pz Army had managed for nine days to preserve a front of sorts by gradually retreating towards Koenigsberg but, on 24 January, Cherniakhovsky's forces broke through south of the Pregel and threatened to cut off Koenigsberg from the south. Two divisions that IV Army had taken out of the line for its own counter-attack were transferred to III Pz Army. Hossbach advised his three corps commanders that they should, without orders from OKH and without informing III Pz Army, try to break out to the west on 26 January. Also, on 24 January Muehlhausen had been taken by 10 Tank Corps, and 2 Shock Army was closing on Marienburg, the town falling two days later. On 25 January, 3 Belorussian Front was 20km from the south-eastern edge of Koenigsberg, and appeared to be intent on pinching off the neck of the 'sack' in which IV Army was caught. IV Army and III Pz Army were by then back-to-back and only 60km apart. On that day, in a rationalisation of army group designations, Army Group North was renamed Army Group Courland and placed under the command of Col-Gen Heinrich Vietinghoff; Army Group Centre was renamed Army Group North; and Army Group A became Army Group Centre. At the same time, II Army and IX Army were transferred to a newly-created Army Group Vistula under Himmler's direct command, an army group tasked with defending Germany along the coastal strip between the Oder and the Vistula. This new army group included XI SS Pz Army – being formed from disparate groups of forces, and based on an upgraded corps staff under Steiner's command. Steiner's 'army' occupied the sector west of II Army, but in fact II Army was the new army group's only substantial force. On 26 January Hossbach's redeployments for the breakout attempt meant that Loetzen was lost, and the Soviets achieved a number of breakthroughs along the IV Army front. Reinhardt reported to Hitler that he was about to order a withdrawal of IV Army to shorter lines. Hitler responded by sacking Reinhardt and replacing him with Rendulic, who had orders to hold Koenigsberg and what was left of East Prussia. On 27 January the breakout attempt by IV Army towards Marienburg by six infantry divisions, a motorised division and a panzer division opened, hitting an unprepared 48 Army. By 29 January the offensive had penetrated 25km into Soviet positions, retaking Muehlhausen and reaching to within 10km of Elbing; but thereafter it could progress no further. The next day Rendulic cancelled the offensive and he replaced Hossbach with General Friedrich-Wilhelm Mueller, formerly the commander of Southeast Theatre's LXVIII Corps. Rendulic was ruthless in his determination to keep his new command in being, and initiated a programme of summary executions of officers and men who were deemed to have retreated or otherwise left the front. Meanwhile 1 Baltic Front had added its weight to the advance on Koenigsberg, taking Memel on 27 January. The Memel garrison was able to withdraw from the city across the Bay of Courland to the Samland Peninsula as the German defenders of Koenigsberg were pushed back into a 60km deep coastal strip along the southern shore of the Vistula Lagoon (the *Frisches Haff*); territory that was packed with elements of twenty-three German divisions.

In its winter offensive the Red Army had solved the difficult problem of breaking through deeply echeloned German defence and overcoming river obstacles, not only through positioning their forces in depth (strong first echelons and large second echelons), but also by decisive massing of manpower and material on the axis of the main attack. By this stage of the war problems of long distance pursuit had also been solved. The 1 Belorussian and 1 Ukrainian Fronts pursued the Germans without a break for more than two weeks, advancing more than 400km at an average rate of 30km per day. Around 35 German divisions were destroyed in the offensive by 1 Belorussian and 1 Ukrainian Fronts alone, and a further 25 lost over half their strength (500,000 killed, wounded and captured). On 29 January the retreating remnants of what had been IX Army and IV Pz Army, organised into battle groups, reached the German defence line on the Oder. On 31 January 5 Shock Army crossed the Oder and seized a bridgehead in the area west of Letschin, while elements of 2 Gds Tank Army also crossed the river. The next day 11 Gds Tank Corps from 8 Gds Army crossed the Oder, and 4 Gds Corps from 8 Gds Army seized a bridgehead south of Kuestrin. Yet the bridgeheads that were secured were not very large, and were subjected to furious German counter-attack. By 3 February the east bank of the lower river had been cleared of German forces south of Zeden. Only at Kuestrin and Frankfurt did the Germans possess a foothold on the east bank.

However, by the beginning of February the Soviet offensive was running out of steam. Zhukov's forces, depleted by losses, were making little further headway on the west bank of the Oder, were having to deal with German forces still fighting at Poznan and Kuestrin, and had a long and vulnerable right flank exposed to German forces in eastern Pomerania.

Budapest and Vienna

When the Soviet encirclement of Budapest was completed in the final week of December 1944, most of the capital's one million inhabitants were trapped in the city. Little provision had been made to sustain the population through a siege, and by the end of 1944 utility services to most parts of the city had failed. On New Year's Day 1945, SS General Herbert Gille and his IV SS Pz Corps began an offensive towards Budapest along the shortest available route – from Tata southeast of Komárno due east through 40km of Soviet-held territory to the capital's defence lines. The first part of this advance would, of necessity, be through the difficult terrain of the Vertes Mountains. Gille deployed two infantry divisions and two SS panzer divisions (*Totenkopf* and *Wiking*) against the right flank of 4 Gds Army, but after five days his corps had advanced little more than 15km, though German infantry operating on his left south of the Danube recaptured Esztergom. Gille's attack was coordinated with an offensive by III Pz Corps into the centre of 4 Gds Army, an offensive launched from south of Mór towards the village of Zamoja 12km north of Székesfehérvár. The aim was to surround part of Zakharov's army, but III Pz Corps' four-day attack was held by 4 Gds Army which had been reinforced with 7 Mech Corps.

See Map 29

By 4 January Malinovsky was preparing to counter IV SS Pz Corps with 6 Gds Tank Army and 7 Gds Army in an offensive north of the Danube towards Komárno. This offensive was to be coordinated with action by Tolbukhin with the aim of encircling IV SS Pz Corps in the Komárno area. On 6 January Gille's advance was stopped half way to its objective. By then Kravchenko's tanks, supported by Shumilov's riflemen, had crossed the Hron to advance west along the left bank of the Danube to threaten Komárno from the northeast. A secondary German relief effort to Budapest was launched on 7 January by I Cav Corps from northwest of Székesfehérvár. This force was nearly 60km from the capital but it was hoped that the attack would catch 4 Gds Army off balance and achieve a rapid breakthrough. The attack did come as a surprise to Zakharov, but he reacted quickly to contain the cavalry corps' penetration.

In Budapest the situation was deteriorating rapidly, particularly in Pest, the eastern half of the city on the left bank of the Danube. An airlift was organised, but it was sporadic and wholly inadequate to meet the supply needs of either the defenders or the civilian population. Yet Hitler continued to refuse permission for a breakout, leaving Woehler no choice but to continue to try to break through to the capital. Woehler decided to try to drive a narrow corridor through to the city from the IV SS Pz Corps sector, to feed in supplies and to provide a possible escape route. By 11 January this renewed relief effort had also failed, though German infantry operating off Gille's left flank had advanced through the Pilis hills northwest of Budapest to reach to within 10km of the capital's defences. At the same time, a counter-attack against 6 Gds Tank Army and 7 Gds Army contained the Soviet advance on Komárno. Both Soviet armies had by then suffered heavy losses, Kravchenko's army being reduced to less than 100 tanks.

On 12 January Hitler ordered IV SS Pz Corps, stalled on the direct approach to Budapest and at risk of encirclement, to withdraw and to deploy to the northern tip of Lake Balaton, from where a renewed effort to relieve Budapest would be made. This offensive was launched on 18 January. It quickly overwhelmed one of 4 Gds Army's rifle corps and made good progress due east. Despite the diversion of 18 Tank Corps and 7 Mech Corps to try to block Gille's advance, by 19 January the panzers had reached the Sárvíz Canal, which ran from Székesfehérvár to the Danube north of Baja. They forced a crossing the next morning and reached the Danube at Dunapentele on the evening of 20 January. Had IV SS Pz Corps turned south from Dunapentele, 57 Army would have been at grave risk of encirclement, but Gille's priority was Budapest to the north. Gille confidently expected to be able to advance along the right bank of the Danube and to reach Budapest with little delay, but Tolbukhin, his entire Front at risk of being split in half, acted quickly to stiffen his defences in the Lake Velence and Ercsi areas. By then Pfeffer-Wildenbruch's forces had been driven out of Pest, retreating across the Danube to the relative safety of Buda. For three days Gille's corps ground its way north, retaking Székesfehérvár on 22 January, reaching Lake Velence and, by 24 January, closing up to the Vali on a 40km front south and west of Ercsi. At its nearest approach IV SS Pz Corps was just 20km from the Budapest defences, but Gille was unable to cross the Vali. On 27 January Tolbukhin launched a counter-attack against Gille's corps, the attack coming from the south between the Danube and the Sárvíz Canal. This action, placing Gille on the defensive, effectively ended any German relief effort towards Budapest from the south, and forced the SS corps back from the Vali and Lake Velence. Yet Hitler, with a newly-devised plan to clear Soviet forces from the right bank of the Danube south of Budapest and to relieve the capital, continued to refuse to sanction any breakout by the beleaguered forces in the city, which by then, with some 300,000 civilians, were crammed into 30 square kilometres in Buda. In the event, long before any renewed relief effort could be mounted, Budapest fell to Soviet forces. On 11 February, in defiance of orders, Pfeffer-Wildenbruch organised a breakout from Buda. Thousands of civilians escaped into the Pilis hills, but of the military personnel, only 700 reached the safety of German lines. The remaining defenders of Buda surrendered unconditionally on 13 February.

The fighting during January between the lower Hron and Lake Balaton had left an S-shaped front that ran down the Hron to Esztergom, to Bicske, east of Mór, east of Székesfehérvár, to Lake Balaton. From there the frontline ran east of Marcali, east See Map 31 of Nagyatád and to the Drava. Woehler deployed VIII Army along the Hron, VI Army with III Hun Army between the Danube and Lake Balaton, and II Pz Army between the lake and the Drava. Late in January, to Guderian's dismay, Hitler decided to move the five panzer divisions of VI SS Pz Army, which had been withdrawn from the Ardennes for refitting in southern Germany, not to Army Group Centre which was falling apart in the Soviet Vistula offensive, nor even to Army Group North, but to Vienna for subsequent deployment in Hungary. Hitler's objective was to launch an offensive with Army Group South, supported by part of Army Group E in Yugoslavia, to split 3 Ukrainian Front in a renewed German drive to the Danube.[10] At the Danube, the offensive would be continued north and south along the right bank of the river.

By early February Hitler had become concerned about the Soviet bridgehead on the Hron, which he feared might be used as the wedge for a thrust on Vienna along the north bank of the Danube. He compromised his desire to keep the location of VI SS Pz Army secret, by agreeing to the first two of the army's divisions to become available, to be used against the Hron bridgehead. On 17 February the German attempt to eliminate the Hron bridgehead began. By then 6 Gds Tank Army had been withdrawn, to leave the bridgehead defended by 7 Gds Army. The German advance went well and, despite the commitment by Malinovsky of 4 Gds Mech Corps, the Soviet bridgehead was eliminated within a week. In light of this, STAVKA revised its plans for 2 Ukrainian Front to strike at Vienna alone in the wake of 1 Ukrainian Front's advances farther north, and it ordered Timoshenko to plan a completely independent offensive by 2 Ukrainian Front and 3 Ukrainian Front.

At this time 3 Ukrainian Front, with just 400 armoured fighting vehicles, included 4 Gds Army, 26 Army, 57 Army, Bulgarian 1 Army, and Yugoslav 3 Army.[11] In reserve Tolbukhin also had 27 Army, transferred from 2 Ukrainian Front, and a number of independent corps. Malinovsky had 40 Army, 53 Army, 7 Gds Army and 46 Army, the latter transferred once again from 3 Ukrainian Front on 21 February. In reserve Malinovsky had 6 Gds Tank Army and Pliev's group which, since January, had been designated 1 Gds Cavalry-Mechanised Group. Also in the vicinity as part of the STAVKA reserve was the newly-formed 9 Gds Army, composed largely of troops from the Red Army's elite airborne forces but re-equipped as a conventional combined arms field army. While fully committed to the offensive against Buda, Malinovsky, on his right flank (40 Army and 53 Army), had been attempting to drive into eastern Slovakia in coordination with 4 Ukrainian Front, where Petrov's forces, having made slow progress to the Ondava, took Košice on 18 January and Presov two days later.

The successful German offensive against the Hron bridgehead, in addition to forcing STAVKA to recast its plans, also had an effect on Army Group South. It eased Woehler's concerns about his left flank and prompted him on 21 February to instruct his staff to revive the earlier planning for an offensive between Lake Balaton and the Danube. The two-stage plan that emerged envisaged Army Group South thrusting south

10   Loehr's Army Group E Headquarters had assumed responsibility for the Balkan defences from Army Group F, which was subsequently disbanded.

11   26 Army had been part of Karelian Front during most of 1944. The army headquarters had been withdrawn into STAVKA reserve in November and, under Gagen's command, subordinated to 3 Ukrainian Front at the end of January 1945. Yugoslav 3 Army was based on the Soviet 12 Rifle Corps, and held the Front's left flank on the lower Drava.

from the Székesfehérvár area in the first phase, and in the second, retaking Budapest and the northern area. This operation (Spring Awakening), to begin on 6 March, would require II SS Pz Corps, the stronger of VI SS Pz Army's two corps, to deploy east of the Sárvíz Canal, which ran southeast from the south of Szekesfehevar, for a thrust to the southeast. On its left III Pz Corps from VI Army would push northeast along the southern shore of Lake Velence to provide flank cover. On the right, VI SS Pz Army's I SS Pz Corps, with help from I Cav Corps, would strike southeast west of the Sárvíz Canal. Between Lake Balaton and the Drava, II Pz Army, by this time composed of four infantry divisions, a motorised brigade, three combat groups and a newly arrived motorised division equipped with assault guns, would attack due west from Nagykanizsa towards Kaposvár. In this attack II Pz Army would be assisted by XCI Corps in the Army Group E zone downstream on the Drava, where a crossing south of Pécs towards Mohács would be made. Gille's corps, by then back on the northern wing of VI Army, and the four divisions of III Hun Army would take no part in the offensive.

Facing Tolbukhin's Front were 31 divisions (11 of which were panzer divisions), five combat groups and motorised brigades, and four assault gun brigades; a force that included 877 tanks. Farther north 2 Ukrainian Front faced a force of nine infantry and two panzer divisions in VIII Army.

The Soviets knew what was coming along the Sárvíz Canal, and deferred their plan for a Vienna offensive along the Danube in the 2 Ukrainian Front sector. Instead they prepared to deploy their main assault force of 6 Gds Tank Army north of Lake Velence, where it could either block a German advance to Budapest or strike the flank of German drive to the southeast. After midnight on 5 March, XCI Corps crossed the Drava south of Pécs and took two bridgeheads. At dawn II Pz Army attacked in appalling weather across boggy ground intersected with watercourses towards Kaposvár, but of SS General Sepp Dietrich's VI SS Pz Army, only I SS Pz Corps was ready. Within three days this corps had advanced 30km, forcing Tolbukhin to commit 27 Army and his reserve corps. On 9 March he asked STAVKA for 9 Gds Army, but, though this army was transferred to Tolbukhin's command, permission to use it in the defensive battle was refused. On 10 March I SS Pz Corps closed to the canal, and the next evening had secured two small bridgeheads on its southern bank. Farther north III Pz Corps had hit the junction of 4 Gds Army and 26 Army and had, by 9 March, despite considerable Soviet reinforcement, penetrated 25km into Soviet lines south of Lake Velence. However, it had become obvious to Woehler that the Soviets had anticipated his offensive and had taken effective counter-measures. In six days of fighting, II SS Pz Corps, which had begun its offensive on 6 March, had only gained 8km against well-prepared defences. On 11 March Tolbukhin, after concentrating his armour, counter-attacked on both sides of the Sárvíz Canal, I SS Pz Corps attracting the heaviest attacks. Woehler concluded that, since II Pz Army and XCI Corps were also making only slow progress against 57 Army, if the offensive were to succeed I SS Pz Corps would have to be pulled back to reinforce II SS Pz Corps for a combined drive east to the Danube. By 15 March Spring Awakening had effectively come to an end, Woehler having reported to OKH the previous day that a Soviet counter-offensive towards Lake Balaton, in the rear of the German advance, appeared to be imminent.

This offensive by 3 Ukrainian Front and the left flank of 2 Ukrainian Front had Vienna as its objective. It opened on 16 March between Lake Velence and Bicske, and was led by Tolbukhin's two Guards armies. The next day Malinovsky launched 46 Army into the offensive. Against Tolbukhin's forces, IV SS Pz Corps held but III Hun Army did not, and Soviet forces pushed through the Vertes Mountains north of Mór. Woehler called off his offensive in order to be able to assemble I SS Pz Corps for a counter-attack near Székesfehérvár, and II SS Pz Corps was also ordered to withdraw. Two days later 4 Gds Army and Glagolev's 9 Gds Army broke through IV SS Pz Corps' line between Mór and Lake Velence. However, 6 Gds Tank Army, which had been subordinated to 3 Ukrainian Front on 16 March, was not ready to commit to the offensive. Kravchenko's mechanised forces were having the same difficulties with mud that had delayed II SS Pz Corps' offensive ten days earlier, and they only went into action on 19 March, by which time the opportunity to close the corridor between the lakes, thereby encircling VI SS Pz Army, was lost. Woehler moved VI SS Pz Army north to cover the gap left by III Hun Army, and Balck's VI Army was given responsibility for the front between the lakes. Hence by 20 March, when 6 Gds Tank Army began its drive towards the tip of Lake Balaton, VI SS Pz Army was gone. Woehler wanted to pull VI Army back too, but Hitler insisted that the bauxite mines in the Székesfehérvár area be protected, which meant VI Army would have to remain east of Lake Balaton. During the next evening, when only a narrow corridor along the lakeshore was still held open, Székesfehérvár, scene of four days of fierce fighting, was given up. For a full day, until the evening of 23 March, VI Army was under threat of complete encirclement south of Székesfehérvár, and ran the gauntlet between the Red Army and the lake. Army headquarters completely lost track of IV SS Pz Corps, and of deserters later rounded up, three-quarters were SS personnel. Meanwhile VI SS Pz Army was trying to establish a front from Pápa northeast to Komárno with staff and troops unaccustomed to improvising under difficult operational conditions. On 23 March, having escaped one encirclement, VI Army was in danger of being caught in another, and Balck submitted an ominous report to Woehler and OKH. His troops, he reported, were losing the will to fight; they were afraid of encirclement, lacking in confidence and seemed unwilling to die for what was increasingly being seen as a lost cause. There were enough weapons and supplies, and they had been in worse situations, but there had developed a crisis of confidence rooted in earlier disasters. The SS in particular needed to adapt to the rapidly changing and sometimes chaotic conditions that often characterised battles on the Eastern Front.

On that same day STAVKA issued formal orders for its armies to strike west towards Austria; 9 Gds Army and 6 Gds Tank Army were to strike towards Kőszeg, 26 Army towards Szombathely and 27 Army towards Zalaegerszeg. By 24 March Tolbukhin's troops were firmly entrenched in Veszprém, a key junction in the Bakony forest 8km west of the northern tip of Lake Balaton, possession of which denied VI Army the ability to retreat westwards. Balck's forces could only angle away southwest along the lakeshore, in continued danger of encirclement. Farther north Malinovsky's forces had demolished the left wing of III Hun Army's front west of Esztergom, forcing the Hungarians north across the Danube. Meanwhile II Pz Army was still advancing slowly eastwards south of Lake Balaton, though XCI Corps' two Drava bridgeheads had been abandoned. Woehler was permitted to take one division from II Pz Army to strengthen his northern flank, a move that brought II Pz Army's advance against 57 Army to an end. By 25 March, 6 Gds Tank Army had emerged from the Bakony forest east of Pápa. VI SS Pz Army had a front to the north but could not be expected to do any more than hold there. VI Army was attempting to keep its right flank on Lake Balaton to protect II Pz Army south of the lake, and at the same time stretch its front west and north to tie in with VI SS Pz Army. East of Pápa the gap between the two armies was 16km wide and Woehler could think of no means of closing it. On that day Malinovsky added to Woehler's problems by attacking across the Hron with a dozen assault battalions from 53 Army and 7 Gds Army against VIII Army, and committing Pliev's group to the exploitation. The next day, without a pause, the Soviets began the drive into Austria. In a single day Tolbukhin's two Guards armies together with 6 Gds Tank Army swept past Pápa between the flanks of VI Army and VI SS Pz Army, and on 27 March they crossed the Raba west of Kőszeg on a broad front. Any German reserves were going to II Pz Army and VIII Army in order to protect the oil fields, though in reality there was little left to protect. II Pz Army reported that its Hungarian contingents were deserting in droves and requested permission to retire to the main defence line between Lake Balaton and the Drava; but because of the 'oil fields' Hitler refused this request.

By 29 March, 6 Gds Tank Army had reached the Austrian border in the Kőszeg – Szombathley area. The next day it crossed the border, turned north towards the corridor between Lake Neusiedler and the mountains, and passed Wiener Neustadt 30km south of Vienna two days later. On its right the two Guards armies also began to wheel northwest towards Vienna, where only 25 Pz Div was available for the defence of the city. Until 30 March, VIII Army still had a tenuous hold on Komárno and II Pz Army, having lost Nagybajom in the centre of its front south of Lake Balaton, and despite having taken command of VI Army's right flank corps at the southern tip of the lake to protect its deep flank and rear, had retreated west of Nagykanizsa to a line that barely contained the oil field. Hitler had allowed VI Army and VI SS Pz Army to go into the Austrian border defences but ordered VIII Army and II Pz Army to remain in position. On 3 April he ordered Woehler to abandon his attempts to oppose the Soviet spearheads frontally, and to attack the flanks of the Soviet penetration. When Woehler objected he was replaced by Rendulic.

Sopron, the last town of any importance in Hungary, fell on 1 April. North of the Danube, 7 Gds Army reached Bratislava on 1 April but circumvented the town, which was well-defended. To support the planned envelopment of Vienna from the north, Malinovsky moved 46 Army, reinforced with 2 Gds Mech Corps and 23 Tank Corps, across the Danube to the north bank to push west across the Morava on the Austrian/Czech border. At the same time Tolbukhin's right flank, south of the river, pushed into the narrows between the Danube at Bratislava and Lake Neusiedler. On 4 April Bratislava fell, the remnants of the German garrison falling back across the Morava, and by 7 April, when Rendulic arrived to take up his new command, 4 Gds Army and 9 Gds Army were already within Vienna and on the Danube to the west. German forces north of the Danube were subordinated to the newly-formed Army Group Austria, to which Woehler was appointed as commander and to which VIII Army was attached. After six days of fighting, Vienna fell to Soviet forces on 13 April.

Farther north Malinovsky sent Pliev's group across the Czech border towards Brno to assist 4 Ukrainian Front's impending attack on the right flank of Army Group Centre. This was scheduled to begin soon after 12 April, for which 60 Army, having been on the extreme left flank of 1 Ukrainian Front, was transferred to 4 Ukrainian Front. STAVKA had been constantly frustrated by the pace of 4 Ukrainian Front's advance through Slovakia. Petrov had begun an offensive towards Ostrava on 10 March, but after eight days had only progressed 10-15 km, resulting in his replacement by Eremenko on 26 March.[12] The offensive by 4 Ukrainian Front had been resumed on 24 March but after a further twelve days the Front had only advanced an additional 30km. In early April Eremenko was ordered to resume the offensive again by mid-month, and it was expected that Pliev's attack towards Brno would subsequently link up with 4 Ukrainian Front in the area of Olomouc.

A Pause on the Oder

After three weeks, the Soviet offensive through Poland and into Germany, an offensive that was intended to have Soviet troops on the Elbe before the end of February, was beginning to stall. Zhukov had faced fierce resistance to the 1 Belorussian Front bridgeheads on the west bank of the Oder, and many of his units were exhausted and under-strength. Yet, given the resources available to him, Zhukov could have broken out of the bridgeheads and taken Berlin in one largely continuous operation as planned at the start of the campaign. It was certainly the expectation of the German General Staff that there would be fighting in the streets of Berlin during February. In October 1944 Hitler had ordered the formation of a national militia, the *Volkssturm*, to be organised locally in units up to battalion size under Nazi party supervision. Its ranks were to be filled with Hitler Youth members, the elderly and men who had otherwise been considered unfit for military service. Hundreds of militia battalions were raised but their training was rudimentary, uniforms were scarce and their weaponry was predominantly the rifle and the *panzerfaust*. The ragged columns of the Berlin militia – elderly men in trilby hats and civilian overcoats, and boys in their Hitler Youth uniforms – did little to inspire the confidence of the capital's population, and the militia would have presented little effective impediment to the battle-hardened troops of Zhukov's armies. Yet as the days of February passed, the Soviet offensive against Berlin mysteriously failed to materialise.

Zhukov's failure to take Berlin in February 1945 stemmed largely from events in East Prussia and on Zhukov's right flank. Cherniakhovsky and Rokossovsky had been unable to clear Army Group North from East Prussia, leaving Rokossovsky with insufficient forces to clear German forces from the Baltic coast west of the Vistula. Consequently Zhukov was left with an extended right flank stretching back from the Oder towards Danzig. Zhukov also had to deal with the substantial German garrison in Poznan, which was tying down a significant Soviet force, and his armies on the Oder were experiencing supply problems, particularly with regard to ammunition and equipment spares. In addition, some of Zhukov's forces were badly under-strength; in Chuikov's army, regiments had been reduced to two battalions with only 22-45 men per company. To be in a position to take Berlin, Zhukov would need to weaken his right flank in order to gain the necessary forces for deployment on the Oder. Yet

See Map 31

12   Govorov was assigned responsibility for the Courland operations thereafter.

by the beginning of February Soviet military intelligence had uncovered evidence of a German plan to counter-attack 1 Belorussian Front and 1 Ukrainian Front from Pomerania and Lower Silesia in order to snip off the western Soviet armies on the Oder. That plan had been suggested by Guderian to take advantage of the extended Soviet flanks. Preparations were begun by OKH to assemble the forces necessary to undertake the offensive, but those preparations were overtaken by events, and they were never to amount to much. Yet STAVKA was uncertain of what resources were available to the *Ostheer* for such an offensive, and, as a result, Zhukov and the Soviet General Staff began to counsel caution.[13]

From 6 February STAVKA made a number of major changes to the organisation and objectives of the Fronts. The forces of 1 Baltic Front facing Army Group Courland were subordinated to 2 Baltic Front. Bagramyan acquired 11 Gds Army and 39 Army from 3 Belorussian Front together with 43 Army, the latter army having been temporarily subordinated to Cherniakhovsky on 20 January. Bagramyan was required to use these armies to eliminate the Koenigsberg garrison and the German forces in Samland. Cherniakhovsky acquired 8 Gds Tank Corps, 48 Army, 50 Army and 5 Gds Tank Army from 2 Belorussian Front in order to focus on the destruction of IV Army south of the Vistula Lagoon between Elbing and Koenigsberg. Although this stripped Rokossovsky of half his operational strength, it left him free to concentrate on the single task of protecting the right flank of 1 Belorussian Front while assisting Zhukov in the clearing of Pomerania. Rokossovsky proposed to shorten his line, change the direction of attack, and to concentrate on a narrow sector in the Koeslin area for a strike north to cut off and destroy II Army and, when Kozlov's 19 Army arrived from STAVKA reserve, the Front was to advance towards Stettin, capture the Danzig – Gotenhafen area, and clear the Baltic coast as far as the Bay of Pomerania. Zhukov proposed that 1 Belorussian Front should make a similar thrust towards the Baltic coast in the directions of Falkenburg and Gollnow. This proposal carried the implicit consequence that an offensive beyond the Oder would have to be delayed. STAVKA was persuaded that the removal of Army Group Vistula from Zhukov's right flank east of the Oder should be a prerequisite for any advance on Berlin, and by mid-February the final decision to suspend the direct drive on Berlin had been taken.

On 2 Belorussian Front's left flank, 70 Army spent the first nine days of February subduing German forces in Thorn on the Vistula, from which only one-tenth of the 30,000 strong defending force was eventually to escape, and subsequently 2 Belorussian Front was to attack west of the Vistula in the Graudenz – Sępólno Krajeńskie area on 10 February to seize a line running from the mouth of the Vistula to Neustettin via Rummelsburg. Rokossovsky's forces made little progress; his 34 divisions were down to an average of 3,250 personnel in each, and the Front had less than 300 tanks in an operational condition. After 10 days, 2 Belorussian Front had gained only 40 to 70 kilometres and was forced to halt on a line running from Gniew to Linde. Meanwhile, though the encircled German garrison at Elbing was wiped out, Graudenz remained in German hands.

---

13   On 1 February IX Army had five infantry divisions and one panzer division, and II Army had thirteen infantry divisions and one panzer division – considerably more than Soviet estimates of German strength; and by 10 February Army Group Vistula had 38 divisions, six of which were panzer divisions.

By early February Konev had packed three field armies and two tank armies into the bridgehead at Steinau, and two field armies supported by two tank corps into the bridgehead at Brieg. At the same time, two more field armies and a cavalry corps were deployed on the left flank southwest of Oppeln. Konev's objective was to break through the German defences along the Oder between Gruenberg and Breslau, and to advance to the Neisse. The offensive would be undertaken against IV Pz Army, which at that time had 18 infantry divisions, four panzer divisions, two mechanised divisions and 'Corps Group Breslau'. The breakout by 3 Gds Tank Army and 4 Tank Army from the Steinau – Keben bridgehead began on 8 February. It was supported by 3 Gds Army, 6 Army, 13 Army, 52 Army and two mechanised corps. After three days 1 Ukrainian Front had forced a 150km gap in the German lines, and 3 Gds Army had advanced 60km, cutting the Berlin – Silesia railway, and surrounding 18,000 German troops in the fortress of Glogau on the east bank of the Oder. On 14 February, 5 Gds Army, supported by two tank corps, joined the offensive by breaking out of its bridgehead at Brieg and heading northwest against XVII Army. The next day, in conjunction with 6 Army, it had surrounded Breslau and had isolated 40,000 German troops. By 24 February the Bober river had been crossed off the march and 100km of the eastern bank of the Neisse north of Penzig had been seized. After 1 Ukrainian Front had joined with 1 Belorussian Front at the confluence of the Oder and the Neisse on 25 February, 4 Tank Army was transferred to the south.

On 15 February XI SS Pz Army began a counter-attack from the Stargard area into the flank of 1 Belorussian Front. The operation, codenamed Solstice, had been anxiously awaited by Zhukov. A simultaneous offensive from the south into the left flank of 1 Ukrainian Front had never been adequately prepared, and such preparations as there were had been overtaken by Konev's Lower Silesian offensive. At Guderian's insistence, the forces for Operation Solstice were subordinated to his second in command at OKH, General Walther Wenck. Wenck was a competent commander but the offensive began and developed in an uncoordinated manner. A one-division attack to relieve a surrounded German detachment in Arnswalde on 15 February was surprisingly successful, and prompted a premature start to the general offensive the next day. It pushed 47 Army and 61 Army of 1 Belorussian Front back around 10km to the south, and took Pyritz from 2 Gds Tank Army. The ill-fated offensive was shortlived, being terminated by Himmler on 18 February after the advance had stalled and Wenck had been hospitalised after an accident. Operation Solstice deserves consideration as one of the most ineptly executed German offensive operations of the war, but it caused considerable nervousness at STAVKA, and it came at the time of the successful German offensive against 7 Gds Army in the Hron bridgehead (see above). Militarily, Operation Solstice may have been inconsequential, but the caution it engendered in STAVKA's strategy was to have enormous repercussions on the future of Europe. During February the Western Allies were still battering their way through the West Wall towards the Rhine, but by the end of March they had brought Hitler's Western armies to the verge of collapse, and were beginning to break out across the Rhine into central Germany. Until mid-February Stalin had confidently assumed that when Germany capitulated, the Red Army, not the Western Allies, would be firmly ensconced in central Germany, and that he would be in a strong position to dictate much of the unresolved detail concerning the future governance of Germany – much as he had, from a position of strength, decided the position of the post-war Polish border. In the event, and to a significant extent as a result of Operation Solstice, it was to be the armies of the Western Allies that occupied central, southern and northern Germany, waiting on the Elbe for the Soviet armies to draw up to their pre-arranged occupation zone boundary.

The second half of February was a chaotic period, both sides suffering reverses, but the Soviet attention to their flanks was beginning to have a positive effect. A German force in Pila, which had been surrounded during January, was eliminated on 14 February, and the siege of Poznan ended on 23 February. In mid-February III Pz Army, which was trapped in the Samland Peninsula, was designated 'Army Detachment Samland', and soon afterwards Raus's III Pz Army Headquarters was reconstituted on the lower Oder, being activated on 23 February and subsequently absorbing the forces of XI SS Pz Army. On 19 February Cherniakhovsky was killed. Vasilevsky took command of 3 Belorussian Front and Antonov, the *de facto* Chief of the General Staff, formally succeeded to the role. At around this time, Army Detachment Samland was able to push 1 Baltic Front back, breaking through to Koenigsberg. STAVKA then merged 1 Baltic Front and 3 Belorussian Front under Vasilevsky whose primary task was to prevent a German withdrawal from the Frische Nehrung peninsula, while preparing for a final operation to clear East Prussia.[14] On 24 February Rokossovsky renewed his offensive north to the east of Kolberg, and within two days a breach 50km wide was made in the German lines, but 19 Army, committed to the exploitation towards Neustettin, lagged behind the armour, prompting Rokossovsky to replace Kozlov with Romanovsky. By 28 February the gap in the German lines was 75km wide and 50km deep, and Rokossovsky's forces had taken Neustettin and Prechlau. Yet 2 Belorussian Front faced a reinforced II Army, which by 1 March consisted of 18 infantry divisions, two panzer divisions and a motorised division – 230,000 men. By the end of February units of 1 Belorussian Front on Zhukov's right flank had eliminating the German garrisons at Deutsch Krone and Arnswalde.[15] By the end of February, Zhukov's right flank armies were ready to join Rokossovsky's offensive towards Kolberg. Zhukov had assembled a force of 18 rifle divisions, four tank corps, a mechanised corps, two cavalry corps and three 'breakthrough' artillery divisions. These were subordinated to the two Guards tank armies and four of his field armies (Polish 1 Army, 3 Shock Army, 47 Army and 61 Army). 1 Belorussian Front faced III Pz Army, which by that time had absorbed XI SS Pz Army's forces, consisting of 11 infantry divisions, one panzer division and two motorised divisions – 200,000 men.

The offensive by 1 Belorussian Front opened on 1 March with Polish 1 Army and 3 Shock Army attacking towards Kolberg, and 1 Gds Tank Army committed to exploiting the breach. Meanwhile 61 Army and 2 Gds Tank Army attacked towards Stargard, while 47 Army attacked towards Altdamm on the east bank of the Oder from Stettin. The offensive quickly broke through the German defences on a broad front, and 1 Gds Tank Army raced north towards the coast, reaching the area northwest of Labes on 3 March. On that day Polish 1 Army took advantage of the success of 2

---

14   The former 1 Baltic Front forces facing the German Samland defences were designated the 'Samland Group' under Bagramyan's command.

15   Polish 2 Army, which had just completed formation, took part in this action and was subsequently subordinated to 1 Ukrainian Front.

Belorussian Front to bypass Polzin and to head north to Kolberg. By 4 March Zhukov's forces had reached the Baltic in the Kolberg area, and by the next day had consolidated a 16km sector of coast west of Kolberg. By 4 March, 1 Gds Tank Army had made contact with 2 Belorussian Front, and four days later was transferred to Rokossovsky's command for use on the left flank of 2 Belorussian Front to assist in the capture of the Danzig – Gotenhafen area. On 5 March, 61 Army broke into Stargard, compromising the German defence of Stettin, and farther east Rokossovsky's assault group took Koeslin and reached the Baltic on a 20km wide sector. The main force of 19 Army then swung east and began to work along the coast towards Gotenhafen. On the left of the breakthrough, 2 Gds Tank Army, with its accompanying 61 Army, made little subsequent progress against stiff opposition in the Stargard area. Similarly 47 Army striking north on the east bank of the Oder was having little success. Southwest of Polzin the Poles and 3 Shock Army had encircled X SS Pz Corps and 'Corps Group Tettau', forces which surrendered on 7 March, while a further 20,000 Germans were trapped southeast of Kolberg.

In the second week of March, after the Polzin pocket had been lost, Rendulic was sent back to command Army Group Courland, Vietinghoff returning to the command of German forces in Italy, and Weiss was appointed to the command of Army Group North, which by then was confined to the Bay of Danzig.[16] From the coast 1 Belorussian Front turned west towards the Stettin lagoon. When on 20 March Altdamm was stormed, the last German foothold on the east bank of the lower Oder had been eliminated. On 28 March Gotenhafen naval base was stormed, splitting Army Group North, and Danzig fell two days later. At that point 1 Gds Tank Army was returned to 1 Belorussian Front.

On 1 Belorussian Front's left, 5 Shock Army and 8 Gds Army had overcome stiff opposition from IX Army on the west bank of the Oder to surround Kuestrin and extend their bridgehead round it so as to form a springboard for a future offensive. The failure to eliminate the Soviet bridgehead at Kuestrin cost Guderian his job at OKH, and on 28 March he was replaced by General Hans Krebbs, a long-serving staff officer. The next day the fortress town of Kuestrin fell to the two Soviet armies after a final attempt by IX Army to break through to the town with a relieving force had failed.

Meanwhile, in early March, Konev had been planning a double assault north and south of Oppeln that would outflank the main part of XVII Army and meet in the Neustadt area so as to encircle it and seize the remaining German-held areas of Upper Silesia. The northern force consisted of 4 Tank Army and 21 Army with part of 5 Gds Army, and 4 Gds Tank Corps was to attack southwest from the Grottkau area. The southern force (59 Army, 60 Army, 31 Tank Corps and 7 Gds Mech Corps) would strike west from the vicinity of Kosel north of Ratibor. This assault began on 15 March and by the fourth day five German divisions near Oppeln had been wiped out. As a result of its actions in this operation, 4 Tank Army was awarded the 'Guards' status. During the last week of March the Front took Nysa, Neustadt and Ratibor, the latter being taken by a heavily reinforced 60 Army, and by the end of the month was approaching the Sudeten mountains, crossing into Czechoslovakia in some places. These actions meant that the entire Oder/Neisse line was cleared of German forces, and the

16 Weiss was succeeded at II Army by Saucken, and II Army was transferred from the command of Army Group Vistula to that of Army Group North.

Soviet armies on the Berlin axis were free from possible flank attack on their left. By the beginning of February the right flank of 4 Ukrainian Front had forced I Pz Army off one position after another in the western Carpathians and was advancing in the direction of Ostrava. By mid February the left flank forces had reached Ružomberok. This represented an advance of up to 160km in which German forces were pushed out of the eastern half of Slovakia.

In the second half of March Vasilevsky's 3 Belorussian Front, with Bagramyan's Samland Group under command, began an offensive to clear German forces from the German bridgehead based on Heiligenbeil. The Heiligenbeil area was strongly defended by IV Army, but once cleared, the offensive was to be followed by a final attack on Koenigsberg and the elimination of German forces in Samland. By 25 March Heiligenbeil had fallen after fierce fighting, and four days later the bridgehead had been eliminated, few German troops escaping to the Vistula Lagoon and Pillau.[17] On 2 April the Army Group North Headquarters was recalled to Germany, and II Army and IV Army came under the direct command of OKH. By 4 April mopping up of the German 'East Pomerania grouping' had been completed, and the threat to the right flank of a Soviet offensive across the Oder had been eliminated. On 6 April, 3 Belorussian Front stormed Koenigsberg with four armies, an assault that lasted three days and which resulted in the city's surrender. After the fall of Gotenhafen, with its 10,000 German prisoners, and Koenigsberg (42,000 Germans killed and 92,000 captured according to Soviet sources), Rokossovsky left just nine divisions to guard the remnants of Army Group North, and moved the rest of his forces west. At the same time IV Army Headquarters was recalled to Germany and the remnants of what had been IV Army were combined with II Army to form the Army of East Prussia under Weiss's command. Vasilevsky's attack on Samland opened on 13 April but it took a week of savage fighting to take Pillau.

The Last Battle

The German forces facing the Red Army on the Oder in April were from Army Group Vistula, by that time under the command of Heinrici, and from Schoerner's Army Group Centre. Heinrici's command included the 11 divisions of III Pz Army under the command of General Hasso von Manteuffel, and Busse's IX Army of 14 divisions.[18] Schoerner's command on the Oder included Graeser's IV Pz Army and XVII Army commanded, since the beginning of April, by Hasse. Army Group Centre was also responsible for the front south of the Oder in Slovakia, where Schoerner deployed I Pz Army – commanded by Nehring after Heinrici's departure to Army Group Vistula. The two army groups contained 4 panzer divisions, 10 motorised divisions, 48 other divisions and many smaller units. For the defence of Berlin there were 200 *Volkssturm* battalions, while OKH held a further eight divisions in reserve – a total of a million men. The Germans began working on the Berlin defences early in February and by mid-April three belts had been set up between the Baltic and the Sudeten foothills in a defensive system up to 40km deep. A major obstacle to a direct Soviet attack on Berlin from the east was the Seelow Heights stretching north to south 8km in front of Zhukov's troops in the Kuestrin bridgehead (3 Shock Army, 5 Shock Army and 8

---

17   During this time the Soviet Samland Group was disbanded.

18   Manteuffel had previously commanded V Pz Army on the Western Front.

Gds Army). Yet during March, Hitler had not been convinced that an offensive would be conducted against Berlin. He had refused to sanction an evacuation of the civilian population from the city and by early April he had transferred half of Army Group Vistula's armoured and mobile forces farther south. He had also made arrangements to establish XII Army, based on staff from tank and officer training schools, in the Harz Mountains to attack US forces moving into central Germany east of the Ruhr, but XII Army Headquarters did not assume command until 12 April. Even as late as 10 April, Schoerner was still predicting that Konev's main offensive would take place southwest of Bunzlau, that is, 80km southeast of where Konev would actually strike six days later; and German military intelligence, having lost track of 3 Gds Tank Army, was in no position to contradict him. To replace the panzer forces transferred south, Hitler promised Heinrici 100,000 additional troops but only delivered 35,000 *Kriegsmarine* and *Luftwaffe* personnel, few of which were adequately trained for ground combat. On 11 April forces from US 9 Army reached the Elbe at Magdeburg and established a small bridgehead on the east bank.

The Soviet offensive against Berlin began on 16 April. STAVKA had originally proposed an assault on Berlin for the second half of May, but the rapid advance of the Western Allies into central Germany in early April prompted an earlier than planned assault from the east. As Soviet forces were frantically redeploying for this offensive, Stalin advised the Western Allies that Berlin had lost its strategic significance and that only secondary forces would be allocated for the Berlin axis. On 14 April a preliminary attack against the Seelow Heights positions west of Kuestrin by five Soviet rifle divisions supported by 200 tanks failed to make any gains. By then it was clear to OKH that a major Soviet offensive against the capital was imminent, and on 15 April responsibility for the defence of the capital was transferred to Army Group Vistula.

Rokossovsky's 2 Belorussian Front, having assumed responsibility for 100km of frontline from 1 Belorussian Front south of Kolberg, held the Oder front from the coast to the river east of Schwedt. Stalin had set the Front's boundary line from Schwedt to Wittenberge on the Elbe. Zhukov's 1 Belorussian Front held the line south to a point southeast of Guben, but Stalin set the Front's boundary due west only as far as Luebben. This suggested that 1 Ukrainian Front, should it reach a point west of Luebben, could potentially strike northwest towards Berlin. Implicit though this was, Konev's actual orders were to destroy IV Pz Army in the Cottbus area and to then drive west to the Elbe on the Spemberg – Belzig axis. Rokossovsky had 19 Army, 2 Shock Army, 65 Army, 70 Army and 49 Army, and he had 5 Gds Tank Army available to exploit the breakthrough. Zhukov had 61 Army, Polish 1 Army, 47 Army, 3 Shock Army, 5 Shock Army, 8 Gds Army, 69 Army, 33 Army, 2 Gds Tank Army, and 1 Gds Tank Army, with 3 Army in reserve. Konev had 3 Gds Army, 3 Gds Tank Army, 4 Gds Tank Army, 13 Army, 5 Gds Army, Polish 2 Army and 52 Army. In reserve Konev had 28 Army, and would acquire 31 Army later. The Soviet forces amounted to 2.5 million men, 41,600 guns and mortars and 6,000 armoured fighting vehicles.

In addition to the main attack out of the Kuestrin bridgehead, Zhukov planned two supporting attacks; in the north 61 Army and Polish 1 Army would attack on the right flank northwest through Liebenwalde; 69 Army and 33 Army would attack in the south from the Frankfurt area in the direction Fuerstenwalde – Potsdam in an offensive that would isolate IX Army from the city; while 47 Army, just north of the

See Map 32

Kuestrin bridgehead, was to outflank Berlin from the northwest. For the offensive Zhukov organised artillery densities in the attack areas of more than 250 tubes per kilometre, the equivalent of four to five artillery regiments to every first-echelon rifle regiment, and he used them to open his offensive in darkness. After the massive half-hour long artillery bombardment of the German front lines, he sent his troops forward using searchlights reflecting off low cloud for illumination. Heinrici had anticipated the timing of the Soviet assault and had withdrawn IX Army from its frontline positions. Consequently the artillery barrage fell on empty trenches, and the Soviet searchlights meant that the advancing Soviet troops were visible to German observation posts on the Seelow Heights. The result was that Zhukov's troops, despite the commitment of 1 Gds Tank Army to support 8 Gds Army, and of 2 Gds Tank Army to support the two shock armies, made little headway against the main German defence line on 16 April. Furious, Zhukov ordered the offensive to be continued throughout the night of 16/17 April. The next morning, after air attacks and a further artillery bombardment, Soviets forces continued the offensive. Despite German reinforcement of the defences with a further seven divisions, the Seelow defence line had been breached by evening. Nevertheless, after two days of the offensive the German lines had only been penetrated by 11km, less than this north and south of the Kuestrin bridgehead.

Konev's forces, with no bridgeheads over the Neisse, had to begin the offensive with a river crossing. The crossing of the Neisse began at 06:30 on 16 April and employed the same level of concentration of artillery as 1 Belorussian Front. Forward elements of 13 Army, 5 Gds Army and 3 Gds Army, the latter with 25 Tank Corps under command, crossed on assault bridges, boats and rafts in the Triebel area. By 10:00 several bridgeheads had been established. Two hours later a sixty-tonne bridge was completed and at 14:00 the armour from 3 Gds Tank Army and 4 Gds Tank Army was committed, Lelyushenko's tanks aiming for the Sonnenwalde area. A gap 25km wide was made in the main German line, and an advance of 13km penetrated the second German line in places. Despite the commitment of four panzer divisions to counter-attack, by the evening of 17 April, with the main Soviet tank forces committed, the penetration had reached 18km into the German lines, and Soviet tanks began to cross the Spree. On 17 April Stalin, concerned at Zhukov's lack of progress, gave Konev permission to turn his two tank armies on Berlin, and that evening Konev ordered 3 Gds Tank Army to move on Berlin, while 4 Gds Tank Army was to force the Spree north of Spemberg and move on Potsdam. On the secondary Dresden axis, in an offensive undertaken by 52 Army and Polish 2 Army, the main German defence line was breached and the second line was penetrated to a depth of 3km in a number of sectors in the first two days. OKH responded by moving formations from reserve and elsewhere in the line to enable IV Pz Army to stand on its third line on the west bank of the Spree. By 18 April the German line had been strengthened, particularly at Cottbus and Spemberg, with another strong force assembling around Goerlitz, but 3 Gds Tank Army had split off the left flank corps of IV Pz Army from the rest of Graeser's army.

Zhukov's troops resumed their offensive on 18 April and succeeded in levering IX Army off the Seelow Heights, but every step continued to be fiercely contested, the Germans bringing in further reserves. Zhukov's forces were most successful on the right where, by the evening of 19 April, 3 Shock Army and 47 Army had advanced

30km and had seized a position from which they could either attack Berlin from the northeast or bypass it to the north; yet even in the south, by the evening of 19 April, 8 Gds Army and 1 Gds Tank Army had taken Muencheberg, midway between Berlin and the Oder. By the next day, Hitler's birthday, 8 Gds Army and 5 Shock Army had penetrated the fourth and final German defensive line behind the Oder, 47 Army had taken Bernau, 3 Shock Army was through the third German defensive belt, 2 Gds Tank Army had reached open country northeast of Berlin, and in the late morning Soviet artillery began to shell the city. IX Army had been split into three parts by the four days of fighting; in the south were V SS Mtn Corps, the Frankfurt garrison and units of II SS Pz Corps transferred from VI SS Pz Army in Austria. These forces had been split off from Berlin by the advance of 33 Army and 69 Army. In the centre was LVI Pz Corps commanded by Weidling. In the north was CI Corps. Meanwhile, Konev's forces had attacked the German third line at its weakest point between Cottbus and Spemberg using the two tank armies. On the morning of 18 April bridgeheads over the Spree had been secured north and south of Spemberg. During the day the two tank armies advanced more than 40km towards Berlin. By 20 April, with 3 Gds Tank Army 30km south of Berlin in the Zossen area, the Germans had committed all their reserves and two SS panzer grenadier divisions were transferred south from III Pz Army. Konev responded by reinforcing 3 Gds Tank Army with 28 Army in preparation for an attack on the outer defensive perimeter of Berlin.

These events on the ground meant that by the time Hitler's muted birthday celebrations were underway on 20 April, OKH's battle to save Berlin had been effectively lost. IX Army, having taken command of the left flank corps of IV Pz Army in the Cottbus area, had held the Soviet offensive from the Frankfurt bridgehead and had managed to prevent a significant breakthrough directly east of Berlin, holding 1 Belorussian Front's penetration to Fuerstenwalde; but elements of 1 Belorussian Front had reached Bernau north of Berlin, Konev's forces had reached to less than 20km from Zossen, and 2 Belorussian Front opened its offensive across the Oder from Schwedt to Stettin. By the next day elements of both 1 Belorussian Front and 1 Ukrainian Front had reached the outer defences of the capital. Heinrici pleaded for IX Army to be pulled back from the Oder to avoid the army's complete encirclement, but Hitler was planning a counter-attack from the north using three divisions of a scratch force, Operational Group Steiner, and he refused permission for Busse to withdraw. Yet, of the forces assigned to Steiner, only two lightly armed SS police battalions were immediately available for the offensive. Nonetheless Steiner was given specific orders to attack the next day (22 April). At Hitler's headquarters, a bunker complex in the heart of Berlin, the febrile atmosphere oscillated between despair and wild optimism. The death of President Roosevelt on 12 April had engendered a short period of elation as Hitler's inner circle speculated on whether a change of leadership in America might mean a change in US policy towards the prospect of what Goebbels described as an 'iron curtain' across central Europe. Hitler's mood changed frequently, from quiet fatalism, to barely coherent bouts of fury as he railed against what he saw as betrayal, cowardice or incompetence. Increasingly Hitler's orders bore no relationship to the reality of the battlefield and, when he learned on 22 April than Steiner had not attacked as ordered, he had something of a hysterical breakdown during which he articulated for the first time his belief that the war was lost. Yet soon afterwards he was issuing orders for Wenck, in command of the seven divisions of the recently formed XII Army (organised into XLI Pz Corps and XX Corps) to turn his army around and to attack east to relieve Berlin from the southwest. This relief effort, on which Hitler was subsequently to pin all his hopes, was to build on a minor German success on the Dresden axis. Niesky, 15km northwest of Goerlitz, had been taken by 1 Ukrainian Front but the Soviet forces approaching Bautzen had, on the night of 22 April, been pushed back several kilometres by the 'Goerlitz Group', a scratch force of two divisions supported by around a hundred tanks. This attack hit Konev's forces where they were weakest and caused him some consternation for a couple of days until 52 Army, 5 Gds Army and Polish 2 Army could coordinate their actions to contain the German penetration towards Spemberg.

Prior to 20 April STAVKA had been concerned at Zhukov's slow progress, and Rokossovsky, not scheduled to launch his offensive until 20 April, and with some of his forces still moving west from Pomerania, was issued with revised orders. He was to bypass Berlin from the north no later than 22 April. However, since by 20 April Zhukov's advance had gained some momentum, these revised orders were rescinded and Rokossovsky was able to pursue his original operational plan. His objectives were to force the Oder north of Schwedt, destroy III Pz Army and to head west and northwest. For this Rokossovsky planned to use his three assault armies (65 Army, 70 Army and 49 Army) simultaneously along a 50km front from Altdamm to Schwedt, and to reinforce the areas of greatest success. Rokossovsky's endeavours were to be aided by the transfer south of two of Manteuffel's best divisions prior to the Soviet attack. By the end of the first day 65 Army and 70 Army had seized three bridgeheads over the Oder south of Stettin, and over the next three days Rokossovsky was able link these bridgeheads into a single lodgement. Attacking nearer to Schwedt, 49 Army was less successful. By late on 25 April, both 65 Army and 70 Army had broken out of their Oder bridgehead and had advanced to the Randow where the Germans were unable to put up a stable defence line and from where III Pz Army was cut off from Berlin.

By 22 April IX Army's position was becoming desperate. It had lost Cottbus to 3 Gds Army, and Soviet forces had broken through south of Frankfurt. STAVKA had ordered Zhukov and Konev to complete the encirclement of the German forces still holding the Oder line between Frankfurt and Guben within the forests to the southeast of Berlin in order to prevent them from reinforcing the city's defences. Late in the day, Busse was given permission to pull back to the Spree in the Beeskow area in order to free up forces for a link up with XII Army. On 23 April Hitler ordered Weidling to assume responsibility for the defence of the capital and to make his forces available for the defence of the eastern and south-eastern approaches, the rest of the city being defended by Hitler Youth, SS and *Volkssturm* formations. Busse had wanted to use Weidling's corps to defend his own northern flank. Hitler's decision meant that IX Army would almost certainly be surrounded, and the next day Zhukov's 8 Gds Army and 1 Gds Tank Army linked up with Konev's 28 Army and 3 Gds Tank Army at Bohnsdorf in the south-eastern suburbs of the capital, isolating 200,000 troops of Busse's command west of Beeskow.

By the evening of 22 April, 1 Ukrainian Front's 4 Gds Tank Army and 1 Belorussian Front's 47 Army were well to the west of the city and only 40km apart; which left not only IX Army but most of IV Pz Army ripe for encirclement. North of the capital Soviet tank forces had reached the Havel below Oranienburg, while to the south, 4 Gds Tank Army had reached Beelitz, and 3 Gds Tank Army had reached Marienfeld and Lankwitz in the southern outskirts of Berlin astride the rear of IV Pz Army. On 25 April the encirclement of Berlin was completed when forces from 1 Belorussian Front and 1 Ukrainian Front met to the northwest of Potsdam. Also on that day elements of Konev's 5 Gds Army crossed the Elbe at Torgau and linked up with US 1 Army, thereby cutting Germany in two.

Berlin was by this time invested on all sides; by 2 Gds Tank Army from the northwest; 3 Shock Army, incorporating 9 Tank Corps, from the northwest and north; 5 Shock Army, incorporating 11 Tank Corps, from the northeast and east; 8 Gds Army and 1 Gds Tank Army from the southeast; 28 Army from the south and 3 Gds Tank Army from the southwest. These forces were organised into mixed battle groups and assault detachments in preparation for the impending street fighting. Weidling, as the Berlin garrison commander, had orders to hold the city at all costs and Hitler, against the strong advice of his inner circle, made the decision to stay in Berlin. Henceforth the *Wehrmacht*'s absolute priority was to be the relief of the capital.

Having split the German armies involved in the defence of Berlin into three isolated groups, STAVKA planned to annihilate them. Zhukov and Konev strengthened their forces to the southeast of Berlin to prevent a breakout by the encircled German divisions of IX Army in the area of forests and lakes west of Beeskow. To deal with the Beeskow grouping Zhukov, on 25 April, committed his reserve 3 Army towards Storkow and Mittenwalde; 69 Army to push south and southeast from the Oder near Frankfurt to the bend of the Spree; and 33 Army to strike due west from Beeskow. Konev had a long and exposed right flank between Guben and Zossen, with only 3 Gds Army and part of 28 Army to secure it; though he did create a reserve from one of 13 Army's rifle corps.

Despite the hopelessness of Germany's position, Hitler continued to issue orders to continue the conflict and to try to restore a viable front in the east. Admiral Karl Doenitz, commander in chief of the *Kriegsmarine*, was given responsibility for all forces in the northern part of Germany; General August Winter, a senior OKW staff officer, was given command of all forces in the south; and Schoerner, while retaining command of Army Group Centre, was appointed commander in chief of the German Army. OKH was disbanded and OKW assumed direct command responsibility for all land forces, east and west. Schoerner was ordered to mount an offensive with Army Group Centre northwards through Bautzen to link up with the eastern flank of IX Army; Steiner was to attack south with his three divisions (25 Pz Gdr Div, 7 Pz Div and 3 Naval Div) from northwest of Oranienburg; and XII Army was to attack to the northeast from Belzig in order to link up with an offensive to the west by IX Army, and from there the two armies were to advance north on a broad front to Berlin. Desperate though these orders were, the offensives had some limited success. Schoerner made some progress at Bautzen, and XII Army successfully defended its staging area around Belzig. Even Steiner, with only 25 Pz Gdr Div immediately available for the offensive, managed to establish a bridgehead over the Havel west of Oranienburg. However, a breakout attempt by IX Army from the Beeskow encirclement on 26 April was contained, and subsequent breakout attempts over the next several days were repulsed. By 27 April Army Group Centre's advance had stalled more than 60km from IX

Army as the strength of Busse's army began to dwindle in its unsuccessful attempts to break out to the west. The next day the last attempt by IX Army to break out of its encirclement failed and the pocket, which had been shrunk to the bend of the Spree southeast of Berlin by 69 Army, 33 Army and 3 Gds Army, was eliminated on 1 May; the Germans losing 60,000 killed. Only 25,000 of the encircled German troops from IX Army had been able to break through the Soviet lines, predominantly from the area of the village of Halbe some 35km west of Beeskow, to link up with XII Army.

In the north Manteuffel, having expended his last reserves, was unable to stop 2 Belorussian Front's forces from breaking through his centre south of Prenzlau and racing west to the Elbe. OKW ordered the XXI Army Headquarters (based on the former IV Army Headquarters staff and commanded by Tippelskirch) to use its two subordinated regiments, neither of which was available, to contain Rokossovsky's breakthrough. Late in the evening of 27 April, Manteuffel reported to Heinrici that, in defiance of orders, half his divisions had stopped fighting, and that 100,000 of his men were fleeing west. In the early hours of 29 April Heinrici, more concerned with saving his men than indulging in unrealistic plans to relieve Berlin with troops that, in large part, had absented themselves from the chain of command, reported to Field Marshal Wilhelm Keitel at OKW that Rokossovsky's forces had reached the Havel on Manteuffels's right flank. Heinrici was then summarily dismissed by Keitel for failing to carry out orders, and command of the disintegrating Army Group Vistula passed to Manteuffel. Manteuffel refused the command, and Tippelskirch, in the process of taking over Steiner's forces northwest of the Berlin encirclement, was prevailed on to accept the army group command temporarily until Col-Gen Kurt Student could be transferred from the west.

Meanwhile the reduction of Berlin's defences had begun. The defence of Berlin was a patchy affair. In some districts fanatical resistance was offered, but in many areas resistance was somewhat perfunctory. On 27 April Zhukov's men alone cleared over 600 city blocks. The devastation of Berlin's infrastructure owed more to months of aerial bombardment by the Western Allies than it did to the ground fighting. By the evening of 27 April, the German defenders had been squeezed into a narrow east-west belt 16 km long and less than 5 km wide; though on this day 4 Gds Tank Army, and in particular its 5 Gds Mech Corps, had difficulty in holding a determined attempt by XII Army to break into Berlin in the Brandenburg – Beelitz – Treuenbrietzen area. By 28 April the Berlin garrison had been pushed back into an area 15km long by a few kilometres wide, and during the course of the next day it was split into three parts. On 29 April, only in the XII Army area was the news less than catastrophic for OKW. XX Corps advanced 25km to edge of Lake Schwielow southwest of Potsdam, but its flanks were not secure and it was still more than 30km from Berlin. The assault on the *Reichstag*, a building viewed by most Russians as the symbolic heart of the 'fascist beast', began early on the morning of 30 April, and was undertaken without a pause by 3 Shock Army's 79 Rifle Corps until the morning of 2 May.[19] Hitler committed suicide on 30 April after learning that XII Army would be unable to break through to the capital. In his 'testament', written in the early hours of the previous day, he had appointed Doenitz as his posthumous successor. The news of Hitler's death did not become widely known until 1 May. That evening XX Corps, after gathering 30,000

---

19 The Soviet victory banner was first raised over the *Reichstag* at 2250 on 30 April.

survivors from IX Army, began to pull back from its forward positions. When Doenitz enquired whether Schoerner could withdraw his forces west, Schoerner advised that if he tried to move, his army group would disintegrate. A surrender delegation from Weidling was received at Chuikov's headquarters in the early hours of 2 May. The Berlin garrison formally surrendered at 07:00. All resistance was supposed to cease by 15:00, but sporadic fighting continued for a further two days.

In the 'Berlin Strategic Offensive Operation' the Red Army, including the Polish contingent, suffered more than 360,000 casualties, 81,000 of them fatalities.

Unconditional Surrender

As the Soviet offensive against Berlin raged, fighting continued on the southern axis. By the end of the second week in April, at the time of the fall of Vienna, VI SS Pz Army, VI Army and II Pz Army had an almost continuous front in the outlying Alps from west of St. Polten to the Drava east of Varaždin. Once the Soviets had crossed the Austrian border, OKH noted a relaxation of the pressure on VI Army and II Pz Army since, in Army Group South's southern sector, there were no further objectives that STAVKA was willing to make a significant effort to take. On the right bank of the Danube the front stabilised from Tullin to St. Polten south across Austria to Bad Gleichenberg, to the Drava at Varaždin and then along the Drava and Danube. In the second half of April, the Soviets shifted the weight of their offensive north of the Danube.

On 15 April, 4 Ukrainian Front resumed its offensive attacking towards Ostrava from north, east and south, aiming to move on southwest into central Czechoslovakia and to capture the important German military arsenal in Olomouc. However, Eremenko's offensive proceeded at a far slower pace than STAVKA had anticipated. On 22 April, badly behind schedule, 60 Army took Opava, and it was not until 30 April that 38 Army and 1 Gds Army took Ostrava, while 18 Army and Czech 1 Corps took the railway junction at Žilina. On the morning of 23 April, Malinovsky launched an offensive towards Brno with 53 Army and Pliev's group. By noon, the depleted 6 Gds Tank Army, with just 164 armoured fighting vehicles, was committed to exploit the breakthrough using 2 Gds Mech Corps and 9 Gds Mech Corps as first echelon. Kravchenko's army moved north of Brno and Pliev's group, only slightly weaker in armour than the tank army, moved south of the town, while 53 Army pushed on Brno from the east. The next day Kravchenko committed 5 Gds Tank Corps to break into the town but the corps lost most of its meagre complement of 44 armoured vehicles to German counter-attacks. It took a further two days for Pliev, Managorov and Kravchenko to clear the town, but its capture broke the back of the German defences in eastern Czechoslovakia, leaving I Pz Army at risk of envelopment east of Olomouc.

After the crossing of the Czech border by elements of US 3 Army on 30 April, and the fall of Berlin a few days later, STAVKA set 1 Ukrainian Front the task of co-operating with 4 Ukrainian Front and 2 Ukrainian Front in a drive on Prague. On 1 May Konev was ordered to hand over his Berlin positions to Zhukov and to concentrate his right flank on the Mulde. The next day Malinovsky was ordered to deploy his forces west in the direction of Prague. STAVKA planned attacks on both flanks of Army Group Centre from northwest of Dresden and from south of Brno in order to take Prague and to isolate Schoerner's forces east of the city. Meanwhile 4

Ukrainian Front and the right flank of 2 Ukrainian Front would squeeze I Pz Army in the Olomouc area where a pocket was developing east of the town, with Soviet forces advancing from north and south, and from which I Pz Army was trying to escape. The operations were scheduled to commence by 7 May but on 4 May, as US troops reached the Enns and cut off Army Group Centre from its most important supply depots, General Dwight Eisenhower advised Antonov that US 3 Army intended to cross the Czech border along the south-western frontier and to advance around 30km to the line Karlsbad – Pilsen – České Budějovice. He added that if circumstances required, US forces would advance to the Vltava (Moldau) river line that ran through Prague. Antonov advised that the latter proposal was unacceptable because the Red Army had prepared an offensive through Dresden and down both banks of the river into Prague. The next day an uprising began in the Czech capital and Konev was ordered to begin his operation on 6 May. By then the German lines had been pushed back south of Torgau, south of Liegnitz through Nysa to south of Opava, west of Brno and down the Jihlava river to the Austrian border. Also on that day the 40,000 strong garrison in the Breslau pocket surrendered.

The decision by Doenitz to continue the war into May when Germany was cut in two, Hitler was dead, Berlin was in Soviet hands and German forces on the southern flank in Italy were in the process of surrendering, is explainable by his knowledge of the Allied delineation lines and his desire to ensure that the maximum number of German troops and civilians would have the opportunity to surrender to the Western Allies. There was little prospect of buying time by military means, but a series of local and partial surrenders involving protracted negotiations over each, might allow a large number of Germans to migrate to the west bank of the Elbe. The area in which an accommodation was most urgently required was in the north, where Army Group Vistula had been pushed almost back-to-back with the new Army Group Northwest command facing the British 21 Army Group. On 2 May the situation became even more critical when an armoured division from British 2 Army, having established a bridgehead over the Elbe at Luneburg upriver from Hamburg at the end of April, broke out and raced almost unopposed to Luebeck on the Baltic, thereby severing Army Group Vistula's line of retreat into Schleswig-Holstein, and refuge in the British zone. By then most of what was left of Army Group Vistula had been squeezed into a narrow corridor between the armies of the Soviets and the Western Allies, and as forward elements of 70 Army made contact with British forces southeast of Wismar on 3 May, Manteuffel and Tippelskirch had already begun the process of surrendering their armies.

Accordingly, on 3 May Doenitz sent Admiral Hans-Georg von Friedeburg to Field Marshal Bernard Montgomery's headquarters on Luneburg Heath to offer the military surrender of all northern Germany in exchange for the continued evacuation by sea of the population from the Baltic coast, for which British goodwill would be required. Friedeburg began by offering the surrender of Army Group Vistula, which Montgomery refused since these forces faced the Soviets, but Montgomery suggested that all forces on his northern and western flank should offer a tactical surrender, which he could accept. Friedeburg also raised the issue of the refugees, and suggested that Montgomery could adjust the speed of his advance in co-ordination with the pace of German westward retreat; this Montgomery also refused. He did however promise to accept the surrender of all Germans appearing from the east, and that he would be 'no monster' over the refugee problem. Friedeburg returned to report to Doenitz, and revisited Montgomery the next day ready to sign the instrument of surrender. Friedeburg then set out for Rheims to meet with Eisenhower on 5 May, where he was joined by Alfred Jodl the next day. Meanwhile, on 4 May, Wenck surrendered the forces under his command on the middle Elbe to US 9 Army; IX Army's and XII Army's forces breaking into small groups to make their way west across the river to surrender piecemeal over the subsequent few days. When it became obvious to the German delegation in Rheims that only unconditional surrender on both the Western and Eastern fronts would be acceptable, they were authorised by Doenitz to sign. The formal surrender was agreed and signed in the early hours of 7 May, and was announced on German radio soon after noon that day. The main clause read, "We the undersigned, acting by authority of the German High Command, hereby surrender unconditionally to the Supreme Commander, Allied Expeditionary Force and simultaneously to the Soviet High Command all forces on land sea and in the air which are at this date under German control. This act of surrender is without prejudice to, and will be superseded by, any general instrument of surrender imposed by, or on behalf of, the United Nations and is applicable to Germany and the German armed forces as a whole."

While these events were taking place, Stalin was taking steps to ensure that Prague would be secured by Soviet forces. Konev's main thrust, launched on schedule on 6 May, was along the west bank of the Elbe and the Vltava towards Dresden and Zatec, the latter town being the headquarters location of Army Group Centre. This thrust was conducted by the two Guards tank armies and by 13 Army, 3 Gds Army and 5 Gds Army; the task of taking Dresden being assigned to 5 Gds Army. Polish 2 Army attacked farther east, outflanking Dresden from the southeast, while still farther east 28 Army and 52 Army would advance on Prague via Zittau. Konev's offensive made rapid progress, with much of Army Group Centre's headquarters staff being captured in Zatec. Schoerner escaped capture and described the universal surrender order from Keitel as enemy propaganda, vowing to go on fighting in the Sudeten Mountains. In fact Schoerner was making plans to desert his troops, change into civilian clothing and, after ordering his forces to cease hostilities against the Americans, to flee to Austria. This he did the next day as the Soviet offensive against Army Group Centre continued and 3 Ukrainian Front joined in, attacking northwest towards Pilsen with 7 Gds Army, 9 Gds Army, 46 Army, Pliev's group and the threadbare 6 Gds Tank Army. Having seen 9 Gds Army diverted to other tasks, Malinovsky was left with just 40 Army and Rumanian 4 Army available for the Olomouc axis, though the main burden of this brief offensive would be borne by the armies of 4 Ukrainian Front.

Although the articles of formal surrender were signed in Rheims in the early hours of 7 May, a second similar formal signing was to be made in the Soviet sector on 8 May, and all active operations were to cease at 23:00 on 8 May 1945. Yet the final surrender, by *Luftwaffe* General Hans-Juergen Stumpff, as Doenitz's representative, was not presented to Zhukov at Karlshorst until 9 May, by which time Soviet forces were firmly in command of Prague. According to OKW records, the strength of the *Ostheer*'s forces at the time of surrender was 1,510,000; 180,000 in the south-eastern theatre, 430,000 in Army Group Austria, 600,000 in Army Group Centre, 100,000 in the Army of East Prussia and 200,000 in Army Group Courland.

Army Group Centre, forced into a pocket approximately 150 kilometres square to the east of Prague, continued the fight through the next day, surrendering only at midnight on 10 May. With this surrender of Germany's last active combat force, the Second World War came to an end in Europe.

12

The Butcher's Bill

The Second World War cost the lives of tens of millions of people and blighted the lives of hundreds of millions more. No precise count of the fatalities resulting from the war will ever be made. Such was the degree of devastation resulting from the war in certain countries and regions that even making an estimate of the deaths wrought by the conflict becomes problematic. Consequently it is not even possible to estimate the total number of fatalities to the nearest million. An estimate in the range 55-60 million, a figure that includes approximately 10 million Chinese deaths from the Sino-Japanese war that began in 1937, could be subject to challenge. Even in countries where the monitoring of the national casualty rate remained robust throughout the conflict, fatality figures depend to some degree on how deaths due directly to the war are defined. If deaths resulting from secondary effects of the conflict, such as regional famines, are included, the above figure could increase by at least 10 million.

It is, however, beyond challenge that the Soviet Union suffered the greatest loss of any nation. Around half the fatalities resulting from the war, some 27 million, were Soviet citizens. In the Soviet Union the majority of the fatalities were civilian.

As a consequence of the need in each combatant nation to maintain accurate information on available military resources, losses of military personnel in Eastern Europe are known with a greater degree of precision than those of civilians. The most detailed published assessment of Soviet military casualties has been that undertaken by G F Krivosheev et al (Soviet Casualties and Combat Losses in the Twentieth Century, London 1997). In this work Krivosheev gives a fairly precise figure for Soviet military fatalities in the Great Patriotic War – 8,668,400. Of this number, which includes deaths among state security and internal service troops, 6,329,600 are ascribed to military personnel killed in action or mortally wounded. The rest are personnel missing in action and prisoners of war who did not return after the war (all presumed dead), and personnel who died from non-combat causes such as illness or accident. Krivosheev's total figure for the Great Patriotic War includes 12,000 personnel lost during the brief Manchurian campaign, but does not include more than 126,000 Soviet fatalities from the Finnish Winter War of 1939/40.

With more than 5 million dead from a pre-war population of 35 million, Poles, in proportional terms, suffered even higher losses than the Soviet Union. The vast majority of the Polish dead were civilians, more than half of them Jews.

Statistics on German losses grew increasingly unreliable during the closing months of the war as Germany's meticulous bureaucracy began to disintegrate. The total number of German war dead was around 6.45 million. This figure includes several hundred thousand Germans who were the victims of Nazi persecution and extermination policies, and it includes German prisoners of war who died in captivity, including those who died after the conclusion of hostilities. Ethnic German civilians killed after the conclusion of hostilities are not included in the total.

The most extensive study of German military casualties that has been undertaken is that of Dr. Ruediger Overmans (*Deutsche Militärische Verluste im Zweiten Weltkrieg*, München, 2000). From this study, a total of 5,318,000 deaths among the *Wehrmacht*, *Waffen* SS, and paramilitary support forces are reported. The military fatalities are for German nationals, Austrians and other ethnic Germans, but excludes more than 200,000 personnel of Soviet origin who died while fighting as part of the German military structure. Of the German military fatalities incurred up to the end of hostilities, around 75% occurred on the Eastern Front.

Among the other nations involved in the fighting on the Eastern Front, Slovak forces fought on the side of the Axis in the early period of the war and Czech forces fought as part of the Red Army in the war's final stages. Yet the great majority of Czechoslovakia's war dead were Jewish civilians numbering more than a quarter of a million. Most of Italy's 450,000 fatalities occurred in the Mediterranean theatre and on home territory. Partisans in Yugoslavia and Greece fought among themselves with as much determination as they fought the Germans. Total Greek and Yugoslav fatalities exceeded 1.3 million. Among Germany's three main allies in Eastern Europe, fatalities exceeded 1.5 million – Finnish war dead, including losses from the Winter War of 1939/40, were less than 100,000, only a small minority of which were civilians; but of the total of Rumanian and Hungarian fatalities approximately half were Jewish non-combatants.

The fighting on the Eastern Front was, from the beginning, particularly brutal, with little quarter being given by either side. In comparison, the fighting that took place in the West was described as 'sport' by some German soldiers who had experienced the war in both theatres. This description was not to suggest that the war in the West was an entertainment, but that it was conducted within the boundaries of certain rules that were largely observed by both sides; rules based on the Geneva Convention that included the treatment of prisoners and the collection of wounded from the battlefield. In the East, other than a tacit agreement not to initiate first use of chemical weapons, there were no rules. The pitiless nature of the war in Eastern Europe extended far beyond the battlefield – it extended to the prisoner-of-war camps, to the wantonly devastated cities, towns and villages, and most particularly to the genocidal persecution by the Nazis of the so-called *Untermenschen*. The brutality of the conflict in the East, in combination with its enormous scale, accounted for the unprecedented magnitude of the death toll in that vast region between the Elbe and the Volga.

Appendix I

Place Names

Pre-war Name	Later Post-war Name
Allenstein	Olsztyn
Altdamm	Dąbie
Akkerman	Bilhorod Dnistrovky
Arnswalde	Choszczno
Belgorod	Białogard
Beltsy	Bălți
Bendery	Tighina
Beuthen	Bytom
Breslau	Wrocław
Bromberg	Bydgoszcz
Bunzlau	Bolesławiec
Danzig	Gdańsk
Deutsch Eylau	Iława
Deutsch Krone	Wałcz
Dunapentele	Dunaújváros
Dvinsk	Daugavpils
Elbing	Elbląg
Falkenburg	Złocieniec
Gotenhafen	Gdynia
Gollnow	Goleniów
Graudenz	Grudziądz
Grottkau	Grodków
Gruenberg	Zielona Góra
Gumbinnen	Gusev
Gzhatsk	Gagarin
Heiligenbeil	Mamonovo
Kalinin	Tver
Karlsbad	Karlovy Vary
Kolberg	Kołobrzeg
Koenigsberg	Kaliningrad
Kosel	Kędzierzyn-Koźle
Kovno	Kaunas
Krasnogvardeisk	Gatchina
Liegnitz	Legnica
Leningrad	Saint Petersburg
Linde	Borne Sulinowo
Loetzen	Giżycko
Marienburg	Malbork

Memel	Klaipėda
Mitau	Jelgava
Mogilev	Mahilyow
Mohrungen	Morąg
Mühlhausen	Gvardeyskoye
Neustadt	Prudnik
Neustettin	Szczecinek
Okuninovo	Kosachivka
Olita	Alytus
Oppeln	Opole
Orjonikidze	Vladikavkaz
Penzig	Pieńsk
Pilkallen	Poltavskoye
Pillau	Baltiysk
Propoisk	Slawharad (Slavograd)
Proskurov	Khmelnitsky
Rummelsburg	Miastko
Šahy	Ipolyság
Schirwindt	Kudirkos Naumiestis
Stalingrad	Volgograd
Stalino	Donetsk
Stalinogorsk	Novomoskovsk
Stanislav	Ivano-Frankovsk
Stary Bykhov	Bykhaw
Steinau	Ścinawa Mała
Stettin	Szczecin
Taipale	Solovevo
Tali	Paltsevo
Thorn	Toruń
Tilsit	Sovetsk
Vilno	Vilnius
Voroshilovgrad	Luhansk
Voroshilovsk	Stavropol
Vyborg	Viipuri
Zeden	Cedynia

Appendix II

Abbreviations

Nationalities

The nationalities of units are German or Soviet unless otherwise stated. The abbreviations used for other nationalities are:

Rum -Rumanian; It -Italian; Hun – Hungarian.

Operational Units

Units below army or corps level have been abbreviated as follows:

Div – Division; Rgt – Regiment; Bgd – Brigade; Btn – Battalion

Operation Unit Types

AA – Anti-aircraft or Aviation Artillery; Abn – Airborne; Cav – Cavalry; Gds – Guards; Gdr – Grenadier; Inf – Infantry; Lt – Light; LwF – *Luftwaffe* Field; Mech – Mechanised; Mot – Motorised; Mtn – Mountain; Pz – Panzer.

Ranks

Senior ranks in the German and Soviet armed forces have been abbreviated. These abbreviations in descending order of rank for land force commanders are tabulated below. Note that in the Red Army the rank of Colonel-General (*General Polkovnick*) is a lower rank than that of Army General (*General Armii*) whereas in the German army Colonel-General (*Generaloberst*) is a higher rank than that of General. In the German army the rank of General is associated with a particular operational function; General of Infantry, General of Artillery, General of Panzer Troops, etc.

Red Army Ground Force Ranks:

Rank	Term used
Marshal Sovetskogo Soyuza,	
Glavnyi Marshal or	Marshal
Marshal	
General Armii	General
General Polkovnick	Col-Gen
General Leytenant	Lt-Gen
General Major	Major-Gen
Polkovnick	Col

German Army Ranks:

Rank	Term Used
Generalfeldmarschall	Field Marshal
Generaloberst	Col-Gen
General der Infanterie etc	General
Generalleutnant	Lt-Gen
Generalmajor	Major-Gen
Oberst	Col

Other services within the armed forces of the main combatants had somewhat different ranking structures. For services involved in ground combat operations, these ranks, where they differ from the above, have been identified as the equivalent army rank.

Other abbreviations and organisational acronyms are explained in the text.

German Divisional Structure 1941

The Panzer Division

At the heart of each panzer division was a panzer regiment of two or three panzer battalions, each panzer battalion being composed of four tank companies. The authorised strength of a tank company was 22 tanks, though actual numbers were generally less than this. A panzer division also contained a motorised infantry brigade of one motorcycle battalion and four infantry battalions, the latter grouped into two motorised infantry regiments of two battalions each. The infantry battalions each had three motorised rifle companies, a machine gun company and a heavy (mortar) company. Regimental support included a headquarters company (motorcycle, engineering and signals platoons) and a motorised infantry gun company (six 7.5cm and two 15cm infantry guns). At divisional level artillery support was provided by a motorised artillery regiment with twenty-four cannons and howitzers. In addition to the usual signals, services and engineering support, panzer divisions also included a reconnaissance battalion of armoured cars and motorcycles, and an anti-tank battalion (typically thirty-six anti-tank guns frequently with a battery of 2cm anti-aircraft guns attached).

During the Polish and French campaigns panzer divisions included two panzer regiments, each of two battalions, subordinated to a panzer brigade headquarters. During 1941 this intermediate headquarters between panzer regiment and panzer division was in the process of being phased out.

The Infantry Division

A German infantry division was based on nine infantry battalions grouped into three infantry regiments. The infantry battalion was composed of three rifle companies with light machine guns and light mortars, and a machine gun company with heavy machine guns and medium mortars. At regimental level there was an engineer platoon; a cavalry platoon, which was primarily for reconnaissance; a fully motorised anti-tank company of twelve 3.7cm *Panzerabwehrkanone* 36 (Pak 36) or 5cm Pak 38 guns; an infantry gun company of six 7.5cm and two 15cm infantry guns; and a supply column. In addition to the usual signals, services and engineering support, infantry divisions also included a reconnaissance company (horses and bicycles), an artillery regiment (typically twenty-four 10.5cm howitzers, twelve 10.5cm cannons, and twelve 15cm howitzers) and an anti-tank battalion similar in composition to that in the panzer divisional structure.

The regimental infantry guns were relatively short-range weapons and were often used in direct fire support of the infantry. Indirect fire support was more generally conducted at divisional level. In the infantry divisions, artillery pieces were generally horse-drawn.

The Motorised Division

The motorised division was essentially an infantry division with a substantial pool of motor vehicles to provide a greater degree of mobility to the division's combat units (infantry and artillery) and to its support services. With 16,400 personnel it was slightly smaller than an infantry division, having only two infantry regiments but incorporating two independent motorcycle battalions.

Typical Soviet Army Structure in the Initial Phase of the War

Army Headquarters
  Rifle Corps
  Rifle Corps
    Rifle Division
    Rifle Division
    Rifle Division
      Rifle Regiment
      Rifle Regiment
      Rifle Regiment
        Rifle Battalion
        Rifle Battalion
        Rifle Battalion
        Regimental Gun Battery
        Heavy Mortar Battery
        Anti-tank Battery
        Companies of personnel for transport, signals, recon, pioneers, AA and medical
      Field Artillery Regiment
        Field Artillery Battalion x 2 (each 12 guns and howitzers)
      Howitzer Regiment
        Light Howitzer Battalion x 2 (each 12 howitzers)
        Medium Howitzer Battalion (12 howitzers)
      Battalions of personnel for transport, signals, recon, pioneers, AA, anti-tank and medical
    Corps Artillery Regiment (48 medium guns and howitzers)
  Mechanised Corps
    Tank Division (up to 375 tanks)
    Tank Division
      Tank Regiment
      Tank Regiment
      Motorised Rifle Regiment
    Motorised Rifle Division
      Motorised Rifle Regiment x 3
      Artillery Regiment
      Battalions of personnel for transport, signals, recon, pioneers, AA, anti-tank and medical
    Motorcycle Regiment

Corps Artillery Regiment
Howitzer (or Heavy Howitzer) Regiment (48 medium or heavy howitzers)
Anti-tank Brigade (120 anti-tank guns)
Anti-Aircraft Battalion x 2
Air Support Division (mixed aircraft)
Engineering Support Regiment (or Battalion)

Appendix V

Axis Order of Battle for Operation Barbarossa 1941

Army Group North – Field Marshal Ritter von Leeb
- XVIII Army – Col-Gen Georg von Kuechler
  - I Corps
    - 11 Inf Div
    - 21 Inf Div
  - XXXVIII Corps
    - 1 Inf Div
    - 58 Inf Div
  - XXVI Corps
    - 291 Inf Div
    - 61 Inf Div
    - 217 Inf Div
- IV Pz Group – Col-Gen Erich Hoepner
  - XLI Pz Corps – General Georg-Hans Reinhardt
    - 1 Pz Div
    - 6 Pz Div
    - 36 Mot Div
    - 269 Inf Div
  - LVI Pz Corps – General Erich von Manstein
    - 8 Pz Div
    - 3 Mot Div
    - 3 SS Mot Div (*Totenkopf*)
    - 290 Inf Div
- XVI Army – Col-Gen Ernst Busch
  - II Corps
    - 121 Inf Div
    - 12 Inf Div
    - 32 Inf Div
    - 253 Inf Div (res)
  - XXVIII Corps
    - 122 Inf Div
    - 123 Inf Div
  - X Corps
    - 30 Inf Div
    - 126 Inf Div
- Army Group Reserve
  - XXIII Corps
    - 206 Inf Div
    - 251 Inf Div
    - 254 Inf Div
  - L Corps from reserves later (two infantry divisions)

Army Group Centre – Field Marshal Fedor von Bock
- III Pz Group – Col-Gen Hermann Hoth
  - XXXIX Pz Corps - General Rudolf Schmidt
    - 7 Pz Div
    - 20 Pz Div
    - 14 Mot Div
    - 20 Mot Div
  - LVII Pz Corps – General Adolf Kuntzen
    - 12 Pz Div
    - 19 Pz Div
    - 18 Mot Div
  - VI Corps
    - 6 Inf Div
    - 26 Inf Div
  - V Corps
    - 5 Inf Div
    - 35 Inf Div
- IX Army – Col-Gen Adolf Strauss
  - XX Corps (subsequently transferred to IV Army)
    - 256 Inf Div
    - 162 Inf Div

304

VIII Corps
  8 Inf Div
  28 Inf Div
  161 Inf Div
XLII Corps
  87 Inf Div
  102 Inf Div
  129 Inf Div
XXIII Corps from reserves later
IV Army – Field Marshal Hans
  Günther von Kluge
  XIII Corps
    17 Inf Div
    78 Inf Div
  VII Corps
    7 Inf Div
    23 Inf Div
    258 Inf Div
    268 Inf Div
  IX Corps
    137 Inf Div
    263 Inf Div
    292 Inf Div
  XLIII Corps
    131 Inf Div
    134 Inf Div
    252 Inf Div
II Pz Group – Col-Gen Heinz
  Guderian
  XLVI Pz Corps - General
    Heinrich von Vietinghoff
    10 Pz Div
    2 SS Mot Div (*Das Reich*)
    Grossdeutschland Inf Rgt
  XLVII Pz Corps – General
    Joachim Lemelsen
    17 Pz Div
    18 Pz Div
    29 Mot Div
    167 Inf Div
  XXIV Pz Corps – General
    Leo Freiherr Geyr von
    Schweppenburg
    3 Pz Div - Lt-Gen Walter
    Model
    4 Pz Div

  10 Mot Div
  267 Inf Div
  1 Cav Div
Reserve
  255 Inf Div
Army Group Reserve
  LIII Corps
    293 Inf Div
  XXXV Corps from reserves later (four
    infantry divisions)
  XLII Corps from reserves later (two
    infantry and one motorised
    light division)

Army Group South – Field Marshal Gerd von Rundstedt
VI Army – Field Marshal Walter von
  Reichenau
  XVII Corps
    56 Inf Div
    62 Inf Div
  XLIV Corps
    9 Inf Div
    297 Inf Div
  Reserve
    LV Corps
    158 Inf Div
I Pz Group – Col-Gen Ewald von
  Kleist
  III Pz Corps – General Eberhard
    von Mackensen
    14 Pz Div
    44 Inf Div
    298 Inf Div
  XIV Pz Corps – General Gustav
    von Wietersheim
    9 Pz Div
    16 Pz Div
    5 SS Mot Div (*Wiking*)
  XLVIII Pz Corps – General
    Werner Kempf
    11 Pz Div
    57 Inf Div
    75 Inf Div
  XXIX Corps
    111 Inf Div

299 Inf Div
Reserve
  13 Pz Div
  16 Mot Div
  25 Mot Div
  1 SS Mot Div (*Leibstandarte SS Adolf Hitler*)
XVII Army – General Karl-Heinrich von Stuelpnagel
IV Corps
  24 Inf Div
  71 Inf Div
  262 Inf Div
  295 Inf Div
  296 Inf Div
XLIX Mtn Corps
  1 Mtn Div
  68 Inf Div
  257 Inf Div
LII Corps
  101 Light Div
Slovakian Expeditionary Corps
  1 Slovak Inf Div
  2 Slovak Inf Div
Reserve
  100 Light Div
  97 Light Div
XI Army – Col-Gen Eugen Ritter von Schobert
Rum Mtn Corps
  7 Rum Inf Div
  1 Rum Mtn Bgd
  2 Rum Mtn Bgd
  4 Rum Mtn Bgd
  8 Rum Cav Bgd
XXX Corps
  198 Inf Div
  14 Rum Inf Div
  5 Rum Cav Bgd
XI Corps
  76 Inf Div
  239 Inf Div
LIV Corps
  50 Inf Div
  170 Inf Div
Reserve

22 Inf Div
99 Light Div
Army Group Reserve
Rum III Army Headquarters – Lt-Gen Petre Dumitrescu
Rum IV Army – Lt-Gen Nicolae Ciupercă
III Rum Corps
  35 Rum Inf Div
  11 Rum Inf Div
  15 Rum Inf Div
V Rum Corps
  Rum Gds Inf Div
  21 Rum Inf Div
  Rum Frontier Gds Div
XI Rum Corps
  1 Rum Fortification Bgd
  2 Rum Fortification Bgd
II Rum Corps
  9 Rum Inf Div
  10 Rum Inf Div

In addition to the above OKH also had in the Army Group South area the headquarters of XXXIV Corps together with 4 Mtn Div and 125 Inf Div, and available for later use were a further four infantry divisions and LI Corps Headquarters. In the Army Group Centre area the headquarters of II Army under Col-Gen Maximilian Freiherr von Weichs would become available after the commencement of operations. Each army group also had available three security divisions but these were neither trained nor equipped for conventional combat duties.

Appendix VI

Red Army Order of Battle 22 June 1941

Northwestern Front – Col-Gen F I Kuznetsov
8 Army – Lt-Gen P P Sobennikov
  10 Rifle Corps (3 rifle divisions)
  11 Rifle Corps (2 rifle divisions)
  12 Mech Corps (2 tank divisions and a motorised rifle division)
11 Army – Lt-Gen V I Morosov
  16 Rifle Corps – Major-Gen M S Shumilov (3 rifle divisions)
  29 Rifle Corps (2 rifle divisions)
  3 Mech Corps (2 tank divisions and a motorised rifle division)
  3 rifle divisions reserve
27 Army – Major-Gen N E Berzarin
  22 Rifle Corps (2 rifle divisions)
  26 Rifle Corps (2 rifle divisions)
  2 rifle divisions reserve
Front Reserve – 5 Abn Corps

Western Front – General D G Pavlov
3 Army – Lt-Gen V I Kuznetsov
  4 Rifle Corps (3 rifle divisions)
  11 Mech Corps Major-Gen D K Mostovenko (2 tank divisions and a motorised rifle division)
10 Army – Major-Gen K D Golubev
  1 Rifle Corps (2 rifle divisions)
  5 Rifle Corps (3 rifle divisions)
  6 Mech Corps – Major-Gen M G Khatskilevich (2 tank divisions and a motorised rifle division)
  13 Mech Corps – Major-Gen P N Akhliustin (2 tank divisions and a motorised rifle division)
  6 Cav Corps (2 cavalry divisions)

4 Army – Major-Gen A A Korobkov
  28 Rifle Corps (4 rifle divisions)
  14 Mech Corps – Major-Gen S I Oborin (2 tank divisions and a motorised rifle division)
13 Army – Col-Gen P M Filatov (Headquarters only; army formed 24 June)
Front Reserve
  2 Rifle Corps (2 rifle divisions)
  21 Rifle Corps (3 rifle divisions)
  44 Rifle Corps (2 rifle divisions)
  47 Rifle Corps (3 rifle divisions)
  17 Mech Corps – Major-Gen M P Petrov (2 tank divisions and a motorised rifle division)
  20 Mech Corps – Major-Gen A G Nikitin (2 tank divisions and a motorised rifle division)
  4 Abn Corps – Major-Gen A S Zhadov
  50 Rifle Div

Southwestern Front – Col-Gen M P Kirponos
5 Army – Lt-Gen M I Potapov
  15 Rifle Corps (2 rifle divisions)
  27 Rifle Corps (3 rifle divisions)
  9 Mech Corps – Major-Gen K K Rokossovsky (2 tank divisions and a motorised rifle division)
  22 Mech Corps – Major-Gen S I Kondrusev (2 tank divisions and a motorised rifle division)
6 Army – Lt-Gen I N Muzychenko
  6 Rifle Corps (3 rifle divisions)
  37 Rifle Corps (3 rifle divisions)

4 Mech Corps – Major-Gen A A
  Vlasov (2 tank divisions and a
  motorised rifle division)
15 Mech Corps – Major-Gen I I
  Karpezo (2 tank divisions and
  a motorised rifle division)
5 Cav Corps (2 cavalry divisions)
26 Army – Lt-Gen F I Kostenko
  8 Rifle Corps Major-Gen M G
    Snegov (2 rifle divisions and a
    mountain rifle division)
  8 Mech Corps – Lt-Gen D I
    Riabyshev (2 tank divisions
    and a motorised rifle division)
12 Army – Major-Gen P G Ponedelin
  13 Rifle Corps Major-Gen N K
    Kirillov (3 mountain rifle
    divisions)
  17 Rifle Corps (2 mountain rifle
    divisions and a rifle division)
  16 Mech Corps – Major-Gen A D
    Sokolov (2 tank divisions and
    a motorised rifle division)
Front Reserve
  31 Rifle Corps (3 rifle divisions)
  36 Rifle Corps (3 rifle divisions)
  49 Rifle Corps – Major-Gen A I
    Kornilov (3 rifle divisions)
  55 Rifle Corps (3 rifle divisions)
  19 Mech Corps – Major-Gen NV
    Feklenko (2 tank divisions and
    a motorised rifle division)
  24 Mech Corps – Major-Gen V I
    Chistiakov (2 tank divisions
    and a motorised rifle division)
  1 Abn Corps – Major-Gen M A
    Usenko

**9 Separate Army – Col-Gen Y T
Cherevichenko**
  14 Rifle Corps (2 rifle divisions)
  35 Rifle Corps (2 rifle divisions)
  48 Rifle Corps (2 rifle divisions and a
    mountain rifle division)

2 Mech Corps Lt-Gen I V Novoselsky
  (2 tank divisions and a
  motorised rifle division)
18 Mech Corps (2 tank divisions and
  a motorised rifle division)
2 Cav Corps (2 cavalry divisions)

**The Operational Reserve, formed by an
order of 13 May 1941 comprised:**
16 Army – Major-Gen M F Lukin
    deploying in the Kiev area
  32 Rifle Corps (2 rifle divisions)
  5 Mech Corps (2 tank divisions and a
    motorised rifle division)
19 Army – Lt-Gen I S Konev deploying
    south of Kiev
  25 Rifle Corps (3 rifle divisions)
  34 Rifle Corps (3 rifle divisions)
  26 Mech Corps (2 tank divisions and
    a motorised rifle division)
  38 Rifle Div
20 Army – Lt-Gen F N Remezov
    deploying in the Moscow area
  61 Rifle Corps (3 rifle divisions)
  69 Rifle Corps (3 rifle divisions)
  7 Mech Corps (2 tank divisions and a
    motorised rifle division)
  18 Rifle Div
21 Army –Lt-Gen V F Gerasimenko
    deploying in the Gomel area
  63 Rifle Corps (3 rifle divisions)
  66 Rifle Corps (3 rifle divisions)
  25 Mech Corps (2 tank divisions and
    a motorised rifle division)
22 Army – Major-Gen F A Ershakov
    from STAVKA reserve in the
    Vitebsk area
  51 Rifle Corps (3 rifle divisions)
  62 Rifle Corps (3 rifle divisions)
24 Army – Major-Gen K I Rakutin
    deploying southeast of
    Smolensk
  52 Rifle Corps (3 rifle divisions)
  53 Rifle Corps (3 rifle divisions)
28 Army – Lt-Gen V I Kachalov in transit
    from Archangel to Bryansk

67 Rifle Corps (3 rifle divisions)
     deploying in the Moscow area
45 Rifle Corps (3 rifle divisions)
     deploying in the Zhlobin area
21 Mech Corps (2 tank divisions and
     a motorised rifle division)
     from STAVKA reserve in the
     Idritsa area

In the north along the Finnish and
Norwegian borders were 23 Army
(Lt-Gen M N Gerasimov with five rifle
divisions and a mechanised corps in the
Karelian isthmus facing two Finnish
corps); 7 Army (Lt-Gen F D Gorolenko
with four divisions in Russian Karelia
facing a further two Finnish corps); and
14 Army (Lt-Gen V A Frolov with five
divisions in the Murmansk area facing a
Finnish corps and two German corps).

On 21 June an order was issued for the
creation of an additional army in the
Ukraine. This was 18 Army based on the
Kharkov Military District Headquarters
commanded by Lt-Gen A K Bryevoy.
At the outbreak of hostilities it was no
more than a headquarters but became
operational on 25 June 1941 and was
composed of two corps drawn from
12 Army (17 Rifle Corps and 16 Mech
Corps), one corps from Southwestern
Front reserve (55 Rifle Corps), and one
corps from 9 Army (18 Mech Corps).

Appendix VII

Axis Order of Battle for Operation Blue 1942

Army Group North – Field Marshal Georg von Kuechler
  XVIII Army – General Georg Lindemann
    XXVI Corps
      227 Inf Div
      223 Inf Div
    I Corps
      254 Inf Div
      61 Inf Div
      291 Inf Div
      225 Inf Div (part)
      215 Inf Div
      212 Inf Div (part)
      4 SS Mot Div (*Polizei*)
      81 Inf Div (part)
      20 Mot Div
      1 Inf Div
      121 Inf Div
    L Corps
      225 Inf Div (part)
      285 Inf Div (part)
      385 Inf Div (part)
      212 Inf Div (most)
      5 Mtn Div (part)
    XXVIII Corps
      296 Inf Div
      96 Inf Div
      11 Inf Div
      217 Inf Div
      93 Inf Div
      5 Mtn Div (part)
      21 Inf Div
      12 Pz Div
    XXXVIII Corps
      58 Inf Div
      126 Inf Div

      250 Spanish Inf Div
  XVI Army – Col-Gen Ernst Busch
    XXXIX Pz Corps
      8 Pz Div (plus four infantry regiments from other divisions)
    II Corps
      12 Inf Div
      123 Inf Div
      32 Inf Div
      30 Inf Div
      290 Inf Div
      3 SS Mot Div (*Totenkopf*)
      218 Inf Div
      225 Inf Div (most)
    X Corps
      329 Inf Div
      8 Lt Div
      5 Lt Div
      18 Mot Div
      81 Inf Div (most)
      122 Inf Div (part)
      7 Mtn Div (part)

Army Group Centre – Field Marshal Hans Gunther von Kluge
  LIX Corps
    83 Inf Div
    218 Inf Div (part)
    205 Inf Div
    328 Inf Div (part)
    330 Inf Div
  IX Army – Col-Gen Walter Model
    XXIII Corps
      1 Pz Div
      102 Inf Div
      253 Inf Div

129 Inf Div
110 Inf Div
VI Corps
  339 Inf Div (part)
  26 Inf Div
  6 Inf Div
  256 Inf Div
XXVII Corps
  86 Inf Div
  206 Inf Div
  251 Inf Div
  14 Mot Div
XLVI Pz Corps
  5 Pz Div
  87 Inf Div
  328 Inf Div
Operational Group Esebeck
  2 Pz Div
  246 Inf Div
  197 Inf Div
III Pz Army – Col-Gen Georg-Hans
  Reinhardt
XLI Pz Corps
  342 Inf Div
  36 Mot Div
  161 Inf Div
IX Corps
  35 Inf Div
  78 Inf Div
  252 Inf Div
  7 Inf Div
XX Corps
  255 Inf Div
  258 Inf Div
  292 Inf Div
  183 Inf Div
Reserve 20 Pz Div
IV Army – General Gotthard Heinrici
XII Corps
  268 Inf Div
  98 Inf Div
  260 Inf Div
  263 Inf Div
XLIII Corps
  31 Inf Div
  34 Inf Div

137 Inf Div
LVI Pz Corps
  267 Inf Div
  331 Inf Div
  10 Mot Div
  19 Pz Div
  52 Inf Div
  131 Inf Div
II Pz Army – Col-Gen Rudolf
  Schmidt
LIII Corps
  25 Mot Div
  296 Inf Div
  112 Inf Div
  56 Inf Div
  134 Inf Div
XXXV Corps
  262 Inf Div
  293 Inf Div
  4 Pz Div
XLVII Pz Corps
  17 Pz Div
  208 Inf Div
  211 Inf Div
  339 Inf Div (most)
  18 Pz Div
  216 Inf Div (part)
Reserve – 707 Inf Div and 102
  Hun Lt Div
Army Group Reserve 108 Hun Lt Div

**Army Group South – Field Marshal
Fedor von Bock**
II Army – Col-Gen Maximilian von
  Weichs
LV Corps
  45 Inf Div
  95 Inf Div
  299 Inf Div
  Reserve 88 Inf Div and 383
  Inf Div
IV Pz Army – Col-Gen Hermann
  Hoth
XLVIII Pz Corps – General
  Werner Kempf
  Grossdeutschland Mot Div

24 Pz Div
XXIV Pz Corps – Lt-Gen
Willibald Freiherr von
Langermann
377 Inf Div
3 Mot Div
9 Pz Div
XIII Corps
385 Inf Div (most)
82 Inf Div
11 Pz Div
II Hun Army – Lt-Gen Gusztáv Vitéz
Jány
VII Corps
387 Inf Div
6 Hun Inf Div
III Hun Corps
7 Hun Lt Div
9 Hun Lt Div
16 Mot Div
VI Army – General Friedrich Paulus
XXIX Corps
75 Inf Div
168 Inf Div
57 Inf Div
XVII Corps
294 Inf Div
79 Inf Div
113 Inf Div
XL Pz Corps – General Georg
Stumme
23 Mot Div
3 Pz Div
29 Mot Div
336 Inf Div
VIII Corps
376 Inf Div
389 Inf Div
305 Inf Div
Reserve 100 Lt Div
I Pz Army – Col-Gen Ewald von
Kleist
LI Corps
384 Inf Div
62 Inf Div
44 Inf Div

71 Inf Div
297 Inf Div
VI Rum Corps
2 Rum Inf Div
20 Rum Inf Div
4 Rum Inf Div
XLIV Mtn Corps
97 Lt Div
101 Lt Div
257 Inf Div
68 Inf Div
III Pz Corps – General Eberhard
von Mackensen
60 Mot Div
14 Pz Div
16 Pz Div
XI Corps
1 Rum Inf Div
1 Mtn Div
XVII Army – Col-Gen Richard Ruoff
LII Corps
111 Inf Div
Italian Expeditionary Corps
(subsequently XXXV It Corps)
52 It Inf Div (*Torino*)
9 It Inf Div (*Pasubio*)
3 It Mot (*Celere*) Div
XLIX Mtn Corps
198 Inf Div
4 Mtn Div
IV Corps
295 Inf Div
76 Inf Div
94 Inf Div
370 Inf Div
9 Inf Div
XI Army – Field Marshal Erich von
Manstein
Rum Mtn Corps
1 Rum Mtn Div
18 Rum Inf Div
4 Rum Mtn Bgd
8 Rum Cav Bgd
LIV Corps
24 Inf Div
22 Inf Div

50 Inf Div
132 Inf Div
4 Rum Mtn Div
46 Inf Div
Rum Cav Corps
  5 Rum Cav Div
  6 Rum Cav Div
  298 Inf Div
VII Rum Corps
  10 Rum Inf Div
  19 Rum Inf Div
  8 Rum Cav Div
XLII Mtn Corps
  19 Rum Inf Div
  10 Rum Inf Div
  22 Pz Div
  132 Inf Div (most)
  8 Rum Cav Div
XXX Corps
  170 Inf Div
  72 Inf Div
  28 Lt Div
Reserve
XIV Pz Corps – General Gustav
von Wietersheim
  13 Pz Div
  1 SS Mot Div (*Leibstandarte
SS Adolf Hitler*)
  5 SS Mot Div (*Wiking*)
  Slovakian Mot Inf Div
  73 Inf Div
  125 Inf Div
323 Inf Div
340 Inf Div
IV Hun Corps
  1 Hun Lt Div
  10 Hun Lt Div
  12 Hun Lt Div
  13 Hun Lt Div

OKH Reserve in the southern theatre
  371 Inf Div
II It Corps
  2 Mtn (*Sforzesca*) Div
  3 Mtn (*Ravenna*) Div
  5 Inf (*Cosseria*) Div

In addition to the above each army group had numerous specialist and independent battalions, regiments and operational groups and each army group also had three security divisions.

Moving into theatre in the south during July were the Italian Alpine Corps of three Alpine divisions (2nd *Tridentina*; 3rd *Julia*; 4th *Cuneense*); VII Hun Corps of three light divisions (19th, 20th and 23rd) and III Rum Army of three cavalry divisions (1st, 7th, 9th), three mountain divisions (2nd, 3rd, 9th) and three security divisions.

Appendix VIII

Red Army Order of Battle at the time of Operation Blue 1942

Leningrad Front – Lt-Gen L A Govorov

23 Army (6 rifle divisions and a tank brigade)

42 Army (5 rifle divisions)

55 Army (4 rifle divisions and a tank brigade)

Two operational groups with a total of 5 rifle divisions and 3 rifle brigades

Front reserve – a rifle division, a rifle brigade and a tank brigade

Volkhov Front – General K A Meretskov

8 Army (3 rifle divisions and a rifle brigade)

54 Army (10 rifle divisions and 4 tank brigades)

4 Army (3 rifle divisions and 2 tank brigades)

59 Army (6 rifle divisions, a rifle brigade and 2 tank brigades)

52 Army (4 rifle divisions)

Reserve – 2 Shock Army (7 rifle divisions and 6 rifle brigades by 1 July)

Front reserve – 3 rifle divisions, a rifle brigade, 3 cavalry divisions and a tank brigade

Northwestern Front – Lt-Gen P A Kurochkin

11 Army (5 rifle divisions, 8 rifle brigades and a tank brigade)

34 Army (4 rifle divisions and 2 rifle brigades)

53 Army (7 rifle divisions, 2 rifle brigades and 3 tank brigades)

1 Shock Army (5 rifle divisions and 9 rifle brigades)

Reserve – 27 Army (6 rifle divisions and a rifle brigade)

Front reserve – 2 rifle divisions and a tank brigade

Kalinin Front – Col-Gen I S Konev

3 Shock Army (6 rifle divisions, 2 rifle brigades and 2 tank brigades)

4 Shock Army (5 rifle divisions, a rifle brigade and a tank brigade)

22 Army (6 rifle divisions, a rifle brigade and a tank brigade)

41 Army (5 rifle divisions and a tank brigade)

39 Army (7 rifle divisions)

30 Army (7 rifle divisions, 3 rifle brigades and 2 tank brigades)

29 Army (4 rifle divisions)

31 Army (3 rifle divisions and 2 tank brigades)

Reserve – 58 Army (4 rifle divisions and 2 tank brigades)

Front reserve – 2 rifle divisions, 4 cavalry divisions, 2 rifle brigades and a tank brigade

Western Front – General G K Zhukov

20 Army (3 rifle divisions, 4 rifle brigades and 3 tank brigades)

5 Army (7 rifle divisions, 3 rifle brigades and a tank brigade)

33 Army (4 rifle divisions and a tank brigade)

43 Army (4 rifle divisions and a tank
brigade)

49 Army (5 rifle divisions and a tank
brigade)

50 Army (9 rifle divisions and 2 tank
brigades)

10 Army (5 rifle divisions and a tank
brigade)

16 Army (7 rifle divisions, a cavalry
division and 3 tank brigades)

61 Army (7 rifle divisions, a rifle
brigade, a tank corps (3rd)
and 2 tank brigades)

Front reserve – 5 tank corps (5th, 6th,
8th, 9th and 10th), a rifle
division, 2 cavalry divisions
and 2 tank brigades

Bryansk Front – Lt-Gen F I Golikov

3 Army (6 rifle divisions, 2 rifle
brigades and 2 tank brigades)

48 Army (4 rifle divisions, 2 rifle
brigades, a cavalry division
and 2 tank brigades)

13 Army – Major-Gen N P Pukhov
(5 rifle divisions and a tank
brigade)

40 Army – Lt-Gen M A Parsegov (6
rifle divisions, 3 rifle brigades
and 2 tank brigades)

Reserve – 5 Tank Army (2 tank corps
(2nd and 11th), a rifle division
and a tank brigade)

Front reserve – 3 tank corps (1st, 16th
and 17th), 2 rifle divisions, 2
rifle brigades and 5 cavalry
divisions

Southwestern Front – Marshal S K Timoshenko

21 Army – Major-Gen V N Gordov (9
rifle divisions, a tank corps
(13th), a motorised rifle
brigade and a tank brigade)

28 Army – Lt-Gen D I Riabyshev (5 rifle
divisions, a tank corps (23rd)
and 3 tank brigades)

38 Army – Major-Gen K S Moskalenko
(6 rifle divisions, a tank corps
(22nd), 4 tank brigades and a
motorised rifle brigade)

9 Army – Lt-Gen A I Lopatin (8 rifle
divisions, 3 cavalry divisions
and a tank brigade)

Front reserve – 57Army Headquarters,
4 rifle divisions, 3 cavalry
divisions, 3 tank corps
(4th, 14th and 24th), 6 tank
brigades and a motorised rifle
brigade

Southern Front – Lt-Gen R I Malinovsky

37 Army – Major-Gen P M Kozlov
(5 rifle divisions and a tank
brigade)

12 Army – Major-Gen A A Grechko
(5 rifle divisions)

18 Army – Lt-Gen F V Kamkov (4
rifle divisions and a tank
brigade)

56 Army – Major-Gen V V Tsyganov
(4 rifle divisions, a rifle brigade
and a tank brigade)

Reserve – 24 Army (4 rifle divisions)

Front reserve – a rifle division and 3
tank brigades

North Caucasian Front – Marshal S M Budenny

47 Army – Major-Gen G P Kotov
(2 rifle divisions and a rifle
brigade)

51 Army – from July 1942 Major-Gen
N I Trufanov (4 rifle divisions,
2 cavalry divisions and a tank
brigade)

Front reserve – 6 cavalry divisions,
2 rifle brigades and 2 tank
brigades

Transcaucasian Front – General I V Tyulenev

44 Army – Lt-Gen A A Khryashchev
(3 rifle divisions and 2 rifle
brigades)

46 Army – Major-Gen V F Sergatskov
(2 mountain divisions, 4 rifle
divisions and a rifle brigade)

Front reserve – a cavalry division and a
tank brigade

In addition to the above, each Front had numerous specialist and independent battalions, regiments and brigades.

46 Army was one of the reserve armies made operational towards the end of 1941. The third formation of 24 Army became operational on 20 May 1942. The second formation of 27 Army became operational on 1 June 1942. 58 Army was formed on 25 June 1942 but was disbanded less than two months later when its forces were absorbed by 39 Army.

Appendix IX

Axis Order of Battle for Operation Citadel 1943

Army Group North – Field Marshal
Georg von Kuechler
  XVIII Army – Col-Gen Georg
    Lindemann
  III LwF Corps
    9 LwF Div
    10 LwF Div
  L Corps
    250 Spanish Inf Div
    170 Inf Div
    215 Inf Div
  LIV Corps
    21 Inf Div
    24 Inf Div
    254 Inf Div
    4 SS Mot Div (*Polizei*)
    58 Inf Div
  XXVI Corps
    212 Inf Div
    1 Inf Div
    11 Inf Div
    69 Inf Div
    290 Inf Div
    23 Inf Div
    5 Mtn Div
  XXVIII Corps
    96 Inf Div
    61 Inf Div
    81 Inf Div
    12 LwF Div
    225 Inf Div
    132 Inf Div
  I Corps
    13 LwF Div
    227 Inf Div
  XXXVIII Corps
    1 LwF Div

    217 Inf Div
    Reserves 121 Inf Div and 28 Light
    Div
  XVI Army – Field Marshal Ernst
    Busch
  X Corps
    5 Lt Div
    30 Inf Div
    8 Lt Div
    126 Inf Div
    329 Inf Div
  VIII Corps
    21 LwF Div
    122 Inf Div
    32 Inf Div
  II Corps
    331 Inf Div
    12 Inf Div
    218 Inf Div
    123 Inf Div
    93 Inf Div
  Army Group Reserve – 18 Pz Gdr Div
    and 223 Inf Div

Army Group Centre – Field Marshal
Hans Gunther von Kluge
  III Pz Army – Col-Gen Georg-Hans
    Reinhardt
  XLIII Corps
    20 Pz Gdr Div
    205 Inf Div
  LIX Corps
    263 Inf Div
    291 Inf Div
  II LwF Corps
    4 LwF Div
    3 LwF Div

6 LwF Div
2 LwF Div
VI Corps
  206 Inf Div
  330 Inf Div
  87 Inf Div
IV Army – Col-Gen Gotthard
  Heinrici
XXVII Corps
  246 Inf Div
  197 Inf Div
  256 Inf Div
  52 Inf Div
XXXIX Pz Corps
  337 Inf Div
  95 Inf Div
  129 Inf Div
IX Corps
  35 Inf Div
  252 Inf Div
  342 Inf Div
XII Corps
  267 Inf Div
  260 Inf Div
  268 Inf Div
LVI Pz Corps
  131 Inf Div
  14 Inf Div
  321 Inf Div
  Reserve – 183 Inf Div and 253 Inf Div
II Pz Army – General Heinrich
  Cloessner
LV Corps
  339 Inf Div
  110 Inf Div
  296 Inf Div
  134 Inf Div
LIII Corps
  211 Inf Div
  293 Inf Div
  25 Pz Gdr Div
  208 Inf Div
XXXV Corps
  34 Inf Div
  56 Inf Div

262 Inf Div
299 Inf Div
Reserve – 112 Inf Div and 707 Inf Div
IX Army – Col-Gen Walter Model
XXIII Corps
  36 Inf Div (part)
  383 Inf Div
  216 Inf Div
  78 Assault Div
XLI Pz Corps
  86 Inf Div
  292 Inf Div
  18 Pz Div
XLVII Pz Corps
  6 Inf Div
  20 Pz Div
  9 Pz Div
  2 Pz Div
  21 Pz Bgd
XLVI Pz Corps
  31 Inf Div
  7 Inf Div
  258 Inf Div
  102 Inf Div
XX Corps
  72 Inf Div
  45 Inf Div
  137 Inf Div
  251 Inf Div
  Reserve – 299 Inf Div and 36 Inf Div (part)
II Army – General Walter Weiss
XIII Corps
  82 Inf Div
  340 Inf Div
  377 Inf Div
  327 Inf Div
VII Corps
  26 Inf Div
  323 Inf Div (part)
  75 Inf Div
  68 Inf Div
  88 Inf Div
Army Group Reserve
  Group Esebeck

10 Pz Gdr Div
12 Pz.Div
VII Hun Corps
    8 Hun Light Div
    2 Hun Light Div
    5 Hun Light Div
LXI Corps
    141 Inf Div
    151 Inf Div
5 Pz.Div
8 Pz Div
83 Inf Div
36 Inf Div (part)
4 Pz Div (from 9 July)

Army Group South – Field Marshal
Erich von Manstein
    IV Pz Army – Col-Gen Hermann
        Hoth
    LII Corps
        57 Inf Div
        255 Inf Div
        332 Inf Div
    XLVIII Pz Corps
        3 Pz Div
        11 Pz Div
        167 Inf Div (most)
        Grossdeutschland Pz Gdr Div
        10 Pz Bgd
    II SS Panzer Corps
        1 SS Pz Gdr Div (*Leibstandarte*
        SS Adolf Hitler)
        2 SS Pz Gdr Div (*Das Reich*)
        3 SS Pz Gdr Div (*Totenkopf*)
        167 Inf Div (part)
    Army Detachment Kempf – General
        Werner Kempf
    III Panzer Corps
        6 Pz Div
        7 Pz Div
        19 Pz Div
        168 Inf Div
    XI Corps (Corps Raus)
        320 Inf Div
        106 Inf Div
    XLII Corps

161 Inf Div
282 Inf Div
39 Inf Div
I Pz Army – Col-Gen Eberhard von
    Mackensen
    LVII Pz Corps
        15 Inf Div
        198 Inf Div
        328 Inf Div
    XL Pz Corps
        333 Inf Div
        46 Inf Div
        257 Inf Div
    XXX Corps
        62 Inf Div
        38 Inf Div
        387 Inf Div
    Reserve – XXIV Pz Corps
        23 Pz Div
        17 Pz Div
        5 SS Pz Gdr Div (*Wiking*)
    VI Army – General Karl Adolf Hollidt
        IV Corps (Group 'Mieth')
        304 Inf Div
        3 Mtn Div
        335 Inf Div
    XVII Corps
        294 Inf Div
        306 Inf Div
        302 Inf Div
    XXIX Corps
        111 Inf Div
        15 LwF Div
        17 Inf Div
        336 Inf Div
    Reserve – 16 Pz Gdr Div
    Army Group Reserve
        24 Rum Inf Div
    LXII Corps
        143 Inf Div
        147 Inf Div

Army Group A – Field Marshal Ewald
von Kleist
    XVII Army – General Erwin Jaenecke
        XLIV Corps

97 Light Div
79 Inf Div
101 Light Div
19 Rum Inf Div (part)
79 Inf Div
3 Rum Mtn Div (part)
10 Rum Inf Div (most)
98 Inf Div
125 Inf Div
V Corps
9 Inf Div
1 Rum Mtn Div
9 Rum Cav Div
19 Rum Inf Div (most)
6 Rum Cav Div
4 Mtn Div
73 Inf Div
XLIX Mountain Corps
370 Inf Div
50 Inf Div
125 Inf Div
3 Rum Mtn Div (most)
10 Rum Inf Div (part)
13 Pz Div (part)
Army Group Reserve
13 Pz Div (most)
5 LwF Div
153 Inf Div
355 Inf Div
381 Inf Div (part)
1 Slov Mot Div
Rum Mtn Corps
4 Rum Mtn Div
2 Rum Mtn Div

In addition to the above each army group had numerous specialist and independent battalions, regiments and operational groups, and each army group included four or five security divisions. The *Ostheer* contained more than thirty independent self-propelled gun battalions and additionally, XLI Pz Corps had an independent 'tank destroyer' regiment.

Moving into theatre in the XVI Army sector were 9 LwF Div and 69 Inf Div.

Red Army Order of Battle at the time of Operation Citadel 1943

Leningrad Front – Col-Gen L A Govorov
23 Army (4 rifle divisions)
42 Army (5 rifle divisions, a tank brigade and a tank regiment)
55 Army (7 rifle divisions and a tank brigade)
67 Army (9 rifle divisions, 2 tank brigades and a tank regiment)
2 Shock Army (5 rifle divisions, 2 rifle brigades, 2 tank brigades and a tank regiment)
Front reserve – a tank brigade and 3 tank regiments

Volkhov Front – General K A Meretskov
8 Army (8 rifle divisions, 3 rifle brigades, a tank brigade and 4 tank regiments)
54 Army (7 rifle divisions, a rifle brigade and a tank brigade)
4 Army (2 rifle divisions and 2 rifle brigades)
59 Army (7 rifle divisions, a tank brigade)
Front reserve – 4 rifle divisions, 3 tank brigades and a tank regiment

Northwestern Front – Lt-Gen P A Kurochkin
34 Army (8 rifle divisions, 3 rifle brigades, a tank brigade and 7 tank regiments)
1 Shock Army (4 rifle divisions, a rifle brigade and 3 tank regiments)

22 Army (3 rifle divisions, 5 rifle brigades and a tank brigade)
Front reserve – 2 rifle divisions and a rifle brigade

Kalinin Front – Col-Gen A I Eremenko
3 Shock Army (3 rifle divisions, a rifle brigade, a mechanised brigade and a tank brigade)
4 Shock Army (5 rifle divisions, a rifle brigade and 2 tank brigades)
43 Army (4 rifle divisions, a rifle brigade and a tank regiment)
39 Army (5 rifle divisions, a rifle brigade and a tank brigade)
Front reserve – 3 rifle divisions, 2 cavalry divisions, a mechanised brigade and a tank regiment)

Western Front – Col-Gen V D Sokolovsky
31 Army (9 rifle divisions and a tank brigade)
5 Army (4 rifle divisions and a tank brigade)
33 Army (5 rifle divisions and a tank brigade)
49 Army (5 rifle divisions and a tank brigade)
10 Army (5 rifle divisions)
50 Army (7 rifle divisions and a tank brigade)
11 Gds Army (12 rifle divisions, 4 tank brigades and 2 tank regiments)
Reserve 10 Gds Army (6 rifle divisions and a tank regiment) and

20 Army (two fortified regions)

Front reserve – 2 tank corps, 4 tank brigades, a rifle division, a rifle brigade and 4 tank regiments

Bryansk Front – Col-Gen M M Popov

61 Army (8 rifle divisions, a tank brigade and a tank regiment)

3 Army (6 rifle divisions and 2 tank regiments)

63 Army (7 rifle divisions, and a tank regiment)

Front reserve – a tank corps, 3 rifle divisions and 5 tank regiments

Central Front – General K K Rokossovsky

48 Army (7 rifle divisions and 3 tank regiments)

13 Army (6 rifle divisions, a cavalry corps, 3 airborne divisions, a tank brigade and 5 tank regiments)

70 Army (8 rifle divisions and 3 tank regiments)

65 Army (9 rifle divisions, a rifle brigade and 4 tank regiments)

60 Army (5 rifle divisions, 3 rifle brigades and a tank brigade)

Reserve 2 Tank Army (2 tank corps and a tank brigade)

Front reserve – 3 fortified regions

Voronezh Front – General N F Vatutin

38 Army (6 rifle divisions and 2 tank brigades)

40 Army (7 rifle divisions, a tank brigade and 2 tank regiments)

6 Gds Army (7 rifle divisions, 2 tank brigades and 2 tank regiments)

7 Gds Army (7 rifle divisions, a tank brigade and 3 tank regiments)

Reserve 1 Tank Army (2 tank corps and a mechanised corps) and 69 Army (5 rifle divisions)

Front reserve – 2 tank corps and 3 rifle divisions

Southwestern Front – General R I Malinovsky

57 Army (8 rifle divisions and 2 tank brigades)

6 Army (11 rifle divisions, a tank brigade and a tank regiment)

1 Gds Army (6 rifle divisions and a rifle brigade)

3 Gds Army (7 rifle divisions, a mechanised brigade, a tank brigade and 2 tank regiments)

Reserve 8 Gds Army (6 rifle divisions a tank regiment) and 12 Army (5 rifle divisions and a tank regiment) and

46 Army (6 rifle divisions)

Front reserve – 2 tank corps, a mechanised corps and a tank brigade

Southern Front – Col-Gen F I Tolbukhin

5 Shock Army (8 rifle divisions and a tank regiment)

28 Army (2 rifle divisions, a tank brigade and 2 fortified regions)

44 Army (7 rifle divisions and 2 tank brigades)

Reserve 2 Gds Army (6 rifle divisions and a mechanised corps)

51 Army (7 rifle divisions and a tank brigade)

Front reserve – a mechanised corps

North Caucasian Front – Lt-Gen I E Petrov

9 Army (2 rifle divisions and 8 rifle brigades)

18 Army (2 rifle divisions and 4 rifle brigade)

37 Army (6 rifle divisions)

56 Army (5 rifle divisions and 6 rifle brigades)

58 Army (4 rifle divisions)
Front reserve – 5 tank regiments

Reserve Front – Col-Gen I S Konev
4 Gds Army (3 rifle divisions, 3
      airborne divisions and a tank
      corps)
5 Gds Army (5 rifle divisions, 2
      airborne divisions and a tank
      corps)
27 Army (6 rifle divisions, a tank
      brigade and a tank regiment)
47 Army (6 rifle divisions)
53 Army (7 rifle divisions and 2 tank
      regiments)
5 Gds Tank Army (a mechanised
      corps and 2 tank corps)
Front reserve – 3 mechanised corps, a
      tank corps, and 3 cavalry corps

In addition to the above, each Front had numerous specialist and independent battalions, regiments and brigades.

STAVKA had further reserves available in the western theatre including Major-Gen E P Zhuravlev's 68 Army and Lt-Gen I I Fedyuninsky's 11 Army, both of which were released from the reserve on 12 July; Lt-Gen V M Badanov's 4 Tank Army, released from the reserve on 20 July; and Lt-Gen P S Rybalko's 3 Gds Tank Army which was still forming up at the beginning of July and which became operational two weeks later.

Appendix XI

Axis Order of Battle at the time of Operation Bagration 1944

Army Group North – Col-Gen Georg Lindemann
Army Detachment Narva – General
    Johannes Friessner
    XXVI Corps
        227 Inf Div
        170 Inf Div
        225 Inf Div
    XLIII Corps
        58 Inf Div
        11 Inf Div
        122 Inf Div
    III SS Pz Corps
        11 SS Pz Gdr Div (*Nordland*)
        20 SS Gdr Div
        SS Brigade (*Nederland*)
    Reserves – 61 Inf Div, nine
        Estonian battalions, a flak
        division and a security division
XVIII Army – General Herbert Loch
    XXVIII Corps
        126 Inf Div
        21 Inf Div
        212 Inf Div
        12 LwF Div
        30 Inf Div
    XXXVIII Corps
        21 LwF Div
        32 Inf Div
        121 Inf Div
    Reserves 215 Inf Div
XVI Army – General Christian
    Hansen
    X Corps
        389 Inf Div
        290 Inf Div
        263 Inf Div

    II Corps
        81 Inf Div
        329 Inf Div
        23 Inf Div
    VI SS Corps
        93 Inf Div
        15 SS Gdr Div
        19 SS Gdr Div
    L Corps
        218 Inf Div
        132 Inf Div
        83 Inf Div
    I Corps
        205 Inf Div
        87 Inf Div
    Reserve – 69 Inf Div, 24 Inf Div
        (part) and a security division
    Army Group Reserve – 12 Pz Div
        (part) and a training division

Army Group Centre – Field Marshal Ernst Busch
    III Pz Army – Col-Gen Georg-Hans
        Reinhardt
    IX Corps
        252 Inf Div
        Corps Detachment 'D'
    LIII Corps
        246 Inf Div
        4 LwF Div
        6 LwF Div
        206 Inf Div
    VI Corps
        197 Inf Div
        299 Inf Div
        256 Inf Div

Reserves – 95 Inf Div and three
  security divisions
IV Army – General Kurt von
  Tippelskirch
  XXVII Corps
    260 Inf Div
    25 Pz Gdr Div
    78 Assault
    55 Inf Div (part)
  XXXIX Pz Corps
    337 Inf Div
    12 Inf Div
    31 Inf Div
    110 Inf Div
  XII Corps
    18 Pz Gdr Div
    267 Inf Div
    57 Inf Div (part)
  Reserve – a security division
IX Army – General Hans Jordan
  XXXV Corps
    383 Inf Div
    45 Inf Div
    6 Inf Div
    296 Inf Div
    134 Inf Div
    129 Inf Div (part)
  XLI Pz Corps
    36 Inf Div
    35 Inf Div
    129 Inf Div (part)
  LV Corps
    292 Inf Div (part)
    102 Inf Div
II Army – Col-Gen Walter Weiss
  XXIII Corps
    7 Inf Div
    203 Security Div and a panzer
    grenadier brigade
  VIII Corps
    211 Inf Div
    5 Light Div
  XX Corps
    Corps Detachment 'E' and a
    cavalry brigade

Reserve – two Hungarian 'reserve'
  divisions, a Hungarian cavalry
  division, and a cavalry brigade
Army Group Reserve
  14 Inf Div
  707 Inf Div

**Army Group North Ukraine – Field
Marshal Walter Model**
IV Pz Army – Col-Gen Josef Harpe
  LVI Pz Corps
    26 Inf Div
    342 Inf Div
    132 Inf Div
    253 Inf Div
    1 Ski Jäger Div
  XIII Corps
    340 Inf Div
    361Inf Div
    Corps Detachment 'C'
    Grossdeutschland Pz Gdr Div
  XLII Corps
    214 Inf Div
    72 Inf Div
    88 Inf Div
    291 Inf Div
  Reserve – 4 Pz Div, 5 Pz Div,
    28 Light Div and a security
    division
I Pz Army – General Erhard Raus
  XLVIII Pz Corps
    349 Inf Div
    357 Inf Div
    96 Inf Div
    359 Inf Div
  XXIV Pz Corps
    100 Light Div
    75 Inf Div
    371 Inf Div
  LIX Corps
    254 Inf Div
    208 Inf Div
    20 Inf Div (part)
  XLVI Pz Corps
    1 Inf Div
    168 Inf Div

367 Inf Div
Reserve
  III Pz Corps
    1 Pz Div
    7 Pz Div
    8 Pz Div
    17 Pz Div
    20 Pz Gdr Div
I Hun Army
  VI Hun Corps
    27 Hun Light Div
    Two Hungarian mountain
    brigades
  XI Corps
    18 Hun 'Reserve' Div
    25 Hun Inf Div
    101 Light Div
    24 Hun Inf Div
  VII Hun Corps
    68 Inf Div
    16 Hun Inf Div
  Reserve
    2 Hun Pz Div
    19 Hun 'Reserve' Div
Army Group Reserve
  II SS Pz Corps
    9 SS Pz Div (*Hohenstaufen*)
    10 SS Pz Div (*Frundsberg*)
    16 Pz Div

Army Group South Ukraine – Col-Gen Ferdinand Schoerner
Armeegruppe Woehler
  VIII Army – General Otto Woehler
    IV Rum Corps
      5 Rum Cav Div and two
      Rumanian brigades
    IV Corps
      376 Inf Div
      79 Inf Div
      11 Rum Inf Div
      3 Rum Inf Div
      23 Pz Div
    Reserve – 18 Rum Mtn Div and
      XL Pz Corps Headquarters

IV Rum Army – Lt-Gen Mihail
  Racovitza
  XVII Corps
    3 Mtn Div
    8 Light Div
  VII Rum Corps
    two Rumanian brigades
  I Rum Corps
    6 Rum Inf Div
    20 Rum Inf Div
  LVII Pz Corps
    14 Pz Div
    1 Rum Inf Div
    46 Inf Div
    13 Rum Inf Div
  VI Rum Corps
    7 Rum Inf Div
    18 Rum Mtn Div
    5 Rum Inf Div
    101 Rum Mtn Div
    4 Rum Inf Div
  Reserve
    24 Pz Div
    1 Rum Cav Div
Armeegruppe Dumitrescu
  VI Army – General Maximilian de
    Angelis
    VII Corps
      14 Rum Inf Div
      370 Inf Div
      106 Inf Div
    LII Corps
      17 Inf Div
      294 Inf Div
      320 Inf Div
      4 Mtn Div
      Corps Detachment 'A'
      97 Light Div
    XXX Corps
      384 Inf Div
      257 Inf Div
      15 Inf Div
      306 Inf Div
    XLIV Corps
      258 Inf Div
      282 Inf Div

10 Pz Gdr Div
Corps Detachment 'F'
Reserve – 3 Pz Div, 13 Pz Div and
335 Inf Div
III Rum Army – Col-Gen Petre
Dumitrescu
XXIX Corps
304 Inf Div
21 Rum Inf Div
4 Rum Mtn Div
III Rum Corps
2 Rum Inf Div
15 Rum Inf Div
Reserves – II Rum Corps
Headquarters and LXXII
Corps Headquarters
Army Group Reserve – XVII Army
Headquarters, V Corps
Headquarters,
XLIX Mtn Corps Headquarters, 8
Rum Cav Div and 1 Rum Pz
Div

In addition to the above each army group
had numerous specialist and independent
units. OKH also held 20 Pz Div as reserve.

Appendix XII

Red Army Order of Battle for Operation Bagration 1944

Leningrad Front – General L A Govorov
23 Army (8 rifle divisions and 2 tank regiments)
21 Army (15 rifle divisions, a tank brigade and 5 tank regiments)
59 Army (4 rifle divisions)
2 Shock Army (3 rifle divisions)
8 Army (12 rifle divisions and a tank regiment)
Front reserve – 5 rifle divisions, 3 tank brigades and 6 tank regiments

3 Baltic Front – Col-Gen I I Maslennikov
42 Army (3 rifle divisions)
67 Army (8 rifle divisions and 3 tank regiments)
54 Army (5 rifle divisions and a tank regiment)
Front reserve – 2 tank brigades

2 Baltic Front – General A I Eremenko
1 Shock Army (10 rifle divisions, a tank brigade and 2 tank regiments)
10 Gds Army (9 rifle divisions, a tank brigade and 2 tank regiments)
22 Army (3 rifle divisions and a tank regiment)
3 Shock Army (6 rifle divisions and a tank brigade)
Front reserve – a rifle division and a tank corps

1 Baltic Front – General I K Bagramyan
6 Gds Army (9 rifle divisions, 2 tank brigades and 3 tank regiments)
4 Shock Army (7 rifle divisions, a rifle brigade and a tank brigade)
43 Army (8 rifle divisions, 2 tank brigades and a tank regiment)
Front reserve – 6 rifle divisions and a tank corps

3 Belorussian Front – Col-Gen I D Cherniakhovsky
39 Army (7 rifle divisions and a tank brigade)
5 Army (9 rifle divisions and 2 tank brigades and a tank regiment)
Group Obukhov (a cavalry corps and a mechanised corps)
5 Gds Tank Army (2 tank corps and a tank regiment)
11 Gds Army (9 rifle divisions, a tank corps, a tank brigade and 4 tank regiments)
31 Army (8 rifle divisions and a tank brigade)

2 Belorussian Front – Col-Gen G F Zakharov
33 Army (5 rifle divisions)
49 Army (2 rifle divisions, 2 tank brigades and a tank regiment)
50 Army (9 rifle divisions)
Front reserve – a rifle division and 2 tank brigades

1 Belorussian Front – General K K Rokossovsky

3 Army (13 rifle divisions and 5 tank regiments)

48 Army (9 rifle divisions and 2 tank regiments)

65 Army (7 rifle divisions, a rifle brigade and a tank regiment)

28 Army (9 rifle divisions and 4 tank regiments)

Group Pliev (a cavalry corps and a mechanised corps)

61 Army (6 rifle divisions and 2 tank regiments)

70 Army (4 rifle divisions)

47 Army (10 rifle divisions, a tank brigade and 2 tank regiments)

69 Army (9 rifle divisions)

Reserve – 2 Tank Army (2 tank corps and a tank brigade)

Reserve – 8 Gds Army (9 rifle divisions)

Reserve – Polish 1 Army (4 rifle divisions and a tank brigade)

Front reserve – 4 tank corps and 2 cavalry corps

1 Ukrainian Front – Marshal I S Konev

3 Gds Army (12 rifle divisions, a tank brigade and a tank regiment)

13 Army (9 rifle divisions, a tank corps)

60 Army (12 rifle divisions and a tank regiment)

38 Army (5 rifle divisions)

1 Gds Army (17 rifle divisions and a tank corps)

18 Army (10 rifle divisions)

Reserve – 5 Gds Army (7 rifle divisions)

Reserve – 4 Tank Army (a tank corps, a mechanised corps and a tank brigade)

Reserve – 1 Gds Tank Army (a tank corps, a mechanised corps, a tank brigade and a tank regiment)

Reserve – 3 Gds Tank Army (2 tank corps, a mechanised corps and a tank brigade)

Front reserve – 2 cavalry corps, a tank corps and a tank regiment

2 Ukrainian Front – General R I Malinovsky

40 Army (8 rifle divisions)

7 Gds Army (7 rifle divisions and a tank brigade)

27 Army (7 rifle divisions and a tank regiment)

52 Army (7 rifle divisions)

53 Army (8 rifle divisions)

4 Gds Army (10 rifle divisions)

Reserve – 6 Tank Army (a tank corps and a mechanised corps)

Front reserve – 6 rifle divisions, 2 tank corps, a mechanised corps and a cavalry corps

3 Ukrainian Front – General F I Tolbukhin

5 Shock Army (8 rifle divisions)

57 Army (8 rifle divisions and a tank brigade)

37 Army (9 rifle divisions)

46 Army (7 rifle divisions)

Front reserve – 3 rifle divisions, a mechanised corps, a motorised rifle brigade, 2 tank regiments and 6 Army Headquarters

In addition to the above, each Front had numerous specialist and independent battalions, regiments and brigades; in particular there were heavy concentrations of High Command artillery units on the main axes of attack.

Select Bibliography

Bellamy, Chris, *Absolute War, Soviet Russia in the Second World War, a modern history* (London: Macmillan, 2007)

Erickson, John, *The Road to Berlin* (London: Weidenfeld & Nicolson, 1983)

Erickson, John, *The Road to Stalingrad* (London: Weidenfeld & Nicolson, 1975)

Fugate, Bryan I. & Lev Divoretsky, *Thunder on the Dnepr: Zhukov-Stalin and the Defeat of Hitler's Blitzkrieg* (Novato CA: Presidio Press, 1997)

Glantz, David M. & Jonathan M. House, *When Titans Clashed. How the Red Army stopped Hitler* (Lawrence KS: University Press of Kansas, 1995)

Glantz, David M., *Barbarossa. Hitler's Invasion of Russia 1941* (Stroud: Tempus, 2001)

Grylev, A.N. (comp. & ed.), *Boyevoi Sostav Sovetskoy Armii* [Combat Strength of the Soviet Army] (Moscow: Voenizdat, 1963-90, 5 volumes)

Krivosheev, G.F. *et al, Soviet Casualties and Combat Losses in the Twentieth Century* (London: Greenhill Books, 1997)

Merridale, Catherine, *Ivan's War. Life and Death in the Red Army 1939-1945* (London: Faber, 2005)

Mitcham, Samuel W., *Crumbling Empire: The German Defeat in the East 1944-45* (Westport CT: Praeger, 2001)

Overmans, Rüdiger, *Deutsche militärische Verluste im Zweiten Weltkrieg* (München: Oldenbourg Verlag, 1999)

Overy, Richard, *Russia's War* (London: Allen Lane, 1998)

Pitt, Barrie (ed.), *Purnell's History of the Second World War* (London: Macdonald, 1968). In particular, the following articles:

> de Beaulie, W. C., *Barbarossa – Drive to Leningrad*
>
> Istomin, Vasily, *The Liberation of Smolensk*
>
> Jukes, Geoffrey, *Drive to Kharkov*
>
> Konev, I. S., *Berlin: The Plan*
>
> Parotkin, I. V., *Berlin: The Battle*
>
> Philippi, Alfred, *Barbarossa – Drive to Smolensk*
>
> Popel N. K., *Barbarossa – The Shock*
>
> Samsonov, A. M. *Stalingrad: The Relief*
>
> Shimansky, A. N., *Drive to Rumania*
>
> Shimansky, A. N., *Drive to Warsaw*
>
> Traktuyev, M. I., *Drive into Poland*
>
> Utkin, Grigory, *Battle for the Dniepr*
>
> Zhabkin, Ivan, *Forgotten Campaign: The Caucasus*

Ryan, Cornelius, *The Last Battle* (London: Collins, 1966)

Shirer W. L., *The Rise and Fall of the Third Reich* (London: Secker & Warburg, 1960)

Shtemenko, S. M., *The Soviet General Staff at War 1941-1945* (Moscow: Progress Publishers, 1970)

Shukman, Harold, *Stalin's Generals* (London: Weidenfeld & Nicolson, 1993)
Glantz, David M., *From the Don to the Dnepr: Soviet Offensive Operations December 1942-August 1943* (London: Cass, 1991)
Taylor, Brian, *Barbarossa to Berlin. A Chronology of the Campaigns on the Eastern Front 1941-45 Volume 1: The Long Drive East 22 June 1941 to 18 November 1942* (Staplehurst: Spellmount, 2003)
Taylor, Brian, *Barbarossa to Berlin. A Chronology of the Campaigns on the Eastern Front 1941-45 Volume 2: The Defeat of Germany 19 November 1942 to 15 May 1945* (Staplehurst: Spellmount, 2004)
Zaloga, Steven J. and Leland S. Ness, *The Red Army Handbook* (Stroud: Sutton, 1998)
Ziemke, Earl M. & Magna E. Bauer, *Moscow to Stalingrad. Decision in the East* (Washington DC: Center of Military History, United States Army, 1987)
Ziemke, Earl M., *Stalingrad to Berlin. The German Defeat in the East* (Washington DC: United States Army Office of the Chief of Military History, 1971)

Index

General Index

Index of Axis Combat Units

Army Groups (*Heeresgruppen*) (German)

Panzer Groups

168 Inf Div : 164, 312, 319, 325
197 Inf Div : 223, 225, 311, 318, 324
205 Inf Div : 229, 310, 317, 324
206 Inf Div : 222, 226, 304, 311, 218, 324
210 Inf Div : 247
211 Inf Div : 223, 311, 318, 325
212 Inf Div : 230, 310, 317, 324
216 Inf Div : 311, 318
246 Inf Div : 222, 311, 318, 324
250 Inf Div (Spanish 'Blue' Div) : 205
251 Inf Div : 163, 304, 311, 318
252 Inf Div : 305, 311, 318, 324
255 Inf Div : 305, 311, 319
256 Inf Div : 223, 225, 304, 311, 318, 324
258 Inf Div : 305, 311, 318, 326
260 Inf Div : 223, 311, 318, 325
267 Inf Div : 39, 223, 305, 311, 318, 325
282 Inf Div : 319, 326
290 Inf Div : 229, 304, 310, 317, 324
292 Inf Div : 163, 223, 305, 311, 318, 325
296 Inf Div : 223, 306, 310, 311, 318, 325
299 Inf Div : 163, 223, 225, 306, 311, 318, 324
304 Inf Div : 319, 327
320 Inf Div : 319, 326
323 Inf Div : 164, 313, 318
327 Inf Div : 164, 318
332 Inf Div : 164, 319
337 Inf Div : 223, 318, 325
340 Inf Div : 313 318, 325
377 Inf Div : 312, 318
383 Inf Div : 318, 325
384 Inf Div : 182, 312, 326
5 Light Div : 223, 325
4 LwF Div : 222, 226, 317, 324
6 LwF Div : 222, 226, 318, 324
3 Mot Div : 37, 304, 312
10 Mot Div : 30-31, 39, 45, 305, 311
16 Mot Div : 113, 118, 306, 312
20 Mot Div : 32, 304, 310
25 Mot Div : 33, 306, 311
29 Mot Div : 28, 30, 113-114, 305, 312
1 Mtn Div : 213, 256-257, 306, 312
2 Mtn Div : 247-249
3 Mtn Div : 126, 252, 319, 326
6 Mtn Div : 247-249
7 Mtn Div : 84, 310
3 Naval Div : 289
1 Pz Div : 25, 55, 182, 185, 304, 310, 326
2 Pz Div : 61-62, 168, 311, 318

3 Pz Div : 23, 39, 44-45, 52, 139, 142, 164, 167, 172, 305, 312 319, 327
4 Pz Div : 39, 52, 134, 168, 305, 311, 319, 325
6 Pz Div : 112, 116, 118, 126-127, 167, 170, 172, 304, 319
7 Pz Div : 26, 38, 62, 130, 138-139, 167, 173, 185, 192, 208, 212, 289, 304, 319, 326
8 Pz Div : 22, 29, 47, 177, 192, 304, 310, 319, 326
9 Pz Div : 44, 141, 168, 196, 305, 312, 318
10 Pz Div : 30, 55, 64, 305
11 Pz Div : 23-24, 33, 118, 126-27, 138-140, 164, 167, 182, 194, 305, 312, 319
12 Pz Div : 29, 47, 70, 163, 200-201, 227-228, 304, 310, 324
13 Pz Div : 24, 33, 252, 306, 313, 320, 327
14 Pz Div : 44-45, 109-110, 182, 194, 305, 312, 326
16 Pz Div : 24, 44-45, 105, 188, 190, 305, 322, 326
17 Pz Div : 23, 26,-7, 59, 61, 64, 118-119, 141, 190, 233, 305, 311, 319, 326
18 Pz Div : 47, 163, 168, 305, 311, 38
19 Pz Div : 30, 37, 41, 126, 164, 238, 240, 242, 304, 311, 319
20 Pz Div : 26, 27, 37, 38, 168, 304, 311, 318, 327
22 Pz Div : 313
23 Pz Div : 89, 94, 118, 196, 319, 326
24 Pz Div : 182, 196, 312, 326
25 Pz Div : 184, 240, 278
27 Pz Div : 126
10 Pz Gdr Div : 163, 319, 327
18 Pz Gdr Div : 223, 317, 325
20 Pz Gdr Div : 317, 326
25 Pz Gdr Div : 289, 318, 325
203 Security Div : 223, 325
1 SS Div (*Leibstandarte*) : 138-139, 142, 164, 167, 173, 182, 185, 208, 212, 306, 313, 319
2 SS Div (*Das Reich*) : 30, 55, 138, 141, 164, 167-168, 172-173, 305,319
3 SS Div (*Totenkopf*) : 138, 141, 164, 167, 172-173, 182, 273, 304, 310, 319
4 SS Div (*Polizei*) : 37, 310, 317
5 SS Div (*Wiking*) : 141, 173, 194, 212, 273, 305, 313, 219
6 SS Mtn Div (*Nord*) : 247
9 SS Pz Div (*Hohenstaufen*) : 212, 214, 326
10 SS Pz Div (*Frundsberg*) : 212, 326
11 SS Div (*Nordland*) : 245, 324

Brigades (Axis)
5 Rum Cav Bgd : 24, 306
6 Rum Can Bgd : 25

Armies (Soviet)

3 Army : 18, 26, 32, 40-41, 43, 51-52, 54, 60, 63-64, 66, 164, 171, 187, 224, 226, 228, 265, 269, 275, 285, 289, 207, 315, 322, 329

4 Army : 19, 21-22, 25-26, 28, 30-31, 58-59, 72, 189, 198, 307, 314, 321

5 Army : 19, 23-24, 33, 35, 38-40, 42-45, 54-55, 60-1, 63, 69, 90, 223, 225-226, 231, 246, 265, 268, 307, 314, 321, 328

6 Army : 19, 23-24, 33-34, 42, 49, 66, 71-72, 89-90, 95-96, 125, 127, 136, 138, 140-142, 180, 208, 213, 266, 281, 307, 322, 329

7 Army : 19, 27, 35-37, 58, 220-221, 309

8 Army : 18, 21-22, 26, 30, 35-37, 47-48, 90, 132, 200, 314, 321, 328

9 Army : 24, 42, 49, 53, 56-57, 66, 72, 89, 90, 93, 101-102, 133-135, 161, 171, 189, 285, 293, 309, 322

10 Army : 19, 55, 62-64, 67, 69-70,74, 216, 315, 321

11 Army : 18, 21-22, 29, 35, 36, 68, 70, 166, 170-171, 189, 314, 323

12 Army : 19, 33-34, 42, 53, 66, 93, 99-100, 102-103, 181, 189, 315, 322

13 Army : 19, 22, 25, 28, 30-31, 39, 40-42, 51-52, 54, 60, 63-64, 66, 79, 93-94, 137, 144, 165-166, 168, 174, 177-178, 184-185, 187, 190-191, 207-208, 210-211, 233, 235, 266, 271, 281, 285-286, 289, 293, 315, 322, 329

14 Army : 19, 27, 36, 247-249

16 Army : 19, 28, 31-32, 38, 51-52, 55, 60-61, 63-65, 67, 144, 160-161, 315

18 Army : 19, 24, 34, 42, 49, 53, 56-57, 66, 93, 99, 103-104, 133, 135, 161, 177, 183, 190, 207, 212, 236, 242, 291, 309, 315, 322, 329

19 Army : 27, 32, 38, 41, 51, 54, 61-62, 247-248, 280, 282-283, 285

20 Army : 19, 26-28, 30, 32, 38, 41, 51, 54, 62-63, 65, 67, 69, 119-123, 164, 216, 314, 322

21 Army : 19, 26-28, 30-31, 38-45, 49, 53, 66, 68, 79, 89, 93, 95-97, 99-101 105, 109, 112-113, 115, 118, 128-129, 144-145, 147, 161, 174, 220-222, 266, 270, 283, 292, 328

22 Army : 19, 25, 27, 33, 41, 51, 55, 60, 69-71, 120-121, 124, 182, 246, 314, 321, 328

23 Army : 27, 35-36, 132, 188, 220-222, 309, 314, 321, 328

24 Army : 19, 28-30, 31, 33, 38, 41, 51-52, 54, 63, 102-103, 105, 107, 109-110, 112, 128, 161, 315

26 Army : 19, 24, 33-34, 44, 54, 60, 63, 66-67, 247-248, 275-276

27 Army : 18, 25, 35-36, 67, 165, 167, 169, 184, 208, 211, 251, 260, 262-263, 275, 277, 314, 316, 323, 329

28 Army : 19, 31, 38, 89, 99-100, 108, 113, 133-134, 183, 208, 210, 224, 226-227, 236, 246, 265, 268, 285, 287-289, 322, 329

29 Army : 27, 29, 33, 41, 51, 55, 63, 65, 67, 69, 71, 74, 119-120, 122-123, 314

30 Army : 29, 41, 51, 55, 60-61, 63-65, 120, 122, 161, 314

31 Army : 33, 51-52, 55, 60, 63-65, 119-120, 122, 227-228, 246, 265, 285, 314, 321, 328

32 Army : 33, 51, 60, 62, 65, 70, 74, 91, 223, 266, 268, 285, 287, 289-290, 314, 321, 328

33 Army : 33, 51, 60, 62, 65, 70-71, 74, 91, 223, 266, 268, 285, 287, 289-290, 314, 321, 328

34 Army : 35-36, 67, 70, 182, 189, 314, 321

37 Army : 34, 40, 44-45, 57, 66, 71-72, 96-97, 99, 102, 133, 135, 161, 182, 208, 251-252, 262, 315, 322, 329

38 Army : 34, 42, 43- 44, 66, 68, 89, 93, 97, 99-100, 130, 137, 165, 173, 179-180, 184, 207, 210-212, 233, 255, 260-261, 269, 291, 322, 329

39 Army : 63, 65, 67, 69, 71, 74, 95, 119-120, 122, 186, 223, 225-226, 230-231, 245-246, 265, 268, 314, 316, 321, 328

40 Army : 41-44, 49, 51, 66, 68, 88-89, 93-95, 131, 135, 137, 139, 165, 172-173, 179, 184, 190-191, 208, 212, 251, 263, 275, 293, 315, 322, 329

41 Army : 120, 122, 123, 314

42 Army : 38, 47, 48, 198, 199, 216, 246, 314, 321, 328

43 Army : 38, 51, 55, 60, 65, 70, 121 186, 223, 225-226, 231-232, 238, 244-246, 265-266, 280, 315, 321, 328

44 Army : 66, 68, 75, 87, 94, 133, 189, 316, 322

46 Army : 94, 102-103, 133, 135, 161, 176, 196, 208, 251, 255, 257, 260-261, 263, 275, 278, 293, 316, 322 329

47 Army : 87-88, 94, 100, 103-104, 133-134, 161, 165, 170, 173, 192, 207, 224, 234, 236, 240-241, 268-269, 281-283, 285-288, 315, 323, 329

48 Army : 36, 47-48, 89, 144, 165, 181, 226, 265, 269, 271-272, 280, 315, 322, 329

49 Army : 38, 51-52, 55, 60-61, 64, 67, 69, 70, 73, 223, 227, 265, 285, 288, 315, 321, 328

50 Army : 39-40, 43, 51-52, 60-61, 64, 67, 69, 73, 164, 187, 216, 223, 227, 265, 271, 280, 315, 321, 328,

51 Army : 39, 49, 53, 56, 66, 68, 75, 87, 94, 99-102, 108-109, 112, 115-116, 118-119, 127-128, 133-134, 181, 183, 214-215, 219, 224, 232, 238, 245-246, 315, 322

Operational Groups (Soviet)